William Whitmee

Lent and holy week in Rome

with the Lenten stations, visit to the seven churches and to the Scala Santa

William Whitmee

Lent and holy week in Rome
with the Lenten stations, visit to the seven churches and to the Scala Santa

ISBN/EAN: 9783742834416

Manufactured in Europe, USA, Canada, Australia, Japa

Cover: Foto ©Lupo / pixelio.de

Manufactured and distributed by brebook publishing software (www.brebook.com)

William Whitmee

Lent and holy week in Rome

Nostra Signora della Speranza
che si venera nella
Chiesa di San Silvestro in Capite, Roma.

LENT
AND
HOLY WEEK

LENT
AND
HOLY WEEK
IN
ROME

WITH

THE LENTEN STATIONS
VISIT TO THE SEVEN CHURCHES
AND TO THE SCALA SANTA

TOGETHER WITH

A COPIOUS GLOSSARY

COMPILED

by the Rev. William Whitmee P. S. M.
Rector of the Ven. Church of St. Silvestro in Capito, Rome.

ROMA
Tipografia Valentini - Via dei Serpenti, 87-88.
1896

Religious Functions

DURING HOLY WEEK

in the principal Churches of Rome

PALM SUNDAY.

St. Peter's.

At 9 a. m., blessing and distribution of the Palms by the Cardinal Archpriest of the Basilica, followed by High Mass, at which the Passion is sung.

At 5 p. m. Solemn Vespers.

St. John Lateran.

At 9 a. m., the Palms are blessed, and distributed among the people by the Cardinal Archpriest. This is followed by High Mass and the singing of the Passion.

At 4 30 p. m., Solemn Vespers, without accompaniment of the organ. The Cardinal Penitentiary hears confessions, if required, seated in the Cathedra.

St. Mary Major.

At 9 a.m., blessing and distribution of the Palms, by His Eminence the Cardinal Archpriest of the Basilica, after which High Mass and Singing of the Passion.

At 4 30 p.m., Solemn Vespers.

San Silvestro in Capite.
(Church for English-speaking Catholics)

At 10 30 a. m., Solemn High Mass in the presence of the Blessed Sacrament, during which the Passion is sung. A choir of trained voices sings the part of the *Turba*. After Mass, a Cardinal carries the Blessed Sacrament in procession.

The Gesù.

At 9 30 a. m., blessing and distribution of the Palms, followed by Solemn High Mass and singing of the Passion.

The students of the German College assist at all the functions.

WEDNESDAY IN HOLY WEEK.
St. Peter's.

At 4 30 p.m., Office of Tenebrae. Lamentation

and Miserere, sung by the Choir of the Cappella Giulia.

St. John Lateran.

At 4 30 p. m. Office of Tenebrae and singing of Lamentations and Miserere.

St. Mary Major's.

At 9 a. m., Solemn High Mass and singing of the Passion.

The Station is held in the Basilica.

At 4 30 p. m., Office of Tenebrae and singing of the Miserere. His Eminence the Cardinal Penitentiary assists and hears confessions.

The Gesù.

At 4 30 p. m., Office of Tenebrae and singing of the Miserere.

San Silvestro in Capite.

At 4 p. m. Office of Tenebrae.

St. Apollinare.

At 4 p m. Office of Tenebrae and singing of the Miserere, by the students of the Roman Seminary.

MAUNDY THURSDAY.

St. Peter's.

At 7 15 a. m. Blessing of the Oils, and Office in Choir. High Mass, and procession to the Altar of Repose.

At 4 30 p. m. Office of Tenebrae, with Solemn Miserere. Washing of the Papal Altar, by the Cardinal Archpriest of the Basilica. — Exposition of the greater relics.

1st. The " Veil " of Veronica.

2nd. The Lance, which pierced our Lord's side.

3rd. A large piece of the True Cross.

The Church is open for the visit to the Altar of Repose till 9 30 p. m. It is the only time in the whole year that St. Peter's can be seen by night. This Basilica is the most frequented to-day. Visits should be made to the altars of repose of the different Churches.

St. John Lateran.

At 8 a. m., His Eminence the Cardinal Vicar of Rome blesses the Oils. Solemn High Mass with procession to the Altar of Repose.

At 4 30 p. m., Office of Tenebrae and Singing of the Lamentations and Miserere.

The table from which our Blessed Lord partook of the Last Supper remains exposed all day over the Blessed Sacrament Altar.

St. Mary Major.

At 9 a. m. High Mass and procession to the Altar of Repose.
At 4 30 p. m. Office of Tenebrae.

San Silvestro in Capite.

At 9 a. m. Solemn High Mass and procession to the Altar of Repose.
Stripping of the altars.
At 4 p. m. Office of Tenebrae and singing of the Miserere.

St. Apollinare.

At 10 30 a. m. Solemn High Mass and procession. After Mass the Cardinal Vicar performs the " lavanda dei piedi " or the washing of feet.
At 4 p. m. Office of Tenebrae and singing of Miserere.
To day it is customary to visit the altars of repose. The most noteworthy are:
S. Pietro Vaticano.
S. Giovanni Laterano.
S. Maria Maggiore.
Chiesa del Gesù.
S. Silvestro in Capite.
Chiesa del Coll. Amer. del Nord (Via Umiltà).
S. Sudario — Via del Sudario.
S. Luigi de' Francesi.

S. Antonino de' Portoghesi.
SS. Apostoli.
SS. Domenico e Sisto (Monte Magnanapoli).
S. Caterina della Rota.
Suore Oblate in Via Tor de' Specchi.
S. Andrea della Valle.
Santa Brigida (Piazza Farnese).
S. Maria sopra Minerva.
S. Ignazio.
Santa Maria in Aquiro — via in Aquiro.
S. Andrea della Valle — P. S' Andrea della Valle.
S. Agostino — Piazza S. Agostino.
S. Marcello — Piazza S. Marcello.

—)o(—

GOOD FRIDAY

St. Peter's.

At 8 a. m. Adoration of the Holy Cross. The Blessed Sacrament is removed from the altar of repose. Afterwards Mass of the Presanctified.

At 4 30. Office of Tenebrae and Singing of the Miserere.

St. John Lateran.

At 8 30 a. m. Sermon on the Passion of our Lord Jesus Christ. Mass of the Presanctified, and removal of the Blessed Sacrament from the altar of repose.

At 4 15 p. m. Office of Tenebrae at which the lamentations of Jeremias and the Miserere are sung.

(This Basilica is the most frequented to-day).

St. Mary Major.

At 9 a. m. The Canons chant Office, after which the Blessed Sacrament is removed from the Altar of Repose.

San Silvestro in Capite.

At 9 a m. Solemn Mass of the Presanctified and singing of the Passion.

At 1 p. m. The sermon of the Three Hours begins

At 4 p. m. Office of Tenebrae and singing of the miserere.

Santa Croce in Gerusalemme.

The station is held in this church to-day. The relics of the Passion are exhibited frequently during the course of the day. The Cardinal Vicar pontificates the Solemn Mass of the Presanctified.

The Passion is chanted before the Mass.

At one o'clock to day begins in several Churches the devotion of the "Three Hours" which consists of Sermons on the seven words of our Lord on the Cross; in the seven intervals into

which the sermon is divided some music is performed, generally the "*Stabat Mater.*" In The Gesù the sermon is in Italian; at San Silvestro in Capite it is in English: the Stabat Mater of Pergolese is sung with accompaniment of instruments. In S Marcello al Corso at 8 p.m. the devotion of the "Desolata" takes place followed by good music.

HOLY SATURDAY.

St. Peter's

At 7 30 a. m. — Blessing of the fire, and paschal candle.

Procession to the baptismal font in which the Water is blessed. Solemn High Mass, at which all the bells are rung.

St. John Lateran.

At 7 a.m. — Blessing of the fire and paschal Candle. Procession to the baptism front, in which the Water is blessed High Mass at which all the bells are rung.

At the Mass, His Eminence the Cardinal Vicar General of the Pope holds an ordination.

The function terminates about 1 30 p.m.

St. Mary Major.

At 8 30 a. m. — Blessing of the fire and paschal Candle, followed by the blessing of the font.

Chanting of the Prophecies. Solemn High Mass with music,

The Gesù.

Blessing of the fire and paschal candle. Chanting of the Litanies and Solemn High Mass.

San Silvestro in Capite.

At 10 a.m. — Blessing of the fire and paschal candle. Singing of the Litanies and Solemn High Mass.

EASTER SUNDAY.

St. Peter's.

At 9. a.m. — Pontifical High Mass, at an altar erected immediately under the Papal Altar. The "Cappella Giulia" executes the music.

At 4 30 p. m. — Service with procession, commonly called Service of the Maries.

St. Silvestro in Capite.

At 10 a.m. Solemn High Mass.

At 4 p.m. Sermon in English followed by Benediction of the Blessed Sacrament.

AN
EXPLANATION
OF THE
CEREMONIES
OBSERVED IN
THE OFFICE OF HOLY WEEK.

HOLY WEEK. The week before Easter was anciently called the Painful Week, or Week of Austerities, also the Week of Sorrows, the Days of the Cross or of Sufferings, but it is now generally distinguished by the name of *Holy Week*, on account of the merciful and great things wrought by God which we yearly commemorate in it. The fast of Lent was observed with even greater austerity during this week than in the preceding weeks. St. Epiphanius assures us, that in his time, in the fourth century, Christians who had least fervour and zeal only eat bread with a little salt, and drank water once a day at evening all Holy Week. The more devout, according to their strength, continued their fasts for two, three or four days, without eating at all; and watchings and meditations, especially all Easter-eve, were general practices. More abundant alms also accompanied the fasts: "many," says St. Chrysostom, "now double their alms, in order to honour so holy a time;" they felt that the nearer they approached the solemn commemorations of Christ's sufferings and Resurrection, mysteries by which all blessings have been conferred on men, the more they were constrained to show

all manner of acts of mercy and love to their brethren. Emperors and princes at this time "often set prisoners at liberty, that they might imitate, as far as in them lay, the example of our Lord, who at this time delivered us from the bonds of our sins, and made us capable of enjoying unappreciable blessings. For we ought as much as possible to imitate His loving kindness."* The imperial laws of Theodosius forbade all judicial acts or legal processes during this and the following week. Servants were exempted from bodily labour at this time, that they might have opportunities of attending to the worship of God and the affairs of their souls. In the Apostolical Constitutions the law is mentioned in the following words: "In the Great Week and the week following, let servants rest from their labour, because the one is the time of our Lord's Passion, and the other of His Resurrection, and servants have need to be instructed now in the knowledge of these mysteries." In a word, believing that the great work of Redemption more nearly concerned them than any worldly business, Christians took care, without listening to excuses, to give up this holy time to devout meditations on the Cross and Passion of our Lord, and to firm purposes of amendment of life. St. Bernard, in a sermon delivered at the beginning of Holy Week, excites his religious in the following words: "Be attentive with all possible watchfulness, and with all the application of your souls, that the memory of these great mysteries may not pass you in vain. God is going to pour forth His most abundant blessings; let, then, your hearts be penetrated with devotion. Restrain your senses under strict discipline, cleanse your con-

---

* St. John Chrysostom, Hom. in Ps.

science, purify and sanctify your affections, and prepare your souls to receive the admirable gifts which now will be plentifully conferred on those who shall be disposed to receive them."*

PALM SUNDAY. On this day the Church honours the triumphant entry of our Divine Redeemer into Jerusalem four days before His Crucifixion. He was pleased, before the humiliation of His Passion, to be acknowledged and received as the Messias, the Saviour of the world and King of souls, and on the very day, too, on which by the appointment of the law (Exodus XII. 3) the lamb was to be conducted into the town to be sacrificed for the Passover. As an emblem of the first fruits of His conquests of souls, He would make a public entry into Jerusalem, which was a kind of triumph, but such a one as suited the spirit of humility and contempt of the world which He came to establish in the hearts of men. Crowds met Him in the suburbs of the city, consisting chiefly of the poorer classes and of innocent children, and then walking before Him they strewed the way which He was to pass with green boughs and repeated the praises of Christ, proclaiming Him the long-expected Messias, the Saviour of the people. In imitation of these devout Jews, this day we carry in our hands palm branches or other green boughs, such as the climate and season afford. These are blessed, because the Church, as we see in the most ancient rituals, makes use of nothing in its ceremonies which has not been first blessed. Receiving them from the priest the Faithful kiss the palms out of respect, and hold them in their hands during the procession, and whilst the history of the Passion and Last Gospel are read. We hold them up as emblems of the share we take in the

---

* Serm. de Passione Domini.

triumphal reception of Christ and in protestation of our joy, love and pain; and also, as the Church teaches by the prayers said over them, as symbols of the honours awaiting us for victories over all our spiritual enemies.

TENEBRAE. On Wednesday, Thursday and Friday evenings is sung the Office now called *Tenebrae*. So long as Christians spent the greatest part of the nights of Holy Week, especially of the four last, in watchings in the churches, this office was said at *midnight*, as was the universal practice in the twelfth century. The name of *Tenebrae*, however, is derived from the ceremony of gradually extinguishing the lights, expressive of the deepest mourning, and in memory of that darkness which covered the whole of the earth at our Lord's Crucifixion. For these three days the Church omits many of those psalms and hymns of jubilation generally recited by her ministers; and only those passages from holy writers and the fathers are read, which give truest utterance to her sighs and lamentations at the death of her Lord.

On the left or epistle side of the altar is placed a triangular candlestick, in which are set fifteen lights, seven on each side and one on the top. At the end of each of the fourteen psalms recited in Matins and Lauds a candle is extinguished and, while the *Benedictus*, or Canticle of Zachary, is being sung, the lights on the altar also are put out. The fifteenth candle, a white one, placed on the top, is afterwards taken down, and concealed for a time, by the side of the altar, until the Fiftieth Psalm, the *Miserere*, and the accompanying prayer are recited, when the light is once more restored to its place. In the works of commentators on the ritual, in the ninth and eleventh centuries, we find various explanations of the meaning of this cere-

mony. By some these lights are understood to represent the Apostles and Evangelists, or other followers of Jesus Christ; and the desolation and abandonment in which our Redeemer is left, is pointed out by the extinction of these lights. Others have considered that the whole refers to Christ only, and the quenching of these lights to the mournful death of Him who is the life and light of the world. All agree that the white candle on the top evidently refers to our Saviour, for it is not extinguished, but hidden only for a time, to signify that He did not long remain a tenant of the tomb, but soon raised His body to life again.

On Wednesday the Jews in their great council agreed on their design to take away the life of Christ by charging Him with crimes before Pilate, the Roman governor. Hence the commencement of the Passion is dated from this day; and hence Wednesday, as well as Friday, was formerly kept as a fast-day.

MAUNDY THURSDAY. The Church on this day commemorates the Last supper of our Divine Redeemer, the establishment of the holy Eucharist, and the washing of the feet of the Apostles. The solemn consecration of the Holy Oils employed in the administration of the sacraments of Baptism, Extreme Unction, etc., also takes place on this day. The rest of the Office of the Church on it refers to the Passion.

In a week in which so many and such affecting instances of the sufferings of Christ, endured for sinful man, are celebrated, it would be quite impossible to give to that mystery of love, the Blessed Sacrament, instituted on this day, the peculiar and continued thanksgiving which it so eminently deserves; hence, the feast of *Corpus Christi*, or of the body of Christ, is observed at a later period,

and among the greatest of the solemnities of religion. The white colour of the vestments, the ornaments of the altar, the ringing of bells at the *Gloria in Excelsis*, or hymn of praise, at the beginning of the Mass, show, however, that the Church cannot refrain from some expression of her joy and gratitude on the day itself, whereon our Lord was pleased to work so great a wonder of his affection. But in the High Mass, the *pax*, or peace, is not given as usual, in detestation of the treacherous kiss of peace, by which Judas on this day betrayed his Divine Master into the hands of His enemies.

After Mass, the Blessed Eucharist is removed from the tabernacle on the altar, and carried in solemn procession to some other altar, (often called erroneously the Sepulchre), which, according to very ancient custom, is adorned with lights, flowers and tapestry. Here it remains until the time of Mass on Friday, and here the Faithful resort during the rest of the day and night, pouring out their souls in adoration, condolence, and contrition. The reason of removing the Blessed Sacrament is to prevent all interruption in devotion to the Passion at the chief altar of the church, which the rubrics require to be left without any ornament whatever. Hence, after Vespers (said directly after Mass) the priest with his attendants takes the linen cloths from the altar while the choir sings the Antiphon, *Diviserunt:* 'They have divided my garments,' and the Psalm, *Deus, Deus meus:* 'O God, my God, why,' etc. The state of desolation in which the sacred places of religion are now left forcibly remind us of the grief and mourning of the Church and the abandonment in which Christ passed the night before and the day of his Passion.

Christ, at his Last Supper, not only washed the

feet of his apostles but gave all his disciples a command to do the same, that is, readily to serve each other in exercising all actions of charity and humility, of which he had set them the example. Such offices performed in the true spirit of those virtues have an incredible efficacy in improving the heart in the strongest sentiments of those virtues, and the occasions of them have been ardently embraced by the saints. In imitation of our blessed Redeemer, Christians, Popes, kings, bishops, superiors of religious houses and others, wash the feet of some poor persons or of their colleagues and fellows on this day, which ceremony is called the *Mandate*, from the first word of the first anthem of it: *Mandatum novum do vobis*, etc. Hence this day is usually called in English, *Maundy* or *Mandy Thursday*. The Greeks styled it the *Holy and Great Fifth Day of the Week of the Passion;* which name is given it by John Moschus, and St. Chrysostom.

GOOD FRIDAY. On this day the precious death of the Divine Redeemer and Spouse of our souls, engrosses all the attention and devotion of the Faithful. The Church in her whole Office expresses the deepest mourning and compunction. The altars are bare, except at the priest's Communion, when the ornaments are black, and the crucifix is covered with a black veil until the prostration: after which it is left uncovered. No Mass is said nor sacrifice offered; only the Holy Sacrament, which was reserved the day before, is received in one kind only by the priest, who recites the Lord's Prayer, and a small part of the prayers of the Mass, without any consecration of the Eucharist; for none is performed on this day, according to the ancient discipline of both the Latin and Greek Churches. No others receive the Holy Communion,

except the priest who celebrates the Divine Office, and the sick in moral danger of death, to whom it is administered by way of Viaticum.

The mourning Office after the canonical hours, is opened by morning versicles from the prophets, the divine promises of mercy through Christ, and a prayer to obtain that mercy. Then is read for an epistle the divine mandate for the sacrifice of the paschal lamb in the Mosaic law, the most noble figure of the bloody sacrifice of Christ on the cross. After this, the history of Christ's Passion from the Gospel of St. John is sung.

The Church, on this day, puts up her prayers for all states and conditions of men, expressly naming heathens and Jews. In private prayers we pray for all by name, without exception. The Church also in her public suffrages, prays for the conversion and salvation of infidels of every denomination, but in order to express her abhorrence of wilful apostates, and to distinguish them from children who live within her pale and enjoy the advantages of her communion, she forbids her ministers publicly to name such at Mass, or at her altar. She makes an exception to this discipline on Good Friday, because on this day Christ died for all men. It is, therefore, reasonable on it to beg publicly by name, and in a more explicit manner, that all reap the fruit of His Death, for which she presents the names of all at His altar, as Alcuin observes. No genuflexion is made before the prayer which is offered for the Jews, as is prescribed for the rest, because the Jews mocked Christ by bending their knees to him. These prayers for all orders and conditions occur in the sacramentary of St. Gregory the Great, and are mentioned by St. Cœlestine I.

On this occasion also takes place what is called the *Exposition*, sometimes *the Adoration, of the Cross*,

a very ancient ceremony, and one which has been much misunderstood and misrepresented by many hostile to our faith. When the priest holds up the crucifix or image of Jesus Christ dying for us on the Cross, and when priest and people kneel down and kiss the representation of His sacred wounds, every Catholic knows and believes that this is done only for the purpose of impressing on the soul, in a more lively and lasting manner the boundless mercies and unutterable sufferings of our Redeemer. As this book, however, may fall into the hands of some who are not members of our Church, and who candidly seek the knowledge of our Faith and ritual, it may be well to write at a little greater length on this particular practice.

And first, we must explain the word *adoration* which is used in the Missal to express this ceremony. In its original meaning the word signifies that mark of respect which is shown to another *by the application of the hand to the mouth* (from the Latin words *ad*, to, and *os*, mouth); it is also extended to denote veneration, salutation and even prostration. In the last sense it is recorded in the Bible that Abraham *adored* the sons of Heth and the angels; that Jacob adored Esau; that Joseph was adored by his brethren; that Moses adored Jethro; that Balaam adored the angel; that Saul adored Samuel; that Miphiboseth and Joab adored David; that Judith adored Holofernes. In all, or at least, in most of these examples, the same Hebrew and Greek words are employed as are used to express Divine worship. From our poverty of language, from the scantiness of our external marks of honour and respect, we are, from necessity, compelled to apply to our fellow-creatures, who may be superior to us in rank or power, the same terms, such as Sovereign Lord, Majesty, Grace,

Honour, Excellence, etc., and to employ towards them the same gestures, such as kneeling, bowing, prostration, etc., as we do to the Supreme Ruler of the universe. *The meaning, then, must be ascertained by the nature of the objects and the intention of the person who employs them,* and this will introduce the grand distinction between Divine homage and civil worship. For example, when you style a magistrate *Worshipful,* or when the bridegroom, in the marriage ceremony of the Church of England, thus addresses the bride, 'With my body I thee *worship,*' no sensible person can be scandalised, or imagine that they are intended to be worshipped as divinities. To apply this reasoning to the crucifix:— When a Catholic kneels before it, he is not taught that an inherent power or divinity exists in the wood or metal; he has learnt from his childhood that he must place no confidence in it; that he can expect nothing from it; that it can neither see, nor hear, nor help him. The Catholic cries aloud, 'Cursed is he that commits idolatry, that prays to relics or images, or worships them for God.' He professes the only true Christ, the only true God; and he therefore repels with contempt the truly pagan and antiChristian imputation of idolatry, for showing decent respect to the Cross of his Redeemer. And why should not the representation of our best and dearest friend, of our Sovereign Lord and future Judge— why should not the sign of the Son of Man challenge that mark of respect and regard which is paid by a subject to the effigy of his prince, or by an affectionate child to the portrait of his deceased parent? If it be thought so great a crime to insult the statue of an earthly monarch, how can it be thought injurious to the Divine honour, to show exterior respect to the representation of the King

of kings and the Lord of lords? If no one is shocked at seeing witnesses in a court of justice kissing the paper and ink, or the leather of the book, in which the word of God is written; if no one thinks it is a scandalous profanation in the peers of the realm to bow to the vacant throne, or for persons at sea to pay salutation and homage to her Majesty's flag, or for Knights of the Garter to wear *the image*, of the holy martyr and Christian knight, St. George, as it is called in the form of installation; if no one charges the members of the Established Church with idolatry for kneeling before the sacramental elements, which they believe to be but mere symbols of Christ; if the Jews were not reproached for showing respect to the Ark, to the Tables of the Law, to Aaron's rod, to the holy vessels, and to the Temple; if the woman mentioned in the 9th chapter of St. Matthew is not rebuked for idolatry and superstition, for reverently touching the hem of Christ's garment, but, on the contrary, is so highly praised and rewarded for her faith, why should Catholics be vilified for venerating the Cross, the sceptre of the Great King? Our respect is referred to and terminates in the original whom it represents; we wish to testify, by external action, the most natural and pathetic of all languages, our interior love and gratitude to Him, who was pleased to die upon it. He chose it as the instrument of our redemption, as the altar of His sacrifice, as the monument of His love, and the trophy of His victory. It is by excellence His sign; and, on the great accounting day, it shall appear in the heavens, brilliant with light, when the sun and moon shall be involved in darkness.

Our respect for the Cross is a profession of our faith and confidence in a crucified Redeemer. Reason, religion and the impulse of a feeling mind will

lead us forward to give him this demonstration of our grateful recollection. The practice of kissing the Cross on this day is immemorial, as is well known to every ecclesiastical antiquarian. We trace it in the pure ages of Christianity, in the very infancy of the Church. The most powerful monarchs, and kings, and princes of Christendom; the most enlightened scholars; some of the greatest and best men scrupled not to pay this tribute of respect to the instrument of Redemption; they gloried with St. Paul in the Cross of our Lord Jesus Christ. It was reserved for modern times to boast of being its enemies.

As to the argument, that the custom of kissing the Cross may be abused, and should, therefore, be laid aside, the answer is very simple; *for by proving too much, it proves nothing.* If every thing is to be laid aside because it is liable to abuse, we must dispense with every Divine and human institution. Society, laws, government, marriage, every thing that is most sacred, the Bible, the Sacraments, the name of God, are perpetually abused by man. What is more impiously abused and insulted than the Divine patience and mercy? Yet, would any man who pretends to the gift of common sense insist that the means and dispensations of Grace should be abolished, or rather that the abuses should be remedied? The distinction between religious respect and divine worship is as distant as the east is from the west, as wide as the earth is from the heavens: and, as no *reasonable* Christian can confound them, no danger can result from the practice, which needs but to be explained, and it is abundantly vindicated.

HOLY SATURDAY. In many parts of the Service of this day, the word *night* is used, clearly showing that some part of the Office and Mass were formerly

said in the night, in order that the Faithful might be found in the church, watching at the very moment of the anniversary of Christ's rising from the dead and joining with the angels and choirs of heaven, at that time, in alleluias and hymns of triumph. The Service usually commenced at three o'clock in the afternoon, by blessing the fire and then the Paschal Candle. Afterwards the ancient prophecies were read for the instruction of those about to receive the holy Sacrament of Baptism, the font was blessed, and Baptism was solemnly administered. When Matins had been said, then the Mass of the Resurrection was celebrated.

The Church has been accustomed to bless most things that the Faithful make use of in common life, hence in ancient rituals we find blessings for a new house, a new ship, first fruits, etc. On this day, all lights and fires being put out, fire is struck anew from a flint, and blessed. This new fire represents Christ rising to kindle in our hearts a new spiritual fire of His love; the old profane fire of our earthly passions being first extinguished in us by His victory over sin. It likewise serves symbolically to put us in mind of our obligation of walking in the newness of a spiritual heavenly life, being now risen with Christ by His Grace.

The *blessing of the Paschal Candle* is performed by the deacon, who in this august ceremony, as the herald of heaven, announces to the Church the glorious Resurrection of Christ, His unutterable triumph in this mystery, the wonderful display of His infinite mercy and goodness, and the happiness of man restored by the accomplishment or seal of the great work of his Redemption. The Paschal Candle and its solemn blessing are mentioned in the most ancient Sacramentary or Missal of Pope Gelasius; and in the fourth council of Toledo,

of 62 bishops, in which St. Isidore of Seville presided.

The Paschal Candle is an illustrious emblem of Christ rising from the dead, the light of the world, and is a sign which announces to us the joy and glory of His Resurrection. The five grains of frankincense fixed in it symbolically represent His Five precious Wounds, and the embalming of His body at His burial, and again in the grave, by the devout persons who brought spices to His monument. This great candle anciently gave light during the watching in the Church on Easter-eve in the night.

The custom of different churches varies as to the time when this candle is lighted: the most usual practice is, that it burns at High Mass and Vespers every day during Easter-week and every Sunday and Holiday to Ascension-day, on which it is taken out of the church immediately after the Gospel is sung at High Mass.

The triple candle arising from one stock, signifies the Trinity of Persons in one God, or the light of the Triune God shining to the world through Christ. This only burns during the Office of Holy Saturday morning, after which it is taken away, and no more made use of, not even on Easter-day, or during the Octave.

In all parish Churches the Baptismal font is blessed; after which Baptism is solemnly administered, if any are presented to receive that Sacrament, according to the ancient discipline on Easter and Whitsun-eve.

The Celebrant with the Deacon and Subdeacon lies prostrate at the foot of the altar, whilst the litany is sung to implore the Divine mercy for the pardon of sin and all Divine graces, through the sacred mysteries of Christ's Death and Resurrection. The prophecies and litany supply the introit of the Mass, which is therefore omitted.

The Solemn Mass of Christ's Resurrection is said after the Litany towards noon, which was still sung at the midnight following in the time of St. Thomas Aquinas. By repeated alleluias we are invited to spiritual joy and praise. *Hallelu-jah* is a compound Hebrew word, which signifies, *Praise ye the Lord*, a usual pious acclamation of spiritual joy and praise.

In the Mass incense is used at the Gospel, to represent the perfumes carried by the holy women to our Saviour's monument: no lights are borne, as at other times, because neither they nor the Apostles as yet believed in His Resurrection: and for the same reason the Creed is not said. The Offertory, the Kiss of Peace, and the Communion, are also omitted, because the Faithful did not receive the Blessed Eucharist.

Palm Sunday

After the sprinkling of holy water the palms are blessed as follows.

The Choir sings:

HOSANNA Filio David: benedictus qui venit in nomine Domini. O Rex Israel: Hosanna in excelsis.

HOSANNA to the Son of David: blessed is he that comes in the name of the Lord. O King of Israel: Hosanna in the highest.

Then the Priest says:

Dominus vobiscum.
R. Et cum spiritu tuo.
Oremus.

The Lord be with you.
R. And with thy spirit.
Let us pray.

DEUS, quem diligere et amare justitia est; ineffabilis gratiæ tuæ in nobis dona multiplica: et qui fecisti nos in morte Filii tui sperare quæ credimus: fac nos eodem resurgente pervenire quo tendimus. Qui tecum vivit et regnat, etc.

O GOD, whom to esteem and love is justice; increase in us the gifts of thy unspeakable grace; and as in the death of thy Son thou madest us hope for what we believe; so by his resurrection make us arrive at the place whither we are going. Who liveth, etc.

The Subdeacon then sings the following Lesson.

Lectio Libri Exodi.
(cap. xv. 27)
IN diebus illis, venerunt filii Israel in

Lesson from the Book of Exodus. *(ch.* xv. 27.)
IN those days the children of Israel came

Elim, ubi erant duodecim fontes aquarum, et septuaginta palmæ; et castrametati sunt juxta aquas. Profectique sunt de Elim, et venit omnis multitudo filiorum Israel in desertum Sin, quod est inter Elim et Sinai, quinto decimo die mensis secundi, postquam egressi sunt de terra Egypti. Et murmuravit omnis congregatio filiorum Israel contra Moysen et Aaron in solitudine. Dixeruntque filii Israel ad eos: Utinam mortui essemus per manum Domini in terra Egypti, quando sedebamus super ollas carnium et comedebamus panem in saturitate: Cur eduxistis nos in desertum istud, ut occideretis omnem multidinem fame? Dixit autem Dominus ad Moysen: Ecce, ego pluam vobis panes de cœlo: egrediatur populus, et colligat quæ sufficiunt per singulos dies, ut tentem eum utrum ambulet in lege mea, an non. Die autem sexto parent quod

into Elim, where there were twelve fountains of water and seventy palm-trees: and they encamped by the waters. And they set forward from Elim, and all the multitude of the children of Israel came into the desert of Sin, which is between Elim and Sinai, the fifteenth day of the second month, after they came out of the land of Egypt. And all the congregation of the children of Israel murmured against Moses and Aaron in the wilderness. And the children of Israel said to them: Would to God we had died by the hand of the Lord in the land of Egypt, when we sat over the flesh pots and ate bread to the full. Why have you brought us into this desert, that you might destroy all the multitude with famine? And the Lord said to Moses: Behold, I will rain bread from heaven for you: let the people go forth, and gather what is sufficient

inferant: et sit duplum quam colligere solebant per singulos dies. Dixeruntque Moyses et Aaron ad omnes filios Israel: Vespere scietis quod Dominus eduxerit vos de terra Ægypti: et mane videbitis gloriam Domini.

for every day, that I may prove them whether they will walk in my law or no. But the sixth day let them provide for to bring in: and let it be double to what they were wont to gather every day. And Moses and Aaron said to the children of Israel. In the evenimg you shall know that the Lord hath brought you forth out of the land of Egypt: and in the morning you shall see the glory of the Lord

R. Collegerunt pontifices et pharisæi consilium, et dixerunt: Quid facimus? quia hic homo multa signa facit. Si dimittimus eum sic, omnes credent in eum: * Et venient Romani, et tollent nostrum locum et gentem. V. Unus autem ex illis, Caiphas nomine, cum esset Pontifex anni illius prophetavit, dicens: Expedit vobis ut unus moriatur homo pro populo, et non tota gens pereat. Ab illo ergo die cogitaverunt interficere eum, dicentes: * Et venient, etc.

R. The chief priests and the Pharisees assembled a council, and said: What are we doing? for this man doth many miracles. If we let him go so, all will believe in him: * And the Romans will come, and destroy our place and nation. V. But one of them called Caiphas being the high-priest of that year, prophesied, saying: It is expedient for you that one man die for the people, and not the whole nation perish. From that day, therefore, they designed to kill him, saying: * And the Romans, etc.

vel,

R. In monte Oliveti, oravit ad Patrem: Pater, si fieri potest transeat a me calix iste. *Spiritus quidem promptus est, caro autem infirma: fiat voluntas tua. ℣. Vigilate, et orate, ut non intretis in tentationem. * Spiritus, etc.

or,

R. On Mount Olivet he prayed to his Father: Father, if it may be, let this cup pass from me. * The spirit indeed is willing, but the flesh is weak: thy will be done. V. Watch and pray, that ye enter not into temptation. * The spirit, etc.

Then the Deacon sings the following Gospel, with the usual ceremonies before and after.

Sequentia Sancti Evangelii secundum Mattheum. (*cap.* 21, v. 1.)

Continuation of the Holy Gospel according to St. Matthew (*ch.* 21 v. 1).

IN illo tempore: cum appropinquasset Jesus Jerosolymis, et venisset Bethphage ad montem Oliveti : tunc misit duos discipulos suos, dicens eis: Ite in castellum, quod contra vos est, et statim invenietis asinam alligatam, et pullum cum ea: solvite, et adducite mihi: et si quis vobis aliquid dixerit, dicite, quia Dominus his opus habet; et confestim dimittet eos. Hoc autem totum

AT that time: when Jesus drew nigh to Jerusalem, and was come to Bethphage, unto Mount Olivet, he sent two disciples, saying to them: Go ye into the village that is over against you, and immediately you shall find an ass tied, and a colt with her: loose them and bring them to me: and if any man shall say any thing to you, say ye, that the Lord hath need of them: and forthwith he will

factum est, ut adimpleretur quod dictum est per prophetam, dicentem: *Dicite filiæ Sion: Ecce Rex tuus venit tibi mansuetus, sedens super asinam, et pullum filium subjugalis.* Euntes autem discipuli fecerunt sicut præcepit illis Jesus. Et adduxerunt asinam et pullum: et imposuerunt super eos vestimenta sua, et eum desuper sedere fecerunt. Plurima autem turba straverunt vestimenta sua in via: alii autem cædebant ramos de arboribus, et sternebant in via: turbæ autem quæ præcedebant et quæ sequebantur clamabant, dicentes: Hosanna Filio David; benedictus qui venit in nomine Domini. saying: *Hosanna to the Son of David: Blessed is he that cometh in the name of the Lord.*

let them go. Now all this was done that the word might be fulfilled which was spoken by the prophet, saying: *Tell ye the daughter of Sion: Behold thy King cometh to thee meek and sitting upon an ass, and a colt, the foal of her that is used to the yoke.* And the disciples going did as Jesus commanded them. And they brought the ass and the colt; and laid their garments upon them, and made him sit thereon. And a very great multitude spread their garments in the way; and others cut down boughs from the trees, and strewed them in the way; and the multitude that went before and that followed, cried,

Dominus vobiscum. The Lord be with you.
R. Et cum spiritu tuo. R. And with thy spirit.

Then the palms are blessed by the Priest standing at the Epistle corner, saying:

Oremus. Let us pray.

AUGE fidem in te sperantium, Deus, et supplicum preces cle-

INCREASE, O God, the faith of them that hope in thee, and mer-

menter exaudi: veniat super nos multiplex misericordia tua; bene✠dicantur et hi palmites palmarum seu olivarum et sicut in figura ecclesiæ multiplicasti Noe egredientem de arca et Moysen exeuntem de Ægypto cum filiis Israel, ita nos portantes palmas et ramos olivarum, bonis actibus occurramus obviam Christo; et per ipsum in gaudium introeamus æternum. Qui tecum vivit et regnat in unitate Spiritus Sancti Deus, per omnia sæcula sæculorum.

R. Amen.
V. Dominus vobiscum.
R. Et cum spiritu tuo.
V. Sursum corda.
R. Habemus ad Dominum.
V. Gratias agamus Domino Deo nostro.
R. Dignum et justum est.

VERE dignum et justum est, æquum et salutare nos tibi semper et ubique gratias

cifully hear the prayers of thy supplicants: let thy manifold mercy come upon us, and let these branches of palm-trees or olive-trees be blessed; and as in a figure of the church thou didst multiply Noah going out of the ark, and Moses going out of Egypt with the children of Israel, so let us, carrying palms and boughs of olive-trees, go and meet Christ with good works, and enter by him into eternal joy. Who with Thee and the Holy Ghost liveth and reigneth.

R. Amen.
V. The Lord be with you.
R. And with thy spirit.
V. Lift up your hearts.
R. We have lifted them up to the Lord.
V. Let us give thanks to the Lord our God.
R. It is fitting and just.

IT is truly fitting and just, right and saving, always and every where to give thee thanks, O

agere, Domine sancte, Pater omnipotens, æterne Deus: qui gloriaris in concilio sanctorum tuorum. Tibi enim serviunt creaturæ tuæ, quia te solum auctorem et Deum cognoscunt. Et omnis factura tua te collaudat, et benedicunt te sancti tui: quia illud magnum Unigeniti tui nomen coram regibus et potestatibus hujus sæculi, libera voce confitentur. Cui assistunt angeli et archangeli, throni et dominationes, cumque omni militia cœlestis exercitus, hymnum gloriæ tuæ concinunt, sine fine dicentes:

holy Lord, Almighty Father, eternal God: who art glorious in the assembly of thy saints. For thy creatures serve thee, because they acknowledge thee for their only Creator and God. All that thou hast made praise thee, and thy saints bless thee; because they confess with freedom, before the kings and powers of this world, the great name of thy only-begotten Son. The angels and archangels, the thrones and dominions, stand before thee, and with all the troops of the heavenly army sing the hymn of thy glory, saying without end:

The Choir sings,

Sanctus, sanctus, sanctus, Dominus Deus Sabaoth. Pleni sunt cœli et terra gloria tua. Hosanna in excelsis. Benedictus qui venit in nomine Domini: Hosanna in excelsis.

Holy, holy, holy, is the Lord God of hosts. The heavens and the earth are full of thy glory. Hosanna in the highest. Blessed is he that comes in the name of the Lord. Hosanna in the highest.

Then the priest says:

Dominus vobiscum.
R. Et cum spiritu tuo.
Oremus.

PEtimus Domine sancte, Pater omnipotens, æterne Deus; ut hanc creaturam olivæ, quam ex ligni materia prodire jussisti, quamque columba rediens ad arcam proprio pertulit ore, bene ✠ dicere et sancti ✠ ficare digneris: ut quicumque ex ea receperint, accipiant sibi protectionem animæ et corporis: fiatque, Domine, nostræ salutis remedium, tuæ gratiæ sacramentum. Per Dominum, etc. R. Amen.

Oremus.

DEUS, qui dispersa congregas et congregata conservas: qui populis obviam Jesu ramos portantibus benedixisti: bene ✠ dic etiam hos ramos palmæ et olivæ, quos tui famuli ad honorem nominis tui fideliter suscipiunt:

The Lord be with you.
R. And with thy spirit.
Let us pray.

WE beseech thee, O holy Lord, Almighty Father, eternal God, that thou wouldst be pleased to bless and sanctify this creature of the olive tree, which thou madest to shoot out of the substance of the wood, and which the dove returning to the ark brought in its bill; that whoever receives it may find protection of soul and body; and that it may prove, O Lord, the remedy of our salvation, and a sacred sign of thy grace. Through etc. R. Amen

Let us pray.

O GOD, who gatherest what is dispersed, and preservest what is gathered; who didst bless the people that carried boughs to meet Jesus: bless also these branches of the palm-tree and olive-tree, which thy servants take

ut in quemcumque locum introducti fuerint, tuam benedictionem habitatores loci illius consequantur: et omni adversitate effugata, dextera tua protegat quos redemit Jesus Christus, Filius tuus, Dominus noster. Qui tecum vivit et regnat etc.

Oremus.

DEUS, qui miro dispositionis ordine, ex rebus etiam insensibilibus dispensationem nostræ salutis ostendere voluisti: da quæsumus; ut devota tuorum corda fidelium salubriter intelligant, quid mystice designent in facto quod hodie cœlesti lumine efflata Redemptori obviam procedens, palmarum atque olivarum ramos vestigiis ejus turba substravit. Palmarum igitur rami de mortis principe triumphos expectant: surculi vero olivarum spiritualem unctionem advenisse quodam modo clamant.

with faith for the honour of thy name: that into whatever place they shall be brought, the inhabitants of that place may obtain thy benediction; and thy right hand preserve from all adversity, and protect those that have been redeemed by our Lord Jesus Christ thy Son, Who liveth. etc.

Let us pray.

O GOD, who by the wonderful order of thy providence wouldst even in insensible things show us the manner of our salvation; grant we beseech thee, that the devout hearts of the faithful may savingly understand the mystical meaning of that ceremony, when the multitude, by direction from heaven, going this day to meet our Redeemer, strewed under his feet palms and olive branches. The palms represent his triumph over the prince of death, and the olive branches proclaim in some manner the

Intellexit enim jam tunc illa hominum beata multitudo præfigurari: quia Redemptor noster humanis condolens miseriis, pro totius mundi vita cum mortis principe esset pugnaturus ac moriendo triumphaturus. Et ideo talia obsequens administravit, quæ in illo et triumphos victoriæ et misericordiæ pinguedinem declararent. Quod nos quoque plena fide, et factum et significatum retinentes, te, Domine sancte Pater omnipotens, æterne Deus, per eundem Dominum nostrum Iesum Christum suppliciter exoramus; ut in ipso atque per ipsum cujus nos membra fieri voluisti, de mortis imperio victoriam reportantes, ipsius gloriosæ resurrectionis participes esse mereamur. Qui tecum vivit et regnat, etc.

coming of a spiritual unction. For that pious multitude knew by them was signified, that our Redeemer compassionating the misery of mankind, was to fight for the life of the whole world with the prince of death, and to triumph over him by his own death. And therefore in that action they made use of such things as might declare, both the triumph of this victory and the riches of his mercy. We also with a firm faith, retaining both the ceremony and its signification, humbly beseech thee, O holy Lord, Almighty Father, eternal God, through the same Lord Jesus Christ that we whom thou hast made his members, gaining by him and in him a victory over the empire of death, may deserve to be partakers of his glorious resurrection. Who liveth.

Oremus.

DEUS, qui per olivæ ramum pacem terris columbam nuntiare jus-

Let us pray.

O GOD, who by an olive branch, didst command the dove to

sisti: præsta, quæsumus, ut hos olivæ, cæterarumque arborum ramos cœlesti bene ✠ dictione sanctifices: ut cuncto populo tuo proficiant ad salutem. Per Christum Dominum nostrum. R. Amen.

Oremus.

BENE✠dic, quæsumus Domine, hos palmarum, seu olivarum ramos; et præsta, ut quod populus tuus, in tui venerationem hodierna die corporaliter agit, hoc spiritualiter summa devotione perficiat, de hoste victoriam reportante, et opus misericordiæ summopere diligendo. Per Dominum nostrum, etc.

proclaim peace to the world; grant us, we beseech thee, the grace to sanctify by thy heavenly benediction those branches of the olive and other trees; that they may be serviceable to all thy people for their salvation. Through etc. R. Amen.

Let us pray.

BLESS, O Lord, we beseech thee, these branches of the palm or olive tree; and grant that what thy people this day act corporally for thy honour, they may perform the same spiritually with the greatest devotion, by gaining a victory over their enemy, and by ardently loving works of mercy. Through etc.

Here the Priest spinkles the palms thrice with holy water, saying the antiphon Asperges me *and fumes them thrice with incense. Then he says:*

Dominus vobiscum.
R. Et cum spiritu tuo.

The Lord be with you.
R. And with thy spirit.

Oremus.

DEUS, qui Filium tuum Jesum Christum Dominum nostrum, pro salute nostra in hunc

Let us pray.

O GOD, who for our salvation didst send into this world thy Son Jesus Christ our Lord,

mundum missisti, ut se humiliaret ad nos, et nos revocaret ad te: cui etiam, dum Jerusalem veniret, ut adimpleret Scripturas, credentium populorun turba, fidelissima devotione vestimenta sua cum ramis palmarum in via sternebant; præsta quæsumus, ut illi fidei viam præparemus, de qua remoto lapide offensionis, et petra scandali, floreant apud te opere nostro justitiæ ramis; ut ejus vestigia sequi mereamur. Qui tecum vivit et regnat, etc.

that he might humble himself to us, and call us back to thee: for whom also, as he was coming to Jerusalem to fulfil the scriptures, a multitude of faithful people, with a zealous devotion, spread their garments together with palm-branches, in the way: grant, we beseech thee, that we may prepare him the way of faith, out of which the stone of offence and rock of scandal being removed, our actions may flourish with branches of justice, so that we may be able to follow his steps. Who, etc.

The palms, when blessed, are distributed by the priest, first to the clergy, and then to the laity, all kneeling and kissing the palm, and also his hand. During the distribution the following anthems are sung:

Ant. Pueri Hebræorum, portantes ramos olivarum, obviaverunt Domino, clamantes et dicentes: Hosanna in excelsis.

Ant. Pueri Hebræorum vestimenta prosternebant in via, et cla-

Ant. The Hebrew children, carrying olive-branches, met our Lord, crying out, and saying: Hosanna in the highest.

Ant. The Hebrew children spread their garments in the way, and cried out, saying:

mabant, dicentes; Hosanna Filio David: benedictus qui venit in nomine Domini.

Hosanna to the Son of David: blessed is he that cometh in the name of the Lord.

Then the priest says.

Dominus vobiscum.
R. Et cum spiritu tuo.

The Lord be with you.
R. And with thy spirit.

Oremus.

OMnipotens sempiterne Deus, qui Dominum nostrum Jesum Christum super pullum asinæ sedere fecisti, et turbas populorum vestimenta, vel ramos arborum in via sternere, et Hosanna decantare in laudem ipsius docuisti: da quaesumus, ut illorum innocentiam imitari possimus, et eorum meritum consequi mereamur. Per eundem Christum Dominum nostrum.
R. Amen.

Let us pray.

Almighty and everlasting God, who wouldst have our Lord Jesus Christ ride on the colt of an ass, and didst inspire the crowds of people to spread their garments or branches of the trees in the way, and to sing Hosanna in his praise: grant, we beseech thee, that we may imitate their innocence, and deserve to partake of their merit. Through the same Christ our Lord.
R. Amen.

Next follows the procession. First, the Priest puts incense in the censer, and the Deacon, turning to the people, says:

Procedamus in pace.
R. In nomine Christi. Amen.

Let us proceed in peace.
R. In the name of Christ. Amen.

The thurifer, or incense-bearer, goes first with the censer smoking; then follows the Sub-deacon with the cross between two acolytes with their candles

burning: next the clergy in order; and last of all, the Priest, with the Deacon on his left hand, all bearing palms in their hands. During the procession the following antiphons are sung:

Ant. Cum appropinquaret Dominus Jerosolymam, misit duos ex discipulis suis, dicens: Ite in castellum quod contra vos est, et invenietis pullum asinæ alligatum, super quem nullus hominum sedit: solvite, et adducite mihi. Si quis vos interrogaverit, dicite: Opus Domino est. Solventes adduxerunt ad Jesum: et imposuerunt illi vestimenta sua, et sedit super eum: alii expandebant vestimenta sua in via: alii ramos de arboribus sternebant: et qui sequebantur clamabant, Hosanna, benedictus qui venit in nomine Domini: benedictum regnum patris nostri David: Hosanna in excelsis: miserere nobis, Fili David.

Ant. When our Lord drew near to Jerusalem, he sent two of his disciples, saying: Go to the village that is over against you, and you will find an ass's colt tied, on which no man ever rode: untie him and bring him to me. If any man shall question you, say: Our Lord hath need of him. They untying him, brought him to Jesus, and put their garments on him and he sat upon him: some spread their garments in the way: some strewed branches cut from trees; and they that followed cried out: Hosanna, blessed is he that comes in the name of the Lord: blessed is the kingdom of our father David: Hosanna in the highest: have mercy on us, O Son of David.

Ant. Cum audisset populus, quia Jesus venit Jerosolymam, acce-

Ant. When the people heard that Jesus was coming to Jerusa-

perunt ramos palmarum: et exierunt ei obviam et clamabant pueri, dicentes: Hic est, qui venturus est in salutem populi. Hic est salus nostra, et redemptio Israel. Quantus est iste, cui throni et dominationes occurrunt? Noli, timere, filia Sion: ecce Rex tuus venit tibi sedens super pullum asinæ; sicut scriptum est: Salve Rex fabricator mundi, qui venisti redimere nos.

lem, they took palm branches, and went out to meet him: and the children cried out, saying: This is he that is come for the salvation of the people. He is our salvation, and the redemption of Israel. How great is he, whom the thrones and dominions go out to meet? Fear not, O daughter of Sion, behold thy king comes to thee sitting on an ass's colt: as it is written: Hail, O King, Creator of the world, who art come to redeem us.

Ant. Ante sex dies solemnis Paschæ, quando venit Dominus in civitatem Jerusalem, occurrerunt ei pueri; et in manibus portabant ramos palmarum; et clamabant voce magna, dicentes: Hosanna in excelsis: benedictus qui venisti in multitudine misericordiæ tuæ: Hosanna in excelsis.

Ant. Six days before the solemnity of the Passover, when our Lord was coming into the city of Jerusalem, the children met him, and carried palm-branches in their hands; and they cried with a loud voice, saying: Hosanna in the highest; blessed art thou who art come in the multitude of thy mercy: Hosanna in the highest.

Ant. Occurrunt turbæ cum floribus et pal-

Ant. The multitude go out to meet our Re-

mis Redemptori obviam: et victori triumphanti digna dant obsequia : Filium Dei ore gentes prædicant: et in laudem Christi voces tonant per nubila: Hosanna in excelsis.

Ant. Cum angelis et pueris fidelis inveniamur, triumphatori mortis clamantes: Hosanna in excelsis.

Ant. Turba multa, quæ convenerat ad diem festum, clamabat Domino: Benedictus qui venit in nomine Domini: Hosanna in excelsis.

deemer with flowers and palms, and pay the homage due to a triumphant conqueror; nations proclaim the Son of God; and their voices rend the skies in the praise of Christ; Hosanna in the highest.

Ant. Let us join in faith with the angels and children, singing to the conqueror of death: Hosanna in the highest.

Ant. A great multitude that was met together at the festival cried out to the Lord: Blessed is he that comes in the name of the Lord: Hosanna in the highest.

At the return of the procession two or four singers enter the church, and shutting the door, stand with their faces towards the procession, singing the two first verses, Gloria, laus; *which are repeated by the priest and others without. Then the other verses following are to be sung by those within, and they that are without, at every second verse, answer,* Gloria, laus.

GLORIA, laus, et honor, tibi sit Rex Christe Redemptor:
Cui puerile decus prompsit Hosanna pium.
R. Gloria laus.

TO thee, O Christ, be glory, praises loud.

To thee Hosanna cried the Jewish crowd.
R. To the, etc.

Israel es tu Rex, Davidis
et inclyta proles:
Nomine qui in Domini
Rex benedicto venis.

R. Gloria, laus.
Cœtus in excelsis te laudat cœlicus omnis,
Et mortalis homo, et cuncta creata simul.
R. Gloria, laus.
Plebs Hebræa tibi cum palmis obvia venit,

Cum prece voto, hymnis, adsumus ecce tibi.
R. Gloria, laus.
Hi tibi passuro solvebant munia laudis:

Nos tibi regnanti pangimus ecce melos.
R. Gloria, laus.
Hi placuere tibi, placeat devotio nostra:

Rex bone, Rex clemens, cui bona cuncta placent.
R. Gloria, laus.

We Israel's monarch, David's Son proclaim:
Thou com'st, blest king, in God's most holy name,
R. To thee, etc.
Angels and men in one harmonious choir,
To sing thy everlasting praise conspire.
R. To thee etc.
Thee Israel's children met with conquering palmes,
To thee our vows we pay in loudest psalms:
R. To thee, etc.
For thee, on earth with boughs they strewed the ways:
To thee in heaven we sing melodious praise.
R. To thee, etc.
Accept this tribute, which to thee we bring,
As thou didst theirs, O good and gracious King. Amen.
R. To thee, etc.

After this the Sub-deacon knocks at the door with the foot of the cross; which being opened, the procession enters the church singing.

Ingrediente Domino in sanctam civitatem Hebræorum pueri

As our Lord entered the holy city, the Hebrew children de-

resurrectionem vitæ pronuntiantes: * Cum ramis palmarum Hosanna clamabant in excelsis. V. Cum audisset populus quod Jesus veniret Jerosolymam, exierunt obviam ei: * Cum ramis, etc.

claring the resurrection of life: * with palm-branches, cried out: Hosanna in the highest. V. When the people heard that Jesus had come to Jerusalem, they went out to meet him: † with palm branches, etc.

Then the Mass is celebrated, and all hold the palms in their hands during the Passion and the Gospel.

MASS FOR PALM SUNDAY.

The Priest at the foot of the altar makes the sign of the cross, saying:

IN nomine Patris, et Filii, et Spiritus Sancti. Amen.

Introibo ad altare Dei.

R. Ad deum, qui lætificat juventutem meam.

V. Adjutorium nostrum in nomine Domini.

R. Qui fecit cœlum et terram.

V. Confiteor Deo omnipotenti, etc.

IN the name of the Father, and of the Son, and of the Holy Ghost. Amen.

I will go to the altar of God.

R. To God who rejoiceth my youth.

V. Our help is in the name of the Lord.

R. Who made heaven and earth.

V. I confess to Almighty God. etc.

PALM SUNDAY. 35

R. Misereatur tui omnipotens Deus, et dimissis peccatis tuis perducat te ad vitam æternam.
V. Amen.
R. Confiteor Deo omnipotenti, beatæ Mariæ, semper virgini, beato Michaeli archangelo, beato Joanni Baptistæ, sanctis apostolis Petro et Paulo, omnibus sanctis et tibi, Pater; quia peccavi nimis cogitatione, verbo, et opere, *mea culpa; mea culpa; mea maxima culpa.* Ideo precor beatam Mariam, semper virginem, beatum Michaelem archangelum, beatum Joannem Baptistam, sanctos apostolos Petrum et Paulum, omnes sanctos, et te, Pater, orare pro me ad Dominum Deum nostrum.

V. Misereatur vestri omnipotens Deus, et dimissis peccatis vestris perducat vos ad vitam eternam.
R. Amen.
V. Indulgentiam, ab-

R. Almighty God be merciful to thee, and having forgiven thee thy sins, bring thee to life everlasting.
V. Amen.
R. I confess to Almighty God, to blessed Mary, ever a virgin, to blessed Michael the archangel, to blessed John the Baptist, to the holy apostles Peter and Paul, to all the saints, and to thee, Father; that I have very much sinned in thought, word, and deed, *through my fault; through my fault; through my most grievous fault.* Therefore I beseech blessed Mary, ever a virgin, blessed Michael the archangel, blessed John the Baptist, the holy apostles Peter and Paul, all the saints, and thee, Father, to pray for me to our Lord God.
V. May Almighty God be merciful to you, and having forgiven you your sins, bring you to life everlasting.
R. Amen.
V. May the Almighty

solutionem et remissionem peccatorum nostrorum tribuat nobis omnipotens et misericors Dominus.

R. Amen.

V. Deus, tu conversus vivificabis nos.

R. Et plebs tua lætabitur in te.

V. Ostende nobis, Domine, misericordiam tuam.

R. Et salutare tuum da nobis.

V. Domine, exaudi orationem meam.

R. Et clamor meus at te veniat.

V. Dominus vobiscum.

R. Et cum spiritu tuo.

Oremus.

and merciful Lord grant us the pardon, absolution, and remission of our sins.

R. Amen.

V. O God, thou being turned towards us, will enliven us.

R. And thy people will rejoice in thee.

V. Show us, O Lord, thy mercy.

R. And grant us thy salvation.

V. Lord, hear my prayer.

R. And let my cry come to thee.

V. The Lord be with you.

R. And with thy spirit.

Let us pray.

The priest says the following prayer in a low voice.

AUFER a nobis, quæsumus Domine, iniquitates nostras; ut ad sancta sanctorum puris mereamur mentibus introire. Per Christum Dominum nostrum. Amen.

TAKE from us our iniquities, we beseech thee, O Lord; that we may deserve to enter into the sanctuary with clean hearts. Through Christ our Lord. Amen.

PALM SUNDAY.

ORAMUS te Domine, per merita sanctorum tuorum, quorum reliquiæ hic sunt, et omnium sanctorum; ut indulgere digneris omnia peccata mea. Amen.

WE beseech thee, O Lord, by the merits of thy saints, whose relics are here, and of all the saints, that thou wouldst vouchsafe to pardon all my sins. Amen.

Then he goes to the book at the corner of the altar, and making the sign of the cross on himself, reads aloud

THE INTROIT.

DOMINE, ne longe facias auxilium tuum a me, ad defensionem meam aspice: libera me de ore leonis et a cornibus unicornium humilitatem meam. *Ps.* Deus, Deus meus, respice in me: quare me dereliquisti? Longe a salute mea verba delictorum meorum. Domine, ne longe, etc.

LORD, keep not thy help far from me; look to my defence; deliver me from the lion's mouth, and my low condition from the horns of unicorns. *Ps.* O God, my God, look on me: Why hast thou forsaken me? The voice of my sins keep salvation far from me. Lord, keep not, etc.

V. KYRIE eleison.
R. Kyrie eleison,
V. Kyrie eleison.
R. Christe eleison.
V. Christe eleison.
R. Christe eleison.
V. Kyrie eleison.
R. Kyrie eleison.

V. LORD, have mercy on us. R. Lord, have mercy on us. V. Lord, have mercy on us. R. Christ, have mercy on us. V. Christ, have mercy on us. R. Christ have mercy on us. V. Lord, have mercy on us. R. Lord, have mercy

PALM SUNDAY.

V. Kyrie eleison.

V. Dominus vobiscum.

R. Et cum spiritu tuo.

Oremus.

OMNIPOTENS sempiterne Deus, qui humano generi ad imitandum humilitatis exemplum, Salvatorem nostrum carnem sumere et crucem subire fecisti: concede propitius, ut patientiæ ipsius habere documenta et resurrectionis consortia mereamur. Per eundem, etc.

Lectio Epistolæ beati Pauli apostoli ad Philippenses.

Cap. ii.

FRATRES, hoc enim sentite in vobis, quod et in Christo Jesu, qui cum in forma Dei esset, non rapinam arbitratus est esse se æqualem Deo sed semetipsum exinanivit, formam servi accipiens, in similitudinem hominum factus, et habitu inven-

V. Lord, have mercy on us.

V. The Lord be with you.

R. And with thy spirit.

Let us pray.

ALMIGHTY and everlasting God, who would have our Saviour become man, and suffer on a cross, to give mankind an example of humility: mercifully grant that we may be instructed by his patience, and partake in his resurrection. Through the same, etc.

Lesson from the Epistle of the apostle St Paul to the Philippians.

Chap. ii.

BRETRHEN, let this mind be in you which was also in Christ Jesus: who being in the form of God, thought it not robbery to be equal with God: but debased himself, taking the form of a servant, being made in the likeness of men, and in fashion found as

tus ut homo. Humiliavit semetipsum, factus obediens usque ad mortem, mortem autem crucis. Propter quod et Deus exaltavit illum, et donavit illi nomen, quod est super omne nomen: ut in nomine Jesu omne genu flectatur, cælestium, terrestrium, et infernorum, et omnis lingua confiteatur, quia Dominus Jesus Christus in gloria est Dei Patris. R. Deo gratias.

a man. He humbled himself, becoming obedient unto death, even the death of the cross. Wherefore God also hath exalted him, and hath given him a name which is above every name; that in the name of Jesus every knee should bow, of those that are in heaven, on earth, and under the earth, and that every tongue should confess that the Lord Jesus Christ is the glory of God the Father. R. Thanks be to God.

Graduale. — Tenuisti manum dexteram meam: et in voluntate tua deduxisti me: et cum gloria assumpsisti me. V. Quam bonus Israel Deus rectis corde! mei autem pene moti sunt pedes, pene effusi sunt gressus mei: quia zelavi in peccatoribus pacem peccatorum videns.

Gradual. — Thou hast held my right hand: and according to thy will thou hast conducted me, and received me with glory. V. How good is God to Israel, to those of an upright heart but my feet were almost gone, my steps were ready to slip: because I was jealous of sinners, seeing the peace of sinners.

Tractus. — Deus, Deus meus, respice in me: quare me dereliquisti? V. Longe a salute mea verba delictorum meo-

Tract. — O God, my God, look on me; why hast thou forsaken me? V. The voice of my sins keep salvation far from

rum. V. Deus meus, clamabo per diem, nec exaudies: in nocte, et non ad insipientiam mihi. V. Tu autem in sancto habitas, laus Israel. V. In te speraverunt patres nostri; speraverunt, et liberasti eos. V. Ad te clamaverunt, et salvi facti sunt; in te speraverunt: et non sunt confusi. V. Ego autem sum vermis et non homo: opprobrium hominum, et abjectio plebis. V. Omnes qui videbant me, aspernabantur me: locuti sunt labiis, et moverunt caput. V. Speravit in Domino, eripiat eum; salvum faciat eum, quoniam vult eum. V. Ipsi vero consideraverunt et conspexerunt me; diviserunt sibi vestimenta mea, et super vestem meam miserunt sortem. V. Libera me de ore leonis: et à cornibus unicornium humilitatem meam. V. Qui timetis Dominum, laudate eum: universum semen Jacob magnificate eum. V. An-

me. V. My God, I shall cry to thee in the day, and thou wilt not hear in the night, and it shall not be my folly, V. But thou dwellest in the holy place, the praise of Israel. V. In thee our fathers have hoped; they have hoped and thou didst save them. V. They cried to thee and were saved: they hoped in thee, and were not confounded V. But I am a worm; and not a man, the reproach of men, and outcast of the people. V. All that saw me, scorned me, and shook their heads. V. He hoped in the Lord, let him save him, because he loves him. V. And they considered and viewed me; they divided my garment amongst them, and upon my coat they cast lots. V. Deliver me from the lion's mouth, and my low condition from the horns of unicorns. V. Ye that fear the Lord, praise him: the whole race of Jacob, magnify him. V. The

nuntiabitur Domino generatio ventura: et annuntiabunt cœli justitiam ejus. V. Populo qui nascetur quem fecit Dominus.

Passio Domini nostri Jesu Christi secundum Matthæum.

Cap. xxvi.

IN illo tempore, dixit Jesus discipulis suis: scitis quid post biduum pascha fiet, et filius hominis tradetur ut crucifigatur. *C.* Tunc congregati sunt principes sacerdotum et seniores populi in atrium principis sacerdotum, qui dicebatur Caiphas: et concilium fecerunt ut Jesum dolo tenerent, et occiderent. Dicebant autem: *S.* non in die festo, ne forte tumultus fieret in populo. *C.* Cum autem Jesus esset in Bethania in domo Simonis leprosi, accessit ad eum mulier habens alabastrum unguenti pretiosi, et effudit super caput ipsius recumbentis. Videntes

generation to come shall be declared to be the Lord's: and the heavens shall declare his justice. V. To the people that shall be born, which the Lord has made.

The Passion of our Lord Jesus Christ according to Matt.

Chap. xxvi.

AT that time: Jesus said to his disciples, you know that after two days shall be the pasch, and the son of man shall be delivered up to be crucified. Then they gathered together the chief priests, and the ancients of the people into the palace of the high-priest, who was called Caiphas: and they consulted together, that by subtilty they might apprehend Jesus, and put him to death. But they said: not on the festival day, lest there should be a tumult among the people. And when Jesus was in Bethania, in the house of Simon the lep-

autem discipuli, indignati sunt dicentes: S. Ut quid perditio hæc? Potuit enim istud venumdari multo, et dari pauperibus. C. Sciens autem Jesus, ait illis: ✠ Quid molesti estis huic mulieri? Opus enim bonum operata est in me. Nam semper pauperes habetis vobiscum: me autem non semper habetis. Mittens enim hæc unguentum hoc in corpus meum, ad sepeliendum me fecit. Amen dico vobis: Ubicumque prædicatum fuerit hoc evangelium in toto mundo, dicetur, et quod hæc fecit in memoriam ejus. C. Tunc abiit unus de duodecim, qui dicebatur Judas Iscariotes, ad principes sacerdotum, et ait illis: S. Quid vultis mihi dare, et ego vobis eum tradam? C. At illi constituerunt ei triginta argenteos. Et exinde quærebat opportunitatem ut eum traderet. Prima autem die Azymorum accesserunt discipuli ad Jesum, dicentes: S. Ubi vis paremus tibi comedere

er, there came to him a woman having an alabaster box of precious ointment, and poured it on his head as he was at table. And the disciples seeing it, had indignation, saying: To what purpose is this waste? For this might have been sold for much, and given to the poor. And Jesus knowing it said to them; Why do you trouble this woman? for she hath wrought a good work upon me. For the poor you have always with you: but me you have not always. For she in pouring this ointment upon my body, hath done it for my burial. Amen, I say to you wheresoever this gospel shall be preached in the whole world, that also which she hath done, shall be told for a memory of her. Then went one of the twelve, who was called Judas Iscariot, to the chief priests: and he said to them: What will you give me, and I will deliver him

Pascha? *C.* At Jesus dixit: ✠ Ite in civitatem ad quemdam, et dicite ei: Magister dicit: Tempus meum prope est; apud te facio Pascha cum discipulis meis. Et fecerunt discipuli sicut constituit illis Jesus, et paraverunt pascha. Vespere autem facto, discumbebat cum duodecim discipulis suis: Et edentibus illis, dixit: ✠ Amen, dico vobis, quia unus vestrum me traditurus est. *C.* Et contristati valde, cœperunt singuli dicere: *S.* Numquid ego sum, Domine? *C.* At ipse respondens, ait: ✠ qui intingit mecum manum in paropside, hic me tradet. Filius quidem hominis vadit, sicut scriptum est de illo: væ autem homini illi per quem Filius hominis tradetur: bonum erat ei, si natus non fuisset homo ille. *C.* Respondens autem Judas, qui tradidit eum dixit: *S.* Numquid ego sum Rabbi? *C.* Ait illi: ✠ Tu dixisti. *C.* Cænantibus autem eis, accepit Jesus panem, et benedixit, ac fre-

unto you? But they appointed him thirty pieces of silver. And from thenceforth he sought an opportunity to betray him. And on the first day of the Azymes the disciples came to Jesus, saying: Where wilt thou that we prepare for thee to eat the pasch? But Jesus said: Go ye into the city to a certain man, and say to him: The master saith: My time is near at hand, I will keep the pasch at thy house with my disciples. And the disciples did as Jesus had appointed them, and they prepared the pasch. Now when it was evening, he sat down with his twelve disciples. And whilst they were eating he said: Amen I say to you, that one of you is about to betray me. And they being very much troubled, began every one to say: Is it I, Lord? But he answering, said: He that dippeth his hand with me in the dish, the same shall betray me. The

git, deditque discipulis suis, et ait: ✠ Accipite et comedite: Hoc est corpus meum. C. Et accipiens calicem, gratias egit, et dedit illis, dicens: ✠ Bibite ex hoc omnes. Hic est enim sanguis meus Novi Testamenti, qui pro multis effundetur in remissionem peccatorum. Dico autem vobis: Non bibam amodo de hoc genimine vitis, usque in diem illum cum illud bibam vobiscum novum in regno Patris mei. C. Et hymno dicto, exierunt in montem Oliveti. Tunc dicit illis Jesus: ✠ Omnes vos scandalum patiemini in me, in ista nocte. Scriptum est enim: *Percutiam pastorem, et dispergentur oves gregis.* Postquam autem resurrexero, præcedam vos in Galilæam. C. Respondens autem Petrus ait illi: S. Et si omnes scandalizati fuerint in te, ego numquam scandalizabor. ✠ Ait illi Jesus: ✠ Amen dico tibi, quia in hac nocte, antequam gallus cantet,

Son of Man indeed goeth, as it is written of him: but wo to that man by whom the Son of Man shall be betrayed: it were better for that man if he had not been born. And Judas that betrayed him, answering, said: Is it I, Rabbi? He saith to him: Thou hast said it. And whilst they were at supper, Jesus took bread, and blessed, and broke, and gave to his disciples, and said: Take ye, and eat: This is my body. And taking the chalice he gave thanks: and gave to them, saying: Drink ye all of this. For this is my blood of the new testament, which shall be shed for many for the remission of sins. And I say to you, I will not drink from henceforth of this fruit of the vine, until that day when I shall drink it new with you in the kingdom of my Father. And when they had sung an hymn, they went out to Mount Olivet. Then Jesus saith to them: All you shall

ter me negabis. *C.* Ait illi Petrus: *S.* Etiam si oportuerit me mori tecum non te negabo. *C.* Similiter et omnes discipuli dixerunt. Tunc venit Jesus cum illis in villam quæ dicitur Gethsemani, et dixit discipulis suis: ✠ Sedete hic, donec vadam illuc, et orem. *C.* Et assumpto Petro, et duobus filiis Zebedæi cœpit contristari et mœstus esse. Tunc ait illis: ✠ Tristis est anima mea usque ad mortem: Sustinete hic, et vigilate mecum. *C.* Et progressus pusillum, procidit in faciem suam, orans, et dicens: ✠ Pater mi, si possibile est, transeat a me calix iste. Verumtamen non sicut ego volo, sed sicut tu. *C.* Et venit ad discipulos suos et invenit eos dormientes; Et dicit Petro: ✠ Sic non potuistis una hora vigilare mecum? Vigilate et orate, ut non intretis in tentationem. Spiritus quidem promptus est, caro autem infirma. *C.* Iterum secundo abiit, et oravit, dicens:

be scandalized in me this night. For it is written: *I will strike the shepherd, and the sheep of the flock shall be dispersed.* But after I shall be risen again I will go before you into Galilee. And Peter answering, said to him: Though all men shall be scandalized in thee, I will never be scandalized. Jesus said to him: Amen I say to thee, that in this night before the cock crow, thou wilt deny me thrice. Peter saith to him: Though I should die with thee, I will not deny thee. And in like manner said all the disciples. Then Jesus came with them to a country-place, which is called Gethsemani, and he said to his disciples: Sit you here, till I go yonder and pray. And taking with him Peter and the two sons of Zebedee, he began to grow sorrowful and to be sad. Then he saith to them: My soul is sorrowful even unto death: stay you here, and

✠ Pater mi, si non potest hic calix transire, nisi bibam illum, fiat voluntas tua. *C.* Et venit iterum, et invenit eos dormientes; erant enim oculi eorum gravati. Et relictis illis, iterum abiit, et oravit tertio, eundem sermonem dicens. Tunc venit ad discipulos suos, et dicit illis: ✠ Dormite jam, et requiescite: ecce appropinquavit hora, et Filius hominis tradetur in manus peccatorum. Surgite, eamus: ecce appropinquavit qui me tradet. *C.* Adhuc eo loquente, ecce Judas unus de duodecim venit, et cum eo turba multa cum gladiis, et fustibus, missi a principibus sacerdotum et senioribus populi. Qui autem tradidit eum, dedit illis signum dicens: *S.* Quemcumque osculatus fuero, ipse est, tenete eum. *C.* Et confestim accedens ad Jesum dixit: *S.* Ave Rabbi, *C.* et osculatus est eum. Dixitque illi Jesus: ✠ Amice, ad quid venisti? *C.* Tunc accesserunt et manus

watch with me. And going a little further, he fell upon his face, praying, and saying: O my father, if it is possible, let this chalice pass from me. Nevertheless, not as I will, but as thou wilt. And he cometh to his disciples, and findeth them asleep, and he saith to Peter: What! could you not watch one hour with me? Watch ye and pray that ye enter not into temptation. The spirit indeed is willing, but the flesh is weak. Again he went the second time and prayed, saying: O my father, if this chalice may not pass away but I must drink it, thy will be done. And he cometh again, and findeth them asleep: for their eyes were heavy. And leaving them he went away again, and he prayed the third time, saying the same words. Then he cometh to his disciples, and saith to them: Sleep on now, and take your rest; behold the hour is at

injecerunt in Jesum, et tenuerunt eum. Et ecce unus ex his qui erant cum Jesu, extendens manum, exemit gladium suum, et percutiens servum principis sacerdotum, amputavit auriculam ejus. Tunc ait illi Jesus: ✠ Converte gladium tuum in locum suum. Omnes enim qui acceperint gladium, gladio peribunt. An putas, quia non possum rogare Patrem meum, et exhibebit mihi modo plusquam duodecim legiones angelorum? Quomodo ergo implebuntur scripturæ quia sic oportet fieri? *C.* In illa hora dixit Jesus turbis ✠ Tamquam ad latronem existis cum gladiis et fustibus comprehendere me: quotidie apud vos sedebam docens in templo, et non me tenuistis. *C* Hoc autem totum factum est, ut adimplerentur Scripturæ prophetarum. Tunc discipuli omnes, relicto eo, fugerunt. At illi tenentes Jesum, duxerunt ad Caipham, prin-

hand, and the Son of Man shall be betrayed into the hands of sinners. Rise, let us go: behold, he is at hand that will betray me. And as he yet spoke, behold Judas, one of the twelve, came, and with him a great multitude, with swords and clubs, sent from the chief priests and the ancients of the people. And he that betrayed him, gave them a sign, saying: Whomsoever I shall kiss, that is he, hold him fast. And forthwith coming to Jesus, he said: Hail, Rabbi. And he kissed him. And Jesus said to him: Friend, whereto art thou come? Then they came up and laid hands on Jesus and held him. And behold one of them that were with Jesus stretching forth his hand, drew out his sword, and striking the servant of the highpriest, cut off his ear, then Jesus saith to him: Put up thy sword again into its place, for all that take the sword

cipem sacerdotum, ubi scribæ et seniores convenerant. Petrus autem sequebatur eum a longe usque in atrium principis sacerdotum. Et ingressus intro, sedebat cum ministris, ut videret finem. Principes autem sacerdotum, et omne concilium, quærebant falsum testimonium contra Jesum, ut eum morti traderent: et non invenerunt, cum multi falsi testes accessissent. Novissime autem venerunt duo falsi testes et dixerunt: *S.* Hic dixit: Possum destruere templum Dei, et post triduum reædificare illud. *C.* Et surgens princeps sacerdotum ait illi: *S.* Nihil respondes ad ea, quæ isti adversum te testificantur? *C.* Jesus autem tacebat. Et princeps sacerdotum ait illi: *S.* Adjuro te per Deum vivum, ut dicas nobis, si tu es Christus Filius Dei. *C.* Dicit illi Jesus: ✠ Tu dixisti. Verumtamen dico vobis, amodo videbitis Filium hominis sedentem a dextris virtu-

shall perish by the sword. Thinkest thou that I cannot ask my Father, and he will give me presently more than twelve legions of angels? How then shall the scriptures be fulfilled, that so it must be done? In that same hour Jesus said to the multitude: You are come out as against a robber with swords and clubs to apprehend me: I sat daily with you teaching in the temple, and you laid not hands on me. Now all this was done, that the scriptures of the prophets might be fulfilled. Then the disciples all leaving him fled away. But they holding Jesus led him to Caiphas the high-priest, where the scribes and the ancients were assembled: But Peter followed him afar off, to the high-priest's palace and going in, he sat with the servants, to see the end. Now the chief priests and the whole council sought

tis Dei, et venientem in nubibus cœli. *C.* Tunc princeps sacerdotum scidit vestimenta sua dicens: *S.* Blasphemavit: quid adhuc egemus testibus? Ecce nunc audistis blasphemiam: quid vobis videtur? *C.* At illi respondentes, dixerunt: *S.* Reus est mortis. *C.* Tunc expuerunt in faciem ejus, et colaphis eum ceciderunt, alii autem palmas in faciem ejus dederunt, dicentes: *S.* Prophetiza nobis, Christe, quis est, qui te percussit? *C.* Petrus vero sedebat foris in atrio: et accessit ad eum una ancilla, dicens: *S.* Et tu cum Jesu Galilæo eras. *C.* At ille negavit coram omnibus dicens: *S.* Nescio quid dicis. *C.* Exeunte autem illo januam, vidit eum alia ancilla, et ait his qui erant ibi: *S.* Et hic erat cum Jesu Nazareno. *C.* Et iterum negavit cum juramento, quia non novi hominem. Et post pusillum accesserunt qui stabant et dixerunt Petro: *S.* Vere

false witness against Jesus, that they might put him to death: And they found not, though many false witnesses had come in. And last of all there came two false witnesses, and they said: This man said, I am able to destroy the temple of God, and in three days to rebuild it. And the high-priest rising up, said to him: Answerest thou nothing to these things which these witness against thee? But Jesus held his peace. And the high priest said to him: I adjure thee by the living God, that thou tell us if thou be the Christ the Son of God. Jesus said to him: thou hast said it. Nevertheless I say to you, hereafter you shall see the Son of Man sitting on the right hand of the power of God, and coming in the clouds of heaven. Then the high priest rent his garments, saying: He hath blasphemed, what farther need have we of witnesses? Behold, now

et tu ex illis es: nam et loquela tua manifestum te facit. *C.* Tunc cœpit detestari et jurare, quia non novisset hominem. Et continuo gallus cantavit. Et recordatus est Petrus verbi Jesu quod dixerat: Priusquam gallus cantet, ter me negabis. Et egressus foras, flevit amare. Mane autem facto, consilium inierunt omnes principes sacerdotum, et seniores populi adversus Jesum, ut eum morti traderent. Et vinctum adduxerunt eum et tradiderunt Pontio Pilato præsidi. Tunc videns Judas, qui eum tradidit quod damnatus esset: pœnitentia ductus retulit triginta argenteos principibus sacerdotum et senioribus, dicens: *S.* Peccavi, tradens sanguinem justum. *C.* At illi dixerunt: *S.* Quid ad nos? Tu videris. *C.* Et projectis argenteis in templo recessit: et abiens, laqueo se suspendit. Principes autem sacerdotum, acceptis argenteis, dixerunt: Non licet eos

you have heard the blasphemy. What think you? But they answering said: He is guilty of death. Then did they spit in his face, and buffet him, and others struck his face with the palms of their hands, saying: Prophesy unto us, O Christ: who is he that struck thee? But Peter sat without in the palace: and there came to him a servant maid, saying: Thou also wast with Jesus the Galilean. But he denied before them all, saying: I know not what thou sayest. And as he went out of the gate another maid saw him, and she said to them that were there: This man also was with Jesus of Nazareth. And again he denied with an oath: I do not know the man. And after a little while they that stood by came, and said to Peter: Surely thou also art one of them: for even thy speech doth discover thee. Then he began to curse and to

mittere in corbonam: quia pretium sanguinis est. *S.* Consilio autem inito emerunt ex illis agrum figuli, in sepulturam peregrinorum, Propter hoc vocatus est ager ille, Haceldama, hoc est, ager sanguinis, usque in hodiernum diem. Tunc impletum est quod dictum est per Jeremiam prophetam, dicentem: « Et acceperunt triginta argenteos pretium appretiati, quem appretiaverunt a filiis Israel; et dederunt eos in agrum figuli, sicut constituit mihi Dominus. » Jesus autem stetit ante præsidem, et interrogavit eum præses, dicens: *S.* Tu es rex Judæorum? *C.* Dicit illi Jesus: ✠ Tu dicis. *C.* Et cum accusaretur a principibus sacerdotum et senioribus, nihil respondit. Tunc dicit illi Pilatus: *S.* Non audis quanta adversum te dicunt testimonia? *C.* Et non respondit ei ad ullum verbum, ita ut miraretur præses vehementer. Per diem autem

svear that he knew not the man. And immediately the cock crew. And Peter remembered the words of Jesus which he had said; Before the cock crow, thou wilt deny me thrice. And going forth, he wept bitterly. And when morning was come, all the chief priests and ancients of the people took council against Jesus to put him to death. And they brought him bound, and delivered him to Pontius Pilate, the governor. Then Judas, who betrayed him, seeing that he was condemned, repenting himself, brought back the thirty pieces of silver to the chief priests and the ancients, saying: I have sinned, in betraying innocent blood. But they said: What is that to us? look thou to it. And casting down the pieces of silver in the temple, he departed; and went and hanged himself with a halter. But the chief priests

PALM SUNDAY.

solemnem consueverat præses populo dimittere unum vinctum, quem voluissent. Habebat autem tunc vinctum insignem, qui dicebatur Barabbas. Congregatis ergo illis, dixit Pilatus: *S.* Quem vultis dimittam vobis, Barabbam an Jesum, qui dicitur Christus? *C.* Sciebat enim quod per invidiam tradidissent eum. Sedente autem illo pro tribunali, misit ad eum uxor ejus, dicens: *S.* Nihil tibi, et justo illi: multa enim passa sum hodie per visum propter eum. Principes autem sacerdotum et seniores persuaserunt populis ut peterent Barabbam, Jesum vero perderent. Respondens autem præses, ait illis: *S.* Quem vultis vobis de duobus dimitti? *C.* At illi dixerunt: *S.* Barabbam. *C.* Dicit illis Pilatus: *S.* Quid igitur faciam de Jesu, qui dicitur Christus? *C.* Dicunt omnes: *S.* Crucifigatur. *C.* Ait illis præses: *S.* Quid enim mali fecit? *C.* At illi magis

having taken the pieces of silver, said: It is not lawful to put them into the corbona, because it is the price of blood. And after they had consulted together, they bought with them the potter's field, to be a burying-place for strangers. Wherefore that field was called Haceldama, that is, the field of blood, even to this day. Then was fulfilled that which was spoken by Jeremias the prophet, saying: *And they took the thirty pieces of silver, the price of him that was priced, whom they priced of the children of Israel. And they gave them unto the potter's field, as the Lord appointed to me.* And Jesus stood before the governor, and the governor, asked him, saying: Art thou the king of the Jews? Jesus saith to him: Thou sayest it. And when he was accused by the chief priests and ancients, he answered nothing. Then Pilate said to him: Dost

PALM SUNDAY.

clamabant, dicentes; *S.* Crucifigatur. *C.* Videns autem Pilatus, quia nihil proficeret; sed magis tumultus fieret: accepta aqua, lavit manus coram populo, dicens: *S.* Innocens ego sum a sanguine justi hujus: vos videritis. *C.* Et respondens universus populus, dixit: *S.* Sanguis ejus super nos, et super filios nostros. *C.* Tunc dimisit illis Barabbam; Jesum autem flagellatum tradidit eis, ut crucifigeretur. Tunc milites præsidis suscipientes Jesum in prætorium, congregaverunt ad eum universam cohortem; et exuentes eum, chlamydem coccineam circumdederunt ei, et plectentes coronam de spinis, posuerunt super caput ejus, et arundinem in dextera ejus. Et genuflexo ante eum, illudebant ei, dicentes: *S.* Ave rex Judæorum. *C.* Et expuentes in eum, acceperunt arundinem, et percutiebant caput ejus. Et postquam illuserunt ei, exuerunt

not thou hear how great testimonies they allege against thee? And he answered him never a word: so that the governor wondered exceedingly. Now upon the solemn day the governor was accustomed to release to the people one prisoner, whom they would. And he had then a notorious prisoner, that was called Barabbas. They therefore being gathered together, Pilate said: Whom will you that I release to you, Barabbas, or Jesus who is called Christ? For he knew that for envy they had delivered him. And as he was sitting on the judgment-seat, his wife sent to him, saying: Have thou nothing to do with that just man. For I have suffered many things this day in a dream because of him. But the chief priests and ancients persuaded the people, that they should ask Barabbas, and make Jesus away. And the

eum chlamyde, et induerunt eum vestimentis ejus, et duxerunt eum ut crucifigerent. Exeuntes autem invenerunt hominem Cyrenæum nomine Simonem : hunc angariaverunt ut tolleret crucem ejus. Et venerunt in locum, qui dicitur Golgotha, quod est, Calvariæ locus. Et dederunt ei vinum bibere cum felle mistum. Et cum gustasset, noluit bibere. Postquam autem crucifixerunt eum, diviserunt vestimenta ejus, sortem mittentes: ut impleretur quod dictum est per prophetam dicentem: « Diviserunt sibi vestimenta mea, et super vestem meam miserunt sortem. » Et sedentes servabant eum. Et imposuerunt super caput ejus causam ipsius scriptam: *Hic est Jesus Rex Judæorum*. Tunc crucifixi sunt cum eo duo latrones: unus a dextris, et unus a sinistris. Prætereuntes autem blasphemabant eum, moventes

governor answering, said to them: Whether will you have of the two to be released unto you? But they said Barabbas. Pilate saith to them: What shall I do then with Jesus that is called Christ? They say all: Let him be crucified. The governor said to them: Why what evil hath he done? but they cried out the more, saying: Let him be crucified. And Pilate seeing that he prevailed nothing; but that rather a tumult was made; taking water washed his hands before the people, saying: I am innocent of the blood of this just man: look you to it. And all the people answering, said: His blood be upon us, and upon our children. Then he released to them Barabbas, and having scourged Jesus, delivered him to them to be crucified. Then the soldiers of the governor taking Jesus into the hall, gathered

capita sua, et dicentes: *S.* Vah! qui destruis templum Dei, et in triduo illud re-ædificas: salva teipsum. Si Filius Dei es, descende de cruce. *C.* Similiter et principes sacerdotum, illudentes cum scribis et senioribus, dicebant: *S.* Alios salvos fecit: seipsum non potest salvum facere: si rex Israel est descendat nunc de cruce, et credimus ei: confidit in Deo: liberet nunc, si vult, eum; dixit enim: quia Filius Dei sum. *C.* Idipsum autem et latrones, qui crucifixi erant cum eo, improperabant ei. A sexta autem hora tenebræ factæ sunt super universam terram usque ad horam nonam. Et circa horam nonam clamavit *Jesus* voce magna, dicens: ✠ *Eli, Eli, lamma Sabacthani?* Hoc est: Deus meus, Deus meus, ut quid dereliquisti me? *C.* Quidem autem illic stantes, et audientes, dicebant: *S.* Eliam vocat iste. *C.* Et continuo currens unus ex eis, accep-

together unto him the whole band: and stripping him, they put a scarlet cloak about him. And platting a crown of thorns, they put it upon his head, and a reed in his right hand. And bowing the knee before him, they mocked him, saying: Hail, king of the Jews. And spitting upon him, they took the reed, and struck his head. And after they had mocked him they took off the cloak from him, and put on him his own garments, and led him away to crucify him. And going out, they found a man of Cyrene, named Simon: him they forced to take up his cross. And they came to the place that is called Golgotha, which is the place of Calvary. And they gave him wine to drink mingled with gall. And when he had tasted, he would not drink. And after they had crucified him, they divided his garments, casting lots: that the word might be

tam spongiam implevit aceto, et imposuit arundini et dabat ei bibere. Cæteri vero dicebant: S. Sine videamus an veniat Elias liberans eum. Jesus autem iterum clamans voce magna, emisit spiritum.

fulfilled which was spoken by the prophet, saying: *They divided my garments among them and upon my vesture they cast lots.* And they sat down and watched him. And they put over his head his cause written: *This is Jesus the King of the Jews.* Then were there crucified with him two thieves: the one on the right hand, and the other on the left. And they that passed by, blasphemed him, wagging their heads and saying: Vah! thou that destroyest the temple of God, and in three days buildest it up again, save thy own self: if thou be the Son of God, come down from the cross. In like manner also the chief priests with the scribes and ancients mocking, said: He saved others; himself he cannot save: if he be the King of Israel, let him now come down from the cross, and we will believe him. He trusted in God, let him deliver him now if he will have him: For he said: I am the son of God. And the self-same thing the thieves also, that were crucified with him, reproached him with. Now from the sixth hour there was darkness over all the earth, until the ninth hour. And about the ninth hour Jesus cried with a loud voice, saying: *Eli, Eli, lamma sabacthani?* that is, My God, my God, why hast thou forsaken me? And some of them that stood there and heard, said: This man calleth for Elias. And immediately one of them running, took a sponge and filled it with vinegar and put it on a reed, and gave him to drink. And the others said: Let be, let us see whether Elias will come to deliver

him. And Jesus again crying with a loud voice, gave up the ghost.*

Here all kneel down and meditate on the redemption of mankind and after a short pause the deacon goes on.

Et ecce velum templi scissum est in duas partes, a summo usque deorsun: et terra mota est et petræ scissae sunt et monumenta aperta sunt: et multa corpora sanctorum qui dormierant surrexerunt. Et exeuntes de monumentis post resurrectionem ejus venerunt in sanctam civitatem, et apparuerunt multis. Centurio autem, et qui cum eo erant, custodientes Jesum, viso terræmotu et his quifiebant, timuerunt valde, dicentes: Vere Filius Dei erat iste. Erant autem ibi mulieres multæ a longe quæ secutæ erant Jesum a Galilæa ministrantes ei: inter quas erat Maria Magdalene, et Maria Jacobi et Joseph mater, et mater filiorum Zebedæi. Cum autem sero factum esset, venit quidam homo dives ab

And behold the veil of the temple was rent in two from the top even to the bottom, and the earth quaked, and the rocks were rent, And the graves were opened: and many of the saints that had slept, arose. And coming out of the tombs after his resurrection, came into the holy city, and appeared to many. Now the centurion, and they that were with him watching Jesus, having seen the earthquake, and the things that were done, were greatly afraid, saying: Indeed this was the Son of God. And there were then many woman afar off, who had followed Jesus from Galilee, ministering unto him; among whom was Mary Magdalen, and Mary the mother of James and Joseph, and the mother of the sons of Zebedee,

Arimathœa nomine Joseph qui et ipse discipulus erat Jesu. Hic accessit ad Pilatum, et petiit corpus Jesu. Tunc Pilatus jussit reddi corpus. Et accepto corpore Joseph involvit illud in sindone munda. Et posuit illud in monumento suo novo, quod exciderat in petra. Et advolvit saxum magnum ad ostium monumenti, et abiit. Erat autem ibi Maria Magdalene, et altera Maria, sedentes contra sepulchrum.

And when it was evening, there came a certain rich man of Arimathea, named Joseph, who also himself was a disciple of Jesus. He went to Pilate, and begged the body of Jesus. Then Pilate commanded that the body should be delivered. And Joseph, taking the body, wrapt it up in a clean linen cloth. And laid it in his own new monument, which he had hewed out in a rock, and he rolled a great stone to the door of the monument, and went his way. And there were there Mary Magdalen, and the other Mary, sitting over against the sepulchre.

In solemn Masses, the rest of the Passion is sung by the Deacon in the tone of the Gospel, with the usual ceremonies before and after it; otherwise the Priest stands at the middle of the altar, and bowing down says, in a low voice:

MUNDA cor meum ac labia mea, omnipotens Deus, qui labia Isaiæ prophetæ calculo mundasti ignito; ita me tua grata miseratione digna e mundare, ut sanctum evangelium tuum digne valeam nun-

CLEANSE my heart and my lips, almighty God, who with a fiery coal didst cleanse the lips of the prophet Isaiah: vouchsafe so to cleanse me by thy gracious mercy, that I may worthily declare thy ho-

PALM SUNDAY.

tiare. Per Christum. Amen.

Jube Domine benedicere. — Dominus sit in corde meo, et in labiis meis: ut digne et competenter annuntiem evangelium suum. Amen.

Iv gospel. Through Christ, our Lord. Amen.

Bless me, O Lord. — The Lord be in my heart and in my lips that I may worthily and fitly proclaim his gospel. Amen.

Then he goes to the book and finishes the Passion.

ALtera autem die quæ est post parasceven convenerunt principes sacerdotum et pharisæi ad Pilatum, dicentes: Domine, recordati sumus quod seductor ille dixit, adhuc vivens: Post tres dies resurgam. Jube ergo custodiri sepulchrum usque in diem tertium: ne forte veniant discipuli eius, et furentur eum et dicant plebi: Surrexit a mortuis. Et erit novissimus error pejor priore. Ait illis Pilatus: Habetis custodiam, ite, custodite sicut scitis. Illi autem abeuntes, munierunt sepulchrum, signantes lapidem cum custodibus.

AND the next day, which followed the day of the Preparation, the chief priests and the pharisees came together to Pilate, saying: Sir, we have remembered, that the seducer said, while he was yet alive: After three days I will rise again. Command therefore the sepulchre to be guarded until the third day: let his disciples come and steal him away, and say to the people; He is risen from the dead; so the last error shall be worse than the first. Pilate said to them: You have a guard: go guard it as you know. And they, departing made the sepulchre sure, sealing the stone, and setting guards.

Here the Priest kisses the Gospel, saying in a low voice:

Per evangelica dicta, deleantur nostra delicta.	By the words of the Gospel may our sins be blotted out.

After which he goes to the middle of the altar, and says or sings aloud:

THE NICENE CREED.

CREDO in unum Deum, Patrem omnipotentem, factorem cœli et terræ, visibilium, omnium et invisibilium Et in unum Dominum Jesum Christum Filium Dei unigenitum, et ex Patre natum ante omnia sæcula. Deum de Deo, Lumen de Lumine, Deum verum de Deo vero. Genitum, non factum, consubstantialem Patri: per quem omnia facta sunt. Qui propter nos homines, et propter nostram salutem descendit de cœlis. Et incarnatus est de Spiritu Sancto ex Maria virgine: ET HOMO FACTUS EST. Crucifixus etiam pro nobis sub Pontio Pilato passus, et sepultus est. Et resurrexit tertia die se-

I Believe in one God, the Father Almighty, maker of heaven and earth, and of all things visible and invisible. And in one Lord Jesus Christ, the only begotten son of God and born of the Father before all ages. God of God, Light of Light, true God of true God. begotten, not made, consubstantial with the Father, by whom all things were made. Who for us men, and for our salvation came down from heaven. And took flesh by the Holy Ghost of the Virgin Mary: AND WAS MADE MAN. Was also crucified for us: suffered under Pontius Pilate, and was buried. And he rose again the third day, according

cundum Scripturas. Et ascendit in cœlum; sedet ad dexteram Patris. Et iterum venturus est cum gloria, judicare vivos et mortuos: cujus regni non erit finis. Et in Spiritum Sanctum, Dominum et vivificantem, qui ex Patre Filioque procedit. Qui cum Patre et Filio simul adoratur, et conglorificatur: qui locutus est per prophetas. Et unam sanctam Catholicam et Apostolicam Ecclesiam. Confiteor unum baptisma in remissionem peccatorum. Et expecto resurrectionem mortuorum. Et vitam venturi sæculi. Amen.

V. Dominus vobiscum.

R. Et cum spiritu tuo.

Oremus.

Offertorium. — Improperium expectavit cor meum, et miseriam : et sustinui qui simul mecum contristaretur, et non fuit: consolantem

to the scriptures. And ascended into heaven: sits on the right hand of the Father. And He shall come again with glory, to judge the living and the dead: of whose kingdom there shall be no end. And in the Holy Ghost, the Lord and giver of life: who proceeds from the Father and the Son. Who with the Father and the Son is equally adored and glorified: who spake by the prophets. And one Holy Catholic and apostolic Church. I confess one baptism for the remission of sins. And I expect the resurrection of the dead. And the life of the world to come. Amen.

V. The Lord be with you.

R. And with thy spirit.

Let us pray.

The Offertory. — My heart looked for reproach and misery; and I expected some one to condole with me, and there was none: I sought

me quæsivi, et non inveni: et dederunt in escam meam fel, et in siti mea potaverunt me aceto.

for a comforter, and found him not: and they gave me gall for my meat, and in my thirst they gave me vinegar to drink.

Here the Priest offers the bread that is to be consecrated, saying:

SUSCIPE, sancte Pater omnipotens æterne Deus, hanc immaculatam hostiam, quam ego indignus famulus tuus offero tibi Deo meo vivo et vero, pro innumerabilibus peccatis et offensionibus et negligentiis meis, et pro omnibus circumstantibus, sed et pro omnibus fidelibus Christianis vivis atque defunctis; ut mihi et illis proficiat ad salutem in vitam æternam. Amen.

RECEIVE, O holy Father, Almighty and eternal God, this unspotted host, which I, thy unworthy servant offer to thee, my true and living God, for my innumerable sins, offences and negligences, and for all here present, as also for all faithful Christians both living and dead: and that it may avail both me and them to salvation and life everlasting. Amen.

Then he blesses the water that is to be put in the chalice, saying:

DEUS, qui humanæ substantiæ dignitatem mirabiliter condidisti, et mirabilius reformasti: da nobis per huius aquæ et vini mysterium, ejus divinitatis esse consortes, qui hu-

O GOD, who didst wonderfully create the dignity of human nature, and more wonderfully reform it: grant by the mystery of this water and wine that we may become partakers

manitatis nostræ fieri dignatus est particeps, Jesus Christus Filius tuus Dominus noster. Qui tecum vivit et regnat in unitate Spiritus Sancti Deus, per omnia sæcula sæculorum. Amen.

of his divinity, who was graciously pleased to partake of our humanity, Jesus Christ thy Son our Lord. Who with these and the Holy Ghost liveth and reigneth, etc. Amen.

Having blessed the water, and poured it after the wine into the chalice, he offers them up, saying:

OFFERIMUS tibi, Domine, calicem salutaris, tuam deprecantes clementiam: ut in conspectu divinæ majestatis tuæ, pro nostra et totius mundi salute cum odore suavitatis ascendat. Amen.

WE offer to thee, O Lord, the cup of salvation, beseeching thy clemency: that it may ascend before thy divine majesty, as a sweet smelling odour, for our salvation, and that of the whole world. Amen.

Then bowing down he says:

IN spiritu humilitatis, et in animo contrito suscipiamur a te, Domine: et sic fiat sacrificium nostrum in conspectu tuo hodie, ut placeat tibi, Domine Deus.

MAY our humble minds and contrite hearts render us acceptable to thee, O Lord, and let our sacrifice be so performed this day in thy sight, that it may be pleasing to thee, O Lord our God.

After which, looking up to heaven he blesses the bread and wine, saying:

VENI, Sanctificator omnipotens æterne Deus, et bene✠dic hoc

COME, O eternal God, the almighty sanctifier, and bless this sa-

sacrificium tuo sancto nomini præparatum.

crifice prepared for the honour of thy holy name.

The four prayers immediately following, which are used for the blessing of the incense and the incensing of the Altar, in Solemn Masses, are omitted in Low Masses.

PER intercessionem Beati Michaelis Archangeli, stantis a dextris altaris incensi, et omnium electorum suorum incensum istud dignetur Dominus bene ✠ dicere, et in odorem suavitatis accipere. Per, etc.

BY the intercession of blessed Michael the Archangel, standing at the right side of the altar of incense, and of all the elect, may the Lord bless this incense and receive it as a sweet smelling odour. Through, etc.

While he incenses the oblations, he says:

INCENSUM istud a te benedictum, ascendat ad te, Domine: et descendat super nos misericordia tua.

MAY this incense, blessed by thee, ascend to thee, O Lord: and may thy mercy descend upon us.

Then he incenses the Altar, saying:

DIRIGATUR Domine, oratio mea, sicut incensum in conspectu tuo: elevatio manuum mearum sacrificium vespertinum. Pone, Domine, custodiam ori meo, et ostium circumstantiæ labiis meis: ut non declinet cor meum in verba

LET my prayer, O Lord, ascend like incense in thy sight: the lifting up of my hands as an evening sacrifice. Place, O Lord, a guard on my mouth, and a gate of prudence before my lips: that my heart may not wander after words

malitiæ, ad excusandas excusationes in peccatis.

ACCENDAT in nobis Dominus ignem sui amoris, et flammam æternæ charitatis. Amen.

of malice to make excuses in sins.

MAY the Lord kindle in us the fire of his love, and the flame of eternal charity. Amen.

Then going to the corner of the altar, he washes his fingers, saying:

LAVABO inter innocentes manus meas, et circumdabo altare tuum, Domine.

Ut audiam vocem laudis, et enarrem universa mirabilia tua.

Domine, dilexi decorem domus tuæ, et locum habitationis gloriæ tuæ.

Ne perdas cum impiis animam meam, et cum viris sanguinum vitam meam.

In quorum manibus iniquitates sunt; dextera eorum repleta est muneribus.

Ego autem in innocentia mea ingressus sum: redime me, et miserere mei.

Pes meus stetit in

I WILL wash my hands among the innocent and encompass thy altar, O Lord.

That I may hear the voice of praise, and publish all thy wonderful works.

Lord, I have loved the beauty of thy house: and the dwelling place of thy glory.

Destroy not my soul with the impious; nor my life with men of blood.

In whose hands are iniquities; their right hand is filled with gifts.

But I have walked in my innocence: redeem me, and have mercy on me.

My foot has stood in the right path: in the

directo: in ecclesiis benedicam te, Domine.
Gloria, etc. Amen.

churches I will bless thee, O Lord.
Glory be, etc.

Inclined before the middle of the altar, the Priest says:

SUSCIPE, santa Trinitas, hanc oblationem, quam tibi offerimus ob memoriam passionis, resurrectionis et ascensionis Jesu Christi Domini nostri: et in honore beatæ Mariæ semper virginis et beati Joannis Baptistæ, et sanctorum apostolorum Petri et Pauli, et istorum, et omnium sanctorum: ut illis proficiat ad honorem, nobis autem ad salutem: et illi pro nobis intercedere dignentur in cœlis, quorum memoriam agimus in terris. Per eundem, etc. Amen.

RECEIVE, O holy Trinity, this oblation which we make to thee in memory of the passion, resurrection, and ascension of our Lord Jesus Christ, and in honour of blessed Mary, ever Virgin, of blessed John the Baptist, of the holy apostles Peter and Paul, and of all the saints: that it may be available to their honour, and to our salvation; and that they may vouchsafe to intercede for us in heaven, whose memory we celebrate on earth. Through the same, etc.

Afterwards he turns to the people, and says aloud the two first words of the following prayer.

ORATE, fratres, ut meum ac vestrum sacrificium acceptabile fiat apud Deum Patrem omnipotentem.

PRAY, brethren, that my sacrifice and yours may be acceptable to God the Father Almighty.

PALM SUNDAY.

Answer.

SUSCIPIAT Dominus sacrificium de manibus tuis, ad laudem et gloriam nominis sui, ad utilitatem quoque nostram, totiusque ecclesiæ suæ sanctæ.

MAY our Lord receive this sacrifice from thy hands, to the praise and glory of his name, for our good also, and that of all his holy church.

The Priest in a low voice says, Amen: *and*

Secreta. *The Secret.*

CONCEDE, quæsumus Domine, ut oculis tuæ majestatis munus oblatum, et gratiam nobis devotionis obtineat et effectum beatæ perennitatis acquirat. Per Dominum.

GRANT, we beseech thee, O Lord, that this gift offered in the presence of thy majesty, may procure us the grace of devotion, and effectually obtain for us a blessed eternity. Through, etc.

What follows he says aloud:

PER omnia sæcula sæculorum.
R. Amen.
V. Dominus vobiscum.

R. Et cum spiritu tuo.
V. Sursum corda.

R. Habemus ad Dominum.
V. Gratias agamus Domino Deo nostro.
R. Dignum et justum est.

FOR ever and ever.
R. Amen.
V. The Lord be with you.
R. And with thy spirit.
V. Lift up your hearts.
R. We have lifted them up to the Lord.
V. Let us give thanks to the Lord our God.
R. It is meet and just.

VERE dignum et justum est, æquum et salutare, nos tibi semper, et ubique gratias agere: Domine sancte, Pater omnipotens, æterne Deus, qui salutem humani generis in ligno crucis constituisti: ut unde mors oriebatur, inde vita resurgeret: et qui in ligno vincebat in ligno quoque vinceretur: per Christum Dominum nostrum. Per quem majestatem tuam laudant angeli, adorant dominationes, tremunt potestates. Cœli, cœlorumque virtutes, ac beata seraphim, socia exultatione concelebrant. Cum quibus et nostras voces ut admitti jubeas deprecamur, supplici confessione dicentes:

Sanctus, sanctus, sanctus Dominus Deus Sabaoth. Pleni sunt cœli et terra gloria tua: Hosanna in excelsis. Benedictus qui venit in nomine Domini: Hosanna in excelsis.

IT is truly meet and just, right and available to salvation, that we should always and in all places give thanks to thee, O holy Lord, Almighty Father, Eternal God, who didst ordain the salvation of mankind on the tree of the cross: that life might spring from whence death arose and that he who overcame by a tree, might also be overcome by a tree: through Christ our Lord. By whom the angels praise, the dominations adore, the powers dread thy majesty. The heavens and heavenly virtues, and the blessed seraphim with united joy glorify it. With whom also we beseech thee to admit our voices with humble praise, saying:

Holy, Holy, Holy, Lord God of Hosts. Heaven and earth are full of thy glory: Hosanna in the highest. Blessed is he that comes in the name of the Lord: Hosanna in the highest.

THE CANON OF THE MASS.

TE igitur clementissime Pater, per Jesum Christum Filium tuum Dominum nostrum, supplices rogamus ac petimus, uti accepta habeas, et benedicas hæc ✠ dona, hæc ✠ munera, hæc ✠ sancta sacrificia illibata, in primis quæ tibi offerimus pro Ecclesia tua sancta Catholica: quam pacificare, custodire, adunare, et regere digneris toto orbe terrarum: una cum famulo tuo Papa nostro *N.* et Antistite nostro *N.* et omnibus orthodoxis, atque catholicæ et apostolicæ fidei cultoribus.

WE therefore humbly pray and beseech thee, most merciful Father, through Jesus Christ thy Son our Lord, to accept and bless these gifts, these presents, these holy unspotted sacrifices, which in the first place we offer to thee for thy holy Catholic Church, to which vouchsafe to grant peace: as also to preserve, unite, and govern it throughout the whole world, together with thy servants. *N.* our Pope, *N.* our Bishop and all orthodox believers and professors of the catholic and apostolic faith.

The Commemoration of the living.

MEMENTO, Domine, famulorum famularumque tuarum *N* et *N.*

REMEMBER, O Lord, thy servants both men and women, *N,* and *N.*

Here he pauses a little, to remember those for whom he intends to pray and then proceeds:

Et omnium circumstantium, quorum tibi fides cognita est, et nota de-

And of all here present, whose faith and devotion are known to thee,

votio pro quibus tibi offerimus: vel qui tibi offerunt hoc sacrificium laudis, pro se, suisque omnibus: pro redemptione animarum suarum, pro spe salutis et incolumitatis suæ; tibique reddunt vota sua æterno Deo, vivo et vero.

COmmunicantes et memoriam venerantes, in primis gloriosæ semper virginis Mariæ, genitricis Dei, et Domini nostri Jesu Christi: sed et beatorum apostolorum ac martyrum tuorum, Petri et Pauli, Andreæ, Jacobi, Joannis, Thomæ, Jacobi, Philippi, Bartholomæi, Matthæi, Simonis et Thaddæi, Lini, Cleti, Clementis, Xysti, Cornelii, Cypriani, Laurentii, Chrisogoni, Joannis et Pauli, Cosmæ et Damiani: et omnium sanctorum tuorum, quorum meritis precibusque concedas, ut in omnibus protectionis tuæ muniamur auxilio. Per eundem Christum Dominum nostrum. Amen.

for whom we offer to thee: or who offer thee this sacrifice of praise for themselves and all theirs: for the redemption of their souls, for the hope of their salvation and safety: and pay their vows to thee, the eternal, living, and true God.

COmmunicating with, and honouring, in the first place, the memory of the glorious ever Virgin Mary, Mother of God and our Lord Jesus Christ; as also of thy blessed apostles and martyrs Peter and Paul, Andrew, James, John, Thomas, James, Philip, Bartholomew, Matthew, Simon and Thaddæus, Linus, Cletus, Clement, Xystus, Cornelius, Cyprian, Laurence, Chrysogonus, John and Paul, Cosmas and Damian: and of all thy saints: by whose merits and prayers grant that we may in all things be defended by the help of thy protection. Through the same Christ our Lord. Amen.

Holding his hands extended over the Oblations, he says:

HANC igitur oblationem servitutis nostræ sed et cunctæ familiæ tuæ, quæsumus Domine, ut placatus accipias: diesque nostros in tua pace disponas, atque ab æterna damnatione nos eripi, et in electorum tuorum jubeas grege numerari. Per Christum Dominum nostrum. Amen.

QUAM oblationem tu Deus in omnibus quæsumus bene ✠ dictam, adscrip ✠ tam, ra ✠ tam, rationabilem, acceptabilemque facere digneris: ut nobis cor ✠ pus et san ✠ guis fiat dilectissimi Filii tui Domini nostri Jesu Christi.

QUI pridie quam pateretur, accepit panem in sanctas ac venerabiles manus suas: et elevatis oculis in cœlum ad te Deum Patrem suum omnipotentem tibi gratias agens, bene✠dixit, fregit, deditque discipulis suis, dicens: Ac-

WE therefore beseech thee, O Lord, graciously to accept this oblation of our service, as also of thy whole family: grant us thy peace in our days; preserve us from eternal damnation, and command us to be nunbered among thy elect. Through Christ our Lord. Amen.

WHICH oblation do thou, O God, vouchsafe in all respects to bless, approve, ratify, and accept: that it may be made for us the body and blood of thy most beloved Son our Lord Jesus Christ.

WHO, the day before he suffered, took bread in his sacred and venerable hands, and with his eyes lifted up towards heaven to thee, O God, his Almighty Father, giving thee thanks, blessed it, broke it, and gave it to his

cipite et manducate ex hoc omnes: Hoc EST ENIM CORPUS MEUM.

disciples, saying: Take and eat ye all of this: For THIS IS MY BODY.

Here he adores the Blessed Sacrament on his knees, and then raises it above his head for the adoration of the people. After which he proceeds to the consecration of the chalice, saying:

SIMILI modo postquam cœnatum est, accipiens et hunc præclarum calicem in sanctas ac venerabiles manus suas, item tibi gratias agens, bene✠dixit, deditque discipulis suis dicens: Accipite et bibite ex eo omnes:
HIC EST ENIM CALIX SANGUINIS MEI, NOVI ET ÆTERNI TESTAMENTI: MYSTERIUM FIDEI, QUI PRO VOBIS ET PRO MULTIS EFFUNDETUR IN REMISSIONEM PECCATORUM.

IN like manner after supper, taking this excellent chalice in his sacred and venerable hands, giving thee also thanks, he blessed it, and gave it to his disciples, saying: Take and drink ye all of this.

FOR THIS IS THE CHALICE OF MY BLOOD, OF THE NEW AND EVERLASTING TESTAMENT: A MYSTERY OF FAITH, WHICH SHALL BE SHED FOR YOU AND FOR MANY FOR THE REMISSION OF SINS.

Then he adores on his knees the Sacred Blood saying:

Hæc quotiescumque feceritis, in mei memoriam facietis.

As often as ye shall do these things ye shall do them in remembrance of me.

After which he shows it to the people for their adoration and then goes on, saying:

UNDE et memores, Domine, nos servi

WHEREFORE, O Lord we thy servants

tui, sed et plebs tua sancta, ejusdem Christi Filii tui Domini nostri tam beatæ Passionis, necnon et ab inferis resurrectionis, sed et in cœlos gloriosæ ascensionis, offerimus preclaræ majestati tuæ de tuis donis ac datis, hostiam ✠ puram, hostiam ✠ sanctam, hostiam ✠ immaculatam, panem ✠ sanctum vitæ æternæ, et calicem ✠ salutis perpetuæ.

SUPRA quæ, propitio ac sereno vultu respicere digneris, et accepta habere, sicuti accepta habere dignatus es munera pueri tui justi Abel, et sacrificium patriarchæ nostri Abrahae: et quod tibi obtulit summus sacerdos tuus Melchisedech, sanctum sacrificium, immaculatam hostiam.

SUPPLICES te rogamus omnipotens Deus: jube hæc perferri per manus sancti angeli tui in sublime altare tuum, in conspectu di-

as also thy holy people, being mindful of the blessed passion of the same Christ thy Son our Lord, and of his resurrection from hell, as also of his glorious ascension into heaven, offer to thy most excellent majesty, of thy own gifts and favours, a pure host: a holy host; an unspotted host; the holy bread of eternal life, and the chalice of everlasting salvation.

ON which vouchsafe to look with a propitious and serene countenance, and to accept, as thou wert pleased to accept the offerings of thy just servant Abel, and the sacrifice of our patriarch Abraham, and that which thy high priest Melchisedech offered to thee, a holy sacrifice and spotless victim.

WE humbly beseech thee, Almighty God, command these offerings to be carried by the hands of thy holy angel to thy altar above

vinæ majestatis tuæ; ut quotquot ex hac altaris participatione, sacrosanctum Filii tui, cor ✠ pus et san ✠ guinem sumpserimus, omni benedictione cœlesti et gratia repleamur. Per eundem Christum Dominum nostrum. Amen.

in the presence of thy divine majesty, that as many as shall partake of the most sacred body and blood of thy Son at this altar, may be filled with all heavenly blessings and grace. Through, etc. Amen.

The commemoration of the dead.

MEmento etiam, Domine, famulorum famularumque tuarum N. et N. qui nos præcesserunt cum signo fidei et dormiunt in somno pacis.

REmember also, O Lord, thy servants, both men and women, N. and N. who are gone before us with the sign of faith and repose in the sleep of peace.

Here he pauses a little, to pray for particular persons.

IPSIS, Domine, et omnibus in Christo quiescentibus, locum refrigerii, lucis et pacis, ut indulgeas, deprecamur. Per eumdem Christum Dominum nostrum. Amen.

TO these, O Lord, and to all that rest in Christ, grant, we beseech thee, a place of refreshment, rest, and peace. Through the same Christ our Lord. Amen.

Then he strikes his breast, saying aloud the three first words of the following prayer:

NOBIS quoque peccatoribus famulis tuis, de multitudine misera-

TO us sinners also, thy servants, hoping in the multitude of thy

PALM SUNDAY. 75

tionum tuarum sperantibus, partem aliquam, et societatem donare digneris cum tuis sanctis apostolis et martyribus, cum Joanne, Stephano, Matthia, Barnaba, Ignatio, Alexandro, Marcellino, Petro, Felicitate, Perpetua, Agatha, Lucia, Agnete, Cæcilia, Anastasia, et omnibus sanctis tuis; intra quorum nos consortium non æstimator meriti, sed veniæ, quæsumus largitor admitte. Per Christum Dominum nostrum. Per quem hæc omnia, Domine, semper bona creas, sancti ✠ ficas, vivi ✠ ficas, bene ✠ dicis, et præstas nobis. Per ip ✠ sum, et cum ip ✠ so, et in ip ✠ so, est tibi Deo Patri ✠ omnipotenti, in unitate Spiritus ✠ Salncti, omnis honor et goria.

mercies, vouchsafe to grant some part and fellowship with thy holy apostles and martyrs, with John, Stephen, Matthias, Barnabas, Ignatius, Alexander, Marcellinus, Peter, Felicitas, Perpetua, Agatha, Lucy, Agnes, Cecily, Anastasia, and all thy saints; into whose company we beseech thee to admit us, not in consideration of our merit, but through thy gratuitous mercy and pardon through Christ our Lord. By whom, O Lord, thou dost always create, sanctify, quicken, bless, and grant us all these good things. By him, and with him, and in him, is to thee, God the Father Almighty, in the unity of the Holy Ghost, all honour and glory.

Then he says as follows:

V. Per omnia sæcula sæculorum. R. Amen.

V. For ever and ever R. Amen.

Oremus.

Let us pray.

PRæceptis salutaribus moniti, et divina in-

INstructed by thy wholesome precepts,

-stitutione formati, audemus dicere:

PATER noster, qui es in cœlis: sanctificetur nomen tuum: adveniat regnum tuum: fiat voluntas tua, sicut in cœlo, et in terra. Panem nostrum quotidianum da nobis hodie: et dimitte nobis debita nostra, sicut et nos dimittimus debitoribus nostris: et ne nos inducas in tentationem.

R. Sed libera nos a malo. *R.* Amen.

and following thy divine directions, we presume to say:

OUR Father, who art in heaven, hallowed be thy name: thy kingdom come: thy will be done on earth, as it is in heaven. Give us this day our daly bread: and forgive us our trespasses, as we forgive them that trespass against us: and lead us not into temptation.

R. But deliver us from evil. *R.* Amen.

Then in a low voice he says as follows:

LIBERA nos, quæsumus Domine, ab omnibus malis, præteritis, prœsentibus, et futuris: et intercedente beata et gloriosa semper Virgine Dei genitrice Maria, cum beatis apostolis tuis Petro et Paulo, atque Andrea, et omnibus sanctis, da propitius pacem in diebus nostris: ut ope misericordiæ tuæ adjuti, et a peccato simus semper liberi, et ab omne perturbatione securi:

DELIVER us, O Lord, we beseech thee, from all past, present, and future evils: and by the intercession of the blessed and glorious Mary ever Virgin, Mother of God, with thy blessed apostles Peter and Paul, with Andrew, and all the saints, mercifully grant peace in our days; that by the assistance of thy mercy we may be always free from sin, and secure from all disturbance.

Here breaking the Host in the middle, he says:

Per eundem Dominum nostrum Jesum Christum Filium tuum.

Through the same Jesus Christ our Lord thy Son.

Then he breaks off a small particle from one of its parts, saying:

Qui tecum vivit et regnat in unitate Spiritus Sancti Deus.

Who liveth and reigneth with thee in the unity of the Holy Ghost one God.

After which, holding the little piece over the Chalice, he says aloud:

V. Per omnia sæcula sæculorum. R. Amen.

V. For ever and ever. R. Amen.

Here he makes the sign of the cross thrice over the Chalice, saying aloud:

V. Pax ✠ Domini sit ✠ semper vobis ✠ cum.
R. Et cum spiritu tuo.

V. The peace of our Lord be always with you.
R. And with thy spirit.

Then he puts the particle of the Host into the Chalice, saying in a low voice:

HÆC commixtio et consecratio corporis et sanguinis Domini nostri Jesu Christi, fiat accipientibus nobis in vitam æternam. Amen.

MAY this mixture and consecration of the body and blood of our Lord Jesus Christ, be to us that receive them everlasting life.

After this, bowing down, he strikes his breast thrice, saying aloud:

AGNUS Dei, qui tollis peccata mundi: miserere nobis.

LAMB of God, that takest away the sins of the world: have mercy upon us.

Agnus Dei, qui tollis peccata mundi: miserere nobis.

Lamb of God, that takest away the sins of the world: have mercy upon us.

Agnus Dei, qui tollis peccata mundi: dona nobis pacem.

Lamb of God, that takest away the sins of the world: grant us peace.

The following prayers are said in a low voice:

DOMINE Jesu Christe, qui dixisti apostolis tuis: Pacem relinquo vobis, pacem meam do vobis: ne respicias peccata mea, sed fidem ecclesiæ tuæ: eamque secundum voluntatem tuam pacificare et coadunare digneris. Qui vivis et regnas Deus, etc. Amen.

LORD Jesus Christ, who didst say to thy apostles: I leave you peace, I give you my peace: regard not my sins, but the faith of thy church; and vouchsafe to grant us peace and union according to thy will. Who livest and reignest God for ever and ever. Amen.

In Solemn Masses, after this prayer, the Priest gives the Pax to the Deacon, saying:

V. Pax tecum.

V. Peace be with thee.

To which the Deacon answers:

Et cum spiritu tuo.

And with thy spirit.

DOMINE Jesu Christe, Fili Dei vivi, qui ex voluntate Patris, cooperante Spiritu Sancto, per mortem tuam mundum vivificasti: libera me per hoc sacrosanctum corpus et sanguinem tuum ab omni-

LORD Jesus Christ Son of the living God, who according to the will of the Father by the co-operation of the Holy Ghost, didst thro' thy death give life to the world: deliver me by this thy most sa-

bus iniquitatibus meis, et universis malis: et fac me tuis semper inhærere mandatis, et a te nunquam separari permittas. Qui cum eodem Deo Patre et Spiritu Sancto vivis et regnas Deus in sæcula sæculorum. Amen.

PErceptio corporis tui, Domine Jesu Christe, quod ego indignus sumere præsumo, non mihi proveniat in judicium et condemnationem; sed pro tua pietate prosit mihi ad tutamentum mentis et corporis, et ad medelam percipiendam. Qui vivis et regnas cum Deo Patre, etc. Amen.

cred body and blood from all my iniquities and from all evils; make me always obedient to thy commandments, and never suffer me to be separated from thee. Who with the same God the Father and Holy Ghost livest, etc. Amen.

LET not the participation of thy body, O Lord Jesus Christ, which I, though unworthy, presume to receive, turn to my judgment and condemnation: but through thy mercy may it become a safeguard and remedy both of my soul and body. Who with God the Father and the Holy Ghost livest. Amen.

Taking the Host in his hands, he says:

PANEM cœlestem accipiam, et nomen Domini invocabo.

I Will take the bread of heaven, and call on the name of the Lord.

Then striking his breast, he says thrice:

DOMINE, non sum dignus, ut intres sub tectum meum; sed tantum dic verbo, et sanabitur anima mea.

LORD, I am not worthy that thou shouldst enter under my roof: but say only the word, and my soul shall be healed.

After which he receives the Blessed Sacrament, saying:

CORPUS Domini nostri Jesu Christi custodiat animam meam in vitam æternam. Amen.

MAY the body of our Lord Jesus Christ preserve my soul to life everlasting. Amen.

Pausing awhile to meditate on the blessing he has received, he gathers up the fragments, and puts them into the Chalice, saying:

QUID retribuam Domino, pro omnibus quae retribuit mihi? Calicem salutaris accipiam, et nomen Domini invocabo. Laudans invocabo Dominum, et ab inimicis meis salvus ero.

WHAT shall I return to the Lord, for all that he has given me? I will take the cup of salvation, and call on the name of the Lord. Praising I will call upon the Lord and I shall be saved from my enemies.

Then he receives the Precious Blood, saying:

SANGUIS Domini nostri Jesu Christi custodiat animam meam in vitam æternam. Amen.

MAY the blood of our Lord Jesus Christ preserve my soul to life everlasting. Amen.

Whilst the servant pours wine into the chalice, the Priest says:

QUOD ore sumpsimus, Domine, pura mente capiamus; et de munere temporali fiat nobis remedium sempiternum.

WHAT we have taken with our mouth, O Lord, may we receive with a pure heart; and grant, that of a temporal gift, it may prove an everlasting remedy.

PALM SUNDAY. 81

Whilst he washes his fingers over the Chalice with wine and water, he says:

CORPUS tuum, Domine, quod sumpsi, et sanguis, quem potavi, adhæreat visceribus meis, et præsta, ut in me non remaneat scelerum macula, quem pura et sancta refecerunt sacramenta. Qui vivis et regnas in sæcula sæculorum. Amen.

MAY thy body, O Lord, which I have received: and thy blood, which I have drunk, cleave to my bowels, and grant that no stain of sin may remain in me, who have been refreshed by thy pure and holy mysteries. Who livest. Amen.

Then the book is moved to the Epistle side of the Altar, where he says as follows:

Communio. — Pater, si non potest hic calix transire, nisi bibam illum: fiat voluntas tua.

The Communion. — Father, if this cup cannot pass away, unless I drink it, thy will be done.

V. Dominus vobiscum.

R. Et cum spiritu tuo.

V. The Lord be with you.
R. And with thy spirit.

Postcommunio.

PER hujus, Domine, operationem mysterii, et vitia nostra purgentur, et justa desideria compleantur. Per Dominum. *R.* Amen.
V. Dominus vobiscum.
R. Et cum spiritu tuo.
V. Benedicamus Domino.
R. Deo gratias.

Postcommunion.

MAY our vices be destroyed, O Lord, and our just desires fulfilled, by virtue of these mysteries. Through our Lord. *R.* Amen.
V. The Lord be with you. *V.* And with thy spirit. *V.* Let us bless the Lord. *R.* Thanks be to God.

After this, bowing in the middle of the Altar, he says in a low voice:

PLACEAT tibi sancta Trinitas, obsequium servitutis meæ: et præsta, ut sacrificium, quod oculis tuæ majestatis indignus obtuli, tibi sit acceptabile, mihique, et omnibus, pro quibus illud obtuli, sit te miserante, propitiabile. Per Christum Dominum nostrum. Amen.

LET the performance of my homage be pleasing to thee, O holy Trinity; and grant, that this sacrifice, which I, though unworthy, have offered to thy divine Majesty, may be acceptable to thee and through thy mercy, be a propitiation for me, and all those for whom it has been offered. Through etc. Amen.

Then kissing the Altar, and turning towards the people, he blesses them, saying aloud:

Benedicat vos omnipotens Deus, Pater et Filius, et Spiritus Sanctus. R. Amen.

May almighty God, Father, Son, and Holy Ghost, bless you. R. Amen.

After which he goes to the Gospel side of the Altar, and there he says aloud:

V. Dominus vobiscum.
R. Et cum spiritu tuo.

V. The Lord be with you.
R. And with thy spirit.

In Low Masses, (instead of the following Gospel according to St. John,) the Gospel according to St. Matthew is read, as above at the blessing of the palms, p. 20.

V. Initium sancti evangelii secundum Joannem.

V. The beginning of the holy Gospel according to St. John.

R. Gloria tibi, Domine.

IN principio erat Verbum, et Verbum erat apud Deum, et Deus erat Verbum. Hoc erat in principio apud Deum. Omnia per ipsum facta sunt: et sine ipso factum est nihil quod factum est: In ipso vita erat, et vita erat lux hominum: et lux in tenebris lucet, et tenebræ eum non comprehenderunt. Fuit homo missus a Deo, cui nomen erat Joannes. Hic venit in testimonium, ut testimonium perhiberet de lumine, ut omnes crederent per illum. Non erat ille lux, sed ut testimonium perhiberet de lumine. Erat lux vera, quæ illuminat omnem hominem venientem in hunc mundum. In mundo erat, et mundus per ipsum factus est, et mundus eum non cognovit. In propria venit et sui eum non receperunt. Quotquot autem receperunt eum, dedit eis potestatem Filios Dei fie-

R. Glory be to thee O Lord.

IN the beginning was the Word, and the Word was with God and the Word was God. The same was in the beginning with God. All things were made by him: and without him was made nothing that was made. In him was life, and the life was the light of men: and the light shineth in darkness, and the darkness did not comprehend it. There was a man sent from God, whose name was John. This man came for a witness, to bear witness of the light, that all men might believe through him. He was not the light, but was to bear witness of the light. That was the true light, which enlighteneth every man that cometh into this world. He was in the world, and the world was made by him, and the world knew him not. He came unto his own, and his own received him not. But as

ri, his qui credunt in nomine ejus: qui non ex sanguinibus, neque ex voluntate carnis, neque ex voluntate viri, sed ex Deo nati sunt. *Et Verbum caro factum est*, et habitavit in nobis: et vidimus gloriam ejus, gloriam quasi unigeniti a Patre, plenum gratiæ et veritatis.

many as received him, to them he gave power to be made the sons of God, to them that believe in his name. Who are born not of blood, nor of the will of the flesh nor of the will of man, but of God. *And the Word was made flesh* and dwelt among us, and we saw his glory, as it were the glory of the only-begotten of the Father, full of grace and truth.

R. Deo gratias.   R. Thanks be to God.

MONDAY IN HOLY WEEK.

The Priest begins Mass at foot of the Altar, as above, p. 34 *till he comes to*

THE INTROIT.

JUDICA, Domine, nocentes me, expugna impugnantes me: apprehende arma et scutum, et exurge in adjutorium meum, Domine, virtus salutis meæ. *Ps.*—Effunde frameam, et conclude adversus eos qui persequuntur me: dic animæ meæ: salus tua ego sum. Judica, Domine, etc.

JUDGE, O Lord, those that hurt me, defeat those that assault me: take thy armour and shield, and come to my assistance, O Lórd, the strength of my salvation. *Ps.*—Draw thy sword, and hold it against those that persecute me: say to my soul: I am thy salvation, Judge, O Lord, etc.

MONDAY IN HOLY WEEK.

Kyrie eleison, *as above p. 37*

Oremus. | Let us pray.

DA, quæsumus, omnipotens Deus, ut qui in tot adversis ex nostra infirmitate deficimus; intercedente unigeniti Filii tui passione respiremus. Qui tecum vivit et regnat in unitate Spiritus Sancti Deus. Per ommia sæcula sæculorum. R. Amen.

GRANT, we beseech thee, almighty God, that we, who through our weakness faint under so many adversities may recover by the passion of thy only begotten Son. Who with thee and the Holy Ghost, liveth and reigneth one God for ever and ever. R. Amen.

Then is said either the following prayer against the persecutors of the Church; or the prayer for the Pope as below.

ECCLESIÆ tuæ, quæsumus Domine, preces placatus admitte: ut destructis adversitatibus et erroribus universis secura tibi serviat libertate. Per Dominum nostrum, etc.

MERCIFULLY hear we beseech thee, O Lord, the prayers of thy church: that being delivered from all adversities and errors, she may serve thee in secure liberty. Through, etc.

The Prayer for the Pope.

DEUS, omnium fidelium pastor et rector, famulum tuum N. quem pastorem Ecclesiæ tuæ præesse voluisti, propitius respice: da ei, quæsumus, verbo et exemplo quibus præest, proficere; ut ad vitam

O GOD, the pastor and governor of all the faithful, mercifully regard thy servant N. whom thou hast been pleased to appoint the supreme pastor of thy church; and grant, we beseech thee, that both

una cum grege sibi credito, perveniat sempiternam. Per Dominum nostrum Jesum Christum, etc.

Lectio Isaiæ Prophetæ, *cap.* 50.

IN diebus illis, dixit Isaias: Dominus Deus aperuit mihi aurem, ego autem non contradico: retrorsum non abii. Corpus meum dedi percutientibus, et genas meas vellentibus: faciem meam non averti ab increpantibus et conspuentibus in me. Dominus Deus auxiliator meus, ideo non sum confusus: ideo posui faciem meam, ut petram durissimam, et scio quoniam non confundar. Juxta est qui justificat me, quis contradicet mihi? Stemus simul, quis est adversarius meus? Accedat ad me. Ecce Dominus Deus auxiliator meus: quis est qui condemnet me? Ecce omnes quasi vestimentum conterentur, tinea comedet eos. Quis

by word and example, he may edify all that are under his charge, and with the flock committed to him arrive at life everlasting. Through.

Lesson from the Prophet Isaias. *chap.* 50.

IN those days, Isaias said: The Lord God hath opened my ear, and I do not resist, I have not gone back. I have given my body to the strikes and my cheeks to them that plucked them: I have not turned away my face from them that rebuked me, and spit upon me. The Lord God is my helper, therefore am I not confounded: therefore have I set my face as a most hard rock, and I know that I shall not be confounded. He that is near justifieth me. Who will contend with me? let us stand together. Who is my adversary? let him come near to me. Behold the Lord God is my helper: who is he that shall condemn me? Lo

ex vobis timens Dominum audiens vocem servi sui? Qui ambulavit in tenebris, et non est lumen ei, speret in nomine Domini, et innitatur super Deum suum.

they shall all be destroyed as a garment, the moth shall eat them up. Who is there among you that feareth the Lord, that heareth the voice of his servant, that hath walked in darkness, and hath no light? let him hope in the name of the Lord, and lean upon his God,

Graduale. — Exurge, Domine, et intende judicio meo.— Deus meus, et Dominus meus, in causam meam. *V.* Effunde frameam: et conclude adversus eos qui me persequuntur.

Gradual. — Arise, O Lord, and attend to my judgment, to my cause, my God and my Lord. *V.* Draw thy sword and hold it against those that persecute me.

Tractus.—Domine non secundum peccata nostra, quæ fecimus nos, neque secundum iniquitates nostras retribuas nobis. *V.* Domine, ne memineris iniquitatum nostrarum antiquarum: cito anticipent nos misericordiæ tuæ, quia pauperes facti sumus nimis. *R.* Adjuva nos. Deus Salutaris noster; et propter gloriam nominis tui, Domine, libera nos: et propitius esto peccatis nostris, propter nomen tuum.

Tract. — O Lord, render not to us according to the sins we have committed, nor according to our iniquities. *V.* O Lord, remember not our former iniquities: let thy mercies speedily prevent us: because we are become exceeding poor. *R.* Help us, O God our Saviour: and for the glory of thy name, O Lord, deliver us: and pardon us our sins for the sake of thy name.

Munda cor meum, *and* Jube Domine benedicere, *as at* p. 58.

Sequentia sancti Evangelii secundum Joannem. *Cap. 12.*

Cotinuation of the holy Gospel according to St. John. *Ch. 12.*

ANTE sex dies pascha, venit Jesus Bethaniam, ubi Lazarus fuerat mortuus, quem suscitavit Jesus. Fecerunt autem ei cœnam ibi: et Martha ministrabat, Lazarus vero unus erat ex discumbentibus cum eo. Maria ergo accepit libram unguenti nardi pistici pretiosi, et unxit pedes Jesu, et extersit pedes ejus capillis suis: et domus impleta est ex odore unguenti. Dixit ergo unus ex discipulis ejus, Judas Iscariotes, qui erat eum traditurus: Quare hoc unguentum non væniit trecentis denariis, et datum est egenis? Dixit autem hoc, non quia de egenis pertinebat ad eum, sed quia fur erat, et loculos habens, ea quæ mittebantur, portabat. Dixit ergo Jesus: Sinite illam, ut in diem sepul-

SIX days before the pasch, Jesus came to Bethania, where Lazarus had been dead, whom Jesus raised to life. And they made a supper there: and Martha served, but Lazarus was one of them that were at the table with him. Mary therefore took a pound of ointment of right spikenard, of great price, and anointed the feet of Jesus, and wiped his feet with her hair: and the house was filled with the odour of the ointment. Then one of his disciples, Judas Iscariot, he that was about to betray him, said: Why was not this ointment sold for three hundred pence, and given to the poor? Now he said this, not because he cared for the poor, but because he was a thief, and having the

MONDAY IN HOLY WEEK.

turæ meæ servet illud. Pauperes enim semper habetis vobiscum: me autem non semper habetis. Cognovit ergo turba multa ex Judæis, quia illic est: et venerunt non propter Jesum tantum, sed ut Lazarum viderent, quem suscitavit a mortuis.

purse carried what was put therein. But Jesus said: Let her alone, that she may keep it against the day of my burial. For the poor you have always with you: but me you have not always. A great multitude therefore of the Jews knew that he was there; and they came, not for Jesus's sake only, but that they might see Lazarus, whom he had raised from the dead.

Offertorium. — Eripe me de inimicis meis, Domine: ad te confugi, doce me facere voluntatem tuam: quia Deus meus es tu.

Offertory. — Deliver me from mine enemies O Lord; to thee have I fled, teach me to do thy will, because thou art my God.

Then he returns to Suscipe, *as above* p. 62, *till he comes to the following prayer called*

THE SECRETA.

HÆC sacrificia nos, omnipotens Deus, potenti virtute mundatos ad suum facient puriores venire principium. Per Dominum nostrum, etc.

GRANT, Almighty God, that being purified by the powerful virtue of these sacrifices. we may arrive with greater purity to their fountain. Through our Lord, etc.

The secret against the persecutors of the Church.

PROTEGE nos, Domine, tuis mysteriis servientes: ut divinis rebus

PROTECT us, O Lord, who celebrate thy mysteries: that apply-

inhærentes, et corpore tibi famulemur, et mente. Per Dominum nostrum, etc.

ing ourselves to divine things, we may serve thee both in soul and body. Through, etc.

Or for the Pope.

OBLATIS, quæsumus Domine, placare muneribus: et famulum tuum N. quem pastorem ecclesiæ tuæ præesse voluisti, assidua protectione guberna. Per Dominum nostrum, etc.

BE appeased, O Lord. we beseech thee, by these offerings: and govern by thy continual protection thy servant N. whom thou hast been pleased to appoint supreme pastor of thy church. Through, etc.

The Preface and Canon from p. 69 to p. 81, till he comes to the

Communio. — Erubescant et revereantur simul, qui gratulantur malis meis: induantur pudore et reverentia, qui maligna loquuntur adversus me.

Communion. — Let them blush and be ashamed together, who rejoice at my evils; let them be clothed with confusion and shame, that speak malicious things against me.

The Post communion.

PRæbeant nobis, Domine, divinum tua sancta fervorem: quo eorum pariter et actu delectemur et fructu. Per Dominum nostrum, etc.

LET thy holy mysteries, O Lord, inspire us with thy divine fervour: that we may delight both in their effect and celebration. Through our Lord, etc.

MONDAY IN HOLY WEEK.

Against the persecutors of the Church.

QUæsumus, Domine Deus noster: ut quos divina tribuis participatione gaudere, humanis non sinas subjacere periculis. Per Dominum nostrum, etc.

PReserve, we beseech thee, O Lord our God, from human dangers, those whom thou rejoicest by the participation of this divine communion. Through, etc.

Or for the Pope.

HÆC nos, quæsumus Domine, divini sacramenti perceptio protegat: et famulum tuum N. quem pastorem ecclesiæ tuæ præesse voluisti, una cum commisso sibi grege, salvet semper et muniat. Per Dominum nostrum, etc.

MAY the participation of this divine sacrament protect us, O Lord, and always procure safety and defence to thy servant N. whom thou hast been pleased to appoint the supreme pastor of thy church, together with the flock committed to his charge. Through our Lord, etc.

The prayer over the people.

Oremus.

Let us pray.

Humiliate capita vestra Deo.

Bow down your heads to God.

ADJUVA nos, Deus Salutaris noster; et ad beneficia recolenda, quibus nos instaurare dignatus es, tribue venire gaudentes. Per Dominum nostrum, etc.

HELP us, O God our Saviour: and grant that we may celebrate with joy the memory of those benefits, by which thou hast been pleased to redeem us. Through our Lord, etc.

The remainder as above, p. 81.

TUESDAY IN HOLY WEEK.

The Priest begins Mass at the foot of the Altar, as above, p. 34 *till he comes to*

THE INTROIT.

NOS autem gloriari oportet in cruce Domini nostri Jesu Christi: in quo est salus, vita et resurrectio nostra: per quem salvati et liberati sumus. *Ps.* — Deus misereatur nostri, et benedicat nobis: illuminet vultum suum super nos, et misereatur nostri. Nos autem, etc.

WE ought to glory in the cross of our Lord Jesus Christ: in Whom is our salvation, life, and resurrection, by whom we have been saved and delivered *Ps.* — May God have mercy on us, and bless us: may he illuminate us with his countenance, and have mercy on us. We ought, etc.

Kyrie eleison, *as before,* p. 37.

Oremus.

Let us pray.

OMnipotens sempiterne Deus, da nobis ita Dominicæ passionis sacramenta peragere: ut indulgentiam percipere mereamur. Per eundem Dominum nostrum, etc.

ALmighty and everlasting God, grant that we may celebrate the mysteries of our Lord's passion in such a manner as to deserve to obtain thy pardon. Through, etc.

Then is said the prayer against the persecutors of the Church, or for the Pope as p. 85.

Lectio Jeremiae Prophetae, *cap.* 11.

The Lesson out of the Prophet Jeremiah, *chap.* 11.

IN diebus illis: dixit Jeremias: Domine demonstrasti mihi, et cognovi: tunc ostendisti mihi studia eorum. Et ego quasi agnus mansuetus, qui portatur ad victimam; et non cognovi quia cogitaverunt super me consilia, dicentes: Mittamus lignum in panem ejus, et eradamus eum de terra viventium, et nomen ejus non memoretur amplius. Tu autem Domine Sabaoth, qui judicas juste, et probas renes et corda, videam ultionem tuam ex eis: tibi enim revelavi causam meam, Domine Deus meus.

Graduale. — Ego autem, cum mihi molesti essent, induebam me cilicio, et humiliabam in jejunio animam meam: et oratio mea in sinu meo convertetur. *V.* Judica, Domine nocentes me: expugna impugnantes me: apprehende arma et scutum, et exurge in adjutorium mihi.

IN those days, Jeremiah said, O Lord thou hast showed me and I have known: then thou showedst me their doings. And I was as a meek lamb, that is carried to be a victim: and I knew not that they had devised counsels against me, saying. Let us put wood on his bread, and cut him off from the land of the living, and let his name be remembered no more. But thou, O Lord of Sabaoth, who judgest justly, and triest the reins and the hearts, let me see thy revenge on them: for to thee have I revealed my cause.

Gradual.—But I, when they were troublesome to me, put on hair cloth, and humbled my soul in fasting: and my prayer will be returned into my bosom. *V.* Judge, O Lord, those that hurt me; defeat those that assault me: take up thy armour and shield, and come to my assistance.

TUESDAY IN HOLY WEEK.

Passio Domini nostri Jesu Christi, secundum Marcum (*Cap.* 14).

The passion of our Lord Jesus Christ, according to Mark. (*Ch.* 14).

IN illo tempore: Erat pascha et azyma post biduum: et quærebant summi sacerdotes et Scribæ, quomodo Jesum dolo tenerent, et occiderent. Dicebant autem: *S.* non in die festo, ne forte tumultus fieret in populo. *C.* Et cum esset Jesus Bethaniæ in domo Simonis leprosi, et recumberet: venit mulier habens alabastrum unguenti nardi spicati pretiosi, et fracto alabastro, effudit super caput ejus. Erant autem quidam indigne ferentes intra semetipsos, et dicentes: *S.* Ut quid perditio ista unguenti facta est? Poterat enim unguentum istud venumdari plus quam trecentis denariis, et dari pauperibus. *C.* Et fremebant in eam, Jesus autem dixit: ✠ Sinite eam, quid illi molesti estis? Bonum opus operata est in me. Semper enim pauperes

AT that time: The feast of the pasch and of the azymes was after two days: and the chief priests, and the scribes, sought how they might by some wile lay hold on him, and kill him. But they said: Not on the festival day, lest there should be a tumult among the people. And when he was in Bethania in the house of Simon the leper, and was at meat, there was a woman having an alabaster box of ointment of precious spikenard: and breaking the alabaster box, she poured it out upon his head. Now there were some that had indignation within themselves, and said: Why was this waste of the ointment made? For this ointment might have been sold for more than three hundred pence, and given to the poor. And they mur-

habetis vobiscum; et cum volueritis, potestis illis benefacere: me autem non semper habetis. Quod habuit hæc, fecit: prævenit ungere corpus meum iu sepulturam. Amen dico vobis, ubicumque prædicatum fuerit evangelium istud in universo mundo, et quod fecit hæc, narrabitur in memoriam ejus. *C.* Et Judas Iscariotes unus de duodecim abiit ad summos sacerdotes, ut proderet eum illis. Qui audientes gavisi sunt: et promiserunt ei pecuniam se daturos. Et quærebat quomodo illum opportune traderet. Et primo die azymorum quando pascha immolabant, dicunt ei discipuli: *S.* Quo vis eamus, et paremus tibi, ut manduces pascha: *C.* Et mittit duos ex discipulis suis, et dicit eis: ✠ Ite in civitatem, et occurret vobis homo lagenam aquæ bajulans, sequimini eum: et quocumque introierit, dicite domino domus, quia magister

mured against her. But Jesus said: Let her alone, why do you molest her? She hath wrought a good work upon me. For the poor you have always with you: and whensoever you will, you may do them good: but me you have not always. She hath done what she could; she is come before-hand to anoint my body for the burial. Amen I say to you, wheresoever this gospel shall be preached in the whole world, that also which she hath done, shall be told for a memorial of her. And Judas Iscariot, one of the twelve, went to the chief priests, to betray him to them. And they hearing it were glad and promised to give him money. And he sought how he might conveniently betray him. Now on the first day of the unleavened bread, when they sacrificed the pasch, the disciples say to him: Whither wilt thou that

dicit: Ubi est refectio mea, ubi pascha cum discipulis meis manducem? Et ipse vobis demonstrabit cœnaculum grande, stratum: et illic parate nobis. *C.* Et abierunt discipuli ejus, et venerunt in civitatem: et invenerunt sicut dixerat illis, et paraverunt pascha. Vespere autem facto, venit cum duodecim. Et discumbentibus eis, et manducantibus, ait Jesus: ✠ Amen dico vobis, quia unus ex vobis tradet me, qui manducat mecum. *C.* At illi cœperunt contristari, et dicere ei singulatim: *S.* Numquid ego? *C.* Qui ait illis:✠Unus ex duodecim qui intingit mecum manum in catino. Et Filius quidem hominis vadit, sicut scriptum est de eo; Væ autem homini illi, per quem Filius hominis tradetur. Bonum erat ei, si non esset natus homo ille.*C.* Et manducantibus illis, accepit Jesus panem, et benedicens fregit, et edit deis, et ait: ✠ Sumite, hoc est corpus me-

we go, and prepare for thee to eat the pasch? And he sendeth two of his disciples, and saith to them: Go ye into the city: and there shall meet you a man carrying a pitcher of water, follow him: and whithersoever he shall go in, say to the master of the house: The master saith: Where is my refectory where I may eat the pasch with my disciples? And he will show you a large dining-room furnished; and there prepare ye for us. And his disciples went their way, and came into the city, and they found as he had told them, and they prepared the pasch. And when evening was come, he cometh with the twelve. And when they were at table and eating, Jesus saith: Amen I say to you, one of you that eateth with me shall betray me. But they began to be sorrowful, and to say to him one by one: It is I? And he said to them:

um. *C.* Et accepto calice, gratias agens, dedit eis: et biberunt ex illo omnes, et ait illis: ✠ Hic est sanguis meus novi testamenti, qui pro multis effundetur. Amen dico vobis, quia iam non bibam de hoc genimine vitis, usque in diem illum, cum illud bibam novum in regno Dei. *C.* Et hymno dicto, exierunt in montem Olivarum. Et ait eis Jesus: ✠ Omnes scandalizabimini in me in nocte ista: quia scriptum est: Percutiam pastorem, et dispergentur oves. Sed postquam resurrexero, præcedam vos in Galilæam. *C.* Petrus autem ait illi: *S.* Et si omnes scandalizati fuerint in te, sed non ego. *C.* Et ait illi Jesus: ✠ Amen dico tibi, quia tu hodie in nocte hac, priusquam gallus vocem bis dederit, ter me es negaturus. *C.* At ille amplius loquebatur: *S.* Et si oportuerit me simul commori tibi, non te negabo. *C.* Similiter autem et omnes dicebant. Et veniunt

One of the twelve who dippeth his hand in the dish with me, and the Son of man indeed goeth, as it is written of him: but wo to that man by whom the Son of Man shall be betrayed. It were better for him, if that man had not been born. And whilst they were eating, Jesus took bread: and blessing broke, and gave to them, and said: take ye: This is my body. And having taken the chalice, and giving thanks, he gave it to them: and they all drank of it. And he said to them: This is my blood of the new testament, which shall be shed for many. Amen I say unto you, that I will drink no more of this fruit of the vine, until that day when I shall drink it new in the kingdom of God. And when they had sung a hymn, they went forth to the mount of Olives. And Jesus saith to them: You will all be scandalized in my

in prædium, cui nomen Gethsemani, et ait discipulis suis: ✠ Sedete hic donec orem. *C.* Et assumit Petrum, et Jacobum, et Joannem secum: et cœpit pavere et tædere. Et ait illis: ✠ Tristis est anima mea usque ad mortem: sustinete hic, et vigilate. *C.* Et cum processisset paululum, procidit super terram: et orabat, ut si fieri posset, transiret ab eo hora: et dixit: ✠ Abba, Pater, omnia tibi possibilia sunt: transfer calicem hunc a me, sed non quod ego volo, sed quod tu. *C.* Et venit, et invenit eos dormientes. Et ait Petro: ✠ Simon, dormis? Non potuisti una hora vigilare? Vigilate, et orate, ut non intretis in tentationem. Spiritus quidem promptus est, caro vero infirma. *C.* Et iterum abiens oravit, eumdem sermonem dicens. Et reversus denuo invenit eos dormientes (erant enim oculi eorum gravati) et ignorabant quid respon-

regard this night: for it is written: *I will strike the shepherd, and the sheep shall be dispersed.* But after I shall be risen again, I will go before you into Galilee. But Peter saith to him: Although all shall be scandalized in thee, yet not I. And Jesus said to him: Amen I say to thee, to-day, even in this night, before the cock crow twice thou shalt deny me thrice. But he spoke the more vehemently: Although I should die together with thee, I will not deny thee. And in like manner also said they all. And they came to a farm called Gethsemani. And he saith to his disciples: Sit you here while I pray. And he taketh Peter, and James, and John with him; and he began to fear and to be heavy. And he saith to them: My soul is sorrowful even unto death: stay you here, and watch. And when he had gone forward a little, he fell flat on the ground: and

TUESDAY IN HOLY WEEK.

deret ei. Et venit tertio, et ait illis: ✠ Dormite jam, et requiescite. Sufficit: venit hora: ecce Filius hominis tradetur in manus peccatorum. Surgite, eamus: ecce qui me tradet, prope est. *C.* Et, adhuc eo loquente, venit Judas Iscariotes, unus de duodecim, et cum eo turba multa cum gladiis et lignis, a summis sacerdotibus, et Scribis, et senioribus. Dederat autem traditor signum eis, dicens: *S.* Quemcumque osculatus fuero, ipse est, tenete eum, et ducite caute. *C.* Et cum venisset, statim accedens ad eum, ait: *S.* Ave, Rabbi *C.* et osculatus est eum. At illi manus injecerunt in eum, et tenuerunt eum. Unus autem quidam de circumstantibus educens gladium, percussit servum summi sacerdotis: et amputavit illi auriculam. Et respondens Jesus, ait illis: ✠ Tamquam ad latronem existis cum gladiis et lignis comprehendere me? quotidie

he prayed, that if it might be, the hour might pass from him: And he said: Abba, Father, all things are possible to thee, take away this chalice from me, but not what I will, but what thou wilt. And he cometh, and findeth them sleeping. And he saith to Peter: Simon, sleepest thou? couldst thou not watch one hour? Watch ye and pray, that you enter not into temptation. The spirit indeed is willing, but the flesh is weak. And going away again, he prayed, saying the same words. And when he returned, he found them again asleep (for their eyes were heavy), and they knew not what to answer him. And he cometh the third time and saith to them: Sleep ye now, and take your rest, it is enough: the hour is come: behold the Son of Man shall be betrayed into the hands of sinners. Rise up, let us go. Behold he that will betray me is at

eram apud vos in templo docens, et non me tenuistis. Sed ut implerentur scripturæ. C. Tunc discipuli ejus, relinquentes eum, omnes fugerunt. Adolescens autem quidam sequebatur eum, amictus sindone super nudo: et tenuerunt eum. At ille, rejecta sindone, nudus profugt ab eis. Et adduxerunt Jesum ad summum sacerdotem: et convenerunt omnes sacerdotes, et Scribæ et seniores. Petrus autem a longe secutus est eum, usque intro in atrium summi sacerdotis: et sedebat cum ministris ad ignem, et calefaciebat se. Summi vero sacerdotes, et omne concilium, quærebant adversus Jesum testimonium, ut eum morti traderent, nec inveniebant. Multi enim testimonium falsum dicebant adversus eum: et con·enientia testimonia non erant. Et quidam surgentes, falsum testimonium ferebant adversus eum, dicentes:

hand. And while he was yet speaking, cometh Judas Iscariot, one of the twelve, and with him a great multitude with swords and staves, from the chief priests and the scribes and the ancients. And he that betrayed him had given them a sign, saying: Whomsoever I shall kiss, that is he, lay hold on him, and lead him away carefully. And when he was come, immediately going up to him, he saith: Hail, Rabbi: and he kissed him. But they laid hands on him and held him. And one of them that stood by, drawing a sword, struck a servant of the chief priest, and cut off his ear. And Jesus answering, said to them: Are you come out as against a robber with swords and staves to apprehend me? I was daily with you in the temple teaching, and you did not lay hands on me. But that the scriptures might be fulfilled. Then his disciples leav·

S. Quoniam nos audivimus eum dicentem: Ego dissolvam templum hoc manufactum, et per triduum aliud non manufactum ædificabo. C. Et non erat conveniens testimonium illorum. Et exurgens summus sacerdos in med um, interrogavit Jesum, dicens: S. Non respondes quidquam ad ea, quæ tibi objiciuntur ab his? C. Ille autem tacebat, et nihil respondit. Rursum summus sacerdos interrogabat eum, et dixit ei: S. Tu es Christus Filius Dei benedicti? C. Jesus autem dixit illi: ✠ Ego sum. Et videbitis Filium hominis sedentem a dextris virtutis Dei, et venientem cum nubibus cœli. C. Summus autem sacerdos scindens vestimenta sua, ait: S. Quid adhuc desideramus testes? Audistis blasphemiam: quid vobis videtur? C. Qui omnes condemnaverunt eum esse reum ,mortis. Et cœperunt quidam conspuere eum, et velare faciem ejus, et co-

ing him, al' fled away. And a certain young man followed him, having a linen cloth cast about his naked body, and they laid hold on him. But he casting off the linen cloth, fled from them naked. And they brought Jesus to the high-priest; and all the priests and the scribes and the ancients were assembled together. And Peter followed him afar off even unto the palace of the high priest: and he sat with the servants at the fire, and warmed himself. And the chief priests and all the council sought for evidence against Jesus, that they might put him to death, and they found none. For many bore false witness against him, and their evidence did not agree. And some rising up, bore false witness against him, saying: We heard him say, I will destroy this temple made with hands, and within three days I will build another not made

laphis eum cædere, et dicere ei: *S.* Prophetiza. *C.* Et ministri alapis eum cædebant. Et cum esset Petrus in atrio deorsum, venit una ex ancillis summi sacerdotis: et cum vidisset Petrum calefacientem se, aspiciens illum, ait: *S.* Et tu cum Jesu Nazareno eras. *C.* At ille negavit, dicens: *S.* Neque scio, neque novi quid dicas. *C.* Et exiit foras ante atrium, et gallus cantavit. Rursus autem cum vidisset illum ancilla, cœpit dicere circumstantibus: *S.* Quia hic ex illis est. *C.* At ille iterum negavit. Et post pusillum rursus qui astabant, dicebant Petro: *S.* Vere ex illis es: nam et Galilæus es. *C.* Ille autem cœpit anathematizare et jurare: quia nescio hominem istum, quem dicitis. Et statim gallus iterum cantavit. Et recordatus est Petrus verbi, quod dixerat ei Jesus: Priusquam gallus cantet bis, ter me negabis. Et cœpit flere. Et confestim, mane concilium facientes summi

with hands. And their witness did not agree. And the high-priest rising up in the midst, asked Jesus, saying: Answerest thou nothing to the things that are laid to thy charge by these men? But he held his peace, and answered nothing. Again the high-priest asked him, and said to him: Art thou the Christ the Son of the Blessed God? And Jesus said to him: I am. And you shall see the Son of Man sitting on the right hand of the power of God, and coming with the clouds of heaven. Then the high-priest rending his garments, saith: What need we any farther witnesses? You have heard the blasphemy. What think you? And they all condemned him to be guilty of death. And some began to spit on him, and to cover his face, and to buffet him, and to say to him: Prophesy: and the servants struck him with the palms of their

sacerdotes, cum senioribus, et Scribis, et universo consilio: vincientes Jesum, duxerunt et tradiderunt Pilato. Et interrogavit eum Pilatus: *S.* Tu es Rex Judæorum? *C.* At ille respondens ait illi: ✠ Tu dicis. *C.* Et accusabant eum summi sacerdotes in multis. Pilatus autem rursum interrogavit eum, dicens: *S.* Non respondes quidquam? Vide in quantis te accusant. *C.* Jesus autem amplius nihil respondit, ita ut miraretur Pilatus. Per diem autem festum solebat dimittere illis unum ex vinctis, quemcumque petissent. Erat autem qui dicebatur Barabbas, qui cum seditiosis erat vinctus, qui in seditione fecerat homicidium. Et cum ascendisset turba, cœpit rogare, sicut semper faciebat illis. Pilatus autem respondit eis, et dixit: *S.* Vultis dimittam vobis Regem Judæorum? Sciebat enim, quod per invidiam tra-

hands. Now when Peter was in the court below, there cometh one of the maid servants of the high-priest: and when she had seen Peter warming himself, looking on him, she saith: Thou also wast with Jesus of Nazareth. But he denied: saying: I know not nor understand what thou sayest. And he went forth before the court; and the cock crew. And again a maid servant seeing him, began to say to the standers-by: This is one of them. But he denied again. And after a while they that stood by, said again to Peter: Surely thou art one of them: for thou also art a Galilean. But he began to curse and to swear, saying: I know not this man of whom you speak. And immediately the cock crew again. And Peter remembered the word that Jesus had said to him: Before the cock crow twice, thou shalt deny me thrice. And

didissent eum summi sacerdotes. Pontifices autem concitaverunt turbam, ut magis Barabbam dimitteret eis. Pilatus autem iterum respondens, ait illis: *S.* Quid ergo vultis faciam regi Judæorum? *C.* Et illi iterum clamaverunt: Crucifige eum. *C.* Pilatus vero dicebat illis: *S.* Quid enim mali fecit? *C.* At illi magis clamabant: *S.* Crucifige eum. *C.* Pilatus autem volens populo satisfacere, dimisit illis Barabbam, et tradidit Jesum flagellis cæsum, ut crucifigeretur. Milites autem duxerunt eum in atrium prætorii, et convocant totam cohortem, et induunt eum purpura, et imponunt ei plectentes spineam coronam. Et cæperunt salutare eum: *S.* Ave Rex Judæorum. *C.* Et percutiebant caput ejus arundine: et conspuebant eum, et ponentes genua, adorabant eum. Et postquam illuserunt ei, exuerunt illum purpura, et induerunt eum vestimentis suis: et eduhe began to weep. And straightway in the morning the chief priests holding a consultation with the ancients and the scribes, and the whole council, bound Jesus and led him away, and delivered him to Pilate, and Pilate asked him: art thou the king of the Jews? But he answering saith to him: Thou sayest it. And the chief priests accused him in many things. And Pilate again asked him, saying: Answerest thou nothing? Behold in how many things they accuse thee. But Jesus still answered nothing; so that Pilate wondered. Now on the festival day he was wont to release unto them one of the prisoners, whomsoever they demanded. And there was one called Barabbas, who was put in prison with some seditious men, who in the sedition had committed murder. And when the multitude was come, they began to desire

cunt illum, ut crucifigerent eum. Et angariaverunt prætereuntem quempiam, Simonem Cyrœneum, venientem de villa, patrem Alexandri et Rufi, ut tolleret crucem ejus. Et perducunt illum in Golgotha locum, quod est interpretatum, Calvariæ locus. Et dabant ei bibere myrrhatum vinum: et non accepit. Et crucifigentes eum, diviserunt vestimenta ejus, mittentes sortem super eis, quis quid tolleret. Erat autem hora tertia: Et crucifixerunt eum. Et erat titulus causæ ejus inscriptus; *Rex Judæorum*. Et cum eo crucifigunt duos latrones: unum a dextris, et alium a sinistris ejus. Et impleta est Scriptura, quæ dicit: Et cum iniquis reputatus est. Et prætereuntes blasphemabant eum moventes capita sua, et dicentes. *S.* Vah. qui destruis templum Dei, et in tribus diebus reædificas: salvum fac temetipsum, descendens de cruce.

that he would do as he had ever done to them. And Pilate answered them, and said: Will you that I release to you the king of the Jews? for he knew that the chief priests had delivered him up out of envy. But the chief priests moved the people that he should rather release Barabbas to them. And Pilate again answering, saith to them: What will you then that I do to the king of the Jews? But they again cried out: Crucify him. And Pilate saith to them: Why, what evil hath he done? But they cried out the more: Crucify him. So Pilate being willing to satisfy the people released to them Barabbas, and delivered up Jesus, when he had scourged him, to be crucified. And the soldiers led him into the court of the palace, and they call together the whole band: and they clothe him with purple, and platting a crown of

C. Similiter et summi sacerdotes illudentes, ad alterutrum cum scribis dicebant: *S.* Alios salvos fecit, seipsum non potest salvum facere. Christus Rex Israel descendat nunc de cruce, ut videamus, et credamus. *C.* Et qui cum eo crucifixi erant, convitiabantur ei. Et facta hora sexta, tenebræ factæ sunt per totam terram usque in horam nonam. Et hora nona exclamavit Jesus voce magna dicens: ✠ *Eloi, Eloi, lamma sabacthani?* *C.* Quod est interpretatum: ✠ Deus meus, Deus meus, ut quid dereliquisti me? *C.* Et quidam de circumstantibus audientes, dicebant: Ecce Eliam vocat. *C.* Currens autem unus, implens spongiam aceto, circumponensque calamo, potum dabat ei dicens: *S.* Sinite, videamus, si veniat Elias ad deponendum eum. *C.* Jesus autem emissa voce magna expiravit.

thorns, they put it upon him. And they began to salute him: Hail, king of the Jews. And they struck his head with a reed: And they did spit on him, and bowing their knees they worshipped him. And after they had mocked him, they took off the purple from him, and put his own garments on him, and they led him out to crucify him. And they forced one Simon, a Cyrenean, who passed by, coming out of the country, and father of Alexander and of Rufus, to take up his cross. And they bring him into the place called Golgotha, which being interpreted is, the place of Calvary: And they gave him to drink wine mingled with myrrh: but he took it not. And crucifying him, they divided his garments, casting lots upon them, what every man should take. And it was the third hour, and they crucified him. And the inscription of his cause was written over, THE KING OF THE JEWS. And

with him they crucify two thieves, the one on his right hand, and the other on his left. And the scripture was fulfilled which saith: *And with the wicked he was reputed.* And they that passed by blasphemed him, wagging their heads, and saying: Vah! thou that destroyest the temple of God, and in three days buildest it up again: save thyself, coming down from the cross. In like manner the chief priests with the scribes mocking said one to another: He saved others, himself he cannot save. Let Christ the king of Israel come down now from the cross, that we may see and believe. And they that were crucified with him, reviled him. And when the sixth hour was come, there was darkness over the whole earth until the ninth hour. And at the ninth hour Jesus cried out with a loud voice, saying: *Eloi, Eloi, lamma sabacthani?* which is, being interpreted, My God, my God, why hast thou forsaken me? And some of the standers-by hearing, said: Behold, he calleth Elias. And one running and filling a sponge with vinegar, and putting it upon a reed, gave him to drink, saying: Stay, let us see if Elias will come and take him down. And Jesus having cried out with a loud voice, gave up the ghost.

Here all kneel to meditate on the Redemption of mankind, and after a short pause the Deacon goes on:

Et velum templi scissum est in duo, a summo usque deorsum. Videns autem centurio, qui ex adverso stabat, quia sic clamans expirasset, ait: *S.* Vere hic homo Filius Dei erat.

And the veil of the temple was rent in two, from the top to the bottom. And the centurion, who stood over against him, seeing that crying out in this manner he had given up

Erant autem et mulieres de longe aspicientes; inter quas erat Maria Magdalene, et Maria Jacobi minoris et Joseph mater, et Salome; et cum esset in Galilæa, sequebantur eum, et ministrabant ei, et aliæ multæ, quæ simul cum eo ascenderant Jerosolymam.

the ghost, said: Indeed this man was the Son of God. And there were also women looking on afar off; among whom was Mary Magdalen, and Mary the mother of James the less and of Joseph and Salome; who also when he was in Galilee, followed him, and ministered unto him, and many other women that came up with him to Jerusalem.

The rest of the Passion is said as directed at p. 58.

ET cum jam sero esset factum (quia erat Parasceve, quod est ante sabbatum) venit Joseph ab Arimathæa nobilis decurio, qui et ipse erat expectans regnum Dei, et audacter introivit ad Pilatum, et petiit corpus Jesu. Pilatus autem mirabatur si jam obiisset. Et accersito centurione, interrogavit eum si jam mortuus esset. Et cum cognovisset a centurione, donavit corpus Joseph. Joseph autem mercatus sindonem, et deponens eum involvit sindone, et posuit eum in monumento, quod

AND when evening was now come (because it was the Parasceve, that is, the day before the Sabbath) Joseph of Arimathea, a noble counsellor, who was also himself looking for the kingdom of God, came and went in boldly to Pilate, and begged the body of Jesus. But Pilate wondered that he should be already dead. And sending for the centurion he asked him if he were already dead. And when he had understood it by the centurion, he gave the body to Jo-

erat excisum de petra, et advolvit lapidem ad ostium monumenti.

seph. And Joseph buying fine linen, and taking him down, wrapped him up in the fine linen, and laid him in a sepulchre which was hewed out of the rock, and he rolled a stone to the door of the sepulchre.

Offertorium.—Custodi me, Domine, de manu peccatoris: et ab hominibus iniquis eripe me.

Offertory. — Preserve me, O Lord, from the hand of the sinner: and from unjust men deliver me.

Suscipe, *as above p. 62, till he comes to the prayer called,*

THE SECRET.

SAcrificia nos, quæsumus Domine, propensius ista restaurent, quæ medicinalibus sunt instituta jejuniis. Per Dominum nostrum.

MAY these sacrifices, O Lord, we beseech thee, which are accompanied with healing fasts, mercifully repair us. Through, etc.

For the Secret against the persecutors of the Church, or for the Pope, see p. 89; for the Preface and Canon see from p. 69 to p. 82.

Communio — Adversum me exercebantur, qui sedebant in porta: et in me psallebant, qui bibebant vinum: ego vero orationem meam ad te, Domine: tempus beneplaciti Deus in multitudine misericordiæ tuæ.

The Communion.— They that sat in the gate spoke against me: and they that drank wine made songs against me: but I made my prayer to thee, O Lord: it is the time, O God, to show thy good-will in the multitude of thy mercy.

The Postcommunion.

SAnctificationibus tuis, omnipotens Deus, et vitia nostra curentur, et remedia nobis sempiterna proveniant. Per Dominum nostrum.

MAY these thy holy mysteries, O Almighty God, both cure our vices, and become our eternal remedies. Through our Lord, etc.

For the Postcommunion against the persecutors of the Church, or for the Pope, see p. 91.

The Prayer over the People.

Oremus.
Humiliate capita vestra Deo.

Let us pray.
Bow down your heads to God.

TUA nos misericordia, Deus, et ab omni subreptione vetustatis expurget, et capaces sanctæ novitatis efficiat. Per Dominum nostrum. *All the rest as above, p. 82.*

MAY thy mercy, O God, purify us from the corruption of the old man, and enable us to put on the new. Through our Lord, etc.

WEDNESDAY IN HOLY WEEK.
The Priest begins the Mass at the foot of the Altar as at p. 34, till he comes to
THE INTROIT.

IN nomine Jesu omne genu flectatur, cœlestium, terrestrium, et infernorum: quia Dominus factus est obediens usque ad mortem, mortem autem crucis: ideo Dominus Jesus Christus in gloria est Dei Patris. *Ps.*—Domine, exaudi orationem

AT the name of Jesus let every knee bow, of things in heaven, earth, and hell: because the Lord became obedient to death, even the death of the cross. Therefore our Lord Jesus Christ is in the glory of God the Father. *Ps.*—O Lord, hear my

meam: et clamor meus ad te veniat. In nomine, etc.

prayer; and let my cry come to thee. In the name, etc.

Kyrie eleison, *as above*, *p. 37.*

Oremus.
Flectamus genua.
R. Levate.

Let us pray.
Let us bend our knees.
R. Rise up.

PRÆSTA, quæsumus omnipotens Deus, ut, qui nostris excessibus incessanter affligimur, per unigeniti Filii tui passionem liberemur: qui tecum vivit, etc.

GRANT, we beseech thee, O Almighty God, that we, who are continually punished for our excesses, may be delivered by the passion of thy only begotten Son: who with thee, etc.

1. Lectio Isaiæ Prophetæ, *cap. 62 et 63.*

1. Lesson out of the Prophet Isaias, *chap. 62 and 63.*

HÆC dicit Dominus Deus: Dicite filiæ Sion: Ecce Salvator tuus venit: ecce merces ejus cum eo. Quis est iste, qui venit de Edom; tinctis vestibus de Bosra? Iste formosus in stola sua, gradiens in multitudine fortitudinis suæ. Ego, qui loquor justitiam, et propugnator sum ad salvandum. Quare ergo rubrum est indumentum tuum, et vestimenta tua sicut calcantium in

THUS sayeth the Lord God: Tell the daughter of Sion: Behold thy Saviour cometh, behold his reward is with him.
Who is this that cometh from Edom, with dyed garments from Bosra? This beautiful one in his robe, walking in the greatness of his strength? I, that speak justice, and am a defender to save. Why then is thy apparel red, and thy garments like theirs

torculari? Torcular calcavi solus: et de gentibus non est vir mecum: calcavi eos in furore meo, et conculcavi eos in ira mea: et aspersus est sanguis eorum super vestimenta mea, et omnia indumenta mea inquinavi. Dies enim ultionis in corde meo, annus redemptionis meæ venit. Circumspexi, et non erat auxiliator: quæsivi, et non fuit qui adjuvaret: et salvavit mihi brachium meum, et indignatio mea ipsa auxiliata est mihi. Et conculcavi populos in furore meo, et inebriavi eos in indignatione mea, et detraxi in terram virtutem eorum. Miserationum Domini recordabor, laudem Domini super omnibus quæ reddidit nobis Dominus Deus noster.

that tread in the wine-press? I have trodden the wine-press alone, and of the gentiles there is not a man with me: I have trampled on them in my indignation, and have trodden them down in my wrath, and their blood is sprinkled upon my garments, and I have stained all my apparel. For the way of vengeance is in my heart, the year of my redemption is come. I looked round about, and there was none to help: I sought, and there was none to give aid: and my own arm hath saved for me, and my indignation itself hath helped me. And I have trodden down the people in my wrath, and have made them drunk in my indignation, and have brought down their strength to the earth.

I will remember the tender mercies of the Lord, the praise of the Lord for all the things that the Lord hath bestowed on us.

Graduale. — Ne avertas faciem tuam a puero tuo, quoniam tribulor; velociter exaudi me. *V.*

Gradual. — Turn not away thy face from thy servant, because I am in tribulation: hear me

WEDNESDAY IN HOLY WEEK.

Salvum me fac, Deus, quoniam intraverunt aquæ usque ad animam meam: infixus sum in limo profundi, et non est substantia.

V. Dominus vobiscum.
R. Et cum spiritu tuo.

Oremus.

DEUS, qui pro nobis Filium tuum crucis patibulum subire voluisti, ut inimici a nobis expelleres potestatem: concede nobis famulis tuis, ut resurrectionis gratiam consequamur. Per eundem Dominum nostrum, etc.

speedily. *V.* Save me O God, because waters of affliction have entered into my soul: I stuck fast in the deep mire, and there is no sure standing.
V. The Lord be with you.
R. And with thy spirit.

Let us pray.

O GOD, who wouldst have thy Son suffer for us on the gibbet of the cross, to deliver us from the power of the enemy; grant to us thy servants, that we may obtain the grace of his resurrection. Through the same our Lord, etc.

Then is said the prayer against the persecutors of the Church, or for the Pope, as p. 85.

ii. Lectio Isaiæ Prophetae.

Cap. 53.

IN diebus illis: dixit Isaias: Domine, quis credidit auditui nostro? et brachium Domini cui revelatum est? Et ascendet sicut virgultum coram eo, et sicut radix de terra sitienti: non

ii. Lesson from the Prophet Isaias.

Chap. 53.

IN those days: Isaias said: Who hath believed our report? and to whom is the arm of the Lord revealed? And he shall grow up as a tender plant before him, and as a root out of a

est species ei, neque decor, et vidimus eum, et non erat aspectus, et desideravimus eum: despectum et novissimum virorum, virum dolorum, et scientem infirmitatem: et quasi absconditus vultus ejus et despectus, unde nec reputavimus eum. Vere languores nostros ipse tulit, et dolores nostros ipse portavit: et nos putavimus eum quasi leprosum et percussum a Deo et humiliatum. Ipse autem vulneratus est propter iniquitates nostras, attritus est propter scelera nostra: disciplina pacis nostræ super eum, et livore ejus sanati sumus. Omnes nos quasi oves erravimus, unusquisque in viam suam declinavit: et posuit Dominus in eo iniquitatem omnium nostrum. Oblatus est quia ipse voluit, et non aperuit os suum: sicut ovis ad occisionem ducetur et quasi agnus coram tondente se obmutescet et non aperiet os suum. De angustia

thirsty ground: there is no beauty in him, nor comeliness: and we have seen him, and there was no sightliness that we should be desirous of him: despised, and the most abject of men, a man of sorrows, and acquainted with infirmity: and his look was as it were hidden and despised, whereupon we esteemed him not. Surely he hath borne our infirmities, and carried our sorrows: and we have thought him as it were a leper, and as one struck by God and afflicted. But he was wounded for our iniquities, he was bruised for our sins: the chastisement of our peace was upon him, and by his bruises we are healed. All we like sheep have gone astray, every one hath turned aside into his own way: and the Lord hath laid on him the iniquity of us all. He was offered because it was his own will, and he opened not his mouth: he shall be

WEDNESDAY IN HOLY WEEK.

et de judicio sublatus est: generationem ejus quis enarrabit? Quia abscissus est de terra viventium: propter scelus populi mei percussi eum. Et dabit impios pro sepultura, et divitem pro morte sua: eo quod iniquitatem non fecerit, neque dolus fuerit in ore ejus. Et Dominus voluit conterere eum in infirmitate: si posuerit pro peccato animam suam, videbit semen longœvum, et voluntas Domini in manu ejus dirigetur. Pro eo quod laboravit anima ejus videbit et saturabitur: in scientia sua justificabit ipse justus servus meus multos, et iniquitates eorum ipse portabit. Ideo dispertiam ei plurimos: et fortium dividet spolia pro eo quod tradidit in mortem animam suam, et cum sceleratis reputatus est: et ipse peccata multorum tulit, et pro transgressoribus rogavit.

led as a sheep to the slaughter, and shall be dumb as a lamb before his shearer, and he shall not open his mouth: he was taken away from distress, and from judgment, who shall declare his generation? because he is cut off out of the land of the living: for the wickedness of my people have I struck him. And he shall give the ungodly for his burial and the rich for his death: because he hath done no iniquity, neither was there deceit in his mouth. And the Lord was pleased to bruise him in infirmity: if he shall lay down his life for sin, he shall see a long-lived seed, and the will of the Lord shall be prosperous in his hand. Because his soul hath laboured, he shall see, and be filled: by his knowledge shall this my just servant justify many, and he shall bear their iniquities. Therefore will I distribute to him very many, and he shall divide the spoils of the strong,

because he hath delivered his soul unto death, and was reputed with the wicked, and he hath borne the sins of many, and hath prayed for the transgressors.

Tractus.—Domine, exaudi orationem meam, et clamor meus ad te veniat. V. Ne avertas faciem tuam a me: in quacumque die tribulor, inclina ad me aurem tuam. V. In quacumque die invocavero te, velociter exaudi me. V. Quia defecerunt sicut fumus dies mei: et ossa mea sicut in frixorio confrixa sunt. V. Percussus sum sicut fœnum, et aruit cor meum: quia oblitus sum manducare panem meum. V. Tu exurgens Domine misereberis Sion: quia venit tempus miserendi ejus.

Tract.—O Lord, hear my prayer, and let my cry come to thee. V. Turn not away thy face from me: in whatever day I am in tribulation, bend thy ear to me. V. In whatever day I shall invoke thee, hear me speedily. V. Because my days have vanished like smoke; and my bones as if they were fried in a frying-pan. V. I was struck like the grass, and my heart withered: because I forgot to eat my bread. V. Thou rising up, O Lord, shalt have mercy on Sion: because the time is come to have mercy on it.

Passio Domini nostri Jesu Christi secundum Lucam. *(cap.* 22, 23)

The Passion of our Lord Jesus Christ according to Luke. *(ch.* 22, 23)

IN illo tempore: appropinquabat dies festus azymorum, qui dicitur Pascha: et quærebant principes sacerdotum et Scribæ, quo-

AT that time: The feast of unleavened bread, which is called the pasch, was at hand: and the chief priests and the scribes sought

modo Jesum interficerent: timebant vero plebem. Intravit autem Satanas in Judam, qui cognominabatur Iscariotes, unum de duodecim. Et abiit et locutus est cum principibus sacerdotum, et magistratibus, quemadmodum illum traderet eis. Et gavisi sunt, et pacti sunt pecuniam illi dare. Et spopondit. Et quærebat opportunitatem ut traderet illum sine turbis. Venit autem dies Azymorum, in qua necesse erat occidi Pascha. Et misit Petrum et Joannem, dicens: ✠ Euntes parate nobis Pascha ut manducemus. *C.* At illi dixerunt: *S.* Ubi vis paremus? *C.* Et dixit ad eos: ✠ Ecce introeuntibus vobis in civitatem, occurret vobis homo quidam amphoram aquæ portans : sequimini eum in domum, in quam intrat, et dicetis patrifamilias domus: Dicit tibi Magister: Ubi est diversorium, ubi Pascha cum discipulis meis mandu-

how they might put Jesus to death: but they feared the people. And Satan entered into Judas, who was surnamed Iscariot, one of the twelve. And he went and discoursed with the chief priests and the magistrates, how he might betray him to them. And they were glad and covenanted to give him money. And he promised. And he sought an opportunity to betray him in the absence of the multitude. And the day of the unleavened bread came, on which it was necessary that the pasch should be killed. And he sent Peter and John: saying: Go and prepare us the pasch, that we may eat. But they said: Where wilt thou that we prepare? And he said to them: Behold, as you go into the city, there shall meet you a man carrying a pitcher of water: follow him into the house where he entereth in: and you shall say to the good

cem? Et ipse ostendet vobis cœnaculum magnum stratum, et ibi parate. *C.* Euntes autem invenerunt sicut dixit illis, et paraverunt Pascha. Et cum facta esset hora, discubuit, et duodecim Apostoli cum eo. Et ait illis: ✠ Desiderio desideravi hoc Pascha manducare vobiscum, antequam patiar. Dico enim vobis, quia ex hoc non manducabo illud, donec impleatur in regno Dei. *C.* Et accepto calice, gratias egit, et dixit. ✠ Accipite et dividite inter vos. Dico enim vobis, quod non bibam de generatione vitis, donec regnum Dei veniat. *C.* Et accepto pane gratias egit, et fregit, et dedit eis, dicens: ✠ Hoc est corpus meum, quod pro vobis datur, hoc facite in meam commemorationem. *C.* Similiter et calicem, postquam cœnavit, dicens: ✠ Hic est calix novum testamentum in sanguine meo, qui pro vobis fundetur. Verumtamen ecce ma-

man of the house: The master saith to thee: Where is the guest-chamber, where I may eat the pasch with my disciples? And he will show you a large dining-room furnished: and there prepare. And they going found as he had said to them, and they made ready the pasch. And when the hour was come, he sat down, and the twelve apostles with him. And he said to them: With desire I have desired to eat this pasch with you before I suffer. For I say to you, that from this time I will not eat it, till it be fulfilled in the kingdom of God. And having taken the chalice, he gave thanks and said: Take and divide it among you. For I say to you, that I will not drink of the fruit of the vine, till the kingdom of God come. And taking bread, he gave thanks, and brake, and gave to them saying: This is my body which is given for you:

nus tradentis me, mecum est in mensa. Et quidem Filius hominis, secundum quod definitum est, vadit: verumtamen væ homini illi, per quem tradetur. *C.* Et ipsi cœperunt quærere inter se, quis esset ex eis, qui hoc facturus esset. Facta est autem et contentio inter eos, quis eorum videretur esse major. Dixit autem eis : ✠ Reges Gentium dominantur eorum: et qui potestatem habent super eos, benefici vocantur. Vos autem non sic, sed qui major est in vobis, fiat sicut minor, et qui præcessor est, sicut ministrator. Nam quis major est, qui recumbit, an qui ministrat ? Nonne qui recumbit ? Ego autem in medio vestrum sum, sicut qui ministrat: vos autem estis qui permansistis mecum in tentationibus meis. Et ego dispono vobis sicut disposuit mihi Pater meus regnum, ut edatis, et bibatis super mensam meam in regno do this for a commemoration of me. In like manner the chalice also. after he had supped, saying: This is the chalice, the new testament in my blood, which shall be shed for you. But yet behold, the hand of him that betrayeth me is with me on the table. And the Son of Man indeed goeth, according to that which is determined : but wo to that man by whom he shall be betrayed. And they began to inquire among themselves, which of them it was that should do this thing. And there was also a strife amongst them, which of them should seem to be greater. And he said to them: The kings of the Gentiles lord it over them ; and they that have power over them, are called beneficent. But you not so: but he that is the greater among you, let him be as the least; and he that is the leader, as he that serveth. For which

meo: et sedatis super thronos, judicantes duodecim tribus Israel *C.* Ait autem Dominus: ✠ Simon, Simon ecce Satanas expetivit vos, ut cribraret sicut triticum: ego autem rogavi pro te, ut non deficiat fides tua: et tu aliquando conversus, confirma fratres tuos. *C.* Qui dixit ei: *S.* Domine, tecum paratus sum, et in carcerem, et in mortem ire. *C.* At ille dixit: ✠ Dico tibi, Petre: Non cantabit hodie gallus, donec ter abneges nosse me. *C.* Et dixit eis: ✠ Quando misi vos sine sacculo, et pera. et calceamentis, numquid aliquid defuit vobis? *C.* At illi dixerunt: *S.* Nihil. *C.* Dixit ergo eis: ✠ Sed nunc, qui habet sacculum, tollat similiter et peram: et qui non habet, vendat tunicam suam, et emat gladium. Dico enim vobis, quoniam adhuc hoc, quod scriptum est, oportet impleri in me: *Et cum iniquis deputatus est.* Etenim, ea quæ sunt de me, finem habent.

is greater, he that sitteth at table, or he that serveth? Is not he that sitteth at table? But I am in the midst of you, as he that serveth: and you are they who have continued with me in my temptations: and I appoint to you, as my Father hath appointed to me, a kingdom: that you may eat and drink at my table in my kingdom: and may sit upon thrones judging the twelve tribes of Israel. And the Lord said: Simon, Simon, behold Satan hath desired to have you, that he may sift you as wheat. But I have prayed for thee that thy faith fail not: and thou being once converted, confirm thy brethren. And he said to him: Lord, I am ready to go with thee both into prison, and into death. And he said: I say to thee, Peter, the cock shall not crow this day, till thou thrice deniest that thou knowest me. And he said to them: When I

C. At illi dixerunt: *S.* Domine, ecce duo gladii hic. *C.* At ille dixit eis: ✠ Satis est. *C.* Et egressus ibat secundum consuetudinem in montem Olivarum. Secuti sunt autem illum et discipuli. Et cum pervenisset ad locum: dixit illis: ✠ Orate, ne intretis in tentationem. *C.* Et ipse avulsus est ab eis, quantum jactus est lapidis: et positis genibus orabat, dicens: ✠ Pater si vis, transfer calicem istum a me: verumtamen non mea voluntas, sed tua fiat. *C.* Apparuit autem illi angelus de cœlo confortans eum. Et factus in agonia, prolixius orabat. Et factus est sudor ejus, sicut guttæ sanguinis decurrentis in terram. Et cum surrexisset ab oratione, et venisset ad discipulos suos, invenit eos dormientes præ tristitia, et ait illis: ✠ Quid dormitis? Surgite, orate, ne intretis in tentationem. *C.* Adhuc eo loquente, ecce turba, et qui vocabatur Judas, unus de duodecim, ante-

sent you without purse and scrip and shoes, did you want any thing? But they said: Nothing. Then he said to them. But now he that hath a purse, let him take it and likewise a scrip, and he that hath no sword, let him sell his coat, and buy one. For I say to you, that this that is written, must yet be fulfilled in me: *And he was reckoned among the wicked:* For the things concerning me have an end. But they said: Lord, behold here are two swords. And he said to them: It is enough. And going out he went according to his custom to the mount of Olives. And his disciples also followed him. And when he was come to the place, he said to them: Pray, lest ye enter into temptation. And he was withdrawn away from them a stone's cast; and kneeling down, he prayed, saying: Father, if thou wilt, remove this chalice from me; but yet

cedebat eos, et appropinquavit Jesu ut oscularetur eum. Jesus autem dixit illi: ✠ Juda, osculo Filium hominis tradis? *C.* Videntes autem hi, qui circa ipsum erant, quod futurum erat, dixerunt ei: *S.* Domine, si percutimus in gladio? *C.* Et percussit unus ex illis servum principis sacerdotum, et amputavit auriculam ejus dexteram. Respondens autem Jesus ait: ✠ Sinite usque huc. *C.* Et cum tetigisset auriculam ejus, sanavit eum. Dixit autem Jesus ad eos, qui venerant ad se, principes sacerdotum, et magistratus templi, et seniores: ✠ Quasi ad latronem existis cum gladiis et fustibus? Cum quotidie vobiscum fuerim in templo, non extendistis manus in me: sed hæc est hora vestra, et potestas tenebrarum. *C.* Comprehendentes autem eum, duxerunt ad domum principis sacerdotum: Petrus vero sequebatur a longe. Ac-

not my will, but thine be done. And there appeared to him an angel from heaven, strengthening him. And being in an agony, he prayed the longer. And his sweat became as drops of blood trickling down upon the ground. And when he rose up from prayer, and was come to his disciples, he found them sleeping for sorrow. And he said to them: Why sleep you? arise, pray, lest you enter into temptation. As he was yet speaking, behold a multitude; and he that was called Judas, one of the twelve, went before them, and drew near to Jesus to kiss him. And Jesus said to him: Judas, dost thou betray the Son of Man with a kiss? And they that were about him, seeing what would follow, said to him: Lord, shall we strike with the sword? And one of them struck the servant of the highpriest, and cut off his right ear. But Jesus

censo autem igne in medio atrii, et circumsedentibus illis, erat Petrus in medio eorum. Quem cum vidisset ancilla quædam sedentem ad lumen et eum fuisset intuita, dixit: *S.* Et hic cum illo erat. *C.* At ille negavit eum, dicens: *S.* Mulier, non novi illum. *C.* Et post pusillum alius videns eum, dixit: *S.* Et tu de illis es. Petrus vero ait: *S.* O homo, non sum. *C.* Et intervallo facto quasi horæ unius alius quidam affirmabat, dicens: *S.* Vere et hic cum illo erat: nam et Galilæus est. *C.* Et ait Petrus: *S.* Homo, nescio quid dicis. *C.* Et continuo adhuc illo loquente cantavit gallus. Et conversus Dominus respexit Petrum. Et recordatus est Petrus verbi Domini, sicut dixerat: Quia priusquam gallus cantet, ter me negabis. Et egressus foras Petrus flevit amare. Et viri qui tenebant illum, illudebant ei, cædentes. Et velaverunt eum, et per-

answering, said: Suffer ye thus far. And when he had touched his ear, he healed him. And Jesus said to the chief-priests, and magistrates of the temple, and the ancients that were come to him: Are you come out as it were against a thief, with swords and clubs? When I was daily with you in the temple, you did not stretch forth your hands against me; but this is your hour, and the power of darkness. Then they laid hold on him, and led him to the high-priest's house: but Peter followed afar off. And when they had kindled a fire in the midst of the hall, and were sitting about it, Peter was in the midst of them. And when a certain servant-maid had seen him sitting at the light, and had earnestly looked upon him, she said: This man was also with him. But he denied him, saying; Woman, I know him not. And after a little

cutiebant faciem ejus, et interrogabant eum, dicentes: Prophetiza, quis est, qui te percussit? Et alia multa blasphemantes dicebant in eum. Et ut factus est dies, convenerunt seniores plebis, et principes sacerdotum et scribæ, et duxerunt illum in concilium suum, dicentes: *S.* Si tu es Christus, dic nobis. *C.* Et ait illis: ✠ Si vobis dixero, non credetis mihi: Si autem et interrogavero, non respondebitis mihi, neque dimittetis. Ex hoc autem erit Filius hominis sedens a dextris virtutis Dei. *C.* Dixerunt autem omnes: *S.* Tu ergo es Filius Dei? *C.* Qui ait: ✠ Vos dicitis, quia ego sum. *C.* At illi dixerunt: *S.* Quid adhuc desideramus testimonium? Ipsi enim audivimus de ore ejus. *C.* Et surgens omnis multitudo eorum duxerunt illum ad Pilatum. Cœperunt autem illum accusare, dicentes: *S.* Hunc invenimus subvertentem gentem

while another seeing him said: Thou also art one of them. But Peter said: O man, I am not. And about the space of one hour after, another man affirmed, saying: Of a truth this man was also with him: for he is also a Galilæan. And Peter said: Man, I know not what thou sayest. And immediately while he was yet speaking, the cock crew. And the Lord turning looked on Peter. And Peter remembered the word of the Lord, how he had said: Before the cock crow, thou shalt deny me thrice. And Peter went out and wept bitterly. And the men that held him, mocked him, and struck him. And they blindfolded him, and smote him on the face. And they asked him, saying: Prophesy, who is it that struck thee? And many other things blaspheming they said against him. And as soon as it was day, the

WEDNESDAY IN HOLY WEEK. 125

nostram, et prohibentem tributa dare Cæsari, et dicentem se Christum regem esse. *C.* Pilatus autem interrogavit eum, dicens: *S.* Tu es rex Judæorum? *C.* At ille respondens, ait: ✠ Tu dicis. *C.* Ait autem Pilatus ad principes sacerdotum et turbas: *S.* Nihil invenio causæ in hoc homine. *C.* At illi invalescebant, dicentes: *S.* Commovet populum, docens per universam Judæam, incipiens a Galilæa usque huc. *C.* Pilatus autem audiens Galilæam, interrogavit si homo Galilæus esset. Et ut cognovit, quod de Herodis potestate esset, remisit eum ad Herodem, qui et ipse Jerosolymis erat illis diebus. Herodes autem, viso Jesu gavisus est valde. Erat enim cupiens ex multo tempore videre eum, eo quod audierat multa de eo, et sperabat signum aliquod videre ab eo fieri. Interrogabat autem eum multis sermonibus. At ipse nihil illi respondebat. Sta-

ancients of the people, and the chief priests and scribes came together, and they brought him into their council, saying: If thou be the Christ, tell us. And he said to them: If I shall tell you, you will not believe me: and if I shall also ask you, you will not answer me, nor let me go. But hereafter the Son of Man shall be sitting on the right hand of the power of God. Then said they all: Art thou then the Son of God? And he said: You say, that I am. Then they said: What need we any farther testimony? For we ourselves have heard it from his own mouth. And the whole multitude of them rose up, and led him away to Pilate. And they began to accuse him, saying: We have found this man perverting our nation, and forbidding to give tribute to Cæsar, and saying that he is Christ the king. And Pilate asked him, say-

bant autem principes sacerdotum et Scribæ constanter accusantes eum. Sprevit autem illum Herodes cum exercitu suo: et illusit indutum veste alba, et remisit ad Pilatum Et facti sunt amici Herodes et Pilatus in ipsa die: nam antea inimici erant ad invicem. Pilatus autem convocatis principibus sacerdotum, et magistratibus, et plebe, dixit ad illos: *S.* Obtulistis mihi hunc hominem quasi avertentem populum, et ecce ego coram vobis interrogans, nullam causam inveni in homine isto ex his, in quibus eum accusatis. Sed neque Herodes: nam remisi vos ad illum, et ecce nihil dignum morte actum est ei. Emendatum ergo illum dimittam. *C.* Necesse autem habebat dimittere eis per diem festum, unum. Exclamavit autem simul universa turba, dicens: *S.* Tolle hunc et dimitte nobis Barabbam. *C.* Qui erat, propter sedi-

ing: Art thou the king of the Jews? And he answered and said: Thou sayest it. Then Pilate said to the chief priests and to the multitude: I find no cause in this man. But they were more earnest, saying: He stirreth up the people, teaching throughout all Judea, beginning from Galilee to this place. And Pilate hearing of Galilee, asked if the man were a Galilean? And when he understood that he belonged to Herod's jurisdiction, he sent him away to Herod, who himself was also at Jerusalem in those days. And Herod seeing Jesus, was very glad, for he was desirous of a long time to see him, because he had heard many things of him: and he hoped to see some miracle wrought by him. And he questioned him with many words. But he answered him nothing. And the chief priests and

tionem quandam factam in civitate et homicidium, missus in carcerem. Iterum autem Pilatus locutus est ad eos, volens dimittere Jesum. At illi succlamabant dicentes: *S.* Crucifige, crucifige eum. *C* Ille autem tertio dixit ad illos: *S:* Quid enim mali fecit iste? Nullam causam mortis invenio in eo: corripiam ergo illum, et dimittam. *C.* At illi instabant vocibus magnis postulantes, ut crucifigeretur. Et invalescebant voces eorum. Et Pilatus adjudicavit fieri petitionem eorum. Dimisit autem illis eum, qui propter homicidium et seditionem missus fuerat in carcerem, quem petebant: Jesum vero tradidit voluntati eorum. Et cum ducerent eum, apprehenderunt Simonem quemdam Cyrenensem venientem de villa, et imposuerunt illi crucem portare post Jesum. Sequebatur autem illum multa turba populi et mulierum: quæ plange-

the scribes stood by earnestly accusing him. And Herod with his soldiers set him at nought: and mocked him, putting on him a white garment, and sent him back to Pilate: And Herod and Pilate were made friends together that same day, for before they were enemies to one another. Then Pilate calling together the chief priests, and the magistrates, and the people, said to them: You have brought this man to me, as one that perverteth the people, and behold I having examined him before you, find no cause in this man touching those things wherein you accuse him. No, nor Herod neither: For I sent you to him, and behold, nothing worthy of death is done to him. I will chastise him therefore, and release him. Now of necessity he was to release them one on the feast day. But the whole multitude cried out at once,

bant et lamentabantur eum. Conversus autem ad illas Jesus, dixit: ✠ Filiæ Jerusalem, nolite flere super me, sed super vos ipsas flete, et super filios vestros. Quoniam ecce venient dies, in quibus dicent: Beatæ steriles, et ventres qui non genuerunt, et ubera quæ non lactaverunt. Tunc incipient dicere montibus: Cadite super nos: et collibus: Operite nos. Quia si in viridi ligno hæc faciunt; in arido quid fiet? *C.* Ducebantur autem et alii duo nequam cum eo, ut interficerentur. Et postquam venerunt in locum, qui vocatur Calvariæ, ibi crucifixerunt eum; et latrones, unum a dextris, et alterum a sinistris. Jesus autem dicebat: ✠ Pater, dimitte illis; non enim sciunt quid faciunt. *C.* Dividentes vero vestimenta ejus, miserunt sortes. Et stabat populus spectans, et deridebant eum principes cum eis, dicentes; *S.* Alios salvos fecit; se

saying: Away with this man, and release unto us Barabbas. Who for a certain sedition made in the city, and for murder, was cast into prison. And Pilate spoke to them again, desiring to release Jesus. But they cried out, saying: Crucify him, crucify him. And he said to them the third time: Why, what evil hath this man done? I find no cause of death in him: I will chastise him therefore, and let him go. But they were instant with loud voices requiring that he might be crucified: and their voices prevailed. And Pilate gave sentence that it should be as they required. And he released unto them him, who for murder and sedition had been cast into prison, whom they had desired: but Jesus he delivered up to their will. And as they led him away they laid hold on one Simon of Cyrene, that was coming out of the

salvum faciat, si hic est Christus Dei electus. *C.* Illudebant autem ei et milites accedentes, et acetum offerentes ei, et dicentes: *S.* Si tu es rex Judæorum, salvum te fac. *C.* Erat autem et superscriptio scripta super eum literis Græcis, et Latinis, et Hebraicis: *Hic est rex Judæorum.* Unus autem de his, qui pendebant, latronibus, blasphemabat eum, dicens: *S.* Si tu es Christus, salvum fac temetipsum et nos. *C.* Respondens autem alter increpabat eum, dicens: *S.* Neque tu times Deum, quod in eadem damnatione es? Et nos quidam juste, nam digna factis recipimus: hic vero nihil mali gessit. *C.* Et dicebat ad Jesum: *S.* Domine, memento mei, cum veneris in regnum tuum. *C.* Et dixit illi Jesus: ✠ Amen dico tibi: Hodie mecum eris in paradiso. *C.* Erat autem fere hora sexta, et tenebræ factæ sunt in universam terram usque in horam nonam. Et obscuratus est country: and they laid the cross on him to carry after Jesus. And there followed him a great multitude of people, and of women: who bewailed and lamented him. But Jesus turning to them, said: Daughters of Jerusalem, weep not over me but weep for yourselves, and for your children. For behold the days shall come, wherein they will say: Blessed are the barren, and the wombs that have not borne, and the paps that have not given suck. Then shall they begin to say to the mountains: Fall upon us: and to the hills: Cover us. For if in the green wood they do these things, what shall be done in the dry? And there were also two other malefactors led with him to be put to death. And when they were come to the place which is called Calvary, they crucified him there; and the robbers, one on the right hand

sol: et velum templi scissum est medium. Et clamans voce magna Jesus ait: ✠ Pater in manus tuas commendo spiritum meum. *C.* Et hæc dicens, expiravit.	and the other on the left. And Jesus said: Father forgive them, for they know not what they do. But they divided his garments, and cast lots. And the people stood

beholding, and the rulers with them deriding him, saying: he saved others, let him save himself, if he be Christ, the chosen of God. And the soldiers also mocked him, coming to him, and offering him vinegar, and saying: If thou be the king of the Jews, save thyself. And there was also a superscription written over him in letters of Greek, and Latin, and Hebrew: THIS IS THE KING OF THE JEWS. And one of those robbers who were hanged, blasphemed him, saying: If thou be Christ, save thyself, and us. But the other answering, rebuked him, saying: Neither dost thou fear God, seeing thou art under the same condemnation. And we indeed justly, for we receive the due reward of our deeds: but this man hath done no evil. And he said to Jesus: Lord, remember me when thou shalt come into thy kingdom. And Jesus said to him: Amen I say to thee, this day thou shalt be with me in paradise. And it was almost the sixth hour: and there was darkness over all the earth until the ninth hour. And the sun was darkened; and the veil of the temple was rent in the midst. And Jesus crying with a loud voice, said: Father, into thy hands I commend my spirit. And saying this he gave up the ghost.

Here all kneel to meditate on the redemption of mankind, and after a short pause, the Deacon goes on:

Videns autem centurio quod factum fuerat,	Now the centurion seeing what was done,

glorificavit Deum, dicens: Vere hic homo justus erat. Et omnis turba eorum, qui simul aderant ad spectaculum istud, et videbant quæ fiebant, percutientes pectora sua revertebantur. Stabant autem omnes noti ejus a longe, et mulieres, quæ secutæ eum erant a Galilæa, hæc videntes.

glorified God, saying: Indeed this was a just man. And all the multitude of them that were come together to that sight, and saw the things that were done, returned striking their breasts. And all his acquaintance, and the women that had followed him from Galilee, stood afar off beholding these things.

The rest of the Passion is said as directed at p. 58.

ET ecce vir nomine Joseph, qui erat decurio vir bonus et justus: hic non consenserat consilio et actibus eorum, ab Arimathæa, civitate Judæa, qui expectabat et ipse regnum Dei. Hic accessit ad Pilatum, et petiit corpus Jesu: et depositum involvit sindone, et posuit eum in monumento exciso, in quo nondum quisquam positus fuerat.

AND behold there was a man named Joseph, who was a counsellor, a good and a just man, (the same had not consented to their counsel and doings) of Arimathea, a city of Judea, who also himself looked for the kingdom of God. This man went to Pilate, and begged the body of Jesus. And taking him down, he wrapped him in fine linen, and laid

him in a sepulchre that was hewed in stone wherein never yet any man had been laid.

Offertorium.—Domine exaudi orationem me-

Offertory. — O Lord, hear my prayer, and let

WEDNESDAY IN HOLY WEEK

am, et clamor meus ad te perveniat: ne avertas faciem tuam a me.

my cry come to thee: turn not thy face from me.

Suscipe, as above, p. 62, *till he comes to*

THE SECRET.

SUSCIPE, quæsumus Domine, munus oblatum, et dignanter operaré, ut quod passionis Filii tui Domini nostri mysterio gerimus, piis affectibus consequamur. Per eundem Dominum nostrum.

ACCEPT, O Lord, we beseech thee this offering, and mercifully grant, that we may receive with pious sentiments what we celebrate in this mystery of the passion of thy Son our Lord. Through the same Lord. etc.

The secret against the persecutors of the Church, or for the Pope, p. 89.
The preface and canon as from p. 69, *to p.* 82, *till he comes to*

Communio. - Potum meum cum fletu temperabam: quia elevans allisisti me: et ego sicut fænum arui: tu autem Domine in æternum permanes: tu exurgens misereberis Sion, quia venit tempus miserendi ejus.

The Communion. — I mingled my drink with tears: because having lifted me up thou hast thrown me down, and I withered like grass: but thou, O Lord, continuest for ever: thou shalt rise up and have mercy on Sion, because the time to have mercy on her is come.

The Prayer called the Post Communion.

LArgire sensibus nostris, omnipotens Deus, ut per temporalem,

GRANT, O Almighty God, that we may sensibly hope, thou hast

Filii tui mortem, quam mysteria veneranda testantur, vitam te nobis dedisse perpetuam concedamus. Per eundem, etc.

given us eternal life by the temporal death of thy Son, represented in these adorable mysteries. Through the same Lord, etc.

Against the persecutors of the Church, or for the Pope, p. 91.

The prayer over the people.

Oremus.
Humiliate capita vestra Deo.

Let us pray.
Bow down your heads to God.

RE spice, quæsumus Domine, super hanc familiam tuam, pro qua Dominus noster Jesus Christus non dubitavit manibus tradi nocentium, et crucis subire tormentum. Qui tecum vivit et regnat, etc.

LOOK down we beseech thee, O Lord, on this thy family, for which our Lord Jesus Christ was pleased to be delivered into the hands of the wicked, and to suffer the torment of the cross. Who liveth, etc.

All the rest as before, p. 82.

The Tenebræ-offices *for* Maundy Thursday, Good Friday, *and* Holy Saturday, *which in the primitive ages were said at a very early hour on the mornings of those days, are now said or sung (by way of anticipation) on* Wednesday, Thursday, *and* Friday *evenings. At the close of each psalm, both in Matins and Lauds,* Gloria Patri *is omitted, and one of the fifteen candles in the triangular candlestick is* extinguished.

ON WEDNESDAY EVENING,
MAUNDY THURSDAY AT MATINS.
THE FIRST NOCTURN.

Antiphona.	The Antiphon.
Zelus domus tuæ comedit me, et opprobria exprobantium tibi ceciderunt super me.	Zeal of thy house hath eaten me up, and the affronts of those that affronted thee fell upon me.

PSALM LXVIII.

Salvum me fac, Deus: * quoniam intraverunt aquæ usque ad animam meam.

2. Infixus sum in limo profundi: * et non est substantia.

3. Veni in altitudinem maris: * et tempestas demersit me.

4. Laboravi clamans, raucæ factæ sunt fauces meæ: * defecerunt oculi mei, dum spero in Deum meum.

5. Multiplicati sunt super capillos capitis mei: * qui oderunt me gratis.

6. Confortati sunt qui persecuti sunt me inimici mei injuste: * quæ non rapui, tunc exolvebam.

Save me, O God: for the waters are come in even unto my soul.

2. I stick fast in the mire of the deep: and there is no sure standing.

3. I am come into the depth of the sea: and a tempest hath overwhelmed me.

4. I have laboured with crying: my jaws are become hoarse: my eyes have failed, whilst I hope in my God.

5. They are multiplied above the hairs of my head, who hate me without cause.

6. My enemies are grown strong, who have wrongfully persecuted me: then did I pay that which I took not away.

7. Deus, tu scis insipientiam meam: * et delicta mea a te non sunt abscondita.
8. Non erubescant in me, qui expectant te, Domine, * Domine virtutum.
9. Non confundantur super me, * qui quærunt te, Deus Israel.
10. Quoniam propter te sustinui opprobrium: * operuit confusio faciem meam.
11. Extraneus factus sum fratribus meis, * et peregrinus filiis matris meæ.
12. Quoniam zelus domus tuæ comedit me: * et opprobria exprobrantium tibi ceciderunt super me.
13. Et operui in jejunio animam meam: * et factum est in opprobrium mihi.
14. Et posui vestimentum meum cilicium; * et factus sum illis in parabolam.
15. Adversum me loquebantur qui sedebant in porta: et in me psal-

7 O God, thou knowest my foolishness, and my offences are not hid from thee.
8. Let them not be ashamed for me, who look for thee, O Lord, the Lord of hosts.
9. Let them not be confounded on my account, who seek thee, O God of Israel.
10. Because for thy sake I have borne reproach: shame hath covered my face.
11. I am become a stranger to my brethren, and an alien to the sons of my mother.
12. For the zeal of thy house hath eaten me up: and the reproaches of them that reproached thee, are fallen upon me.
13. And I covered my soul in fasting: and it made a reproach to me.
14. And I made haircloth my garment: and I became a bye word to them.
15. They that sat in the gate spoke against me and they that drank

lebant qui bibebant vinum.

16. Ego vero orationem meam ad te, Domine: * tempus beneplaciti Deus.

17. In multitudine misericordiæ tuæ exaudi me, * in veritate salutis tuæ.

18. Eripe me de luto, ut non infigar; * libera me ab iis qui oderunt me, et de profundis aquarum.

19. Non me demergat tempestas aquæ, neque absorbeat me profundum: * neque urgeat super me puteus os suum.

20. Exaudi me, Domine, quoniam benigna est misericordia tua: * secundum multitudinem miserationum tuarum respice in me.

21. Et ne avertas faciem tuam a puero tuo: * quoniam tribulor, velociter exaudi me.

22. Intende animæ meæ et libera eam: * propter inimicos meos eripe me.

wine made me their song.

16. But as for me, my prayer is to thee, O Lord: for the time of thy good pleasure, O God.

17. In the multitude of thy mercy hear me in the truth uf thy salvation.

18. Draw me out of the mire, that I may not stick fast: deliver me from them that hate me, and out of the deep waters.

19. Let not the tempest of water drown me, nor the deep swallow me up: and let not the pit shut her mouth upon me.

20. Hear me, O Lord, for thy mercy is kind: look upon me according to the multitude of thy tender mercies.

21. And turn not away thy face from thy servant: for I am in trouble, hear me speedily.

22. Attend to my soul, and deliver it; save me because of my enemies.

23. Tu scis improperium meum, et confusionem meam, * et reverentiam meam.

24. In conspectu tuo sunt omnes qui tribulant me, * improperium expectavit cor meum, et miseriam.

25. Et sustinui qui simul contristaretur, et non fuit: * et qui consolaretur, et non inveni.

26. Et dederunt in escam meam fel: * et in site mea potaverunt me aceto.

27. Fiat mensa eorum coram ipsis in laqueum, * et in retributiones, et in scandalum,

28. Obscurentur oculi eorum ne videant: * et dorsum eorum semper incurva.

29. Effunde super eos iram tuam: et furor iræ tuæ comprehendat eos.

30. Fiat habitatio eorum deserta: * et in tabernaculis eorum non sit qui inhabitet.

31. Quoniam quem tu

23. Thou knowest my reproach, and my confusion, and my shame.

24. In thy sight are all they that afflict me; my heart hath experienced reproach and misery.

25. And I looked for one that would grieve together with me, but there was none: and for one that would comfort me, and I found none.

26. And they gave me gall for my food, and in my thirst they gave me vinegar to drink.

27. Let their table become as a snare before them, and a recompense and a stumbling block.

28. Let their eyes be darkened that they see not: and their back bow thou down always.

29. Pour out thy ire upon them: and let thy wrathful anger take hold of them.

30. Let their habitation be made desolate, and let there be none to dwell in their tabernacles.

31. Because they have

percussisti, persecuti sunt; *et super dolorem vulnerum meorum addiderunt.

32. Appone iniquitatem super iniquitatem eorum et non intrent in justitiam tuam.

33. Deleantur de libro viventium: *et cum justis non scribantur.

34. Ego sum pauper et dolens; *salus tua Deus suscepit me.

35. Laudabo nomen Dei cum cantico: et magnificabo eum in laude.

36. Et placebit Deo super vitulum novellum: *cornua producentem et ungulas

37. Videant pauperes et lætentur: *quærite Deum, et vivet anima vestra

38 Quoniam exaudivit pauperes Dominus: *et vinctos suos non despexit.

39. Laudent illum cœli et terra: *mare et omnia reptilia in eis.

persecuted him whom thou hast smitten: and they have added to the grief of my wounds

32. Add thou iniquity upon their iniquity: and let them not come into thy Justice.

33. Let them be blotted out of the book of the living: and with the just let them not be written.

34. But I am poor and sorrowful: thy salvation, O God hath set me up.

35. I will praise the name of God with a canticle: and I will magnify him with praise.

36. And it shall please God better than a young calf: that bringeth forth horns and hoofs.

37. Let the poor see redress: seek you God and your souls shall live.

38. For the Lord hath heard the poor, and hath not despised his prisoners.

39. Let the heavens and the earth praise him; the sea, and every

40. Quoniam Deus salvam faciet Sion; * et ædificabuntur civitates Juda.
41. Et inhabitabunt ibi * et hereditate acquirent eam.
42. Et semen servorum ejus possidebit eam: * et qui diligunt nomen ejus habitabunt in ea.

Ant. Zelus domus tuæ comedit me, et opprobria exprobantium tibi ceciderunt super me.

Ant. Avertantur retrorsum et erubescant, qui cogitant mihi mala.

40, For God will save Sion; and the cities of Juda shall be build up.
41. And they shall dwell there, and acquire it by inheritance.
42. And the seed of his servants shall possess it; and they that love his name shall dwell therein.

Ant. A zeal of thy house hath eaten me; and the affronts of those that affronted thee fell upon me.

Ant. Let those that intend me harm, be driven backward, and be ashamed.

PSALM LXIX

DEUS in adjutorium meum intende: * Domine ad adjuvandum me festina.
2. Confundantur et revereantur, * qui quærunt animam meam:
3. Avertantur retrorsum, et erubescant, * qui volunt mihi mala:
4. Avertantur statim

O God, come to my assistance; O Lord, make haste to help me.
2. Let them be confounded and ashamed that seek my soul:
3. Let them be turned backward, and blush for shame, that desire evil to me:
4. Let them be pre-

erubescentes, * qui dicunt mihi: Euge, euge.

5. Exultent et lætentur in te omnes qui quærunt te, * et dicant semper: Magnificetur Dominus, qui diligunt salutare tuum.
6. Ego vero egenus, et pauper sum: * Deus adjuva me.
7. Adjutor meus et liberator meus es tu: * Domine ne moreris.

Ant. Avertantur retrorsum, et erubescant, * qui cogitant mihi mala.

Ant. Deus meus, eripe me de manu peccatoris.

sently turned away blushing for shame that say to me: 'Tis well, 'tis well.

5. Let all that seek thee rejoice and be glad in thee: and let such as love thy salvation say always: The Lord be magnified.
6. But I am needy and poor; O God, help me.
7. Thou art my helper and my deliverer: O Lord, make no delay.

Ant. Let those that intend me harm be turned backward and be ashamed.

Ant. O my God, deliver me out of the hand of the sinner.

PSALM LXX.

IN te Domine speravi, non confundar in æternum: * in justitia tua libera me, et eripe me.
2. Inclina ad me aurem tuam. * et salva me.
3. Esto mihi in Deum protectorem et in locum munitum: * ut salvum me facias.

IN thee, O Lord, I have hoped, let me never be put to confusion: deliver me in thy justice, and rescue me.
2. Incline thine ear unto me, and save me.
3. Be thou unto me a God, a protector, and a place of strength, that thou mayest make me safe.

4. Quoniam firmamentum meum * et refugium meum es tu.

5. Deus meus eripe me de manu peccatoris, * et de manu contra legem agentis et iniqui.

6. Quoniam tu es patientia mea, Domine: * Domine, spes mea a juventute mea.

7. In te confirmatus sum ex utero: * de ventre matris meæ tu es protector meus.

8. In te cantatio mea semper: * tamquam prodigium factus sum multis; et tu adjutor fortis.

9. Repleatur os meum laude, ut cantem gloriam tuam: * tota die magnitudinem tuam.

10. Ne projicias me in tempore senectutis: * cum defecerit virtus mea, ne derelinquas me.

11. Quia dixerunt inimici mei mihi: * et qui custodiebant animam

4. For thou art my firmament, and my refuge.

5. Deliver me, O my God, out of the hand of the sinner, and out of the hand of the transgressor of the law, and of the unjust.

6. For thou art my patience, O Lord: my hope, O Lord, from my youth.

7. By thee have I been confirmed from the womb: from my mother's womb thou art my protector.

8. Of thee shall I continually sing: I am become unto many as a wonder: but thou art a strong helper.

9. Let my mouth be filled with praise, that I may sing thy glory: thy greatness all the day long.

10. Cast me not off in the time of old age, when my strength shall fail, do not thou forsake me.

11. For my enemies have spoken against me: and they that watched

meam consilium fecerunt in unum.

12. Dicentes: Deus dereliquit eum, persequimini et comprehendite eum: * quia non est qui eripiat.

13. Deus ne elongeris a me: * Deus meus in auxilium meum respice.

14. Confundantur et deficiant detrahentes animæ meæ * operiantur confusione et pudore qui quærunt mala mihi.

15. Ego autem semper sperabo: * et adjiciam super omnem laudem tuam.

16. Os meum annuntiavit justitiam tuam: * tota die salutare tuum.

17. Quoniam non cognovi literaturam, introibo in potentias Domini: * Domine memorabor justitiæ tuæ solius.

18. Deus docuisti me a juventute mea: * et usque nunc pronuntiabo mirabilia tua.

19. Et usque in senec-

my soul have consulted together.

12. Saying: God hath forsaken him; pursue and take him, for there is none to deliver him.

13. O God, be not thou far from me: O my God, make haste to my help.

14. Let them be confounded and come to nothing that detract my soul: let them be covered with confusion and shame that seek my hurt.

15. But I will always hope: and will add to all thy praise.

16. My mouth shall show forth thy justice: thy salvation all the day long.

17. Because I have not known learning, I will enter into the powers of the Lord: O Lord, I will be mindful of thy justice alone.

18. Thou hast taught me, O God, from my youth, and till now I will declare thy wonderful works.

19. And unto old age

tam et senium: * Deus ne derelinquas me.

20. Donec annuntiem brachium tuum: * generationi omni, quæ ventura est.

21. Potentiam tuam, et justitiam tuam Deus usque in altissima, quæ fecisti magnalia: * Deus quis similis tibi?

22. Quantas ostendisti mihi tribulationes multas et malas: et conversus vivificasti me: * et de abyssis terræ iterum reduxisti me.

23. Multiplicasti magnificentiam tuam: * et conversus consolatus es me.

24. Nam et ego confitebor tibi in vasis psalmi veritatem tuam: * Deus, psallam tibi in cithara, sanctus Israel.

25. Exultabunt labia mea cum cantavero tibi: * et anima mea, quam redemisti.

26. Sed et lingua mea

and grey hairs, O God, forsake me not.

20. Until I show forth thy arm to all the generation that is to come.

21. Thy power, and thy justice, O God, even to the highest, great things thou hast done; O God, who is like to thee?

22. How great troubles hast thou showed me, many and grievous: and turning thou hast brought me to life, and hast brought me back again from the depths of the earth.

23. Thou hast multiplied thy magnificence: and turning to me thou hast comforted me.

24. I will also give praise to thee: I will extol thy truth with the instruments of psaltery: O God, I will sing to thee with the harp, thou holy one of Israel.

25. My lips shall greatly rejoice when I shall sing to thee: and my soul which thou hast redeemed.

26. Yea and my tongue

tota die meditabitur justitiam tuam: *cum confusi et reveriti fuerint qui quærunt mala mihi.

Ant. Deus meus, eripe me de manu peccatoris.

V. Avertantur retrorsum et erubescant.
R. Qui cogitant mihi mala.

Pater noster, *secreto.*
Incipit Lamentatio Jeremiæ Prophetæ, *cap. I.*

LECTIO I.

Aleph. QUOMODO sedet sola civitas plena populo: facta est quasi vidua domina gentium: princeps provinciarum facta est sub tributo.

Beth. Plorans ploravit in nocte, et lacrymæ ejus in maxillis ejus: non est qui consoletur eam ex omnibus caris ejus omnes amici ejus spreverunt eam, et facti sunt ei inimici.

Ghimel. Migravit Ju-

also shall meditate on thy justice all the day; when they shall be confounded and put to shame that seek evils to me.

Ant. O my God, deliver me out of the hand of the sinner.

V. Let them be driven backward and ashamed.
R. That intend me harm.

Our Father, *in secret.*
Beginning of the Lamentation of Jeremiah the Prophet, *chap I.*

LESSON I.

Aleph. HOW doth the city sit solitary that was full of people: how is the mistress of nations become as a widow: the princess of provinces made tributary.

Beth. Weeping she hath wept in the night, and her tears are on her cheeks; there is none to comfort her among all them that were dear to her: all her friends have despised her, and are become her enemies.

Ghimel. Judah hath

das propter afflictionem, et multitudinem servitutis: habitavit inter gentes, nec invenit requiem: omnes persecutores ejus apprehenderunt eam inter angustias.

Daleth. Viæ Sion lugent, eo quod non sint qui veniant ad solemnitatem: omnes portæ ejus destructæ: sacerdotes ejus gementes, virgines ejus squalidæ, et ipsa oppressa amaritudine.

He. Facti sunt hostes ejus in capite, inimici ejus locupletati sunt: quia Dominus locutus est super eam propter multitudinem iniquitatum ejus: parvuli ejus ducti sunt in captivitatem, ante faciem tribulantis.

Jerusalem, Jerusalem, convertere ad Dominum Deum tuum.

R. In monte Oliveti oravit ad Patrem: Pater, si fieri potest, tran-

removed her dwelling-place because of her affliction, and the greatness of her bondage: she hath dwelt among the nations, and she hath found no rest: her persecutors have taken her in the midst of straits.

Daleth. The ways of Sion mourn, because there are none that come to the solemn feast: all her gates are broken down: her priests sigh, her virgins are in affliction, and she is oppressed with bitterness.

He. Her adversaries are become her lords, her enemies are enriched: because the Lord hath spoken against her for the multitude of her iniquities: her children are led into captivity, before the face of the oppressor.

Jerusalem, Jerusalem, be converted to the Lord thy God.

R. He prayed to his Father on mount Olivet; Father if it be pos-

seat a me calix iste: *Spiritus quidem promptus est, caro autem infirma. V. Vigilate et orate, ut non intretis in tentationem. *Spiritus quidem.

sible, let this cup pass away from me: *The spirit indeed is ready but the flesh is weak. *Watch and pray that ye may not enter into temptation. *The spirit indeed.

LECTIO II.

Vau. ET egressus est a filia Sion omnis decor ejus facti sunt principes ejus velut arietes non invenientes pascua, et abierunt absque fortitudine ante faciem subsequentis.

Zain. Recordata est Jerusalem dierum afflictionis suæ, et prævaricationis omnium desiderabilium suorum, quæ habuerat a diebus antiquis, cum caderet populus ejus in manu nostili, et non esset auxiliator: viderunt eam hostes, et deriserunt sabbata ejus.

Heth. Peccatum peccavit Jerusalem, propterea instabilis facta est: omnes qui glorificabant eam spreverunt illam, quia viderunt i-

LESSON II.

Vau. AND from the daughter of Sion all her beauty is departed: her princes are become like rams that find no pasture, and they are gone away without strength before the face of the pursuer.

Zain. Jerusalem hath remembered the days of her affliction and transgression of all her desirable things, which she had from the days of old, when her people fell in the enemy's hand, and there was no helper: the enemies have seen her, and have mocked at her Sabbaths.

Heth. Jerusalem hath grievously sinned, therefore is she become vagabond: all that honoured her, have despised her, because they have

gnominiam ejus: ipsa autem gemens conversa est retrorsum.

Teth. Sordes ejus in pedibus ejus nec recordata est finis sui : deposita est vehementer; non habens consolatorem vide Domine afflictionem meam, quoniam erectus est inimicus.

Jerusalem, Jerusalem, convertere ad Dominum Deum tuum.

R. Tristis est anima mea usque ad mortem: sustinete hic, et vigilate mecum: nunc videbitis turbam, quæ circumdabit me: * Vos fugam capietis, et ego vadam immolari pro vobis. *V.* Ecce appropinquat hora, et Filius hominis tradetur in manus peccatorum. * Vos fugam capietis.

LECTIO III.

Jod. MANUM suam misit hostis ad omnia desiderabilia ejus: quia vidit gentes ingressas sanctuarium suum, de quibus præceperas ne intrarent in ecclesiam tuam.

seen her shame: but she sighed and turned backward.

Teth. Her filthiness is on her feet, and she hath not remembered her end: she is wonderfully cast down, not having a comforter: behold, O Lord, my affliction, because the enemy is lifted up.

Jerusalem, Jerusalem, be converted to the Lord thy God.

R. My soul is sorrowful to death: stay here and watch with me: now ye shall see a multitude, that will surround me: * Ye shall run away, and I will go to be sacrificed for you. *V.* Behold the time draws near, and the Son of Man shall be delivered into the hands of sinners. *Ye shall.

LESSON III.

Jod. THE enemy hath put out his hand to all her desirable things: for she hath seen the Gentiles enter into her sanctuary, of whom thou gavest commandment that they

Caph. Omnis populus ejus gemens et quærens panem: dederunt pretiosa quæque pro cibo ad refocillandam animam. Vide Domine, et considera quoniam facta sum vilis.

Lamed. O vos omnes, qui transitis per viam, attendite, et videte si est dolor sicut dolor meus: quoniam vindemiavit me, ut locutus est Dominus in die iræ furoris sui.

Mem. De excelso misit ignem in ossibus meis, et erudivit me: expandit rete pedibus meis, convertit me retrorsum: posuit me desolatam, tota die mœrore confectam.

Nun. Vigilavit jugum iniquitatum mearum: in manu ejus convolutæ sunt, et impositæ collo meo: infirmata est virtus mea: dedit me Dominus in manu de qua non potero surgere.

should not enter into thy church.

Caph. All her people sigh they seek bread: they have given all their precious things for food to relieve the soul. See, O Lord, and consider, for I am become vile.

Lamed. O all ye that pass by the way, attend, and see if there be any sorrow like to my sorrow: for he hath made a vintage of me, as the Lord spoke in the day of his fierce anger.

Mem. From above he hath sent fire into my bones, and hath chastised me: he hath spread a net for my feet, he hath turned me back, he hath made me destitute, and spent with sorrow all the day long.

Nun. The yoke of my iniquities hath watched for me: they are folded together in his hand, and put on my neck: my strength is weakened: the Lord hath delivered me into a hand out of which I am not able to rise.

Jerusalem, Jerusalem convertere ad Dominum Deum tuum.

℟. Ecce vidimus eum non habentem specimen, neque decorem: aspectus ejus in eo non est: hic peccata nostra portavit et pro nobis dolet: ipse autem vulneratus est propter iniquitates nostras, * cujus livore sanati sumus. ℣. Vere languores nostros ipse tulit, et dolores nostros ipse portavit. * Cusus livore. Ecce vidimus.

Jerusalem, Jerusalem, be converted to the Lord thy God.

℟. Behold we have seen him disfigured and without beauty: his aspect is gone from him: he has borne our sins and suffers for us: and he was wounded for our iniquities, * and by his stripes we are healed. ℣. He has truly borne our infirmities, and carried our sorrows. * And by his stripes. Behold we have seen him, etc.

THE SECOND NOCTURN.

Ant. Liberavit Dominus pauperem a potente, et inopem, cui non erat adjutor.

Ant. The Lord has delivered from the mighty the poor and needy man that had no helper.

PSALM LXXI.

DEUS judicium tuum regi da: * et justitiam tuam filio regis.

2. Judicare populum tuum in justitia: * et pauperes tuos in judicio.

3. Suscipiant montes pacem populo, * et colles justitiam.

GIVE to the king thy judgment, O God: and to the king's son thy justice.

2. To judge thy people with justice, and thy poor with judgment.

3. Let the mountains receive peace for the people, and the hills justice.

4. Judicabit pauperes populi, et salvos faciet filios pauperum: * et humiliabit calumniatorem.

5. Et permanebit cum sole, et ante lunam, * in generatione et generationem.

6. Descendet sicut pluvia in vellus: * et sicut stillicidia stillantia super terram.

7. Orientur in diebus ejus justitia, et abundantia pacis; * donec auferatur luna.

8. Et dominabitur a mari usque ad mare: * et a flumine usque ad terminos orbis terrarum.

9. Coram illo procident Æthiopes: * et inimici ejus terram lingent.

10. Reges Tharsis et insulæ munera offerent: * reges Arabum et Saba dona adducent.

11. Et adorabunt eum omnes reges terræ: * omnes gentes servient ei.

4. He shall judge the poor of the people, and he shall save the children of the poor, and he shall humble the oppressor.

5. And he shall continue with the sun; and before the moon, throughout all generations.

6. He shall come down like rain upon the fleece: and as showers falling gently upon the earth.

7. In his days justice shall spring up, and abundance of peace: till the moon be taken away.

8. And he shall rule from sea to sea: and from the river to the ends of the earth.

9. Before him the Ethiopians shall fall down: and his enemies shall lick the ground.

10. The kings of Tharsis and the islands shall offer presents: the kings of the Arabians and of Saba shall bring gifts.

11. And all the kings of the earth shall adore him; all nations shall serve him.

12. Quia liberabit pauperem a potente: * et pauperem cui non erat adjutor.

13. Parcet pauperi et inopi: * et animas pauperum salvas faciet.

14. Ex usuris et iniquitate redimet animas corum: * et honorabile nomem eorum coram illo.

15. Et vivet et dabitur ei de auro Arabiæ, et adorabunt de ipso semper: * tota die benedicent ei.

16. Et erit firmamentum in terra in summis montium, superextolletur super Libanum fructus ejus: * et florebunt de civitate sicut fœnum terræ.

17. Sit nomen ejus benedictum in sæcula: * ante solem permanet nomen ejus.

18. Et benedicentur in ipso omnes tribus terræ: * omnes gentes magnificabunt eum.

12. For he shall deliver the poor from the mighty: and the needy that had no helper.

13. He shall spare the poor and needy: and he shall save the souls of the poor.

14. He shall redeem their souls from usuries and iniquity: and their name shall he honourable in his sight.

15. And he shall live and to him shall be given of the gold of Arabia: for him they shall always adore; they shall bless him all the day.

16. And there shall be a firmament on the earth, on the tops of mountains: above Libanus shall the fruit thereof be exalted: and they of the city shall flourish like the grass of the earth.

17. Let his name be blessed for evermore: his name continueth before the sun.

18. And in him shall all the tribes of the earth be blessed: all nations shall magnify him.

19. Benedictus Dominus Deus Israel, * qui facit mirabilia solus.

20. Et benedictum nomen majestatis ejus in æternum: * et replebitur majestate ejus omnis terra: Fiat, Fiat.

Ant. Liberavit Dominus pauperem a potente, et inopem cui non erat adjutor.

Ant. Cogitaverunt impii, et locuti sunt nequitiam: iniquitatem in excelso locuti sunt.

19. Blessed be the Lord, the God of Israel, who alone doth wonderful things.

20. And blessed be the name of his majesty for ever: and the whole earth shall be filled with his majesty. So be it, so be it.

Ant. The Lord has delivered from the mighty the poor and needy man, that hath no helper.

Ant. The impious have thought and spoken wickedness: they have spoken iniquity from the high place.

PSALM LXXII.

QUAM bonus Israel Deus * his, qui recto sunt corde.

2. Mei autem pene moti sunt pedes: * pene effusi sunt gressus mei:

3. Quia zelavi super iniquos, * pacem peccatorum videns.

4. Quia non est respectus morti eorum: * et firmamentum in plaga eorum.

5. In labore hominum non sunt, * et cum ho-

HOW good is God to Israel: to them that are of a right heart!

2. But my feet were almost moved, my steps had well nigh slipt:

3. Because I had a zeal on occasion of the wicked, seeing the prosperity of sinners.

4. For there is no regard to their death; nor is there strength in their stripes.

5. They are not in the labour of men; neither

minibus non flagellabuntur.

6. Ideo tenuit eos superbia, * operti sunt iniquitate et impietate sua.

7. Prodiit quasi ex adipe iniquitas eorum: * transierunt in affectum cordis.

8. Cogitaverunt, et locuti sunt nequitiam: * iniquitatem in excelso locuti sunt.

9. Posuerunt in cœlum os suum: * et lingua eorum transivit in terra.

10. Ideo convertetur populus meus hic * et dies pleni invenientur in eis.

11. Et dixerunt, Quomodo scit Deus, * et si est scientia in excelso?

12. Ecce ipsi peccatores, et abundantes in seculo, * obtinuerunt divitias.

13. Et dixi: Ergo sine causa justificavi cor me-

shall they be scourged like other men.

6. Therefore pride hath held them fast: they are covered with their iniquity and their wickedness.

7. Their iniquity hath come forth, as it were, from fatness: they have passed into the affection of the heart.

8. They have thought and spoken wickedness: they have spoken iniquity on high.

9. They have set their mouth against heaven: and their tongue hath passed through the earth.

10. Therefore will my people return here: and full days shall be found in them.

11. And they said: How doth God know, and is there knowledge in the Most High?

12. Behold these are sinners; and yet abounding in the world, they have obtained riches.

13. And I said: Then have I in vain justified

um, * et lavi inter innocentes manus meas:

14. Et fui flagellatus tota die, * et castigatio mea in matutinis.

15. Si dicebam: Narrabo sic: * ecce nationem filiorum tuorum reprobavi.
16. Existimabam ut cognoscerem hoc, * labor est ante me:

17. Donec intrem in sanctuarium Dei; * et intelligam in novissimis eorum.
18. Verumtatmen propter dolos posuisti eis: * dejecisti eos dum allevarentur.

19. Quomodo facti sunt in desolationem, subito defecerunt; * perierunt propter iniquitatem suam.

20. Velut somnium surgentium, Domine, * in civitate tua imaginem ipsorum ad nihilum rediges.
21. Quia inflammatum est cor meum, et renes

my heart, and washed my hands among the innocent.
14. And I have been scourged all the day, and my chastisement hath been in mornings.
15. If I said: I will speak thus: behold I should condemn the generation of thy children.
16. I studied that I might know this thing: it is as labour in my sight.
17. Until I go into the sanctuary of God, and understand concerning their last ends.
18. But indeed for deceits thou hast put it to them: when they were lifted up thou hast cast them down.
19. How are they brought to desolation: they have suddenly ceased to be: they have perished by reason of their iniquity.
20. As the dream of them that awake, O Lord, so in thy city thou shalt bring their image to nothing.
21. For my heart hath been inflamed, and

mei commutati sunt: * et ego ad nihilum redactus sum, et nescivi.

22. Ut jumentum factus sum apud te, * et ego semper tecum.
23. Tenuisti manum dexteram meam: et in voluntate tua deduxisti me, * et cum gloria suscepisti me.

24. Quid enim mihi est in cœlo? * et a te quid volui super terram?

25. Defecit caro mea, et cor meum; * Deus cordis mei, et pars mea Deus in æternum.

26. Quia ecce, qui elongant se a te, peribunt: * perdidisti omnes qui fornicantur abs te.

27. Mihi autem adhærere Deo bonum est: * ponere in Domino Deo spem meam.
28. Ut annuntiem omnes prædicationes tuas, * in portis filiæ Sion.

Ant. Cogitaverunt im-

my reins have been changed: and I am brought to nothing, and I know not.

22. I am become as a beast before thee: and I am always with thee.
23. Thou hast held me by my right hand: and by thy will thou hast conducted me: and with glory thou hast received me.

24. For what have I in heaven? and besides thee what do I desire upon earth?

25. For thee my flesh and my heart hath fainted away: thou art the God of my heart and the God that is my portion for ever.

26. For behold they that go far from thee shall perish: thou hast destroyed all them that are disloyal to thee.

27. But it is good for me to stick close to my God, to put my hope in the Lord God.

28. That I may declare all thy praises in the gates of the daughter of Sion.

Ant. The impious

pii, et locuti sunt nequitiam: iniquitatem in excelso locuti sunt.

Ant. Exurge Domine, et judica causam meam.

have thought and spoken wickedness: they have spoken iniquity on high.

Ant. Arise, O Lord, and judge my cause.

PSALM LXXIII.

UT qui Deus repulisti in finem ? * iratus est furor tuus super oves pascuæ tuæ.

2. Memor esto congregationis tuæ, * quam possedisti ab initio.

3. Redemisti virgam hereditatis tuæ: mons Sion in quo habitasti in eo.

4. Leva manus tuas in superbias eorum in finem : * quanta malignatus est inimicus in sancto.

5. Et gloriati sunt qui oderunt te. * in medio solemnitatis tuæ.

6. Posuerunt signa sua signa: * et non cognoverunt sicut in exitu super summum.

O GOD, why hast thou cast us off unto the end ? why is thy wrath enkindled against the sheep of thy pasture?

2. Remember thy congregation, which thou hast possessed from the beginning.

3. The sceptre of thy inheritance which thou hast redeemed: Mount Sion, in which thou hast dwelt.

4. Lift up thy hands against their pride unto the end: see what things the enemy hath done wickedly in the sanctuary.

5. And they that hate thee have made their boasts, in the midst of thy solemnity.

6. They have set up their ensigns for signs; and they knew not both in the going out and on the highest top.

7. Quasi in silva lignorum securibus exciderunt januas ejus in idipsum: * in securi et ascia dejecerunt eam.

8. Incenderunt igni sanctuarium tuum: * in terra polluerunt tabernaculum nominis tui.

9. Dixerunt in corde suo cognatio eorum simul: * Quiescere faciamus omnes dies festos Dei a terra.

10. Signa nostra non vidimus, jam non est propheta: * et nos non cognoscet amplius.

11. Usquequo Deus improperabit inimicus * irritat adversarius nomen tuum in finem?

12. Ut quid avertis manum tuam, et dexteram tuam, * de medio sinu tuo in finem?

13. Deus autem Rex noster ante sæcula: * operatus est salutem in medio terræ.

14. Tu confirmasti in virtute tua mare: * con-

7. As with axes in a wood of trees, they have cut down at once the gates thereof: with axe and hatchet they have brought it down.

8. They have set fire to thy sanctuary: they have defiled the dwelling-place of thy name on the earth.

9. They said in their heart, the whole kindred of them together. Let us abolish all the festival days of God from the land.

10. Our signs we have not seen, there is now no prophet: and he will know us no more.

11. How long, O God, shall the enemy reproach? is the adversary to provoke thy name for ever?

12. Why dost thou turn away thy hands and thy right hand out of the midst of thy bosom for ever?

13. But God is our king before ages: he hath wrought salvation in the midst of the earth.

14. Thou by thy strength didst make the

tribulasti capita draconum in aquis.

15. Tu confregisti capita draconis: * dedisti eum escam populis Æthiopum.

16. Tu dirupisti fontes et torrentes: * tu siccasti fluvios Ethan.

17. Tuus est dies, et tua est nox: * tu fabricatus es auroram et solem.

18. Tu fecisti omnes terminos terræ: * æstatem et ver tu plasmasti ea.

19. Memor esto hujus, inimicus improperavit Domino: * et populus insipiens incitavit nomen tuum.

20. Ne tradas bestiis animas confitentes tibi: * et animas pauperum tuorum ne obliviscaris in finem.

21. Respice in testamentum tuum : * quia repleti sunt, qui obscurati sunt, terræ domibus iniquitatum.

sea firm: thou didst crush the heads of the dragons in the waters.

15. Thou hast broken the heads of the dragon: thou hast given him to be meat for the Ethiopian people.

16. Thou hast broken up the fountains, and the torrents: thou hast dried up the Ethan rivers.

17. Thine is the day, and thine is the night: thou hast made the moon and the sun.

18. Thou hast made all the borders of the earth: the summer and the spring were formed by thee.

19. Remember this, the enemy hath reproached the Lord: and a foolish people hath provoked thy name.

20. Deliver not up to beasts the souls that confess thee: and forget not to the end the souls of thy poor.

21. Have regard to thy covenant: for they that are obscure of the earth have been filled with the dwellings of iniquity.

22. Ne avertatur humilis factus confusus: * pauper et inops laudabunt nomen tuum.

23. Exurge Deus, judica causam tuam: * memor esto improperiorum tuorum, eorum quæ ab insipiente sunt tota die.

24. Ne obliviscaris voces inimicorum tuorum: * superbia eorum qui te oderunt ascendit semper.

Ant. Exurge Domine, et judica causam meam.
V. Deus meus eripe me de manu peccatoris.

R. Et de manu contra legem agentis, et iniqui.
Pater noster, secreto.

Ex tractatu Sancti Augustini Episcopi super Psalmos. Ps. liv.

LECTIO IV.

*E*Xaudi Deus orationem meam et ne despexeris deprecationem meam: intende mihi, et exaudi me.

22. Let not the humble be turned away with confusion: the poor and needy shall praise thy name.

23. Arise, O God, judge thy own cause: remember the reproaches with which the foolish man hath reproached thee all the day.

24. Forget not the voices of thy enemies: the pride of them that hate thee ascendeth continually.

Ant. Arise, O Lord, and judge my cause.
V. O God deliver me out of the hand of the sinner.
R. And out of the hand of the law breaker and the unjust man.
Our Father, in secret.

From the treatise of St. Augustine the Bishop upon the Psalms. Ps. liv.

LESSON IV.

*H*EAR my prayer, O God, and despise not my petition: attend to me and hear me. These are

Satagentis solliciti, in tribulatione positi, verba sunt ista. Orat multa patiens, de malo liberari desiderans. Superest ut videamus in quo malo sit: et cum dicere cœperit, agnoscamus ibi nos esse: ut communicata tribulatione, conjungamus orationem. *Contristatus sum,* inquit, *in exercitatione mea, et conturbatus sum.* Ubi contristatus? Ubi conturbatus? *In exercitatione mea,* inquit. Homines malos, quos patitur commemoratus est: eamdemque passionem malorum hominum, exercitationem suam dixit. Ne putetis gratis esse malos in hoc mundo, et nihil boni de illis agere Deum. Omnis malus aut ideo vivit, ut corrigatur: aut ideo vivit, ut per illum bonus exerceatur.

R. Amicus meus osculi me tradidit signo: quem osculatus fuero, ipse est, tenete eum: hoc malum fecit signum, qui per osculum adim-

the words of a man in trouble, solicitude, and affliction. He prays in his great sufferings, desiring to be freed from some evil. Let us now see what evil he lies under: and having told us, let us acknowledge ourselves in it: that by partaking of the affliction we may join in his prayer. *I am become sorrowful in my exercise,* says he, *and I am troubled.* Where is he become sorrowful? where is he troubled? He says, *In my exercise.* He speaks of the wicked men whom he suffers, and calls such suffering of wicked men his exercise. Think not that the wicked are in the world for nothing, and that God does no good with them. Every wicked man lives, either to amend his life, or to exercise the good.

R. The sign by which my friend betrayed me was a kiss: whom I shall kiss, that is he: hold him fast: he that committed murder by a

plevit homicidium. Infelix prætermisit pretium sanguinis, et in fine laqueo se suspendit

℣. Bonum erat ei, si natus non fuisset homo ille. * Infelix prætermisit.

LECTIO V.

Utinam ergo qui nos modo exercent, convertantur, et nobiscum exerceantur : tamen quamdiu ita sunt ut exerceant, non eos oderimus : quia in eo quod malus est quis eorum, utrum usque in finem perseveraturus sit, ignoramus. Et plerumque cum tibi videris odisse inimicum, fratrem odisti, et nescis. Diabolus, et angeli ejus in scripturis sanctis manifestati sunt nobis, quod ad ignem æternum sint destinati. Ipsorum tantum desperanda est correctio, contra quos habemus occultam luctam, ad quam luctam nos armat apostolus, dicens, *Non est nobis colluctatio adversus carnem et san-*

kiss gave this wicked sign. * The unhappy wretch returned the price of blood, and in the end hanged himself.

℣. It had been good for that man, if he had never been born. * The unhappy wretch.

LESSON V.

Would to God then they that now exercise us were converted and exercised with us: but let us not hate them, tho' they continue to exercise us; for we know not whether they will persevere to the end in their wickedness. And many times when you imagine that you hate your enemy, it is your brother you hate, though you are ignorant of it. The holy scriptures plainly show us that the devil and his angels are doomed to eternal fire. It is only their amendment we may despair of, with whom we wage an invisible war; for which the apostle arms us, saying: *Our conflict is not*

guinem: id est, non adversus homines, quos videtis, *sed adversus principes, et potestates, et rectores mundi tenebrarum harum.* Ne forte cum dixisset, *mundi*, intelligeres dæmones esse rectores cœli et terræ, *mundi* dixit, *tenebrarum harum.* Mundi dixit, amatorum mundi: *mundi* dixit, impiorum et iniquorum: *mundi* dixit, de quo dicit Evangelium: *Et mundus eum non cognovit.*

R. Judas mercator pessimus osculo petiit Dominum: ille ut agnus innocens non negavit Judæ osculum; * Denariorum numero Christum Judæis tradidit.

V. Melius illi erat, si natus non fuisset: * Denariorum.

LECTIO VI.

*Q*Uoniam vidi iniquitatem, et contradictionem in civitate. Attende gloriam crucis ipsius. Jam in fronte regum

with *flesh and blood*, that is, not with the men you see before your eyes, but with the princes, and powers, and rulers of the world of this darkness. And lest by his saying, *of the world*, you might think perhaps, that the devils are rulers of heaven and earth, he added, *of this darkness.* By the *world* then, he meant the lovers of the world: by the *world*, he meant the impious and the wicked: by the *world*, he meant that which the gospel speaks of: *And the world knew him not.*

R. The wicked merchant Judas kissed our Lord: he like an innocent Lamb refused not the kiss to Judas. * For a few pence he delivered Christ to the Jews.

V. It had been better for him if he had never been born: * For a few pence.

LESSON VI.

*F*OR I have seen injustice and strife in the city. See the glory of the cross. That cross that was the derision of

crux illa fixa est, cui inimici insultaverunt. Effectus probavit virtutem: domuit orbem non ferro, sed ligno. Lignum crucis contumeliis dignum visum est inimicis, et ante ipsum lignum stantes caput agitabant, et dicebant: *Si Filius Dei est descendat de cruce.* Extendebat ille manus suas ad populum non credentem, et contradicentem. Si enim justus est qui ex fide vivit, iniquus est qui non habet fidem. Quod ergo hic ait *iniquitatem*, perfidiam intellige. Videbat ergo Dominus in civitate iniquitatem, et contradictionem, et extendebat manus suas ad populum non credentem, et contradicentem: et tamen et ipsos expectans, dicebat: *Pater ignosce illis*; *quia nesciunt quid faciunt.*

R. Unus ex discipulis meis tradet me hodie: væ illi per quem tradar ego: * Melius illi erat,

his enemies, is now placed on the foreheads of kings. The effect is a proof of his power: he conquered the world not by the sword, but by the wood. The wood of the cross was thought a subject of scorn by his enemies, who as they stood before it, shook their heads and said: *If he is the Son of God, let him come down from the cross.* He stretched forth his hand to an unbelieving and seditious people. For if he is just that lives by faith, he is unjust that has not faith. By *injustice* then here you must understand infidelity. Our Lord therefore saw injustice and strife in the city, and stretched forth his hands to an unbelieving and seditious people; and yet he waited for them, saying, *Father, forgive them, for they know not what they do.*

R. One of my disciples will this day betray me: wo to him by whom I am betrayed: * It had

si natus non fuisset. *V.* Qui intingit mecum manum in paropside, hic me traditurus est in manus peccatorum. * Melius illi, etc. *R.* Unus ex discipulis, etc.

been better for him if he had never been born. *V.* He that dips his hand with me in the dish, is the man that will deliver me into the hands of sinners. * It had been etc. *R.* One of my disciples, etc.

THE THIRD NOCTURN.

Ant. Dixi iniquis: Nolite loqui adversus Deum iniquitatem.

Ant. I said to the wicked: Speak not iniquity against God.

PSALM LXXIV.

COonfitebimur tibi Deus: * confitebimur, et invocabimus nomen tuum.

2. Narrabimus mirabilia tua: * cum accepero tempus, ego justitias judicabo.

3. Liquefacta est terra, et omnes qui habitant in ea: * ego confirmavi columnas ejus.

4. Dixi iniquis: Nolite inique agere: * et delinquentibus: Nolite exaltare cornu.

5. Nolite extollere in altum cornu vestrum: * Nolite loqui adversus Deum iniquitatem.

6. Quia neque ab oriente, neque ab occi-

WE will praise thee, O God: we will praise, and we will call upon thy name.

2. We will relate thy wondrous works: when I shall take a time, I will judge justice.

3. The earth is melted and all that dwell therein: I have established the pillars thereof.

4. I said to the wicked: Do not act wickedly: and to the sinners; Lift not up the horn.

5. Lift not up your horn on high: speak not iniquity against God.

6. For neither from the east, nor from the west,

dente, neque a desertis montibus: * quoniam Deus judex est.

7. Hunc humiliat, et hunc exaltat: * quia calix in manu Domini vini meri plenus mixto.

8. Et inclinavit ex hoc in hoc: verumtamen fæx ejus non est exinanita: * bibent omnes peccatores terræ.

9. Ego autem annuntiabo in sæculum: * cantabo Deo Jacob.

10. Et omnia cornua peccatorum confringam: * et exaltabuntur cornua justi.

Ant. Dixi iniquis: Nolite loqui adversus Deum iniquitatem.

Ant. Terra tremuit et quievit, dum exurgeret in judicio Deus.

nor from the desert hills: for God is the judge.

7. One he putteth down, and another he lifteth up. For in the hand of the Lord there is a cup of strong wine full of mixture.

8. And he hath poured it out from this to that: but the dregs thereof are not emptied: all the sinners of the earth shall drink.

9. But I will declare for ever: I will sing to the God of Jacob.

10. And I will break all the horns of sinners, but the horns of the just shall be exalted.

Ant. I said to the wicked: Speak not iniquity against God.

Ant. The earth trembled and was silent, while God arose to judgment.

PSALM LXXV.

NOTUS in Judæa Deus: * in Israel magnum nomen ejus.

2. Et factus est in pace locus ejus: * et habitatio ejus in Sion.

IN Judea God is known, his name is great in Israel.

2. And his place is in peace, and his abode in Sion.

3. Ibi confregit potentias arcuum, * scutum, gladium, et bellum.

4. Illuminas tu mirabiliter a montibus æternis: * turbati sunt omnes insipientes corde.

5. Dormierunt somnum suum: * et nihil invenerunt omnes viri divitiarum in manibus suis.

6. Ab increpatione tua Deus Jacob, * dormitaverunt qui ascenderunt equos.

7. Tu terribilis es, et quis resistet tibi? * ex tunc ira tua.

8. De cœlo auditum fecisti judicium: * terra tremuit et quievit.

9. Cum exurgeret in judicium Deus, * ut salvos faceret omnes mansuetos terræ.

10. Quoniam cogitatio hominis confitebitur tibi: * et reliquiæ cogitationis diem festum agent tibi.

11. Vovete et reddite Domino Deo vestro

3. There hath he broken the power of bows, the shield, the sword and the battle.

4. Thou enlightenest wonderfully from the everlasting hills: all the foolish of heart were troubled.

5. They have slept their sleep: and all the men of riches have found nothing in their hands.

6. At thy rebuke, O God of Jacob, they have all slumbered that mounted on horseback.

7. Thou art terrible, and who shall resist thee? from that time thy wrath.

8. Thou hast caused judgment to be heard from heaven: the earth trembled and was still.

9. When God arose in judgment, to save all the meek of the earth.

10. For the thought of man shall give praise to thee: and the remainders of the thought shall keep holyday to thee.

11. Vow ye, and pay to the Lord your God:

* omnes qui in circuitu ejus affertis munera.

12. Terribili et ei qui aufert spiritum principum, * terribili apud reges terræ.

Ant. Terra tremuit et quievit, dum exurgeret in judicio Deus.

Ant. In die tribulationis meæ Deum exquisivi manibus meis.

all you that round about him bring presents.

12. To him that is terrible, even to him who taketh away the spirit of princes; to the terrible with the kings of the earth.

Ant. The earth trembled and was silent, while God arose to judgment.

Ant In the day of my tribulation I sought God with my hands lifted up to him.

PSALM LXXVI.

VOCE mea ad Dominum clamavi: * voce mea ad Deum, et intendit mihi.

2. In die tribulationis meæ Deum exquisivi, manibus meis nocte contra eum: * et non sum deceptus.

3. Renuit consolari anima mea, * memor fui Dei, et delectatus sum, et exercitatus sum, et defecit spiritus meus.

4. Anticipaverunt vigilias oculi mei: * turbatus sum, et non sum locutus.

I Cried to the Lord with my voice: to God with my voice, and he gave ear to me.

2. In the day of my trouble I sought God: with my hands lifted up to him in the night, and I was not deceived.

3. My soul refused to be comforted; I remembered God, and was delighted, and was exercised, and my spirit swooned away.

4. My eyes prevented the watches: I was troubled, and I spoke not.

5. Cogitavi dies antiquos: * et annos æternos in mente habui.

6. Et meditatus sum nocte cum corde meo,* et exercitabar, et scopebam spiritum meum.

7. Numquid in æternum projiciet Deus? * Aut non apponet ut complacitior sit adhuc?

8. Aut in finem misericordiam suam abscindet, * a generatione in generationem?

9. Aut obliviscetur misereri Deus? * aut continebit in ira sua misericordias suas?

10. Et dixi: nunc cœpi: * hæc mutatio dexteræ Excelsi.

11. Memor fui operum Domini: * quia memor ero ab initio mirabilium tuorum.

12. Et meditabor in omnibus operibus tuis: * et in adinventionibus tuis exercebor.

13. Deus in sancto via tua: quis Deus magnus sicut Deus noster? * Tu

5. I thought upon the days of old: and I had in my mind the eternal years.

6. And I meditated in the night with my own heart, and I was exercised, and I swept my spirit.

7. Will God then cast off for ever? or will he never be more favourable again?

8. Or will he cut off his mercy for ever, from generation to generation?

9. Or will God forget to show mercy? or will he in his anger shut up his mercies?

10. And I said: Now have I begun: this is the change of the right-hand of the Most High.

11. I remembered the works of the Lord: for I will be mindful of thy wonders from the beginning.

12. And I will meditate on all thy works: and will be employed in thy inventions.

13. Thy way, O God, is in the holy place: who is the great God like our

es Deus, qui facis mirabilia.
14. Notum fecisti in populis virtutem tuam : * redemisti in brachio tuo populum tuum, filios Jacob et Joseph.

15. Viderunt te aquæ Deus, viderunt, te aquæ: * et timuerunt, turbatæ sunt abyssi.

16. Multitudo sonitus aquarum: * vocem dederunt nubes.
17. Etenim sagittæ tuæ transeunt: vox tonitrui tui in rota.
18. Illuxerunt coruscationes tuæ orbi terræ: * commota est et contremuit terra.
19. In mari via tua, et semitæ tuæ in aquis multis: * et vestigia tua non cognoscentur.

20. Deduxisti sicut oves populum tuum, * in manu Moysi et Aaron.
Ant. In die tribulationes meæ, Deum exquisivi manibus meis.

God? Thou art the God that dost wonders.
14. Thou hast made thy power known among the nations: with thy arm thou hast redeemed thy people, the children of Jacob and Joseph.
15. The waters saw thee, O God, the waters saw thee ; and they were afraid, and the depths were troubled.
16. Great was the noise of the waters: the clouds sent out a sound.
17. For thy arrows pass: the voice of thy thunder in a wheel.
18. Thy lightnings enlightened the world; the earth shook and trembled.
19. Thy way is in the sea, and thy paths in many waters; and thy footsteps shall not be known.
20. Thou hast conducted thy people like sheep, by the hand of Moses and Aaron.
Ant. In the day of my tribulation, I sought after God with my hands lifted up to him.

℣ Exurge Domine.
℟ Et judica causam meam:
Pater noster, *secreto.*

De Epistola prima beati Pauli Apostoli ad Corinthios, *cap.* xi. 17.

LECTIO VII.

HOC autem præcipio: non laudans quod non in melius, sed in deterius convenitis. Primum quidem convenientibus vobis in ecclesiam audio scissuras esse inter vos, et ex parte credo. Nam oportet et hæreses esse, ut et qui probati sunt, manifesti fiant in vobis. Convenientibus ergo vobis in unum, jam non est Dominicam cœnam manducare. Unusquisque enim suam cœnam præsumit ad manducandum. Et alius quidem esurit, alius autem ebrius est. Numquid domos non habetis ad manducandum et bibendum? Aut ecclesiam Dei contemnitis, et confunditis eos qui non habent? Quid dicam

℣ Arise, O Lord.
℟ And judge my cause.
Our Father, *in secret.*

From the first epistle of St. Paul the Apostle to the Corinthians, *ch.* xi.

LESSON VII.

NOW this I ordain not praising you that you come together not for the better, but for the worse. For first of all I hear that when you come together in the church, there are divisions among you and in part I believe it. For there must be also heresies; that they also who are approved may be made manifest among you. When you come together therefore into one place, it is not now to eat the Lord's supper. For every one taketh before his own supper to eat. And one indeed is hungry, and another is drunk. What, have you not houses to eat and drink in? Or despise ye the church of God, and put

vobis? Laudo vos? In hoc non laudo.

℟. Eram quasi agnus innocens: ductus sum ad immolandum, et nesciebam: consilium fecerunt inimici mei adversum me dicentes; * Venite, mittamus lignum in panem ejus, et eradamus eum de terra viventium. ℣. Omnes inimici mei adversum me cogitabant mala mihi: verbum iniquum mandaverunt adversum me, dicentes; * Venite.

LECTIO VIII.

EGO enim accepi a Domino, quod et tradidi vobis, quoniam Dominus Jesus in qua nocte tradebatur, accepit panem et gratias agens fregit, et dixit: Accipite, et manducate, hoc est corpus meum, quod pro vobis tradetur: hoc facite in meam commemorationem. Similiter et calicem postquam cœnavit dicens: Hic calix novum testa-

them to shame that have not? What shall I say to you? Do I praise you? In this I praise you not.

℟. I was like an innocent lamb: I was led to be sacrificed and I knew it not: my enemies conspired against me, saying: * Come, let us put wood into his bread, and root him out of the land of the living. ℣. All my enemies contrived mischief against me, they uttered a wicked speech against me, saying: * Come.

LESSON VIII.

FOR I have received that which also I delivered to you, that the Lord Jesus, the same night in which he was betrayed, took bread, and giving thanks, broke *it*, and said: Take ye, and eat: this is my body which shall be delivered for you: this do for the commemoration of me. In like manner also the chalice, after he had

mentum est in meo sanguine. Hoc facite quotiescumque bibetis, in meam commemorationem. Quotiescumque enim manducabitis panem hunc et calicem bibetis: mortem Domini annuntiabitis donec veniat.

R. Una hora non potuistis vigilare mecum, qui exhortabamini mori pro me? * Vel Judam non videtis, quomodo non dormit, sed festinat tradere me Judæis? V. Quid dormitis? Surgite, et orate, ne intretis in tentationem. * Vel Judam.

LECTIO IX.

ITAQUE quicumque manducaverit panem hunc, vel biberit calicem Domini indegne, reus erit corporis, et sanguinis Domini. Probet autem seipsum homo; et sic de pane illo edat, et de calice bibat. Qui enim manducat et bibit indigne, judicium sibi manducat et bibit,

supped, saying: This chalice is the new testament in my blood: this do ye (as often at you shall drink it) for the commemoration of me. For as often as you shall eat this bread, and drink this chalice, you shall show the death of the Lord until he comes.

R. Could ye not watch one hour with me, ye that were resolved to die for me? * Or do you not see Judas, how he sleeps not, but makes haste to betray me to the Jews? V. Why do ye sleep? Arise and pray, lest ye fall into temptation. * Or do ye not see.

LESSON IX.

WHEREFORE whosoever shall eat this bread or drink the chalice of the Lord unworthily, shall be guilty of the body and of the blood of the Lord. But let a man prove himself: and so let him eat of that bread, and drink of the chalice. For he that eateth and drinketh un-

non dijudicans corpus Domini. Ideo inter vos multi infirmi et imbecilles, et dormiunt multi. Quod si nosmetipsos dijudicaremus, non utique judicaremur. Dum judicamur autem, a Domino corripimur, ut non cum hoc mundo damnemur. Itaque fratres mei, cum convenitis ad manducandum invicem expectate. Si quis esurit, domi manducet: ut non in judicium conveniatis. Cætera autem, cum venero disponam.

worthily, eateth and drinketh judgment to himself, not discerning the body of the Lord. Therefore are there many infirm and weak among you, and many sleep. But if we would judge ourselves, we should not be judged. But whilst we are judged, we are chastised by the Lord, that we be not condemned with this world. Wherefore, my brethren, when you come together to eat, wait for one another. If any man be hungry let him eat at home; that you come not together unto judgment. And the rest I will set in order when I come.

R. Seniores populi consilium fecerunt: * Ut Jesum dolo tenerent, et occiderent, cum gladiis et fustibus exierunt tamquam ad latronem. *V.* Collegerunt pontifices et pharisæi concilium. * Ut Jesum dolo tenerent, et occiderent. *R.* Seniores, etc.

R. The elders of the people consulted together: * how they might by some craft apprehend Jesus and kill him: they went out with swords and clubs as to a thief. *V.* The priests and pharisees held a council. * How they might. *R.* The elders ec.

AT LAUDS.

Ant. Justificeris Domine in sermonibus

Ant. Mayest thou be justified, O lord, in thá

tuis, et vincas cum judicaris.

words, and overcome when thou art judged.

PSALM L.

MISERERE mei, Deus, * secundum magnam misericordiam tuam.

2. Et secundum multitudinem miserationum tuarum, * dele iniquitatem meam.

3. Amplius lava me ab iniquitate mea; * et a peccato meo munda me.

4. Quoniam iniquitatem meam ego cognosco: * et peccatum meum contra me est semper.

5. Tibi soli peccavi, et malum coram te feci: * ut justificeris in sermonibus tuis, et vincas cum judicaris.

6. Ecce enim in iniquitatibus conceptus sum: * et in peccatis concepit me mater mea.

7. Ecce enim veritatem dilexisti: * incerta et occulta sapientiæ tuæ manifestasti mihi.

8. Asperges me hyssopo et mundabor: * la-

HAVE mercy on me O God, according to thy great mercy.

2. And according to the multitude of thy tender mercies, blot out my iniquities.

3. Wash me yet more from my iniquity: and cleanse me from my sin.

4. For I know my iniquity: and my sin is always before me.

5. To thee only have I sinned, and have done evil before thee: that thou mayest be justified in thy words, and mayest overcome when thou art judged.

6. For behold I was conceived in iniquities and in sins did my mother conceive me.

7. For behold thou hast loved truth: the uncertain and hidden things of thy wisdom thou hast made manifest to me.

8. Thou shalt sprinkle me with hyssop, and I

vabis me et super nivem dealbabor.

9. Auditui meo dabis gaudium et lætitiam: * et exultabunt ossa humiliata.

10. Averte faciem tuam a peccatis meis: * et omnes iniquitates meas dele.

11. Cor mundum crea in me, Deus: * et spiritum rectum innova in visceribus meis.

12. Ne projicias me a facie tua: * et spiritum sanctum tuum ne auferas a me.

13. Redde mihi lætitiam salutaris tuæ: * et spiritu principali confirma me.

14. Docebo iniquos vias tuas: * et impii ad te convertentur.

15. Libera me de sanguinibus Deus, Deus salutis meæ: * et exultabit lingua mea justitiam tuam.

16. Domine, labia mea aperies: et os meum an-

shall be cleansed: thou shalt wash me, and I shall be made whiter than snow.

9. To my hearing thou shalt give joy and gladness: and the bones that have been humbled shall rejoice.

10. Turn away thy face from my sins: and blot out all my iniquities.

11. Create a clean heart in me, O God: and renew a right spirit within my bowels.

12. Cast me not away from thy face: and take not thy holy Spirit from me.

13. Restore unto me the joy of thy salvation: and strengthen me with a perfect spirit.

14. I will teach the unjust thy ways: and the wicked shall be converted to thee.

15. Deliver me from blood, O God, the God of my salvation: and my tongue shall extol thy justice.

16. O Lord, thou wilt open my lips: and my

nuntiabit laudem tuam.

17. Quoniam si voluisses sacrificium dedissem utique: * holocaustis non delectaberis.

18. Sacrificium Deo spiritus contribulatus: * cor contritum et humiliatum, Deus, non despicies.

19. Benigne fac Domine in bona voluntate tua Sion: * ut ædificentur muri Jerusalem.

20. Tunc acceptabis sacrificium justitiæ, oblationes, et holocausta: * tunc imponent super altare tuum vitulos.

Ant. Justificeris Domine in sermonibus tuis, et vincas cum judicaris.

Ant. Dominus tamquam ovis ad victimam ductus est, et non aperuit os suum.

mouth shall declare thy praise.

17. For if thou hadst desired sacrifice, I would indeed have given it: with burnt-offerings thou wilt not be delighted.

18. A sacrifice to God is an afflicted spirit: a contrite and humble heart, O God, thou will not despise.

19. Deal favourably, O Lord, in thy good-will with Sion: that the walls of Jerusalem may be built up.

20. Then shalt thou accept the sacrifice of justice, oblations and whole burnt-offering, then shall they lay calves upon thy altar.

Ant. Mayst thou be justified, O Lord, in thy words, and overcome when thou art judged.

Ant. The Lord was led like a sheep to the slaughter, and he opened not his mouth.

PSALM LXXXIX.

DOMINE refugium factus es nobis: * a generatione in generationem.

LORD, thou hast been our refuge: from generation to generation.

2. Priusquam montes fierant, aut formaretur terra et orbis: * a sæculo et usque in sæculum tu es Deus.

3. Ne avertas hominem in humilitatem: * et dixisti: Convertimini, filii hominum.

4. Quoniam mille anni ante oculos tuos: * tanquam dies hesterna quæ præteriit.

5. Et custodia in nocte: * quæ pro nihilo habentur, eorum anni erunt.

6. Mane sicut herba transeat, mane floreat, et transeat: * vespere decidat, induret et arescat.

7. Quia defecimus in ira tua: * et in furore tuo turbati sumus.

8. Posuisti iniquitates nostras in conspectu tuo * sæculum nostrum in illuminatione.

9. Quoniam omnes dies

2. Before the mountains were made, or the earth and the world was formed; from eternity and to eternity thou art God.

3. Turn not man away to be brought low; and thou hast said: Be converted, O ye sons of men.

4. For a thous and years in thy sight are but as yesterday which is past and gone.

5. And as a watch in the night: as things that are counted nothing, so shall thy years be.

6. In the morning man shall grow up like grass, in the morning he shall flourish and pass away: in the evening he shall fall, grow dry and wither.

7. For in thy wrath we are quickly consumed: and are troubled in thy indignation.

8. Thou hast set our iniquities before thy eyes: our life in the light of thy countenance.

9. For all our days are

nostri defecerunt: * et in ira tua defecimus.

10. Anni nostri sicut aranea meditabuntur: * dies annorum nostrorum in ipsis, septuaginta anni:

11. Si autem in potentatibus, octoginta anni: * et amplius eorum labor et dolor.

12. Quoniam supervenit mansuetudo: * et corripiemur.

13. Quis novit potestatem iræ tuæ: * et præ timore tuo iram tuam dinumerare?

14. Dexteram tuam sic notam fac: * et eruditos corde in sapientia.

15. Convertere, Domine, usquequo? * et deprecabilis esto super servos tuos.

16. Repleti sumus mane misericordia tua: * et exultavimus, et delectati sumus omnibus diebus nostris.

17. Lætati sumus pro diebus, quibus nos humiliasti: * annis, quibus vidimus mala.

spent: and in thy wrath we have fainted away.

10. Our years shall be considered as a spider: the days of our years in them are threescore and ten years:

11. But if in the strong they be fourscore years: and what is more of them is labour and sorrow.

12. For mildness is come upon us; and we shall be corrected.

13. Who knoweth the power of thy anger: and for thy fear can number thy wrath?

14. So make thy right hand known: and make us learned in heart in wisdom.

15. Return, O Lord, how long, and be entreated in favour of thy servants.

16. We are filled in the morning with thy mercy: and we are rejoiced, and are delighted all our days.

17. We have rejoiced for the day in which thou hast humbled us: for the years in which we have seen evils.

18. Respice in servos tuos, et in opera tua: * et dirige filios eorum.

19. Et sit splendor Domini Dei nostri super nos, et opera manuum nostrarum dirige super nos: * et opus manuum nostrarum dirige.

Ant. Dominus tamquam ovis ad victimam ductus est, et non aperuit os suum.

Ant. Contritum est cor meum in medio mei, contremuerunt omnia ossa mea.

18. Look upon thy servants, and upon their works: and direct their children.

19. And let the brightness of the Lord our God be upon us, and direct thou the works of our hands over us: yea, the work of our hands do thou direct.

Ant. The Lord was led like a sheep to the slaughter, and he opened not his mouth.

Ant. My heart is broken within me, all my bones have trembled.

PSALM LXII.

DEUS, Deus meus, * ad te de luce vigilo.

2. Sitivit in te anima mea, * quam multipliciter tibi caro mea.

3. In terra deserta, et in via, et inaquosa: * sic in sancto apparui tibi, ut viderem virtutem tuam, et gloriam tuam.

4. Quoniam melior est

O God, my God, to thee do I watch at break of day.

2. For thee my soul hath thirsted: for thee my flesh, O how many ways!

3. In a desert land, and where there is no way, and no water: so in the sanctuary have I come before thee, to see the power and thy glory.

4. For thy mercy is

misericordia tua super vitas: * labia mea laudabunt te.

5. Sic benedicam te in vita mea: * et in nomine tuo levabo manus meas.

6. Sicut adipe et pinguedine repleatur anima mea: * et labiis exultationis laudabit os meum.

7. Si memor fui tui super stratum meum, in matutinis meditabor in te: * quia fuisti adjutor meus.

8. Et in velamento alarum tuarum exultabo, adhæsit anima mea post te: * me suscepit dextera tua.

9. Ipsi vero in vanum quæsierunt animam meam, introibunt in inferiora terræ: * tradentur in manus gladii, partes vulpium erunt.

10. Rex vero lætabitur in Deo, laudabuntur omnes qui jurant in eo: * quia obstructum est os loquentium iniqua.

better than lives: thee my lips shall praise.

5. Thus will I bless thee all my life long: and in thy name I will lift up my hands.

6. Let my soul be filled as with marrow and fatness: and my mouth shall praise thee with joyful lips.

7. If I have remembered thee on my bed, I will meditate on thee in the morning: because thou hast been my helper.

8. And I will rejoice under the covert of thy wings: my soul hath stuck close to thee: thy right hand hath received me.

9. But they have sought my soul in vain, they shall go into the lower parts of the earth: they shall be delivered into the hands of the sword, they shall be the portions of foxes.

10. But the king shall rejoice in God: all they shall be praised that swear by him: because the mouth is stopped of

them that speak wicked things.

PSALM LXVI.

DEUS misereatur nobis, et benedicat nobis: * illuminet vultum suum super nos, et misereatur nostri.

2. Ut cognoscamus in terra viam tuam: * in omnibus gentibus salutare tuum.

3. Confiteantur tibi populi Deus: « confiteantur tibi populi omnes.

4. Lætentur et exultent gentes: * quoniam judicas populos in æquitate, et gentes in terra dirigis.

5. Confiteantur tibi populi Deus; confiteantur tibi populi omnes; * terra dedit fructum suum.

6. Benedicat nos Deus, Deus noster, benedicat nos Deus: * et metuant eum omnes fines terræ.

Ant. Contritum est cor

MAY God have mercy on us, and bless us: may he cause the light of his countenance to shine upon us, and may he have mercy on us.

2. That we may know thy way upon earth: thy salvation in all nations.

3. Let people confess to thee, O God: let all people give praise to thee.

4. Let the nations be glad and rejoice: for thou judgest the people with justice, and directest the nations upon earth.

5. Let the people, O God, confess to thee, let all the people give praise to thee: the earth hath yielded her fruit.

6. May God, our own God, bless us, may God bless us; and all the ends of the earth fear him.

Ant. My heart is bro-

meum in medio mei, contremuerunt omnia ossa mea.

Ant. Exhortatus es in virtute tua, et in refectione sancta tua, Domine.

Canticum Moysi.
(*Exod.* xv)

CANTEMUS Domino; gloriose enim magnificatus est: * equum et ascensorem dejecit in mare.

2. Fortitudo mea et laus mea Dominus: * et factus est mihi in salutem

3. Iste Deus meus et glorificabo eum: * Deus patris mei, et exaltabo eum.

4. Dominus quasi vir pugnator, Omnipotens nomen ejus. * Currus Pharaonis, et exercitum ejus projecit in mare.

5. Electi principes ejus submersi sunt in mari rubro: * abyssi operuerunt eos, descenderunt in profundum quasi lapis.

6. Dextera tua, Domine, magnificata est in fortitudine: dextera tua,

ken within me, all my bones have trembled.

Ant. Thou hast encouraged us with thy power and thy holy refreshment, O Lord.

The Canticle of Moses.
(*Exod.* xv)

LET us sing to the Lord; for he is gloriously magnified; the horse and the rider he hath thrown into the sea.

2. The Lord is my strength and my praise and he is become salvation to me.

3. He is my God, and I will glorify him: the God of my father, and I will exalt him.

4. The Lord is as a man of war, Almighty is his name. Pharaoh's chariots and his army he hath cast into the sea.

5. His chosen captains are drowned in the Red Sea. The depths have covered them, they are sunk to the bottom like a stone.

6. Thy right hand, O Lord, is magnified in strength; thy right hand,

Domine, percussit inimicum. * Et in multitudine gloriæ tuæ deposuisti adversarios tuos.

7. Misisti iram tuam, quæ devoravit eos sicut stipulam. * Et in spiritu furoris tui congregatæ sunt aquæ.

8. Stetit unda fluens, * congregatæ sunt abyssi in medio mari.

9. Dixit inimicus: persequar et comprehendam, * dividam spolia, implebitur anima mea.

10. Evaginabo gladium meum, * interficiat eos manus mea.

11. Flavit spiritus tuus, et operuit eos mare; * submersi sunt quasi plumbum in aquis vehementibus.

12. Quis similis tui in fortibus, Domine? quis similis tui, magnificus in sanctitate, terribilis atque laudabilis, faciens mirabilia?

13. Extendisti manum tuam, et devoravit eos terra. * Dux fuisti in

O Lord, hath slain the enemy. And in the multitude of thy power thou hast put down thy adversaries.

7. Thou hast sent thy wrath, which hath devoured them like stubble. And with the blast of thy anger the waters were gathered together:

8. The flowing water stood, the depths were gathered together in the midst of the sea.

9. The enemy said: I will pursue and overtake, I will divide the spoils, my soul shall have its fill.

10. I will draw my sword, my hand shall slay them.

11. Thy wind blew, and the sea covered them; they sunk as lead in the mighty waters.

12. Who is like to thee among the strong, O Lord? who is like to thee, glorious in holiness, terrible and praiseworthy, doing wonders?

13. Thou stretchedst forth thy hand, and the earth swallowed them.

misericordia tua populo quem redemisti:

14. Et portasti eum in fortitudine tua, * ad habitaculum sanctum tuum.
15. Ascenderunt populi et irati sunt: * dolores obtinuerunt habitatores Philisthiim.
16. Tunc conturbati sunt principes Edom, robustos Moab obtinuit tremor: * obriguerunt omnes habitatores Canaan.
17. Irruat super eos formido et pavor, * in magnitudine brachii tui.
18. Fiant immobiles quasi lapis, donec pertranseat populus tuus, Domine: * donec pertranseat populus tuus iste, quem possedisti.
19. Introduces eos, et plantabis in monte hæreditatis tuæ, * firmissimo habitaculo tuo quod operatus es, Domine:
20. Sanctuarium tuum,

In thy mercy thou hast been a leader to the people whom thou hast redeemed:

14. And in thy strength thou hast carried them to thy holy habitation.
15. Nations rose up, and were angry: sorrows took hold of the inhabitants of Philisthiim.
16. Then were the princes of Edom troubled, trembling seized on the stout men of Moab: all the inhabitants of Canaan became stiff.
17. Let fear and dread fall upon them, in the greatness of thy arm.
18. Let them become immovable as a stone, until thy people, O Lord, pass by; until this thy people pass by which thou hast possessed.
19. Thou shalt bring them in, and plant them in the mountain of thy inheritance, in thy most firm habitation, which thou hast made, O Lord:
20. Thy sanctuary, O

Domine, quod firmaverunt manus tuæ. * Dominus regnabit in æternum, et ultra.

21. Ingressus est enim eques Pharao cum curribus et equitibus ejus in mare: * et reduxit super eos Dominus aquas maris.

22. Filii autem Israel ambulaverunt per siccum * in medio ejus.

Ant. Exhortatus es in virtute tua, et in refectione sancta tua, Domine.

Ant. Oblatus est, quia ipse voluit, et peccata nostra ipse portavit.

Lord, which thy hands have established. The Lord shall reign for ever and ever.

21. For Pharaoh went in on horseback with his chariots and horsemen into the sea: and the Lord brought back upon them the waters of the sea.

22. But the children of Israel walked on dry ground in the midst thereof.

Ant. Thou hast encouraged us with thy power and thy holy refreshment, O Lord.

Ant. He was offered up, because he himself desired it, and he himself bore our sins.

PSALM CXLVIII.

LAUDATE Dominum de cœlis: * laudate eum in excelsis.

2. Laudate eum omnes angeli ejus: * laudate eum omnes virtutes ejus.

3. Laudate eum sol et luna: * laudate eum omnes stellæ et lumen.

4. Laudate eum cœli cœlorum: * et aquæ om-

PRAISE ye the Lord from the heavens praise ye him in the high places.

2. Praise ye him, all his angels praise ye him all his hosts.

3. Praise ye him, O sun and moon: praise him all ye stars and light.

4. Praise him ye heavens of heavens; and let

nes quæ super cœlos sunt, laudent nomen Domini.

5. Quia ipse dixit, et facta sunt: * ipse mandavit, et creata sunt.

6. Statuit ea in æternum et in sæculum sæculi: * præceptum posuit, et non præteribit.

7. Laudate Dominum de terra: * dracones et omnes abyssi.

8. Ignis, grando, nix, glacies. spiritus procellarum: * quæ faciunt verbum ejus.

9. Montes et omnes colles: * ligna fructifera et omnes cedri,

10. Bestiæ et universa pecora: serpentes et volucres pennatæ.

11. Reges terræ, et omnes populi: * principes et omnes judices terræ.

12. Juvenes et virgines; senes cum junioribus laudent nomen Domini * quia exaltatum est nomen ejus solius.

13. Confessio ejus super cœlum et terram:

all the waters that are above the heavens praise the name of the Lord.

5. For he spoke, and they were made; he commanded, and they were created.

6. He hath established them for ever, and for ages of ages; he hath made a decree, and it shall not pass away.

7. Praise the Lord from the earth, ye dragons, and all ye deeps.

8. Fire, hail, snow, ice, stormy winds, which fulfil his word.

9. Mountains and all hills: fruitful trees and all cedars.

10. Beasts and all cattle: serpents and feathered fowls.

11. Kings of the earth, and all people: princes and all judges of the earth.

12. Young men and maidens: let the old with the younger praise the name of the Lord: for his name alone is exalted.

13. The praise of him is above heaven and

* et exaltavit cornu populi sui.

14. Hymnus omnibus sanctis ejus: * filiis Israel, populo appropinquanti sibi.

earth; and he hath exalted the horn of his people.

14. A hymn to all his saints; to the children of Israel, a people approaching to him.

PSALM CXLIX.

CANTATE Domino canticum novum: * laus ejus in ecclesia sactorum.
2. Lætetur Israel in eo qui fecit eum: * et filii Sion exultent in rege suo.
3. Laudent nomen ejus in choro: * in tympano, et psalterio psallant ei.
4. Quia beneplacitum est Domino in populo suo: et exaltabit mansuetos in salutem.
5. Exultabunt sancti in gloria: * lætabuntur in cubilibus suis.
6. Exultationes Dei in gutture eorum: * et gladii ancipites in manibus eorum.
7. Ad faciendam vindictam in nationibus: * increpationes in populis.

SING ye to the Lord a new canticle: let his praise be in the church of the saints.
2. Let Israel rejoice in him that made him; and let the children of Sion be joyful in their king.
3. Let them praise his name in choir: let them sing to him with the timbrel and the psaltery.
4. For the Lord is well pleased with his people and he will exalt the meek unto salvation.
5. The saints shall rejoice in glory: they shall be joyful in their beds.
6. The high praises of God shall be in their mouth: and two-edged swords in their hands.
7. To execute vengeance upon the nations, chastisements among the people.

8. Ad alligandos reges eorum in compedibus: * et nobiles eorum in manicis ferreis.

9. Ut faciant in eis judicium conscriptum: * gloria hæc est omnibus sanctis ejus.

8. To bind their kings with fetters, and their nobles with manacles of iron.

9. To execute upon them the judgment that is written: this glory is to all his saints.

PSALM CL.

LAUDATE Dominum in sanctis ejus: * laudate eum in firmamento virtutis ejus.

2. Laudate eum in virtutibus ejus: * laudate eum secundum multitudinem magnitudinis ejus.

3. Laudate eum in sono tubæ: * laudate eum in psalterio et cithara.

4. Laudate eum in tympano et choro: * laudate eum in chordis et organo.

5. Laudate eum in cymbalis bene-sonantibus: laudate eum in cymbalis jubilationis: * omnis spiritus laudet Dominum.

Ant. Oblatus est quia ipse voluit, et peccata nostra ipse portavit.

PRAISE ye the Lord in his holy places: praise ye him in the firmament of his power.

2. Praise ye him for his mighty acts: praise ye him according to the multitude of his greatness.

3. Praise him with sound of trumpet: praise him with psaltery and harp.

4. Praise him with timbrel and choir: praise him with strings and organs.

5. Praise him on high-sounding cymbals: praise him on cymbals of joy: let every spirit praise the Lord.

Ant. He was offered up, because he himself desired it, and he himself carried our sins.

V. Homo pacis meæ, in quo speravi.

R. Qui edebat panes meos, ampliavit adversum me supplantationem.

Ant. Traditor autem dedit eis signum, dicens: Quem osculatus fuero, ipse est, tenete eum.

Canticum Zachariæ.
Luc. 1. 68.

BENEDICTUS Dominus Deus Israel: * quia visitavit, et fecit redemptionem plebis suæ:

2. Et erexit cornu salutis nobis, * in domo David pueri sui.

3. Sicut locutus est per os sanctorum, * qui a sæculo sunt prophetarum ejus:

4. Salutem ex inimicis nostris, * et de manu omnium qui oderunt nos.

5. Ad faciendam misericordiam cum patribus nostris: * et memorari testamenti sui sancti.

6. Jusjurandum, quod juravit ad Abraham pa-

V. The man of my affection, in whom I confided.

R. He who has eaten my bread, hath most wickedly supplanted me.

Ant. The traitor gave them a sign, saying: He that I shall kiss, that is he, hold him fast.

The Canticle of Zachary.
Luke 1. 68.

BLESSED be the Lord God of Israel, because he hath visited and wrought the redemption of his people:

2. And hath raised up a horn of salvation to us, in the house of David his servant.

3. As he spoke by the mouth of his holy prophets, who are from the beginning.

4. Salvation from our enemies, and from the hand of all that hate us.

5. To perform mercy to our fathers; and to remember his holy covenant.

6. The oath which he swore to Abraham our

trem nostrum, * daturum se nobis.

7. Ut sine timore, de manu inimicorum nostrorum liberati, * serviamus illi.

8. In sanctitate et justitia coram ipso, omnibus diebus nostris.

9. Et tu puer, propheta Altissimi vocaberis: * præibis enim ante faciem Domini parare vias ejus.

10. Ad dandam scientiam salutis plebi ejus: * in remissionem peccatorum eorum.

11. Per viscera misericordiæ Dei nostri: * in quibus visitavit nos Oriens ex alto:

12. Illuminare his, qui in tenebris et in umbra mortis sedent; * ad dirigendos pedes nostros in viam pacis.

Ant. Traditor autem dedit eis signum, dicens: Quem osculatus fuero, ipse est, tenete eum.

father, that he would grant to us.

7. That being delivered from the hands of our enemies, we may serve him without fear.

8. In holiness and justice before him, all our days.

9. And thou, child, shalt be called the prophet of the Highest: for thou shalt go before the face of the Lord to prepare his ways.

10. To give knowledge of salvation to his people, unto the remission of their sins:

11. Through the bowels of the mercy of our God: in which the Orient from on high hath visited us:

12. To enlighten them that sit in darkness, and in the shadow of death: to direct our feet in the way of peace.

Ant. The traitor gave them a sign, saying: He that I shall kiss, that is he, hold him fast.

All the candles in the triangular candlestick being extinguished, except that at the top, whilst the Benedictus is being sung, the six candles on the

altar are also extinguished, one by one, at every alternate verse, so that all may be put out at the last verse. In like manner all the lamps and lights about the church are put out. When the Ant. Traditor, is repeated, the white candle is taken from the top of the triangular candlestick and hidden under the Epistle side of the Altar, whilst all kneel and say.

V. Christus factus est pro nobis obediens usque ad mortem.
Pater noster, *silentio.*

V. Christ became obedient for us unto death.
Our Father, *in silence.*

Then is said, in a little more audible tone of voice, the Psalm Miserere, p. 174 and at the end of it without Oremus, the following prayer:

RESPICE, quæsumus Domine, super hanc familiam tuam, pro qua Dominus noster Jesus Christus non dubitavit manibus tradi nocentium et crucis subire tormentum. Qui tecum, etc., *silentio.*

LOOK down, O Lord, we beseech thee, on this thy family, for which our Lord Jesus Christ was pleased to be delivered into the hands of the wicked, and suffer the torments of the cross. Who liveth, etc., *in silence.*

The foregoing prayer having been read, a noise is made, to represent the confusion of nature at the death of its Author: and when the lighted candle, is brought from beneath the Altar, to denote Christ's Resurrection from the dead, all rise up and depart in silence.

THE MASS FOR MAUNDY THURSDAY.

The Priest begins Mass by reciting the Ps. Judica me Deus. *etc., in the usual manner at the foot of the Altar, till he comes to,*

THE INTROIT.

NOS autem gloriari oportet in cruce Domini nostri Jesu Christi: in quo est salus, vita et resurrectio nostra: per quem salvati et liberati sumus. *Ps.* Deus misereatur nostri et benedicat nobis: illuminet vultum suum super nos, et misereatur nostri. Nos autem.

WE ought to glory in the cross of our Lord Jesus Christ: in whom is our salvation, life, and resurrection: by whom we are saved and delivered. *Ps.* Let God have mercy on us, and bless us; let his countenance enlighten us, and let him have mercy on us. We ought.

Kyrie eleison, *as before*, p. 37.

GLORIA in excelsis Deo, et in terra pax hominibus bonæ voluntatis. Laudamus te, benedicimus te, adoramus te, glorificamus te. Gratias agimus tibi propter magnam gloriam tuam; Domine Deus, Rex cœlestis, Deus Pater omnipotens. Domine Fili unigenite Jesu Christe. Domine Deus, Agnus Dei, Filius Patris. Qui

GLORY be to God on high and peace on earth to men of goodwill. We praise thee, we bless thee, we adore thee, we glorify thee. We give thee thanks for thy great glory, O Lord God, heavenly king. O God the Father Almighty. O Lord, only begotten Son Jesus Christ. O Lord God, Lamb of God, Son of the Father.

THE MASS FOR MAUNDY THURSDAY.

tollis peccata mundi, miserere nobis. Qui tollis peccata mundi suscipe deprecationem nostram. Qui sedes ad dexteram Patris, miserere nobis. Quoniam tu solus sanctus: tu solus Dominus: tu solus Altissimus, Jesu Christe, cum Sancto Spiritu in gloria Dei Patris. Amen.

Who takest away the sins of the world, have mercy upon us. Who takest away the sins of the world, receive our petition. Who sittest at the right hand of the Father, have mercy upon us. For thou only art holy: thou only art the Lord: thou only art the Most High, O Jesus Christ, with the Holy Ghost, in the glory of God the Father. Amen.

The bells are rung during the Gloria in excelsis, *and not rung again until the* Gloria in excelsis *of Holy Saturday.*

THE PRAYER.

DEUS, a quo et Judas reatus sui pœnam, et confessionis suæ latro præmium sumpsit: concede nobis tuæ propitiationis effectum: ut sicut in passione sua Jesus Christus Dominus noster diversa utrisque intulit stipendia meritorum: ita nobis, ablato vetustatis errore, resurrectionis suæ gratiam largiatur. Qui tecum vivit et regnat in unitate Spiritus Sancti.

O GOD, from whom Judas received the punishment of his sin and the thief the reward of his confession; grant us the effect of thy mercy: that as our Lord Jesus Christ in his passion bestowed on both different rewards for their merits; so having destroyed the old man in us, he may give us the grace of his resurrection. Who liveth and reigneth.

Lectio Epistolæ beati Pauli Apostoli ad Corinthios. *(1 Cor. 11)*

Fratres, convenientibus vobis in unum, jam non est Dominicam cœnam manducare. Unusquisque enim suam cœnam præsumit ad manducandum. Et alius quidem esurit, alius autem ebrius est. Numquid domos non habetis ad manducandum et bibendum? Aut ecclesiam Dei contemnitis et confunditis eos qui non habent? Quid dicam vobis? Laudo vos? In hoc non laudo. Ego enim accepi a Domino, quod et tradidi vobis, quoniam Dominus Jesus in qua nocte tradebatur, accepit panem et gratias agens fregit, et dixit: Accipite et manducate; hoc est corpus meum, quod pro vobis tradetur; hoc facite in meam commemorationem. Similiter et calicem, postquam cœnavit, dicens: Hic calix novum testamentum est in meo sanguine: hoc facite quotiescum-

Lesson out of the first Epistle of St. Paul the Apostle to the Corinthians. *(1 Cor. 11)*

Brethren, when you come together therefore into one place, it is not now to eat the Lord's supper. For every one taketh before his own supper to eat. And one indeed is hungry, and another is drunk. What, have you not houses to eat and drink in? Or despise ye the church of God, and put them to shame that have not? What shall I say to you? Do I praise you? In this I praise you not. For I have received of the Lord, that which also I delivered to you, that the Lord Jesus, the same night in which he was betrayed, took bread, and giving thanks, broke, and said: Take ye, and eat: This is my body which shall be delivered for you: this do for the commemoration of me. In like manner also the chalice, after he had

que bibetis, in meam commemorationem. Quotiescumque enim manducabitis panem hunc, et calicem bibetis: mortem Domini annuntiabitis donec veniat. Itaque quicumque manducaverit panem hunc, vel biberit calicem Domini indigne, reus erit corporis et sanguinis Domini. Probet autem seipsum homo, et sic de pane illo edat, et de calice bibat. Qui enim manducat et bibit indigne, judicium sibi manducat et bibit: non dijudicans corpus Domini. Ideo inter vos multi infirmi et imbecilles, et dormiunt multi. Quod si nosmetipsos dijudicaremus, non utique judicaremur. Dum judicamur autem a Domino corripimur: ut non cum hoc mundo damnemur.

supped, saying: This chalice is the new testament in my blood: this do ye as often as ye shall drink it, for the commemoration of me. For as often as you shall eat this bread, and drink this chalice, you shall show the death of the Lord until he come. Wherefore whosoever shall eat this bread, or drink the chalice of the Lord unworthily, shall be guilty of the body and of the blood of the Lord: but let a man prove himself, and so let him eat of that bread, and drink of the chalice. For he that eateth and drinketh unworthily, eateth and drinketh judgment to himself, not discerning the body of the Lord. Therefore are there many infirm and weak among you, and many sleep. But if we would judge ourselves, we should not be judged. But while we are judged, we are chastised by the Lord: that we be not condemned with this world.

Graduale. — Christus factus est pro nobis obediens usque ad mortem,

The Gradual. — Christ became obedient for us unto death, even the

mortem autem crucis. *V.* Propter quod et Deus exaltavit illum, et dedit illi nomen, quod est super omne nomen.

death of the cross. *V.* For which God has exalted him and given him a name, that is above every name.

Munda cor meum *is said as above, p.* 58.

Sequentia sancti Evangelii secundum Joannem. (*cap.* xiii)

Continuation of the Holy Gospel according to St. John (*chap.* xiii).

ANTE diem festum Pascha. sciens Jesus quia venit hora eius ut transeat ex hoc mundo ad Patrem: cum dilexisset suos, qui erant in mundo, in finem dilexit eos. Et cœna facta, cum diabolus jam misisset in cor ut traderet eum Judas Simonis Iscariotæ: sciens quia omnia dedit ei Pater in manus, et quia a Deo exivit, et ad Deum vadit, surgit a cœna, et ponit vestimenta sua: et cum accepisset linteum, præcinxit se. Deinde mittit aquam in pelvim et cœpit lavare pedes discipulorum, et extergere linteo, quo erat præcinctus. Venit ergo ad Simonem Petrum. Et dicit ei Pe-

BEFORE the festival day of the pasch Jesus knewing that his hour was come, that he should pass out of this world to the Father having loved his own who were in the world he loved them to the end. And when supper was done, (the devil having now put it into the heart of Judas, the son of Simon the Iscariot, to betray him) knowing that the Father had given him all things into his hands, and that he came from God, and goeth to God: he riseth from supper and layeth aside his garments: and having taken a towel he girded himself. After that he poureth water into a basin, and began

trus: Domine tu mihi lavas pedes? Respondit Jesus, et dixit ei: Quod ego facio, tu nescis modo, scies autem postea. Dicit ei Petrus: Non lavabis mihi pedes in æternum. Respondit ei Jesus: Si non lavero te non habebis partem mecum. Dicit ei Simon Petrus: Domine, non tantum pedes meos, sed et manus, et caput. Dicit ei Jesus: Qui lotus est non indiget nisi ut pedes lavet, sed est mundus totus. Et vos mundi estis, sed non omnes. Sciebat enim quisnam esset qui traderet eum: propterea dixit: non estis mundi omnes. Postquam ergo lavit pedes eorum, et accepit vestimenta sua: cum recubuisset iterum, dixit eis: Scitis quid fecerim vobis? Vos vocatis me, Magister et, Domine: et bene dicitis: sum etenim. Si ergo ego lavi pedes vestros, Dominus et Magister: et vos debetis alteralterius lavare pedes? Exemplum enim dedi vo-

to wash the feet of the disciples, and to wipe them with a towel, wherewith he was girded. He cometh therefore to Simon Peter. And Peter saith to him: Lord, dost thou wash my feet? Jesus answered and said to him: What I do, thou knowest not now, but thou shalt know hereafter. Peter saith to him: Thou shalt never wash my feet. Jesus answered him: If I wash thee not, thou shalt have no part with me. Simon Peter saith to him: Lord, not only my feet, but also my hands, and my head. Jesus saith to him: He that is washed, needeth not but to wash his feet, but is clean wholly. And you are clean, but not all: for he knew who he was that would betray him: therefore he said: you are not all clean.. Then after he had washed their feet, and taken his garments, having sat down again, he said to them: Know you

bis, ut quemadmodum ego feci vobis, ita et vos faciatis.

what I have done to you? You call me Master and Lord: and you say well, for so I am. If then I, being your Lord and Master, have washed your feet; you also ought to wash one another's feet. For I have given you an example, that as I have done to you, so you do also.

Credo, *as before p.* 60.

The Offertory.

Dextera Domini fecit virtutem, dextera Domini exaltavit me: non moriar, sed vivam et narrabo opera Domini.

The right hand of the Lord has shown his power, the right hand of the Lord has exalted me: I shall not die, but live, and declare the works of the Lord.

Suscipe, *as above, p.* 62, *till he comes to the prayer called,*

The segret.

IPSE tibi, quæsumus Domine sancte, Pater omnipotens, æterne Deus, sacrificium nostrum reddat acceptum, qui discipulis suis in sui commemorationem hoc fieri hodierna traditione monstravit, Jesus Christus Filius tuus Dominus noster. Qui tecum vivit et regnat.

WE beseech thee, O holy Lord, almighty Father, eternal God, that our Lord Jesus Christ thy Son may make our sacrifice acceptable to thee, who on this day commanded his disciples to celebrate it in memory of him. Who liveth and reigneth.

The Preface and Canon as before, from p. 66 *to p.* 70.

THE MASS FOR MAUNDY THURSDAY.

COmmunicantes, et diem sacratissimum celebrantes, quo Dominus noster Jesus Christus pro nobis est traditus: sed et memoriam venerantes in primis gloriosæ semper virginis Mariæ, genitricis ejusdem Dei et Domini nostri Jesu Christi: sed et beatorum apostolorum, ac martyrum tuorum Petri et Pauli, Andreæ, Jacobi, Joannis, Thomæ, Jacobi, Philippi, Bartholomæi, Mathæi, Simonis et Thadæi: Lini, Cleti, Clementis, Xysti, Cornelii, Cypriani, Laurentii, Chrysogoni, Joannis et Pauli, Cosmæ et Damiani, et omnium sanctorum tuorum: quorum meritis precibusque concedas, ut in omnibus protectionis tuæ muniamur auxilio. Per eundem Christum Dominum nostrum.

HANC igitur oblationem servitutis nostræ, sed et cunctæ familiæ tuæ, quam tibi offerimus ob diem, in qua Dominus noster Jesus Christus tradidit

COmmunicating and celebrating this most sacred day, in which our Lord Jesus Christ was betrayed for us: and also honouring in the first place the memory of the ever glorious Virgin Mary, Mother of the same God, and our Lord Jesus Christ: as also of thy blessed apostles and martyrs, Peter and Paul, Andrew, James, John, Thomas, James, Philip, Bartholomew, Matthew, Simon and Thaddeus: Linus, Cletus, Clement, Xystus, Cornelius, Cyprian, Laurence, Chrysogonus, John and Paul, Cosmas and Damian, and of all thy saints: by whose merits and prayers, grant that we may in all things be defended by the help of thy protection. Through the same Christ our Lord.

WE therefore beseech thee, O Lord, graciously to accept this offering of our service, and of thy whole family, which we make to thee in memory of the day

discipulis suis corporis et sanguinis sui mysteria celebranda, quæsumus Domine, ut placatus accipias, diesque nostros in tua pace disponas: atque ab æterna damnatione nos eripi, et in electorum tuorum jubeas grege numerari. Per eundem Christum Dominum nostrum.

QUAM oblationem tu Deus in omnibus quæsumus, bene ✠ dictam, adscrip ✠ tam, ra- ✠ tam, rationabilem, acceptabilemque facere digneris: ut nobis cor ✠ pus et san ✠ guis fiat dilectissimi Filii tui Domini nostri Jesu Christi.

QUI pridie quam pro nostra omniumque salute pateretur, hoc est hodie, accepit panem, etc., *as p. 71.*

on which our Lord Jesus Christ commanded his disciples to celebrate the mysteries of his body and blood: order also our days in thy peace, and command us to be preserved from eternal damnation, and to be numbered in the flock of thy elect. Through the same.

WHICH offering be pleased, O God, we beseech thee, to render in all things blessed, approved, ratified, reasonable, and acceptable: that it may be made to us the body and blood of thy most beloved Son our Lord Jesus Christ.

WHO the day before he suffered for the salvation of us and of all men, that is, on this day, took bread, etc.

The rest of the Canon to the Communion as at p. 72, except that the Pax is not given, in detestation of the treacherous kiss of Judas.

On this day the Priest consecrates two Hosts, reserving one for the next day, on which there is no Consecration. Before he washes his fingers he puts the reserved Host into another Chalice, which he covers with the pall, paten, and veil and places in the middle of the Altar.

Communio. Dominus Jesus, postquam cœnavit cum discipulis suis, lavit pedes eorum, et ait illis: Scitis quid fecerim vobis ego Dominus et Magister? Exemplum dedi vobis, ut et vos ita faciatis.

The Communion. Our Lord Jesus, after he had supped with his disciples, washed their feet, and said to them: Do ye know what I your Lord and Master have done to you? I have given you an example, that ye may do the same.

The Postcommunion.

REfecti vitalibus alimentis, quæsumus Domine Deus noster; ut quod tempore nostræ mortalitatis exequimur, immortalitatis tuæ munere consequamur. Per Dominum nostrum Jesum Christum.

WE beseech thee, O Lord our God, that being nourished with this life-giving food, we may receive by thy grace in immortal glory, what we celebrate in this mortal life. Through our Lord.

V. Dominus vobiscum.
R. Et cum spiritu tuo.

V. The Lord be with you.
R. And with thy spirit.

V. Ite missa est.
R. Deo gratias.

V. Go, Mass is said.
R. Thanks be to God.

All the rest as above, p. 82.

At the end of the Mass, the Priest carries the reserved consecrated Host to the place prepared for its reception, accompanied with lights and incense. During the procession the following hymn is sung.

HYMN.

PANGE lingua, gloriosi,
   Corporis mysterium,

SING, O my tongue, the mystic rite,
   Contriv'd by wisdom infinite,

Sanguinisque pretiosi,
Quem in mundi pretium,
Fructus ventris generosi,
Rex effudit Gentium.

2. Nobis datus, nobis natus,
Ex intacta virgine;

Et in mundo conversatus,
Sparso verbi semine;

Sui moras incolatus

Miro clausit ordine.

3. In supremæ nocte cœnæ,
Recumbens cum fratribus,
Observata lege plene,

Cibis in legalibus,

Cibum turbæ duodenæ
Se dat suis manibus.

4. Verbum caro panem verum,
Verbo carnem efficit:

Containing, in the shape of food,
The glorious flesh and precious blood,
Shed by the fruit of noblest womb,
The Gentiles' King, to stop our doom.

2. For man He came, was born for man;
From virgin chaste His life began;
On earth He liv'd and preach'd to sow,
The seeds of heav'nly truth below;
And then with lasting love to close
His life, this wond'rous way He chose.

3. That ev'ning, when that supper past,
Which with His brethren was His last,
The paschal victim having eat,
And clos'd the law with legal meat,
He with his hands for food bestows
Himself to twelve His wisdom chose.

4. The Word made flesh by words He said,
Turns into flesh substantial bread:

Fitque sanguis Christi merum,
  Et si sensus deficit:

Ad firmandam cor sincerum,
  Sola fides sufficit.

5. Tantum ergo Sacramentum
  Veneremur cernui:

Et antiquum documentum
  Novo cedat ritui:

Præstet fides supplementum
  Sensuum defectui.

6. Genitori, Genitoque,
  Laus et jubilatio,

Salus, honor, virtus quoque
  Sit et benedictio:

Procedenti ab utroque
  Compar sit laudatio. Amen.

Wine too He makes His blood divine,
  Tho' sense cry out:
  'Tis bread and wine:
But hearts sincere are here secur'd.
  By faith in words of truth assur'd.

5. To this mysterious table now
  Let knees and heart, and senses bow:
  Let ancient rites resign their place
To nobler elements of grace:
  What our weak senses can't descry,
  Let stronger faith the want supply.

6. To th' undivided Three in One,
  To God the Father and the Son,
  Salvation, honour, jubilee,
  Praise, glory, benediction be:
  To th' Holy Ghost, whose equal rays
  From both proceed, be equal praise. Amen.

After the procession, Vespers are said in the Choir as follows:

AT VESPERS.

Ant. Calicem saluta-

Ant. I will drink the

ris accipiam, et nomen Domini invocabo.

cup of salvation, and call upon the name of the Lord.

PSALM CXV.

CREDIDI, propter quod locutus sum: * ego autem humiliatus sum nimis.

2. Ego dixi in excessu meo: * omnis homo mendax.

3. Quid retribuam Domino, * pro omnibus quæ retribuit mihi?

4. Calicem salutaris accipiam: * pretiosa in conspectu Domini mors sanctorum ejus.

5. Vota mea Domino reddam coram omni populo ejus: * pretiosa in conspectu Domini mors sanctorum ejus.

6. O Domine, quia ego servus tuus: * ego servus tuus, et filius ancillæ tuæ

7. Dirupisti vincula mea: * tibi sacrificabo hostiam laudis, et nomen Domini invocabo.

8. Vota mea Domino reddam in conspectu

I HAVE believed, therefore have I spoken: but I have been humbled exceedingly.

2. I said in my excess: every man is a liar.

3. What shall I render to the Lord for all the things that he hath rendered to me?

4. I will take the chalice of salvation: and I will call upon the name of the Lord.

5. I will pay my vows to the Lord before all his people: precious in the sight of the Lord is the death of his saints.

6. O Lord, for I am thy servant; I am thy servant, and the son of thy handmaid.

7. Thou hast broken my bonds: I will sacrifice to thee the sacrifice of praise, and I will call upon the name of the Lord.

8. I will pay my vows to the Lord in the sight

omnis populi ejus: * in atriis domus Domini, in medio tui Jerusalem.

Ant. Calicem salutaris accipiam et nomen Domini invocabo.

Ant. Cum his qui oderunt pacem, eram pacificus: dum loquebar illis impugnabant me gratis.

of all his people: in the courts of the house of the Lord, in the midst of thee, O Jerusalem.

Ant. I will drink the cup of salvation, and call upon the name of the Lord.

Ant. I was peaceable with those that hated peace: whilst I spoke to them, they attacked me without a cause.

PSALM CXIX.

AD Dominum cum tribularer, clamavi: * et exaudivit me.
2. Domine, libera animam meam a labiis iniquis, * et a lingua dolosa.
3. Quid detur tibi, aut quid apponatur tibi, * ad linguam dolosam?
4. Sagittæ potentis acutæ * cum carbonibus desolatoriis.
5. Heu mihi quia incolatus meus prolongatus est: habitavi cum habitantibus Cedar: * multum incola fuit anima mea.
6. Cum his qui oderunt pacem, eram pacificus: * cum loquebar

IN my trouble, I cried to the Lord, and he heard me.
2. O Lord, deliver my soul from wicked lips, and a deceitful tongue.
3. What shall be given to thee, or what shall be added to thee, to a deceitful tongue?
4. The sharp arrows of the mighty, with coals that lay waste.
5. Wo is me that my sojourning is prolonged: I have dwelt with the inhabitants of Cedar: my soul has been long a sojourner.
6. With them that hated peace I was peaceable: when I spoke to

illis, impugnabant me gratis.

Ant. Cum his qui oderunt pacem, eram pacificus: dum loquebar illis impugnabant me gratis.

Ant. Ab hominibus iniquis libera me, Domine.

PSALM CXXXIX.

ERIPE me, Domine, ab homine malo: a viro iniquo eripe me.

2. Qui cogitaverunt iniquitates in corde: * tota die constituebant prælia.

3. Acuerunt linguas suas sicut serpentis: * venenum aspidum sub labiis eorum.

4. Custodi me, Domine de manu peccatoris: * et ab hominibus iniquis eripe me.

5. Qui cogitaverunt supplantare gressus meos: * absconderunt superbi laqueum mihi.

6. Et funes extenderunt in laqueum: * juxta iter scandalum posuerunt mihi.

them, they fought against me without cause.

Ant. I was peaceable with those that hated peace: whilst I spoke to them, they attacked me without cause.

Ant. From unjust men deliver me, O Lord.

DELIVER me, O Lord, from the evil man: rescue me from the unjust man.

2. Who have devised iniquities in their hearts: all the day long they designed battles.

3. They have sharpened their tongues like a serpent: the venom of asps is under their lips.

4. Keep me, O Lord, from the hands of the wicked: and from unjust men deliver me.

5. Who have proposed to supplant my steps: the proud have hid a net for me.

6. And they have stretched out cords for a snare: they have laid for me a stumbling block by the way-side.

7. Dixi Domino: Deus meus es tu: * exaudi, Domine, vocem deprecationis meæ.
8. Domine, Domine, virtus s a l u t i s meæ obumbrasti super caput meum in die belli.

9. Ne tradas me Domine, a desiderio meo peccatori: * cogitaverunt contra me, ne derelinquas me, ne forte exaltentur.

10. Caput circuitus eorum: * labor labiorum ipsorum operiet eos.

11. Cadent super eos carbones, in ignem dejicies eos: * in miseriis non subsistent.

12. Vir linguosus non dirigetur in terra: * virum injustum malacapient in interitu.

13. Cognovi quia faciet Dominus judicium inopis * et vindictam pauperum.
14. Verumtamen justi

7. I said to the Lord: Thou art my God: hear O Lord, the voice of my supplication.
8. O Lord, O Lord, the strength of my salvation: thou hast overshadowed my head in the day of battle.

9. Give me not up, O Lord, from my desire to the wicked: they have plotted against me; do not thou forsake me, lest they should triumph.

10. The head of their compassing me about: the labour of their lips shall overwhelm them.

11. Burning coals shall fall upon them; thou wilt cast them down into the fire: in miseries they shall not be able to stand.

12. A man full of tongue shall not be established in the earth: evils shall catch the unjust man unto destruction.

13. I know that the Lord will do justice to the needy, and will revenge the poor.
14. But as for the just,

confitebuntur nomini tuo: * et habitabunt recti cum vultu tuo.

Ant. Ab hominibus iniquis libera me, Domine.

Ant. Custodi me a laqueo quem statuerunt mihi, et a scandalis operantium iniquitatem.

they shall give glory to thy name: and the upright shall dwell with thy countenance.

Ant. From unjust men deliver me, O Lord.

Ant. Keep me from the snare which they have laid for me, and from the stumblingblocks of those that work iniquity.

PSALM CXL

DOMINE, clamavi ad te, exaudi me: * intende voci meæ cum clamavero ad te.

2. Dirigatur oratio mea sicut incensum in conspectu tuo: * elevatio manuum mearum, sacrificium vespertinum.

3. Pone, Domine, custodiam ori meo: * et ostium circumstantiæ labiis meis.

4. Non declines cor meum in verba malitiæ, * ad excusandas excusationes in peccatis,

5. Cum hominibus operantibus iniquitatem: * et non communicabo cum electis eorum.

I HAVE cried out to thee, O Lord, hear me: hearken to my voice when I cry to thee.

2. Let my prayer be directed as incense in thy sight: the lifting up of my hands as an evening sacrifice.

3. Set a watch, O Lord, before my mouth: and a door round my lips.

4. Incline not my heart to evil words: to make excuses for sins,

5. With men that work iniquity: and I will not communicate with the choicest of them.

6. Corripiet me justus in misericordia, et increpabit me: * oleum autem peccatoris non impinguet caput meum.

7. Quoniam adhuc et oratio mea in beneplacitis eorum: * absorpti sunt juncti petræ judices eorum.

8. Audient verba mea quoniam potuerunt: * sicut crassitudo terræ erupta est super terram.

9. Dissipata sunt ossa nostra sicut infernum: * quia ad te Domine, Domine, oculi mei: in te speravi, non auferas animam meam.

10. Custodi me a laqueo quem statuerunt mihi * et a scandalis operantium iniquitatem.

11. Cadent in retiaculo ejus peccatores: * singulariter sum ego, donec transeam.

Ant. Custodi me a laqueo quem statuerunt

6. The just man shall correct me in mercy, and reprove me: but let not the oil of the sinner fatten my head.

7. For my prayer also shall still be against the things with which they are well pleased: their judges falling upon the rock have been swallowed up.

8. They shall hear my words, for they have prevailed; as when the thickness of the earth is broken up upon the ground.

9. Our bones are scattered by the side of hell: but on thee, O Lord, Lord, are my eyes; in thee have I put my trust, take not away my soul.

10. Keep me from the snare, which they have laid for me, and from the stumbling-blocks of them that work iniquity.

11. The wicked shall fall in his net: I am alone until I pass.

Ant. Keep me from the snare which they have

mihi, et a scandalis operantium iniquitatem.

Ant. Considerabam ad dexteram, et videbam, et non erat qui cognosceret me.

laid for me, and from the stumbling-blocks of those that work iniquity.

Ant. I looked about on my right hand, and beheld, and there was none that knew me.

PSALM CXLI.

VOCE mea ad Dominum clamavi * voce mea ad Dominum deprecatus sum.

2. Effundo in conspectu ejus orationem meam: * et tribulationem meam ante ipsum pronuntio.

3. In deficiendo ex me spiritum meum: * et tu cognovisti semitas meas.

4. In via hac qua ambulabam: * absconderunt laqueum mihi.

5. Considerabam ad dexteram et videbam: * et non erat qui cognosceret me.

6. Periit fuga a me * et non est qui requirat animam meam.

7. Clamavi ad te Domine, * dixi: Tu es spes mea, portio mea in terra viventium.

I Cried to the Lord with my voice; with my voice I made supplication to the Lord.

2. In his sight I pour out my prayer: and before him I declare my trouble.

3. When my spirit failed me, then thou knowest my paths.

4. In this way wherein I walked, they have had a snare for me.

5. I looked on my right hand, and beheld: and there was no one that would know me.

6. Flight hath perished from me: and there is no one that hath regard to my soul.

7. I cried to thee, O Lord; I said: Thou art my hope, my portion in the land of the living.

8. Intende ad deprecationem meam: * quia humiliatus sum nimis.

9. Libera me a persequentibus me: * quia confortati sunt super me.

10. Educ de custodia animam meam ad confitendum nomini tuo: * me expectant justi, donec retribuas mihi.

Ant. Considerabam ad dexteram et videbam, et non erat qui cognosceret me.

Ant. Cœnantibus autem illis, accepit Jesus panem, et benedixit, ac fregit deditque discipulis suis.

Canticum Beatæ Mariæ Virginis.

Lucæ, 1

Magnificat * anima mea Dominum:

2. Et exultavit spiritus meus * in Deo salutari meo.

3. Quia respexit humilitatem ancillæ suæ: * ecce enim ex hoc beatam me dicent omnes generationes.

4. Quia fecit mihi ma-

8. Attend to my supplication: for I am brought very low.

9. Deliver me from my persecutors, for they are stronger than I.

10. Bring my soul out of prison, that I may praise thy name: the just wait for me until thou reward me.

Ant. I looked about on the right hand, and beheld, and there was none that knew me.

Ant. As they were at supper, Jesus took bread, and blessed it, and broke it, and gave it to his disciples.

The Canticle of the Blessed Virgin Mary.

Luke 1.

My soul doth magnify the Lord:

2. And my spirit hath rejoiced in God my Saviour.

3. Because he hath regarded the humility of his hand-maid: for behold from henceforth all generations shall call me blessed.

4. For he that is migh-

gna qui potens est: * et sanctum nomen ejus.

5. Et misericordia ejus a progenie in progenies * timentibus eum.

6. Fecit potentiam in brachio suo: * dispersit superbos mente cordis sui.

7. Deposuit potentes de sede: * et exaltavit humiles.

8. Esurientes implevit bonis: * et divites dimisit inanes.

9. Suscepit Israel puerum suum: * recordatus misericordiæ suæ.

10. Sicut locutus est ad patres nostros, * Abraham: et semini ejus in sæcula.

Ant. Cœnantibus autem illis, accepit Jesus panem et benedixit, ac fregit deditque discipulis suis.

V. Christus factus est pro nobis obediens usque ad mortem.

Pater noster *secreto.*

ty hath done great things to me, and holy is his name.

5. And his mercy is from generation to generation, to them that fear him.

6. He hath showed might in his arm: he hath scattered the proud in the conceit of their heart.

7. He hath put down the mighty from their seat: and hath exalted the humble.

8. He hath filled the hungry with good things: and the rich he hath sent empty away.

9. He hath received Israel his servant, being mindful of his mercy.

10. As he spoke to our fathers, to Abraham, and his seed for ever.

Ant. As they were at supper, Jesus took bread, and blessed it, and broke it, and gave it to his disciples.

V. Christ became obedient for us unto death.

Our Father *in secret.*

THE WASHING OF THE FEET.

After the Psalm, Miserere p. 174 and the prayer Respice, p. 191, the Priest with his Ministers uncovers the Altars, saying the antiphon, Diviserunt, with the Psalm, Deus, Deus meus, respice in me p. 220.

THE WASHING OF THE FEET.

This ceremony generally takes place after the uncovering of the Altars. The number of persons whose feet are to be washed is generally thirteen, for which various reasons are assigned, see Glossary. The Priest assumes a stole and cope of violet and is assisted by the Deacon and Subdeacon, in the vestments of the Mass (white): The Deacon sings the Gospel, Ante diem festum Paschæ, with the usual ceremonies. Then the Priest laying aside the Cope puts a towel about him and with head uncovered and on his knees washes the right foot of each one of the thirteen, the Deacon holding it; wipes it with another towel, and kisses it. In the meantime the Choir sings as follows:

ANTIPHONA.	ANTIPHON.
Mandatum novum do vobis: ut diligatis invicem, sicut dilexi vos, dicit Dominus. *Ps.* Beati immaculati in via: qui ambulant in lege Domini. Mandatum, etc., *repetitur.* *Ant.* Postquam surrexit Dominus a cœna, misit aquam in pelvim, et cœpit lavare pedes discipulorum suorum:	I give you a new commandment: that ye love one another, as I have loved you, says our Lord. *Ps.* Blessed are the immaculate in the way; who walk in the law of the Lord. I give you, etc., *repeated.* *Ant.* After our Lord was risen from supper, he put water into a basin, and began to wash

hoc exemplum reliquit eis. *Ps.* Magnus Dominus et laudabilis nimis: in civitate Dei nostri, in monte sancto ejus.

Postquam, etc.

Ant. Dominus Jesus, postquam cœnavit cum discipulis suis, lavit pedes eorum, et ait illis: Scitis quid fecerim vobis ego Dominus et Magister? Exemplum dedi vobis: ut et vos ita faciatis. *Ps.* Benedixisti, Domine terram tuam: avertisti captivitatem Jacob.

Dominus, etc.

Ant. Domine, tu mihi lavas pedes? Respondit Jesus, et dixit ei: Si non lavero tibi pedes, non habebis partem mecum. *V.* Venit ergo ad Simonem Petrum, et dixit ei Petrus.

Domine, etc. *V.* Quod ego facio, tu nescis modo: scies autem postea.

Domine, etc. *V.* Si ego Dominus et Magis-

the feet of his disciples; to whom he gave that example. *Ps.* Great is the Lord, and exceedingly to be praised: in the city of our God, in his holy mountain.

After, etc.

Ant. Our Lord Jesus, after he had supped with his disciples, washed their feet, and said to them: Know you what I your Lord and Master have done to you? I have given you an example, that ye also may do the same. *Ps.* Thou hast blessed, O Lord, thy land thou hast delivered Jacob from captivity.

Ant. Lord, dost thou wash my feet? Jesus answered, and said to him: If I shall not wash thy feet, thou shalt have no part with me. *V.* He came to Simon Peter, and Peter said to him.

Lord, etc. *V.* What I do thou knowest not now: but thou shalt know it afterwards.

Lord, etc. *V.* If I your Lord and Master have

ter vester lavi vobis pedes: quanto magis debetis alter alterius lavare pedes? *Ps.* Audite hæc, omnes gentes: auribus percipite qui habitatis orbem.

Ant. In hoc cognoscent omnes quia discipuli mei estis, si dilectionem habueritis ad invicem. *V.* Dixit Jesus discipulis suis. In hoc, etc.

Ant. Maneant in vobis fides, spes, charitas, tria hæc, major autem horum est charitas. *V.* Nunc autem manent fides, spes, charitas, tria hæc: major horum est charitas.

Ant. Benedicta sit sancta Trinitas atque indivisa Unitas: confitebimur ei, quia fecit nobiscum misericordiam suam. *V.* Benedicamus Patrem, et Filium, cum Sancto Spiritu. *Ps.* Quam dilecta tabernacula tua, Domine virtutum! concupiscit et deficit anima mea in atria Domini.

Benedicta, etc.

washed your feet: how much more ought you to wash the feet of one another? *Ps.* Hear these things, all ye nations: hearken to them, all ye that inhabit the world.

Ant. In this all shall know that ye are my disciples, if ye have a love for one another. *V.* Said Jesus to his disciples. In this etc.

Ant. Let these three, Faith, Hope and Charity, remain in you: but the greatest of them is Charity. *V.* But now remain Faith, Hope and Charity, these three: but the greatest of them is charity.

Ant. Blessed be the holy Trinity and undivided Unity: we will praise It because It has shown us its mercy. *V.* Let us bless the Father and the Son, with the Holy Ghost. *Ps.* How lovely are thy tabernacles, O Lord of Hosts! my soul desires and longs after the house of the Lord.

Blessed be, etc.

THE WASHING OF THE FEET.

Ant. Ubi charitas et amor, Deus ibi est. *V.* Congregavit nos in unum Christi amor. *V.* Exultemus et in ipso jucundemur. *V.* Timeamus et amemus Deum vivum. *V.* Et ex corde diligamus nos sincero.

Ubi charitas, etc. *V.* Simul ergo cum in unum congregamur. *V.* Ne nos mente dividamur caveamus. *V.* Cessent jurgia maligna, cessent lites. *V.* Et in medio nostri sit Christus Deus.

Ubi charitas, etc. *V.* Simul quoque cum beatis videamus. *V.* Glorianter vultum tuum, Christe Deus. *V.* Gaudium quod est immensum atque probum. *V.* Per infinita sæcula sæculorum. Amen.

Ant. Where charity and love are, there is God. *V.* The love of Christ has gathered us together, *V.* Let us rejoice in him and be glad. *V.* Let us fear and love the living God. *V.* And let us love one another with a sincere heart.

Where charity etc. *V.* When therefore we are assembled. *V.* Let us take heed, we be not divided in mind. *V.* Let malicious quarrels and contentions cease. *V.* And let Christ our God dwell among us.

Where charity, etc. *V.* Let us also with the blessed see. *V.* Triumphantly thy countenance, O Christ our God. *V.* Joy that is exceeding and unadulterated. *V.* For infinite ages of ages. Amen.

After the washing of the feet, the Priest washes and wipes his hands. Then having re-assumed the Cope he says.

Pater noster, *secreto.*
V. Et ne nos inducas in tentationem.

Our Father, *in silence.*
V. And lead us no. into temptation.

THE WASHING OF THE FEET.

R. Sed libera nos a malo.
V. Tu mandasti mandata tua, Domine.

R. Custodiri nimis.

V. Tu lavasti pedes discipulorum tuorum.
R. Opera manuum tuarum ne despicias.
V. Domine, exaudi orationem meam.
R. Et clamor meus ad te veniat.
V. Dominus vobiscum.
R. Et cum spiritu tuo.

Oremus.

ADESTO, Domine quæsumus, officio servitutis nostræ, et quia discipulis tuis pedes lavare dignatus es, ne despicias opera manuum tuarum, quæ nobis retinenda mandasti: ut sicut hic nobis, et a nobis exteriora abluuntur inquinamenta; sic a te omnium nostrum interiora laventur peccata. Quod ipse præstare digneris, qui vivis et regnas

R. But deliver us from evil.
V. Thou hast commanded thy precepts, O Lord.
R. To be exactly observed.
V. Thou hast washed the feet of thy disciples.
R. Despise not the works of thy hands.
V. O Lord, hear my prayer.
R. And let my cry come to thee.
V. The Lord be with you.
R. And with thy spirit.

Let us pray.

BE present, O Lord, we beseech thee, with the office of our service: and since thou didst vouchsafe to wash the feet of thy disciples, despise not the work of thy hands, which thou hast commanded to be retained by us; that as here outward impurities are washed away by us and from us, so the inward sins of us all may be washed away by thee.

Deus per omnia sæcula sæculorum. R. Amen.

Which be thou pleased to grant who livest. R. Amen.

ON THURSDAY EVENING.
GOOD FRIDAY AT MATINS.
THE FIRST NOCTURN.

ANTIPHONA.
Astiterunt reges terræ, et principes convenerunt in unum, adversus Dominum, et adversus Christum ejus.

THE ANTIPHON.
The kings of the earth stood up, and the princes met together, against the Lord, and against his Christ.

PSALM II.

QUARE fremuerunt Gentes, * et populi meditati sunt inania?

2. Astiterunt reges terræ, et principes convenerunt in unum * adversus Dominum, et adversus Christum ejus.

3. Dirumpamus vincula eorum: * et projiciamus a nobis jugum ipsorum.

4. Qui habitat in cœlis, irridebit eos: * et Dominus subsannabit eos.

5. Tunc loquetur ad eos in ira sua: * et in

WHY have the Gentiles raged, and the people devised vain things?

2. The kings of the earth stood up and the princes met together, against the Lord, and against his Christ.

3. Let us break their bonds asunder: and let us cast away their yoke from us.

4. He that dwelleth in heaven shall laugh at them: and the Lord shall deride them.

5. Then shall he speak to them in his anger:

furore suo conturbabit eos.

6. Ego autem constitutus sum rex ab eo super Sion montem sanctum ejus, * prædicans præceptum ejus.

7. Dominus dixit ad me: * Filius meus es tu, ego hodie genui te.

8. Postula a me, et dabo tibi Gentes hæreditatem tuam: * et possessionem tuam terminos terræ.

9. Reges eos in virga ferrea, * et tanquam vas figuli confringes eos.

10. Et nunc reges intelligite: * erudimini qui judicatis terram.

11. Servite Domino in timore: et exultate ei cum tremore.

12. Apprehendite disciplinam, ne quando irascatur Dominus: * et pereatis de via justa.

13. Cum exarserit in brevi ira ejus, * beati

and trouble then in his rage.

6. But I am appointed king by him over Sion his holy mountain, preaching his commandment.

7. The Lord hath said to me: Thou art my son, this day have I begotten thee.

8. Ask of me, and I will give thee the Gentiles for thy inheritance: and the utmost parts of the earth for thy possession.

9. Thou shalt rule them with a rod of iron: and shalt break them in pieces like a potter's vessel.

10. And now, O ye kings, understand: receive instruction, you that judge the earth.

11. Serve ye the Lord with fear: and rejoice unto him with trembling.

12. Embrace discipline, lest at any time the Lord be angry: and you perish from the just way.

13. When his wrath shall be kindled in a

omnes qui confidunt in eo.

Ant. Astiterunt reges terræ, et principes convenerunt in unum, adversus Dominum, et adversus Christum ejus.

Ant. Diviserunt sibi vestimenta mea: et super vestem meam miserunt sortem.

short time: blessed are all they that trust in him.

Ant. The kings of the earth stood up, and the princes met together, against the Lord, and against his Christ.

Ant. They divided my garments amongst them: and they cast lots upon my vesture.

PSALM XXI.

DEUS, Deus meus, respice in me: quare me dereliquisti ? * Longe a salute mea verba delictorum meorum.

2. Deus meus, clamabo per diem, et non exaudies: * et nocte, et non ad insipientiam mihi.

3. Tu autem in sancto habitas, * laus Israel.

4. In te speraverunt patres nostri: * speraverunt et liberasti eos.

5. Ad te clamaverunt, et salvi facti sunt: * in te speraverunt, et non sunt confusi.

6. Ego autem sum ver-

O God, my God, look upon me: why hast thou forsaken me? Far from my salvation are the words of my sins.

2. O my God, I shall cry by day, and thou wilt not hear: and by night, and it shall not be reputed as folly in me.

3. But thou dwellest in the holy place, the praise of Israel.

4. In thee have our fathers hoped: they have hoped and thou hast delivered them.

5. They cried to thee, and they were saved: they trusted in thee, and were not confounded.

6. But I am a worm,

mis, et non homo: * opprobrium hominum, et abjectio plebis.

7. Omnes videntes me deriserunt me: * locuti sunt labiis, et moverunt caput.

8. Speravit in Domino, eripiat eum: * salvum faciat eum, quoniam vult eum.

9. Quoniam tu es, qui extraxisti me de ventre: * spes mea ab uberibus matris meæ. In te projectus sum ex utero.

10. De ventre matris meæ Deus meus es tu: * ne discesseris a me.

11. Quoniam tribulatio proxima est: * quoniam non est qui adjuvet.

12. Circumdederunt me vituli multi: * tauri pingues obsederunt me.

13. Aperuerunt super me os suum, * sicut leo rapiens et rugiens.

14. Sicut aqua effusus sum: * et dispersa sunt omnia ossa mea.

15. Factum est cor meum tamquam cera li-

and no man: [the reproach of men, and the outcast of the people.

7. All they that saw me have laughed me to scorn: they have spoken with the lips, and wagged the head.

8. He hoped in the Lord, let him deliver him: let him save him, seeing he delighted in him.

9. For thou art he that hast drawn me out of the womb: my hope from the breasts of my mother. I was cast upon thee from the womb.

10. From my mother's womb thou art my God, depart not from me.

11. For tribulation is very near: for there is none to help me.

12. Many calves have surrounded me: fat bulls have besieged me.

13. They have opened their mouths against me, as a lion ravening and roaring.

14. I am poured out like water: and all my bones are scattered.

15. My heart is become like wax melting

quescens * in medio ventris mei.

16. Aruit tamquam testa virtus mea, et lingua mea, adhæsit faucibus meis: * et in pulverem mortis deduxisti me.

17. Quoniam circumdederunt me canes multi: * concilium malignantium obsedit me.

18. Foderunt manus meas et pedes meos: * dinumeraverunt omnia ossa mea.

19. Ipse vero consideraverunt et inspexerunt me: * diviserunt sibi vestimenta mea, et super vestem meam miserunt sortem.

20. Tu autem, Domine, ne elongaveris auxilium tuum a me: * ad defensionem meam conspice.

21. Erue a framea, Deus, animam meam: * et de manu canis unicam meam.

22. Salva me ex ore leonis: * et a cornibus unicornium humilitatem meam.

23. Narrabo nomen tu-

in the midst of my bowels.

16. My strength is dried up like a potsherd, and my tongue hath cleaven to my jaws: and thou hast brought me down into the dust of death.

17. For many dogs have encompasssed me: the council of the malignant hath besieged me.

18. They have dug my hands and feet: they have numbered all my bones.

19. And they have looked and stared upon me: they parted my garments amongst them, and upon my vesture they cast lots.

20. But thou, O Lord, remove not thy help to a distance from me: look towards my defence.

21. Deliver, O God, my soul from the sword: my only one from the hand of the dog.

22 Save me from the lion's mouth and my lowness from the horns of the unicorns.

23. I will declare thy

um fratribus meis: * in medio ecclesiæ laudabo te.

24. Qui timetis Dominum, laudate eum: * universum semen Jacob, glorificate eum.

25. Timeat eum omne semen Israel: * quoniam non sprevit, neque despexit deprecationem pauperis.

26. Nec avertit faciem suam a me: et cum clamarem ad eum, exaudivit me.

27. Apud te laus mea in ecclesia magna: * vota mea reddam in conspectu timentium eum.

28. Edent pauperes et saturabuntur: et laudabunt Dominum qui requirunt eum: * vivent corda eorum in sæculum sæculi.

29. Reminiscentur et convertentur ad Dominum * universi fines terræ.

30. Et adorabunt in conspectu ejus * universæ familiæ Gentium.

name to my brethren: in the midst of the church will I praise thee.

24. Ye that fear the Lord, praise him: all ye the seed of Jacob, glorify him.

25. Let all the seed of Israel fear him: because he hath not slighted nor despised the supplication of the poor man:

26. Neither hath he turned away his face from me: and when I cried to him he heard me.

27. With thee is my praise in the great church: I will pay my vows in the sight of them that fear him.

28. The poor shall eat and shall be filled: and they shall praise the Lord that seek him: their hearts shall live for ever and ever.

29. All the ends of the earth shall remember and shall be converted to the Lord.

30. And all the kindreds of the Gentiles shall adore in his sight.

31. Quoniam Domini est regnum: * et ipse dominabitur Gentium.

32. Manducaverunt et adoraverunt omnes pingues terræ: * in conspectus ejus cadent omnes qui descendunt in terram.

33. Et anima mea illi vivet: * et semen meum serviet ipse.

34. Annuntiabitur Domino generatio ventura: * et annuntiabunt cœli justitiam ejus populo qui nascetur, quem fecit Dominus.

Ant. Diviserunt sibi vestimenta mea: et super vestem meam miserunt sortem.

Ant. Insurrexerunt in me testes iniqui, et mentita est iniquitas sibi.

31. For the kingdom is the Lord's: and he shall have dominion over the nations.

32. All the fat ones of the earth have eaten and have adored: all they that go down to the earth shall fall before him.

33. And to him my soul shall live: and my seed shall serve him.

34. There shall be declared to the Lord a generation to come: and the heavens shall show forth his justice to a people that shall be born, which the Lord hath made.

Ant. They divided my garments amongst them: ad upon my vesture they cast lots.

Ant. Unjust witnesses have risen up against me, and iniquity hath lied to itself.

PSALM XXVI.

DOMINUS illuminatio mea, et salus mea, * quem timebo.

2. Dominus protector vitæ meæ, * a quo trepidabo?

THE Lord is my light and my salvation whom shall I fear?

2. The Lord is the protector of my life, of whom shall I be afraid?

3. Dum appropriant super me nocentes, * ut edant carnes meas.
4. Qui tribulant me inimici mei: * ipsi infirmati sunt et ceciderunt.

5. Si consistant adversum me castra, * non timebit cor meum.

6. Si exsurgat adversum me prælium: * in hoc ego sperabo.
7. Unam petii a Domino, hanc requiram, * ut inhabitem in domo Domini omnibus diebus vitæ meæ.

8. Ut videam voluptatem Domini et visitem templum ejus.

9. Quoniam abscondit me in tabernaculo suo: * in die malorum protexit me in abscondito tabernaculi sui.

10. In petra exaltavit me: * et nunc exaltavit caput meum super inimicos meos.

11. Circuivi, et immolavi in tabernaculo ejus hostiam vociferationis:

3. Whilst the wicked draw near against me to eat my flesh.
4. My enemies that troubled me have been weakened, and have fallen.

5. If armies in camp should stand together against me, my heart shall not fear.

6. If a battle should rise up against me, in this will I be confident.
7. One thing have I asked of the Lord, this will I seek after, that I may dwell in the house of the Lord all the days of my life.

8. That I may see the delight of the Lord, and may visit his temple.

9. For he hath hid me in his tabernacle: in the day of evils he hath protected me in the secret place of his tabernacle.

10. He hath exalted me upon a rock: and now he hath lifted up my head above my enemies.

11. I have gone round and have offered up in his tabernacle a sacri-

cantabo, et psalmum dicam Domino.

12. Exaudi, Domine, vocem meam, qua clamavi ad te: * miserere mei, et exaudi me.

13. Tibi dixit cor meum, exquisivit te facies mea: * faciem tuam, Domine, requiram.

14. Nec avertas faciem tuam a me: * ne declines in ira a servo tuo.

15. Adjutor meus esto: * ne derelinquas me, neque despicias me, Deus salutaris meus.

16. Quoniam pater meus et mater mea dereliquerunt me: * Dominus autem assumpsit me.

17. Legem pone mihi, Domine, in via tua: * et dirige me in semitam rectam propter inimicos meos.

18. Ne tradideris me in animas tribulantium me: * quoniam insurrexerunt in me testes iniqui, et mentita est iniquitas sibi.

19. Credo videre bona Domini: * in terra viventium.

fice of jubilation: I will sing, and recite a psalm to the Lord.

12. Hear, O Lord, my voice, with which I have cried to thee: have mercy on me, and hear me.

13. My heart hath said to thee, my face hath sought thee: thy face, O Lord, will I still seek.

14. Turn not away thy face from me: decline not in thy wrath from thy servant.

15. Be thou my helper: forsake me not, do not thou despise me, O God my Saviour.

16. For my father and my mother have left me: but the Lord hath taken me up.

17. Set me, O Lord, a law in the way: and guide me in the right path, because of my enemies.

18. Deliver me not over to the will of them that trouble me: for unjust witnesses have risen up against me and iniquity hath lied to itself.

19. I believe to see the good things of the Lord in the land of the living.

20. Expecta Dominum viriliter age: et confortetur cor tuum, et sustine Dominum.

Ant. Insurrexerunt in me testes iniqui, et mentita est iniquitas sibi.

V. Diviserunt sibi vestimenta mea.
R. Et super vestem meam miserunt sortem.
Pater noster, *secreto.*

De Lamentatione Jeremiæ Prophetæ. (*cap.* ii, *p.* 8)

LECTIO I.

Heth. COGITAVIT Dominus dissipare murum filiæ Sion: tetendit funiculum suum, et non avertit manum suam a perditione: luxitque antemurale, et murus pariter dissipatus est.

Teth. Defixæ sunt in terra portæ ejus: perdidit et contrivit vectes ejus: Regem ejus et principes ejus in Gentibus: non est lex, et pro-

20. Expect the Lord, do manfully: and let thy heart take courage and wait thou for the Lord.

Ant. Unjust witnesses have risen up against me, and iniquity hath lied to itself.

V. They divided my garments amongst them.
R. And upon my vesture they cast lots.
Our Father, *in secret.*

From the Lamentations of the Prophet Jeremias. (*ch.* ii. *p.* 8)

LESSON I.

Heth. THE Lord hath purposed to destroy the wall of the daughter of Sion: he hath stretched out his line, and hath not withdrawn his hand from destroying: and the bulwark hath mourned, and the wall hath been destroyed together.

Teth. Her gates are sunk into the ground: he hath destroyed and broken her bars: her king and her princes among the Gentiles:

phetæ ejus non invenerunt visionem a Domino.

Jod. Sederunt in terra, conticuerunt senes filiæ Sion: consperserunt cinere capita sua, accincti sunt ciliciis: abjecerunt in terram capita sua virgines Jerusalem.

Caph. Defecerunt præ lacrymis oculi mei, conturbata sunt viscera mea, effusum est in terra jecur meum super contritione filiæ populi mei, cum deficeret parvulus, et lactens in plateis oppidi.

Jerusalem, Jerusalem, convertere ad Dominum Deum tuum.

R. Omnes amici mei dereliquerunt me, et prævaluerunt insidiantes mihi: tradidit me quem diligebam: * Et terribilibus oculis plaga crudeli percutientes, aceto potabant me. *V.* Inter iniquos projece-

the law is no more, and her prophets have not found vision from the Lord.

Jod. The ancients of the daughter of Sion sit upon the ground, they have held their peace: they have sprinkled their heads with dust, they are girded with hair-cloth: the virgins of Jerusalem hang down their heads to the ground.

Caph. My eyes have failed with weeping, my bowels are troubled: my liver is poured out upon the earth, for the destruction of the daughter of my people, when the children and the sucklings fainted away in the streets of the city.

Jerusalem, Jerusalem, be converted to the Lord thy God.

R. All my friends have forsaken me, and they that lay in ambush for me prevailed: He whom I love has betrayed me: * And they with terrible looks striking me with a cruel wound, gave me

runt me, et non pepercerunt animæ meæ. * Et terribilibus oculis.

LECTIO II.

Lamed. MAtribus suis dixerunt: Ubi est triticum et vinum? cum deficerent quasi vulnerati in plateis civitatis: cum exhalarent animas suas in sinu matrum suarum.

Mem. Cui comparabo te? vel cui assimilabo te, filia Jerusalem? cui exæquabo te, et consolabor te, virgo filia Sion? magna est enim velut mare contritio tua: quis medebitur tui?

Nun. Prophetæ tui viderunt tibi falsa et stulta, nec aperiebant iniquitatem tuam, ut te ad pœnitentiam provocarent: viderunt autem tibi assumptiones falsas et ejectiones.

Samech. Plauserunt super te manibus om-

vinegar to drink. *V.* They cast me out among the wicked, and spared not my life. * And they.

LESSON II.

Lamed. THEY said to their mother: Where is corn and wine? when they fainted away as the wounded in the streets of the city: when they breathed out their souls in the bosoms of their mothers.

Mem. To what shall I compare thee? or to what shall I liken thee, O daughter of Jerusalem? to what shall I equal thee, that I may comfort thee, O virgin daughter of Sion? For great as the sea is thy destruction: who shall heal thee?

Nun. Thy prophets have seen false and foolish things for thee and they have not laid open thy iniquity, to excite thee to penance: but they have seen for thee false revelations and banishments.

Samech. All they that passed by the way have

nes transeuntes per viam: sibilaverunt, et moverunt caput suum super filiam Jerusalem: Hæccine est urbs dicentes perfecti decoris, gaudium universæ terræ.

Jerusalem, Jerusalem, convertere ad Dominum Deum tuum.

R. Velum templi scissum est. * Et omnis terra tremuit: latro de cruce clamabat, dicens: Memento mei, Domine, dum veneris in regnum tuum. V. Petræ scissæ sunt, et monumenta aperta sunt, et multa corpora sanctorum, qui dormierant, surrexerunt. * Et omnis terra tremuit.

clapped their hands at thee: they have hissed and wagged their heads at the daughter of Jerusalem saying: Is this the city of perfect beauty, the joy of all the earth?

Jerusalem, Jerusalem, be converted to the Lord thy God.

R. The veil of the temple was rent. * And all the earth shook: the thief from the cross cried out, saying: Remember me, O Lord, when thou shalt come into thy kingdom. The rocks were split, and the monuments opened, and many bodies of the saints that were dead rose out of them. * And all the earth shook.

LECTIO III.

cap. 3

Aleph. EGO vir videns paupertatem meam in virga indignationis ejus.

Aleph. Me minavit, et adduxit in tenebras, et non in lucem.

LESSON III.

ch. 3

Aleph. I AM the man that see my poverty by the rod of his indignation.

Aleph.. He hath led me, and brought me into darkness, and not into light.

Aleph. Tantum in me vertit, et convertit manum suam tota die.

Beth. Vetustam fecit pellem meam et carnem meam, contrivit ossa mea.

Beth. Ædificavit in gyro meo, et circumdedit me felle et labore.

Beth. In tenebrosis collocavit me, quasi mortuos sempiternos.

Ghimel. Circumædificavit adversum me, ut non egrediar: aggravavit compedem meum.

Ghimel. Sed et cum clamavero et rogavero exclusit orationem meam.

Ghimel. Conclusit vias meas lapidibus quadris, semitas meas subvertit.

Jerusalem, Jerusalem, convertere ad Dominum Deum tuum.

R. Vinea mea electa, ego te plantavi: ' Quomodo conversa es in amaritudinem, ut me crucifigeres, et Barabbam dimitteres? *V.* Se-

Aleph. Only against me he hath turned, and turned his hand all the day.

Beth. My skin and my flesh he hath made old, he hath broken my bones.

Beth. He hath built round about me, and he hath compassed me with gall and labour.

Beth. He hath set me in dark places as those that are dead for ever.

Ghimel. He hath built against me round about that I may not get out: he hath made my fetters heavy.

Ghimel. Yea, and when I cry and entreat, he hath shut out my prayer.

Ghimel. He hath shut up my ways with square stones, he hath turned my paths upside down.

Jerusalem, Jerusalem, be converted to the Lord thy God.

R. O my chosen vineyard. I have planted thee: How art thou become so bitter that thou shouldst crucify me, and release

pivi te, et lapides elegi ex te, et ædificavi turrim. Quomodo conversa es. Vinea.

Barabbas? ℣. I have hedged thee in, and picked the stones out of thee, and have built a tower. How art thou, O my chosen.

THE SECOND NOCTURN.

Ant. Vim faciebant qui quærebant animam meam.

Ant. They used violence that sought my soul.

PSALM XXXVII

DOMINE, ne in furore tuo arguas me: * neque in ira tua corripias me.

2. Quoniam sagittæ tuæ infixæ sunt mihi: * et confirmasti super me manum tuam.

3. Non est sanitas in carne mea a facie iræ tuæ: non est pax ossibus meis a facie peccatorum meorum.

4. Quoniam iniquitates meæ supergressæ sunt caput meum: * et sicut onus grave gravatæ sunt super me.

5. Putruerunt, et corruptæ sunt cicatrices meæ, * a facie insipientiæ meæ.

6. Miser factus sum, et curvatus sum usque in

REBUKE me not, O Lord, in thy indignation: nor chastise me in thy wrath.

2. For thy arrows are fastened in me: and thy hand hath been strong upon me.

3. There is no health in my flesh, because of thy wrath: there is no peace for my bones, because of my sins.

4. For my iniquities are gone over my head: and as a heavy burthen are become heavy upon me.

5. My sores are putrified and corrupted, because of my foolishness.

6. I am become miserable, and am bowed

finem * tota die contristatus ingrediebar.

7. Quoniam lumbi mei impleti sunt illusionibus: * et non est sanitas in carne mea.

8. Afflictus sum, et humiliatus sum nimis: * rugiebam a gemitu cordis mei.

9. Domine, ante te omne desiderium meum: * et gemitus meus a te non est absconditus.

10. Cor meum conturbatum est, dereliquit me virtus mea: * et lumen oculorum meorum, et ipsum non est mecum.

11. Amici mei et proximi mei: * adversum me appropinquaverunt et steterunt.

12. Et qui juxta me orant, de longe steterunt: * et vim faciebant qui quærebant animam meam.

13. Et qui inquirebant mala mihi, locuti sunt vanitates: * et dolos tota die meditabantur.

14. Ego autem tamquam surdus non audiebam: * et sicut mutus non aperiens os suum.

down even to the end: I walked sorrowful all the day long.

7. For my loins are filled with illusions: and there is no health in my flesh.

8. I am afflicted and humbled exceedingly: I roared with the groaning of my heart.

9. Lord, all my desire is before thee: and my groaning is not hid from thee.

10. My heart is troubled, my strength hath left me: and the light of my eyes itself is not with me.

11. My friends and my neighbours have drawn near, and stood against me.

12. And they that were near me stood afar off: and they that sought my soul used violence.

13. And they that sought evils to me spoke vain things: and studied deceits all the day long.

14. But I, as a deaf man, heard not: and was as a dumb man not opening his mouth.

15. Et factus sum sicut homo non audiens: * et non habens in ore suo redargutiones.

16. Quoniam in te Domine speravi: * tu exaudies me, Domine Deus meus.

17. Quia dixi: Nequando supergaudeant mihi inimici mei: * et dum commoventur pedes mei super me magna locuti sunt.

18. Quoniam ego in flagella paratus sum: * et dolor meus in conspectu meo semper.

19. Quoniam iniquitatem meam annuntiabo: et * cogitabo pro peccato meo.

20. Inimici autem mei vivunt, et confirmati sunt super me: * et multiplicati sunt qui oderunt me inique.

21. Qui retribuunt mala pro bonis, detrahebant mihi: * quoniam sequebar bonitatem.

22. Ne derelinquas me, Domine Deus meus: * ne discesseris a me.

23. Intende in adjutorium meum, Domine, * Deus salutis meæ.

15. And I became as a man that heareth not: and that hath no reproofs in his mouth.

16. For in thee, O Lord, have I hoped: thou wilt hear me, O Lord my God.

17. For I said: Lest at any time my enemies rejoice over me: and whilst my feet are moved, they speak great things against me.

18. For I am ready for scourges: and my sorrow is continually before me;

19. For I will declare my iniquity: and I will think for my sin.

20. But my enemies live, and are stronger than I: and they that hate me wrongfully are multiplied.

21. They that render evil for good, have detracted me, because I followed goodness.

22. Forsake me not, O Lord my God: do not thou depart from me.

23. Attend unto my help, O Lord, the God of my salvation.

Ant. Vim faciebant qui quærebant animam meam.

Ant. Confundantur et revereantur, qui quærunt animam meam, ut auferant eam.

Ant. They used violence that sought my soul.

Ant. Let them be confounded and ashamed that seek to take away my life.

PSALM XXXIX.

EXpectans expectavi Dominum * et intendit mihi.

2. Et exaudivit preces meas : * et eduxit me de lacu miseriæ et de luto fæcis.

3. Et statuit super petram pedes meos : * et direxit gressus meos.

4. Et immisit in os meum canticum novum, carmen Deo nostro.

5. Videbunt multi, et timebunt: * et sperabunt in Domino.

6. Beatus vir, cujus est nomen Domini spes ejus: * et non respexit in vanitates et insanias falsas.

7. Multa fecisti tu Domine Deus meus, mirabilia tua: * et cogitatio-

WITH waiting I have waited for the Lord, and he was attentive to me.

2. And he heard my prayers and he brought me out of the pit of misery, and the mire of dregs.

3. And he set my feet upon a rock, and directed my steps.

4. And he put a new canticle into my mouth, a song to our God.

5. Many shall see this, and shall fear: and they shall hope in the Lord.

6. Blessed is the man whose trust is in the name of the Lord: and who hath not had regard to vanities and lying follies.

7. Thou hast multiplied thy wonderful works, O Lord my God:

nibus tuis non est qui similis sit tibi.

8. Annuntiavi, et locutus sum: * multiplicati sunt super numerum.

9. Sacrificium et oblationem noluisti: * aures autem perfecisti mihi.

10. Holocaustum et pro peccato non postulasti: * tunc dixi: Ecce venio.

11. In capite libri scriptum est de me, ut facerem voluntatem tuam: * Deus meus, volui, et legem tuam in medio cordis mei.

12. Annuntiavi justitiam tuam in ecclesia magna; * ecce labia mea non prohibebo: Domine tu scisti.

13. Justitiam tuam non abscondi in corde meo: veritatem tuam et salutare tuum dixi.

14. Non abscondi misericordiam tuam, et veritatem tuam concilio multo.

15. Tu autem, Domine, ne longe facias misera-

and in thy thoughts there is no one like to thee.

8. I have declared, and I have spoken: they are multiplied above number.

9. Sacrifice and oblation thou didst not desire: but thou hast pierced ears for me.

10. Burnt-offerings and sin-offerings thou didst not require: then said I: Behold I come.

11. In the head of the book it was written of me, that I should do thy will: O my God, I have desired it, and thy law in the midst of my heart.

12. I have declared thy justice in the great church; lo, I will not restrain my lips: O Lord, thou knowest it.

13. I have not hid thy justice within my heart I have declared thy truth and thy salvation.

14. I have not concealed thy mercy and thy truth from the great council.

15. With-hold not thou, O Lord, thy tender

tiones tuas a me * misericordia tua et veritas tua semper susceperunt me.

16. Quoniam circumdederunt me mala, quorum non est numerus: * comprehenderunt me iniquitates meæ, et non potui ut viderem.

17. Multiplicatæ sunt super capillos capitis mei: * et cor meum dereliquit me.

18. Complaceat tibi Domine ut eruas me: * Domine, ad adjuvandum me respice.

19. Confundantur et revereantur simul, qui quærunt animam meam, * ut auferant eam.

20. Convertantur retrorsum et revereantur, * qui volunt mihi mala.

21. Ferant confestim confusionem suam, * qui dicunt mihi: Euge, euge.

22. Exultent et lætentur super te omnes quærentes te: * et dicant semper: Magnificentur Dominus, qui diligunt salutare tuum.

23. Ego autem mendi-

mercies from me: thy mercy and thy truth have always upheld me.

16. For evils without number have surrounded me: my iniquities have overtaken me, and I was not able to see.

17. They are multiplied above the hairs of my head: and my heart hath forsaken me.

18. Be pleased, O Lord, to deliver me, look down, O Lord, to help me.

19. Let them be confounded and ashamed together, that seek after my soul, to take it away.

20. Let them be turned backward, and be ashamed, that desire evils to me:

21. Let them immediately bear their confusion that say to me: 'Tis well, 'tis well.

22. Let all that seek thee rejoice and be glad in thee: and let such as love thy salvation, say always, The Lord be magnified.

23. But I am needy

cus sum et pauper: * Dominus solicitus est mei.

24. Adjutor meus et protector meus, tu es: * Deus meus, ne tardaveris.

Ant. Confundantur et revereantur, qui quærunt animam meam, ut auferant eam.

Ant. Alieni insurrexerunt in me, et fortes quæsierunt animam meam.

and poor: the Lord is careful for me.

24. Thou art my helper and my protector: O my God, be not slack.

Ant. Let them be confounded and ashamed, that seek to take away my soul.

Ant. Strangers have risen up against me, and the powerful have sought my soul.

PSALM LIII.

DEUS, in nomine tuo salvum me fac: * et in virtute tua judica me.

2. Deus, exaudi orationem meam: * auribus percipe verba oris mei.

3. Quoniam alieni insurrexerunt adversum me, et fortes quæsierunt animam meam: * et non proposuerunt Deum ante conspectum suum.

4. Ecce enim Deus adjuvat me: * et Dominus susceptor est animæ meæ.

5. Averte mala inimicis meis: * et in veritate tua disperde illos.

SAVE me, O God, by thy name, and judge me in thy strength.

2. O God, hear my prayer: give ear to the words of my mouth.

3. For strangers have risen up against me: and the mighty have sought after my soul: and they have not God before their eyes.

4. For behold God is my helper: and the Lord is the protector of my soul.

5. Turn back the evils upon my enemies: and cut them off in thy truth.

6. Voluntarie sacrificabo tibi: * et confitebor nomini tuo, Domine. quoniam bonum est.

7. Quoniam ex omni tribulatione eripuisti me: * et super inimicos meos despexit oculus meus.
Ant. Alieni insurrexerunt in me, et fortes quæsierunt animam meam.
V. Iusurrexerunt in me testes iniqui.

R. Et mentita est iniquitas sibi.
Pater noster, *secreto.*

Ex Tractatu Sancti Augustini Episcopi super Psalmos.
(*in Ps.* 63. ad v. 2)

LECTIO IV.

PRotexisti me, Deus, a conventu malignantium, a multitudine in operantium iniquitatem. Jam ipsum caput nostrum intueamur. Multi martyres talia passi sunt, sed nihil sic elucet, quomodo caput martyrum:

6. I will freely sacrifice to thee, and will give praise, O God, to thy name: because it is good.

7. For thou hast delivered me out of all trouble: and my eye hath looked down upon my enemies.
Ant. Strangers have risen up against me, and the powerful have sought my soul.
V. Unjust witnesses have risen up against me.

R. And iniquity has lied to itself.
Our Father, *in silence.*

From the Treatise of St. Augustine, Bishop, on the Psalms.
(no Ps. 63. v. 2)

LESSON IV.

THOU hast protected me, O God, from the assembly of the wicked, from the multitude of those that work iniquity. Now let us behold our head himself. Many martyrs have suffered such things, but nothing is so

ibi melius intuemur, quod illi experti sunt. Protectus est a multitudine malignantium, protegente se Deo, protegente carnem suam ipso Filio, et homine, quem gerebat: quia Filius hominis est, et Filius Dei est. Filius Dei propter formam Dei. Filius hominis propter formam servi, habens potestatem ponere vitam suam, et recipere eam. Quid ei potuerunt facere inimici? Occiderunt corpus, animam non occiderunt. Intendite. Parvum ergo erat Dominum hortari martyres verbo, nisi firmaret exemplo.

conspicuous as the head of the martyrs; there we see better what they endured. He was protected from the multitude of the wicked: God protecting himself, the Son, and, the manhood whichle bore protecting his flesh: for he is the Son of Man, and the Son of God: the Son of God because of the form of God. the Son of Man, because of the form of a servant, having it in his power to lay down his life, and tak it up again. What could his enemies do against him? They killed his body, but they did not kill his soul. Take notice. It were little then for the Lord to exhort martyrs by word, without fortifying them by example.

R. Tamquam ad latronem existis cum gladiis et fustibus comprehendere me: * Quotidie apud vos eram in templo docens, et non me tenuistis: et ecce flagellatum ducitis ad crucifigendum. *V.* Cumque injecisseut manus in

R. Ye come to take me like a thief, with swords, and clubs: * I was every day among you, teaching in the temple, and ye did not apprehend me: yet now ye scourge me and lead me to be crucified. *V.* And when they had

Jesum, et tenuissent eum, dixit ad eos. * Quotidie apud vos.

LECTIO V.

NOSTIS qui conventus erat malignantium Judæorum, et quæ multitudo erat operantium iniquitatem. Quam iniquitatem? Quia voluerunt occidere Dominum Jesum Christum. Tanta opera bona, inquit, ostendi vobis: propter quod horum me vultis occidere? Pertulit omnes infirmos eorum, curavit omnes languidos eorum, prædicavit regnum cœlorum, non tacuit vitia eorum, ut ipsa potius eis displicerent, non medicus a quo sanabantur. His omnibus curationibus ejus ingrati, tamquam multa febre phrenetici insanientes in medicum, qui venerat curare eos, excogitaverunt consilium perdendi eum: tanquam ibi volentes probare, utrum vere homo sit qui mori possit, an aliquid super homines sit, et mori se non permit-

laid hands on Jesus, and taken him, he said to them. * I was every day.

LESSON V.

YE know what was the assembly of the wicked Jews, and what the multitude of those that work iniquity. But what was that iniquity? It was that they intended to kill the Lord Jesus Christ. I have done, saith he, so many good works among you: for which of them will you kill me? He bore with all their weaknesses, he cured all their sick, he preached the kingdom of heaven, he concealed not their crimes that they might rather hate them, than the physician that healed them. Yet such was their ingratitude for all these cures, that like men raving in a high fever, they raged against the physician that came to cure them, and formed the design of destroying him: as if they had a mind to try whether he was a real man that

17

tat. Verbum ipsorum ignoscimus in Sapientia Salomonis: Morte turpissima, inquiunt, condemnemus eum: interrogemus eum: erit enim respectus in sermonibus illius. Si enim vere Filius Dei est, liberet eum.

could die, or something above men, and would not die. We find their words in Solomon's Book of Wisdom 'Let us condemn him,' say they, 'to a most shameful death. Let us examine him: for regard will be had to his words. If he is truly the Son of God, let him deliver him.'

R. Tenebræ factæ sunt dum crucifixissent Jesum Judæi: et circa horam nonam exclamavit Jesus voce magna: Deus meus, ut quid me dereliquisti? * Et inclinato capite emisit spiritum. V. Exclamans Jesus voce magna, ait: Pater, in manus tuas commendo spiritum meum. * Et inclinato.

R. Darkness covered the earth, whilst the Jews crucified Jesus: and about the ninth hour Jesus cried out with a loud voice: My God, why hast thou forsaken me? * And bowing down his head, he gave up the ghost. V. Jesus crying out with a loud voice, saith: Father, into thy hands I commend my spirit. * And bowing down, etc.

LECTIO VI.

*E*Xacuerunt tamquam gladium linguas suas. Non dicant Judæi: non occidimus Christum: etenim propterea eum dederunt judici Pilato, ut quasi ipsi a morte ejus

LESSON VI.

*T*HEY sharpened their tongues like a sword. Let not the Jews say: We did not kill Christ: under that pretence therefore they delivered him up to Pilate, the

viderentur immunes. Nam cum dixisset eis Pilatus: *Vos eum occidite:* responderunt: *Nobis non licet occidere quemquam.* Iniquitatem facinoris sui in judicem hominem refundere volebant: sed numquid Deum judicem fallebant? Quod fecit Pilatus, in eo ipso quod fecit aliquantum particeps fuit: sed in comparatione illorum multo ipse innocentior. Institit enim quantum potuit, ut illum ex eorum manibus liberaret: nam propterea flagellatum produxit ad eos. Non persequendo Dominum flagellavit, sed eorum furori satisfacere volens: ut vel sic jam mites erant, et desinerent velle occidere, cum flagellatum viderent. Fecit et hoc. At ubi perseveraverunt, nostis illum lavisse manus, et dixisse, quod ipse non fecisset, mundum se esse a morte illius. Fecit tamen. Sed si reus, quia fecit vel invitus: illi innocentes, qui coëgerunt ut faceret? Nullo

judge, that they might seem innocent of his death: for when Pilate had said to them: *Put him to death yourselves,* they answered: *It is not lawful for us to put any man to death.* Thus they pretended to throw the injustice of their crime upon a Judge that was a man: but could they deceive a judge that is God? What Pilate did, made him partaker of their crime: but in comparison of them he was much more innocent. For he laboured what he could to get him out of their hands; and for that reason ordered him to be scourged and shown to them. This he did to our Lord, not by way of persecution, but to satisfy their rage: that the sight of him in that condition might move them to pity, and make them desist from desiring his death. All this he did. But when they still persisted, ye knew that he washed his hands, and said, that he would not do it, that

modo. Sed ille dixit in eum sententiam, et jussit eum crucifigi, et quasi ipse occidit: et vos, O Iudæi occidistis: Unde occidistis? Gladio linguæ, acuistis enim linguas vestras. Et quando percussistis, nisi quando clamastis: Crucifige, Crucifice.

he was innocent of his death. And yet he put him to death. But if he was guilty for doing so against his will: are they innocent that forced him to it? Not at all. He pronounced sentence upon him, and commanded him to be crucified, and so might be said to kill him: but ye also, O Jews, have killed him. How have ye killed him? With the sword of your tongues: for *ye sharpened your tongues.* And when gave ye the stroke, but when ye cried out: *Crucify him, Crucify him?*

R. Animam meam dilectam tradidi in manus iniquorum, et facta est mihi hæreditas mea sicut leo in silva: dedit contra me voces adversarius dicens: Congregamini, et properate ad devorandum illum: posuerunt me in deserto solitudinis et luxit super me omnis terra: * Quia non est inventus qui me agnosceret, et faceret bene.

R. I delivered my beloved Son into the hands of the wicked, and my inheritance is become to me like a lion in the forest: my adversary gave out voices against me, saying: Come together, and make haste to devour him: they placed me in a solitary desert, and all the earth mourned for me. * Because there was none that would know me, and do me any good.

V. Insurrexerunt in me viri absque misericordia, et non peperce-

V. Men without mercy rose up against me, and they spared not my

runt animæ meæ. * Quia non est. R. Animam.

life. * Because. R. I delivered.

THE THIRD NOCTURN.

Ant. Ab insurgentibus in me libera me, Domine: quia occupaverunt animam meam.

Ant. From those that rise up against me, O Lord, deliver me: for they are in possession of my soul.

PSALM LVIII.

ERIPE me de inimicis meis Deus meus: * et ab insurgentibus in me libera me.

2. Eripe me de operantibus iniquitatem: * et de viris sanguinum salva me.

3. Quia ecce ceperunt animam meam: * irruerunt in me fortes.

4. Neque iniquitas mea, neque peccatum meum, Domine: * sine iniquitate cucurri, et direxi.

5. Exurge in occursum meum, et vide: * et tu, Domine, Deus virtutum, Deus Israel.

6. Intende ad visitandas omnes Gentes: * non miserearis omnibus qui operantur iniquitatem.

DEliver me from my enemies, O my God, and defend me from them that rise up against me.

2. Deliver me from them that work iniquity: and save me from bloody men.

3. For behold they have caught my soul the mighty have rushed in upon me.

4. Neither is it for my iniquity, nor for my sin, O Lord: without iniquity have I run and directed my steps.

5. Rise up thou to meet me, and behold: even thou, O Lord the God of hosts, the God of Israel.

6. Attend to visit all the nations: have no mercy on all them that work iniquity.

7. Convertentur ad vesperam, et famem patientur ut canes: * et circuibunt civitatem.

8. Ecce loquentur in ore suo, et gladius in labiis eorum: * quoniam quis audivit?

9. Et tu, Domine, deridebis eos: * ad nihilum deduces omnes Gentes.

10. Fortitudinem meam ad te custodiam, quia Deus, susceptor meus es: * Deus meus, misericordia ejus præveniet me.

11. Deus ostendit mihi super inimicos meos, ne occidas eos: * nequando obliviscantur populi mei.

12. Disperge illos in virtute tua: * et depone eos, protector meus Domine:

13. Delictum oris eorum, sermonem labiorum ipsorum: * et comprehendantur in superbia sua.

14. Et de execratione et mendacio annuntiabuntur in consummati-

7. They shall return at evening and shall suffer hunger like dogs: and shall go round about the city.

8. Behold they shall speak with their mouth, and a sword is in their lips: for who, say they, hath heard us?

9. But thou, O Lord, shalt laugh at them, thou shalt bring all the nations to nothing.

10. I will keep my strength to thee, for thou art my protector: my God, his mercy shall prevent me.

11. God shall let me see over my enemies; slay them not, lest at any time my people forget.

12. Scatter them by thy power: and bring them down, O Lord, my protector.

13. For the sin of their mouth, and the word of their lips: and let them be taken in their pride.

14. And for their cursing and lying they shall be talked of when they

one: * in ira consummationis, et non erunt.

15. Et scient quia Deus dominabitur Jacob: * et finium terræ.

16. Convertentur ad vesperam: et famem patientur ut canes: * et circuibunt civitatem.

17. Ipsi dispergentur ad manducandum: * si vero non fuerint saturati, et murmurabunt.

18. Ego autem cantabo fortitudinem tuam: * et exultabo mane misericordiam tuam.

19. Qui factus es susceptor meus: * et refugium meum, in die tribulationis meæ.

20. Adjutor meus tibi psallam, quia Deus susceptor meus es: * Deus meus, misericordia mea.

Ant. Ab insurgentibus in me libera me, Domine: quia occupaverunt animam meam.

Ant. Longe fecisti no-

are consumed: when they are consumed by wrath, and they shall be no more.

15. And they shall know that God will rule Jacob: and all the ends of the earth.

16. They shall return at evening, and shall suffer hunger like dogs: and shall go round about the city.

17. They shall be scattered abroad to eat: and shall murmur if they be not filled.

18. But I will sing thy strength: and will extol thy mercy in the morning.

19. For thou art become my support and my refuge, in the day of my trouble.

20. Unto thee, O my helper, will I sing, for thou art God, my defence: my God, my mercy.

Ant. From those that rise up against me, O Lord, deliver me: for they are in possession of my soul.

Ant. Thou hast re-

tos meos a me: traditus sum, et non egrediebar.

moved my acquaintance far from me: I was delivered up, and did not come out.

PSALM LXXXVII.

DOMINE, Deus salutis meæ, * in die clamavi, et nocte coram te.

2. Intret in conspectu tuo oratio mea: * inclina aurem tuam ad precem meam.

3. Quia repleta est malis anima mea: * et vita mea inferno appropinquavit.

4. Æstimatus sum cum descendentibus in lacum: * factus sum sicut homo sine adjutorio, inter mortuos liber.

5. Sicut vulnerati dormientes in sepulchris, quorum non es memor amplius: * et ipsi de manu tua repulsi sunt.

6. Posuerunt me in lacu inferiori: * in tenebrosis, et in umbra mortis.

7. Super me confirmatus est furor tuus: * et omnes fluctus tuos induxisti super me.

O LORD, the God of my salvation, I have cried in the day, and in the night before thee.

2. Let my prayer come in before thee: incline thy ear to my petition.

3. For my soul is filled with evils: and my life hath drawn nigh to hell.

4. I am counted among them that go down into the pit: I am become as a man without help, free among the dead.

5. Like the slain sleeping in the sepulchres, whom thou rememberest no more: and they are cast off from thy hand.

6. They have laid me in the lower pit: in the dark places, and in the shadow of death.

7. Thy wrath is strong over me: and all thy waves thou hast brought in upon me.

8. Longe fecisti notos meos a me: * posuerunt me abominationem sibi.

9. Traditus sum, et non egrediebar: * oculi mei languerunt præ inopia.

10. Clamavi ad te, Domine tota die: * expandi ad te manus meas.

11. Numquid mortuis facies mirabilia: * aut medici suscitabunt, et confitebuntur tibi?

12. Numquid narrabit aliquis in sepulchro misericordiam tuam, * et veritatem tuam in perditione?

13. Numquid cognoscentur in tenebris mirabilia tua: * et justitia tua in terra oblivionis?

14. Et ego ad te, Domine, clamavi: * et mane oratio mea præveniet te.

15. Ut quid, Domine, repellis orationem meam: * avertis faciem tuam a me?

16. Pauper sum ego, et in laboribus a juven-

8. Thou hast put away my acquaintance far from me: they have set me an abomination to themselves.

9. I was delivered up, and came not forth: my eyes languished through poverty.

10. All the day I cried to thee, O Lord: I stretched out my hands to thee.

11. Wilt thou show wonders to the dead: or shall physicians raise to life, and give praise to thee?

12. Shall any one in the sepulchre declare thy mercy, and thy truth in destruction?

13. Shall thy wonders be known in the dark: and thy justice in the land of forgetfulness?

14. But I, O Lord, have cried to thee: and in the morning my prayer shall prevent thee.

15. Lord, why castest thou off my prayer: why turnest thou away thy face from me.

16. I am poor, and in labours from my youth:

tute mea: * exaltatus autem, humiliatus sum et conturbaverunt me.

17. In me transierunt iræ tuæ: * et terrores tui conturbaverunt me.

18. Circumdederunt me sicut aqua tota die: * circumdederunt me simul.

19. Elongasti a me amicum et proximum: * et notos meos a miseria.

Ant. Longe fecisti notos meos a me: traditus sum, et non egrediebar.

Ant. Captabunt in animam justi, et sanguinem innocentem condemnabunt.

and being exalted, have been humbled and troubled.

17. Thy wrath hath come upon me: and thy terrors have troubled me.

18. They have come round about me like water all the day: they have compassed me about together.

19. Friend and neighbour thou hast put far from me: and my acquaintance because of misery.

Ant. Thou hast removed my acquaintance far from me: I was delivered up, and did not come out.

Ant. They will conspire against the soul of the just man, ad condemn innocent blood.

PSALM XCIII.

DEUS ultionum Dominus: * Deus ultionum libere egit.

2. Exaltare qui judicas terram: * redde retributionem superbis.

THE Lord is the God to whom revenge belongeth: the God of revenge hath acted freely.

2. Lift up thyself, thou that judgeth the earth: render a reward to the proud.

3. Usquequo peccatores Domine, * usquequo peccatores gloriabuntur:
4. Effabuntur et loquentur iniquitatem: * loquentur omnes qui operantur injustitiam?
5. Populum tuum, Domine, humiliaverunt: * et hæreditatem tuam vexaverunt.
6. Viduam et advenam interfecerunt: * et pupillos occiderunt.
7. Et dixerunt: Non videbit Dominus: * nec intelliget Deus Jacob.
8. Intelligite insipientes in populo: * et stulti aliquando sapite.
9. Qui plantavit aurem, non audiet: * aut qui finxit oculum, non considerat?
10. Qui corripit gentes, non arguet: * qui docet hominem scientiam?
11. Dominus scit cogitationes hominum, * quoniam vanæ sunt.

3. How long shall the wicked, O Lord, how long shall the wicked make their boast:
4. How long shall they utter and speak wrong things: how long shall all the workers of iniquity talk?
5. Thy people, O Lord, they have brought low and they have afflicted thy inheritance.
6. They have slain the widow and the stranger: and they have murdered the fatherless.
7. And they have said: The Lord shall not see neither shall the God of Jacob understand.
8. Understand, ye senseless among the people: and you fools, be wise at last.
9. He that planted the ear, shall he not hear: or he that formed the eye, doth he not consider?
10. He that chastiseth nations, shall he not rebuke: he that teacheth man knowledge?
11. The Lord knoweth the thoughts of man, that they are vain.

12. Beatus homo, quem tu erudieris, Domine: * et de lege tua docueris eum.

13. Ut mitiges ei a diebus malis: * donec fodiatur peccatori fovea.

14. Quia non repellet Dominus plebem suam: * et hereditatem suam non derelinquet.

15. Quoadusque justitia convertatur in judicium: * et qui juxta illam omnes qui recto sunt corde.

16. Quis consurget mihi adversus malignantes? * aut quis stabit mecum adversus operantes iniquitatem?

17. Nisi quia Dominus adjuvit me: * paulo minus habitasset in inferno anima mea.

18. Si dicebam: Motus est pes meus: * misericordia tua, Domine, adjuvabat me.

19. Secundum multitudinem dolorum meorum in corde meo: * consolationes tuæ lætificaverunt animam meam.

20. Numquid adhæret

12. Blessed is the man whom thou shalt instruct, O Lord: and shalt teach him out of thy law.

13. That thou mayest give him rest from the evil days: till a pit be dug for the wicked.

14. For the Lord will not cast off his people: neither will he forsake his own inheritance.

15. Until justice be turned into judgment: and they that are near it are all the upright in heart.

16. Who shall rise up for me against the evildoers? or who shall stand with me against the workers of iniquity?

17. Unless the Lord had been my helper: my soul had almost dwelt in hell.

18. If I said: My foot is moved: thy mercy, O Lord assisted me.

19. According to the multitude of my sorrows in my heart: thy comforts have given joy to my soul.

20. Doth the seat of

tibi sedes iniquitatis: *
qui fingis laborem in
præcepto?

21. Captabunt in animam justi: * et sanguinem innocentem condemnabunt.

22. Et factus est mihi Dominus in refugium: * et Deus meus in adjutorium spei meæ.

23. Et reddet illis iniquitatem ipsorum: et in malitia eorum disperdet eos * disperdet illos Dominus Deus noster.

Ant. Captabunt in animam justi: et sanguinem innocentem condemnabunt.

V. Locuti sunt adversum me lingua dolosa. *R.* Et sermonibus odii circumdederunt me, et expugnaverunt me gratis.

Pater noster, *secreto.*
De Epistola beati Pauli Apostoli ad Hebræos.

(*cap.* IV. v)

LECTIO VII.

FEstinemus ingredi in illam requiem: ut ne

iniquity stick to theer vho framest labour in commandment?

21. They will hunt after the soul of the just: and will condemn innocent blood.

22. But the Lord is my refuge: and my God, the help of my hope.

23. And he will render to them their iniquity, and in their malice he will destroy them: yea, the Lord our God will destroy them.

Ant. They will conspire aganst the soul of the just man: and condemn innocent blood.

V. They have spoken against me with a deceitful tongue. *R.* And with words of hatred they have encompassed me, and assaulted me without cause.

Our Father, *in secret.*
Out of the Epistle of Blessed Paul the Apostle to the Hebrews.

(*ch.* IV. v)

LESSON VII.

LET us haste therefore to enter into

in idipsum quis incidat incredulitatis exemplum. Vivus est enim sermo Dei, et efficax, et penetrabilior omni gladio ancipiti: et pertingens usque ad divisionem animæ ac spiritus, compagum quoque ac medullarum, et discretor cogitationum et intentionum cordis. Et non est ulla creatura invisibilis in conspectu ejus: omnia autem nuda et aperta sunt oculis ejus, ad quem nobis sermo. Habentes ergo pontificem magnum, qui penetravit cœlis, Jesum Filium Dei, teneamus confessionem. Non enim habemus pontificem qui non possit compati infirmitatibus nostris: tentatum autem per omnia pro similitudine absque peccato.

R. Tradiderunt me in manus impiorum, et inter iniquos projecerunt me, et non pepercerunt animæ meæ: congregati sunt adversum me for-

that rest: lest any man fall into the same example of unbelief. For the word of God is living and effectual, and more piercing than any two-edged sword, and reaching unto the division of the soul and the spirit, of the joints also, and the marrow, and is a discerner of the thoughts and intents of the heart. Neither is there any creature invisible in his sight: but all things are naked and open to the eyes of him, to whom our speech is. Seeing then that we have a great high-priest that hath passed into the heavens, Jesus the Son of God: let us hold fast our confession. For we have not a high-priest who cannot have compassion on our infirmities: but one tenpted in all things like as we are, yet without sin.

R. They delivered me into the hands of the impious, and cast me out amongst the wicked, and spared not my life: the powerful gathered

tes: * Et sicut gigantes steterunt contra me. V. Alieni insurrexerunt adversum me, et fortes quæsierunt animam meam. * Et sicut gigantes.

LECTIO VIII.

Adeamus ergo cum fiducia ad thronum gratiæ: ut misericordiam consequamur, et gratiam inveniamus in auxilio opportuno. Omnis namque pontifex ex hominibus assumptus pro hominibus constituitur in iis quæ sunt ad Deum, ut offerat dona et sacrificia pro peccatis: qui condolere possit iis qui ignorant et errant: quoniam et ipse circumdatus est infirmitate: et propterea debet quamadmodum pro populo ita etiam et pro semetipso offerre pro peccatis.

R. Jesum tradidit impius summis principibus sacerdotum, et senioribus populi: * Petrus autem sequebatur eum a longe, ut videret

together against me: * And like giants they stood against me. V. Strangers have risen up against me, and the mighty have sought my life. * And like giants.

LESSON VIII.

Let us go therefore with confidence to the throne of grace: that we may obtain mercy, and find grace in seasonable aid. For every high-priest taken from among men, is appointed for men in the things that appertain to God, that he may offer up gifts and sacrifices for sins: who can have compassion on them that are ignorant, and that err: because he himself also is compassed with infirmity: and therefore he ought, as for the people, so also for himself, to offer for sins.

R. The wicked man betrayed Jesus to the chief priests and senators of the people: * but Peter followed him afar off, to see what would

finem. ℣. Adduxerunt autem eum ad Caipham principem sacerdotum, ubi Scribæ et Pharisæi convenerant * Petrus autem.

LECTIO IX.

NEC quisquam sumit sibi honorem sed qui vocatur a Deo, tanquam Aaron. Sic et Christus non semetipsum clarificavit ut pontifex fieret: sed qui locutus est ad eum: *Filius meus es tu, ego hodie genui te.* Quémadmodum et in alio loco dicit: *Tu es sacerdos in æternum secundum ordinem Melchisedech.* Qui in diebus carnis suæ preces supplicationesque ad eum, qui possit illum salvum facere a morte, cum clamore valido et lacrymis offerens, exauditus est pro sua reverentia. Et quidem cum esset Filius Dei, didicit ex iis, quæ passus est, obedientiam: et consummatus, factus est omnibus obtemperantibus sibi causa salutis æternæ appellatus a Deo Pontifex juxta ordinem Melchisedech.

be the end. ℣. And they led him to Caiphas the high-priest, where the Scribes and Pharisees were met together, * But Peter.

LESSON IX

NEither doth any man take the honour to himself, but he that is called by God, as Aaron was. So also Christ did not glorify himself to be made a high-priest, but he that said to him. *Thou art my Son, this day have I begotten thee.* As he saith also in another place: *Thou art a priest for ever according to the order of Melchisedech.* Who in the days of his flesh, offering up prayers and supplications, with a strong cry and tears, to him that was able to save him from death, was heard for his reverence: and whereas indeed he was the Son of God, he learned obedience by the things which he suffered: and being consummated, he became the cause of eternal salvation to all that obey him, called

by God a high-priest according to the order of Melchisedech.

℟. Caligaverunt oculi mei a fletu meo: * quia elongatus est a me, qui consolabatur me. Videte omnes populi, * Si est dolor similis sicut dolor meus. ℣. O vos omnes qui transitis per viam, attendite et videte. * Si est dolor. Caligaverunt.

℟. My eyes are darkened by my tears: for he is far from me that comforted me. See all ye people. * If there be sorrow like to my sorrow. ℣. O all ye that pass by the way, behold and see. * If there be. My eyes.

AT LAUDS.

Ant. Proprio Filio suo non pepercit Deus, sed pro nobis omnibus tradidit illum.

Ant. God spared not his own Son, but delivered him up for us all.

PSALM L.

MISERERE mei, Deus etc. *p.* 174.

HAVE mercy on me, etc. *p.* 174.

Ant. Proprio Filio suo non pepercit Deus, sed pro nobis omnibus tradidit illum.

Ant. God spared not his own Son, but delivered him up for us all.

Ant. Anxiatus est super me spiritus meus, in me turbatum est cor meum.

Ant. My spirit is in anguish, my heart is troubled within me.

PSALM CXLII.

DOMINE, exaudi orationem meam: auribus percipe obsecrationem meam in veritate tua: * exaudi me in tua justitia.

HEAR, O Lord, my prayer, give ear to my supplication in thy truth: hear me in thy justice.

2. Et non intres in judicium cum servo tuo: * quia non justificabitur in conspectu tuo omnis vivens.

3. Quia persecutus est inimicus animam meam: * humiliavit in terra vitam meam.

4. Collocavit me in obscuris sicut mortuos sæculi: * et anxiatus est super me spiritus meus, in me turbatum est cor meum.

5. Memor fui dierum antiquorum, meditatus sum in omnibus operibus tuis: * in factis manuum tuarum meditabar.

6. Expandi manus meas ad te: * anima mea sicut terra sine aqua tibi.

7. Velociter exaudi me, Domine: * defecit spiritus meus.

8. Non avertas faciem tuam a me: * et similis ero descendentibus in lacum.

9. Auditam fac mihi mane misericordiam tuam: * quia in te speravi.

2. And enter not into judgment with thy servant: for in thy sight no man living shall be justified.

3. For the enemy hath persecuted my soul: he hath brought down my life to the earth.

4. He hath made me to dwell in darkness, as those that have been dead of old; and my spirit is in anguish within me, my heart within me is troubled.

5. I remembered the days of old, I meditated on all thy works: I mused upon the works of thy hands.

6. I stretched forth my hands to thee: my soul is as earth without water unto thee.

7. Hear me speedily, O Lord: my spirit hath fainted away.

8. Turn not away thy face from me: lest I be like unto them that go down into the pit.

9. Cause me to hear thy mercy in the morning: for in thee have I hoped.

10. Notam fac mihi viam in qua ambulem: * quia ad te levavi animam meam.

11. Eripe me de inimicis meis, Domine, ad te confugi: * doce me facere voluntatem tuam, quia Deus meus es tu.

12. Spiritus tuus bonus deducet me in terram rectam: * propter nomen tuum, Domine, vivificabis me in æquitate tua.

13. Educes de tribulatione animam meam: * et in misericordia tua disperdes inimicos meos.

14. Et perdes omnes qui tribulant animam meam: * quoniam ego servus tuus sum.

Ant. Anxiatus est super me spiritus meus, in me turbatum est cor meum.

Ant. Ait latro ad latronem: Nos quidem digna factis recipimus; hic autem quid fecit? Memento mei, Domine, dum veneris in regnum tuum.

10. Make the way known to me wherein I should walk: for I have lifted up my soul to thee.

11. Deliver me from my enemies, O Lord, to thee have I fled: teach me to do thy will, for thou art my God.

12. Thy good spirit shall lead me into the right land: for thy name's sake, O Lord thou wilt quicken me in thy justice.

13. Thou wilt bring my soul out of troubles: and in thy mercy thou wilt destroy my enemies.

14. And thou wilt cut off all them that afflict my soul: for I am thy servant.

Ant. My spirit is in anguish, my heart is troubled within me.

Ant. One thief said to the other: We indeed receive what our actions deserve: but what has this man done? Remember me, O Lord, when thou shalt come into thy kingdom?

PSALM LXII.

DEUS, Deus meus, etc. p. 179

O GOD my God, etc. p. 179

PSALM LXVI.

DEUS misereatur etc. p. 175.

MAY God have mercy, etc. p. 175.

Ant. Ait latro ad latronem: Nos quidem digna factis recipimus; hic autem quid fecit? Memento mei, Domine, dum veneris in regnum tuum.

Ant. One thief said to the other: We indeed receive what our actions deserve; but what has this man done? Remember me, O Lord, when thou shalt come into thy kingdom.

Ant. Cum conturbata fuerit anima mea, Domine, misericordiæ memor eris.

Ant. When my soul shall be in trouble, O Lord, thou wilt be mindful of thy mercy.

Canticum Habacuc.
(*cap.* III)

The Canticle of Habacuc.
(*ch.* III)

DOMINE, audivi auditionem tuam, * et timui.

O LORD, I heard what thou madest me hear, and was afraid.

2. Domine, opus tuum * in medio annorum vivifica illud.

2. Lord, thy work in the midst of the years, bring it to life.

3. In medio annorum notum facies: * cum iratus fueris, misericordiæ recordaberis.

3. In the midst of the years thou shalt make it known: when thou art angry, thou wilt remember mercy.

4. Deus ab austro veniet, * et Sanctus de monte Pharan.

4. God will come from the south, and the Holy One from mount Pharan.

5. Operuit cœlos gloria

5. His glory covered

ejus: * et laudis ejus plena est terra.

6. Splendor ejus ut lux erit: * cornua in manibus ejus.

7. Ibi abscondita est fortitudo ejus: * ante faciem ejus ibit mors.

8. Et egredietur diabolus ante pedes ejus: * stetit, et mensus est terram.

9. Aspexit, et dissolvit Gentes: * et contriti sunt montes sæculi.

10. Incurvati sunt colles mundi, * ab itineribus æternitatis ejus.

11. Pro iniquitate vidi tentoria Æthiopiæ:* turbabuntur pelles terræ Madian.

12. Numquid in fluminibus iratus es, Domine? * aut in fluminibus furor tuus? vel in mari indignatio tua?

13. Qui ascendes super equos tuos: * et quadrigæ tuæ salvatio.

14. Suscitans suscitabis arcum tuum: jura-

the heavens: and the earth is full of his praise.

6. His brightness shall be as the light: horns are in his hands.

7. There is his strength hid: death shall go before his face.

8. And the devil shall go forth before his feet: he stood and measured the earth.

9. He beheld, and melted the nations: and the ancient mountains were crushed to pieces.

10. The hills of the world were bowed down, by the journeys of his eternity.

11. I saw the tents of Æthiopia for their iniquity: the curtains of the land of Madian shall be troubled.

12. Wast thou angry, O Lord, with the rivers? or was thy wrath upon the rivers? or thy indignation in the sea?

13. Who will ride upon thy horses, and thy chariots are salvation.

14. Thou wilt surely take up thy bow, ac-

menta tribubus, quæ locutus es.

15. Fluvios scindes terræ: viderunt te et doluerunt montes: * gurges aquarum transiit.

16. Dedit abyssus vocem suam: * altitudo manus suas levavit.

17. Sol et luna steterunt in habitaculo suo, * in luce sagittarum tuarum, ibunt in splendore fulgurantis hastæ tuæ.

18. In fremitu conculcabis terram: * et in furore obstupefacies Gentes.

19. Egressus es in salutem populi tui, * in salutem cum Christo tuo.

20. Percussisti caput de domo impii: * denudasti fundamentum ejus usque ad collum.

21. Maledixisti sceptris ejus, capiti bellatorum ejus, * venientibus ut turbo ad dispergendum me.

cording to the oaths which thou hast spoken to the tribes.

15. Thou wilt divide the rivers of the earth: the mountains saw thee and were grieved: the great body of waters passed away.

16. The deep put forth its voice: the deep lifted up its hands.

17. The sun and the moon stood still in their habitation, in the light of thy arrows, they shall go in the brightness of thy glittering spear.

18. In thy anger thou wilt tread the earth under foot: in thy wrath thou wilt astonish the nations.

19. Thou wentest forth for the salvation of thy people, for salvation with thy Christ.

20. Thou struckedst the head of the house of the wicked: thou hast laid bare his foundation even to the neck.

21. Thou hast cursed their sceptres, the head of his warriors, them that came out as a whirlwind to scatter me.

22. Exultatio eorum * sicut ejus qui devorat pauperem in abscondito.

23. Viam fecisti in mari equis tuis, * in luto aquarum multarum.

24. Audivi, et conturbatus est venter meus: * a voce contremuerunt labia mea.

25. Ingrediatur putredo in ossibus meis, * et subter me scateat.

26. Ut requiescam in die tribulationis: * ut ascendam ad populum accinctum nostrum.

27. Ficus enim non florebit: * et non erit germen in vineis.

28. Mentietur opus olivæ: * et arva non afferent cibum.

29. Abscindetur de ovili pecus: * non erit armentum in præsepibus.

30. Ego autem in Domino gaudebo: * et exultabo in Deo Jesu meo.

31. Deus Dominus fortitudo mea: * et ponet

22. Their joy was like that of him that devoureth the poor man in secret.

23. Thou madest a way in the sea for thy horses, in the mud of many waters.

24. I have heard, and my bowels were troubled: my lips trembled at the voice.

25. Let rottenness enter into my bones, and swarm under me.

26. That I may rest in the day of tribulation: that I may go up to our people that are girded.

27. For the fig-tree shall not blossom: and there shall be no spring in the vines.

28. The labour of the olive-tree shall fail: and the fields shall yield no food.

29. The flock shall be cut off from the fold: and there shall be no herd in the stalls.

30. But I will rejoice in the Lord: and I will rejoice in God my Jesus.

31. The Lord God is my strength: and he

pedes meos quasi cervorum.
  32. Et super excelsa mea deducet me victor: * in psalmis canentem.

Ant. Cum conturbata fuerit anima mea, Domine, misericordiæ memor eris.

Ant. Memento mei, Domine, dum veneris in regnum tuum.

will make my feet like the feet of harts.
  32. And he, the conqueror, will lead me upon my high places singing psalms.

Ant. When my soul shall be in trouble, O Lord, thou wilt be mindful of thy mercy.

Ant. Remember me, O Lord, when thou shalt come into thy kingdom.

PSALM CXLVII.

LAUDATE Dominum de cœlis, etc. *p.* 185.

PRAISE ye the Lord, etc. *p.* 185.

PSALM CXLIX.

CANTATE Domino, etc. *p.* 187.

SING to the Lord, etc. *p.* 187.

PSALM CL.

LAUDATE Dominum in sanctis ejus, *p.* 188.

PRAISE ye the Lord in his holy places, *p.* 188.

Ant. Memento mei, Domine, dum veneris in regnum tuum.

  V. Collocavit me in obscuris.
  R. Sicut mortuos sæculi.

Ant. Posuerunt super caput ejus causam ipsius scriptam: Jesus Nazarenus, Rex Judæorum.

Ant. Remember me O Lord, when thou shalt come into thy kingdom.

  V. He has placed me in obscure places.
  R. Like the dead of the world.

Ant. They put over his head the cause of his death, written thus: Jesus of Nazareth, King of the Jews.

Canticum Zachariæ.   *The Canticle of Zachary.*
(*Luc* i.)   (*Luke* i.)

Benedictus, etc. p. 189.   Blessed be etc., *p.* 189.

Ant. Posuerunt super caput ejus causam ipsius scriptam: Jesus Nazarenus, Rex Judæorum.

Ant. They put over his head his sentence, written thus: Jesus of Nazareth, King of the Jews.

V. Christus factus est pro nobis obediens usque ad mortem: mortem autem crucis.

V. Christ became obedient for us unto death: even the death of the cross.

Then are said the Pater noster (*in silence*), the Psalm, Miserere, *p.* 174, *and the Prayer*, Respice, *p.* 191.

MASS OF THE PRESANCTIFIED.

The Priest and Ministers come to the Altar in black vestments, without lights or incense, and prostrate themselves before it, whilst the accolytes cover it with the altar-cloth. They then go up to it and the Priest reads the following Prophecy which is read aloud at the same time by a Reader.

(*Osee* vi)   (*Osee* vi)

Hæc dicit Dominus: In tribulatione sua mane consurgent ad me. Venite, et revertamur ad Dominum: quia ipse cepit et sanabit nos: percutiet et curabit nos. Vivificabit nos post duos dies: in die tertia susci-

Thus saith the Lord: In their affliction they will rise early to me. Come, and let us return to the Lord: for he hath taken us, and he will heal us: he will strike, and he will cure us. He will revive us

tabit nos, et vivemus in conspectu ejus. Sciemus, sequemurque ut cognoscamus Dominum. Quasi diluculum præparatus est egressus ejus, et veniet quasi imber nobis temporaneus et serotinus terræ. Quid faciam tibi Ephraim? Quid faciam tibi Juda? Misericordia vestra quasi nubes matutina: et quasi ros mane pertransiens. Propter hoc dolavi in prophetis, et occidi eos in verbis oris mei: et judicia tua quasi lux egredientur. Quia misericordiam volui, et non sacrificium: et scientiam Dei plusquam holocausta.

after two days: on the third day he will raise us up, and we shall live in his sight. We shall know, and we shall follow on, that we may know the Lord. His going forth is prepared as the morning light and he will come to us as the early and the latter rain to the earth. What shall I do to thee, O Ephraim? what shall I do to thee, O Juda? Your mercy is as a morning cloud, and as the dew that goeth away in the morning. For this reason have I hewed them by the prophets, I have slain them by the words of my mouth: and thy judgments shall go forth as the light. For I desired mercy, and not sacrifice; and the knowledge of God more than holocausts.

Tractus. — Domine, audivi auditum tuum, et timui: consideravi opera tua, et expavi. V. In medio duorum animalium innotesceris: dum appropinquaverint anni cognosceris: dum advenerit tempus, ostenderis. V. In eo, dum

The Tract. — Lord, I heard what thou madest me hear, and I was afraid. I considered thy works, and trembled. V. Thou wilt appear between two animals: when thy years shall be accomplished, thou wilt make thyself

MASS OF THE PRESANCTIFIED.

conturbata fuerit anima mea, in ira misericordiæ memor eris. *V.* Deus a Libano veniet, et Sanctus de monte umbroso et condenso. *V.* Operuit cœlos majestas ejus: et laudis ejus plena est terra.

known: when the time shall come, thou wilt be manifested. *V.* When my soul shall be in trouble, thou wilt remember thy mercy even in thy wrath. *V.* God will come from Libanus, and the Holy one from the shady and dark mountain. *V.* His majesty overspread the heavens: and the earth is full of his praise

Oremus.

Let us pray.

Flectamus genua.
Levate.

Let us bend our knees.
Rise up.

Oratio.

The Prayer.

DEUS, a quo et Judas reatus sui pœnam, et confessionis suæ latro præmium sumpsit: concede nobis tuæ propitiationis effectum: ut sicut in passione sua Jesus Christus Dominus noster diversa utrisque intulit stipendia meritorum: ita nobis, ablato vetustatis errore, resurrectionis suæ gratiam largiatur. Qui tecum vivit et regnat in unitate, etc.

O GOD, from whom Judas received the punishment of his sin, and the thief the reward of his confession: grant us the effect of thy mercy: that as our Lord Jesus Christ in his passion bestowed on each a different recompense of his merits: so having destroyed the old man in us, he may give us the grace of his resurrection. Who liveth, etc.

The following Lesson is sung by the Subdeacon.

(*Exod.* xii)

IN diebus illis: Dixit Dominus ad Moysen et Aaron in terra Ægypti: Mensis iste vobis principium mensium: primus erit in mensibus anni. Loquimini ad universum cœtum filiorum Israel, et dicite eis: Decima die mensis hujus tollat unusquisque agnum per familias et domos suas. Sin autem minor est numerus, ut sufficere possit ad vescendum agnum, assumet vicinum suum qui junctus est domui suæ, juxta numerum animarum, quæ sufficere possunt ad esum agni. Erit autem agnus absque macula, masculus anniculus: juxta quem ritum tolletis et hœdum. Et servabitis eum usque ad quartam-decimam diem mensis hujus: immolabitque eum universa multitudo filiorum Israel ad vesperam. Et sument de sanguine ejus, ac ponent super utrumque postem, et in superliminaribus domo-

(*Exod.* xii)

IN those days: The Lord said to Moses and Aaron in the land of Egypt: this month shall be to you the beginning of months: it shall be the first in the months of the year. Speak ye to the whole assembly of the children of Israel, and say to them: on the tenth day of this month let every man take a lamb by their families and houses. But if the number be less than may suffice to eat the lamb, he shall take unto him his neighbour that joineth to his house, according to the number of souls which may be enough to eat the lamb. And it shall be a lamb without blemish, a male of one year: according to which rite also you shall take a kid. And you shall keep it until the fourteenth day of this month: and the whole multitude of the children of Israel shall sacrifice it in the even-

rum, in quibus comedent illum. Et edent carnes nocte illa assas igni, et azymos panes, cum lactucis agrestibus. Non comedetis ex eo crudum quid, nec coctum acqua, sed tantum assum igni: caput cum pedibus ejus et intestinis vorabitis. Nec remanebit quidquam ex eo usque mane. Si quid residuum fuerit, igne comburetis. Sic autem comedetis illum: renes vestros accingetis et calceamenta habebitis in pedibus, tenentes baculos in manibus, et comedetis festinanter. Est enim Phase, id est, tranitus Domini.

ing. And they shall take of the blood thereof, and put it upon both the side-posts, and upon the upper door-posts of the houses, wherein they shall eat it. And they shall eat the flesh that night roasted at the fire, and unleavened bread, with wild lettuce. You shall not eat thereof any thing raw, nor boiled in water, but only roasted at the fire. You shall eat the head with the feet and the entrails thereof: neither shall there remain anything of it until morning. If there shall be anything left, you shall burn it with fire. And thus you shall eat it: you shall gird your reins, and you shall have shoes on your feet, holding staves in your hands, and you shall eat in haste. For it is the *Phase*, that is, the passage, of the Lord.

Tractus. — Eripe me, Domine, ab homine malo: a viro iniquo libera me. *V.* Qui cogitaverunt malitias in corde, tota die constituebant prælia. *V.* Acuerunt linguas suas sicut serpentis: venenum aspi-

Tract. — Rescue me, O Lord, from the wicked man: from the unjust man deliver me. *V.* They that have thought mischief in their hearts made war against me all the day. *V.* They sharpened

dum, sub labiis eorum. *V.* Custodi me, Domine de manu peccatoris: et ab hominibus iniquis libera me. *V.* Qui cogitaverunt supplantare gressus meos: absconderunt superbi laqueum mihi. *V.* Et funes extenderunt in laqueum pedibus meis: juxta iter scandalum posuerunt mihi. *V.* Dixi Domino, Deus meus es tu: exaudi Domine vocem orationis meæ. *V.* Domine, Domine virtus salutis meæ, obumbra caput meum in die belli. *V.* Ne tradas me a desiderio meo peccatori: cogitaverunt adversus me: ne derelinquas me, ne unquam exaltentur. *V.* Caput circuitus eorum: labor labiorum ipsorum operiet eos. *V.* Verumtamen justi confitebuntur nomini tuo: et habitabunt recti cum vultu tuo.

their tongues like that of a serpent: the venom of asps is under their lips. *V.* Keep me, O Lord, out of the sinner's hands: and from unjust men deliver me. *V.* Who have designed to supplant my steps, the proud have laid a hidden snare for me. *V.* And they have stretched out ropes for a snare for my feet: they have made a stumbling block for me near the way. *V.* I said to the Lord, thou art my God: hear, O Lord, the voice of my prayer. *V.* O Lord, O Lord, the strength of my salvation, do thou overshadow my head in the day of battle. *V.* Deliver me not to the sinner against my desire: they have formed designs against me: forsake me not, that they may never be exalted *V.* The chief of those that are round me: the works of their lips will overwhelm them. But the just shall praise thy name, and the righteous shall dwell in thy presence.

MASS OF THE PRESANCTIFIED.

Passio Domini nostri Jesu Christi secundum Joannem. *(cap.* xviii)

IN illo tempore: Egressus est Jesus cum discipulis suis trans torrentem Cedron, ubi erat hortus, in quem introivit ipse et discipuli ejus. Sciebat autem et Judas qui tradebat eum, locum: quia frequenter Jesus convenerat illuc cum discipulis suis. Judas ergo cum accepisset cohortem, et a Pontificibus et Pharisæis ministros, venit illuc cum laternis, et facibus, et armis. Jesus itaque sciens omnia, quæ ventura erant super eum, processit, et dixit eis: ✠ Quem quæritis? *C.* Responderunt ei: *S.* Jesum Nazarenum. *C.* Dicit eis Jesus: ✠ Ego sum. *C.* Stabat autem et Judas, qui tradebat eum, cum ipsis. Ut ergo dixit eis: Ego sum: Abierunt retrorsum, et ceciderunt in terram. Iterum ergo interrogavit eos: ✠ Quem quæritis? *C.* Illi autem dixerunt. *S.* Jesum Nazarenum. *C.* Re-

The Passion of our Lord Jesus Christ, according to St. John. *(c.*xviii)

AT that time: Jesus went forth with his disciples over the brook Cedron, where there was a gard/en, into which he entered with his disciples. Now Judas also, who betrayed him' knew the place: because Jesus had often resorted thither, together with his disciples. Judas therefore having received a band of men and servants from the chief priests and the Pharisees, cometh thither with lanterns, and torches, and weapons. Jesus therefore knowing all things that should come upon him, went forth and said to them: Whom seek ye? They answered him: Jesus of Nazareth. Jesus said to them: I am he. And Judas also, who betrayed him, stood with them. As soon then as he had said to them: I am he: they went backward, and fell to the ground.

spondit Jesus: ✠ Dixi vobis quia ego sum. Si ergo me quæritis, sinite hos abire. *C.* Ut impleretur sermo, quem dixit: Quia quos dedisti mihi, non perdidi ex eis quemquam. Simon ergo Petrus habens gladium, eduxit eum: et percussit Pontificis servum: et abscidit auriculam ejus dexteram. Erat autem nomen servo Malchus. Dixit ergo Jesus Petro: ✠ Mitte gladium tuum in vaginam. Calicem, quem dedit mihi Pater, non bibam illum? *C.* Cohors ergo, et tribunus et ministri Judæorum comprehenderunt Jesum, et ligaverunt eum: et adduxerunt eum ad Annam primum, erat enim socer Caiphæ, qui erat Pontifex anni illius. Erat autem Caiphas, qui consilium dederat Judæis; quia expedit unum hominem mori pro populo. Sequebatur autem Jesum Simon Petrus, et alius discipulus. Discipulus autem ille erat notus

Again therefore ha said to them: Whom seek ye? And they said: Jesus of Nazareth. Jesus answered, I have told you, that I am he. If therefore you seek me, let these go their way. That the word might be fulfilled which he said. Of them whom thou hast given me, I have not lost any one. Then Simon Peter having a sword, drew it, and struck the servant of the high-priest, and cut off his right ear. And the name of the servant was Malchus. Then Jesus said to Peter. Put up thy sword into the scabbard. The chalice which my Father hath given me, shall I not drink it? Then the band, and the tribune, and the servants of the Jews took Jesus, and bound him: and they led him away to Annas first, for he was father-in-law to Caiphas, who was the high-priest of that year. Now Caiphas was he who had given

Pontifici, et introivit cum Jesu in atrium Pontificis. Petrus autem stabat ad ostium foris. Exivit ergo discipulus alius, qui erat notus Pontifici, et dixit ostiariæ: et introduxit Petrum. Dixit ergo Petro ancilla ostiaria: *S.* Numquid et tu ex discipulis es hominis istius? *C.* Dicit ille: *S.* Non sum *C.* Stabant autem servi et ministri ad pruinas quia frigus erat, et calefaciebant se. Erat autem cum eis et Petrus stans, et calefaciens se. Pontifex ergo interrogavit Jesum de discipulis suis et de doctrina ejus. Respondit ei Jesus ✠ Ego palam locutus sum mundo: ego semper docui in synagoga, et in templo quo omnes Judæi conveniunt et in occulto locutus sum nihil. Quid me interrogas? interroga eos qui audierunt quid locutus sum ipsis: Ecce hi sciunt quæ dixerim ego. *C.* Hæc autem cum dixisset, unus assistens ministrorum

counsel to the Jews: that it was expedient that one man should die for the people. And Simon Peter followed Jesus, and so did another disciple. And that disciple was known to the high priest, and went in with Jesus into the palace of the high-priest. But Peter stood at the door without. Then the other disciple, who was known to the high-priest, went out, and spoke to the porteress, and brought in Peter. And the maid that was porteress saith to Peter: Art not thou also one of this man's disciples? He saith: I am not. Now the servants and officers stood at the fire of coals, because it was cold, and warmed themselves. And with them was Peter also standing, and warming himself. The high-priest then asked Jesus of his disciples, and of his doctrine. Jesus answered him: I have spoken openly to the world: I have always taught in

dedit alapam Jesu, dicens: *S.* Sic respondes Pontifici? *C.* Respondit ei Jesus: ✠ Si male locutus sum testimonium perhibe de malo: Si autem bene, quid me cædis? *C.* Et misit eum Annas ligatum ad Caipham Pontificem. Erat autem Simon Petrus stans et calefaciens se. Dixerunt ergo ei. *S.* Numquid et tu ex discipulis ejus es? *C.* Negavit ille, et dixit: *S.* Non sum. Dicit ei unus ex servis Pontificis, cognatus ejus, cujus abscidit Petrus auriculam: *C.* Nonne ego te vidi in horto cum illo? *S.* Iterum ergo negavit Petrus: et statim gallus cantavit. Adducunt ergo Jesum a Caipha in prætorium. Erat autem mane; et ipsi non introierunt in prætorium, ut non contaminarentur, sed ut manducarent Pascha. Exivit ergo Pilatus ad eos foras, et dixit: *S.*Quam accusationem affertis adversus hominem hunc? *C.* Responderunt et dixerunt ei: *S.* Si non

the synagogue, and in the temple whither all the Jews resort: and in secret I have spoken nothing. Why askest thou me? ask them who have heard what I have spoken to them: behold they know what things I have said. And when he had said these things, one of the officers standing by gave Jesus a blow, saying: Answerest thou the high-priest so? Jesus answered him: If I have spoken evil, give testimony of the evil: but if well, why strikest thou me? And Annas sent him bound to Caiphas the high-priest. And Simon Peter was standing warming himself. They said therefore to him: Art not thou also one of his disciples? He denied it, and said: I am not. One of the servants of the high-priest (a kinsman to him whose ear Peter cut off) saith to him: Did not I see thee in the garden with him? Then Peter again denied: and im-

esset hic malefactor, non tibi tradidissemus eum: *C.* Dixit ergo eis Pilatus: *S.* Accipite eum vos, et secundum legem vestram judicate eum. *C.* Dixerunt ergo ei Judæi: *S.* Nobis non licet interficere quemquam. *C.* Ut sermo Jesu impleretur, quem dixit, significans qua morte esset moriturus. Introivit ergo iterum in prætorium Pilatus, et vocavit Jesum, et dixit ei: *S.* Tu es Rex Judæorum? *C.* Respondit Jesus: ✠ A temetipso hoc dicis, an alii dixerunt tibi de me? *C.* Respondit Pilatus: *S.* Numquid ego Judæus sum? Gens tua, et Pontifices tradiderunt te mihi: Quid fecisti? *C.* Respondit Jesus: ✠ Regnum meum non est de hoc mundo. Si ex hoc mundo esset regnum meum, ministri mei adhuc decertarent ut non traderer Judæis. Nunc autem regnum meum non est hinc. *C.* Dixit itaque ei Pilatus. Ergo rex es tu. Respondit Jesus: ✠ Tu dicis quia rex sum ego.

mediately the cock crew. Then they led Jesus from Caiphas to the governor's hall. And it was morning: and they went not into the hall, that they might not be defiled, but that they might eat the Pasch. Pilate therefore went out to them, and said: What accusation bring you against this man? They answered and said to him: If he were not a malefactor we would not have delivered him unto thee. Pilate then said to them: Take him you, and judge him according to your law. The Jews therefore said to him: It is not lawful for us to put any man to death. That the word of Jesus might be fulfilled, which he said, signifying what death he should die. Pilate therefore went into the hall again, and called Jesus, and said to him: Art thou the king of the Jews? Jesus answered: Sayest thou this thing of thyself, or have others told it thee

Ego in hoc natus sum, et ad hoc veni in mundum, ut testimonium perhibeam veritati. Omnis qui est ex veritate, audit vocem meam. *C.* Dicit ei Pilatus: *S.* Quid est veritas? *C.* Et cum hoc dixisset, iterum exivit ad Iudæos, et dicit eis: *S.* Ego nullam invenio in eo causam. Est autem consuetudo vobis ut unum dimittam vobis in pascha: vultis ergo dimittam vobis regem Judæorum? *C.* Clamaverunt ergo rursum omnes, dicentes: *S.* Non hunc, sed Barabbam. *C.* Erat autem Barabbas latro. Tunc ergo apprehendit Pilatus Jesum, et flagellavit. Et milites plectentes coronam de spinis, imposuerunt capiti ejus: et veste purpurea circumdederunt eum. Et veniebant ad eum, et dicebant: *S.* Ave rex Judæorum: *C.* Et dabant ei alapas. Exivit ergo iterum Pilatus foras, et dicit eis *S.* Ecce adduco vobis eum foras, ut cognoscatis quia nullam invenio in eo causam.

of me: Pilate answered: Am I a Jew? Thy own nation and the chief priests have delivered thee up to me: what hast thou done? Jesus answered: My kingdom is not of this world. If my kingdom were of this world my servants would certainly strive that I should not be delivered to the Jews: but now my kingdom is not from hence. Pilate therefore said to him: art thou a king then? Jesus answered: Thou sayest that I am a king. For this was I born, and for this came I into the world, that I should give testimony to the truth. Every one that is of the truth, heareth my voice. Pilate saith to him: What is truth. And when he had said this, he went out again to the Jews, and saith to them: I find no cause in him. But you have a custom that I should release one unto you at the pasch; will you therefore that I release unto you the king of the

C. (Exivit ergo Jesus portans coronam spineam et purpureum vestimentum.) Et dicit eis: S. Ecce homo. C. Cum ergo vidissent eum Pontifices, et ministri, clamabant, dicentes: S. Crucifige, crucifige eum. C. Dicit eis Pilatus: S. Accipite eum vos, et crucifigite: ego enim non invenio in eo causam. C. Responderunt ei Judæi: S. Nos legem habemus, et secundum legem debet mori, quia Filium Dei se fecit. C. Cum ergo audisset Pilatus hunc sermonem: magis timuit. Et ingressus est prætorium iterum: et dixit ad Jesum: S. Unde es tu? C. Jesus autem responsum non dedit ei. Dicit ergo ei Pilatus: S. Mihi non loqueris? Nescis, quia potestatem habeo crucifigere te, et potestatem habeo dimittere te? C. Respondit Jesus: *Non haberes potestatem adversum me ullam, nisi tibi datum esset desuper. Propterea qui me tradidit tibi, majus peccatum habet. C. Et exin-

Jews? Then cried they all again, saying: Not this man but Barabbas. Now Barabbas was a robber. Then therefore Pilate took Jesus and scourged him. And the soldiers platting a crown of thorns, put it upon his head: and they put on him a purple garment. And they came to him, and said: Hail king of the Jews: and they gave him blows. Pilate therefore went forth again, and saith to them: Behold I bring him forth to you, that you may know that I find no cause in him. (So Jesus came forth bearing the crown of thorns, and the purple garment.) And he saith to them: Behold the man. When the chief priests therefore and the officers had seen him, they cried out, saying: Crucify him, crucify him. Pilate saith to them: Take him you, and crucify him; for I find no cause in him. The Jews answered him: We have

de quærebat Pilatus dimittere eum. Judæi autem clamabant, dicentes: *S.* Si hunc dimittis, non es amicus Cæsaris. Omnis enim qui se regem facit contradicit Cæsari. *C.* Pilatus autem cum audisset hos sermones, adduxit foras Jesum: et sedit pro tribunali, in loco qui dicitur Lithostrotos, Hebraice autem Gabbatha. Erat autem parasceve paschæ, hora quasi sexta, et dicit Judæis: *S.* Ecce rex vester. Illi autem clamabant: *S.* Tolle, tolle, crucifige eum. *C.* Dicit eis Pilatus: *S.* Regem vestrum crucifigam? *C.* Responderunt pontifices: *S.* Non habemus regem nisi Cæsarem. *C.* Tunc ergo tradidit eis illum ut crucifigeretur. Susceperunt autem Jesum, et eduxerunt, et bajulans sibi crucem exivit in eum, qui dicitur Calvariæ locum, Hebraice autem Golgotha: ubi crucifixerunt eum, et cum eo alios duos, hinc et hinc, medium autem Jesum.

a law, and according to the law he ought to die, because he made himself the Son of God. When Pilate therefore had heard this saying, he feared the more. And he entered into the hall again; and he said to Jesus: Whence art thou? But Jesus gave him no answer. Pilate therefore saith to him: Speakest thou not to me? knowest thou not that I have power to crucify thee, and I have power to release thee? Jesus answered: Thou shouldest not have any power against me, unless it were given thee from above. Therefore he that hath delivered me to thee hath the greater sin. And from thenceforth Pilate sought to release him. But the Jews cried out, saying: If thou release this man, thou art not Cæsar's friend. For whosoever maketh himself a king, speaketh against Cæsar. Now when Pilate had heard these words, he brought

MASS OF THE PRESANCTIFIED. 279

Scripsit autem et titulum Pilatus: et posuit super crucem. Erat autem scriptum: *Jesus Nazarenus, Rex Judæorum.* Hunc ergo titulum multi Judæorum legerunt, quia prope civitatem erat locus, ubi crucifixus est Jesus. Et erat scriptum Hebraice, Græce, et Latine. Dicebant ergo Pilato pontifices Judæorum, *S.* Noli scribere, rex Judæorum: sed quia ipse dixit: rex sum Judæorum. *C.* Respondit Pilatus: *S.* Quod scripsi, scripsi. *C.* Milites ergo cum crucifixissent eum, acceperunt vestimenta ejus (et fecerunt quatuor partes: unicuique militi partem) et tunicam. Erat autem tunica inconsutilis, desuper contexta per totum. Dixerunt ergo ad invicem: *S.* Non scindamus eam sed sortiamur de illa cujus sit. *C.* Ut scriptura impleretur dicens: Partiti sint vestimenta mea sibi: et in vestem meam miserunt sortem. Et milites quidem hæc fecerun. Stabant autem Jesus forth: and sat down in the judgment-seat, in the place that is called Lithostrotos, and in Hebrew Gabbatha. And it was the parasceve of the pasch, about the sixth hour, and he saith to the Jews: Behold your king. But they cried out: Away with him, away with him, crucify him. Pilate saith to them: Shall I crucify your king? The chief priest answered: We have no king but Cæsar. Then therefore he delivered him to them to be crucified. And they took Jesus and led him forth. And bearing his own cross, he went forth to that place which is called Calvary, but in Hebrew Golgotha. Where they crucified him, and with him two others one on each side, and Jesus in the midst. And Pilate wrote a title also: and he put it upon the cross. And the writing was: JESUS OF NAZARETH THE KING OF THE JEWS. This title there-

juxta crucem Jesu mater ejus, et soror matris ejus Maria Cleophæ, et Maria Magdalene. Cum vidisset ergo Jesus matrem, et discipulum stantem quem diligebat, dicit matri suæ : ✠ Mulier, ecce filius tuus. Deinde dicit discipulo: ✠ Ecce mater tua. *C.* Et ex illa hora accepit eam discipulus in sua. Postea sciens Jesus, quia omnia consummata sunt, ut consummaretur scriptura, dixit : ✠ Sitio. *C.* Vas ergo erat positum aceto plenum. Illi autem spongiam plenam aceto hyssopo circumponentes, obtulerunt ori ejus. Cum ergo accepisset Jesus acetum, dixit: ✠ Consummatum est. Et inclinato capite, tradidit spiritum.

fore many of the Jews did read, because the place where Jesus was crucified, was righ to the city. And it was written in Hebrew, in Greek, and in Latin. Then the chief priest of the Jews said to Pilate: Write not, the King of the Jews: but that he said, I am the king of the Jews. Pilate answered : What I have written, I have written. Then the soldiers, when they had crucified him, took his garments (and they made four parts, to every soldier a part) and also his coat. Now the coat was without seam, woven from the top throughout. They said then one to another: Let us not cut it, but let us cast lots for it whose it shall be: that he scripture might be fulfilled which saith: *They have parted my garments among them: and upon my vesture they have cast lots.* And the soldiers indeed did these things. Now there stood by the cross of Jesus, his mother, and his mother's sister. Mary of Cleophas and Mary Magdalen. When Jesus therefore saw his mother, and the disciple standing, whom he loved, he saith to his mother, Woman, behold thy son. After that, he saith to

the disciple: Behold thy mother. And from that hour the disciple took her to his own. Afterwards Jesus knowing that all things were now accomplished, that the scripture might be fulfilled, said: I thirst. Now there was a vessel set there full of vinegar. And they put a sponge full of vinegar about hyssop, and put it to his mouth. When Jesus therefore had taken the vinegar, he said: It is consummated. And bowing his head, he gave up the ghost.

Here all kneel and pause a little, to meditate on the redemption of mankind.

Judæi ergo (quoniam parasceve erat) ut non remanerent in cruce corpora sabbato (erat enim magnus dies ille sabbati), rogaverunt Pilatum ut frangerentur eorum crura et tollerentur. Venerunt ergo milites: et primi quidem fregerunt crura, et alterius qui crucifixus est eum eo. Ad Jesum autem cum venissent ut viderunt eum jam mortuum, non fregerunt ejus crura. Sed unus militum lancea latus ejus aperuit et continuo exivit sanguis et aqua. Et qui vidit, testimonium perhibuit, et verum est testimomium ejus, Et ille scit quia vera dicit: ut et vos creda-

Then the Jews (because it was the parasceve) that the bodies might not remain upon the cross on the sabbath day (for that was a great sabbath day) besought Pilate that their legs might be broken, and that they might be taken away. The soldiers therefore came, and they broke the legs of the first, and of the other that was crucified with him. But after they were come to Jesus, when they saw that he was already dead, they did not break his legs. But one of the soldiers opened his side with a spear, and immediately there came out blood and water. And

tis. Facta sunt enim hæc ut scriptura impleretur: Os non comminuetis ex eo. Et iterum alia scriptura dicit: Videbunt in quem transfixerunt.

he that saw it gave testimony: and his testimony is true. And he knoweth that he saith true: that you also may believe. For these things were done that the Scripture might be fulfilled: *You shall not break a bone of him.* And again another Scripture saith: *They shall look on him whom they pierced.*

Here Munda cor meum *is said, as p. 58, but the blessing is not asked, nor the lights used, as at other Gospels, nor does the Priest kiss the book.*

Post hæc autem rogavit Pilatum Joseph ab Arimathea (eo quod esset discipulus Jesu, occultus autem propter metum Judæorum) ut tolleret corpus Jesu. Et permisit Pilatus. Venit ergo, et tulit corpus Jesu. Venit autem et Nicodemus, qui venerat ad Jesum nocte primum, ferens mixturam myrræ et aloes quasi libras centum. Acceperunt ergo corpus Jesu et ligaverunt illud linteis cum aromatibus, sicut mos est Judæis sepelire. Erat autem in loco, ubi crucifixus est, hortus: et in horto monumentum novum, in

And after these things, Joseph of Arimathea (because he was a disciple of Jesus, but secretly, for fear of the Jews) besought Pilate that he might take away the body of Jesus. And Pilate gave him leave. He came therefore and took away the body of Jesus. And Nicodemus also came, he who at the first came to Jesus by night, bringing a mixture of myrrh and aloes, about a hundred pound weight. They took therefore the body of Jesus, and wound it in linen cloths with the spices, as the manner of the Jews is to bury.

quo nondum quisquam positus erat. Ibi ergo propter parasceven Judæorum, quia juxta erat monumentum, posuerunt Jesum.

Now there was a garden in the place, where he was crucified: and in the garden a new sepulchre. wherein no man yet had been laid. There, therefore, because of the parasceve of the Jews, they laid Jesus, because the sepulchre was nigh at hand.

Then the Priest at the Epistle corner says the following prayers.

OREMUS dilectissimi nobis, pro ecclesia sancta Dei: ut eam Deus et Dominus noster pacificare, adunare, et custodire dignetur toto orbe terrarum: subjiciens ei principatus, et potestates: detque nobis quietam et tranquillam vitam degentibus glorificare Deum Patrem omnipotentem.

LET us pray, beloved brethren, for the holy church of God: that our God and Lord would be pleased to give it peace, maintain it in union, and preserve it over the earth: subjecting to it the princes and potentates of the world: and grant us that live in peace and tranquillity, grace to glorify God the Father Almighty.

Oremus.

Flectamus genua.

Levate.

Let us pray.

Let us bend our knees.

Rise up.

OMNIPOTENS sempiterne Deus, qui gloriam tuam omnibus in Christo gentibus revelasti: custodi opera misericordiæ tuæ: ut ecclesia tua toto orbe diffusa,

ALmighty and everlasting God, who by Christ hast revealed thy glory to all nations: preserve the works of thy mercy: that thy church spread over all

stabili fide in confessione tui nominis perseveret. Per eumdem Dominum nostrum Jesum Christum Filium tuum. Qui. R. Amen.

OREMUS et pro beatissimo Papa nostro N. ut Deus et Dominus noster, qui elegit eum in ordine episcopatus, salvum atque incolumem custodiat ecclesiæ suæ sanctæ, ad regendum populum sanctum Dei.

Oremus.
Flectamus genua.
Levate.

OMNIPOTENS sempiterne Deus, cujus judicio universa fundantur: respice propitius ad preces nostras, et electum nobis antistitem tua pietate conserva ut christiana plebs, quæ te gubernatur auctore, sub tanto pontifice, credulitatis suæ meritis augeatur. Per Dominum nostrum Jesum Christum. R. Amen.

OREMUS, et pro omnibus episcopis, pres-

the world, may persevere with a constant faith in the confession of thy name. Through the same our Lord Jesus Christ. R. Amen.

LET us pray also for our holy Father Pope N. that our Lord God, who elected him to the order of the episcopacy, may preserve him in health and safety for the good of his holy church, to govern the holy people of God.

Let us pray.
Let us kneel.
Rise up.

ALMIGHTY and everlasting God, by whose judgment all things are founded: mercifully regard our prayers, and by thy goodness preserve our bishop chosen for us: that the christian people that are governed by thy authority, may increase the merit of their faith under so great a prelate. Through. R. Amen.

LET us pray also for all bishops, priests,

MASS OF THE PRESANCTIFIED.

sum Christum Filium tuum. R. Amen.

OREMUS, dilectissimi nobis, Deum Patrem omnipotentem, ut cunctis mundum purget erroribus: morbos auferat: famem depellat: aperiat carceres: vincula dissolvat: peregrinantibus reditum, infirmantibus sanitatem, navigantibus portum salutis indulgeat.
 Oremus
 Flectamus genua.
 Levate.

OMnipotens, sempiterne Deus, mœstorum consolatio: laborantium fortitudo: perveniat ad te preces de quacumque tribulatione clamantium: ut omnes sibi in necessitatibus suis misericordiam tuum gaudeant adfuisse. Per Dominum nostrum. Jesum Christum Filiuum tuum. Qui tecum. R. Amen.

OREMUS et pro hæreticis et schismaticis: ut Deus et Dominus noster eruat eos ab erroribus universis et ad

the society of thy adopted children. Through our Lord. R. Amen.

LET us pray, beloved brethren, to God the Father Almighty, that he would purge the world of all errors: cure diseases: drive away famine: open prisons, break chains: grant a safe return to travellers: health to tke sick and a secure haven to such as are at sea.
 Let us pray.
 Let us bend our knees
 Rise up.

ALmighty and everlasting God, the comfort of the afflicted, and the strength of those that labour: let the prayers of those that call upon thee in any trouble, be heard by thee: that all may with joy find the effects of thy mercy in their necessities. Through our Lord. R. Amen.

LET us pray also for heretics and schismatics: that our Lord God would be pleased to deliver them from all

sanctam Matrem Ecclesiam Catholicam atque Apostolicam revocare dignetur.
Oremus.
Flectamus genua
Levate.

Omnipotens, sempiterne Deus, qui salvas omnes, et neminem vis perire: respice ad animas diabolica fraude deceptas: ut omni hæretica pravitate deposita, errantium corda resipiscant et ad veritatis tuæ redeant unitatem. Per Dominum nostrum, etc. Filium tuum. Qui tecum. R. Amen.

Oremus et pro perfidis Judæis: ut Deus et Dominus noster auferat velamen de cordibus eorum: ut et ipsi agnoscant Jesum Christum Dominum nostrum. Filium tuum.

Omnipotens sempiterne Deus, qui etiam Judaicam perfidiam a tua misericordia non repellis exaudi preces nostras quæ pro illius populi obcæcatione deferimus ut agnita veri-

their errors: and recall them to our holy Mother the Catholic and Apostolic Church.
Let us pray.
Let us bend our knees
Rise up.

Almighty and everlasting God, who savest all, and wilt have no one perish: look on the souls that are seduced by the deceit of the devil: that the hearts of those that err, having deposed all heretical malice, may repent and return to the unity of thy truth. Through our Lord, ecc.
R. Amen.

Let us pray also for the perfidious Jews: that our Lord God would withdraw the veil from their hearts: that they also may acknowlege our Lord Jesus Christ.

Almighty and everlasting God, who deniest not thy mercy even to the perfidious Jews: hear our prayers, which we pour forth for the blindness of that people, that acknow-

tatis tuæ luce, quæ Christus est, a suis tenebris eruantur. Per eundem Dominum nostrum.

R. Amen.

OREMUS et pro Paganis: ut Deus omnipotens auferat iniquitatem a cordibus eorum: ut relictis idolis suis, convertantur ad Deum vivum et verum, et unicum Filium ejus Jesum Christum Deum et Dominum nostrum.

Oremus.
Flectamus genua.
Levate.

OMnipotens sempiterne Deus, qui non mortem peccatorum, sed vitam semper inquiris: suscipe propitius orationem nostram, et libera eos ab idolorum cultura et aggrega ecclesiæ tuæ sanctæ, ad laudem et gloriam nominis tui. Per Dominum nostrum.

R. Amen.

ledging the light of thy truth, which is Christ, they may be brought out of their darkness. Through the same Lord. R. Amen.

LET us pray also for the Pagans: that Almighty God would take iniquity out of their hearts: that by quitting their idols, they may be converted to the true and living God, and his only Son Jesus Christ, our God and Lord.

Let us pray.
Let us bend our knees.
Rise up.

ALmighty and everlasting God, who seekest not the death, but the life of sinners: mercifully hear our prayers, and deliver them from the worship of idols: and for the praise and glory of thy name admit them into thy holy church. Through our Lord.

R. Amen.

After reading the foregoing prayers, the Priest lays aside his Chasuble and receiving the Cross, covered

19

with a veil, from the Deacon, goes with the Deacon and Subdeacon to the Epistle corner of the Altar, where he uncovers the top of the Cross and shows it to the people, singing with the Deacon and Subdeacon the following Anthem:

Ant. Ecce lignum crucis, in quo salus mundi pependit.

Ant. Behold the wood of the cross, on which hung the salvation of the world.

To which the Choir answers.

Venite adoremus.

Come, let us adore.

Then the Priest advances to the front corner, where he uncovers the right arm of the Cross, and elevates it, singing a second time, Ecce lignum, *but a little louder; the others singing and kneeling. Lastly he goes to the middle of the Altar, and uncovers the whole cross, singing still louder, a third time,* Ecce lignum, *etc., and the Choir answers as before. After which he carries it to a place prepared before the Altar, where he first kisses it, and then all the clergy and laity, two and two, kneeling thrice on both knees, and kissing the feet of the crucifix.*

During this ceremony, two chanters in the middle of the Choir sing the following verses, wherein the Redeemer of the world is represented as reproaching the Jews for their ingratitude.

POPULE meus quid feci tibi? aut in quo contristavi te? Responde mihi.

V. Quia eduxi te de terra Ægypti: parasti crucem Salvatori tuo.

MY people, what have I done to thee? or in what have I grieved thee? Answer me.

V. Because I brought thee out of the land of Egypt: thou hast prepared a cross for thy Saviour.

One side of choir sings:

Agios o Theos.	Holy God.

The other side answers:

Sanctus Deus.	Holy God.

The first side:

Agios ischyros.	Holy and strong God.

The second side:

Sanctus fortis.	Holy and strong God.

The first side:

Agios athanatos, eleison imas.	Holy and immortal God, have mercy upon us.

The second side.

Sanctus immortalis, miserere nobis.	Holy and immortal God, have mercy upon us.

After this, two of the second side sing:

V. Quia eduxi te per desertum quadraginta annis: et manna cibavi te, et introduxi te in terram satis bonam, parasti crucem Salvatori tuo.	V. Because I have led thee through the desert forty years: and fed thee with manna, and brought thee into an excellent land thou hast prepared a cross for thy Saviour.

Then Agios o Theos *is repeated as above, and two of the first side sing:*

V. Quid ultra debui facere tibi, et non feci? Ego quidem plantavi te vineam meam speciosis-	V. What more could I do for thee, that I have not done? I planted thee a most beautiful

simam: et tu facta es mihi nimis amara: aceto namque sitim meam potasti: et lancea perforasti latus Salvatori tuo.

vine: and thou hast proved exceeding bitter to me: for in my thirst thou gavest me vinegar to drink: and with a spear thou hast pierced the side of thy Saviour.

Agios ò Theos *is repeated as before.*

The following Responses are sung alternately by two chanters on each side of the choir, both sides repeating V. Popule meus, *p.* 290, *after each verse.*
Two of the second side:

V. Ego propter te flagellavi Ægyptum cum primogenitis suis: et tu me flagellatum tradidisti.

V. For thy sake I have scourged Egypt with her first born: and thou hast delivered me to be scourged.

Both sides repeat Popule meus.
Two of the first side:

V. Ego eduxi te de Egypto, demerso Pharaone in mare Rubrum: et tu me tradidisti principibus sacerdotum.

V. I brought thee out of Egypt, having drowned Pharaoh in the Red Sea: and thou hast delivered me over to the chief priests.

Both sides repeat Popule meus.
Two of the second side:

V. Ego ante te aperui mare: et tu aperuisti lancea latus meum.

V. I opened the sea before thee: and thou with a spear hast opened my side.

Both sides repeat Popule meus.
Two of the first side:

V. Ego ante te præivi in columna nubis: et tu

V. I went before thee in a pillar of a cloud:

ne duxisti ad prætorium Pilati.

and thou hast brought me to the palace of Pilate.

Both sides repeat Popule meus.
Two of the second side:

V. Ego te pavi manna per desertum: et tu me cecidisti alapis et flagellis.

V. I fed thee with manna in the desert: and thou hast beaten me with buffets and scourges.

Both sides repeat Popule meus.
Two of the first side:

V. Ego te potavi aqua salutis de petra: et tu me potasti felle et aceto.

V. I gave thee wholesome water to drink out of the rock: and thou hast given me gall and vinegar.

Both sides repeat Popule meus.
Two of the second side:

V. Ego propter te Chananæorum reges percussi: et tu percussisti arundine caput meum.

V. For thy sake I struck the kings of the Chananites: and thou hast struck my head with a reed.

Both sides repeat Popule meus.
Two of the first side:

V. Ego dedi tibi sceptrum regale: et tu dedisti capiti meo spineam coronam.

V. I gave thee a royal sceptre: and thou has given me a crowned thorns.

Both sides repeat Popule meus.
Two of the second side:

V. Ego te exaltavi magna virtute: et tu

V. I have exalted thee with great strength

me suspendisti in patibulo crucis.

and thou hast hanged me on the gibbet of the cross.

Both sides repeat Popule meus, *and then sing the following Antiphon:*

CRUCEM tuam adoramus, Domine: et sanctam resurrectionem tuam laudamus, et glorificamus: ecce enim propter lignum venit gaudium in universo mundo. *Psalmus.* Deus misereatur nostri, et benedicat nobis: illuminet vultum suum super nos, et misereatur nostri. *Ant.* Crucem tuam.

We adore thy cross, O Lord: and we praise and glorify thy holy resurrection, for by the wood of the cross the whole world is filled with joy. *The Psalm.* Let God have mercy on us, and bless us: let his countenance enlighten us: and let him have mercy on us. We adore.

After this is sung ✠ Crux fidelis *and* * Dulce lignum, *which are alternately repeated after each verse of the succeeding hymn,* PANGE LINGUA.

✠ CRUX fidelis inter omnes!
Arbor una nobilis:

Nulla silva talem profert
Fronde, flore, germine.

* DULCE lignum, dulces clavos,
Dulce pondus sustinet.

O Faithful cross! O noblest tree!
In all our woods there is none like thee·

No earthly groves, no shady bow'rs
Produce such leaves, such fruit, such flow'rs.

Sweet are the nails, and sweet the wood,
That bears a weight so sweet and good.

MASS OF THE PRESANCTIFIED.

HYMNUS.	THE HYMN.
PANGE, lingua, gloriosi Lauream certaminis.	SING, O my tongue, devoutly sing, The glorious laurels of our king.
Et super crucis trophæo	Sing the triumphant victory
Dic triumphum nobilem: Qualiter Redemptor orbis Immolatos vicerit. ✠ Crux fidelis. De parentis protoplasti	Gain'd on a cross erected high; Where man's Redeemer yields his breath, And dying conquers hell and death. With pity our Creator saw
Fraude Factor condolens. Quando pomi noxialis	His noble work transgress his law, When our first parents rashly eat
In necem morsu ruit;	The fatal tree's forbidden meat:
Ipse lignum tunc notavit, Damna ligni ut solveret. * Dulce lignum. Hoc opus nostræ salutis,	He then resolv'd the cross' wood Should make that wood's sad damage good. By this wise method God design'd,
Ordo depoposcerat;	From sin and death to save mankind;
Multiformis proditoris	Superior art with love combines,
Ars ut artem falleret:	And arts of Satan countermines:
Ut medelam ferret inde,	And where the traitor gave the wound,
Hostis unde læserat. ✠ Crux fidelis.	There healing remedies are found.

Quando venit ergo sacri Plenitudo temporis,	When the full time decreed above Was come, to show this work of love,
Missus est ab arce Patris	Th'eternal Father sends his Son,
Natus, orbis conditor;	The world's Creator from the throne;
Atque ventre virginali	Who on our earth, this vale of tears,
Carne amictus prodiit. *Dulce lignum.*	Cloth'd with a Virgin's flesh appears.
Vagit infans inter arcta	Thus God made man an infant lies,
Conditus præsepia:	And in sordid manger cries:
Membra pannis involuta	His sacred limbs by Mary bound,
Virgo mater alligat:	The poorest tatter'd rags surround:
Et Dei manus, pedesque	And God's incarnate feet and hands
Stricta cingit fascia. ✠ *Crux fidelis.*	Are closely wrapped in swathing bands.
Lustra sex qui jam peregit,	Full thirty years were freely spent
Tempus implens corporis:	In this our mortal banishment:
Sponte libera Redemptor	And then the Son of Man decreed:
Passioni deditus;	For the lost sons of men to bleed;
Agnus in crucis levatur	And on the cross a victim laid,

MASS OF THE PRESANCTIFIED.

Immolandus stipite.	The solemn expiation made.
⁘ Dulce lignum.	
Felle potus ecce languet;	Gall was his drink; his flesh they tear
Spina, clavi, lancea	With thorns and nails; a cruel spear
Mite corpus perforarunt,	Pierces his side, from whence a flood
Unda manat, et cruor:	Streams forth of water mixed with blood:
Terra pontus, astra, mundus,	With what a tide are wash'd again;
Quo lavantur flumine?	The sinful earth, the stars and main?
✠ Crux fidelis.	
Flecte ramos arbor alta,	Bend, tow'ring tree, thy branches bend,
Tensa laxa viscera,	Thy native stubbornness suspend;
Et rigor lentescat ille,	Let not stiff nature use its force,
Quem dedit nativitas:	To weaker sap have now recourse:
Et superni membra Regis,	With softest arms receive thy load,
Tende miti stipite.	And gently bear our dying God.
⁘ Dulce lignum.	
Sola digna tu fuisti	On thee alone the Lamb was slain,
Ferre mundi victimam;	That reconcil'd the world again;
Atque portum præparare	And when on raging seas was tost
Arca mundo naufrago,	The shipwreck'd world and mankind lost,

Quam sacer cruor perunxit.	Besprinkled with his sacred gore.
Fusus agni corpore.	Thou safely brought'st them to the shore.
✠ Crux fidelis.	
Sempiterna sit beatæ	All glory to the sacred Three.
Trinitati gloria;	One undivided Deity:
Æqua Patri, Filioque,	To Father, Holy Ghost, and Son.
Par decus Paraclito:	Be equal praise and homage done.
Unius, Trinique nomen	Let the whole universe proclaim
Laudet universitas. Amen.	Of One and Three the glorious name. Amen.

When the ceremony is almost finished, the candles are lighted, and the Cross is placed again upon the Altar. Then the Priest with his Ministers and clergy go in procession to the place where the Blessed Sacrament was put the day before, from whence he brings it back. During the procession the following hymn is sung

HYMN.

VExilla regis prodeunt,	BEhold the royal ensigns fly,
Fulget crucis mysterium:	Bearing the cross mystery:
Qua vita mortem pertulit,	Where life itself did death endure.
Et morte vitam protulit.	And by that death did life procure.
2. Quæ vulnerata lanceæ.	2. A cruel spear let out a flood
Mucrone diro, criminum,	Of water mixed with saving blood.

Ut nos lavaret sordibus,

Manavit unda, et sanguine.

3. Impleta sunt, quæ concinit
David fideli carmine,

Dicendo nationibus:

Regnavit a ligno Deus.

4. Arbor decora, et fulgida,
Ornata regis purpura,

Electa digno stipite

Tam sancta membra tangere.

5. Beata, cujus brachiis

Pretium pependit sæculi,
Statera facta corporis,

Tulitque prædam tartari.

6. O crux ave spes unica,
Hoc passionis tempore

Piis adauge gratiam,

Reisque dele crimina.

Which gushing from the Saviour's side,
Drown'd our offences in the tide.

3. The mystery we now unfold
Which David's faithful verse foretold.
Of our Lord's kingdom, whilst we see
God ruling nations from a tree.

4. O lovely tree, whose branches wore
The royal purple of his gore.
How glorious does thy body shine,
Supporting members so divine.

5. The world's blest balance thou wert made,
Thy happy beam its purchase weigh'd,
And bore his limbs, when snatch'd away
Devouring hell's expected prey.

6. Hail, cross, our hope, on thee we call,
Who keep this mournful festival:
Grant to the just increase of grace,
And every sinner's guilt efface.

7. Te, fons salutis Trinitas, Collaudet omnis spiritus. Quibus crucis victoriam Largiris adde præmium. Amen.	7. Blest Trinity, we praises sing To thee, from whom all graces spring: Celestial crowns on those bestow. Who conquer by the cross below. Amen.

The Priest having placed the chalice containing the Consecrated Host on the Altar, incenses it on his knees, and taking the Host out lays it on the corporal. Wine and water are put into the chalice, which is also placed on the corporal. Putting incense into the censer the Priest says.

INcensum istud a te benedictum, ascendat ad te, Domine: et descendat super nos misericordia tua.	LET this incense blessed by thee, ascend to thee, O Lord: and let thy mercy descend upon us.

The he incenses the Altar, saying:

DIrigatur Domine, oratio mea, sicut incensum in conspectu tuo: elevatio manuum mearum sacrificium vespertinum. Pone, Domine, custodiam ori meo, et ostium circumstantiæ labiis meis: ut non declinet cor meum in verba malitiæ, ad excusandas excusationes in peccatis.	LET my prayer, O Lord, ascend like incense in thy sight: let the lifting up of my hands be an evening sacrifice. Set, O Lord, a guard on my mouth, and a door of prudence on my lips: that my heart may not incline to words of malice, to make excuses for my sins.

When he gives the censer to the Deacon, he says:

ACcendat in nobis Dominus ignem sui	MAY the Lord kindle in us the fire of his

MASS OF THE PRESANCTIFIED.

amoris et flammam æternæ charitatis. Amen.

love, and the flame of eternal charity Amen.

After this he goes down from the Altar on the Epistle side, and there washes his hands: then returning to the middle thereof, bowing down, he says:

IN spiritu humilitatis, et in animo contrito suscipiamur a te, Domine: et sic fiat sacrificium nostrum in conspectu tuo hodie, ut placeat tibi, Domine Deus.

ACcept us, O Lord, in the spirit of humility, and with a contrite heart: and make our sacrifice be so performed this day in thy sight, as to please thee, O Lord God.

Then he turns to the people, and says:

ORATE fratres ut meum ac vestrum sacrificium acceptabile fiat apud Deum Patrem omnipotentem.

BRethren, pray that my sacrifice and yours may be acceptable to God the Father Almighty.

Then he turns back the same way, and says:

Oremus.

PRæceptis salutaribus moniti, et divina institutione formati audemus dicere:

PATER noster etc.

R. Sed libera nos a malo.

Let us pray.

INstructed by thy wholesome precepts, and following thy divine institution, we presume to say:

OUR Father, etc.

R. But deliver us from evil.

Then the Priest says to himself Amen, and then aloud.

LIbera nos quæsumus, Domine, ab omnibus malis, præteritis, præsentibus et futuris:

DEliver us O Lord we beseech thee from all evils, past present, and to come: and

et intercedente beata et gloriosa semper Virgine Dei Genitrice Maria, cum beatis Apostolis tuis Petro et Paulo, atque Andrea, et omnibus sanctis, da propitius pacem in diebus nostris: ut ope misericordiæ tuæ adjuti, et a peccato simus semper liberi, et ab omni perturbatione securi. Per eumdem, etc.

R. Amen.

by the intercession of the blessed and ever glorious Virgin Mary Mother of God, with the blessed Apostles Peter and Paul, and Andrew, and all the saints, mercifully grant peace in our days; that by the assistance of thy mercy we may be always free from sin, and secure from all disturbance. Through, etc.

R. Amen.

Having adored the Host on his knees, he puts the paten beneath it and elevates it, that it may be adored by the people. Then dividing it into three parts, he puts the least part into the Chalice and says the following prayer:

PErceptio corporis tui, Domine Jesu Christe, quod ego indignus sumere præsumo, non mihi proveniat in judicium et condemnationem sed pro tua pietate prosit mihi ad tutamentum mentis et corporis, et ad medelam percipiendam. Qui vivis. Amen.

LET not the receiving of thy body, O Lord Jesus Christ, which I unworthy presume to take, turn to my judgment and condemnation: but through thy mercy let it be an effectual security and cure of my soul and body. Who livest.

Taking the paten with the body of Christ, he says:

Panem cœlestem accipiam et nomen Domini invocabo.

I will take the heavenly bread, and will call on the name of the Lord.

Here he strikes his breast, and says thrice.

Domine, non sum dignus, ut intres sub tectum meum: sed tantum dic verbo, et sanabitur anima mea.

Lord, I am not worthy thou shouldst enter under my roof: but say only the word, and my soul shall be healed.

After which, he signs himself with the Blessed Sacrament, saying:

COrpus Domini nostri Jesu Christi custodiat animam meam in vitam æternam. Amen.

MAY the body of our Lord Jesus Christ preserve my soul to life everlasting. Amen.

Then he reverently receives the Host and immediately after the particle of the sacred Host with the wine in the chalice: and having, as usual, washed his fingers, and taken the ablutions in the middle of the Altar, with his hands joined, he says:

QUOD ore sumpsimus, Domine pura mente capiamus: et de munere temporali fiat nobis remedium sempiternum.

GRANT, O Lord, that what we have taken with our mouth, we may receive with a pure heart: and that, of the temporal gift, it may become to us an eternal remedy.

After the departure of the Priest from the Altar, the same Vespers are recited as yesterday, except the following Ant. at the Magnificat.

Ant. Cum accepisset acetum, dixit: Consummatum est: et inclinato capite, emisit spiritum.

Ant When he had taken the vinegar, he said: It is finished: and bowing down his head he expired.

Magnificat *ut supra.*

Ant. Cum accepisset acetum, dixit: Consummatum est: et inclinato capite, emisit spiritum.

V. Christus factus est pro nobis obediens usque ad mortem: mortem autem crucis.

MY soul magnifies.

Ant. When he had taken the vinegar, he said: It is finished: and bowing down his head he expired.

V. Christ became obedient for us to death: even the death of the cross.

Pater noster *in secret, the Psalm Miserere, p.* 174 *and the prayer* Respice, *p.* 191.

ON GOOD FRIDAY EVENING.

HOLY SATURDAY AT MATINS.

THE FIRST NOCTURN

ANTIPHONA

In pace in idipsum dormiam et requiescam

THE ANTIPHON.

In peace, in the selfsame I will sleep and rest.

PSALM IV.

CUM invocarem, exaudivit me Deus justitiæ meæ: * in tribulatione dilatasti mihi.

2. Miserere mei * et exaudi orationem meam.

3. Fili hominum usquequo gravi corde? * ut quid diligitis vanitatem, et queritis mendacium.

WHEN I called upon him, the God of my justice heard me: when I was in distress thou hast enlarged me.

2. Have mercy on me, and hear my prayer.

3. O ye sons of men, how long will ye be dull of heart? why do you love vanity, and seek after lying?

4. Et scitote quoniam mirificavit Dominus sanctum suum: * Dominus exaudiet me, cum clamavero ad eum.

5. Irascimini, et nolite peccare: * quæ dicitis in cordibus vestris, in cubilibus vestris compungimini.

6. Sacrificate sacrificium justitiæ, et sperate in Domino: * multi dicunt: Quis ostendit nobis bona?

7. Signatum est super nos lumen vultus tui, Domine: * dedisti lætitiam in corde meo.

8. A fructu frumenti, vini et olei sui, * multiplicati sunt.

9. In pace in idipsum dormiam et requiescam;

10. Quoniam tu, Domine, singulariter in spe * constituisti me.

Ant. In pace in idipsum dormiam et requiescam.

Ant. Habitabit in tabernaculo tuo, requiescet in monte sancto tuo.

4. Know ye also that the Lord hath made his Holy One wonderful: the Lord will hear me when I shall cry unto him.

5. Be ye angry and sin not: the things you say in your hearts, be sorry for them on your beds.

6. Offer up the sacrifice of justice and trust in the Lord: many say: Who showeth us good things?

7. The light of thy countenance, O Lord, is signed upon us: thou hast given gladness in my heart.

8. By the fruit of their corn, their wine and oil they are multiplied.

9. In peace, in the self same I will sleep.

10. For thou, O Lord singularly hast settled me in hope.

Ant. In peace, in the self-same I will sleep and rest.

Ant. He shall dwell in thy tabernacle, he shall rest on thy holy mountain.

PSALM XIV.

DOMINE, quis habitabit in tabernaculo tuo? * aut quis requiescet in monte sancto tuo?

2. Qui ingreditur sine macula, * et operatur justitiam:

3. Qui loquitur veritatem in corde suo, * qui non egit dolum in lingua sua:

4. Nec fecit proximo suo malum, * et opprobrium non accepit adversus proximos suos.

5. Ad nihilum deductus est in conspectu ejus malignus: * timentes autem Dominum glorificat.

6. Qui jurat proximo suo, et non decipit: * qui pecuniam suam non dedit ad usuram, et munera super innocentem non accepit:

7. Qui facit hæc, * non movebitur in æternum.

Ant. Habitabit in tabernaculo tuo, requiescet in monte sancto tuo.

Ant. Caro mea requiescet in spe.

LORD, who shall dwell in thy tabernacle? or who shall rest in thy holy hill?

2. He that walketh without blemish, and worketh justice:

3. He that speaketh truth in his heart, who hath not used deceit in his tongue:

4. Nor hath done evil to his neighbour, nor taken up a reproach against his neighbours.

5. In his sight the malignant is brought to nothing: but he glorifieth them that fear the Lord.

6. He that sweareth to his neighbour, and deceiveth not: he that hath not put out his money to usury, nor taken bribes against the innocent:

7. He that doth these things shall not be moved for ever.

Ant. He shall dwell in thy tabernacle, he shall rest on thy holy mountain.

Ant. My flesh shall rest in hope.

PSALM XV.

CONSERVA me, Domine, quoniam speravi in te. * Dixi Domino: Deus meus es tu: quoniam bonorum meoram non eges.

2. Sanctis qui sunt in terra ejus, * mirificavit omnes voluntates meas in eis.
3. Multiplicatæ sunt infirmitates eorum: * postea acceleraverunt.
4. Non congregabo conventicula eorum de sanguinibus; * nec memor ero nominum eorum per labia mea.
5. Dominus pars hereditatis meæ et calicis mei: * tu es qui restitues hereditatem meam mihi.
6. Funes ceciderunt mihi in præclaris: etenim hereditas mea præclara est mihi.
7. Benedicam Dominum, qui tribuit mihi intellectum: * insuper et usque ad noctem increpuerunt me renes mei.
8. Providebam Dominum in conspectu meo

PRESERVE me, O Lord, for I have put my trust in thee. I have said to the Lord: thou art my God, for thou hast no need of my goods.

2. To the saints who are in his land, he hath made wonderful all my desires in them.
3. Their infirmities were multiplied: afterwards they made haste.
4. I will not gather together their meetings for blood offerings: nor will I be mindful of their names by my lips.
5. The Lord is the portion of my inheritance and of my cup: it is thou that wilt restore my inheritance to me.
6. The lines are fallen unto me in goodly places: for my inheritance is goodly to me.
7. I will bless the Lord who hath given me understanding: moreover my reins also have corrected me even till night.
8. I set the Lord always in my sight: for

semper: *quoniam a dextris est mihi ne commovear.

9. Propter hoc lætatum est cor meum, et exultavit in lingua mea: *insuper et caro mea requiescet in spe.

10. Quoniam non derelinques animam meam in inferno: *nec dabis Sanctum tuum videre corruptionem.

11. Notas mihi fecisti vias vitæ, adimplebis me lætitia cum vultu tuo: *delectationes in dextera tua usque in finem.

Ant. Caro mea requiescet in spe.
V. In pace in idipsum.
R. Dormiam et requiescam.
Pater noster, *secreto*.

LECTIO I.

De Lamentatione Jeremiæ Prophetæ *cap.* iii.

Heth. Misericordiæ Domini quia non sumus consumpti: quia non defecerunt miserationes ejus.

he is at my right-hand that I be not moved.

9. Therefore my heart hath been glad and my tongue hath rejoiced: moreover my flesh also shall rest in hope.

10. Because thou wilt not leave my soul in hell: nor wilt thou give thy Holy One to see corruption.

11. Thou hast made known to me the ways of life, thou shalt fill me with joy with thy countenance: at thy right-hand are delights even to the end.

Ant. My flesh shall rest in hope.
V. In peace I will.
R. Both sleep and rest.
Our Father, *in silence*.

LESSON I.

From the Lamentations of the Prophet Jeremias, *chap.* iii.

Heth. THE mercies of the Lord that we are not consumed: because his tender mercies have not failed.

Heth. Novi diluculo, multa est fides tua.

Heth. Pars mea Dominus dixit anima mea: propterea expectabo eum.

Teth. Bonus est Dominus sperantibus in eum, animæ quærenti illum.

Teth. Bonum est præsolari cum silentio saluare Dei.

Teth. Bonum est viro, cum portaverit jugum ab adolescentia sua.

Jod. Sedebit solitarius, et tacebit: qui levavit super se.

Jod. Ponet in pulvere os suum, si forte sit spes.

Jod. Dabit percutienti se maxillam, saturabitur opprobriis.

Jerusalem, Jerusalem, convertere ad Dominum Deum tuum.

R. Sicut ovis ad occisionem ductus est, et dum male tractaretur, non aperuit os suum: traditus est ad mortem,

Heth. They are new every morning, great is thy faithfulness.

Heth. The Lord is my portion, said my soul: therefore will I wait for him.

Teth. The Lord is good to them that hope in him, to the soul that seeketh him.

Teth. It is good to wait with silence for the salvation of God.

Teth. It is good for a man, when he hath borne the yoke from his youth.

Jod. He shall sit solitary, and hold his peace: because he hath taken it upon himself.

Jod. He shall put his mouth in the dust, if so be there may be hope.

Jod. He shall give his cheek to him that striketh him, he shall be filled with reproaches.

Jerusalem, Jerusalem, be converted to the Lord thy God.

R. He was led like a sheep to the slaughter and whilst he was illused he opened not his mouth: he was con-

* Ut vivificaret populum suum. V. Tradidit in mortem animam suam, et inter sceleratos reputatus est. * Ut vivificaret, etc.

LECTIO II. CAP. IV.

Aleph. QUOMODO obscuratum est aurum, mutatus est color optimus, dispersi sunt lapides sanctuarii in capite omnium platearum?

Beth. Filii Sion inclyti, et amicti auro primo: quomodo reputati sunt in vasa testea, opus manuum figuli.

Ghimel. Sed et lamiæ nudaverunt mammam, lactaverunt catulos suos: filia populi mei crudelis, quasi struthio in deserto.

Daleth. Adhæsit lingua lactentis ad palatum ejus in siti; parvuli petierunt panem, et non erat qui frangeret eis.

demned to death, ' That he might give life to his people. V. He delivered up himself to death, and was reckoned among the wicked. That he might.

LESSON II CHAP IV.

Aleph. HOW is the gold become dim, the finest colour is changed, the stones of the sanctuary are scattered in the top of every street?

Beth. The noble sons of Sion, and they that were clothed with the best gold: how are they esteemed as earthen vessels, the work of the potter's hands?

Ghimel. Even the sea-monsters have drawn out the breast, they have given suck to their young: the daughter of my people is cruel, like the ostrich in the desert.

Daleth. The tongue of the sucking child hath stuck to the roof of his mouth for thirst: the litle ones have asked for bread, and there was none to break it unto them.

He. Qui vescebantur voluptuose, interierunt in viis: qui nutriebantur in croceis, amplexati sunt stercora.

Vau. Et major effecta est iniquitas filiæ populi mei peccato Sodomorum, quæ subversa est in momento, et non ceperunt in ea manus.

Jerusalem, Jerusalem, convertere ad Dominum Deum tuum.

R. Jerusalem, surge, et exue te vestibus jucunditatis: induere cinere et cilicio. * Quia in te occisus est Salvator Israel. V. Deduc quasi torrentem lacrymas per diem et noctem, et non taceat pupilla oculi tui. * Quia in te.

LECTIO III.

Incipit Oratio Jeremiæ Prophetæ. *(cap. v)*

Recordare, Domine, quid acciderit nobis: intuere et respice opprobrium nostrum. Hereditas nostra versa est ad alienos: domus nostræ ad extraneos.

He. They that were fed delicately have died in the streets: they that were brought up in scarlet have embraced the dung.

Vau. And the iniquity of the daughter of my people is made greater than the sin of Sodom, which was overthrown in a moment, and hands took nothing in her.

Jerusalem, Jerusalem, be converted to the Lord thy God.

R. Arise, Jerusalem, and put off thy garments of joy: put on lashes and hair-cloth. * For in thee was slain the Saviour of Israel. V. Shed tears like a torrent, day and night, and let not the apple of thy eye be dry * For in thee.

LESSON III.

Here begins the Prayer of the Prophet Jeremias. *(ch. v)*

Remember, O Lord, what is come upon us: consider and behold our reproach. Our inheritance is turned to aliens: our houses to strangers. We are be-

Pupilli facti sumus absque patre, matres nostrae quasi viduae. Aquam nostram pecunia bibimus: ligna nostra pretio comparavimus. Cervicibus nostris minabamur, lassis non dabatur requies. Ægypto dedimus manum, et Assyriis, ut saturaremur pane. Patres nostri peccaverunt, et non sunt: et nos iniquitates eorum portavimus. Servi dominati sunt nostri: non fuit qui redimeret de manu eorum. In animabus nostris afferebamus panem nobis, a facie gladii in deserto. Pellis nostra quasi clibanus exusta est a facie tempestatum famis. Mulieres in Sion, humiliaverunt, et virgines in civitatibus Juda.

come orphans without a father, our mothers are as widows. We have drunk our water for money: we have bought our wood. We were dragged by the necks, we were weary and no rest was given us. We have given our hand to Egypt, and to the Assyrians, that we might be satisfied with bread. Our fathers have sinned and are not: and we have borne their iniquities. Servants have ruled over us: and there was none to redeem us out of their hand. We fetched our bread at the peril of our lives, because of the sword in the desert. Our skin was burnt as an oven, by reason of the violence of the famine. They oppressed the women in Sion, and the virgins in the cities of Juda.

Jerusalem, Jerusalem, convertere ad Dominum Deum tuum.

Jerusalem, Jerusalem, be converted to the Lord thy God.

R. Plange quasi virgo plebs mea: ululate pastores, in cinere et cilicio: * Quia veniet dies Domini magna, et amara

R. Mourn as a virgin, my people: howl, ye pastors, in ashes and sackcloth: * For the great and exceeding bit-

valde. V. Accingite vos sacerdotes, et plangite ministri altaris, aspergite vos cinere. * Quia veniet, etc. R. Plange quasi virgo, etc.

ter day of the Lord is coming. V. Gird yourselves, ye priests, and mourn, ye ministers of the altar, sprinkle yourselves with ashes. * For the great, etc. R. Mourn as a virgin.

SECOND NOCTURN.

Ant. Elevamini portæ eternales, et introibit Rex gloriæ.

Ant. Be ye lifted up, O eternal gates, and the King of glory will enter in.

PSALM XXIII.

Domini est terra, et plenitudo ejus: * orbis terrarum, et universi qui habitant in eo.

2. Quia ipse super maria fundavit eum: * et super flumina præparavit eum.

3. Quis ascendet in montem Domini? * aut quis stabit in loco sancto ejus?

4. Innocens manibus et mundo corde, * qui non accepit in vano animam suam, nec juravit in dolo proximo suo.

5. Hic accipiet benedictionem a Domino: * et misericordiam a Deo salutari suo.

The earth is the Lord's and the fulness thereof: the world, and all they that dwell therein.

2. For he hath founded it upon the seas: and hath prepared it upon the rivers.

3. Who shall ascend into the mountain of the Lord? or who shall stand in his holy place?

4. The innocent in hands, and clean of heart, who hath not taken his soul in vain, nor sworn deceitfully to his neighbour.

5. He shall receive a blessing from the Lord: and mercy from God his Saviour.

6. Hæc est generatio quærentium eum, * quæaentium faciem Dei Jacob.

7. Attolite portas principes vestras, et elevamini portæ æternales : * et introibit Rex gloriæ.

8. Quis est iste Rex gloriæ ? * Dominns fortis et potens, Dominus potens in praelio.

9. Attollite portas principes vestras, et elevamini port æ æternales : * et introibit Rex gloriæ.

10. Quis est iste Rex gloriæ ? * Dominus virtutum, ipse est Rex gloriæ.

Ant. Elevamini portæ æternales, et introibit Rex gloriæ.

Ant. Credo videre bona Domini in terra viventium.

6. This is the generation of them that seek him, of them that seek the face of the God of Jacob.

7. Lift up your gates, O ye princes, and be ye lifted up, O eternal gates: and the King of glory shall enter in.

8. Who is this King of glory? the Lord, who is strong and mighty, the Lord, mighty in battle.

9. Lift up your gates, O ye princes, and be ye lifted up, O eternal gates, and the King of glory shall enter in.

10. Who is this King of glory? the Lord of hosts. he is the King of glory.

Ant. Be ye lifted up, O eternal gates. and the King of glory will enter in.

Ant. I believe that I shall see the good things of the Lord in the land of the living.

PSALM XXVI.

Dominus illuminatio mea, etc. *p.* 216.
Ant. Credo videre bo-

THE Lord is my light, etc. *p.* 216.
Ant. I believe that I

na Domini in terra viventium.

Ant. Domine, abstraxisti ab inferis animam meam.

shall see the good things of the Lord in the land of the living.

Ant. Lord, thou hast brought my soul out of hell.

PSALM XXIX.

EXaltabo te Domine, quoniam suscepisti me: * nec delectasti inimicos meos super me.

2. Domine Deus meus, clamavi ad te, * et sanasti me.

3. Domine eduxisti ab inferno animam meam: * salvasti me a descendentibus in lacum.

4. Psallite Domino sancti ejus: * et confitemini memoriæ sanctitatis ejus.

5. Quoniam ira in indignatione ejus: * et vita in voluntate ejus.

6. Ad vesperum demorabitur fletus: * et ad matutinum lætitia.

7. Ego autem dixi in abundantia mea: * Non movebor in æternum.

I Will extol thee, O Lord, for thou hast upheld me: and hast not made my enemies to rejoice over me.

2. O Lord my God, I have cried to thee, and thou hast hea'ed me.

3. Thou hast brought forth O Lord, my soul from hell: thou hast saved me from them that go down into the pit.

4. Sing to the Lord, O you his saints: and give praise to the memory of his holiness.

5. For wrath is in his indignation: and life in his good-will.

6. In the evening weeping shall have place: and in the morning gladness.

7. And in my abundance I said: I shall never be moved.

8. Domine in voluntate tua, * præstitisti decori meo virtutem.

9. Avertisti faciem tuam a me, * et factus sum conturbatus.

10. Ad te, Domine, clamabo : * et ad Deum meum deprecabor.

11. Quæ utilitas in sanguine meo, * dum descendo in corruptionem?

12. Numquid confitebitur tibi pulvis, * aut annuntiabit veritatem tuam?

13. Audivit Dominus, et misertus est mei : * Dominus factus est adjutor meus.

14. Convertisti planctum meum in gaudium mihi : * conscidisti saccum meum, et circumdedisti me lætitia.

15. Ut cantet tibi gloria mea, et non compungar : * Domine Deus meus, in æternum confitebor tibi.

Ant. Domine, abstraxisti ab inferis animam meam.

8. O Lord, in thy favour, thou gavest strength to my beauty.

9. Thou turnedst away thy face from me, and I became troubled.

10. To thee, O Lord, will I cry : and I will make supplication to my God.

11. What profit is there in my blood, whilst I go down to corruption.

12. Shall dust confess to thee, or declare thy truth?

13. The Lord hath heard, and hath had mercy on me: the Lord became my helper.

14. Thou hast turned for me my mourning into joy: thou hast cut my sackcloth, and hast compassed me with gladness.

15. To the end that my glory may sing to thee, and I may not regret: O Lord my God, I will give praise to thee for ever.

Ant. Lord, thou hast brought my soul out of hell.

℣. Tu autem, Domine, miserere mei.

℟. Et resuscita me, et retribuam eis.

Pater noster, *secreto*.

LECTIO IV.

Ex Tractatu sancti Augustini Episcopi super Psalmos.

In Psalmum. lxiii. v. 7.

*A**CCEDIT homo ad cor altum, et exaltabitur Deus. Illi dixerunt, Quis nos videbit? Defecerunt scrutantes scrutationes consilia mala.* Accessit homo ad ipsa consilia, passus est se teneri ut homo. Non enim teneretur nisi homo, aut videretur, nisi homo, aut cæderetur, nisi homo, aut crucifigeretur, aut moreretur nisi homo. Accessit ergo homo ad illas omnes passiones, quæ in illo nihil valerent, nisi esset homo. Sed si ille non esset homo, non liberaretur homo. Accessit homo ad cor altum, id est cor secretum, objiciens aspectibus humanis hominem, servans intus

℣. But do thou, O Lord, have mercy on me.

℟. And raise me up again, and I will repay them.

Our Father, *in secret*.

LESSON IV.

Out of the Treatise of St. Augustin, Bishop, upon the Psalms.

On. Ps. lxiii v. 7.

*M**AN shall come to the deep heart, and God shall be exalted. They said: Who will see us? They failed in making diligent search for wicked designs.* Man came to those designs, and suffered himself to be seized on as a man. For he could not be seized on, if he were not man; nor seen, if he were not man, nor scourged, if he were not man; nor crucified, nor die if he were not man. Man therefore came to all these sufferings which could have no effect on him if he were not man. But if he had not been man, man could not have been redeemed. Man came to the deep

Deum: celans formam Dei, in qua æqualis est Patri: et offerens formam servi, qua minor est patre.

℟. Recessit Pastor noster, fons aquæ vivæ, ad cujus transitum sol obscuratus est: * Nam et ille captus est, qui captivum tenebat primum hominem: hodie portas mortis et seras pariter Salvator noster disrupit. ℟. Destruxit quidem claustra inferni et subvertit potentias diaboli. * Nam et ille, etc.

LECTIO V.

QUO perduxerunt illas scrutationes suas, quas perscrutantes defecerunt, ut etiam mortuo Domino et sepulto, custodes ponerent ad sepulchrum? Dixerunt enim Pilato: Seductor ille: hoc appellabatur nomine Dominus Jesus Christus, ad solatium servorum suorum, quando dicuntur seductores. Ergo illi Pilato: *Seduc-*

heart, that is, the secret heart, exposing his humanity to human view, but hiding his divinty: concealing the form of God, by which he is equal to the Father: and offering the form of a servant, by wich he is inferior to the Father.

℟. Our shepherd, the fountain of living water, is gone, at whose departure the sun was darkened. * For he is taken, who made the first man a prisoner: to day our Saviour broke both the locks and gates of death. ℟. He destroyed the prisons of hell, and overthrew the powers of the devil.
For he, etc.

LESSON V.

HOW far did they carry this their diligent search, in which they failed so much, that when our Lord was dead and buried, they placed guards at the sepulchre? For they said to Pilate: This seducer: by which name our Lord Jesus Christ was called, for the comfort of his servants when they are called sedu-

tor ille inquiunt, *dixit adhuc vivens: Post tres dies resurgam. Jube itaque custodiri sepulchrum usque in diem tertium, ne forte veniant discipuli ejus, et furenter eum, et dicunt plebi surrexit a mortuis: et erit novissimus error pejor priore.* Ait illis Pilatus: *Habetis custodiam, ite, custodite sicut scitis.* Illi autem abeuntes munierunt sepulchrum, signantes lapidem cum custodibus. away and secured the sealing up the stone.

℟. O vos omnes qui transitis per viam, attendite et videte. * Si est dolor similis sicut dolor meus. ℣. Attendite, universi populi, et videte dolorem meum. * Si est dolor similis. etc.

cers. *This seducer,* say they to Pilate, *whilst he was yet living, said: After three days I will rise again. Command therefore the sepulchre to be guarded until the third day, lest perhaps his disciples come and steal him away, and say to the people, he is risen from the dead: and the last error will be worse than the first:* Pilate saith to them: *Ye have a guard, go, and guard him as ye know.* And they went sepulchre with guards,

℟. O all ye that pass by this way, attend and see, * If there be any grief like unto my grief. ℣. Attend all ye people, and see my grief.

LECTIO VI.

POSUERUNT custodes milites ad sepulchrum. Concussa terra, Dominus resurrexit, miracula facta sunt talia circa sepulchrum, ut et ipse milites, qui custodes advenerant, testes

LESSON VI.

THEY placed soldiers to guard the sepulchre. The earth shook, and the Lord rose again: such miracles were done at the sepulchre, that the very soldiers that came as guards might

fierent, si vellent vera nuntiare. Sed avaritia illa quæ captivavit discipulum comitem Christi, captivavit et militem, custodem sepulchri. *Damus, vobis pecuniam et dicite, quia vobis dormientibus venerunt discipuli ejus, et abstulerunt eum:* Vere defecerunt scrutantes scrutationes. Quid est quod dixisti, O infelix astutia? Tantumne deseris lucem consilii pietatis, et in profunda versutia demergeris, ut hoc dicas: *Dicite, quia vobis dormientibus venerunt discipuli ejus, et abstulerunt eum?* Dormientes testes adhibes? Vere tu ipse obdormisti qui scrutando talia defecisti.

be witnesses of it, if they would declare the truth. But that covetousness which possessed the disciple that was the companion of Christ, blinded also the soldiers that were the guards of his sepulchre. *We will give you money,* said they: *and say, that whilst ye were asleep, his disciples came and took him away:* They truly failed in making diligent search. What is it thou hast said, O wretched craft? Dost thou shut thy eyes against the light of prudence and piety, and plunge thyself so deep in cunning, as to say this: *say that whilst ye were asleep, his disciples came and took him away?* Dost thou produce sleeping witnesses? Certainly thou thyself sleepest, that faitest in making search after such things.

V. Ecce quomodo moritur justus, et nemo percipit corde; et viri justi tollentur, et nemo considerat: a facie iniquitatis sublatus est justus: ' Et erit in pace memoria ejus. *V*. Tam-

R. Behold how the just man dies, and no body takes it to heart and just men are taken away and no one considers it: the just man is taken away from the face of iniquity: ' And

HOLY SATURDAY AT MATINS.

quam agnus coram tondente se obmutuit, et non aperuit os suum: de angustia et de judicio sublatus est. * Et erit in pace memoria ejus. R. Ecce quomodo, etc.

his memory shall be in peace. V. He was dumb like the lamb under his shearer; and opened not his mouth: He was taken away from distress, and from judgment. * And his memory shall be in peace. R. Behold, etc.

THIRD NOCTURN.

Ant. Deus adjuvat me, et Dominus susceptor est animæ meæ.

Ant. God help me, and the Lord is the protector of my soul.

PSALM LIII.

DEUS in nomine tuo salvum, etc, *p.* 229.

SAVE me, O God, etc. *p.* 229.

Ant. Deus adjuvat me et Dominus susceptor est animæ meæ.

Ant. God helps me, and the Lord is the protector of my soul.

Ant. In pace factus est locus ejus, et in Sion habitatio ejus.

Ant. His dwelling is in peace, and his habitation is in Sion.

PSALM LXXV.

NOTUS in Judæa Dominus, etc. *p.* 161.

IN Judea God is known, *p.* 161.

Ant. In pace factus est locus ejus, et in Sion habitatio ejus.

Ant. His dwelling is in peace, and his habitation is in Sion.

Ant. Factus sum sicut homo sine adjutorio, inter mortuos liber.

Ant. I am become like a man without help, free among the dead.

PSALM LXXXVII.

DOMINE, Deus salutis meæ, etc *p.* 248.

O Lord, the God of my salvation, etc, *p.* 248.

Ant. Factus sum sicut homo sine adjutorio inter mortuos liber.

V. In pace factus est locus ejus,
R. Et in Sion habitatio ejus.
Pater noster, *secreto.*

LECTIO VII.
De Epistola Beati Pauli Apostoli ad Hebræos.
cap. ix.

CHRISTUS assistens pontifex futurorum bonorum, per amplius et perfectius tabernaculum non manufactum, id est, non hujus creationis: neque per sanguinem hircorum aut vitulorum, sed per proprium sanguinem introivit semel in sancta, æterna redemptione inventa. Si enim sanguis hircorum et taurorum, et cinis vitulæ aspersus inquinatos sanctificat ad emundationem carnis: quanto magis sanguis Christi, qui per Spiritum Sanctum semetipsum obtulit immaculatum Deo, emundabit conscientiam nostram ab operibus mortuis, ad

Ant. I am become like a man without help, free among the dead.

V. His dwelling is in peace.
R. And his habitation is in Sion.
Our Father, *in secret.*

LESSON VII.
Out of the Epistle of Blessed Paul the Apostle to the Hebr. *ch.* ix.

CHRIST being come a high priest of the good things to come: by a greater and more perfect tabernacle, not made with hands, that is, not of this creation: neither by the blood of goats, nor of calves, but by his own blood, entered once into the holies having obtained eternal redemption. For if the blood of goats and of oxen, and the ashes of an heifer being sprinkled sanctify such as are defiled, to the cleansing of the flesh: how much more shall the blood of Christ, who through the Holy Gost offered himself without spot to God, cleanse our

serviendum Deo viventi?

℟. Astiterunt reges terræ, et principes convenerunt in unum. * Adversus Dominum, et adversus Christum ejus. ℣. Quare fremuerunt Gentes: et populi meditati sunt inania? * Adversus Dominum, etc,

LECTIO VIII.

ET ideo novi testamenti mediator est: ut morte intercedente, in redemptionem earum prævaricationum, quæ erant sub priori testamento repromissionem accipiant, qui vocati sunt æternæ hereditatis. Ubi enim testamentum est, mors necesse est intercedat testatoris. Testamentum enim in mortuis confirmatum est: alioquin nondum valet, dum vivit qui testatus est. Unde nec primum quidem sine sanguine dedicatum est.

℟. Æstimatus sum

conscience from dead works, to serve the living God?

℟. The kings of the earth stood up, and the princes assembled together. * Against the Lord, and against his Christ. ℣. Why have the nations raged: and the people meditated vain things? * Against, etc.

LESSON VIII.

AND therefore he is the mediator of the new testament: that by means of his death, for the redemption of those transgressions which were under the former testament, they that are called may receive the promise of eternal inheritance. For where there is a testament, the death of a testator must of necessity come in. For a testament is of force after men are dead: otherwise it is as yet of no strength, whilst the testator liveth. Wherefore neither was the first dedicated without blood.

℟. I am reckoned

cum descendentibus in lacum: * Factus sum sicut homo sine adjutorio, inter mortuos liber. V. Posuerunt me in lacu inferiori: in tenebrosis, et in umbra mortis. * Factus sum, etc.

LECTIO IX.

LECTO enim omnimandato legis a Moyse universo populo, accipiens sanguinem vitulorum et hircorum, cum aqua et lana coccinea et hyssopo, ipsum quoque librum et omnem populum aspersit, dicens: Hic sanguis testamenti, quod mandavit ad vos Deus. Etiam tabernaculum, et omnia vasa ministerii sanguine similiter aspersit. Et omnia pene in sanguine secundum legem mundantur: et sine sanguinis effusione non fit remissio.

R. Sepulto Domino, signatum est monumentum, volventes lapidem ad ostium monumenti.

among those that descend into the pit: * I am become like a man without help, free among the dead. V. They laid me in the lower lake: in dark places, and in the shadow of death. * I am.

LESSON IX.

FOR when every commandment of the law had been read by Moses to all the people, he took the blood of calves and goats, with water and scarlet wool and hyssop, and sprinkled both the book itself and all the people, saying: This is the blood of the testament, which God hath enjoined on you. The tabernacle also, and all the vessels of the ministry, in like manner, he sprinkled with blood. And almost all things, according to the law, are cleansed with blood and without shedding of blood there is no remission.

R. When the Lord was buried, they sealed up the sepulchre, rolling a stone before the mouth

Ponentes milites, qui custodirent illum. Accedentes principes sacerdotum ad Pilatum, petierunt illum. Ponentes. R. Sepulto Domino, etc.

of the sepulchre, and placing * soldiers to guard him. V. The chief priest went to Pilate and asked of him to place soldiers. R. When our Lord,

AT LAUDS.

Ant. O mors, ero mors tua, morsus tuus ero inferne.

Ant. O death, I will be thy death: O hell, I will be thy ruin.

PSALM L.

MISERERE mei, Deus, etc. *p.* 174.

HAVE mercy on me, etc. *p.* 174.

Ant. O mors, ero mors tua, morsus tuus ero inferne.

Ant. O death, I will be thy death: O hell, I will be thy ruin.

Ant. Plangent eum quasi unigenitum, quia innocens Dominus occisus est.

Ant. They shall mourn for him as for an only son, because the innocent Lord is slain.

PSALM XLII.

JUDICA me, Deus, et discerne causam meam de gente non sancta: * ab homine iniquo et doloso erue me.

JUDGE me, O God, and distinguish my cause from the nation that is not holy: deliver me from the unjust and deceiful man.

2. Quia tu es Deus fortitudo mea: * quare me repulisti? et quare tristis incedo, dum affligit me inimicus?

2. For thou art God my strength: why hast thou cast me off? and why do I go sorrowful whilst the enemy afflicteth me?

3. Emitte lucem tuam et veritatem tuam: * ip-

3. Send forth thy light and thy truth: they

sa me deduxerunt, et adduxerunt in montem sanctum tuum, et in tabernacula tua.

4. Et introibo ad altare Dei: * ad Deum qui lætificat juventutem meam.

5. Confitebor tibi in cithara Deus, Deus meus: * quare tristis es anima mea? et quare conturbas me?

6. Spera in Deo quoniam adhuc confitebor illi: * salutare vultus mei, et Deus meus.

Ant. Plangent eum quasi unigenitum, quia innocens Dominus occisus est.

Ant. Attendite universi populi, et videte dolorem meum.

have conducted me, and brought me unto thy holy hill, and into thy tarbernacles.

4. And I will go in to the altar of God: to God who giveth joy to my youth.

5. To thee, O God, my God, I will give praise upon the harp: why art thou sad, O my soul, and why dost thou disquiet me?

6. Hope in God, for I will still give praise to him: the salvation of my countenance and my my God.

Ant. They shall mourn for him as for an only son, because the innocent Lord is slain.

Ant. Behold, all ye people, and see my grief.

PSALM LXII.

DEUS, Deus meus. etc. p. 179.

O God my God, etc. p. 179.

PSALM LXVI.

DEUS misereatur nostri, etc. p. 181.

Ant. Attendite, universi populi, et videte dolorem meum.

MAY God have mercy, etc. p. 181.

Ant. Behold, all ye people, and see my grief.

Ant. A porta inferi erue, Domine, animam meam.

Canticum Ezechiæ
Isa. xxxviii.

EGO dixi: in dimidio dierum meorum * vadam ad portas inferi.

2. Qæsivi residuum annorum meorum: * dixi: Non videbo Dominum Deum in terra viventium.

3. Non aspiciam hominem ultra, * et habitatorem quietis.

4. Generatio mea ablata est, et convoluta est a me, * quasi tabernaculum pastorum.

5. Precisa est velut a texente, vita mea, dum adhuc ordirer, succidit me: * de mane usque ad vesperam finies me.

6. Sperabam usque ad mane: * quasi leo sic contrivit omnia ossa mea.

7. De mane usque ad vesperam finies me: * sicut pullus hirundinis sic clamabo, meditabor ut columba.

Ant. From the gate of hell, O Lord, delives my soul.

The Canticle of Ezechias
Isa. xxxviii.

I Said: in the midst of my days I shall go to the gates of hell.

2. I sought for the residue of my years: I said, I shall not see the Lord God in the land of the living.

3. I shall behold man no more, nor the inhabitant of rest.

4. My generation is at an end, and it is rolled away from me as a shepherd's tent.

5. My life is cut off as by a weaver; whilst I was but beginning, he cut me off: from morning even till night thou wilt make an end of me.

6. I hope till morning: as a lion so hath he broken my bones.

7. From morning even till night thou wilt make an end of me: I will cry like a young swallow. I will meditate like a dove.

8. Attenuati sunt oculi mei: * suspicientes in excelsum.

9. Domine vim patior, responde pro me * Quid dicam, aut quid respondebit mihi, cum ipse fecerit?

10. Recogitabo tibi omnes annos meos, * in amaritudine animæ meæ.

11. Domine, si sic vivitur, et in talibus vita spiritus mei, corripies me, et vivificabis me. * Ecce in pace amaritudo mea amarissima.

12. Tu autem eruisti animam meam ut non periret: * projecisti post tergum tuum omnia peccata mea.

13. Quia non infernus confitebitur tibi, neque mors laudabit te: * non expectabunt qui descendunt in lacum, veritatem tuam.

14. Vivens, vivens, ipse confitebitur tibi, sicut et ego hodie: * Pa-

8 My eyes are weakened with looking upward.

9. Lord, I suffer violence, answer thou for me. What shall I say, or what shall he answer for me, whereas he himself hath done it?

10. I will recount to thee all my years, in the bitterness of my soul.

11. O Lord, if man's life be such, and the life of my spirit be in such things as these, thou shalt correct me, and make me to live. Behold in peace is my bitterness most bitter.

12. But thou hast delivered my soul that I should not perish: thou hast cast all my sins behind thy back.

13. For hell shall not confess to thee, neither shall death praise thee: nor shall they that go down into the pit look for thy truth.

14. The living, the living, he shall give praise to thee, as I do

ter filiis notam faciet veritatem tuam.

15. Domine, salvum me fac, * et psalmos nostros cantabimus cunctis diebus vitæ nostræ in domo Domini.

Ant. A porta inferi erue, Domine, animam meam.

Ant. O vos omnes qui transitis per viam, attendite et videte, si est dolor sicut dolor meus.

this day: the father shall make thy truth known to the children.

15. O Lord, save me, and we will sing our psalms all the days of our life in the house of the Lord.

Ant. From the gate of hell, O Lord, deliver my soul.

Ant. O all ye that pass by the way, behold and see, if there be sorrow like my sorrow.

PSALM CXLVIII.

LAUDATE Dominum de cœlis, etc. *p. 185.*

PRAISE ye the Lord from the heavens, *p. 185.*

PSALM CXLIX.

CANTATE Domino canticum, etc. *p. 187.*

SING ye to the Lord, etc. *p. 187.*

PSALM CL.

LAUDATE Dominum in sanctis, etc. *p. 182.*

Ant. O vos omnes qui transitis per viam, attendite et videte, si est dolor sicut dolor meus.

V. Caro mea requiescet in spe.

R. Et non dabis Sanctum tuum videre corruptionem.

PRAISE ye the Lord, in his holy, *p. 182.*

Ant. O all ye that pass by the way, behold and see, if there be sorrow like to my sorrow.

V. My flesh shall rest in hope.

R. And thou wilt not let thy Holy One see corruption.

Ant. Mulieres sedentes ad monumentum lamentabantur, flentes Dominum.

Canticum Zachariæ.

Benedictus Dominus Deus, *p. 183.*

Ant. Mulieres sedentes ad monumentum lamentabantur, flentes Dominum.

V. Christus factus est pro nobis obediens usque ad mortem, mortem autem crucis: propter quod et Deus exaltavit illum, et dedit illi nomen, quod est super omne nomen.

Ant. The women sitting at the sepulchre lamented, weeping for the Lord.

The Canticle of Zachary.

Blessed be the Lord God, etc. *p. 183.*

Ant. The women sitting at the sepulchre lamented, weeping for the Lord.

V. Christ became obedient to death, even the death of the cross: wherefore God hath exalted him, and given him a name that is above all names.

Pater noster, *in secret; the Psalm* Miserere, *p.* 174, *and the Prayer* Respice, *p.* 191.

MORNING OFFICE ON HOLY SATURDAY.

At the outside of the church, fire is struck from a flint, and coals are lighted with it; after which the Priest (accompanied by his Ministers with the Cross, holy water, and incense, before the church gate, if it can be conveniently done, otherwise in the very entrance of the church), blesses the new fire, saying:

V. Dominus vobiscum.

R. Et cum spiritu tuo.

V. The Lord be with you.

R. And with thy spirit.

MORNING OFFICE OF HOLY SATURDAY. 331

Oremus.

DEUS, qui per Filium tuum, angularem scilicet lapidem, claritatis tuæ ignem fidelibus contulisti: productum e silice, nostris profuturum usibus, novum hunc ignem san ✠ ctifica: et concede nobis, ita per hæc festa paschalia cœlestibus desideriis inflammari, ut ad perpetuæ claritatis. puris mentibus valeamus festa pertingere. Per eundem Christum. etc.
R. Amen.

Oremus.

DOMINE Deus, Pater Omnipotens, lumen indeficiens, qui es conditor omnium luminum, bene ✠ dic hoc lumen, quod a te sanctificatum atque benedictum est, qui illuminasti omnem mundum: ut ab eo lumine accendamur, atque illuminemur igne claritatis tuæ: et sicut illuminasti Moysen exeuntem de Ægypto, ita illumines corda et sensus nostros: ut ad vitam et lucem æternam pervenire mereamur. Per

Let us pray.

O GOD, who by thy Son, the corner stone, hast bestowed on the faithful the fire of thy brightness, sanctify this new fire produced from a flint for our useg and grant that durin this paschal festival, we may be so inflamed with heavenly desires, that with pure minds we may come to the solemnity of eternal splendour. Through the same Christ our Lord.
R. Amen.

Let us pray.

O LORD God, Almighty Father, never failing light, who art the author of all light: bless this light, that is blessed and sanctified by thee, who hast enlightened the whole world: that we may been lightened by that light, and inflamed with the fire of thy brightness: and as thou didst give light to Moses, when he went out of Egypt, so illuminate our hearts and senses, that we may obtain light and life ever-

Christum Dominum nostrum.
R. Amen.
Oremus.

DOMINE sancte, Pater Omnipotens, æterne, Deus: benedicentibus nobis hunc ignem in nomine tuo, et unigeniti Filii tui Dei ac Domini nostri Jesu Christi, et Spiritus Sancti, cooperari digneris: et adjuva nos contra ignita tela inimici, et illustra gratia cœlesti. Qui vivis et regnas cum eodem unigenito tuo et Spiritu Sancto, Deus, per omnia sæcula sæculorum.

R. Amen.

lasting. Through Christ our Lord.
R. Amen.
Let us pray.

O Holy Lord, Almighty Father eternal God: vouchsafe to cooperate with us, who bless this fire in thy name, and in that of thy only Son Christ Jesus, our Lord and God and of the Holy Ghost: assist us against the fiery darts of the enemy, and illuminate us with thy heavenly grace. Who livest and reignest with the same only Son and Holy Ghost, one God, for ever and ever.

R. Amen.

Then he blesses the five grains of incense, that are to be fixed in the Paschal Candle, saying:

VENIAT, quæsumus, Omnipotens Deus, super hoc incensum larga tuæ bene ✠ dictionis infusio: et hunc nocturnum splendorem invisibilis regenerator accende: ut non solum sacrificium, quod hac nocte litatum est, arcana luminis tui admixtione,

POUR forth, we beseech thee, Almighty God, thy abundant blessing on this incense, and kindle, O invisible regenerator, the brightness of this night: that not only the sacrifice that is offered this night, may shine by the secret mixture of thy

refulgeat: sed in quocumque loco ex hujus sanctificationis mysterio aliquid fuerit deportatum, expulsa diabolicæ fraudis nequitia, virtus tuæ majestatis assistat. Per Christum Dominum nostrum.

R. Amen.

light: but also into whatever place anything of this mysterious sanctification shall be brought, there, by the power of thy majesty all the malicious artifices of the devil may be defeated. Through Christ our Lord.

R. Amen.

During this prayer an acolyte puts some of the blessed fire into the censer, and the Priest, after the prayer, puts incense into it, blessing it as usual, saying:

Ab illo benedicaris, in cujus honore cremaberis. Amen.

Be thou blessed by him, in whose honour thou shalt be burnt. Amen.

Then he sprinkles the five grains of incense and the fire with holy water, saying:

Asperges me Domine, hyssopo, et mundabor: lavabis me, et super nivem dealbabor.

Thou wilt sprinkle me, O Lord, with hyssop, and I shall be cleansed: thou wilt wash me, and I shall be made whiter than snow.

Then he censes them thrice:

The Deacon having put on a white dalmatic, takes the rod with the triple candle and all enter the Church. The thurifer goes first with an acolyte carrying on a plate the five grains of incense; the Subdeacon with the Cross follows, with the clergy; then the Deacon with the triple candle and last the priest. When the Deacon has entered the

Church an acolyte, who carries a candle lighted from the new fire, lights one of the three candles and the Deacon, holding up the rod, kneels, as do all, except the Subdeacon, and sings:

V. Lumen Christi

R. Deo gratias.

V. Behold the light of Christ.

R. Thanks be to God.

Having arrived in the middle of the Church and the second candle having been lighted, he sings the same in a louder voice; before the Altar, the third candle is lighted and the Lumen Christi is sung still louder.

The Priest then goes to the Epistle side of the Altar; the Deacon gives the Triple Candle to an acolyte, takes the Missal and asks the Blessing of the Priest.

Jube Domne benedicere.

Pray, father bless me,

Then the Priest says:

Dominus sit in corde tuo, et in labiis tuis: ut digne et competenter annunties suum Paschale præconium. In nomine Patris, et Filii, ✠ et Spiritus Sancti.

R Amen.

The Lord be in thy heart and lips, that thou mayest worthily and fitly proclaim his paschal praise. In the name of the Father, and of the Son, and of the Holy Ghost.

R. Amen.

The Deacon goes to the lectern on the Gospel side, places the Missal on it and proceeds to the Blessing of the Paschal Candle, having previously incensed the Missal as at the singing of the Gospel,

Exultet jam angelica turba cœlorum: ex-

LET now the heavenly troops of angels

MORNING OFFICE OF HOLY SATURDAY. 335

ultent divina mysteria: et pro tanti regis victoria, tuba insonet salutaris. Gaudeat et tellus tantis irradiata fulgoribus: et æterni regis splendore illustrata, totius orbis se sentiat amisisse caliginem. Lætetur et mater Ecclesia tanti luminis adornata fulgoribus: et magnis populorum vocibus hac aula resultet. Qua propter adstantes vos, fratres charissimi, ad tam miram hujus sancti luminis claritatem una mecum, quæso, Dei omnipotentis misericordiam invocate. Ut qui me non meis meritis intra Levitarum numerum dignatus est aggregare, luminis sui claritatem infundens, cerei hujus laudem implere perficiat. Per Dominum nostrum Jesum Christum Filium suum: qui cum eo vivit et regnat in unitate Spiritus Sancti, Deus. Per omnia sæcula sæculorum. R. Amen.

rejoice: let the divine mysteries be joyfully celebrated: and let a sacred trumpet proclaim the victory of so great a king. Let the earth also be filled with joy, being illuminated with such resplendent rays: and let it be sensible that the darkness, which overspread the whole world, is chased away by the splendour of our eternal king. Let our mother the church be also glad, finding herself adorned with the rays of so great a light: and let this temple resound with the joyful acclamations of the people. Wherefore, beloved brethren, you who are now present at the admirable brightness of this holy light, I beseech you to invoke with me the mercy of Almighty God. That he, who has been pleased above my desert to admit me into the number of his Levites, will by an infusion of his light upon me, enable me to celebrate the praises of this candle. Through

MORNING OFFICE OF HOLY SATURDAY.

our Lord Jesus Christ his Son, who with him and the Holy Ghost liveth and reigneth one God for ever and ever. R. Amen.

V. Dominus vobiscum.
R. Et cum spiritu tuo.
V. Sursum corda.
R. Habemus ad Dominum.
V. Gratias agamus Domino Deo nostro.
R. Dignum et justum est.

VERE dignum et justum est, invisibilem Deum Patrem omnipotentem, Filiumque ejus Unigenitum, Dominum nostrum Jesum Christum, toto cordis ac mentis affectu, et vocis ministerio personare. Qui pro nobis æterno Patri, Adæ debitum solv.t: et veteris piaculi cautionem pio cruore detersit. Hæc sunt enim festa paschalia, in quibus verus ille Agnus occiditur cujus sanguine postes fidelium consecrantur. Hæ nox est in qua primum patres nostros filios Israel eductos de Ægypto, mare Rubrum sicco vestigio tran-

V. The Lord be with you.
R. And with thy spirit.
V. Lift up your hearts.
R. We have lifted them up to the Lord.
V. Let us give thanks to the Lord our God.
R. It is meet and just.

IT is truly meet and just to proclaim with all the affection of our heart and soul, and with the sound of our voice, the invisible God the Father Almighty, and his only Son our Lord Jesus Christ. Who paid for us to his eternal Father, the debt of Adam: and by his sacred blood cancelled the guilt contracted by original sin. For this is the paschal solemnity, in which the true Lamb was slain, by whose blood the doors of the faithful are consecrated. This is the night in which thou formerly broughtest forth our

sire fecisti. Hæc igitur nox est quæ peccatorum tenebras, columnæ illuminatione purgavit. Hæc nox est, quæ hodie per universum mundum, in Christo credentes, a vitiis sæculi, et caligine peccatorum segregatos, reddit gratiæ, sociat sanctitati. Hæc nox est, in qua destructis vinculis mortis, Christus ab inferis victor ascendit. Nihil enim nobis nasci profuit, nisi redimi profuisset. O mira circa nos tuæ pietatis dignatio! O inæstimabilis dilectio charitatis: ut servum redimeres, Filium tradidisti! O certe necessarium Adæ peccatum, quod Christi morte deletum est! O felix culpa, quæ talem ac tantum meruit habere redemptorem! O vere beata nox, quæ sola meruit scire tempus et oram, in qua Christus ab inferis resurrexit! Hæc nox est, de qua scriptum est: Et nox sicut dies illuminabitur: et nox illuminatio mea in deliciis meis. Hujus igi-

forefathers the children of Israel out of Egypt, leading them dry-foot through the Red Sea. This then is the night, which dissipated the darkness of sin, by the light of the pillar. This is the night, which now delivers all over the world those that believe in Christ, from the vices of the world, and darkness of sin, restores them to grace, and clothes them with sanctity. This is the night in which Christ broke the chains of death, and ascended conqueror from hell. For it availed us nothing to be born, unless it had availed us to be redeemed. Oh how admirable is thy goodness towards us! O how inestimable is thy love! Thou hast delivered up thy Son to redeem a slave. O truly necessary sin of Adam. which the death of Christ has blotted out: O happy fault, that merited such and so great a Redeemer! O truly blessed night, which

tur sanctificatio noctis fugat scelera, culpas lavat: et reddit innocentiam plasis. et mœstis lætitiam. Fugat odia, concordiam parat, et curvat imperia.

alone deserves to know the time and hour when Christ rose again from hell. This is the night of which it is written: And the night shall be as light as the day, and the night is my illumination in my delights. Therefore the sanctification of this night blots out crimes, washes away sins, and restores innocence to sinners, and joy to the sorrowful. It banishes enmities, produces concord and humbles empires.

Here the Deacon fixes the five grains of incense in the candle, in the form of a cross.

In hujus igitur noctis gratia suscipe, sancte Pater, incensi hujus sacrificium vespertinum: quod tibi in hac cerei oblatione solemni, per ministrorum manus, de operibus apum, sacrosancta reddit ecclesia. Sed jam columnæ hujus præconia novimus, quam in honorem Dei rutilans ignis accendit.

Therefore on this sacred night, receive, O holy Father, the evening sacrifice of this incense, which thy holy church by the hands of her ministers presents to thee in the solemn oblation of this wax candle made out of the labour of bees. And now we know the excellence of this pillar, which the sparking fire lights for the honour of God.

Here he lights the Candle from the triple Candle.

Qui licet sit divisus in partes mutuati tamen luminis detrimenta non novit. Alitur enim li-

Which fire, though now divided, suffers no loss from the communication of its light. Be-

quantibus ceris, quas in substantiam pretiosæ hujus lampadis, apis mater eduxit.

cause it is fed by the melted wax, which its mother the bee made for the composition of the precious lamp.

Here the lamps are lighted.

O vere beata nox, quæ expoliavit Ægyptios, ditavit Hebræos: nox, in qua terrenis cœlestia, humanis divina junguntur. Oramus ergo te, Domine: ut cereus iste in honorem tui nominis consecratus, ad noctis hujus caliginem destruendam, indeficiens perseveret. Et in odorem suavitatis acceptus, supernis luminaribus misceatur. Flammas ejus lucifer matutinus inveniat. Ille, inquam, lucifer, qui nescit occasum. Ille, qui regressus ab inferis humano generi serenus illuxit. Precamur ergo te Domine: ut nos famulos tuos, omnemque clerum, et devotissimum populum: una cum beatissimo Papa nostro *N.* et Antistite nostro *N* quiete temporum concessa, in his

O truly blessed night which plundered the Egyptians, and enriched the Hebrews. A night in which heaven is united to earth, and God to man. We beseech thee therefore, O Lord that this candle, consecrated to the honour of thy name, may continue burning to dissipate the darkness of this night. And being accepted as a sweet-smelling savour may be united with the celestial lights. Let the morning star find it burning. I mean that star which never sets. Who being returned from hell, shone with brightness on mankind. We beseech thee therefore, O Lord, to grant us peaceable times during these paschal solemnities, and with thy constant protection to rule, govern and pre-

paschalibus gaudiis, assidua protectione regere, gubernare, et conservare digneris. Respice etiam ad devotissimum Imperatom nostrum cujus tu Deus, desiderii vota prænoscens, ineffabili pietatis et misericordiæ tuæ munere, tranquillum perpetuæ pacis accomoda: et cœlestem victoriam cum omni populo suo. Per eumdem Dominum nostrum Jesum Christum Filium tuum: qui tecum vivit et regnat in unitate Spiritus Sancti. Deus, per omnia sæcula seculorum.

R. Amen.

serve us thy servants, all the clergy, and the devout laity, together, with our holy Father Pope N, and our Bishop N. Regard also our most devout Imperor, and since thou knowest, O heart, God, the desires of his grant by the ineffable grace of thy goodness and mercy, that he may enjoy with all his people the tranquillity of perpetual peace and heavenly victory. Through the same Lord Jesus Christ thy Son: who with thee and the Holy Ghost, liveth and reigneth one God for ever and ever

R. Amen.

Here the Deaon changes his white vestments for violet and goes to the side of the Priest, who lays aside his Cope and assumes a maniple and Chasuble of violet and reads the Prophecies in a low voice at the Epistle corner, whilst they are read aloud in the chnrch. At this time formerly the Catechumens were prepared for Baptism.

Prophetia prima.
Gen. i. ii

IN principio creavit Deus cœlum et terram. Terra autem erat inanis et vacua, et tene-

The first Prophecy.
Gen. i. ii.

IN the beginnig God created heaven and earth. And the Earth was void and empty,

bræ erant super faciem abyssi: et spiritus Dei ferebatur super aquas. Dixitque Deus: Fiat lux. Et facta est lux. Et vidit Deus lucem quod esset bona: et divisit lucem a tenebris. Appellavitque lucem Diem, et tenebras Noctem: Factumque est vespere et mane, dies unus. Dixit quoque Deus: Fiat firmamentum in medio aquarum, et dividat aquas ab aquis. Et fecit Deus firmamentum: divisitque aquas, quæ erant sub firmamento ab his quæ erant super firmamentum. Et factum est ita. Vocavitque Deus firmamentum. Cælum: Et factum est vespere et mane, dies secundus. Dixit vero Deus: Congregentur aquæ, quae sub cœlo sunt, in locum unum, et appareat Arida. Et factum est ita. Et vocavit Deus aridam, Terram: congregationesque aquarum appellavit Maria. Et vidi Deus quod esset bonum. Et ait:

and darkness was upon the face of the deep, and the spirit of God moved over the waters. And God said: Be light made. And light was made. And God saw the light that it was good: and he divided the light from the darkness. And he called the light Day, and the darkness Night: and there was evening and morning one day. And God said: Let there be a firmament made amidst the waters: and let it divide the waters from the waters. And God made a firmament, and divided the waters that were under the firmament from those that were above the firmament. And it was so. And God called the firmament Heaven: and the evening and morning were the second day. God also said: Let the waters that are under the heaven be gathered together into one place: and let the dry land appear. And it was so done. And God called

Germinet terra herbam virentem, et facientem semen, et lignum pomiferum faciens fructum juxta genus suum, cujus semen in semetipso sit super terram. Et factum est ita. Et protulit terra herbam virentem, et facientem semen juxta genus suum lignumque faciens fructum, et habens unumquodque sementem secundum speciem suam. Et vidit Deus, quod esset bonum. Et factum est vespere et mane, dies tertius. Dixit autem Deus: Fiant luminaria in firmamento cœli, et dividant diem ac noctem, et sint in signa et tempora, et dies et annos: ut luceant in firmamento cœli, et illuminent terram. Et factum est ita. Fecitque Deus duo luminaria magna: luminare majus, ut præesset diei: et luminare minus, ut præesset nocti: et stellas. Et posuit eas in firmamento cœli, ut lucerent super terram, et præessent diei ac nocti, et

the dry land, Earth: and the gathering together of the waters he called Seas. And God saw that it was good. And he said: Let the earth bring forth the green herb, and such as may seed, and the fruit tree yielding fruit after its kind, which may have seed in itself upon the earth. And it was so done. And the earth brought forth the green herb, and such as yielded seed according to its kind, and the tree that beareth fruit, having seed each one according to its kind. And God saw that it was good. And the evening and the morning were the third day. And God said: Let there be lights made in the firmament of heaven, to divide the day and the night, and let them be for signs, and for seasons and for days and years: to shine in the firmament of heaven and to give light upon the earth. And it was so done. And God made two great

dividerent lucem ac tenebras. Et vidit Deus, quod esset bonum. Et factum est vespere et mane, dies quartus. Dixit etiam Deus: Producant aquæ reptile animæ viventis, et volatile super terram sub firmamento cœli Creavitque Deus cete grandia et omnem animam viventem atque motabilem, quam produxerant aquæ in species suas, et omne volatile, secundum genus suum. Et vidit Deus, quod esset bonum. Benedixitque eis, dicens: Crescite, et multiplicamini, et replete aquis maris: avesque multiplicentur super terram. Et factum est vespere et mane, dies quintus. Dixit quoque Deus: Producat terra animam viventem in genere suo: jumenta, et reptilia, et bestias terræ secundum species suas. Factumque est ita. Et fecit Deus bestias terræ juxta species suas, et jumenta et omne reptile terræ in genere suo. Et vidit De-

lights: a greater light to rule the day; and a lesser light to rule the night: and stars. And he set them in the firmament of heaven, to shine upon the earth, and to rule the day and the night, and to divide the light and the darkness. And God saw that it was good. And the evening and the morning were the fourth day. God also said: Let the waters bring forth the creeping creature having life, and the fowl that may fly over the earth under the firmament of heaven. And God created the great whales, and every living and moving creature, which the waters brought forth, according to their kinds, and every winged fowl according to its kind. And God saw that it was good. And he blessed them, saying: Increase and multiply, and fill the waters of the sea and let the birds be multiplied upon the earth. And the even-

us, quod esset bonum, et ait: Faciamus hominem ad imaginem et similitudinem nostram: Et præsit piscibus maris et volatilibus cœli, et bestiis universæque terræ, omnique reptili quod movetur in terra. Et creavit Deus hominem ad imaginem suam: ad imaginem Dei creavit illum, masculum et feminam creavit eos. Benedixitque illis Deus, et ait: Crescite, et multiplicamini, et replete terram, et subjicite eam, et dominamini piscibus maris, et volatilibus cœli, et universis animantibus, quæ moventur super terram. Dixitque Deus: Ecce dedi vobis omnem herbam afferentem semen super terram et universa ligna, quaæ habent in semetpsis sementem generis sui, ut sint vobis in escam, et cunctis animantibus terræ, omnique volucri cœli, et universis quæ moventur in terra, et in quibus est anima vivens, ut habeant ad vescendum. Et

ing and the morning were the fifth day. And God said: Let the earth bring forth the living creature in its kind, cattle, and creeping things, and beasts of the earth according to their kinds: and it was so done. And God made the beasts of the earth according to their kinds, an cattle, and every thing that creepeth on the earth after its kind. And God saw that it was good. And he said: Let us make man to our image and likeness: and let him have dominion over the fishes of the sea, and the fowls of the air, and the beasts, and the whole earth, and every creeping creature that moveth upon the earth. And God created man to his own image: to the image of God he created him, male and female he created them. And God blessed them, saying: Increase and multiply, and fill the earth, and subdue it, and rule over the fishes of the sea,

factum est ita. Viditque Deus cuncta quæ fecerat: et erant valde bona. Et factum est vespere et mane, dies sextus. Igitur perfecti sunt cœli et terra, et omnis ornatus eorum. Complevitque Deus die septimo opus suum, quod fecerat: et requievit die septimo ab universo opere quod patrarat.

and the fowls of the air, and all living creatures that move upon the earth. And God said: Behold I have given you every herb bearing seed upon the earth, and all trees that have in themselves seed of their own kind, to be your meat: and to all beasts of the earth, and to every fowl of the air and to all that move upon the earth, and

wherein there is life, that they may have to feed upon. And it was so done. And God saw all the things that he had made, and they were very good. And the evening and morning were the sixth day. So the heavens and the earth were finished, and the furniture of them. And on the seventh day God ended his work which he had made: and he rested on the seventh day from all his work which he had done.

Oremus.

Let us pray.

Flectamus genua.

Let us bend our knees.

Levate.

Rise up.

Oratio.

The prayer.

DEUS, qui mirabiliter creasti hominem, et mirabilius redemisti: da nobis, quæsumus, contra oblectamenta peccati, mentis ratione

O God, who hast wonderfully created man and more wonderfuly redeemed him: grant us, we beseech thee such strength of mind

persistere; ut mereamur ad æterna gaudia pervenire. Per Dominum nostrum Jesum Christum, etc.
R. Amen.

Prophetia secunda.

(Gen. v-viii.)

NOE vero cum quingentorum esset annorum genuit Sem, Cham et Japhet. Cumque cœpissent homines multiplicari super terram, et filias procreassent, videntes filii Dei filias hominum, quod essent pulchræ, acceperunt sibi uxores ex omnibus, quas elegerant. Dixitque Deus: Non permanebit spiritus meus in homine in æternum, quia caro est: Eruntque dies illius centum viginti annorum. Gigantes autem erant super terram in diebus illis. Postquam enim ingressi sunt filii Dei ad filias hominum, illæque genuerunt, isti sunt potentes a sæculo viri famosi. Videns autem Deus, quod multa malitia hominum esset

and reason against the allurements of sin, that we may deserve to obtain eternal joys. Throug Jesus Christ our Lord, etc. R. Amen.

The second Prophecy.

(Gen. v-viii.)

NOE, when he was five hundred years old, begat Sem, Cham, and Japheth. And after that men began to be multiplied upon the earth, and daughters were born to them, the sons of God seeing the daughters of men, that they were fair, took to themselves wives of all which they chose. And God said: My spirit shall not remain in man for ever, because he is flesh: his days shall be a hundred and twenty years. Now giants were upon the earth in those days. For after the sons of God went in to the daughters of men, and they brought forth children, these are the mighty men of old, men of renown. And God seeing that the wicked-

in terra, et cuncta cogitatio cordis intenta esset ad malum omni tempore, pœnituit eum, quod hominem fecisset in terra. Et actus dolore cordis intrinsecus: Delebo, inquit, hominem quem creavi, a facie terræ, ab homine usque ad animantia, a reptili usque ad volucres cœli. Pœnitet enim me fecisse eos. Noe vero invenit gratiam coram Domino. Hæ sunt generationes Noe: Noe vir justus atque perfectus fuit in generationibus suis, cum Deo ambulavit. Et genuit tres filios, Sem, Cham, et Japheth. Corrupta est autem terra coram Deo, et repleta est iniquitate. Cumque vidisset Deus terram esse corruptam (omnis quippe caro corruperat viam suam super terram) dixit ad Noe: Finis universæ carnis venit coram me: repleta est terra iniquitate a facie eorum, et ego disperdam eos cum terra. Fac tibi arcam de

ness of man was great on the earth, and that all the thought of their heart was bent upon evil at all times, it repented him that he had made man on the earth. And being touched inwardly with sorrow of heart, he said: I will destroy man, whom I have created, from the face of the earth, from man even to beasts, from the creeping thing even to the fowls of the air, for it repenteth me that I have made them. But Noe found grace before the Lord. These are the generations of Noe: Noe was a just and perfect man in his generations, he walked with God. And he begot three sons, Sem, Cham, and Japheth. And the earth was corrupted before God, and was filled with iniquity. And when God had seen that the earth was corrupted (for all flesh had corrupted its way upon the earth) he said to Noe: The end of all flesh is come before me,

lignis levigatis. Mansiunculas in arca facies. Et bitumine linies intrinsecus et extrinsecus. Et sic facies eam: Trecentorum cubitorum erit longitudo arcæ, quinquaginta cubitorum latitudo et triginta cubitorum altitudo illius. Fenestram in arca facies, et in cubito consummabis summitatem ejus. Ostium autem arcæ pones ex latere, deorsum, cœnacula, et tristega facies in ea. Ecce ego adducam aquas diluvii super terram, ut interficiam omnem carnem, in qua spiritus vitæ est subter cœlum. Universa quæ in terra sunt consumentur. Ponamque fœdus meum tecum: et ingredieris arcam tu et filii tui, uxor tua, et uxores filiorum tuorum tecum. Et ex cunctis animantibus universæ carnis bina induces in arcam, ut vivant tecum, masculini sexus et feminini. De volucribus juxta genus suum, et de jumentis in genere suo, et ex omni

the earth is filled with iniquity through them, and I will destroy them with the earth. Make thee an ark of timber planks: thou shalt make little rooms in the ark, and thou shalt pitch it within and without. And thus shalt thou make it. The length of the ark shall be three hundred cubits: the breadth of it fifty cubits, and the height of it thirty cubits. Thou shalt make a window in the ark, and in a cubit thou shalt finish the top of it: and the door of the ark thou shalt set in the side: with lower and middle chambers, and third stories shalt thou make it. Behold I will bring the waters of a great flood upon the earth, to destroy all flesh, wherein is the breath of life under heaven. All things that are in the earth shall be consumed. And I will establish my covenant with thee: and thou shalt enter into the ark, thou and thy sons,

reptili terræ secundum genus suum: bina de omnibus ingredientur tecum, ut possint vivere. Tolles igitur tecum ex omnibus escis, quæ mandi possunt, et comportabis apud te: et erunt tam tibi quam illis in cibum. Fecit igitur Noe omnia quæ præceperat illi Deus. Eratque sexcentorum annorum, quando diluvii aquæ inundaverunt super terram. Rupti sunt omnes fontes abyssi magnæ, et cataractæ coeli apertæ sunt, et facta est pluvia super terram quadraginta diebus et quadraginta noctibus. In articulo diei illius ingressus est Noe, et Sem, et Cham, et Japheth, filii ejus: uxor illius, et tres uxores filiorum ejus cum eis in arcam: ipsi et omne animal secundum genus suum, universaque jumenta in genere suo, et omne quod movetur super tersam in genere suo cunctumque volatile secundum genus suum. Porro arca fere-

and thy wife, and the wives of thy sons with thee. And of every living creature of all flesh, thou shalt bring two of a sort into the ark, that they may live with thee: of the male sex, and the female. Of fowls according to their kind, and of beasts in their kind, and of every thing that creepeth on the earth according to its kind: two of every sort shall go in with thee, that they may live. Thou shalt take unto thee of all food, that may be eaten, and thou shalt lay it up with thee: and it shall be food for thee and them. And Noe did all things which God commanded him. And he was six hundred years old when the waters of the flood overflowed the earth. All the fountains of the great deep were broken up, and the flood gates of heaven were opened. And the rain fell upon the earth forty days and forty nights. In the self-same day Noe, and

batur super aquas. Et aquæ prevaluerunt nimis super terram: pertique sunt omnes montes excelsi sub universo cœlo. Quindecim cubitis altior fuit acqua super montes quos operuerat. Consumptaque est omni caro quae movebatur super terram, volucrum, animantium, bestiarum, omniumque reptilium, quæ reptant super terram. Remansit autem solus Noe, et qui cum eo erant in arca. Obtinueruntque aquæ terram centum quinquaginta diebus. Recordatus autem Deus Noe, cunctorumque animantium, et omnium jumentorum, quæ erant cum eo in arca, adduxit spiritum super terram, et imminutæ sunt aquæ. Et clausi sunt fontes abyssi et cataractæ cœli: et prohibitæ sunt pluviæ de cœlo. Reversæque sunt aquæ de terra, euntes et redeuntes: et cœperunt minui post centum quinquaginta dies. Cumque transissent quadraginta

Sem, and Cham, and Japhet, his sons: his wife, and the three wives of his sons with them, went into the ark. They and every beast according to its kind, and all the cattle in their kind, and every thing that moveth upon the earth according to its kind, and every soul according to its kind, all birds, and all that fly. And the ark was carried upon the waters. And the waters prevailed beyond measure upon the earth: and all the high mountains under the whole heaven were covered. The water was fifteen cubits higher than the mountains, which it covered. And all flesh was destroyed that moved upon the earth, both of fowl, and of cattle, and of beasts, and of all creeping things that creep upon the earth: and Noe only remained, and they that were with him in the ark. And the waters prevailed upon the earth a hundred and

dies, aperiens Noe fenestram arcæ, quam fecerat, dimisit corvum: qui egrediebatur, et non revertebatur, donec siccarentur aquæ super terram. Emisit quoque columbam post eum, ut videret si jam cessassent aquæ super faciem terræ. Quæ cum non invenisset ubi requiesceret pes ejus, reversa est ad eum in arcam. Aquæ enim erant super universam terram. Extenditque manum, et apprehensam intulit in arcam. Expectatus autem ultra septem diebus aliis, rursum dimisit columbam ex arca. At illa venit ad eum ad vesperam, portans ramum olivæ virentibus foliis in ore suo. Intellexit ergo Noe, quod cessassent aquæ super terram. Expectavitque nihilominus septem alios dies: et emisit columbam, quæ non est reversa ultra ad eum. Locutus est autem Deus ad Noe, dicens: Egredere de arca, tu et uxor tua, filii tui, et uxo-

fifty days. And God remembered Noe, and all the living creatures, and all the cattle which were with him in the ark, and brought a wind upon the earth, and the waters were abated. The fountains also of the deep, and the floodgates of heaven, were shut up: and the rain from heaven was restrained. And the waters returned from off the earth, going and coming: and they began to be abated after a hundred and fifty days. And after that forty days were passed. Noe opening the window of the ark which he had made, sent forth a raven: which went forth and did not return, till the waters were dried up upon the face of the earth. He sent forth also a dove after him, to see if the waters had ceased upon the face of the earth. But she not finding where her foot might rest, returned to him into the ark: for the waters were upon

res filiorum tuorum tecum. Cuncta animantia, quæ sunt apud te, ex omni carni, tam in volatilibus, quam in bestiis, et universis reptilibus, quæ reptant super terram educ tecum, et ingredimini super terram: Crescite, et multiplicamini super eam Egressus est ergo Noe, et filii ejus, uxor illius et uxores filiorum ejus cum eo. Sed et omnia animantia, jumenta, et reptilia quæ reptant super terram, secundum genus suum, egressa sunt de arca. Ædificavit autem Noe altare Domino: et tollens de cunctis pecoribus et volucribus mundis obtulit holocausta super altare. Odoratusque est Dominus odorem suavitatis.

the whole earth: and he put forth his hand, and caught her and brought her into the ark. And having waited yet seven other days, he again sent forth the dove out of the ark. And she came to him in the evening, carrying a bough of an olive tree, with green leaves in her mouth. Noe therefore understood that the waters were ceased upon the earth. And he stayed yet other seven days: and he sent forth the dove, which returned not any more unto him. And God spoke to Noe, saying, Go out of the ark, thou and thy wife, thy sons, and the wives of thy sons with thee. All living things that are with thee of all flesh, as well in fowls as beasts, and all creeping things that creep upon the earth, bring out with thee, and go ye upon the earth: increase and multiply upon it. So Noe went out, he and his sons; his wife, and the wives of his sons with him: and all living things, and cattle, and creeping things that creep upon the earth, according to their kinds, went out of the ark. And Noe built an altar unto the Lord: and taking of all cattle

and fowls that were clean, offered holocausts upon the altar, And the Lord smelled a sweet savour.

Oremus.	Let us pray.
Flectamus genua	Let us bend our knees.
Levate.	Rise up.
Oratio.	*The Prayer.*

DEUS, incommutabilis virtus, et lumen æternum: respice propitius ad totius Ecclesiæ tuæ mirabile sacramentum; et opus salutis humanæ, perpetuæ dispotitionis effectu tranquillius operare: totusque mundus experiatur et videat, dejecta erigi, inveterata renovari, et per ipsum redire omnia in integrum, a quo sumpsere principium Dominum nostrum, Jesum Christum Filium tuum, qui tecum vivit et regnat, etc.

O GOD whose power is unchangeable and light eternal: mercifully regard the wonderful sacrament of thy whole church, and by an effect of thy perpetual providence perform with tranquillity the work of human salvation: and let the whole world experience and see, that what is fallen is raised up, what was old is made new, and all things are re-established through him that gave them their first being, our Lord Jesus Christ, who liveth, etc.

Prophetia tertia.
Gen. xxii.

IN diebus illis: tentavit Deus Abraham, et dixit ad eum: Abraham, Abraham. At ille respondit: Adsum. Ait illi: Tolle filium tuum unigenitum, quem dili-

The third Prophecy.
Gen. xxii.

IN those days: God tempted Abraham, and said to him: Abraham, Abraham. And he answered: Here I am. He said to him; Take thy only begotten

gis, Isaac, et vade in terram visionis: atque ibi offeres eum in holocaustum super unum montium, quem monstravero tibi. Igitur Abraham de nocte consurgens, stravit asinum suum, ducens secum duos juvenes, et Isaac filium suum: Cumque concidisset ligna in holocaustum, abiit ad locum quem præceperat ei Deus. Die autem tertio, elevatis oculis vidit locum procul: dixitque ad pueros suos: Expectate hic cum asino: Ego et puer illuc usque properantes, postquam adoraverimus, revertemur ad vos. Tulit quoque ligna holocausti, et imposuit super Isaac filium suum: ipse vero portabat in manibus ignem et gladium. Cumque duo pergerent simul, dixit Isaac patri suo: Pater mi. At ille respondit: Quid vis, fili? Ecce, inquit, ignis et ligna: ubi est victima holocausti? Dixit autem Abraham: Deus providebit sibi victimam holocausti, fili mi

son Isaac, whom thou lovest, and go into the land of Vision: and there thou shalt offer him for a holocaust upon one of the mountains, which I will show thee. So Abraham, rising up in the night, saddled his ass: and took with him two young men, and Isaac his son. And when he had cut wood for the holocaust, he went his way to the place which God had commanded him. And on the third day, lifting up his eyes, he saw the place afar off. And he said to his young men: Stay you here with the ass: I and the boy will go with speed as far as yonder, and after we have worshiped, will return to you. And he took the wood for the holocaust, and laid it upon Isaac his son: and he himself carried in his hands fire and a sword. And as they went on together, Isaac said to his father: My father. And he answered: What wilt

Pergebant ergo pariter: et venerunt ad locum quem ostenderat ei Deus, in quo ædificavit altare, et desuper ligna composuit: cumque alligasset Isaac filium suum, posuit eum in altare super struem lignorum.. Extenditque manum, et arripuit gladium, ut immolaret filium suum. Et ecce angelus Domini de cœlo clamavit, dicens: Abraham, Abraham. Qui respondit: Adsum. Dixitque ei: Non extendas manum tuam super puerum, neque facias illi quidquam: nunc cognovi quod timas Deum, et non pepercisti unigenito filio tuo propter me. Levavit Abraham oculos suos, viditque post tergum arietem inter vepres hærentem cornibus, quem assumens, obtulit holocaustum pro filio. Appellavitque nomen loci illius. *Dominus videt.* Unde usque hodie dicitur: In monte *Dominus videbit.* Vocavit autem angelus Domini Abraham secundo

thou, son? Behold, saith he, fire and wood: where is the victim for the holocaust? And Abraham said: God will provide himself a victim for a holocaust, my son. So they went on together: and they came to the place which God had showed him, where he built an altar and laid the wood in order upon it: and when he had bound Isaac his son, he laid him on the altar upon the pile of wood. And he put forth his hand, and took the sword to sacrifice his son. And behold an angel of the Lord from heaven called to him, saying: Abraham, Abraham. And he answered: Here I am. And he said to him: Lay not thy hand upon the boy, neither do thou any thing to him: now I know that thou fearest God, and hast not spared thy only begotten son for my sake. Abraham lifted up his eyes, and saw behind his back a ram amongst

de cœlo, dicens: Per memetipsum juravi, dicit Dominus: quia fecisti hanc rem, et non pepercisti filio tuo unigenito propter me, benedicam tibi, et multiplicabo semen tuum sicut stellas cœli, et velut arenam, quae est in littore maris. Possidebit semen tuum portas inimicorum suorum, et benedicentur in semine tuo omnes gentes terræ, quia obedisti voci meæ. Reversus est Abraham ad pueros suos, abieruntque Bersabee simul. et habitavit ibi.

the briars, sticking fast by the horns, which he took and offered for a holocaust instead of his son. And he called the name of that place, *The Lord seeth*. Whereupon even to this day it is said: In the mountain, the Lord will see. And the angel of the Lord called to Abraham a second time from heaven saying: By my own self have I sworn, saith the Lord, because thou hast done this thing, and hast not spared thy only begotten son for my sake: I will bless thee and I will multiply thy seed as the stars of heaven, and as the sand that is by the sea-shore: thy seed shall possess the gates of their enemies, and in thy seed shall all the nations of the earth be blessed, because thou hast obeyed my voice. Abraham returned to his young men, and they went to Bersabee together and he dwelt there.

<table>
<tr><td>Oremus.</td><td>Let us pray.</td></tr>
<tr><td>Flectamus genua.</td><td>Let us bend our knees.</td></tr>
<tr><td>Levate.</td><td>Rise up.</td></tr>
<tr><td>Oratio.</td><td>The Prayer.</td></tr>
</table>

DEUS fidelium Pater summe, qui in toto orbe terrarum, promis-

O GOD, the sovereign Father of all the faithful, who all over the

sionis tuæ filios diffusa adoptionis gratia multiplicas: et per paschale sacramentum, Abraham puerum tuum universarum, sicut jurasti, gentium efficis patrem: da populis tuis digne ad gratiam tuæ vocationis introire. Per Dominum nostrum Jesum Christum, etc.

Prophetia quarta.
Exod. xiv.

IN diebus illis: Factum est in vigilia matutina et ecce respiciens Dominus super castra Ægyptiorum per columnam ignis et nubis, interfecit exercitum eorum: et subvertit rotas curruum, ferebanturque in profundum. Dixerunt ergo Ægyptii: Fugiamus Israelem: Dominus enim pugnat pro eis contra nos. Et ait Dominus ad Moysen: Extende manum tuam super mare, ut revertantur aquæ ad Ægyptios super currus et equites eorum. Cumque extendisset Moyses manum contra mare, re-

world multiplies the children of thy promise by the grace of thy adoption: and makest thy servant Abraham, according to thy oath, the father of all nations: by this paschal sacrament grant that thy people may worthily receive the grace of thy vocation. Through our Lord, etc.

The fourth Prophecy.
Exod. xiv.

IN those days: It came to pass in the morning watch, and behold the Lord looking upon the Egyptian army through the pillar of fire and of the cloud, slew their host: and overthrew the wheels of the chariots, and they were carried into the deep. And the Egyptians said: Let us flee from Israel: for the Lord fighteth for them against us. And the Lord said to Moses: Stretch forth thy hand over the sea, that the waters may come again upon the Egyptians upon their chariots and

versum est primo diluculo ad priorem locum: fugientibusque Ægyptiis occurrerunt aquæ: et involvit eos Dominus in mediis fluctibus. Reversæque sunt aquæ, et operuerunt currus et equites cuncti exercitus Pharaonis, qui sequentes ingressi fuerant mare: nec unus quidem superfuit ex eis. Filii autem Israel perrexerunt per medium sicci maris, et aquæ eis erant quasi pro muro a dextris et a sinistris. Liberavitque Dominus in die illa Israel de manu Ægyptiorum. Et viderunt Ægyptios mortuos super littus maris, et manum magnam quam exercuerat Dominus contra eos: timuitque populus Dominum, et crediderunt Domino, et Moysi servo ejus. Tunc cecinit Moyses, et filii Israel carmen hoc Domino, et dixerunt.

horsemen. And when Moses had stretched forth his hand towards the sea, it returned at the first break of day to the former place: and as the Egyptians were fleeing away, the waters came upon them, and the Lord shut them up in the middle of the waves. And the waters returned, and covered the chariots and the horsemen of all the army of Pharaoh, who had come into the sea after them, neither did there so much as one of them remain. But the children of Israel marched through the midst of the sea upon dry land, and the waters were to them as a wall on the right hand and on the left: and the Lord delivered Israel in that day out of the hands of the Egyptians. And they saw the Egyptians dead upon the seashore, and the mighty hand that the Lord had used against them: and the people feared the Lord, and they believed the Lord, and Moses his servant. Then Moses and the children of Israel sung this canticle to the Lord, and said:

Tractus. — Cantemus Domino gloriose enim honorificatus est: equum et ascensorem projecit in mare: adjutor et protector factus est mihi in salutem. *V.* Hic Deus meus, et honorificabo eum: Deus patris mei, et exaltabo eum. *V.* Dominus conterens bella: Dominus nomen est illi.

Oremus.
Flectamus genua.
Levate.
Oratio.

DEUS, cujus antiqua miracula etiam nostris sæculis coruscare sentimus: dum quod uni populo a persecutione Ægyptiaca liberando, dexteræ tuæ potentia contulisti, id in salutem Gentium per aquam regenerationis operaris: præsta, ut in Abrahæ filios, et in Israeliticam dignitatem: totius mundi transeat plenitudo. Per Dominum nostrum, etc.

The Tract. — Let us sing to the Lord, for he is gloriously honoured: he has thrown the horse and his rider into the sea: he became my helper and protector for my safety. *V.* This is my God and I will honour him: the God of my father, and I will extol him. *V.* He is the Lord that destroys wars: the Lord is his name.

Let us pray.
Let us bend our knees.
Rise up.
The Prayer.

O GOD, whose ancient miracles we see renewed in our days, whilst by the water of our regeneration thou workest for the salvation of the Gentiles, that which by the power of thy right hand thou didst for the delivery of one people from the Egyptian persecution: grant that all the nations of the world may become the children of Abraham, and partake of the dignity of the people of Israel. Through our Lord, etc.

Prophetia quinta.
Isa. liv. lv.

HÆC est hereditas servorum Domini, et justitia eorum apud me, dicit Dominus. Omnes sitientes venite ad aquas: et qui non habetis argentum, properate, emite, et comedite: venite, emite absque argento, et absque ulla commutatione, vinum et lac. Quare appenditis argentum non in panibus, et laborem vestrum non in saturitate? Audite audientes me, et comedite bonum, et delectabitur in crassitudine anima vestra. Inclinate aurem vestram et venite ad me: audite, et vivit anima vestra, et feriam vobis cum pactum sempiternum, misericordias David fidelis. Ecce testem populis dedi eum, ducem ac præceptorem Gentibus. Ecce Gentem, quam nesciebas, vocabis: et Gentes, quæ te non cognoverunt ad te current, propter Dominum Deum tuum et sanctum Israel: quia

The fifth Prophecy.
Isa. liv. lv.

THIS is the inheritance of the servants of the Lord, and their justice with me saith the Lord. All you that thirst, come to the waters; and you that have no money, make haste, buy and eat: come ye, buy wine and milk without money, and without any price. Why do you spend money, for that which is not bread, and you labour for that which doth not satisfy you? Hearken diligently to me, and that which is good, and your soul shall be delighted in fatness. Incline your ear and come to me: hear and your soul shall live and I will make an everlasting convenant with you, the faithful mercies of David. Behold I have given him for a witness to the people, for a leader and a master to the Gentiles. Behold thou shalt call a nation, which thou knewest not: and the nations that knew not

glorificavit te. Quærite Dominum, dum inveniri potest: invocate eum dum prope est. Derelinquat impius viam suam, et vir iniquus cogitationes suas, et revertutur ad Dominum, et miserebitur ejus: et ad Deum nostrum: quoniam multus est ad ignoscendum. Non enim cogitationes meæ, cogitationes vestræ: neque viæ vestræ, viæ meæ dicit Dominus. Quia sicut exaltantur cœli a terra: sic exaltatæ sunt viæ meæ a viis vestris, et cogitationes meæ cogitationibus vestris. Et quomodo descendit imber, et nix de cœlo, et illuc ultra non revertitur, sed inebriat terram, et infundit eam, et germinare eam facit, et dat semen serenti, et panem comedenti: sic erit verbum meum, quod egredietur de ore meo: non revertetur ad me vacuum, sed faciet quæcumque volui et prosperabitur in his, ad quæ misi

thee shall run to thee, because of the Lord thy God, and for the Holy One of Israel: for he hath glorified thee. Seek ye the Lord, while he may be found, call upon him while he is near. Let the wicked forsake his way, and the unjust man his thoughts, and let him return to the Lord, and he will have mercy on him: and to our God, for he is bountiful to forgive. For my thoughts are not your thoughts, nor your ways my ways, saith the Lord. For as the heavens are exalted above the earth, so are my ways exalted above your ways, and my thoughts above your thoughts. And as the rain and the snow come down from heaven, and return no more thither, but soak the earth, and water it, and make it to spring, and give seed to the sower, and bread to the eater: so shall my word be which shall go forth from my mouth:

illud: dicit Dominus Omnipotens.

it shall not return to me void but it shall do whatever I please, and shall prosper in the things for which I sent it.

Oremus.

Let us pray.

Flectamus genua.

Let us bend our knees.

Levate.

Rise up.

Oratio.

The Prayer.

OMnipotens sempiterne Deus multiplica in honorem nominis tui quod patrum fidei spopondisti, et promissionis filios sacra adoptione dilata· ut quod priores sancti non dubitaverunt futurum ecclesia tua magna jam ex parte cognoscat impletum, Per Dominum nostrum Jesum Christum.

ALmighty and eternal God, multiply for the honour of thy name what thou didst promise to the faith of our forefathers: and increase by the sacred adoptions the children of that promise: that what the ancient saints doubted not would come to pass thy church may now find in a great part accomplished. Through our Lord Jesus Christ.

Prophetia sexta.

The Sixth Prophecy.

Baruch III.

Baruch III.

AUDI, Israel, mandate vitæ auribus percipe, ut scias prudentiam. Quid est, Israel, quod in terra inimicorum es? Inveterasti in terra aliena, coinquinatus es cum mortuis: de-

HEAR O Israel, the commandments of life: give ear that thou mayest learn wisdom. How happeneth it, O Israel, that thou art in thy enemies' land. Thou art grown old in a

putatus es cum descendentibus in infernum. Derelinquisti fontem sapientæ. Nam si in via Dei ambulasses, habitasses utique in pace sempiterna. Disce, ubi sit prudentia, ubi sit virtus, ubi sit intellectus: ut scias simul, ubi sit longiturnitas vitæ et victus, ubi sit lumen oculorum, et pax Quis invenit locum ejus: et quis intravit in thesauros ejus? Ubi sunt principes gentium, et qui dominantur super bestias, quæ sunt super terram? Qui in avibus cœli ludunt, qui argentum thesaurisant et aurum, in quo confidunt homines, et non est finis acquisitionis eorum? Qui argentum fabricant et soliciti sunt, nec est inventio operum illorum? Exterminati sunt, et ad inferos descenderunt, et alii loco eorum surrexerunt. Juvenes viderunt lumen et habitaverunt super terram: viam autem disciplinæ ignoraverunt, neque intellexerunt se-

strange country, thou art defiled with the dead: thou art counted with them that go down into hell. Thou hast forsaken the fountain of wisdom. For if thou hadst walked in the way of God, thou hadst surely dwelt in peace for ever. Learn where is wisdom, where is strength, where is understanding: that thou mayest know also where is length of days and life, where is the light of the eyes and peace. Who hath found out her place? and who hath gone into her treasures? Where are the princes of the nations, and they that rule over the beasts, that are upon the earth. That take their pastime with the birds of the air, that hoard up silver and gold, wherein men trust, and there is no end of their getting, who work in silver and are solicitous, and their works are unsearchable? They are cut off, and are gone down to hell, and others

mitas ejus neque, filii eorum susceperunt eam: a facie ipsorum longe facta est: non est audita in terra Chanaan, neque visa est in Theman. Filii quoque Agar, qui exquirunt prudentiam quæ de terra est, negotiatores Merrhæ, et Theman, et fabulatores, et exquisitores prudentiæ et intelligentiæ: viam autem sapientiæ nescierunt neque commemorati sunt semitas ejus. O Israel, quam magna est domus Dei, et ingens locus possessionis ejus! Magnus est, et non habet finem: excelsus et immensus. Ibi fuerunt gigantes nominati illi, qui ab initio fuerunt, statura magna, scientes bellum. Non hos elegit Dominus, neque viam disciplinæ invenerunt: propterea perierunt. Et quoniam non habuerunt sapientiam, interierunt propter suam insipientiam. Quis ascendit in cœlum, et accepit eam, et eduxit eam de nubibus? Quis transfretavit mare, et invenit

are risen up in their place. Young men have seen the light, and dwelt upon the earth: but the way of knowledge they have not known, nor have they understood the paths thereof, neither have their children received it, it is far from their face: it hath not been heard of in the land of Chanaan, neither hath it been seen in Theman. The children of Agar also, that search after the wisdom that is of the earth, the merchants of Merrah, and of Theman, and the tellers of fables, and searchers of prudence and understanding: but the way of wisdom they have not known, neither have they remembered her paths. O Israel, how great is the house of God, and how vast is the place of his possession! It is great and hath no end, it is high and immense. There were the giants, those renowned men that were from the begin-

illam: et attulit illam super aurum electum? Non est qui possit scire vias ejus, eque qui exquirat semitas ejus: sed qui scit universa, novit eam, ad adinvenit eam prudentia sua. Qui præparavit terram in æterno tempore: et replevit eam pecudibus et quadrupedibus: qui emittit lumen, et vadit: et vocavit illud, et obedit illi in tremore. Stellæ autem dederunt lumen in custodiis suis, et lætatæ sunt: vocatæ sunt, et dixerunt: Adsumus: et luxerunt ei cum jucunditate, qui fecit illas. Hic est Deus noster, et non estimabitur alius adversus eum. Hic adinvenit omnem viam disciplinæ, et tradidit illam Jacobo puero suo, et Israel dilecto suo. Post hæc in terris visus est, et cum hominibus conversatus est.

ning, of great stature expert in war. The Lord chose not them neither did they find the way of knowledge therefore did they perish. And because they had not wisdom they perished through their folly. Who hath gone up into heaven, and taken her, and brought her down from the clouds? Who hath passed over the sea, and found her, and brought her preferably to chosen gold? There is none that is able to know her ways, nor that can search out her paths: but he that knoweth all things knoweth her, and hath found her out with his understanding. He that prepared the earth for evermore, and filled it with cattle and four-footed beasts: he that sendeth forth light, and it goeth: and hath called it, and it obeyed him with trembling. And the stars have given light in their watches, and rejoiced: they were called, and they said: Here we are: and with cheerfulness they have shined forth to him that made them. This is our God, and there shall be no

other accounted of in comparison of him. He found out all the way of knowledge, and gave it to Jacob his servant, and to Israel his beloved. Afterwards he was seen upon earth and conversed with men.

   Oremus.
  Flectamus genua.
   Levate
   Oratio.

DEUS, qui ecclesiam tuam semper Gentium vocatione multiplicas: concede propitius, ut quos aqua baptismatis abluis, continua protectione tuearis. Per Dominum nostrum.

  Prophetia septima.
   Ezech. xxxvii.

IN diebus illis: Facta est super me manus Domini: eduxit me in spiritu Domini: et dimisit me in medio campi, qui erat plenus ossibus. Et circumduxit me per ea in gyro. Erant autem multa valde super faciem campi, siccaque vehementer. Et dixit ad me: Fili hominis, putasne vivent ossa ista? Et dixit: Domine Deus, tu nosti. Et dixit ad me: Vaticinare de ossibus istis: et dices eis:

   Let us pray.
  Let us bend our knees.
   Rise up.
   The Prayer.

O GOD, who continuest thy church by the vocation of the Gentiles: mercifully grant thy perpetual protection to those whom thou washest with the water of baptism. Through

  The seventh Prophecy.
   Ezech. xxxvii.

IN those days: The hand of the Lord was upon me, and brought me forth in the spirit of the Lord: and set me down in the midst of a plain, that was full of bones: and he led me about through them on every side. Now they were very many upon the face of the plain and they were exceeding dry. And he said to me: Son of man, dost thou think these bones shall live? And I an-

Ossa arida audite verbum Domini. Hæc dicit Dominus Deus ossibus his. Ecce ego intromittam in vos spiritum, et vivetis. Et dabo super vos nervos, et succrescere faciam super vos carnes, et superextendam in vobis cutem: et dabo vobis spiritum, et vivetis et scietis quia ego Dominus. Et prophetavi sicut præceperat mihi: factus est autem sonitus, prophetante me, et ecce commotio: et accesserunt ossa ad ossa, unumquodque ad juncturam suam. Et vidi, et ecce super ea nervi, et carnes ascenderunt: et extenta est in eis cutis desuper, et spiritum non habebant. Et dixit ad me: Vaticinare ad spiritum, vaticinare, fili hominis, et dices ad spiritum: Hæc dicit Dominus Deus: A quatuor ventis veni, spiritus, et insuffla super interfectos istos, et reviviscant. Et prophetavi sicut præceperat mihi: et ingressus est in ea spiritus, et vixerunt: steteruntque

swered: O Lord God thou knowest. And he said to me: Prophecy concerning these bones and say to them: Ye dry bones hear the word of the Lord. Thus saith the Lord God to these bones: Behold I will send spirit into you, and you shall live. And I will lay sinews upon you, and will cause flesh to grow over you, and will cover you with skin: and I will give you spirit, and you shall live, and you shall know that I am the Lord. And I prophesied as he had commanded me: and as I prophesied there was a noise, and behold a commotion: and the bones came together, each one to its joint. And I saw, and behold the sinews and the flesh came upon them: and the skin was stretched out over them, but there was no spirit in them. And he said to me: Prophesy to the spirit, prophesy, O son of man, and say to the spirit: Thus saith

super pedes suos exercitus grandis nimis valde. Et dixit ad me: Fili hominis, ossa hæc universa, domus Israel est: ipsi dicunt: Aruerunt ossa nostra, et periit spes nostra, et abscissi sumus. Propterea vaticinare, et dices ad eos: Hæc dicit Dominus Deus: Ecce ego, aperiam tumulus vestros, et educam vos de sepulchris vestris, populus meus: et inducam vos in terram Israel. Et scietis, quia ego Dominus, cum aperuero sepulchra vestra, et eduxero vos de tumulis vestris, popule meus: et dedero spiritum meum in vobis, et vixeritis, et requiescere vos faciam super humum vestram: dicit Dominus Omnipotens.

the Lord God: Come, spirit, from the four winds, and blow upon those slain, and let them live again. And I prophesied as he had commanded me: and the spirit came into them, and they lived: and they stood up upon their feet, an exceeding great army. And he said to me: Son of man, all these bones are the house of Israel. They say: Our bones are dried up, and our hope is lost, and we are cut off. Therefore prophesy, and say to them: Thus saith the Lord God: Behold, I will open your graves, and will bring you out of your sepulchres, O my people: and will bring you into the land of Israel. And you shall know that I am the Lord, when I shall have opened your sepulchres, and shall have brought you out of your graves, O my people: and shall have put my spirit in you, and you shall live, and I shall make you rest upon your own land: saith the Lord Almighty.

MORNING OFFICE OF HOLY SATURDAY.

Oremus.
Flectamus genua.
Levate.
Oratio.

DEUS, qui nos ad celebrandum paschale sacramentum, utriusque Testamenti paginis instruis: da nobis intelligere misericordiam tuam, ut ex perceptione presentium munerum, firma sit expectatio futurorum. Per Dominum nostrum, etc.

Prophetia octava.
Isa. iv.

APprehendent septem mulieres virum unum in die illa, dicentes: Panem nostrum comendemus, et vestimentis nostris operiemur: tantummodo invocetur nomem tuum super nos, aufer opprobrium nostrum. In die illa erit germen Domini in magnificentia et gloria, et fructus terræ sublimis et exultatio his qui salvati fuerint de Israel. Et erit: Omnis qui relictus fuerit in Sion, et residuus in Jerusalem, sanctus vocabitur, omnis qui scriptus

Let us pray.
Let us bend our knees.
Rise up.
The Prayer.

O GOD, who by thy scriptures of both Testaments teachest us to celebrate the paschal sacrament: give us such a sense of thy mercy that by receiving thy present graces, we may have a firm hope of thy future blessings. Through our Lord, etc.

The eighth Prophecy.
Isa. iv.

AND in that day seven women shall take hold of one man, saying: We will eat our own bread, and wear our own apparel: only let us be called by thy name, take away our reproach. In that day the bud of the Lord shall be in magnificence and glory, and the fruit of the earth shall be high, and a great joy to them that have escaped of Israel. An it shall come to pass that every one that shall be left in Sion, and that shall remain in Jerusalem, shall

est in vita in Jerusalem. Si abluerit Dominus sordes filiarum Sion, et sanguinum Jerusalem laverit de medio ejus, in spiritu judicii, in spiritu ardoris. Et creavit Dominus super omnem locum montis Sion, et ubi invocatus est, nubem per diem, et fumum et splendorem ignis flammantis in nocte: super omnem enim gloriam protectio. Et tabernaculum erit in umbraculum diei ab æstu, et in securitatem, et absconsionem a turbine, et a pluvia.

be called holy, every one that is written in life in Jerusalem. If the Lord shall wash away the filth of the daughters of Sion, and shall wash away the blood of Jerusalem out of the midst thereof, by the spirit of judgment, and by the spirit of burning. And the Lord will create upon every place of Mount Sion, and where he is called upon, a cloud by day, and a smoke and the brightness of a flaming fire in the night: for over all the glory shall be a protection. And there shall be a tabernacle for a shade in the daytime from the heat, and for a security a covert from the whirlwind, and from rain.

Tractus.—Vinea facta est dilecto in cornu, in loco uberi. V. Et maceriam circumdedit, et circumfodit: et plantavit vineam Sorec, et ædificavit turrim in medio ejus. V. Et torcular fodit in ea: vinea enim Domini Sabaoth, domus Israel est.

The Tract. — My beloved has a vineyard on a very fruitful hill V. And he inclosed it with a fence, and made a ditch round it, and planted it with the choicest vine, and built a tower in the middle of it. V. And he made a wine-press in it: for the house of Israel is the vineyard of the Lord of Hosts.

Oremus.
Flectamus genus.
Levate.
Oratio.

DEUS, qui in omnibus Ecclesiæ tuæ filiis sanctorum prophetarum voce manifestasti, in omni loco dominationis tuæ, satorem te bonorum seminum, et electorum palmitum esse cultorem: tribue populis tuis, qui et vinearum apud te nomine censentur et segetum * ut spinarum et tribulorum squalore resecato, digna efficiantur fruge fæcundi. Per Dominum nostrum Jesum Christum, etc.

Prophetia nona.
Exod. xii.

IN diebus illis: dixit Dominus ad Moysen et Aaron, etc. p. 257.

Oremus.
Flectamus genua.
Levate.
Oratio.

OMNIPOTENS sempiterne Deus, qui in omnium operum tuorum dispensatione mirabilis es: intelligant redempti

Let us pray.
Let us bend our knees.
Rise up.
The Prayer.

O GOD, who by the mouths of thy holy prophets hast declared, that through the whole extent of thy empire thou sowest the good seed, and improvest the choicest branches that are found in all the children of thy church: grant to thy people who are called by the name of vines and corn: that they may root out all thorns and briars, and bring forth good fruit in abundance. Through our Lord Jesus Christ, etc.

The ninth Prophecy.
Exod. xii.

IN those days: the Lord said to Moses and Aaron, etc. p. 257.

Let us pray.
Let us bend our knees.
Rise up.
The Prayer.

ALMIGHTY and everlasting God, who art wonderful in the performance of all thy works: let thy redeem

tui, non fuisse excellentius quod initio factus est mundus quam quod in fine sæculorum pascha nostrum immolatus est Christus. Qui tecum vivit et regnat, etc.

Prophetia decima.
Jonæ iii.

IN diebus illis: Factum est verbum Domini ad Jonam prophetam secundo, dicens: Surge et vade in Niniven civitatem magnam: et prædica in ea prædicationem, quam ego loquor ad te. Et surrexit Jonas, et abiit in Niniven, juxta verbum Domini. Et Ninive erat civitas magna, itinere dierum trium. Et cœpit Jonas introire in civitatem itinere diei unius: et clamavit, et dixit: Adhuc quadraginta dies, et Ninive subvertetur. Et crediderunt viri Ninivitæ in Deum: et prædicaverunt jejunium, et vestiti sunt saccis a majore usque ad minorem. Et pervenit verbum ad regem Ni-

ed servants understand, that the creation of the world in the beginning was not more excellent than the immolation of Christ our passover at the latter end of the world. Who with thee, etc.

The tenth Prophecy.
Jonas iii.

IN these days: The word of the Lord came to Jonas the second time, saying: Arise, and go to Ninive, the great city: and preach in it the preaching that I bid thee. And Jonas arose and went to Ninive, according to the word of the Lord. Now Ninive was a great city, of three days' journey. And Jonas began to enter into the city one day's journey: and he cried and said: Yet forty days, and Ninive shall be destroyed. And the men of Ninive believed in God: and they proclaimed a fast, and put on sackcloth, from the greatest to the least. And the word came to the king of Ninive: and

nive: et surrexit de solio suo: et abjecit vestimentum suum a se, et indutus est sacco, et sedit in cinere. Et clamavit, et dixit in Ninive, ex ore regis, et principum ejus, dicens: Homines et jumenta, et boves, et pecora non gustent quidquam: nec pascantur, et aquam non bibant. Et operiantur saccis homines, et jumenta, et clament ad Dominum in fortitudine, et convertatur vir a via sua mala et ab iniquitate, quæ est in manibus eorum. Quis scit, si convertatur, et ignoscat Deus, et revertatur a furore iræ suæ, et non peribimus? Et vidit Deus opera eorum, quia conversi sunt de via sua mala: et misertus est populo suo Dominus Deus noster.

he rose up out of his throne, and cast away his robe from him, and was clothed with sackcloth, and sat in ashes. And he caused it to be proclaimed and published in Ninive from the mouth of the king, and of his princes, saying: Let neither man nor beasts, oxen nor sheep, taste anything, let them not feed, nor drink water. And let men and beasts be covered with sackcloths, and cry to the Lord with all their strength, and let them turn every one from his evil way, and from the iniquity that is in their hands. Who can tell if God will turn, and forgive, and will turn away from his fierce anger, and we shall not perish? And God saw their works, that they were turned from their evil way: and the Lord God had mercy on his people.

      Oremus.   Let us pray.
   Flectamus genua.   Let us bend our knees.
      Levate.   Rise up.

Oratio.

DEUS, qui diversitatem Gentium in confessione tui nominis adunasti: da nobis et velle et posse quæ præcipis: ut populo, ad æternitatem vocato, una sit fides mentium, et pietas actionum. Per Dominum nostrum Jesum Christum. etc.

Prophetia undecima.
Deut. xxxi.

IN diebus illis: Scripsit Moyses canticum, et docuit filios Israel. Precepitque Dominus Josue filio Nun, et ait: Confortare, et esto robustus: tu enim introduces filios Israel in terram, quam pollicitus sum, et ego ero tecum. Postquam ergo scripsit Moyses verba legis hujus in volumine, atque complevit, præcepit Levitis, qui portabant arcam fœderis Domini, dicens: Tollite librum istum, et ponite eum in latere arcæ fœderis Domini

The prayer.

O GOD, who hast united the several nations of the Gentiles in the profession of thy name: give us both the will and the power to obey what thou commandest: that thy people called to eternity, may have the same faith in their minds, and piety in their action. Through. etc.

The eleventh Prophecy.
Deut. xxxi.

IN those days: Moses wrote the canticle, and taught it to the children of Israel. And the Lord commanded Josue the son of Nun, and said: Take courage, and be valiant: for thou shalt bring the children of Israel into the land which I have promised, and I will be with thee. Therefore after Moses had wrote the words of this law in a volume, and finished it, he commanded the Levites, who carried the ark of the covenant of the

Dei vestri: ut sit ibi contra te in testimonium. Ego enim scio contentionem tuam, et cervicem tuam durissimam. Adhuc vivente me, et ingrediente vobiscum, semper contentiose egistis contra Dominum : quanto magis cum mortuus fuero ? Congregate ad me omnes majores natu per tribus vestras, atque doctores et loquar audientibus eis sermones istos, et invocabo contra eos cœlum et terram. Novi enim, quod post mortem meam inique agetis, et declinabitis cito de via, quam præcepi vobis. Et occurrent vobis mala in extremo tempore, quando feceritis malum in conspectu Domini, ut irritetis eum per opera manuum vestrarum. Locutus est ergo Moyses, audiente universo cœtu Israel, verba carminis hujus, et ad finem usque complevit.

Lord, saying: Take this book, and put it in the side of the ark of the covenant of the Lord our God, that it may be there for a testimony against thee. For I know thy obstinacy and thy most stiff neck. While I am yet living and going in with you you have always been rebellious against the Lord: how much more when I shall be dead: Gather unto me all the ancients of your tribes, and your doctors, and I will speak these words in their hearing, and I will call heaven and earth to witness against them. For I know, that after my death you will do wickedly, and will quickly turn aside from the way that I have commanded you: and evils shall come upon you in the latter times, when you shall do evil in the sight of the Lord, to provoke him by the works of your hands. Moses therefore spoke, in the hearing of the whole assembly of Israel, the words of this canticle, and finished it even to the end.

Tractus. — Attende cœlum, et loquar: et audiat terra verba ex ore meo. *V.* Expectetur sicut pluvia eloquium meum: et descendant sicut ros verba mea. *V.* Sicut imber super gramen, et sicut nix super fœnum, quia nomen Domini invocabo. *V.* Date magnitudinem Deo nostro: Deus, vera opera ejus, et omnes viæ ejus judicia. *V.* Deus fidelis, in quo non est iniquitas: justus et sanctus Dominus.

The Tract. — Attend, O heaven, and I will speak: and let the earth hear the words that come out of my mouth. *V.* Let my speech be expected like the rain: and let my words fall like the dew. *V.* Like the flower upon the grass, and like the moss upon the dry herb, because I will invoke the name of the Lord. *V.* Confess the greatness of our God: the works of God are perfect, and all his ways are justice. *V.* God is faithful, in whom there is no iniquity: the Lord is just and holy.

Oremus.

Flectamus genua.

Levate.

Oratio.

Let us pray.

Let us bend our knees.

Rise up.

The Prayer.

DEUS, celsitudo humilium, et fortitudo rectorum, qui per sanctum Moysen puerum tuum, ita erudire populum tuum sacri carminis tui decantatione voluisti, ut illa legis iteratio, fieret etiam nostra directio: exeita in

O God, the exaltation of the humble, and the fortitude of the righteous, who by thy holy servant Moses didst please so to instruct thy people by the singing of thy sacred canticle, that the repetition of the law should

omnem justificaturum Gentium plenitudinem potentiam, tuam, et da lætitiam, mitigando terrorem: ut omnium peccatis tua remissione deletis quod denuntiatum est in ultionem, transeat in salutem: Per Dominum nostrum, etc.

be also our direction: show thy power to all the multitude of Gentiles justified by thee, and by mitigating thy terror, grant them joy that, all their sins being pardoned by thee, the threatened vengence may contribute to their salvation. Through.

Prophetia duodecima.
Dan. III.

IN diebus illis: Nabuchodonosor rex fecit statuam auream, altitudine cubitorum sexaginta, latitudine cubitorum sex, et statuit eam in campo Dura provinciæ Babylonis. Itaque Nabuchodonosor rex misit ad congregandos satrapas magistratus, et judices, duces, et tyrannos, et præfectos, omnesque principes regionum, ut convenirent ad dedicationem statuæ, quam erexerat Nabuchodonosor rex. Tunc congregati sunt satrapæ, magistratus, et judices, duces, et tyranni, et optimates, qui erant in potestatibus consti-

The twelfth Prophecy.
Dan. III.

IN those days: King Nabuchodonosor made a statue of gold of sixty cubits high, and six cubits broad, and he set it up in the plains of Dura of the province of Babylon. Then Nabuchodonosor the king sent to call cogether the nobles, the magistrates, and the judges, the captains, the rulers, and governors, and all the chief men of the provinces, to come to the dedication of the statue which king Nabuchodonosor had set up. Then the nobles, the magistrates, and the judges, the captains, and rulers, and the

tuti, et universi principes regionum, ut convenirent ad dedicationem statuæ, quam erexerat Nabuchodonosor rex Stabant autem in conspectu statuæ, quam posuerat Nabuchodonosor rex: et præco clamabat valenter: Vobis dicitur populis, tributus, et linguis: in hora, qua audieritis sonitum tubæ, et fistulæ, et citharæ, sambucæ, et psalterii, et symphoniæ, et universi generis musicorum, cadentes adorate statuam auream, quam constituit Nabuchodonosor rex. Si quis autem non prostratus adoraverit eadem hora mittetur in fornacem ignis ardentis. Post hæc igitur statim ut audierunt omnes populi sonitum tubæ, fistulæ, et citharæ, sambucæ, et psalterii, et symphoniæ, et omnis generis musicorum, cadentes omnes populi, tribus, et linguæ adoraverunt statuam auream, quam constituerat Nabuchodonosor rex. Statimque in ipso

great men that were placed in authority, and all the princes of the provinces, were gathered together to come to the dedication of the statue, which king Nabuchodonosor had set up. And they stood before the statue which king Nabuchodonosor had set up. Then a herald cried with a strong voice: To you it is commanded, O nations, tribes, and languages; that in the hour that you shall hear the sound of the trumpet, and of the flute, and of the harp, of the sackbut, and of the psaltery and of the symphony, and of all kinds of mpsic, ye shall fall down and adore the golden statue, which Nabuchodonosor hath set up. But if any man shall not fall down and adore he shall the same hour be cast into a furnace of burning fire. Upon this, therefore, at the time when all the people heard the sound of the trumpet, the flute,

tempore accedentes viri Chaldæi accusaverunt Judæos: dixeruntque Nabuchodonosor regi: rex in æternum vive: Tu rex nosuisti decretum, ut omnis homo, qui audierit sonitum tubæ, fistulæ, et citharæ, sambucæ, et psalterii, et symponiæ, et universi generis musicorum, prosternat se, et adoret statuam auream: Si quis autem non procideas adoraverit, mittatur in fornacem ignis ardentis. Sunt ergo viri Judæi, quos constituisti super opera regionis Babylonis, Sidrach, Misach, et Abdenago: viri isti contempserunt, rex, decretum tuum: deos tuos non colont, et statuam auream, quam erexisti, non adorant. Tunc Nabuchodonosor in furore et in ira præcepit ut daducerentur Sidrach, Misach, et Abdenago: qui confestim adducti sunt in conspectu regis. Pronuntiansque Nabuchodonosor rex ait eis: Verene Sidrach, Misach, et Ab-

and the harp, of the sackbut, and the psaltery, of the symphony and of all kinds of music, all the nations, tribes and languages fell down and adored the golden statue, which king Nabuchodonosor had set up. And presently at that very time some Chaldans came and accused the Jews, and said to king Nabuchodonosor: O king, live for ever: thou, O king hast made a decree, that every man that shall hear the sound of the trumpet, the flute, and the harp, of the sackbut, and the psaltery, of the symphony and of all kinds of music shall prostrate himself and adore the golden statue: and that if any man shall not fall down and adore, he should be cast into a furnace of burning fire. Now there are certain Jews whom thou hast set over the works of the province of Babylon, Sidrach, Misach, and Abdenago: these men, O

denago, does meos non colitis et statuam auream, quam constitui non adoratis? Nunc ergo, si estis parati, quacumqua hora audieritis sonitum tubæ, fistulæ, citharæ, sambucæ, et psalterii, et symphoniæ, omnisque generis musicorum, prosternite vos, et adorate statuam quam feci. Quod si non adoraveritis, eadem hora mittemini in fornacem ignis ardentis: et quis est Deus qui eripiet vos de manu mea? Respondentes Sidrach, Misach, et Abdenago, dixerunt regi Nabuchodonosor: Non oportet nos de hac re respondere tibi. Ecce enim Deus noster quem colimus, potest eripere nos de camino ignis ardentis, et de manibus tuis, O rex, liberare. Quod si noluerit, notum sit tibi rex; quod deos tuos non colimus, et statuam auream, quam erexisti non adoramus Tunc Nabuchodonosor repletus est furore: et aspectus faciei illius im-

king, have slighted thy decree: they worship not thy gods, nor do they adore the golden statue which thou hast set up. Then Nabuchodonosor, in fury and in wrath, commanded that Sidrach, Misach, and Abdenago should be brought: who immediately were brought before the king. And Nabuchodonosor the king spoke to them, and said: Is it true, O Sidrach. Misach, and Abdenago, that you do not worship my gods, nor adore the golden statue that I have set up? Now therefore if you be ready, at what hour soever you shall hear the sound of the trumpet, flute, harp, sackbut, and psaltery, and symphony, and of all kinds of music, protrate yourselves, and adore the statue which I have made: but if you do not adore, you shall be cast the same hour, into the furnace of burning fire: and who is the God that shall deliver

mutatus est super, Sidrach, Misach, et Abdenago, et præcepit ut succenderetur fornax septuplum quam succendi consueverat. Et viris fortissimis de exercitu suo jussit, ut ligatis pedibus Sidrach, Misach, et Abdenago, mitterent eos in fornacem ignis ardentis. Et confestim viri illi vincti, cum braccis suis, et tiaris et calceamentis, et vestibus, missi sunt in medium fornacis ignis ardentis. Nam jussio regis urgebat: fornax autem succensa erat nimis. Porro viros illos qui miserant Sidrach, Misach, et Abdenago, interfecit flamma ignis. Viri autem hi tres, id est, Sidrach, Misach, et Abdenago, ceciderunt in medio camino ignis ardentis, colligati. Et ambulabant in medio flammæ, laudantes Deum, et benedicentes Domino.

you out of my hand? Sidrach, Misach, and Abdenago answered and said to the king Nabuchodonosor: We have no occasion to answer thee concerning this matter. For behold our God, whom we worship, is able to save us from the furnace of burning fire, and to deliver us out of thy hands, O king. But if he will not, be it known to thee, O king. that we will not worship thy gods, nor adore the golden statue which thou hast set up. Then was Nabuchodonosor filled with fury: and the countenance of his face was changed against Sidrach, Misach, and Abdenago, and he commanded that the furnace should be heated seven times more than it had been accustomed to be heated. And he commanded the strongest men that were in his army, to bind the feet of Sidrac, Misach, and Abdenago, and to cast them into the furnace of burning fire. And immediately these men were bound and

were cast into the furnace of burning fire, with their coats, and their caps, and their shoes, and their garments. For the king's commandment was urgent, and the furnace was heated exceedingly. And the flame of the fire slew those men that had cast in Sidrach, Misach, and Abdenago. But these three men, that is, Sidrach, Misach, and Abdenago, fell down bound in the midst of the furnace of burning fire. And they walked in the midst of the flame, praising God, and blessing the Lord.

Oremus.
Oratio.

OMnipotens sempiterne Deus, spes unica mundi, qui prophetarum tuorum præconio præsentium temporum declarasti mysteria: auge populi tui vota placatus, quia in nullo fidelium, nisi ex tua inspiratione, proveniunt quarumlibet incrementta virtutum. Per Dominum nostrum Jesum Christum, etc.

Let us pray.
The Prayer.

ALmighty and everlast,ng God, the only hope of the word, who by the voice of thy prophets, hast, manifested the mysteries of this present time: graciously increase the desires of the people, since none of the faithful can advance to any virtue without thy inspiration. Through our Lord, etc.

If the Church has no Baptismal Font, the following Benediction of the Font is omitted and the Litanies are said immediately after the Prophecies, in the manner hereafter directed. But where there is a font, the priest with his ministers and the clegy go in procession to the font, singing:

Tractus. — Sicut cervus desiderat ad fontes aquarum, ita de-

The Tract. — As the hart pants after the fountains of water, so

siderat anima mea ad te, Deus. *V.* Sitivit anima mea ad Deum vivum: quand veniam et appareho ante faciem Dei? *V.* Fuerunt mihi lacrymæ meœ panes die ac nocte, dum dicitur mihi per singulos dies: Ubi est Deus tuus?

my soul pants after thee, O God. *V.* My soul has thirsted for the living God: when shall I come and appear before the face of God? *V.* My tears have been my bread day and night, while they say to me every day: Where is thy God?

Before the blessing of the font, the priest says the following prayer:

V. Dominus vobiscum.
R. Et cum spiritu tuo.

V. The Lord be with you.
R. And with thy spirit.

Oremus
Oratio.

Let us pray.
The Prayer.

OMnipotens sempiterne Deus, respice propitius ad devotionem populi renascentis, qui sicut cervus, aquarum tuarum expetit fontem: et concede propitius, ut fidei ipsius sitis, baptismatis mysterio, animam corpusque sanctificet. Per Dominum nostrum, etc.

ALmighty and evealasting God, look mercifully on the devotion of the people desiring a new birth, that as the hart pants after the fountain of thy waters; so mercifully grant that the thirst of their faith may, by the sacrament of baptism, sanctify their souls and bodies. Through our Lord, etc.

R. Amen.
R. Amen.

Then the Priest begins the Blessing of the font, saying.

V. Dominus, vobiscum.

V. The Lord be with you.

R. Et cum spiritu tuo.

Oremus.

Oratio.

OMnipotens sempiterne Deus, adesto magnæ pietatis tuæ mysteriis, adesto sacramentis: et ad recreandos novos populos, quos tibi fons baptismatis parturit, spiritum adoptionis emitte: ut quod nostræ humilitatis gerendum est ministerio, virtutis tuæ impleatur effectu. Per Dominum nostrum Jesum Christum Filium tuum, qui tecum vivit et regnat in unitate ejusdem Spiritus Santi Deus. *V.* Per omnia sæcula sæculorum.

R. Amen.
V. Dominus vobiscum.
R. Et cum spiritu tuo.

V. Sursum corda.
R. Habemus ad Dominum.
V. Gratias agamus Domino Deo nostro.
R. Dignum et justum. est.

R. And with thy spirit.

Let us pray.

The Prayer.

Almighty and everlasting God, be present at these mysteries, be present at these sacraments of thy great goodness: and send forth the spirit of adoption to regenerate the new people, whom the font of baptism brings forth: that what is to be done by our weak ministry, may be acomplished by the effect of thy power. Through our Lord Jesus Christ thy Son, who with thee and the same Holy Spirit lives and reigns one God. *V.* For ever and ever.

R. Amen.
V. The Lord be with you,
R. And with thy spirit.

V. Lift up your hearts.
R. We have lifted them up to the Lord.
V. Let us give thanks to the Lord our God.
R. It is meet and just.

VERE dignum et justum est, æquum et salutare, nos tibi semper et ubique gratias agere Domine sancte, Pater omn.potens, æterne Deus. Qui invisibili potentia, sacramentorum tuorum mirabiliter operaris effectum: et licet nos tantis myrteriis exequendis simus indigni: tu tamen gratiæ tuæ dona non deserens, etiam ad nostras preces, aures tuæ pietatis inclina. Deus cujus spiritus super aquas, inter ipsa mundi primordia ferebatur: ut jam tunc virtutem sanctificationis, aquarum natura conciperet. Deus, qui nocentis mundi crimina per aquas abluens, regenerationis speciem in ipsa diluvii effusione signasti: ut unius ejusdemque elementi mysterio, et finis esset vitiis, et origo virtutibus. Respice, Domine, in faciem ecclesiæ tuæ, et multiplica in ea regenerationes tuas, qui gratiæ tuæ affluentis impetu lætificas civitatem tu-

IT is truly meet and just, equitable and wholesome, to give the thanks always and in all places, O holy Lord, Almighty Father, eternal God. Who by thy invisible power dost wonderfully produce the effect of thy sacraments: and though we are unworthy to administer so great mysteries: yet as thou dost not forsake the gifts of thy grace, so thou inclinest the ears of thy goodness, even to our prayers. O God, whose Spirit is the very beginning of the world moved over the waters, that even then the nature of water might receive the virtue of sanctification. O God, who by water didst wash away the crimes of the guilty world, and by the overflowing of the deluge didst give a figure of regeneration, that one and the same element might in a mystery be the end of vice and the origin of virtue. Look, O Lord, on the face of thy

am, fontemque baptismatis aperis toto orbe terrarum Gentibus innovandis: ut tuæ majestatis imperio, sumat Unigeniti tui gratiam de Spiritu Sancto.

Here the Priest divides the water in the form of a cross.

Qui hanc aquam regenerandis hominibus præparatam, arcana sui numinis admixtione fæcundet, ut sanctificatione concepta, ab immaculato divini fontis utero, in novam renata creaturam, progenies cœlestis emergat: et quos aut sexus in corpore, aut ætas discernit in tempore, omnes in unam pariat gratia mater infantiam. Procul ergo hinc, jubente te, Domine; omnis spiritus immundus abscedat: procul tota nequitia diabolicæ fraudis absistat. Nihil hic loci habeat contrariæ virtutis admixtio: non insidiando circumvolet: non latendo subrepat: non inficiendo corrumpat.

church, and multiply in her thy regenerations who by the streams of thy abundant grace fillest thy city with joy and openest the fonts of baptism all over the world, for the renovation of the Gentiles: that by the command of thy Majesty she may receive the grace of thy only Son from the Holy Ghost.

Who by a secret mixture of his divine virtue may render this water fruitful for the regeneration of men, to the end that those who have been sanctified in the immaculate womb of this divine font, being born again a new creature, may come forth a heavenly offspring: and that all that are distinguished either by sex in body, or by age in time, may be brought forth to the same infancy by grace, their spiritual mother. Therefore may all unclean spirits, by thy command, O Lord, depart far from hence: may the whole malice of diabolical deceit be entirely banished: may

no power of the enemy prevail here: may he not fly about to lay his snares: may he not creep in by his secret artifice: may he not corrupt with his infection.

Here he touches the water with his hand.

Sit hæc sancta et innocens creatura, libera ab omni impugnatoris incursu, et totius nequitiæ purgata discessu. Sit fons vivus, aqua regenerans, unda purificans: ut omnes hoc lavacro salutifero diluendi, operante in eis Spiritu Sancto, perfectæ purgationis indulgentiam consequantur.

May this holy and innocent creature be free from all the assaults of the enemy, and purified by the destruction of all his malice. May it be a living fountain, a regenerating water, a purifying stream: that all those that are to be washed in this saving bath, may obtain, by the operation of the Holy Ghost, the grace of a perfect purification.

Here he makes the sign of the cross thrice over the font, saying:

Unde benedico te, creatura aquæ, per Deum ✠ vivum, per Deum ✠ verum, per Deum ✠ sanctum: per Deum qui te in princio verbo separavit ab arida, cujus spiritus super te ferebatur.

Therefore I bless thee O creature of water, by the living God, by the true God by the holy God: by that God who in the beginning separated thee by his word from the dry land, whose spirit moved over thee.

He divides the water with his hands, and throws some of it towards the four quarters of the world, saying:

Qui te de paradisi fonte manare fecit, et in quatuor fluminibus totam terram, rigare præcepit. Qui te in deserto amaram, suavitate indita fecit esse potabilem, et sitienti populo de petra produxit. Be✠nedico te et per Jesum Christum Filium ejus unicum, Dominum nostrum qui te in Cana Galileæ, signo admirabili, sua potentia convertit in vinum. Qui pedibus super te ambulavit: et a Joanne in Jordane in te baptizatus est. Qui te una cum sanguine de latere suo produxit: et discipulis suis jussit, ut credentes baptizarentur in te, dicens: *Ite, docete, omnes gentes, baptizantes eos in nomine Patris, et Filii, et Spiritus Sancti.*

Who made thee flow from the fountain of paradise, and commanded thee to water the whole earth with thy four rivers. Who changing thy bitterness in the desert into sweetness, made thee fit to drink, and produced thee out of a rock to quench the thirst of the people. I bless thee also by our Lord Jesus Christ, his only Son: who in Cana of Galileee changed thee into wine by a wonderful miracle of his power. Who walked upon thee dry foot, and was baptised in thee by John in the Jordan. Who made thee flow out of his side together with his blood, and commanded his disciples, that such as believed should be baptised in thee: saying: *Go, teach all nations, baptising them in the name of the Father, and of the Son, and of the Holy Ghost.*

Hæc nobis præcepta servantibus, tu Deus Omnipotens clemens adesto: tu benignus aspira.

Do thou, Almighty God, mercifully assist us that observe this command: do thou graciously inspire us,

He breathes thrice upon the water in the form of a cross, saying:

Tu has simplices aquas tuo ore benedicito; ut præter naturalem emundationem, quam lavandis possunt adhibere corporibus, sint etiam purificandis mentibus efficaces.	Do thou with thy mouth bless these clear waters: that besides their natural virtue of cleansing the body, they may also be effectual for the purifying of the soul.

Here the Priest immerses the Pascal Candle in the water, at three different times, saying each time:

Descendat in hanc plenitudinem fontis virtus Spiritus Sancti.	May the virtue of the Holy Ghost descend into all the water of this font.

Then breathing thrice upon the water: he goes on:

Totamque hujus aquæ substantiam regenerandi fæcundet effectu.	And make the whole substance of this water fruitful and capable of regenerating.

Here the Paschal Candle is taken out of the water and he goes on:

Hic omnium peccatorum maculæ deleantur: hic natura, ad imaginem tuam condita, et ad honorem sui reformata principii cunctis vetustatis squaloribus emuudetur: ut omnis homo sacramentum hoc regenerationis ingressus, in veræ innocentiæ novam	Here may the stains of all sins be washed out: here may human nature, created to thy image, and reformed to the honour of its author, be cleansed from all the filth of the old man: that all who receive this sacrament of regeneration, may be-

infantiam renascatur. Per Dominum nostrum Jesum Christum Fiulium tuum: qui venturus est judicare vivos et mortuos, et sæculum per ignem. R. Amen.	born again new children of true innocence. Through our Lord Jesus Christ thy Son: who shall come to judge the living and the dead, and the world by fire. R. Amen.

Then the people are sprinkled with the blessed water; some of it is reserved for the blessing of the houses and other places. After this the Priest pours some of the oil of catechumens into the water, in the form of a cross, saying:

Sanctificetur et fœcundetur fons iste oleo salutis, renascentibus ex eo, in vitam æternam. R. Amen.	May this font be sanctified and made fruitful by the oil of salvation, for such as are regenerated therein unto life everlasting. R. Amen.

Then he pours chrism into it in the same manner, saying:

Infusio chrismatis Domini nostri Jesu Christi, et Spiritus Sancti Paracliti, fiat in nomine sanctæ Trinitatis. R. Amen.	May this infusion of the chrism of our Lord Jesus Christ, and of the Holy Ghost the Comforter, be made in the name of the Holy Trinity. R. Amen.

Lastly, he pours the oil and chrism both together into the water in the form of a cross, saying:

Commixtio chrismatis sanctificationis, et olei unctionis et aquæ baptismatis pariter fiat	May this mixture of the chrism of sanctification, and of the oil of unction, and of the wa-

in nomine Pa ✠ tris et Fi ✠ lii, et Spiritus ✠ Sancti.

R. Amen.

ter of baptism, be made in the name of the Father, and of the Son, and of the Holy Gost.

R. Amen.

Then he mingles the oil with the water, and with his hands spreads it all over the font: and if there are any to be baptised, he baptises them after the usual manner. After the Blessing of the font, he returns with the Deacon and Subdeacon to the altar, where they lie prostrate, and all the rest kneel, while the Litanies are sung by two chanters in the middle of the Choir, both sides repeating the same.

KYRIE eleison.

Christe eleison.

Kyrie eleison.

Christe audi nos.
Christe exaudi nos.

Pater de cœlis Deus, miserere nobis.

Filii Redemptor mundi Deus, miserere nobis.

Spiritus Sancte Deus miserere nobis.
Sancta Trinitas, unus Deus, miserere nobis.
Sancta Maria, ora pro nobis.

LORD, have mercy on us.

Christ, have mercy upon us.

Lord, have mercy upon us.

Christ, hear us.
Christ, graciously hear us.

God the Father of heaven, have mercy upon us.

God the son, Redeemer of the world, have mercy upon us.

God the Holy Ghost, have mercy upon us.
Holy Trinity, one God, have mercy upon us.
Holy Mary, pray for us.

Sancta Dei Genitrix, ora pro nobis.
Sancta virgo virginum, ora pro nobis.
Sancte Michæl, ora.
Sancte Gabriel, ora.
Sancte Raphael, ora.
Omnes sancti angeli et archangeli, orate pro nobis.
Omnes sancti beatorum spitituum ordines. orate pro nobis.
S. Joannes Baptista, ora pro nobis.
S. Joseph, ora pro nobis.
Omnes sancti patriarchæ, et prophetæ, orate pro nobis.
S. Petre, ora.
S. Paule, ora.
S. Andrea, ora pro nobis.
S. Joannes, ora pro nobis.
Omnes sancti apostoli et evangelistæ, orate pro nobis.
Omnes sancti discipuli Domini, orate pro nobis.
S. Stephane, ora pro nobis.
S. Laurenti, ora pro nobis.
S. Vincenti, ora pro nobis.

Holy Mother of God. pray for us.
Holy Virgin of virgins, pray for us.
St. Michael, pray.
St. Gabriel, pray.
St. Raphael, pray.
All ye holy angels and archangels, pray for us.
All ye holy orders of blessed spirits, pray for us.
St. John the Baptist, pray for us.
St Joseph, pray for us
All ye holy patriarchs and prophets, pray for us.
St. Peter, pray.
St. Paul, pray.
St. Andrew, pray for us.
St. John, pray for us.
All ye holy apostles evangelists, pray for us.
All ye holy disciples of the Lord, pray for us.
St. Stephen, pray for us.
St. Laurence, pray for us.
St. Vincent, pray for us.

Omnes sancti martyres, orate pro nobis.	All ye holy martyrs' pray for us.
S. Silvester, ora pro nobis.	St. Sylvester, pray, for us.
S. Gregori, ora pro nobis.	St. Gregory, pray for us.
S. Augustine, ora pro nobis.	St. Augustin, pray for us.
Omnes sancti pontifices et confessores, orate pro nobis.	All ye holy bishops and confessors, pray of us.
Omnes sancti doctores, orate pro nobis.	All ye holy doctors, pray for us.
S. Antoni, ora pro nobis.	St. Antony, pray for us.
S. Benedicte, ora pro nobis.	St. Benedict, pray for us.
S. Dominice, ora pro nobis.	St. Dominic, pray for us.
S. Francisce, ora pro nobis.	St. Francis, pray for us.
Omnes sancti sacerdotes et levitae, orate pro nobis.	All ye holy priests and levites, pray for us.
Omnes sancti monachi et eremitæ, orate pro nobis.	All ye holy monks and hermits, pray for us.
Sancta Maria Magdalena, ora pro nobis.	St. Mary Magdalen, pray for us.
S. Agnes, ora pro nobis.	St. Agnes, pray for us.
S. Cæcilia, ora pro nobis.	St. Cecily, pray for us.
S. Agatha, ora pro nobis.	St. Agatha, pray for us.
S. Anastasia, ora pro nobis.	St. Anastasia, pray for us.

Omnes sanctæ virgines et viduæ, orate.	All ye holy virgins and widows, pray for us.
Omnes sancti et sanctæ Dei, intercedite pro nobis!	All ye saints of God, men and women, intercede for us.
Propitius esto, parce nobis Domine.	Be merciful unto us, spare us, O Lord.
Propitius esto, exaudi nos domine	Be merciful unto us, hear us, O Lord.
Ab omni malo libera nos, Domine.	From all evil, O Lord, deliver us.
Ab omni peccato, libera nos Domine.	From all sin, O Lord, deliver us.
A morte perpetua, libera nos Domine.	From everlasting death, O Lord, deliver us.
Per mysterium sanctæ incarnationis tuæ, libera nos, Domine.	Through the mystery of thy holy incarnation, O Lord, deliver us.
Per adventum tuum libera nos Domine.	Through thy coming O Lord, deliver us.
Per nativatem tuam libera nos Domine.	Through thy nativity, O Lord, deliver us.
Per baptismum et sanctum jejunium tuum, libera nos, Domine.	Through thy baptism and holy fasting, O Lord deliver us.
Per crucem et passionem tuam, libera nos Domine.	Through thy cross and passion, O Lord, deliver us.
Per mortem et sepulturam tuam, libera nos Domine.	Through thy death and burial, O Lord deliver us.
Per sanctam resurectionem tuam, libera nos Domine.	Through thy holy resurrection, O Lord deliver us.
Per admirabilem ascensionem tuam, libera, me Domine.	Through thy admirable cension, O Lord, deliver us,

Per adventum Spiritus Sancti Paracliti, libera nos Domine.	Through the coming of the Holy Ghost the Comforter, O Lord, deliver us.
In die judicii, libera nos Domine.	In the day of judgment, O Lord, deliver us,
Peccatores, te rogamus audi nos.	We sinners beseech thee hear us.

Here the Priest and Ministers rise and go to the sacristy, to vest themselves in white for the celebration of Mass; and whilst the candles are being lighted upon the Altar, the Litanies are continued by the Choir.

Ut nobis parcas, te rogamus audi nos.	That thou spare us, we beseech thee hear us.
Ut ecclesiam tuam sanctam regere et conservare digneris, te rogamus audi nos.	That thou vouchsafe to govern and preserve thy holy church, we beseech thee hear us.
Ut domnum apostolicum, et omnes ecclesiasticos ordines in sancta religione conservare digneris, te rogamus audi nos.	That thou vouchsafe to preserve our apostolic lord and all ecclestical orders in holy religion we beseech thee, hear us.
Ut regibus et principibus christianis pacem et veram concordiam donare digneris, te rogamus audi nos.	That thou vouchsafe to grant peace and true concord to christian kings and princes, we beseech thee, hear us.
Ut nosmetipsos in tuo sancto servitio confortare et conservare digneris, te rogamus audi nos.	That thou vouchsafe to strengthen and keep us in thy holy service we beseech thee, hear us.

Ut omnibus benefactoribus nostris sempiterna bona retribuas, te rogamus audi nos.	That thou render eternal good things to all our benefactors, we beseech thee, hear us.
Ut fructus terræ dare et conservare digneris, te rogamus audi nos.	That thou vouchsafe to give and preserve the fruits of the earth, we beseech thee, hear us.
Ut omnibus fidelibus defunctis requiem æternam donare digneris, te rogamus audi nos.	That thou vouchsafe to grant eternal rest to all the faithful departed, we beseech thee, hear us.
Ut nos exaudire digneris, te rogamus audi nos.	That thou vouchsafe graciously to hear us, we beseech thee hear us.
Agnus Dei, qui tollis peccata mundi, parce nobis Domine.	Lamb of God, that takest away the sins of the world, spare us, O Lord.
Agnus Dei, qui tollis peccata mundi, exaudi nos Domine.	Lamb of God, that takest away the sins of the world, hear us, O Lord.
Agnus Dei, qui tollis peccata mundi, miserere nobis.	Lamb of God, that takest away the sins of the world, have mercy upon us.
Christe, audi nos.	Christ, hear us.
Christe, exaudi nos.	Christ, graciously hear us.

The Choir here commences the Kyrie *of the Mass.*

MASS FOR HOLY SATURDAY.

Whilst the Choir sings the Kyrie, *the Priest arrives at the steps of the Altar and begins Mass in the accustomed manner, as at p. 34, with the Ps.,* Judica, *etc.*

Having ascended to the Altar and incensed it, he intones the Gloria in excelsis, *p. 192, and the bells, which remained silent from this part of the Mass on Maundy Thursday, are now rung again. After which he turns towards the people, and says:*

V. Dominus vobiscum.	V. The Lord be with you.
R. Et cum spiritu tuo.	R. And with thy spirit.
Oremus.	Let us pray.
Oratio.	The Prayer.
DEUS, qui hanc sacratissimam noctem gloria Dominicæ resurrectionis illustras: conserva in nova familiæ tuæ progenie adoptionis spiritum quem dedisti: ut corpore et mente renovati, puram tibi exhibeant servitutem. Per eumdem Dominum nostrum Jesum Christum.	O GOD, who makest this most sacred night illustrious by the solemnity of the resurrection of our Lord. preserve in the new children of thy family, the spirit of adoption given by thee: that being renewed in body and soul, they may serve thee with purity of heart. Through, etc.
R. Amen.	R. Amen.
Lectio Epistolæ beati Pauli Apostoli ad Colossenses. *(cap. iii.)*	The Lesson from the Epistle of Blessed Paul the Apostle to the Colossians. *(ch. iii.)*

Fratres: Si consurrexistis cum Christo, quæ sursum sunt quærte, ubi Christus est in dextera Dei sedens: quæ sursum sunt sapite, non quæ super terram. Mortui enim estis, et vita vestra est abscondita cum Christo in Deo. Cum Christus apparuerit vita vestra, tunc et vos apparebitis cum ipso in gloria.

Brethren: if you be risen with Christ, seek the things that are above, where Christ is sitting at the right hand of God: mind the things that are above, not the things that are on the earth. For you are dead, and your life is hid with Christ in God. When Christ shall appear, who is your life, then shall you also appear with him in glory.

After the Epistle, the Priest sings three times Alleluia, which is three times repeated by the Choir, which, after the third time, sings the following versicle:

V. Confitemini Domino, quoniam bonus: quoniam in sæculum misericordia ejus.
Tractus. — Laudate Dominum omnes Gentes: et collaudate eum omnes populi. V. Quoniam confirmata est super nos misericordia ejus: et veritas Domini manet in æternum.

V. Praise ye the Lord, because he is good: because his mercy continues for ever.
The Tract.—Praise the Lord, all ye Gentiles: and praise him, all ye people. V. Because his mercy is established on us: and the truth of the Lord remains for ever.

Munda cor meum, *and* Jube Domine, *as at p. 58. At the Gospel, lights are not carried; only incense.*

Sequentia sancti Evan-   Continuation of the Gos-

gelii secundum Matthæum. *(cap. 38.)*

VEspere autem sabbati, quæ lucescit in prima sabbati, venit Maria Magdalene, et altera Maria, videre sepulchrum. Et ecce terræmotus factus est magnus. Angelus enim Domini descendit de cœlo, et accedens revolvit lapidem, et sedebat super eum: erat autem aspectus ejus sicut fulguri et vestimentum ejus sicut nix. Præ timore autem ejus exterriti sunt custodes, et facti sunt velut mortui. Respondens autem angelus, dixit mulieribus: Nolite timere vos; scio enim quod Jesum, qui crucifixus est, quæritis: non est hic: surrexit enim, sicut dixit. Venite, et videte locum, ubi positus erat Dominus. Et cito euntes, dicite discipulis ejus, quia surrexit: et ecce præcedet vos in Galilæam: ibi eum videbitis. Ecce prædixi vobis.

pel according to St. Matthew. *(cap. 38.)*

AND in the end of the sabbath, when it began to dawn towards the first day of the week came Mary Magdalem and the other Mary, to see the sepulchre. And behold there was a great earthquake. For an angel of the Lord descended from heaven, and coming, rolled back the stone, and sat upon it: and his countenance was as lightning; and his raiment as snow. And for fear of him, the guards were struck with terror, and became as dead men. And the angel answering said to the woman: Fear not you: for I know that you seek Jesus who was crucified. He is not here, for he is risen, as he said. Come, and see the place where the Lord was laid. And going quickly, tell ye his disciples that he is risen: and behold he will go before you into Galilee: there you shall see him.

MASS FOR HOLY SATURDAY.

V. Dominus vobiscum.
R. Et cum spiritu tuo.

V. The Lord be with you.
R. And with thy spirit.

THE SECRET.

Oremus.

SUSCIPE, quæsumus, Domine, preces populi tui, cum oblationitus hostiarium: ut paschalibus initiata mysteriis, ad æternitatis nobis medelam, te operante, proficiant. Per Dominum nostrum Jesum Christum Filium tuum: qui tecum, etc.
Per omnia sæcula seculorum.
R. Amen.
V. Dominus vobiscum.
R. Et cum spiritu tuo.
V. Sursum corda.
R. Habemus ad Dominum.
V. Gratias agamus Domino Deo nostro.
R. Dignum et justum est.

VERE dignum et justum est, æquum et salutare, te quidem Do-

Let us pray.

RECEIVE, O Lord, we beseech thee, the prayers of thy people, together with the offerings of these hosts: that being initiated in the paschal mysteries, they may, by thy operation, obtain us eternal life, Through our Lord Jesus Christ thy Son: Who with thee and the Holy Ghost. For ever and ever. R. Amen.
V. The Lord be with you.
R. And with thy spirit.
V. Lift up your hearts.
R. We have lifted them up to the Lord.
V. Let us give thanks to the Lord our God.
R. It is meet and just.

IT is truly meet and just, right and profitable to salvation, to

mine omni tempore, sed in hac potissimum nocte gloriosius prædicare; cum pascha nostrum immolatus est Christus. Ipse enim verus est Agnus, qui abstulit peccata mundi. Qui mortem nostram moriendo destruxit, et vitam resurgendo reparavit. Et ideo cum angelis et archangelis, cum thronis et dominationibus, cumque omni militia cœlestis exercitus, hymnum gloriæ tuæ canimus, sine fine dicentes:

publish thy praise, O Lord, at all times: but chiefly and more gloriously on this night, when Christ our paschal Lamb is sacrificed. For he is the true Lamb that has taken away the sins of the world. Who by dying destroyed our death, and by rising again restored us to life. And therefore with the angels and archangels, with the thrones and dominations, and with all the hosts of the celestial army, we sing the hymn of thy glory, incessantly saying:

Sanctus, etc., *as at p.* 68, *to* Communicantes, *p.* 70.

COmmunicantes, et noctem sacratissimam celebrantes resurrectionis Domini nostri Jesu Christi secundum carnem sed et memoriam venerantes in primis gloriosae semper Virginis Mariæ, Genitricis ejusdem Dei et Domini nostri Jesu Christi, etc.

HANC igitur oblationem servitutis nos-

COmmucicating with and celebrating the most sacred night of the resurrection of our Lord Jesus Christ according to the flesh; and also honouring the memory in the first place of the ever-glorious Virgin Mary, Mother of the same God and our Lord Jesus Christ.

WE therefore beseech thee, O Lord, gra-

trae, sed et cunctæ familiæ tuæ, quam tibi offerimus pro his quoque quos regenerare dignatus es ex aqua et Spiritu Sancto, tribuens eis remissionem omnium peccatorum, quæsumus, Domine, ut placatus accipias: diesque nostros in tua pace disponas, atque ab æterna damnatione nos eripi, et in electorum tuorum jubeas grege numerari Per Christum Dominum nostrum. Amen.

ciously to accept this offering of our service as also of thy whole family, which we offer to thee for these also whom thou hast been pleased to regenerate by water and the Holy Ghost, granting them the remission of all their sins: and to order our days, in thy peace: and to command us to be preserved from eternal condemnation: and to be numbered in the fold of thy elect. Through Jesus Christ our Lord. Amen.

Quam oblationem, *with the rest from p. 71 to Agnus Dei, which is not said, but the Priest says the three prayers before the Communion, and the rest to the washing of his fingers inclusive, as from p. 78 to p. 81, after ablutions Vespers are sung by the Choir.*

VESPERS.

Ant. Alleluia, alleluia, alleluia.

Ant. Alleluia, alleluia, alleluia.

PSALM CXIV.

LAUDATE Dominum, omnes Gentes: * laudate eum omnes populi.

PRAISE the Lord, all ye Nations: praise him, all ye people.

Quoniam confirmata est super nos misericordia ejus: * et veritas Domini manet in æternum.

Because his mercy is established on us: and the truth of the Lord remains for ever,

Gloria Patri, etc.

Ant. Alleluia, alleluia, alleluia.

Glory be to the Father, etc.

Ant. Alleluia, alleluia, alleluia.

Here the Priest sings the three first words of the following anthem, which is continued by the Choir:

Ant. Vespere autem sabbati, quæ lucescit in prima sabbati, venit Maria Magdalene, et altera Maria, videre sepulchrum. Alleluia.

Ant. In the evening of the sabbath, which dawns, in the first day of the week, came Mary Magdalen, and the other Mary, to see the sepulchre. Alleluia.

Afterwards the Magnificat *is sung, as at p.* 211, *with* Gloria Patri *at the end, and the Altar is incensed as usual at Vespers.*

Vespere autem sabbati, *is then repeated, and the Priest at the Altar turns to the people, saying:*

V. Dominus vobiscum.

R. Et cum spiritu tuo.

V. The Lord be with you.

R. And with thy spirit.

Oremus.

Oratio.

Let us pray.

The Prayer.

SPiritum nobis, Domine, tuæ charitatis infunde, et quos sacramentis paschalibus satiasti, tua facias pietate concordes. Per Dominum, etc. in unitate ejusdem Spiritus Sancti Deus.

POUR into us, O Lord, the spirit of thy charity, and whom thou hast replenished with the paschal mysteries do Thou make, by thy goodness, concordant. Through our Lord.

HOLY SATURDAY AT VESPERS.

Then he says:

V. Dominus vobiscum.
R. Et cum spiritu tuo.

V. The Lord be with you.
R. And with thy spirit.

Here the Deacon turning to the people sings:

V. Ite, missa est. Alleluia, alleluia.
R. Deo gratias. Alleluia, alleluia.

V. Go, Mass is said. Alleluia, alleluia.
R. Thanks be to God. Alleluia, alleluia.

MASS FOR EASTER SUNDAY.

The Priest begins by reciting the Psalm Judica *etc. at as. p, 34.*

THE INTROIT.

REsurrexi, et adhuc tecum sum, alleluia: posuisti super me manum tuam, alleluia. Mirabilis facta est scientia tua. Alleluia, alleluia.
Psalm. Domine, probasti me, et cognovisti me: tu cognovisti sessionem meam, et resurrectionem meam V. Gloria Patri, et Filio, et Spiritui Sancto. Sicut erat in principio, et nunc, et semper, et in sæcula sæculorum. Amen. Resurrexi, etc., usque ad *Ps.*

I AM risen, and am yet with thee, alleluia: Thou hast put thy right hand upon me, alleluia. Thy knowledge is become marvellous, alleluia, alleluia.
Psalm. Lord, thou hast proved me, and hast known me: thou hast known my sitting down and my uprising. V. Glory be to the Father, and to the Son, and to the Holy Ghost. As it was in the beginning, is now, and ever shall be, world without end. Amen. I am risen, etc., to *Psalm.*

Kyrie eleison, as p. 37, Gloria in excelsis, as at p. 192.

Oremus.

DEUS, qui hodierna die per unigenitum tuum, æternitatis nobis aditum devicta morte reserasti: vota nostra quæ præveniendo aspiras, etiam adjuvando prosequere. Per eundem Dominum nostrum, etc.

Lectio Epistolæ beati Pauli Apostoli ad Corinthios. (1 *Cor.* 5.)

FRATRES: expurgate vetus fermentum ut sitis nova conspersio, sicut estis azymi. Etenim pascha nostrum immolatus est Christus. Itaque epulemur, non in fermento veteri, neque in fermento malitiæ et nequitiæ: sed in azymis sinceritatis et veritatis.

Graduale. — Hæc dies quam fecit Dominus: exsultemus et lætemur in ea.

V. Confitemini Domino, quoniam bonus: quoniam in sæculum misericordia ejus.

Let us pray.

O God, who on this day, by thy only begotten Son's victory over death, hast opened for us a passage to eternity: grant that our prayers, which thy preventing grace inspires, may, by thy help, become effectual. Through.

The Lesson out of the Epistle of Blessed Paul the Apostle to the Corinthians. (1 *Cor.* 5.)

BRethren, purge out the old leaven, that ye may be a new paste, as ye are unleavened. For Christ our passover is sacrificed. Let us therefore feast not with the old leaven, nor with the leaven of malice and wickedness: but with the unleavened bread of sincerity and truth.

Gradual. — This day which the Lord hath made: let us be glad and rejoice in it.

V. Praise the Lord, for he is good: because his mercy continues for ever.

Alleluia, alleluia.
V. Pascha nostrum immolatus est Christus.

Alleluia, alleluia.
V. Christ our passover is sacrificed.

THE PROSE.

VICTIMÆ paschali laudes

Immolent Christiani.

Agnus redemit oves.

Christus innocens Patri

Reconciliavit peccatores.

Mors et vita duello.

Conflixere mirando:

Dux vitæ mortuus.

Regnat vivus.

Dic nobis Maria,

Quid vidisti in via?

Sepulchrum Christi viventis:
Et gloriam vidi resurgentis:

YE dear-bought Christians, come and sing.
The paschal praises of your King,
That spotless lamb, who more than due
Paid for his sheep, and those sheep you.
The guiltless Son has wrought your peace,
And made his Father's anger cease.
Life has with death the battle fought
And each to strange extremes were brought:
Life died, but soon reviv'd again,
And by itself even death was slain.
Say happy Magdalen, O say.
What objects saw'st thou by the way?
I saw himself, and him ador'd;
I saw the napkin and the sheet
That bound his head and wrapt his feet:

Angelicos testes,	I heard the angels witness bear.
Sudarium et vestes.	That Christ is risen. He is not here.
Surrexit Christus spes mea:	Go tell his brethren they shall see.
	Thine and their hope in Galilee,
Præcedet vos in Galilæam.	We, Lord, with faithful heart, and cheerful voice.
Scimus Christum surrexisse	On this thy glorious rising day rejoice:
A mortuis vere.	O thou, whose conqu'ring power o'ercame the grave,
Tu nobis victor	By thy victorious grace us sinners save. Amen Alleluia.
Rex miserere. Amen. Alleluia.	

Continuation of the Holy Gospel according to St. Mark (ch. 16.)

AT that time: Mary Magdalen and Mary the mother of James and Salome bought sweet spices, that coming they might annoint Jesus. And very early in the morning the first day of the week, they came to the sepulchre, the sun being now risen. And they said one to another: Who shal roll us back the stone from the door of the sepulchre? And looking, they saw thes tone rolled back. For it was very great. And entering into the sepulchre, they saw a young man sitting on the right side clothed with a white robe: and they were astonished. And he saith to them: Be not affrighted; you seek Jesus of Nazareth who was crucified: he is risen, he is not here. Behold the place where they laid him. But go tell his

disciples, and Peter, that he goeth before you into Galilee: there you shall see him, as he told you.

OFFERTORY.

Terra tremuit, et quievit, dum resurgeret in judicio Deus. Alleluia.	The earth trembled, and was still, whilst God arose in judgment. Alleluia.

Suscipe, *as before, p. 62, till he comes to*

THE SECRET.

REceive, O Lord, we beseech thee, the prayers of thy people, together with the offerings of victims: that being initiated in the paschal mysteries, they may, through thy help, obtain us eternal life. Through our Lord.

THE PREFACE.

IT is truly meet and just, right and profitable to salvation, to publish thy praises, O Lord, at all times, but chiefly and more gloriously on this day when Christ our Paschal Lamb is sacrificed. For he is the true Lamb that has taken away the sins of the world. Who by dying destroyed our death, and by rising again restored our life. And therefore with the angels and archangels, with the thrones and dominations, and with all the hosts of the celestial army, we incessantly sing a hymn to thy glory, saying: Holy, holy, Lord God of Hosts. Heaven and earth are full of thy glory. Blessed, etc.

COmmunicating together and celebrating the most sacred day of the Resurrection of our Lord Jesus Christ according to the flesh: and also honouring the memory, in the first place, of the glorious ever Virgin Mary, Mother of the same God and our Lord Jesus Christ, etc., *as at p 64.*

WE therefore beseech thee, O Lord graciously to accept this offering of our service as also of thy whole family, which we offer to thee for

those also, whom thou hast been pleased to regenerate by water and the Holy Ghost, granting them the remission of all their sins: grant us also peace in our days and by thy command preserve us from eternal damnation, and number us amongst thy elect. Through Christ our Lord. Amen.

The Communion.

CHRIST our passover is sacrificed, alleluia; therefore let us feast on the unleavened bread of sincerity and truth. Alleluia, alleluia, alleluia.

The Post Communion.

POUR forth on us, O Lord, the spirit of thy charity: that those whom thou hast replenished with the paschal sacraments, may, by thy goodness, live in perfect concord. Through our Lord Jesus Christ.

V. Dominus vobiscum.
R. Et cum spiritu tuo.
V. Ite, missa est. Alleluia, alleluia.
R. Deo gratias. Alleluia, alleluia.

V. The Lord be with you.
R. And with thy spirit.
V. Go, Mass is said, Alleluia, alleluia.
R. Thanks be to God. Alleluia, alleluia.

VISIT TO THE BLESSED SACRAMENT.

My Lord Jesus Christ, who for the love which Thou bearest to men dost remain day and night in this Sacrament, full of mercy and of love, inviting, expecting, receiving all them who come to visit Thee. I believe that Thou art present in the Blessed Sacrament of the Altar: I adore Thee, confessing my own misery and nothingness, and I thank Thee for all the mercies which Thou hast bestowed upon me, especially for having given me Thyself in this Sacrament, for having given me Thy most Holy Mother Mary for my advocate, and for having called me to visit Thee at this time. I salute Thy most loving Heart, and I desire to do so for three ends: first, in thanksgiving for this great gift; second, to atone for all the injuries Thou hast received from Thy enemies in this Sacrament; third, to adore Thee in all places in which Thou art least honoured and most abandoned in this Holy Sacrament. O my Jesus, I love Thee with all my heart. I am sorry for having hitherto displeased Thy infinite goodness; I resolve, with the assistance of Thy grace, never more to offend Thee; and at this moment, miserable as I am, I desire to consecrate my whole being to Thee. I give Thee my will, my affections, my desires, and all that I have. From this day forward, do with me and whatever belongs to me what Thou pleasest; I ask and desire only Thy love, the gift of final perseverance, and the perfect accomplishment of Thy holy will. I recommend to Thee the souls in purgatory, particularly those who were most devout to the Blessed Sacrament and to Holy

Mary, and I recommend to Thee all poor sinners. Finally, my dear Saviour, I unite all my affections with those of Thy most loving Heart; and thus united, I offer them to Thy eternal Father, and I beseech Him in Thy name, and for Thy sake, to accept them. Amen.

A Prayer at Benediction of the Most Holy Sacrament.

O divine Redeemer of our souls, who of Thy great goodness hast been pleased to leave us Thy precious body and blood in the blessed Sacrament of the Altar, I adore Thee with the most profound reverence. I humbly thank Thee for all the favours Thou hast bestowed upon us, especially for the institution of this most holy Sacrament. And as Thou art the source of every blessing, I entreat Thee to pour down Thy benediction this day upon us and upon all those for whom we offer up our prayers. And that nothing may interrupt the course of Thy blessing, I beseech Thee to banish from my heart all that displeases Thee: pardon me my sins, O my God, since I sincerely detest them for love of Thee; purify my heart, sanctify my soul, bestow on me a blessing like that which Thou didst grant to Thy disciples at Thy ascension into heaven; grant me a blessing that may change, consecrate and unite me perfectly to Thee, and may fill me with Thy Spirit, and be to me in this life a foretaste of those blessings which Thou reservest for Thy elect in heaven. All this I beg in the name of the Father, Son, and Holy Ghost. Amen.

An Act of Spiritual Communion.

I believe in Thee, O my Jesus, present in the most holy Sacrament of the Altar; I love Thee

above all things; and I desire to receive Thee into my soul. Since I cannot now receive Thee sacramentally, come at least spiritually into my heart. I embrace Thee and I unite myself to Thee as if Thou wert already there. Oh never permit me to be separated from Thee.

An Act of Adoration to the Most Holy Trinity.

I most humbly adore Thee, O uncreated Father, and Thee, O only-begotten Son, and Thee, O Holy Ghost the Paraclete, one almighty, everlasting and unchangeable God, Creator of heaven and earth, and of all things visible and invisible. I acknowledge in Thee a true and ineffable Trinity of Persons, a true and indivisible Unity of substance. I glorify thee, O ever-serene effulgent Trinity, one only Deity, my most compassionate Lord, my sweetest hope, my dearest light, my most desired repose, my joy, my life, and all my good. To thy most merciful goodness I commend my soul and body; to thy most sacred Majesty I wholly devote myself, and to thy divine will resign and yield myself eternally. All honour and glory be to thee for ever and ever. Amen.

O heavenly Father, O most forgiving Father, O Lord God, have mercy upon me a wretched sinner, have mercy upon all men. In fullest reparation, expiation, and satisfaction for all my iniquities and negligences, and for the sins of the whole world, and perfectly to supply the deficiency of my good works and merits, I offer to thee thy beloved Son, Christ Jesus, in union with that sovereign charity with which thou didst send him to us, and didst give him to us as our Saviour. I offer his transcendent virtues, and all that he did and suffered for us. I offer his labours, sorrows, torments, and most precious blood. I offer the

merits of the most blessed Virgin Mary, and of all thy Saints. Assist me, I beseech thee, O most merciful Father, through the same thy Son, by the power of thy Holy Spirit. Have mercy on all unhappy sinners, and graciously call them back to the way of salvation. Grant to all living pardon and grace, and to the faithful departed eternal light and rest. Amen.

O Holy Spirit, sweetest Comforter, who proceedest from the Father and the Son in an ineffable manner, come, I beseech thee, and enter into my heart. Purify and cleanse me from all sin, and sanctify my soul. Wash away its defilements, moisten its dryness, heal its wounds, subdue its stubborness, melt its coldness, and correct its wanderings. Make me truly humble and resigned, that I may be pleasing to thee, and thou mayest abide with me for ever. O most blessed light, O most amiable light, enlighten me. O ravishing joy of Paradise, O fount of purest delights, O my God, give thyself to me, and kindle vehemently in my inmost soul the fire of thy love. O my Lord, instruct, direct, and defend me in all things. Give me strength against all immoderate fears and a pusillanimous spirit; bestow upon me a right faith, a firm hope, and a sincere and perfect charity; and grant that I may ever do thy most gracious will. Amen.

Prayer for our Country.

O Lord Jesus Christ, infinite goodness, who by the divine Sacrament of thy Body and Blood dost refresh, comfort, and nourish thy Church, and daily offerest thyself a sacrifice of praise and propitiation to the eternal Father; look graciously upon our beloved country, shut out from the sweet delights of this banquet; mercifully pardon

all that hath been done or said, through impiety or ignorance, against these most holy mysteries in this land; inspire the minds of all men with faith and reverence for them, that they may become thy children, and be as olive-plants round about thy table. Who livest and reignest world without end. Amen.

Vouchsafe, O Lord Jesus Christ, with the Father and the Holy Ghost, to pour down upon me thy most holy benediction, that I may be enabled always to love thee, and seek to accomplish thy divine will in all things; and grant, O bread of angels, that I may deserve to receive thee during life, to be comforted by thee in death, and to enjoy thee eternally in thy heavenly kingdom. Amen.

Acts of Adoration before the Most Holy Sacrament.

[Hail, Salvation of the world, Word of the Father, holy Host, true Life, living Flesh, perfect Deity, true Man, Body of our Lord Jesus Christ; thou who didst form me from the dust of the earth, have mercy upon me a sinner. Amen.

Hail, most merciful Jesus, Son of God and of the Virgin Mary, who didst so love me as to be pleased to die for me, and to give thyself to me as my support, my sacrifice, and my reward; be thou, with the Father and the Holy Ghost, blessed by all and above all for ever.

I grieve for all my sins, purely because they have displeased thee, and I resign myself to thee, and annihilate myself before thee. Supply, O merciful Jesus, for all the imperfections of us thy people, for whom thou didst deign to die, through the merits of the most blessed Virgin Mary and of all the Saints, which I offer thee in union with thine own most sacred merits, to be repre-

sented before the eternal Father. O holy Father, look upon the face of thy Christ, and grant us the grace to know thee, to love thee, and to praise thee, together with thy beloved Son and the Holy Spirit, now and for ever.

All my holy patrons, and thou first, O most Blessed Mother of God, praise the Lord with me, and let us exalt his name for ever. Amen.

O Lord Jesus Christ, true God and man, I humbly adore and invoke thee, now present in the verity of thy flesh and blood, thy body and soul. Would that I could truly contemplate and know thee, that I could love, praise, and glorify thee, even as do thousands of holy angels who contemplate thee with the highest joy, who know thee, love, praise, and glorify thee perfectly without weariness or interruption. All creatures justly celebrate with praise and thanksgiving that ardent love of thine by which thou didst offer thy innocent and precious body upon the altar of the cross, and didst so lovingly, so graciously, so affectionately leave us in this holy Sacrament the same body, living and immortal, as a remembrance of thy departure, and as a pledge of thine infinite love.

Thou, therefore, O Lamb of God, who takest away the sins of the world, have mercy upon us, and give us peace; and so refresh our souls continually with this spiritual food, that we may never, in life or death, be separated from thee and from thine infinite mercy. Who livest and reignest for ever. Amen.

O infinite Wisdom, which cannot be deceived; O immense Goodness, which cannot deceive; great and eternal Truth my Lord and God I believe in thee and I believe thee in all which thou hast revealed, and which thou proposest to me to be believed through thy holy spouse the Church; and for this

holy faith I am ready, by thy grace, to die. I hope in thee, O our eternal Beatitude, and through thy infinite mercy and most precious merits, I trust that thou wilt grant me the pardon, grace, and glory which thou hast promised, with all the necessary means for attaining them; and I acknowledge and profess that I depend wholly upon thee, that I can do nothing without thee, but that through thee I can do all things, I love, and will love thee and all things that thou lovest, O infinite fountain of all good, because thou art good in thyself, and infinitely to be loved. I rejoice in thy infinite perfection, beatitude, and loveliness; and in all the homage, praise, honour, and glory which has been, is, or can be rendered to thee by thy elect and by all creatures. All these I offer to thee, along with every service and affection of my heart and my life itself.

I firmly embrace thee and thy blessed will in all things with the arms of love and resignation; I venerate thee with every possible feeling of reverence, affection, and gratitude; and I desire to embrace, love, and venerate thee for ever, if thou wilt mercifully grant that I may not be separated from thy grace and love here, or fail in attaining thy happy vision hereafter.

I believe in thee, O supreme truth.
I revere thee, O infinite majesty.
I adore thee, O tremendous power.
I bless thee, O most liberal benignity.
I hope in thee, O eternal felicity.
I love thee, O incomprehensible goodness.
I glorify thee, O most holy godhead.
I grieve from my inmost heart that I have ever offended thee!

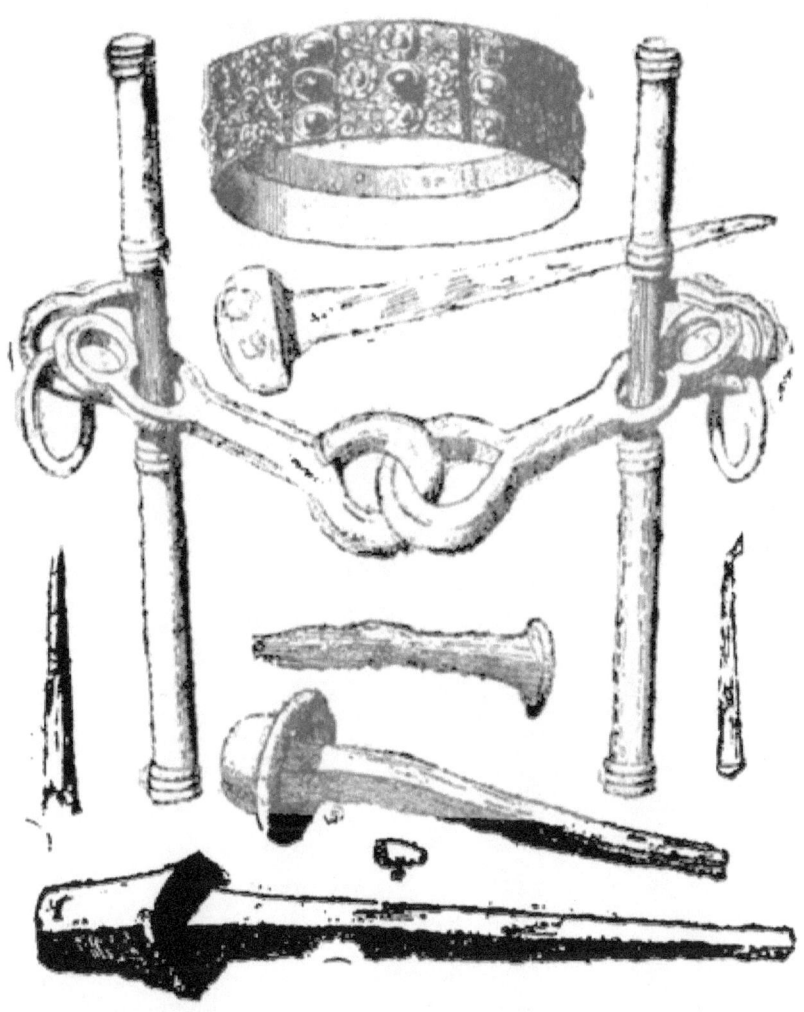

1. Iron Crown of Monza containing Nail of True Cross. — 2. Horse's bit made from Nail of Cross. — 3. Nail of the Cross preserved at Venice. — 4. Nail preserved in S. Maria in Campitelli, Rome. — 5. Nail of Cross preserved in the Church of Santa Croce in Gerusalemme, Rome. — 6. Nail preserved at Treves. — 7. Nail preserved at Arras. — 8. Piece of Nail preserved at Colle. — 9. Piece of Nail preserved at Toul.

THE SACRED STATIONS

WITH

A SHORT HISTORY OF THE

STATIONAL CHURCHES

OF ROME

AND A LIST OF THE BODIES OF THE SAINTS

AND THE OTHER PRINCIPAL RELICS

CONTAINED IN THEM

ALSO

THE PRAYERS IN LATIN AND ENGLISH

RECITED

IN THE CHURCH OF THE STATIONS

THE STATIONS OF LENT

INTRODUCTORY NOTICE

The stations, in olden times, were solemn processions of the clergy and people on certain fixed days to certain churches, for the purpose of prayer and religious exercises.

Their institution is lost in antiquity. In Tertullian, who wrote at the end of the second century, we find an apparent allusion to them. St. Hilary who assumed the pontificate in 461, and St. Gregory the Great, who died in 604, may both be mentioned for their ordinances concerning these religious functions.

The ceremonial is described by many ancient writers. The clergy and people met first in a church not far from that appointed for the station. Here the procession was formed. In front went the cross-bearer, with the particular cross, of which two are still preserved at St. John Lateran's. Next came the clergy in order of rank, with the Supreme Pontiff, however, last and barefooted. The people followed.

Arrived at the Church of the station (the word is of military origin, the early Christians constantly keeping before themselves the metaphors of warfare), the Pope entered the sacristy, where his feet were washed. Then he sang Holy Mass, during which the officiating Subdeacon announced the station for the following day. The Mass finished, one of the acolytes took some cotton or tow, dipped it in the oil of the lamp, and presented it to the Holy Father, who reverently kissed it. Afterwards this tow was carried to the pontifical residence, and the several pieces were there preserved till the pope's death, when they were employed to form a cushion for his head.

This ceremony over, the Holy Father made a sermon to his people. A great number of remarkable homilies of illustrious popes were made in this way, amongst others those of St. Gregory the Great.

This ceremonial was continued down to the fourteenth century. During the Popes' absence at Avignon it was altered, and the procession was never afterwards re-established. The popes, however, have never ceased to encourage the practice of the stations, and, even to the most recent times, have issued continual exortations for their due fulfilment.

Of the stational churches we have four ancient lists; one of about the seventh century, a second of the eleventh, and two others of the twelfth. In all substantial points these lists are at one. We know, consequently, that the stations of the present day are nearly always in the same locality, as those of the most ancient times.

Below we append the list of the Station Churches and the indulgences attached to their visit. It is to be noted however that, according to an indult of Pope Leo XII., a plenary indulgence may be gained by three visits made on three distinct days.

LIST OF THE STATIONS
as they are at present

Note. Churches in brackets no longer exist.

LENTEN STATIONS.

ASH WEDNESDAY — St Sabina; St Mary in Cosmedin; St Alexis.

THURSDAY — St George in Velabrum; Jesus and Mary (Corso).

FRIDAY — SS. John and Paul; St Gregory on the Celian.

SATURDAY — (S. Trifone); St Augustine.

FIRST SUNDAY IN LENT — St John Lateran.

LENTEN STATIONS

MONDAY — St Peter in Chains; St John of the Pigna.
TUESDAY — St Anastasia.
WEDNESDAY — St Mary Major.
THURSDAY — St Laurence in Panisperna.
FRIDAY — Holy Apostles.
SATURDAY — St Peter's
SECOND SUNDAY IN LENT — St. Mary in Domnica (la Navicella); St Mary Major; St Gregory on the Celian.
MONDAY — St Clement.
TUESDAY — St Balbina.
WEDNESDAY — St Cecilia.
THURSDAY — St Maria in Trastevere.
FRIDAY — St Vitalis.
SATURDAY — SS. Marcellinus and Peter (Lateran.)
THIRD SUNDAY IN LENT — St Laurence (Campo Verano.
MONDAY — St Mark.
TUESDAY — St Pudentiana.
WEDNESDAY — St Sixtus; SS. Nereus and Achilleus.
THURSDAY — SS. Cosmas and Damian.
FRIDAY — St Laurence in Lucina.
SATURDAY — St Susanna; (St Caius); St Mary of the Angels.
FOURTH SUNDAY IN LENT — Holy Cross of Jerusalem.
MONDAY — SS. Quattro Coronati.
TUESDAY — St Laurence in Damaso; St Andrew della Valle.
WEDNESDAY — St Paul's (outside the City.)
THURSDAY — St Sylvester in Capite; St Martin ai Monti.
FRIDAY — St Eusebius; St Bibiana.
SATURDAY — St Nicholas in Carcere; St Nicholas dei Lorenesi.
PASSION SUNDAY — St Peter's; St Lazarus.
MONDAY — St Chrysogonus.
TUESDAY — (St Cyriacus); St Mary in Via Lata; St Quiricus (Tor dei Conti).

LENTEN STATIONS

WEDNESDAY — St Marcellus.
THURSDAY — St Apollinaris.
FRIDAY — St Stephen (Rotondo).
SATURDAY — St John before the Latin Gate; St Caesarius.
PALM SUNDAY — St John Lateran.
MONDAY — St Praxedes.
TUESDAY — St Prisca; St Mary del Popolo.
WEDNESDAY — St Mary Major.
HOLY THURSDAY — St John Lateran.
GOOD FRIDAY — Holy Cross of Jerusalem.
HOLY SATURDAY — St John Lateran.

EASTER STATIONS.

EASTER SUNDAY — St Mary Major.
EASTER MONDAY — St Peter's; St Onofrio.
EASTER TUESDAY — St Paul's (outside the walls).
WEDNESDAY — St Laurence (Campo Verano).
THURSDAY — Holy Apostles.
FRIDAY — St Mary ad Martyres (Pantheon); St Mary sopra Minerva.
SATURDAY — St John Lateran.
SUNDAY " IN ALBIS " — St Pancras; St Mary della Scala.

ASCENSION STATION.

ASCENSION THURSDAY — St Peter's.

PENTECOST STATIONS.

VIGIL OF PENTECOST — St John Lateran.
WHIT SUNDAY — St Peter's.
VHIT MONDAY — St Peter in Chains.
TUESDAY — St Anastasia.
WEDNESDAY — St Mary Major.
THURSDAY — St Laurence (Campo Verano).
FRIDAY — Holy Apostles.
SATURDAY — St Peter's.

ADVENT STATIONS, DOWN TO LENTEN ONES.

First Sunday of Advent — St Mary Major.
Second Sunday of Advent — Holy Cross of Jerusalem.
Third Sunday of Advent — St Peter's
Fourth Sunday of Advent — Holy Apostles.
Christmas Eve — St Mary Major.
Christmas Morning — St Anastasia.
Christmas Day — St Mary Major.
St Stephen's Day — St Stephen (Rotondo).
Feast of St John Evang. — St Mary Major.
Feast of Holy Innocents — St Paul's (outside of City).
New Year's Day — St Mary in Trastevere.
Epiphany — St Peter's.
Septuagesima Sunday — St Laurence (Campo Verano).
Sexagesima Sunday — St Paul's (outside of City).
Quinquagesima Sunday — St Peter's.

QUARTER TENSE STATIONS.

Wednesday — St Mary Major.
Friday — Holy Apostles.
Saturday — St Peter's.

STATIONS OF ROGATION DAYS.

Feast of St Mark — St Peter's.
Rogation Monday — St Mary Major.
Rogation Tuesday — St John Lateran.
Rogation Wednesday — St Peter's

INDULGENCES ON DAYS OF STATION.

LENT.

Ash Wednesday, and Fourth Sunday in Lent — Indulgence of 15 years and 15 quarantines.
Palm Sunday — Indulgence of 25 yrs. and 25 quar.
Holy Thursday — Plenary Indulgence.
Good Friday and Holy Saturday — Indulgence of 30 yrs. and 30 quar.
On the other days — 10 years and 10 quar.

EASTER STATIONS.

Easter Sunday — Plenary Indulgence.
On the other days — 30 yrs. and 30 quar.

ASCENSION STATION.

Ascension Thursday — Plenary Indulgence.

PENTECOST STATIONS.

Vigil of Pentecost — 10 yrs. and 10 quar.
On the other days — 30 yrs. and 30 quar.

ADVENT AND OTHER STATIONS.

First, Second and Fourth Sundays of Advent — 10 years and 10 quar.
Third Sunday of Advent — 15 yrs. and 15 quar.
Christmas Eve, Christmas night and Christmas morning — 15 y. and 15 q.
Christmas Day — Plenary Indulgence.
St Stephen's; St John's; Holy Innocents' — 30 y. and 30 q.
Circumcision; Epiphany; Septuagesima — 30 y. and 30 q.
Sexagesima and Quinquagesima Sundays — 30 y. and 30 q.
Days of Quarter Tense — 10 y. and 10 q.
Feast of St Mark, and Rogation Days — 30 y. and 30 q.

Note. When the Station is in several Churches on the same day, it suffices to visit one of these Churches in order to gain the indulgence.

PRAYERS

TO BE RECITED IN VISITING THE CHURCHES OF STATION.

A visit is first of all made to a church in the neighbourhood. There make an Act of Adoration to the Blessed Sacrament and recite the following prayers:

Actiones nostras, quaesumus Domine, aspirando praeveni, et adjuvando prosequere, ut cuncta nostra oratio et operatio a te semper incipiat, et per te coepta finiatur. Per Christum Dominum nostrum.
R. Amen.
Veni, Sancte Spiritus, reple tuorum corda fidelium, et tui amoris in eis ignem accende.

V. Emitte Spiritum tuum, et creabuntur.
R. Et renovabis faciem terrae.

Oremus
Deus, qui corda fidelium Sancti Spiritus illustratione docuisti; da nobis in eodem Spiritu recta sapere, et de ejus semper consolatione gaudere. Per Christum Dominum nostrum. R. Amen.

Anticipate, O Lord, we beseech Thee, our actions, and accompany them by Thy help, so that our every prayer and work may in Thee have its beginning and in Thee its end. Through Christ our Lord. Amen.
Come, O Holy Spirit, fill the hearts of Thy faithful and enkindle in them the fire of Thy love.
V. Send forth Thy Spirit, and they shall be created.
R. And Thou shalt renew the face of he earth.

Let us pray
O God, who hast taught the hearts of Thy fai hful by the light of the Holy Spirit, grant us by the same 'Spirit to think the things that be right, and ever to rejoice in His consolation; through Christ our Lord. Amen.

HYMNUS

Pange lingua gloriosi
Corporis mysterium,
Sanguinisque pretiosi,
Quem in mundi pretium
Fructus ventris generosi
Rex effudit gentium.

HYMN

Sing, my tongue, the Saviour's glory,
Of his Flesh the mystery sing;
Of the Blood, all price exceeding,
Shed by our immortal King,
Destined for the world's redemption,

Nobis datus, nobis natus
Ex intacta Virgine,
Et in mundo conversatus,
Sparso verbi semine,
Sui moras incolatus
Miro clausit ordine.

In supremae nocte coenae,
Recumbens cum fratribus,
Observata lege plene
Cibis in legalibus,
Cibum turbae duodenae
Se dat suis manibus.

Verbum caro, panem verum
Verbo carnem efficit :
Fitque sanguis Christi merum:
Et si sensus deficit,
Ad firmandum cor sincerum
Sola fides sufficit.

Tantum ergo Sacramentum
Veneremur cernui :
Et antiquum documentum
Novo cedat ritui ;
Praestet fides supplementum
Sensuum defectui.

Genitori, Genitoque
Laus et jubilatio,

From a noble womb to spring.
Of a pure and spotless Virgin,
Born for us on earth below,
He as Man with man conversing,
Stayed, the seeds of truth to sow;
Then He closed in solemn order
Wondrously his life of woe.

On the night of that Last Supper,
Seated with his chosen band,
He the paschal victim eating,
First fulfils the law's command;
Then as food to all his brethren,
Gives himself with his own hand.

Word made flesh, the bread of nature
By his Word to flesh he turns;
Wine into his blood he changes:
What, though sense no change discerns,
Only be the heart in earnest,
Faith her lesson quickly learns.

Lowly bending, deep adoring,
Lo! the Sacrament we hail;
Types and shadows have their ending,
Newer rites of grace prevail;
Faith for all defects supplying
Where the feeble senses fail.

Glory, honour, might, dominion,

Salus, honor, virtus quoque
Sit et benedictio:
Procedenti ab utroque
Compar sit laudatio. Amen.

Be unto our God most high;
To the Father, Son, and Spirit,
Ever blessed Trinity,
Praise be given, and power eternal,
Unto all eternity.

O Sacrum convivium, in quo Christus sumitur: recolitur memoria Passionis ejus: mens impletur gratia; et futurae gloriae nobis pignus datur.

V. Panem de coelo praestitisti eis.

R. Omne delectamentum in se habentem.

Oremus

Deus, qui nobis sub Sacramento mirabili, passionis tuae memoriam reliquisti: tribue, quaesumus, ita nos corporis et sanguinis tui sacra mysteria venerari, ut redemptionis tuae fructum in nobis jugiter sentiamus. Qui vivis, etc. Amen.

Ant. Sancta Maria succurre miseris, juva pusillanimes, refove flebiles, ora pro populo, interveni pro Clero, intercede pro devoto foemineo sexu: sentiant omnes tuum juvamen, quicumque celebrant tuam sanctam commemorationem.

V. Dignare me laudare te, Virgo sacrata.

R. Da mihi virtutem contra hostes tuos.

O sacred banquet in which Christ is received: the memory of His Passion is renewed; the mind is filled with grace, and a pledge of future glory is given unto us.

V. Thou didst give them bread from heaven.

R. Containing in itself all sweetness.

Let us pray

O God, who, under a wonderful Sacrament, hast left us a memorial of thy passion; grant us, we beseech thee, so to venerate the sacred mysteries of thy body and blood, that we may ever feel within us the fruit of thy redemption. Who livest, etc. Amen.

Ant. Holy Mary, come to the aid of the wretched, help the wavering, cherish the tearful, pray for the people, intervene for the clergy, intercede for the devout female sex: let all who celebrate thy holy commemoration experience thy assistance.

V. Grant me to praise thee, O Holy Virgin.

R. Give me strength against thy enemies.

Oremus

Concede, misericors Deus, fragilitati nostrae praesidium; ut, qui Sanctae Dei Genitricis memoriam agimus, intercessionis ejus auxilio a nostris iniquitatibus resurgamus. Per eumdem Christum Dominum nostrum. Amen.

Ant. Gaudent in coelis animae Sanctorum, qui Christi vestigia sunt sequuti; et quia pro ejus amore sanguinem suum fuderunt, ideo cum Christo exultant sine fine, et quotidie intercedunt pro nobis.

V. Exsultabunt Sancti in gloria.

R. Laetabuntur in cubilibus suis.

Oremus

Deus, qui nos perpetua sanctorum Martyrum tuorum protectione custodis, concede propitius, ut in aeterna beatitudine de eorum societate gaudere mereamur. Per Christum Dominum nostrum. Amen.

Let us pray

Grant, O merciful God, strength to our weakness; that we who celebrate the commemoration of the Holy Mother of God, may by the help of her intercession be freed from our iniquities. Through Christ our Lord. Amen.

Ant. In heaven rejoice the souls of those Saints, who following in Christ's footsteps, poured out their blood for love of Him. Therefore they exult with Him for ever.

V. The Saints shall rejoice in glory.

R. They shall be glad in their resting place.

Let us pray

O God who dost guard us by the constant protection of thy Martyrs, grant we beseech Thee, that we may enjoy their company in the life to come. Through Christ our Lord. Amen.

Leaving this church and on the way to the church of Station, say:

THE MISERERE

Miserere mei, Deus: * secundum magnam misericordiam tuam.

Et secundum multitudinem miserationum tuarum: * dele iniquitatem meam.

Amplius lava me ab iniqui-

1 Have mercy upon me, O God: according to thy great mercy.

2 And according to the multitude of thy tender mercies: blot out my iniquity.

3 Wash me yet more from

tate mea : * et a peccato meo munda me.

Quoniam iniquitatem meam ego cognosco : * et peccatum meum contra me est semper.

Tibi soli peccavi, et malum coram te feci : * ut justificeris in sermonibus tuis, et vincas cum judicaris.

Ecce enim in inquitatibus conceptus sum : * et in peccatis concepit me mater mea.

Ecce enim veritatem dilexisti : * incerta et occulta sapientiae tuae manifestasti mihi.

Asperges me hyssopo, et mundabor ; * lavabis me, et super nivem dealbabor.

Auditui meo dabis gaudium et laetitiam : et exultabunt ossa humiliata.

Averte faciem tuam a peccatis meis : * et omnes iniquitates meas dele.

Cor mundum crea in me, Deus : * et spiritum rectum innova in visceribus meis.

Ne projicias me a facie tua : * et Spiritum sanctum tuum ne auferas a me.

Redde mihi laetitiam salutaris tui : * et spiritu principali confirma me.

Docebo iniquos vias tuas : *

my iniquity; and cleanse me from my sin.

4 For I acknowledge my iniquity: and my sin is always before me.

5 Against thee only have I sinned, and done evil in thy sight : that thou mayest be justified in thy words, and mayest overcome when thou art judged.

6 For behold, I was conceived in iniquities: and in sins did my mother conceive me.

7 For behold, thou hast loved truth: the uncertain and hidden things of thy wisdom thou hast made manifest unto me.

8 Thou shalt sprinkle me with hyssop, and I shall be cleansed : thou shalt wash me and I shall be made whiter than snow.

9 Thou shalt make me hear of joy and gladness: and the bones that were humbled shall rejoice.

10 Turn away thy face from my sins: and blot out all my iniquties.

11 Create in me a clean heart, O God: and renew a right spirit within my bowels.

12 Cast me not away from thy presence: and take not thy holy Spirit from me.

13 Restore unto me the joy of thy salvation : and strengthen me with a perfect spirit.

14 I will teach the unjust

et impii ad te convertentur.

Libera me de sanguinibus, Deus, Deus salutis meae : * et exultabit lingua mea justitiam tuam.

Domine, labia mea aperies:* et os meum annuntiabit laudem tuam.

Quoniam si voluisses sacrificium, dedissem utique: * holocausis non delectaberis.

Sacrificium Deo spiritus contribulatus : * cor contritum et humiliatum, Deus, non despicies.

Benigne fac, Domine, in bona voluntate tua Sion : * ut aedificen ur muri Jerusalem.

Tunc acceptabis sacrificium justitiae, oblationes, et holocausta : * tunc imponent super altare tuum vitulos.

Gloria, etc.

thy ways: and the wicked shall be converted unto thee.
15 Deliver me from blood, O God, thou God of my salvation: and my tongue shall extol thy justice.
16 Thou shalt open my lips, O Lord: and my mouth shall declare thy praise.
17 For if thou hadst desired sacrifice, I would surely have given it: with burnt-offerings thou wilt not be delighted.
18 The sacrifice to God is an afflicted spirit: a contrite and humble heart, O God, thou wilt not despise.
19 Deal favourably, O Lord, in thy good will with Sion: that the walls of Jerusalem may be built up.
20 Then shalt thou accept the sacrifices of justice, oblations, and whole burnt-offerings; then shall they lay calves upon thine altar.

Glory, etc.

Five *Pater, Ave* and *Glorias*, in honour of the Five Wounds of our Lord.

THE " STAGES OF THE PASSION "

Jesu dulcissime, in horto moestus; Patrem orans: et in agonia positus; sanguineum sudorem effundens: Miserere nobis,

℟. Miserere nostri, Domine miserere nostri.

Jesu dulcissime, osculo traditoris in manus impiorum traditus; et tamquam latro

Most sweet Jesus, sad and sorrowful in the garden, praying to the father, entering into agony, and pouring forth a sweat of blood, have mercy on us.

℟. Have mercy on us, O Lord, have mercy on us.

Most sweet Jesus, betrayed by a traitor's kiss into the hands of the impious, seized

captus, et ligatus: et a Discipulis derelictus: Miserere nobis.

℟. Miserere nostri, Domine, miserere nostri.

Jesu dulcissime, ab iniquo Judaeorum concilio reus mortis acclamatus; ad Pilatum tamquam malefactor ductus: ab iniquo Herode spretus, et delusus: Miserere nobis.

℟. Miserere nostri, Domine, miserere nostri.

Jesu dulcissime, spinis coronatus: colaphis caesus: arundine percussus: facie velatus: veste purpurea circumdatus: multipliciter derisus: et opprobriis saturatus: Miserere nobis.

℟. Miserere nostri, Domine, miserere nostri.

Jesu dulcissime, latroni Barabbae postpositus: a Judaeis reprobatus: et ad mortem Crucis injuste condemnatus: Miserere nobis.

℟. Miserere nostri, Domine, mirerere nostri.

Jesu dulcissime, ligno Crucis oneratus: et ad locum supplicii, tamquam ovis ad occisionem, ductus: Miserere nobis.

℟. Miserere nostri, Domine, miserere nostri.

Jesu dulcissime, inter latrones deputatus: blasphematus et derisus: felle et aceto

and bound as a robber, abandoned by Thy disciples, have mercy on us.

℟. Have mercy on us, O Lord, have mercy on us.

Most sweet Jesus, pronounced deserving of death by the impious council of the Jews, led as a malefactor to Pilate, despised and mocked at by the impious Herod, have mercy on us.

℟. Have mercy on us, O Lord, have mercy on us.

Most sweet Jesus, crowned with thorns, wounded with blows, struck with a reed, blind-folded, covered with a purple garment, in many ways derided, and overwhelmed with insults, have mercy on us.

℟. Have mercy on us, O Lord, have mercy on us.

Most sweet Jesus, esteemed less than the robber Barabbas, rejected by the Jews, and unjustly condemned by them to the death of the cross, have mercy on us.

℟. Have mercy on us, O Lord, have mercy on us.

Most sweet Jesus, burdened with the wood of the cross, and led to the place of execution, like a sheep to the slaughter, have mercy on us.

℟. Have mercy on us, O Lord, have mercy on us.

Most sweet Jesus, reputed amongst robbers, blasphemed and derided, slaked with vin-

potatus, et ab hora sexta usque ad horam nonam in ligno cruciatus: miserere nobis.

℟. Miserere nostri, Domine, miserere nostri.

Jesu dulcissime, in patibulo Crucis mortuus: et coram tua sancta Matre lancea perforatus: simul sanguinem et aquam emittens: miserere nobis.

℟. Miserere nostri, Domine, miserere nostri,

Jesu dulcissime, de Cruce depositus: et lacrymis moestissime Virginis Matris tuae perfusus, miserere nobis.

℟. Miserere nostri, Domine, miserere nostri,

Iesu dulcissime, plagis circumdatus: quinque vulneribus conditus et in sepulchro repositus: miserere nobis.

℟. Miserere nostri, Domine, miserere nostri.

egar and gall, and tortured on the tree of the cross with the most horrible torments, from the sixth to the ninth hour, have mercy on us.

℟. Have mercy ou us, O. Lord, have mercy on os.

Most sweet Jesus, dead on the gibbet of the cross, and in the presence of the Holy Mother, pierced with a lance, giving forth from the wound both blood and water, have mercy on us.

℟. Have mercy on us, O Lord, have mercy on us.

Most sweet Jesus, taken down from the cross, and covered with the tears of Thy most sorrowful Virgin Mother, have mercy on us.

℟. Have mercy on us, O Lord, have mercy on us.

Most sweet Jesus, covered with sores and marked with five wounds, embalmed with unguents and laid in the sepulchre, have mercy on us.

℟. Have mercy on us, O Lord, have mercy on us.

In the church of the Station, before the Altar of the Blessed Sacrament recite the Litany of the Saints with the following Verses, Responses and Prayers.

Ant. Sancta Maria, et omnes Sancti tui, quaesumus Domine, nos ubique adjuvent: ut, dum eorum merita recolimus, patrocinia sentiamus, et pacem tuam nostris concede temporibus, et ab ec-

May the Blessed Virgin and all thy Saints, O Lord, we beseech thee, help us in every place. that while we celebrate their merits we may experience their protection ; grant peace in our time. O Lord,

LENTEN STATIONS

clesia tua cunctam repelle nequitiam.	and drive all malice far from thy Church.
Kyrie eleison.	Lord have mercy.
Kyrie eleison.	*Lord have mercy.*
Christe eleison.	Christ have mercy.
Christe eleison.	*Christ have mercy.*
Kyrie eleison.	Lord have mercy.
Kyrie eleison.	*Lord have mercy.*
Christe audi nos.	Christ hear us.
Christe exaudi nos.	*Christ graciously hear us.*
Pater de coelis Deus, *miserere nobis.*	God the Father of heaven,
Fili Redemptor mundi Deus,	God the Son, Redeemer of the world,
Spiritus Sancte Deus,	God the Holy Ghost,
Sancta Trinitas, unus Deus,	Holy Trinity, one God,
Sancta Maria, *ora pro nobis.*	Holy Mary,
Sancta Dei Genitrix,	Holy Mother of God,
Sancta Virgo virginum,	Holy Virgin of virgins,
Sancte Michael,	St. Michael,
Sancte Gabriel,	St. Gabriel,
Sancte Raphael,	St. Raphael,
Omnes sancti Angeli et Archangeli, *Orate, etc.*	All ye holy Angels and Archangels,
Omnes sancti beatorum Spirituum ordines, *Orate, etc.*	All ye holy orders of blessed Spirits,
Sancte Joannes Baptista, *Ora, etc.*	St. John the Baptist,
Sancte Joseph, *Ora, etc.*	St. Joseph,
Omnes sancti Patriarchae et Prophetae, *Orate, etc.*	All ye holy Patriarchs and Prophets,
Sancte Petre, *ora.*	St. Peter,
Sancte Paule,	St. Paul,
Sancte Andrea,	St. Andrew,
Sancte Jacobe,	St. James,
Sancte Joannes,	St. John,
Sancte Thoma,	St. Thomas,
Sancte Jacobe,	St. James,
Sancte Philippe,	St. Philip,
Sancte Bartholomaee,	St. Bartholomew,
Sancte Matthaee,	St. Matthew,
Sancte Simon,	St. Simon,
Sancte Thaddaee,	St. Thaddeus,

Have mercy, etc.

Pray for us.

Sancte Mathia,	St. Matthias,
Sancte Barnaba,	St. Barnabas,
Sancte Luca,	St. Luke,
Sanc e Marce,	St. Mark,
Omnes sancti Apostoli et Evangelistae, *Orate, etc.*	All ye holy Apostles and Evangelists,
Omnes sancti Discipuli Domini, *Orate, etc.*	All ye holy Disciples of our Lord,
Omnes sancti Innocentes, *Orate etc.*	All ye holy Innocents,
Sancte Stephane, *Ora, etc.*	St. Stephen,
Sancte Laurenti, *Ora, etc.*	St. Lawrence,
Sancte Vincenti, *Ora, etc.*	St. Vincent,
Sancti Fabiane et Sebastiane. *Orate.*	SS. Fabian and Sebastian,
Sancti Joannes et Paule,	SS. John and Paul,
Sancti Cosma et Damiane,	SS. Cosmas and Damian,
Sancti Gervasi et Protasi,	SS. Gervase et Protase,
Omnes sancti Martyres,	All ye holy Martyrs,
Sancte Sylvester, *ora*	St. Silvester,
Sancte Gregori,	St. Gregory,
Sancte Ambrosi,	St. Ambrose,
Sancte Augustine,	St. Augustine,
Sancte Hieronyme,	St. Jerome,
Sancte Martine,	St. Martin,
Sancte Nicolae,	St. Nicholas,
Omnes sancti Pontifices et Confessores, *Orate, etc.*	All ye holy Bishops and Confessors,
Omnes sancti Doctores, *Orate, etc.*	All ye holy Doctors,
Sancte Antoni,	St. Anthony,
Sancte Benedicte,	St. Benedict,
Sancte Bernarde,	St. Bernard,
Sancte Dominice,	St. Dominic,
Sancte Francisce,	St. Francis,
Omnes sancti Sacerdotes et Levitae, *Orate, etc.*	All ye holy Priests and Levites,
Omnes sancti Monachi et Eremitae, *Orate, etc.*	All ye holy Monks and Hermits,
Sancta Maria Magdalena,	St. Mary Magdalene,
Sancta Agatha,	St. Agatha,
Sancta Lucia,	St. Lucy,
Sancta Agnes,	St. Agnes,

Pray for us.

Sancta Caecilia,	St. Cecily,
Sancta Catharina,	St. Catherine,
Sancta Anastasia,	St. Anastasia,
Omnes sanctae Virgines et Viduae, *Orate, etc.*	All ye holy Virgins and Widows,
Omnes Sancti et Sanctae Dei,	All ye holy men and women, Saints of God,
Intercedite pro nobis.	*Make intercession for us.*
Propitius esto,	Be merciful,
Parce nobis, Domine.	*Spare us, O Lord.*
Propitius esto,	Be merciful,
Exaudi nos, Domine.	*Hear us, O Lord.*
Ab omni malo, *Li'era nos Domine.*	From all evil,
Ab omni peccato,	From all sin,
Ab ira tua,	From thy wrath,
Ab imminentibus periculis,	From all dangers that threaten us,
A peste, fame, et bello,	From plague, famine, and war,
A subitanea et improvisa morte,	From a sudden and unprovided death,
Ab insidiis diaboli,	From the snares of the devil,
Ab ira, et odio, et omni mala voluntate,	From anger, and hatred, and every evil will,
A spiritu fornicationis,	From the spirit of fornication,
A fulgore et tempestate,	From lightning and tempest,
A morte perpetua,	From everlasting death,
Per mysterium sanctae Incarnationis tuae,	Through the mystery of thy holy Incarnation,
Per Adventum tuum,	Through thy Coming,
Per Nativitatem tuam,	Through thy Nativity,
Per Baptismum et sanctum Jejunium tuum,	Through thy Baptism and holy Fasting,
Per Crucem et Passionem tuam,	Through thy Cross and Passion,
Per Mortem et Sepulturam tuam,	Through thy Death and Burial,
Per sanctam Resurrectionem tuam,	Through thy holy Resurrection,

O Lord, deliver us.

Per admirabilem Ascensionem tuam,
Per adventum Spiritus Sancti Paracliti,

In die judicii,
Peccatores,
Te rogamus audi nos.
Ut nobis parcas,

Ut nobis indulgeas,

Ut ad veram poenitentiam nos perducere digneris,
Ut ecclesiam tuam sanctam regere et conservare digneris,
Ut domnum Apostolicum, et omnes ecclesiasticos ordines in sancta religione conservare digneris,
Ut inimicos sanctae Ecclesiae humiliare digneris,

Ut Turcarum, et haereticorum conatus reprimere et ad nihilum redigere digneris,

Ut regibus et principibus Christianis pacem et veram concordiam donare digneris,

Ut cuncto populo Christiano pacem et unitatem largiri digneris,

Ut nosmetipsos in tuo sancto servitio confortare et conservare digneris,

Through thine admirable Ascension,
Through the coming of the Holy Ghost the Paraclete,

In the day of judgment,
We sinners,
Beseech thee hear us.
That thou wouldst spare us,

That thou wouldst pardon us,

That thou wouldst bring us to true penance.
That thou wouldst vouchsafe to govern and preserve thy holy Church.
That thou wouldst vouchsafe to preserve our Apostolic Prelate, and all orders of the Church,
That thou wouldst vouchsafe to humble the enemies of holy Church,

That thou wouldst vouchsafe to defeat the attempts of all Turks and heretics, and bring them to nought,

That thou wouldst vouchsafe to grant true concord to Christian kings and princes,

That thou wouldst vouchsafe to grant peace and unity to all Christian people.
That thou wouldst vouchsafe to confirm and preserve us in thy holy desires,

Te rogamus audi nos.

We beseech thee, hear us.

Ut mentes nostras ad coelestia desideria erigas.	That thou wouldst lift up our minds to heavenly desires,
Ut omnibus benefactoribus nostris sempiterna bona retribuas.	That thou wouldst render eternal blessings to all our benefactors.
Ut animas nostras, fratrum, propinquorum, et benefactorum nostrorum ab aeterna damnatione eripias.	That thou wouldst deliver our souls, and the souls of our brethren, relations, and benefactors, from eternal damnation,
Ut fructus terrae dare et conservare digneris,	That thou wouldst vouchsafe to give and preserve the fruits of the earth,
Ut omnibus fidelibus defunctis requiem aeternam donare digneris,	That thou wouldst vouchsafe to grant eternal rest to all the faithful departed,
Ut nos exaudire digneris,	That thou wouldst vouchsafe graciously to hear us.

Te rogamus audi nos.

Fili Dei,
Agnus Dei qui tollis peccata mundi,
Parce nobis, Domine.
Agnus Dei, qui tollis peccata mundi,
Exaudi nos, Domine.
Agnus Dei, qui tollis peccata mundi,
Miserere nobis.
Christe audi nos.
Christe exaudi nos.
Kyrie eleison.
Christe eleison.
Kyrie eleison.
    Pater noster *(secreto)*.
    V. Et ne nos inducas in tentationem.
    R. Sed libera nos a malo.
V. Exaudi, Domine, suppli-

Son of God,
Lamb of God, who takest away the sins of the world,
Spare us, O Lord.
Lamb of God, who takest away the sins of the world,
Graciously hear us, O Lord.
Lamb of God, who takest away the sins of the world,
Have mercy on us.
Christ hear us.
Christ graciously hear us.
Lord have mercy.
Christ have mercy.
Lord have mercy.
    Our Father *(secretly)*.
    V. And lead us not into temptation.
    R. But deliver us from evil.
V. Hearken, O Lord, to

cum preces.
R. Et confitentium tibi parce peccatis.

V. Respice Domine ad humilitatem nostram.
R. Et non deseras nos in tempore tribulationis.
V. Gregem tuum, Pastor aeterne, non deseras.
R. Sed per Beatos Apostolos tuos perpetua defensione custodias.
V. Ostende nobis, Domine, misericordiam tuam.
R. Et salutare tuum da nobis.

V. Oremus pro Pontifice nostro N.
R. Dominus conservet eum, et vivificet eum, et beatum faciat eum in terra, et non tradat eum in animam inimicorum ejus.
V. Fiat pax in virtute tua.

R. Et abundantia in turribus tuis.
V. Domine exaudi orationem meam.
R. Et clamor meus ad te veniat.
V. Dominus vobiscum.
R. Et cum spiritu tuo.

Oremus
Deus refugium nostrum, et virtus, adesto piis Ecclesiae tuae precibus, auctor ipse pietatis, et praesta; ut intercedente Beata, et gloriosa semper Virgine Dei Genitrice Maria, cum Beatis Apostolis tuis Petro, et Paulo et om-

the prayers of thy suppliants.
R. And mercifully forgive the sins of them that confess to thee.
V. O Lord, look down on our humility.
R. And leave us not in the day of tribulation.
V. Forsake not thy flock, O Eternal Father.
R. But grant them eternal protection through thy holy Apostles.
V. O Lord, have mercy upon us.
R. And grant us thy salvation.
V. Let us pray for our Sovereign Pontiff N.
R. The Lord preserve him and give him life and make him blessed upon the earth; and deliver him not up to the will of his enemies.
V. Let there be peace by thy strength.
R. And plenty in thy towers.
V. O Lord hear my prayer.

R. And let my cry come to thee.
V. The Lord be with you
R. And with thy spirit.

Let us pray
O God, our refuge and strength, who art the author of all piety, hearken unto the devout prayers of Thy Church, and vouchsafe by the intercession of the Glorious and Blessed Mother of God Mary ever Virgin, with

nibus Sanctis, quod in praesentibus Ecclesiae necessitatibus fideliter petimus, efficaciter consequamur.

Ecclesiae tuae quaesumus Domine preces placatus admitte, ut destructis adversitatibus, et erroribus universis, secura tibi serviat libertate.

Libera quaesumus Domine a peccatis, et hostibus famulos tuos tibi supplicantes; ut in sancta conversatione viventes, nullis afficiantur adversitatibus.

Deus omnium Fidelium Pastor, et Rector, Famulum tuum N. quem Pastorem Ecclesiae tuae praeesse voluisti, propitius respice; da ei quaesumus, verbo, et exemplo, quibus praeest proficere; ut ad vitam una cum grege sibi credito perveniat sempiternam.

Omnipotens sempiterne Deus, qui vivorum dominaris simul et mortuorum, omniumque misereris, quos tuos fide et opere futuros esse praenoscis: te supplices exoramus; ut pro quibus effundere preces decrevimus, quosque vel praesens saeculum adhuc in carne retinet,

Thy Blessed Apostles Peter and Paul and all Thy Saints, that what we ask in the present necessities of Thy Church we may obtain effectually. Amen.

O Lord we beseech thee mercifully hear the prayers of thy Church, that being preserved from the assaults of her enemies and from all errors, she may serve thee in all freedom.

O Lord we beseech thee, deliver thy servants that cry unto thee, from sin and from all their enemies that, walking in the paths of righteousness, they may be preserved from all adversity.

O God, the Pastor and ruler of all the faithful, mercifully look upon thy servant N. whom thou hast been pleased to appoint the pastor of thy Church; grant, we beseech thee, that both by word and example he may edify those over whom he is placed; and, together with the flock committed to his care, may obtain everlasting life: Through, etc.

Almighty, everlasting, God, who hast dominion over the living and the dead, and art merciful to all, who thou foreknowest will be thine by faith and works; we humbly beseech thee that they for whom we intend to pour forth our prayers, whether this present world still detain them

vel futurum jam exutos corpore suscepit, intercedentibus omnibus Sanctis tuis, pietatis tuae clementia omnium delictorum suorum veniam consequantur. Per Dominum nostrum.

℣. Exaudiat nos omnipotens et misericors Dominus.
℟. Et custodiat nos semper Amen.

in the flesh, or the world to come hath already received them stripped of their mortal bodies, may, by the grace of thy loving kindness, and by the intercession of all the Saints, obtain the remission of all their sins. Through thy Son Jesus Christ our Lord, who liveth and reigneth with Thee, in the unity of the Holy Spirit, God, for ever and ever. ℟. Amen.

℣. May the almighty and merciful God hear us.
℟. And preserve us always. Amen.

On leaving the church recite the following

Psalmus 129.

De profundis clamavi ad te Domine: * Domine exaudi vocem meam.

Fiant aures tuae intendentes, * in vocem deprecationis meae.

Si iniquitates observaveris Domine: * Domine quis sustinebit?

Quia apud te propitiatio est: * et propter legem tuam sustinui te Domine.

Sustinuit anima mea in verbo ejus: * speravit anima mea in Domino.

A custodia matutina usque ad noctem; * speret Israel in Domino.

Quia apud Dominum misericordia: * et copiosa apud eum redemptio.

Psalm 129.

Out of the depths have I cried unto thee O Lord: Lord hear my voice.

Oh, let thine ears consider well: the voice of my supplication.

If thou, O Lord, shalt mark iniquities: Lord, who shall abide it?

For with thee there is propitiation; and because of thy law I have waited for thee, O Lord.

My soul hath waited on his word: my soul hath hoped in the Lord.

From the morning watch even until night; let Israel hope in the Lord.

For with the Lord there is mercy: and with him is plenteous redemption.

Et ipse redimet Israel, *
ex omnibus iniquitatibus ejus.

Requiem aeternam dona eis Domine:

Et lux perpetua luceat eis.

A porta inferi.

Erue Domine animas eorum.

Requiescant in pace.
Amen.

Domine exaudi orationem meam.

Et clamor meus ad te veniat.

Oremus

Fidelium, Deus, omnium Conditor et Redemptor animabus famulorum famularumque tuarum, remissionem cunctorum tribue peccatorum; ut indulgentiam, quam semper optaverunt, piis supplicationibus consequantur. Qui vivis et regnas.

Rèquiem aeternam dona eis Domine:

Et lux perpetua luceat eis.

Requiescant in pace.

Amen.

And he shall redeem Israel: from all his iniquities.

Eternal rest give unto them, O Lord.

And let eternal light shine upon them.

From the gates of hell.

Deliver, O Lord, their souls.

May they rest in peace.
Amen.

O Lord, hear my prayer.

And let my cry come unto thee.

Let us pray

Oh God, the Creator and Redeemer of all the faithful, grant to the souls of thy servants departed the remission of all their sins, that they may obtain through pious supplications, that mercy which they have always desired. Who livest and reignest world without end. Amen.

Eternal rest give unto them O Lord:

And let eternal light shine upon them.

May they rest in peace.
Amen.

SHORT HISTORY
OF THE
CHURCHES OF ROME
ASSIGNED FOR LENTEN STATIONS

ASH WEDNESDAY.

(1) ST. SABINA ON THE AVENTINE.

Supposed to occupy the site of the Temple of Juno Regina. Saint Sabina was a widow of noble Roman family, martyred under the Emperor Hadrian. This church is supposed to be on the site of her house. From the fine inscription in mosaic over the principal door, we learn that it was constructed at the expense of an Illyrian priest, Peter, in the pontificate of S. Celestine I., that is, in the beginning of the fifth century. It was restored by Leo III., (800) and Gregory II. (825), given to St. Dominic for his new Order by Honorius III. (1216). Eugene III., Gregory IX. and other Popes also embellished it. Sistus V. changed it to its present form. Gregory the Great, in a time of pestilence, gathered there the faithful and established the famous Litany or procession. The same Pope chose this church for the station of the first day of Lent.

The adjoining monastery is remarkable as having been the abode of St. Dominic and of several illustrious Saints, amongst them St. Hyacinth, St. Raimond of Pennafort, St. Thomas of Aquin and St. Pius V.

The principal front is hidden against the monastery. On the side are to be seen the celebrated doors of carved wood, supposed to be coeval with the church itself, and representing in bas-reliefs scenes from the Old and New Testament. These doors are unique of their kind in Rome. The church is rich in marbles and mosaics. In the adjoining garden is an orange tree, planted by Saint Dominic. The rooms

occupied by St. Dominic and St. Pius V., since turned into chapels, can be seen in the monastery. The Church contains the Bodies of St. Sabina, St. Serapia and St. Alexander.

(2) S. MARIA in COSMEDIN. (Bocca della Verità)

Built on the ruins of a temple of Ceres, this church is supposed to have been in existence from the very first centuries of our era. We find it mentioned in the sixth century under the title of St. Mary of Greeks. The name was changed to St. Mary in Cosmedin, when the church was rebuilt, in 872, by Pope Adrian I. It was restored in the early part of the 12th century by Pope Callixtus II.

The church has many remarkable ornaments: mosaic pavement, elegant marble ambones, episcopal chair with mosaics. The tower is probably of the eighth or ninth century. The portico contains many inscriptions of much interest to scholars.

Most remarkable is the venerated picture of the Madonna over the high altar. It is said to have been brought from Bysantium to save it from the fury of the Iconoclasts, in the time of Leo the Isaurian. It is declared by judges one of the most beautiful of the sacred paintings in Rome. The church contains the bodies of St. Hilry and SSt. Coronat MM. The room inhabited by St. John Baptiste de Rossi is in the home annexed to the Church.

(3) ST. ALEXIS, ON THE AVENTINE.

Was constructed and dedicated to St. Boniface in the first years of the fourth century. At the end of the tenth century the contiguous monastery became the seat in Rome of the missions for the Slav countries, and at this time, in the title of the Church, we find associated the name of St. Alexis. At the present day it is the latter name which has predominated.

The story of St. Alexis is well known, and in the church is shown the picture of our Lady, which in Edessa pointed out the merits of the holy pilgrim, who thereupon took the resolution of returning to Rome and living unknown in his father's house. The stairs too are shown under which he spent his 17 years of hidden life. The bodies of St. Alexis and St. Boniface are preserved under the High Altar. The body of St. Aglae is buried in the confession. At the Altar of the Crypt are preserved the relics of Saints Thomas of Canterbury, Sebastian, Boniface, Agapito, Anastasia, Hermes, Panuce, Nereus and Achilleus.

2. THURSDAY

(1) ST. GEORGE IN VELABRUM.

Velabrum was the old designation of the locality where the church rises, and probably comes from an Italic root, meaning marshy ground. The church is very old, and still preserves its primitive basilica form. Gregory the Great placed it amongst the Cardinal-deacon titles, since which period it has been the Titular church of many famous men, the last of the number being John Henry Cardinal Newman. Leo II., in the seventh century, restored it, and added in the dedication the name of St. Sebastian. Popes Zachary and Gregory IV., rebuilt and adorned it, and Cardinal Stephaneschi under Boniface VIII., had the shell of the apse painted by Giotto. This painting however has been so barbarously retouched, that the skill of the master-hand is no longer visible.

This St. George is the soldier of Cappadocia, the Patron Saint of England, who was martyred in the time of Diocletian, and around whom has sprung a whole Christian literature; and whose name, in the days of chivalry, and the crusades, was associated with those of Saints Maurice and Sebastian. The church contains various relics of St. George; amongst them are a part of his head, his lance, and a banner used by him.

(2) THE HOLY NAMES OF JESUS AND MARY.
(Gesù e Maria-Corso).

Little is known of this church other than that it was originally called the Church of St. Anthony the Abbot, in Via Paulina, and that in later times it was reconstructed by the Augustinian monks, who still have charge of it.

3. FRIDAY.

(1) SS. JOHN AND PAUL (on the Celian).

The Roman martyrs, John and Paul, were in the service of Constantia, daughter of Constantine the Great. Refusing to abandon their religion, under Julian the Apostate, they were beheaded and interred in their own dwelling on the Celian hill. This was in the year 362. Over their bodies was constructed this church, now in the hands of the Passionist Fathers. A learned member of the pious community, F. German, a few years ago made the remarkable discovery of the dwelling-house of the Saints, under that Basilica. In conformity with his plans, excavations were made, and the rooms discovered. In the ignorance of past centuries, they had been used for burying purposes, and the frescoes that have been found are exceedingly interesting.

The interior of the church has lost the old basilica form, but the outer walls show architecture of the fourth century.

In the pavement of the church is seen a stone, on which the martyr brothers are said to have been beheaded. In this church are the bodies of SS. John and Paul, S. Saturninus, Pammachius, eleven Scillitan brothers Saints Crispus, Crispinian, and Benedicta, the body of S. Paul of the Cross. The room in which he died is shown in the adjoining Monastery, together with many relics of the Saint.

(2) ST. GREGORY (on the Celian Hill).

Tradition gives this ground as the place where the house of St. Gregory the Great existed.

St. Gregory was of a noble Roman family, son of the Senator Gordian and his wife St. Silvia. Before becoming a monk he had held the high charge of Urban Pretor. On his father's death, he used his wealth to found monasteries; six he built in Sicily and this one, the seventh, in Rome. Here he lived for many years and was elected Abbot. Being named Cardinal, he was sent as Nuncio to Constantinople, where he converted from his error the patriarch Eutyches. Later on he was elected Pope, and, as history relates, wrought glorious deeds for the spiritual and temporal welfare of his subjects. All his life he was of delicate health, but the strength of the spirit upheld the weakness of the body. He died in 604, and his remains now lie in St. Peter's, beneath the altar dedicated to him, off the left transept.

This church, erected by St. Gregory himself to the memory of St. Andrew, has many times been rebuilt and restored. It contains the following souvenirs of Saint Gregory: the pavement on which he used to sleep, his episcopal chair, the privileged altar at which he said Mass. One of his arms is kept there for veneration. To his mother, St. Silvia, one of the contiguous oratories is dedicated. In one of the chapels of the monastery is the marble table, on which Gregory is said to have served the poor, and where, as a reward for his charity, he received the visit of an angel, under a pilgrim's guise.

In the Salviati chapel is preserved a ciborium of exquisite artistic work, dating from the year 1469. On it are represented the processions of the greater Litanies, instituted by Gregory, and the apparition of the Angel over Adrian's Mole (Castle St. Angelo).

The church was given to the Camaldolese monks in 1573. It was from this place that St. Gregory, more than thirteen centuries ago, sent under the direction of St. Augustine the missionaries for the conversion of England. On a marble tablet affixed to the left pillar of the arcade near the central entrance are recorded the names of the apostolic band : St. Augustine, first Archbishop of Canterbury, St. Paulinus, first Archbishop of York, St. Melitus, first Bishop of London, Justus first Bishop of Rochester, and several others. In the church, besides the relics already named, there are the bodies of St. Tarsillus and St. Pantaleon, the mitre of St. Rinaldus, a volume of the Council of Trent which belonged to St. Pius V. the cross of St. Gregory, a breviary in manuscript of St Bernardine, and part of the hairshirt of St. Francis of Assisi. Among the many famous titular cardinals of St. Gregory's may be mentioned Cardinals Manning and Vaughan.

4. SATURDAY.

(1) St. TRYPHONIUS (no longer in existence).

This church was situated on the site of the Augustinian Monastery in Via della Scrofa. Little is now known about it, inasmuch as after the construction of the neighbouring church of St. Augustine — whither the Lenten Station was transferred — it was first reduced to the condition of a private oratory, and finally demolished.

(2) St. AUGUSTINE

This Church was built in the year 1484. The façade is in travertine, taken from the masses that had fallen from the Coliseum. The interior has three naves upheld not by columns but by pilasters. On the third of these to the left, in the middle of the naves, is the famous fresco by Raphael, representing the prophet Isaias. The high altar,

exceedingly rich in marbles was designed by Bernini, and there is the famous picture of the Blessed Virgin, brought from Constantinople after the fall of that city into the hands of Mahomet II.

To the right of the principal entrance is the celebrated statue of Our Lady — sculptured by Gatti da Sansovino — so much venerated by the Roman people, as is attested by the numerous votive offerings around and by the number of suppliants praying at all hours before the Shrine.

The adjoining library takes its name, Angelica, from its founder, the distinguished scholar Angelo Rocca, whose body reposes in the church. In the church are preserved the bodies of St. Monica (mother of St. Augustine) of St. Silvius and of St. Tryphonius and the relics of St. William, St. Longinus, S. Nicholas of Tolentino and of St. Valentine.

5. First Sunday in Lent.

St. JOHN OF LATERAN.

The « Mother Church of the Universe » — Ecclesiarum Urbis et Orbis Mater et Caput — was first erected by Constantine in the Imperial palace (formerly the property of the Laterani family, whence the name) and dedicated by Pope Sylvester I. This basilica is also called: « Constantinian, » after its founder; « of our Saviour, » to whom it was originally dedicated; « of St. John » — including both the Baptist, and the Evangelist — to whom it was likewise dedicated some time after the fourth century. It has been thrice rebuilt in its entirety by Sergius III (904—911), by Clement V. and again by Urban V. in the fourteenth century. Magnificent restorations have recently been completed, at the expense of some five millions of francs, by Leo XIII.

This church contains some most sacred relics; amongst them the table that served at the Last Supper, and on which

our Saviour instituted the Holy Eucharist; the heads of the holy Apostles, Peter and Paul, placed here by Urban V; the movable wooden chest on which St. Peter and his successors in the Apostolic See used to celebrate the Holy Mass, during the time of persecution.

In this basilica were celebrated several œcumenical Councils — amongst others, that under Innocent III, in which the Emperor Otho was deposed, and the Fourth Crusade decided on.

Inestimable is the treasure of indulgences attached to this church, and of sacred relics which it contains.

The Corsini Chapel — first to the left of the principal entrance — is remarkable for its magnificence; and in the crypt immediately beneath it is the exquisite Pietà by A. Montauti. Remarkable too is the adjoining cloister. In addition to the relics mentioned above, the following are some of the more notable of the vast collection here:

1. Bones of Saint John of God.
2. Relics of the Blessed Cardinal Barbadigo.
3. Arm of St Helena.
4. Bones of St Mary Salome.
5. A finger of St Catherine of Sienna, bones of St Mary Magdalene, and of St Mary of Egypt, enclosed in a " flowered gothic reliquary " of the 15th century.
6. Bones, and some of the Veil of St. Barbara.
7. Part of the finger of St Joseph of Leonissa.
8. Relic of St Vincent of Paul, and bones of St Francis Regis.
9. Relic St Philip Neri.
10. Head of St Zachary.
11. Some blood of St Charles Borromeo.
12. Miraculous head of St Pancras.
13. Some bones of St Sylvester, Pope.
14. Some bones of St Alexander, Pope, of Saints Eventius and Theodulus, and of Saints Sabina and Serapia.
15. Portion of the shoulder of St Laurence.
16. Cup in which poison was presented to St John, the Beloved Disciple, by order of Domitian.
17. The miraculous tunic of St John.
18. Some of the chain which bound St John, when he was brought from Ephesus to Rome.

19 Some of the bones of St Andrew.
20 Portion of the lower part of the head of St John the Baptist.
21 Some of the hair, and garment of the Blessed Virgin Mary.
22 Some of the Crib of the Infant Jesus.
23 Some linen with which our Lord Jesus Christ wiped his hands after the last Supper.
24 Some linen with which our Lord Jesus Christ wiped the feet of his Disciples.
25 A piece of the Column of Flagellation.
26 A thorn from the Crown of thorns.
27 Some of the purple garment stained with blood, given to our Lord in derision.
28 Piece of the sponge with which gall and vinegar was given to our Lord on the Cross.
29 Linen with which the head of our Lord was covered in the sepulchre.
30 Piece of the wood and Title of the Cross.

6. Monday.

(1) St. PETER IN VINCULIS (S. Pietro in Vincoli).

This church was built by the younger Eudoxia, wife of Valentinian III., about the year 442. Her mother, when on a pilgrimage in Palestine, had received from the Christians of Jerusalem the Chains that St Peter had borne in that city. She sent them to Rome, and her daughter made a present of them to Pope Leo the Great who to those, joined the chains that had bound the Apostle in Rome, under Nero — and raised a basilica to hold them.

The church was twice reconstructed, in the eighth and in the fifteenth and sixteenth centuries; and though it still retains much of its original basilica form, the bad taste of the last-mentioned period is but too visible.

Besides the Chains, the remarkable possessions of the church are: the tomb and bodies of the Maccabees, under the central altar; a very ancient mosaic portrait of St. Sebastian, in the left side nave, placed there in the seventh century to commemorate the delivery of the city from a pestilence. The heads of Saints Constance and Emerentia; a finger and arm of Saint Agnes; several large pieces of the crosses of St. Peter and Saint Andrew; an embroidered mitre of St. Ubaldo (13th century), the Epitaph of Pope John II, dating from the year 532; the majestic statue of Moses, by Michael Angelo; and works of art by Domenechino and Guercino.

(2) St. GIOVANNI DELLA PIGNA (Piazza della Pigna).

This church was formerly dedicated to the martyrs SS. Eleutherius and Genesius, and the body of the latter still reposes there. It was rebuilt in the time of Sixtus V., by the Archconfraternity of Mercy towards prisoners, when it received the new dedication.

7. TUESDAY.

St. ANASTASIA.

This interesting church, at the foot of the Palatine, is of very ancient foundation. Its priests are mentioned as taking part in the Synod of 492. Saint Jerome is said to have lived there and a chalice is still shown in which he is believed to have consecrated.

To this church, the Popes in former times used to be borne with great ceremony, to celebrate the second Mass at dawn on Christmas mornings, Christmas being the anniversary of St. Anastasia's martyrdom.

The veneration for this Saint was formerly very great amongst the people, and to this day her name is very common amongst the lower classes.

The church was repaired in 1210, and again in 1722, when its form was considerably altered. Among the many relics which this church possesses are the bodies of Saints Faustina and Anastasia, under the high altar, formerly the site of their house; altar and chalice of Saint Jerome; veil of the Blessed Virgin, Mantle of St. Joseph and an arm of St. Eugenie.

9. WEDNESDAY.

St. MARY MAJOR.

This magnificent basilica is the oldest solemnly dedicated to the Blessed Virgin. Erected about the year 353, it has had various designations: the *Basilica of Liberius*, from the Pope who consecrated it; the *Basilica major*, or of *S. Maria Major*, as being the largest of those dedicated to our Lady; *Basilica ad praesepe*, from the crib, still preserved, in which our Saviour was born; and finally, after the tenth century, we find the title *S. Maria ad nives*, 'Our Lady of the Snow,' from the miracle of a snow-fall

that had taken place in the middle of summer, to indicate the spot on which the church was to be erected.

St. Mary Major's is said to be the finest type of basilica extant. The objects of worth and interest it contains, are innumerable. We have mentioned the sacred crib. We may add: the body of St Jerome, that also of Pope Pius V. To the right of the high altar, is the magnificent chapel of the Blessed Sacrament. To the left, and opposite that one, is the Borghese Chapel, of unusual splendour. It contains the venerated picture of the Madonna, said to have been painted by the Evangelist, St Luke. The beautifully carved ceiling of the basilica is gilded with the first gold that came from America. Among the relics preserved in this basilica are: the side of St Charles Borromeo: ring of Blessed Cardinal Nicolas Albergati: Tooth of St. Philip Neri: bones of St. Pudentiana: part of the cincture and veil of St. Scholastica and relics of SS. Catherine, Euphemia, Anne, Paulina, and Felicita: Head of St. Bibiana: Tunic stained with the blood of St. Thomas of Canterbury: Body of St. Innocentiola: chin of St. Zachary: Head of St. Marcellino, Pope: Relics of the cross of St. Andrew: Arm of St. Luke: Arm of St. Matthew: Relics of St. Mark: Relics of St. John the Evangelist: Relics of the holy Apostles Peter, Paul, James, Thomas and Bartholomew. Head of St. Matthias: Relics of St. Vincent Ferrer: Relics of SS. Lucia, Apollonia and Barbara: Part of a mantle of St. Joseph; Part of the veil and hair of the Blessed Virgin: Some hay from the manger of our Lord: Relics of the purple garment, the sponge, the towel and the grave of our Lord: Wood of the true cross.

8. THURSDAY.

ST. LAURENCE IN PANISPERNA.

Tradition holds that on the site of this church took place the torture of St. Laurence, one of Rome's great

martyrs. The church is of very ancient date. It was reconstructed as far back as the eighth century.

Here was kept the body of St. Brigid, until its transfer to Sweden; for to this church the Saint used to come to pray, and was accustomed to mix with the crowd of indigent and needy-to receive the food of charity from the hands of the distributing monks.

In the chapel dedicated to SS. Crispin and Crispinian are preserved their heads and part of their bodies.

In this church his Holiness Pope Leo XIII. was consecrated Bishop.

10. FRIDAY.

CHURCH OF THE TWELVE APOSTLES.

The Church of the Apostles, has been attributed to Constantine, but it probably was not erected before the seventh century. The present vast edifice has nothing in common with the original one, except the site. The latter was on a much lower level, but was itself of ample proportions, as we learn from a letter of Pope Adrian I. to the Emperor Charlemagne. In the portico may be admired one of the marble lions that upheld the columns. It is the work of the great master of the thirteenth century, Vassalletto.

The church was rebuilt in the year 891. In the earthquake of 1348 it was overthrown. It remained a ruin for nearly a century, when Martin V. reconstructed it. Other rebuildings and restorations took place and the front of the edifice was finished only in the present century.

The church was originally dedicated to the Apostles Philip and James (the Minor,) but from the sixteenth century it became commonly designated after the Twelve Apostles.

The bodies of SS. Philip and James repose under the high altar. Under the altar of St. Antony lie those of

SS. Claudia and Eugenia, mother and daughter. And beneath the aperture in the centre of the flooring are the bodies of many holy martyrs, brought thither in the eighth century by Pope Stephen II.

The subterranean chapels are at present adorned with copies of frescoes from the Catacombs.

RELICS PRESERVED AT THE CHURCH OF THE HOLY APOSTLES.

1. Bones of Blessed Andrew Caccioli of Spello, O.S.F.
2. Bones of Blessed Bonaventure of Potenza, O.S.F.
3. Bones, some blood and some of the Girdle of Blessed Giles, O.S.F.
4. Bones and some of the skull of Blessed Andrew Conti, O.S.F.
5. Bones of St Othon, Martyr. O.S.F.
6. Relics of St Eugenia, Virgin and Martyr.
7. The heads of Sts. Felicissimus and Agapetus, Martyrs.
8. Part of a leg of St Erasmus, Martyr.
9. Some of the haircloth and bones of St Catherine of Sienna, some of the blood of St Catherine of Alexandria, and bones of St Felice, Martyr.
10. Some of the garments of St. Bonaventure, Cardinal and Doctor.
11. Some relics of St. Martha, and bones of the Empress St. Helena.
12. Relics of Sts. Chrysanthus and Daria, Martyrs.
13. Bones of St. Vincent, Martyr.
14. An arm of St. Anastasia, bones of St. Agatha, and of St. Demetrius, Bishop and Martyr.
15. An arm of St Blaise.
16. The head of St. Benedicta.
17. Bones of St. Guido.
18. Jaw bone and three teeth of St. Nicholas.
19. Two teeth of St. Mary Magdalene.
20. The head of St. Agapa, Virgin and Martyr.
21. Relics of Blessed Crispin of Viterbo, of Blessed Francis of Poxadas, of St. Hyacinth Mariscotti, of St Collete, of St. Rose of Viterbo, of St. Catherine of Bologna, of St Louis, Bishop of Toulouse, of St. Benedict, of St. Emig-

dius, some relics of St Philip Neri, Bones of St Francis Caraccioli, and of St Charles Borromeo.

Relics of Sts. Apollina, Lucia, Ursula, Barbara, Elisabeth, Queen of Hungary, Margaret Cortona, some of the hair of St Clare, relics of Sts. Liborius, Stephen, Gregory the Great, and Joseph Calasancius.

23. Bones of St Clement and Sabina, Martyrs.
24. A relic of St Joseph a Cupertino.
25. Some of the tunic of St Bernard of Sienna.
26. Relics of St. Gregory and St. Roch.
27. A rib of St Laurence.
28. Some of the hood, and Ashes of St Antony of Padua.
29. Some blood of the Stigmas of St Francis of Assisi.
30. Some of his Hair Shirt.
31. Some of his Ashes.
32. Some of his Coffin.
33. A jaw bone of St Barnabas.
34. Relics of the holy Apostles Matthew, Matthias, Simon, Thaddeus, and Thomas.
35. Some of the Arm of St Bartholomew.
36. Some of the blood of St James the Greater.
37. Relics from the leg, arm, and cross of St Andrew.
38. Some of the garments of St John Evangelist.
39. Part of a finger of St Paul.
40. One of the nails of the Crucifixion of St Peter.
41. The right foot of St Philip.
42. Part of an arm of St James the Less.
43. Bones of St Anne.
44. Some of the Mantle of St Joseph.
45. Some of the hairshirt of St John Baptist.
46. Some of the garments of the Blessed Virgin Mary.
47. Some of the Crib, the Cradle, the Table of the Last Supper, and the Tomb of our Lord Jesus Chris .
48. Some of the Wood of the true Cross.

11. SATURDAY.

ST. PETER'S.

The body of St. Peter was buried at the foot of the Vatican hill, near the spot where he was crucified in the Circus of Nero wihch corresponds more or less to the site of the present sacrisy.

LENTEN STATIONS

This circus was the scene of the martyrdom of the first Christians in Rome, described by Tacitus: *Annals*, xv. 45. Those first converts who shed their blood for the Christian Faith were martyred in this circus at the bidding of Nero, who was present in person. Some of the Christians were covered with the skins of wild animals so that ferocious dogs might tear them to pieces in the presence of the Pagan populace. Whilst some were crucified, others were smeared with grease and tar and tied to poles and raised on high; then set fire to, in order to give light to the orgies of Nero, who was present, dressed as a common driver and ran his races around the goals. Two years later A. D. 67, St. Peter was martyred in the same place. He was crucified with his head downwards and from immemorial tradition it appears that he suffered martyrdom between two 'metae' or goals — *inter duas metas* — that is to say, at the foot of the obelisk which now stands in the Piazza of St. Peters, to which position it was moved by Sixtus V. from its place in the middle of Nero's Circus *inter duas metas*. The body of St. Peter was buried quite near where he was crucified, on the right side of the Via Cornelia, which ran parallel with the northern and outer wall of the circus. On the opposite and right side was a long line of tombs; hence the Christians had only to go a few yards to find a suitable burial place for their great treasure, the body of the Prince of the Apostles.

Over the body, very shortly after its deposition, St. Anacletus erected a shrine. This shrine remained till the time of Constantine, who, on the same spot, raised a basilica of unrivalled splendour. It consisted of five naves, like that of St. Paul's outside the Walls. It became at once the centre of Christian devotion. From the fourth century, as we learn from St. Jerome, the feast of St. Peter was celebrated with the same rejoicing as Christmas itself.

For eleven centuries this Basilica remained. It was suffering, however, from the hand of time. Nicholas V. conceived the idea of reconstructing the edifice in its

entirety, and Julius II. put his hand to the work. Succeeding pontiffs carried on the labour, a .d at length was completed that temple, which is the vastest erected to the Living God. This wonderful basilica must be a source of everlasting satisfaction. And yet it is not without some shadow of regret, that we reflect on the loss of the one it has replaced. The Constantinian edifice was a world's store-house of Christian souvenirs and traditions.

The body of the Prince of the Apostles was never moved from its first resting-place since the building of the first Basilica; so great has been the scruple in this respect, that the present Confession, or Papal Altar, in order to be exactly over the tomb, is not perfectly in the centre of the Church.

The treasures of the church are exceedingly interesting and valuable. In the apse, elevated over the altar called " of the Cathedra, " is St. Peter's episcopal chair, encased in a master-piece of bronze work, upheld by four fathers of the Church. In a chapel within one of the pillars supporting the dome is a large part of the true Cross, the spear that opened our Saviour's Side, and the veil with which the holy woman wiped his Face.

The bodies of many of the Popes, from St. Linus, were preserved in different parts of the basilica. Innumerable is the number of persons who have visited it, coming from the most distant parts of the earth; it is said over fifty Saints, not counting St. Peter Damian, St. Bridget, St. Catherine of Sienna, St. Bernard, St. Francis of Assisi, St. Dominic, St. Thomas Aquinas, St. Ignatius, St. Joseph Calasantius, St. Philip Neri, St. Aloysius, St. Stanislaus Kostka and so many others, have visited it during the last two or three centuries.

Amongst the royal personages who have visited this holy spot may be mentioned the Emperors Theodosius and Valentian with Eudosia, and Galla Placidia his mother; the Emperors Otho I., II. and III. St. Henry Emp. S. Cunegunda his wife,; Agnes the wife of Emp. Henry, II.

Emperor Charles IV., King Canute and Richard I of England, besides many others too numerous to mention. Charlemagne came four times to visit this sacred spot and was here crowned Emperor by S. Leo III. Twenty emperors and kings have been crowned by the Sovereign Pontiffs within its precincts.

The basilica contains the following Saints: the Apostles Simon and Jude, SS. Processus and Martiniam; S. Petronilla; S. Gregory Nazianzan St. Gregory the Great; SS. Leo I., II., III., IV., IX.; St. John Chrysostom.

Underneath the GROTTE VATICANE, may be visited parts of the ancient building, rich in treasures of antiquity.

LIST OF THE RELICS PRESERVED
IN THE VATICAN BASILICA.

1. A relic of Blessed Margaret Mary Alacoque.
2. A relic of St Peter Canisius, S. J.
3. Bones of Blessed John Leonard.
4. Bones of St. John Baptist de Rossi.
5. A Tooth of St. Benedict Joseph Labre.
6. A bone of Blessed Santander, Martyr.
7. A relic of Blessed Victoria Fornari.
8. A relic of Blessed Mary of the Incarnation.
9. A relic of St. Germaine Cousin.
10. A relic of St. Mary Anne of Parédès.
11. A relic of St. Mary Frances of the Five Wounds of Jesus Crucified.
12. A relic of St. Jane of Chantal.
13. A relic of St. Mary of Egypt.
14. Bones of St Mary Magdalene.
15. A relic of St. Veronica Giuliani.
16. A relic of St. Hyacinth Mariscotti.
17. Head of St. Petronilla.
18. A rib of St. Judith, Virgin and Martyr.
19. Relics of Sts. Theodora and Bibiana, Virgins and Martyrs.
20. Relics of Sts. Colomba and Susanna, Virgins, and of St. Rufina, Virgin and Martyr.
21. Relics of Sts. Barbara and Lucy, Virgins and Martyrs.

22 Relics of Sts. Catherine, Agatha, Pudentiana, and Margaret, Virgins and Martyrs.
23 Relics of Blessed John Grande.
24 Relics of St. Paul of the Cross.
25 Relics of St. John Berchmans
26 Relics of St. Peter Claver.
27 Relics of Blessed Martin of Porres.
28 Relics of Blessed John Massias.
29 Relics of Blessed Sebastian Valfré.
30 Relics of Blessed Angelus of Aeri.
31 Relics of Blessed Hypolitus Galantini.
32 A rib of St. Alphonsus Rodriguez.
33 A relic of St. Julian of St. Augustine.
34 Bones of Blessed John Baptist of the Conception.
35 Relics of Blessed Francis of Posadas.
36 A Finger of Blessed Joseph Oriol.
37 A relic of Blessed Crispin of Viterbo.
38 A relic of Blessed Cardinal Tommasi.
39 A relic of Blessed Leonard of Port Maurice.
40 A relic of Blessed Bernard of Ophida.
41 A relic of Blessed Andrew Hibernon.
42 A relic of Blessed Sebastian Apparizi.
43 A relic of Blessed Nicholas of the Lombards.
44 A relic of Blessed Gaspard of Bono.
45 A relic of Saint Michael de Sanctio.
46 A relic of Blessed Bonaventure of Potenza.
47 A relic of Blessed John of Ribeira, Patriarch of Antioch, and Archbishop of Valence.
48 Relic of the Blessed Antony Fatati, Canon and Vicar of the Vatican Basilica.
49 A relic of Blessed Cardinal Gregory Barbadigo.
50 A relic of Blessed Andrea Bobola, Martyr.
51 A relic of Blessed John de Britto, Martyr.
52 A relic of St. John Joseph of the Cross.
53 A relic of St. Francis Girolamo.
54 A relic of St. Joseph of Cupertino.
55 Relic of St. Alexius and Aloysius Gonzaga.
56 An Arm of St. William of Aquitaine, and a leg of St. Peter of Alcantara.
57 A relic of St. Philip Neri.
58 A relic of St. Bernardine of Sienna.
59 A relic of St. Roch.
60 A relic of St. Thomas of Aquin.

61 Some skin of the head, and some hair of St. Antony of Padua.
62 A relic, and some blood of the Stigmas of St. Francis of Assisi.
63 A relic of St. Alphonsus Liguori.
64 Bones and hair of St. Pius V.
65 A relic of St. Charles Borromeo.
66 A relic of St. Hormisdas, Pope.
67 A relic of St. Boniface IV.
68 A relic of Sts. Leo I., II., III., and IV., Pop's.
69 A shoulder of St John Chrysostom, an arm of St. Gregory of Nazianzen an and arm of St. Joseph of Arimathea.
70 Relies of St. hilary of Poitiers of St. Martin of Tours, St. Paul the first hermit anc of St. Antony, Abbot.
71 Relics of SS. Ursus Abbot, of St. Jerome, of St. Basil, and of St. Gregory of Nazianzen.
72 A leg or St. Severus, Bishop of Ravenna.
73 Head of St. Damacuso, Pope
74 A relic of St. Nicholas of Bari.
75 A henee-cap of St. Rufillus, Bishop of Forlimpopoli,
76 Bones of St. Gregory Haumatuyus.
77 A relic of St. Trophimus of Arles.
78 A leg of St. Langarus, Beshop of Marseilles.
79 Pincers with which the early Christians were tormented.
80 A piece of cloth which covered the lodies of the martyrs.
81 A relic of St. Tryphon.
82 The heads of St. Lambert, Bishop of Utrecht and of St. Quirinus, martyrs.
83 A relic of St. Silverius, Pope.
84 The head of St. James, martyr and an arm of St. Longinus.
85 The throat of St. Blaise.
86 The head of St. Menna.
87 A part of the head of St. Sebastian.
88 A relic of St, Thrasimus, Bishop and martyr.
89 A relic of St. Venantius and an arm of St. Vincent.
90 The head of St. Magnus.
91 Relic of Sts. Sixtus the Q.na, and Rohn the St. Pope.
92 Relic of St. Polycarp, Bishop and martyr, and of Sts. Agapitus, Neopolytus and Vincent Martyrs.
93 Relic of St. Sixtus the St. Pope.
94 Relic of St. Laurence,
95 Relic of St. Stephen.

96. A finger of St. Luke.
97. The head of St. Luke.
98. Relics of St. Bartholomew, Sebastian, Hippolytus and Jerome.
99. Relics of SS. John the Baptist, Simon, Jude, Philip and James the Less.
100. The head of St Andrew.
101. A very ancient representation of the Apostles St. Peter and Paul.
102. A Relic of St. Paul.
103. A finger of St. Peter.
104. Some of the Mantle and Cincture of St. Joseph.
105. Some of the bones of St. Anne.
106. Some of the hair of the Blessed Virgin.
107. Some of the Crib, and Hay from the Stable, where Christ was born, and some of the veil of our Lady.
108. Two Thorns from the Holy Crown of our Lord Jesus Christ.
109. Reliquary, and Wood of the True Cross, which the Emperor Justin gave to the Vatican Basilica.
110. Relic of the True Cross kept in a golden tripod, which Constantine wore on his breast, in peace and in war.
111. The Lance which pierced the side of our Lord Jesus Christ
112. The Wood of the True Cross.
113. The Veil of St. Veronica, on which is imprinted the Face of our Saviour.

12. SECOND SUNDAY IN LENT.

Sta MARIA IN DOMNICA (Sta. Maria della Navicella).

This church is supposed to be on the site of the house of St. Cyriaca, a noble Roman matron; where St. Laurence used to distribute alms to the poor.

Its origin is obscure; it was restored by S. Paschal I. in the early part of the ninth century, and even before then it was dedicated to the B. Virgin and called Domnica. The body of the building and the apse remain as con-

structed by St. Paschal, and the striking mosaic in the latter part bears the monogram PASCHALIS.

Leo X. restored the church on plans by Raphael, Bramante, and Michael Angelo. The same Pontiff removed from before the church the ancient navicella, or boat (the precise symbolism of which is not clear) and replaced it by one on the same model, but not ina very artistic manner.

It is now served by the Greek Melchite Priests of Mount Lebanon.

(2) St. MARY MAJOR (See page 452)

(3) St. GREGORY (See page 446)

13. MONDAY.

St. CLEMENT.

The church of St. Clement is one of the most remarkable in all Rome from an antiquarian point of view. On this ground is believed to have existed the house of St. Clement, the disciple of St. Peter, the fellow-labourer of S. Paul and fourth bishop of Rome. Of the basilica erected in his memory, we have mention in a work of St. Jerome, written abont 385.

Here St. Gregory in 540 preached his 32nd and 38th homilies; a Council was held within its walls in 417, to condemn the Pelagian Celestius; a celebrated passage in the above-mentioned work of St. Jerome represents Celestius as feeding on porridge (" pultibus Scotorum ").

The lower church was built on this spot probably abont 385 A. D.; it was restored by Adrian I. in 772 but was destroyed by the Normans, under Robert Guiscard in 1084. The upper church was almost rebuilt by Pascal I. in 1108 and at the same time the choir and very fine ambones were removed thither from the lower church.

The original edifice was discovered under the present one in the year 1857, by the learned Fr. Mulhooly, then

prior of the Irish Dominicans, to whom the adjoining convent belongs.

The paintings and inscriptions found on the walls are exceedingly remarkable.

But these two sacred edifices are not all that is of interest here, from the point of view of antiquity. Underneath them, again, are the remains of a building, which the experts judge to have been a Roman dwelling of the time of the kings.

In the church repose the bodies of St. Clement, Pope; St. Ignatius, bishop of Antioch. SS. Cyrillus and Methodius, apostles of the Slav countries, in whose honour a new chapel has been handsomely decorated by Leo XIII.

14 Tuesday

S. BALBINA.

Is situated on the summit of the hill, above the baths of Caracalla. The precise date of construction of this church is no known. We can trace it back to the times of St. Gregory the Great, but it was probably built by St. Mark, Pope, A. D. 336 and dedicated to our Saviour. It was repaired by St. Leo III. in the 8th century, according to Anastasius Bibliothecarius.

It was restored in the 15th century, and retouched twice in the present century.

St. Balbina was the daughter of St. Quirinus; the tribune, who, in the middle of the second century, was guardian of the prisons. In this capacity he became acquainted with Pope Alexander. The tribune promised that he would become a Christian, if the Pope cured his daughter of a scrofulous affection with which she was afflicted. This was done, and father and daughter were converted. The latter spent her life in works of mercy and charity.

The body of the Saint reposes in the beautiful urn beneath the high altar; under the same altar is the body of St. Quirinus, her father.

15 WEDNESDAY.

St. CECILIA.

At the extremity of the Trastevere, near the Quay of la Ripa Grande, built on the site of the house of the patron saint. Its foundation dates from 230, in the pontificate of Urban I. It was rebuilt by Paschal I., in the form of one of the smaller basilicas, in 822, and entirely restored and reduced to its present form by Card. Sfrondati in 1599, and subsequently redecorated by Card. Doria, as we now see it, in 1725, when the ranges of columns which formed the nave of the original church, were built round and converted into the present heavy pilasters to support the roof.

In the fore court is an antique marble or cantharus, which stood in the quadriporticus of the primitive basilica. The portico, which precedes the ch., has on the frieze some early arabesques in mosaic, with portraits of saints, supposed to date from the 9th century. On each side of the cross which forms the centre are rude likenesses of St. Cecilia. Entering the ch., and on the rt. of the door, is the tomb of Cardinal Adam, of Hertford, who was administrator of the diocese of London (ob. 1398) and titular cardinal of this church. This prelate, a very learned man, took part in the opposition to Urban VI., and having been arrested, with five other cardinals, at Lucera, was carried to Genoa: he alone was saved by the interference of the English crown, the others being put to death in the convent of S. Giovanni di Pre, On the sarcophagus are the arms of England, at that time 3 leopards and fleurs-de lis quartered. The body of St. Cecilia, which lay originally in the catacombs St. Calisto, from which it was removed bF Paschal I. to this church is deposited in the confession beneath the high altar; the silver urn in which it had been placed disappeared during the first French occupation. The recumbent statue of St.

Cecilia, by Stefano Moderno, is one of the most expressive and beautiful specimens of sculpture which the 17th century has produced. It represents the body of the saint in her grave-clothes, in the position in which it is described to have been found when her tomb was opened by Paschal I in 822. He found the body inteat, inclosed in a cypress coffin, and laid it in a marble sarcophagus under the altar, in this church, already long existing.

In the year 1595, all Rome was moved at the discovery that was made when this sarcophagus was re-opened. Baronius and Bosius have left us an interesting description of how St. Cecilia appeared in the cypress coffin, leaning on her side, her arms stretched along her body, and her face towards the ground, such identically, and without the slightest alteration, as she must have been on the moment of breathing.

The history of St. Cecilia: of her conversion of her spouse Valerian, and his brother Tiburtius, by the miracle of the apparition of the Angel, who guarded her body, her torture and death under the prefect Almachius, are too well known to need further mention. In the church is shown the bath, in which, it is said her executioners tried to soffocate her.

Out of it flowed the water, destined for the ablutions of the faithful and it was at the same time, a symbol of the refreshment enjoyed by the blessed in the next life.

Sta. Francesca Romana, who dwelt near frequented this Church.

The sacristy was formely the Chapel of the Ponziani family to which St. Frances of Rome belonged; on the floor is seen the sepulchre of Paul Palugio de Ponziani, the son St. Frances.

Besides the Body of St. Cecilia under the high Altar, there is the body of St. Urban, Bishop; a part of the body of St. Lucius,; the body of St. Tiburtius, of St. Valerian, and St. Maximus; and at the Altar of the Confession under

the high Altar is seen an inscription which shows it was consecrated by St. Gregory VII.

16. THURSDAY.

S. MARIA IN TRANSTEVERE.

Built by St Calixtus about 220, restored by Julius I in 340 and by Gregory IV in 828, this Church was brought to its present magnificent dimensions by Innocent II in the twelfth century.

Elegant embellishments were added to it by Pius IX, and while they were in progress important discoveries of antiquities were made beneath the Church.

Under the high altar repose the bodies of SS. Callixtus, Cornelius, Julius, popes, and of St Calepodius, priest and martyr. Likewise are there preserved relics of St. Peter and St. Appollonia.

Under the high altar is shown the spot where the fountain of oil, or naphta, is said to have flowed (the story is told also by Dion Cassius) shortly before the coming of our Saviour, and as a symbol of that event.

This is said to have been the first church dedicated to Our Lady.

The interior is in the three naves, divided by fine granite columns, some of which — those of ionic style — are supposed to have come from a temple of the Egyptian gods, Isis and Serapis.

The fine mosaics are of the eleventh and twelfth centuries. The Assumption on the ceiling, a painting of rare beauty, is by Domenichino.

LIST OF RELICS PRESERVED AT ST. MARY IN TRASTEVERE.

1. Relics of the Saints, Pacificus, Crispin of Viterbo, and Leonard of Port Maurice.
2. Relics of St Margaret of Cortona, and of St Mary Magdalen.
3. A relic of St Frances, of Rome.
4. Relics of Sts Elizabeth and Bridget.
5. A relic of St Rose of Viterbo.
6. Relics of Sts Aurelia, Balbina, and Constance.
7. Relics of Sts Basilidas, Praxedes, Pudentiana, Mary Magdalen of Pazzi, and Teresa of Jesus.
8. The body of. St Eutropus Martyr.
9. Relics of the Holy Martyrs Victoria, Restitua, Theophilus, Verecundus, Trutenus, Januarius, Vincent, Faustinus, Candida, Felicitas, Generosa, Tranquillina, Aureus, Severus, Valerius, Victorina, Severina and Hospita.
10. The body of St Fortunula Martyr.
11. A relic of St Theodora Martyr.
12. An arm of St Margaret Virgin Martyr.
13. The head of St Dorothea Virgin Martyr.
14. Relics of Sts Agnes, Barbara, Cordula, Hilaria, Gemina, Colomba, Rufina, Romula, Milta, and one of the Companions of St Ursula.
15. An arm and rib of St Justina Virgin and Martyr.
16. The head of St Apollina Virgin Martyr.
17. Relics of Sts Galgair of Sienna, Alexis, Philip Neri and Francis of Assisi, some of his habit and haircloth, and blood of his Stigmas.
18. A relic of St Francis of Paul.
19. Relics of Sts John of the Cross, Albert, Aloysius, Vincent Ferrer, Andrew Avellin, Camillus of Lellis, and Bernard.
20. A relic of St Paulinus, Bishop.
21. A relic of St Francis of Sales.
22. Relics of Sts Martin, Severin, Constance, Remi, and Gregory, Bishop.
23. A relic of St Charles Borromeo.
24. Relics of Sts Vitalian, Nicholas, John Crysostom, and Jerome.
25. Relics of Sts Damasus, and Pius V, Popes.
26. An arm and tooth of St Julius Pope.

27 The head of St Bricius, Martyr, and relics of St Eurania, and Exuperancia.
28 Relics of Sts Magnus, Constance, Maximus, Simplician, Theophilus, Celestin, and Justin Martyr.
29 Relics of Sts Valentine, Augustus, Corpus, Apre, Cypriaca, Ursula, Vital, Mamertin, Nectar, Mercury, Dextera, Anastasia Martyrs.
30 The head of St Fermus, Martyr.
31 Relics of Sts Zenon, Theodore, Maurice, Felician, Eustace, Chrysantus Modestus and other saints.
32 The body of St Aurelius Martyr.
33 Relics of Sts Dalmac, Chaste, Firmin, Victor, Felicissimus, and Hypercius. Their bodies rest under the Altar of the Crucifix.
34 The body of St Hermogen, Martyr.
35 Relics of the holy Martyrs Alexis, Savinian, Florentin, and Cornelius. Their bodies rest under the Altar of the Virgin " di Strada Cupa."
36 Relics of Sts George, Gallican, Hippolyte, Pantaleon, Romanus, Hilarius, Cosmas, Damian, and Justin Martyrs.
37 A part of the body of St Pastor the Martyr, and relics of the holy Martyrs Julius, Claudius, Leo, Titian, Abondius, Domitius, Simplicius, Agapitus and Asterus.
38 Portion of the shoulder and head of St Calepodius, his body is under the high Altar
39 An arm of St Quirin, Bishop and Martyr.
40 Relics of Sts Blaise, Emidius, Felix, Ignatius, Sixtus, Telesphorus, and Stephen.
41 An arm and bones of St Cornelius, Pope and Martyr.
42 Relics of Sts Antherus, Alexander, Fabian, and Caius, Pope, and Martyrs.
43 An arm, the head and a tooth of St Calixtus, Pope.
44 Bones of St Laurence.
45 Relics of the Holy Apostles Simon, Matthew, Thaddeus, and Barnabas.
46 Relics of St Stephen the First Martyr.
47 Some of the arm of St James the Less.
48 Some of a leg of St Bartholomew.
49 Relics of the Holy Apostles Andrew, James the Greater Thomas, Philip and Bartholomew.
50 Some bones of St Paul and a piece of the pillar on which he was beheaded.
51 A tooth of St Peter.

52 An arm of St Peter.
53 A relic of St Joachim.
54 Some relics and a bone of St Anne.
55 Some of the Mantle of St Joseph.
56 Relics of St John the Baptist, of St Zachary, and St Elizabeth.
57 Some of the Tomb, the Garment and the veil, and hair of the Blessed Virgin.
58 Some of the stable, and crib where our Lord Jesus Christ was born.
59 Some of the Table of the Supper.
60 Some of the Pillar of the Scourging.
61 Part of a Thorn from the Holy Crown.
62 Some of the Sponge steeped with Gall and Vinegar.
63 Some of the winding sheet.
64 Some of the Sepulchre of our Lord J. C.
65 Some of the wood of the True Cross.

17. FRIDAY.

S. VITALE (Via Nazionale).

This church, one of the most precious christian monuments in Rome, was dedicated to St. Vitalis, and his sons, SS. Gervasius and Protasius. It was built at the expense of a noble Roman lady, named Vestina, and was dedicated in the year 402 by Innocent I.

It was restored by Sixtus IV (in 1475) and by Clement VIII (1595). The latter gave it into the hands of the Jesuit fathers of St. Andrew al Quirinale. The door of carved walnut wood are well worthy of notice. S. Vitale is at present a parish Church and the principal sacred building of the great artery of modern Rome, the Via Nazionale. It was the Titular Church of the Blessed Cardinal Fisher, Bishop of Rochester.

18. SATURDAY

SS. MARCELLINUS AND PETER (Lateran).

Marcellinus was a priest, and Peter an exorcist. For having converted and baptized Artemius a goaler, they

were tried and beheaded by the judge Severus. Their executioner was alive, when Pope Damusus was a youth; and the latter gained from him many details on these saints, and inserted them in one of the poems he composed.

Another church was erected to these saints by Constantine. It is in the cemetery of S. Tiburtius on the Labican way, whither their bodies had been transferred.

The first historical mention of the present church is in a Synod held by St Gregory the Great. It was restored in the eighth, ninth and thirteenth centuries, and was finally repaired, from the foundations by Benedict XIV from designs of the Marquis Jerome Theodoli.

19. THIRD SUNDAY IN LENT.

ST. LAURENCE OUTSIDE THE WALLS.

This church over the tomb of St. Laurence was constructed by Constantine the great.

This basilica was amplified in the sixth century, by Pope Pelagius. In the early part of the seventh century, a second and greater basilica, was erected in the same ground that is over the cemetery of St. Ciriaca. These two edifices were afterwards united and gave the building the somewhat irregular form that we have to day; the entrance to the older and smaller one having been exactly opposite to the present entrance, and precisely where the tomb of Pius IX now lies.

It was restored in the thirteenth century by Honorius III. and reduced to its actual state by the Canons Regular of St. John Lateran who have had it under their care from the time of Sixtus IV; it is now served temporarily by the Capuchin Fathers. Piux IX erected the red granite column in front of the church. His exceedingly beautiful tomb is an object of striking interest.

The High Altar, above the confession is a papal one and only the Pope can celebrate mass there.

Near the basilica is the public cemetery, consecrated in 1834. It has a Church, an ornamented portico, and many note worthy monuments.

The Church contains the following relics, viz the Body of St. Stephen, protomartir, St. Laurence, St. Cyriaca, St. Justin and St. Hippolite, the marble slab upon which St. Laurence was martyred, the stones used at the stoning of St. Stephen; the body of St. Severus, St. Claudius, subdeacon; St. Roman, ostiarius; Crescentis, lector: also the bodies of St. Zosimus, Sextus III, Welarius, Concordia, Cirineus, Abondius, Cyrilla and Trefonia, Martyrs.

20 MONDAY

ST. MARK (near Piazza Venezia).

Founded by St. Mark, Pope, and dedicated by him in honour of St. Mark, the evangelist. Rebuilt in the ninth century by Gregory IV, who had been one of its priests; it was again restored and improved in the fifteenth by Paul II, who erected the present roof, the oldest gilded ceiling still existing in Rome. In the last century it was again altered and enriched.

Amongst the many Saints who have hallowed this church by their presence is St. Dominic of whom it is related the interesting fact, that whilst preaching in the church, to a large concourse of people who always followed him wherever he went, amongst them was a pious woman who on account of the crowd had left her little son at home. On her return from the sermon she found her little child dead. She was distracted with grief. Yet that motherly instinct, and love combined with Christian faith, caused her to take up the little one and hurry after the great and holy preacher, who had gone to San Sisto where he was residing. Distraught by her great loss she hurried breathlessly on and waited not until she arrived, not only at the Church but at the very Chapter hall at which St. Dominic then was. Surprise was on the face of

the brethren, she saw it not, but cast her dead burden at the feet of the Saint crying out, Father he is dead, but you can bring him to life. She prayed and besought the Saint to give her back her child. St. Dominic was moved to compassion at the sight, and began to pray, afterwards made the sign of the cross over the dead child, took it by the hand, raised it up and gave it alive to its mother, commanding her not to tell anyone of what he had done.

Under the high altar are the bodies of St. Mark, the Pope, and of the Holy Martyrs Abdon and Sennen.

THE FOLLOWING RELICS ARE PRESERVED IN THE CHURCH.

1 The ring finger of the Blessed Cardinal Gregory Barbadigo.
2 Bones of Sts Procula and Benerosa, and teeth of St Colombana Martyrs.
3 Bones of the holy Martyrs Thecla, and Mary and a finger of St. Anastasia.
4 Teeth, hair, some of the tunic, and cloth stained with the blood of her heart, and other relics of St Veronica Giuliani. Silk which enveloped her body, tissue made by her hands, garment made by her, flowers found on her body, morsel of the wooden casket in which her body was placed, three lines written by her.
5 Bones of St. Nemenia Martyr.
6 Bones of St. Meresria Martyr.
7 Some of the head of St. John Crysostom, of St Damien Martyr, and of St. Abondantius Martyr.
8 Bones of the holy Martyrs Fortissima, and Soriolone, and of the holy Martyrs Ingenua, Vitalin, Boniface and Flavius Castinus.
9 Some of the head of St. Ursula.
10 Some of the bones of St. Lucina Roman matron.
11 A hair shirt of St. Bridget
12 Jaw-bone and a tooth of St. Nympha Virgin and Martyr.
13 Some of the head of St. Ennes. (His body rests under the High Altar).
14 Spinal bones of St. Francis Girolamo, and St Joseph Calasanctius, and some of the head of St Marcellin Martyr

15 Portion of an arm of St. Patrick, Apostle of Ireland.
16 The head of St Adrien Martyr.
17 The head of St Lucilla Martyr.
18 Bones and some of the Coffin and Cape of St. Charles Borromeo.
19 Bones of Sts. Urbain, Stratonic, Petrius, and Fausta, Martyrs.
20 Bones of Sts. Hyacinth, Cyrill, and Lupercill, Martyrs.
21 The head of St. Julian Martyr.
22 Bones of St. Julius Senator, Martyr.
23 Some of the arm of St Leonin, Martyr.
24 A tooth of St Dominic Martyr.
25 Bones of Saints Sylvester I., Boniface I., Telesphorns, Urban, Eleutherius, Silverius, Sixtus, and Clement, and some of the head of St Marcellus.
26 Bones of Sts Alexander, Theodulus, Eventurus, and of Sts Sabina, and Serapia, some of the head of St George, and head of St Agapitus, Martyrs.
27 Cape in red velvet, and relics of St Pius the 5th,
28 An arm of St Livius, Martyr.
29 Bones of Sts Abdon and Sennen.
30 Some of the head of St Sebastian, and Bones of St Longinus.
31 Bones of Sts Helena, Praxedes, Pudentiana, and Lucia. Also of Sts Romain Hippolyte, and Justin.
32 Bones of Sts Large, Smaragdus, Vincent and Anastasius; some of the head of St Cyriaco and St Stephen.
33 Some of the blood of St Valentine.
34 Hair stained with the blood of St Vincent, Martyr.
35 Hair stained with the blood of St Florida, Virgin Martyr.
36 Bones of St Mark, Martyr.
37 An Arm of St Guido.
38 Bones, ash, flesh, coals and iron from the spit of St Laurence.
39 Some of the head, and a tooth of St Mark, Pope.
40 A finger of St Mary Magdalene.
41 Bones of Sts Bartholomew, Philip, James the Less, Thomas, James the Greater, and Matthew, bones and a tooth of St Andrew, some of the Chain and bones of St Paul.
42 Bones of St Luke, Barnabas, Matthias, Thaddeus, and Simon; some of a garment, girdle, the tomb, and chain of St John Evangelist; some of the altar, cross, and bones of St Peter.

43 Some of the head of St Mark, Evangelist.
44 Bones of St John the Baptist, of St Zachary, of St Elizabeth, of Sts Anne, and Joachim.
45 Some of the mantle of St Joseph.
46 Some of the veil, gaments, hair, and tomb of the B. Virgin Mary.
47 Some of the cradle of our Lord Jesus Christ, and some of the straw from the Crib.
48 Some of the clothes of our Lord Jesus Christ.
49 Some of His Tomb.
50 Some of the Title of the Cross.
51 Some of the Pillar of the Flagellation.
52 Some of the Sponge of His Passion.
53 A remarkable part of the Winding Sheet, still stained with Blood, which covered His Sacred Head in the Tomb.
54 Some of the Veil which covered Him on the Cross.
55 Some of the Coffin in which Joseph of Arimathea placed our Divine Lord.
56 Three thorns from the Holy Crown.
57 A Stational Cross (end of the 15th cent.) with some wood of the True Cross.
58 A Veil stained with the Blood and Water which flowed from the pierced Side of our Lord after His Death.

21 TUESDAY.

S. PUDENTIANA

(near St Mary Major's)

This ancient church is situated in the once aristocratic Vicus Patricius of Imperial Rome, now the Via Urbana. The Saint to whom it is dedicated was the daughter of the Senator Pudens, and of Claudia a British lady, who had accompanied her father, the famous Caractacus.

Claudia became the wife of Pudens and the mother of St. Novatus, St Timothy, St Praxedes and St Pudentiana. She and her husband Pudens are mentioned by St. Paul in his second Epistle to Timothy, chap. 4 verse 21.

Pudens received St Peter into his house where he remained about seven years. From this sacred spot St.

Peter sent forth the first Christian missionaries; here he baptized the whole family of Pudens. St Pius I., about the year 145; converted the house into a church; it was first called Ecclesia Pudentis, or Ecclesia Pudentiana. In a well close by St Pudentiana is said to have deposed the blood and relics of over 3000 martyrs.

Most remarkable is the very ancient mosaic, which dates back, to the fourth century.

The paintings on the cupola are by Pomarancio.

In the chapel to the left of the high altar is a portion of the table on which St Peter is said to have celebrated the Holy Sacrifice.

Cardinal Gaetani in 1588 restored and improved the church to its present form. In the Gaetani chapel are rich marble columns and sculptures, and two magnificent tombs. This was the Titular church of Cardinal Wiseman. It contains the body of St Pudenziana, St Novatus her brother, besides the relics of the above 3000 Martyrs.

22 WEDNESDAY.

ST SIXTUS.

(on the road to Porta San Sebastiano)

This very ancient church once known under Titulus Tigridis is dedicated to Pope Sixtus II., who assumed the pontificate in the hear 257, and who figures so prominently in the touching history of St Laurence.

Restored by Innocent III in 1200, it was given by his successor. Honorius III., to St Dominic, who lived here several years until he went to reside at Santa Sabina. It was in this church that St Dominic began the devotion of the Rosary that has since spread to the furthest parts of the earth; it was here that it was recited publicly.

A miraculous image that was preserved here was transferred by the Dominican nuns to the church of SS. Dominic and Sixtus, Via Magnanapoli.

In the church which now belongs to the Irish Domi-

nicans of San Clemente are frescoes representing the miracles operated there by St Dominic.

The church contains the body of St. Sixtus II. and relics of SS. Secundus, Felix, Zepherinus, Anterus, Lucius and Lucianus.

(2) SS. NEREUS AND ACHILLEUS.

Of this church there is mention as far back as the year 377. It was also known as the church *de Fasciola*, or "of the bandage," from a dressing that St Peter the Apostle had on the wounds caused him by his chains, when he fled from Rome before meeting our Lord, according to very ancient tradition, near the spot where afterwards was erected the little church, *Domine quo vadis*, and which (as we read in the acts of the Martyrs SS. Marcellinus and Peter) fell off on the road, it is supposed, about this spot.

SS. Nereuss and Achilleus were servants of St. Flavia Domitilla, a relative of the Emperor Diocletian. They converted her to the faith, for which they were exiled, tortured and put to death.

The church was several times restored. The illustrious Baronius optated to this church from that of San Silvestro in Capite, which was then undergoing extensive restorations; and he repaired and improved it to a great extent.

He brought hither the bodies of the titular Saints and of S. Flavia Domitilla, and placed them under the high altar and obtained from the then reigning Pontiff the permission to take the very beatiful pulpit and ambone from the church of San Silvestro in Capite to this church.

23 THURSDAY.

SS. COSMAS AND DAMIAN.

(Forum)

One of the most remarkable churches in Rome, erected by Felix IV. in 528, has been formed by joining together

the Temple of Romulus and the *Aedes Sacrae Urbis* by making an arch in the hall which separated them.

The ancient temple of Romulus serves as a vestibule.

Urban VIII. raised the level of the church. This accounts for the very fine mosaics on the arch being cut off on both sides, and for the fact that the bodies of the titular saints no longer repose in the church, but in the subterranean vaults.

In the ancient temple is its old bronze door, and in the church are some columns taken from it.

SS. Cosmas and Damian, martyrs, were Arabians by birth and doctors by profession. Their bodies are in the church together with those of St. Tranquillinus, St. Felix II St. Victor, St. Mark an Marcellinus; and the arm of St. Lucina, and the hand of Tobias, the just man of the Old Testament.

24 FRIDAY.

ST LAURENCE IN LUCINA.

The present church has very little in common with the ancient one, constructed by Sixtus III. in 435. The portico alone is old; the interior is mostly the result of the renovations made in the beginning of the seventeenth century.

Part of St. Laurence's iron bed of torture, part of his chains two teeth and other relics of the Saint are here preserved.

Over the high altar is the celebrated picture of the Crucifixion of Guido Reni. The church contains the relics of St Lucy, the heads of St. Alexander P. St. Restitutus; SS. Vincent, Eusebius, Hyacinth, St. Valentine, Liberatus, Antoninus, Pelegrinus, Pontius, Eugenius, Abondius, Diodorus, Florianus, Adrianus, Modestus, Quirinus, Rusticus, and the Crib of our Lord.

25. SATURDAY.

S. SUSANNA.
(Via Venti Settembre)

This church is supposed to have been built on the site of the paternal dwelling of St. Susanna, the daughter of St. Galbinius, a relation of Dioclesian. St. Susanna was also the niece of Pope Caius. We find mention of the church so far back as the fourth century. It was more than once rebuilt; by Leo III., in the year 800, by Sixtus V. in 1475, and (in part) by Cardinal Rusticucci in 1103. It now differs considerably from its ancient form, which was in three naves with a large apse.

The bodies of St. Susanna, Sts. Eleutherius and Genesius and of her father, St. Gabinius repose under the high altar.

The church also contains the head of St Theodora, of St Pudicissima, a tooth of St. Fabian and relics of Sts. Peter, Paul, Luke the Evangelist, Laurence, Praxedes, of the Holy Innocents, Sts. Andrew, Maur, Sebastian, Bartholomew, James the Greater, Simon, Pamphilius, Aurél, Fabian, Gertrude, Clement, and also a relic of the mantle of St Joseph.

(2) ST CAIUS.

This remarkable historical monument of the Great Pope and martyr of the third century was destroyed after 1870, to make room for the construction of the War Office (Ministero della Guerra, Via Venti Settembre). In the time of Urban VIII., it had fallen into decay, and that Pope rebuilt it in the year 1631.

(3) ST. MARY OF THE ANGELS.

This magnificent temple of Christian Rome is a transformation made by Michael Angelo (under Pius IV) of one of the vastest apartments of the Diocletian baths.

Still upright are the eight colossal columns of Oriental granite. They are each of a single block, forty-five feet high, and sixteen in girth. Part of their base is buried in the soil, as, to combat the dampness of the locality, the great architect raised the level of the flooring.

Michael Angelo's entrance was in the right side of the edifice, towards the south. The façade was of splendid proportions, and built of travertine. It was walled up in 1749, to make a new chapel.

Near the present entrance are the tombs of the Painters, Carlo Maratta and Salvator Rosa, and also the fine statue of S. Bruno by Handon.

The paintings in the church are very remarkable. Near the high altar, to the right, the Presentation in the Temple is by Romanelli; the Martyrdom of St. Sebastian is a celebrated fresco by Domenichino; to the left, the Baptism of our Saviour is by Maratta, and the Punishment of Ananias and Sapphira, by Pomarancio. The tombs of Pius IV. and of Cardinal Serbelloni are after plans of Michael Angelo. Other strikng pictures are by Muziano, Ricciolini, Graziani, Trevisani and Odazzi. The Evangelists on the vault are by Procaccini.

This church contains relics of 730 martyrs, of whom the following are the most precious.

Saints Liberatus, Boniface, Columba, Vincent, Marcellinus, Prosper, Aurelia, Smaragdus, Cyriacus, Maximus, Januarius, Valentine, Felicita, Felix, Irene, Laurence, Anastasius, Priscus, Nectarus, Quintiola, Victor and others.

26 FOURTH SUNDAY IN LENT.

HOLY CROSS OF JERUSALEM.

Constructed by St. Helena, mother of Constantine, to hold the relics of the True Cross, which she brought from Jerusalem and was consecrated by St. Silvester on the 20th March; hence on this day only during the year women are allowed to enter the Chapel or Oratory of St. Helena.

Facsimile of the Title of the Cross as preserved in the Church of Santa Croce in Gerusalemme, Rome.

It was rebuilt by Benedict XIV. after plans by Gregorini.

There have been two Councils held here, one under Sixtus III. and the other under Pope Symmachus.

Hither, from a very ancient date, the Pope used to go on this Sunday (called *Laetare* Sunday), and, according to the ceremonial, hold in his hand the golden rose, that was the symbol of the joys of Heaven, the mystical Jerusalem.

The church is divided by pillars and columns of Egyptian granite. The altar is of basalt with columns of rich marble.

Under the high altar are the bodies of the Martyrs SS. Anastasius and Cesarius. In a chapel apart are preserved very remarkable relics; part of the true Cross and the Title that was put over it in three languages, two of the Thorns from our Saviour's Crown, a nail that pierced His Sacred Hand, and the finger with which St. Thomas probed His Side.

In the underground chapel of St Helena are paintings by Pomarancio, and mosaics by Peruzzi and there too is said to be deposed a quantity of earth brought from Mount Calvary.

The fresco over the apse of the basilica is by Pinturicchio.

The church contains a Reliquary, said to have belonged to St. Gregory the Great, containing 213 Relics, the principal of which are: a bone of St. Gelasius, Pope; relics of St. James (Ap.) and of SS. Elisabeth, Anastasia, Nereus, John the Baptist, Paul, Laurence; of the cross of St. Peter. There are also many other relics preserved here, notably of St. Thomas of Canterbury, St. Catherine of Sienna, Sts. Bridgid, Praxedes, Sixtus, Nicholas, Christopher, Innocent, Blaise, Agapitus and many others.

27. MONDAY.

SS. QUATTRO CORONATI.

This church stands on a spur of the Caelian hill, near the site of *Paedagogium Capitis Africae* — the High School for the boys of Imperial Rome, dates back very probably to the fifth century. It was burned by Robert Guiscard about 1084, and rebuilt, but in much smaller proportions, by Paschal II. in 1112.

Under the altar of St. Sebastian a staircase goes down to a subterranean chapel, where the relics of the titular Saints and the head of St. Sebastian are kept.

The four martyrs to whom the church is dedicated were put to death by Diocletian (or perhaps by Galerian) for refusing to worship an idol of Esculapius. Their names remained unknown, and they have wrongfully been confounded with four Saints buried at Albano (SS. Severus, Severianus, Carpophorus and Victorinus). Amongst the relics preserved in this church are the bodies of Saints Claud, Nicostratus, Symphronius, Casturius, Simplicius, Justus, Fabian, Antoninus, Hippolytus, Clementia, Celestine and Fortunatus.

28 TUESDAY.

St. LAURENCE AND DAMASUS.

This illustrious basilica was erected in the fourth century by St. Damasus, in memory of St. Laurence. The modern building, however, dates from 1495 only, Bramante being its architect.

Amongst the persons buried in it are, Annibale Caro; Cardinal Sadoleto, the famous secretary of Leo X.; Caccianiga, the painter; General Caprara, Pius the Sixth's Captain of Arms; and Pellegrino Rossi, who was treacherously assassinated in the neighbouring palace, during the pontificate of Pius IX.

Under the French domination, this church was used as a court of justice. It was reopened for divine worship after the return of Pius VII. and restored in 1820 by Valvadier.

Here is a facsimile of the celebrated statue of St. Hippolytus, found, in the sixteenth century, in his cemetery on the Tiburtine Way, and now in the Lateran Museum.

The adjoining building, known as the Cancelleria, is built on the site of an older house, once inhabited by St. Jerome, also by St. Brigid. St. Francis Xavier once preached in this church.

(TUESDAY after fourth Sunday)

(2) ST ANDREA DELLA VALLE.

Where this magnificent edifice stands, existed formerly a chapel in honour of St Sebastian. The Duchess Costanza Piccolomini d'Amalfi gave the ground and her contiguous palace to the Theatine Fathers that they might there establish their house and build a church in honour of St Andrew.

The work was begun in 1591 and finished in 1608, the façade being added fifty years later. Obarin and Maderno were the architects of the building. Rainaldi planned the façade. The latter part is truly of magnificent effect.

The cupola is the largest in Rome after that of St Peter's. The frescoes beneath it, representing the Four Evangelists, as well as those above the apse or tribune, are by Domenichino.

The church is rich in works of art. Note especially the first chapel to the left, called the Barberini chapel, from Matthew Barberini, afterwards Urban VIII., who adorned it. The image of his parents is there sculptured in porphyry. The Assumption and other paintings are by Passignano; and the statuary is due to Mochi, Buonvicino, Bernini and Stati.

Amonget other relics here preserved are: — the chains of St Sebastian, an autograph letter of St. Gaetano (founder of the Theatines) and relics of Saints Anastasius, Felix, Lelius, Albert, Benedict (martyr), Julius, Aurelius, Antigonus, Gaudentius, Victor Donatus, Crescens, Columba, Celestinus, Zozimus, Innocent, Theodore, Candidus and Clement.

29. WEDNESDAY.

ST PAUL'S.
(outside the Walls)

Over the tomb of the Apostle Paul, as over that of St Peter, was erected a Shrine, from the very time of his martyrdom. Constantine, here likewise constructed a basilica. Valentinian II. undertook to enlarge it, and for that purpose to reconstruct it anew, and the work was carried out, after his death in 392, by his successors Theodosius, Arcadius and Honorius. Restorations were made at various epochs, but no special mention need be made of them, since the whole edifice was reduced to ashes on July 16th, 1823. Little was preserved, save part of the ancient mosaics and the central altar.

Leo XII. undertook the reconstruction, and Pius IX. dedicated the marvellous temple we now behold.

The principal façade is towards the north, has seven doors, and is adorned with magnificent mosaics and statuary. There is another façade towards the east, upheld by 12 columns of Greek marble. The campanile on the south-west is in Travertine stone.

At the ends of the transepts are two altars in malachite, a present to Gregory XVI. from the Czar Nicholas I. The Gothic baldachino over the Papal altar is upheld by four columns of Oriental alabaster. Under the altar are parts of the bodies of the Apostles Peter and Paul, the heads being in St John Lateran and

the rest of the bodies in St Peter's. At the Gospel side is the immense marble candelabrum of the ancient basilica, enriched with bas-reliefs. In the apse are mosaics of the 13th century, and, engraved on marble slabs, the names of the ecclesiastical dignitaries who were present at the consecration.

Four chapels are to the right and left of the apse or tribune. They are rich with marbles, sculptures, and paintings. In that immediately to the right, the chapel of the Blessed Sacrament, is the second of the miraculous crucifixes, which is said to have conversed with St. Bridget.

The body of the basilica is divided into five naves by eighty Corinthian columns of granite, and the impression of richness and chaste magnificence which it makes on the spectator is marvellous. Near the Altar are two colossal statues of the great Apostles, that of St. Peter by Jacometti, and that of St Paul by Revelli and Doppieri.

Very fine modern frescoes adorn the walls, retracing the events of St Paul's life. There are likewise mosaic portraits of the Popes, from St Peter to Leo XIII., which are not fanciful nor imaginary but are faithful copies of ancient likenesses, which date as far back as the 6th century: this is a magnificent testimony to the Apostolicity of the Catholic Church.

The library of the monks, formerly in the convent of S. Callixtus in Trastevere, has been transferred here. Amongst the precious documents in it is the celebrated copy of the Vulgate or Latin version of the Bible, a MS. written on vellum, and long supposed to have been given to the convent by Charlemagne. There is reason to suppose, however, that it does not date farther back than the 11th century. The printed books number about 12,000, and are chiefly on divinity, canon law and ecclesiastical subjects. The visitor will not fail to remark that the shield bearing the arms of the abbot of this convent, a hand grasping a sword, is surrounded by the

ribbon of the Order of the Garter, with the motto, *Honi soit qui mal y pense*, a remnant of the connection of the monastery, of which, as well as of the adjoining basilica, the kings of England were the royal patrons and protectors.

This basilica, together with that of St Peter's, was from the earliest times a centre of devotion; a covered way (or arcade) once joined the two basilicas together. Thus pilgrims could visit the two principal churches of Rome, protected from the sun and rain. Nothing now remains, exceping, a few traces in the Via dei Pelegrini which street still retains the name, though it has lost its former charm and utility.

Amongst the relics of the basilica are: the Madonna before which St. Ignatius and his first companions pronounced their vows, an arm of St Anne, part of the clothing of our Lady, head of St Chrysanthus (martyr), head of St Gordian (martyr), the chains of Saint Paul, part of St Paul's staff, and relics of Sts. Ananias, Laurence, Blaise, Lucy, Julian, Andrew (apostle) Matthew, (ap.) Bartholomew (ap.) Stephen, Augustine (of Hippo) Epaphras, the Holy Innocents, and the head of St Photinus, the Samaritan.

The relics include SS. Damasus, Eutychus, Hippolytus, Vincent, Carissimus. Primus, Natalis, Justinia, Leopard, Lorentina, Felicita, Silvanus, Pontianus, Montanus, Maximianus, Lucian, Calixtus, Lucius, Liberatus, Clement, Largus, Alexis, Dulcissimus, Bassa, Alexander, Castorius, Justin, Sergius, and many others; also the chains of Saint Lawrence, the body of St Maur, and relics of St John the Baptist and of St Paul. In the Massimo chapel the crucifix which spoke to St. Bridget is exposed.

THURSDAY

S. MARTINO AI MONTI.

This church was erected at a very remote epoch, when shrines were not dedicated to this or that saint in particular, but were simply places of assembly for the Faithful. It was consecrated by Pope Sylvester. Later it would appear that it was dedicated to St. Martin, bishop of Tours, and two centuries later to St Martin the Pope, who died a martyr in the Chersonese.

Restored in 1650 by Fr. de Cortona, it has three naves with 24 Corinthian columns. The landscape paintings on the side walls are by G. Poussin, and the portraits by N. P. Nicholas Poussin.

The chapel of our Lady of Carmel, in the left aisle, is adorned with sculptures and paintings by Cavallucci. Undergroud are remnants of the old basilica, where Pope Sylvester held two councils. Cardinal Alan was titular of this church.

It contains, amongst other relics, the bodies of St. Martin, Pope, of St. Sisinnius, of St. Soter, of St. Anastasius, of St. Artemius and of his daughter St. Paulina, together with relics of St. Sylvester, Pope and of St. Andrew Corsini,

(2) S. SILVESTRO IN CAPITE,

This church is said to have been built by St. Dionysius in 261. Paul I., after erecting a monastery and oratory in honour of Popes Sylvester and Stephen, on the site of his own house adjoining, rebuilt the church which was within the same grounds, and dedicated it, as it would appear, to St. Dionysius or Denis.

This was about the year 760. Paul I. brought to this church from the catacombs of St. Callixtus vast numbers of bodies of the saints and martyrs, hence the church was called for a long time by various authors, the " Ce-

metery of Cemeteries," on account of the enormous number of relics. Nine Popes are buried here. Amongst the large number of Saints whose names we give below, is the martyr Saint of the Blessed Sacrament, St. Tharcisius whom Cardinal Wiseman graphically describes in his historical work "Fabiola." The saint Denis was probably the patron of France, for Paul I had dwelt some time in France, and had been given hospitality by King Pepin, in a monastery dedicated to St. Denis.

The title of St. Denis likely fell into disuse, after the transfer, later on, of the bodies of SS. Sylvester and Stephen from the oratory to the Church. The name of Sylvester prevailed and in the course of time became the only one used.

This church was also called; *Cata Pauli* (i. e. "near Paul's house" a mixture of Greek and Latin, cfr. *catacumbas*); *inter duos hortos* (i. e. the church "between the two gardens,") from its position in the Middle Ages; and *in capite*, a name that still adheres to it from the fact that the head of St John the Baptist, which was formerly kept in the little neighbouring church of St. John in Capite, now desecrated, has been kept here for many centuries. After the 20th of September, 1870, it was by the order of Pius IX. taken to the Vatican for safety, together with the other celebrated relic of the Holy Face of our Lord called of "Abgarus" formerly preserved in the church of Edessa.

The façade of the church was considerably modified in the restorationi under Clement XI. It still has the atrium and portico common to the old basilicas. In the portico are three interesting inscriptions, two with the names of the saints whose bodies were brought here by Pope Paul I., and the third, dated 1119 containing an interdiction and excomunication with regard to all interference with the neighbouring Antonine Column, now standing in the Piazza Colonna, which belongs to this church.

In the Sacristy are some fifteenth century and earlier frescoes, taken from the monastery and placed here by

the Italian Government, at the time of transforming the monastery into the General Post Office, when the building was deformed with the architecture we now behold.

The church was given by Leo XIII. to the Pallotine Fathers for the use of English-speaking Catholics. Sermons in English are preached every Sunday at 4 p. m., from Advent till Easter. The church is well frequented and the Services exceedingly-well carried out. Little is seen of the ancient edifice; the church is rich in associations, Nicolas I was elected Pope in it: St. Gregory the Great preached here his homily on the raising of the Widow's son. It is a titular church.

Among the many bodies of Saints possessed by this church, besides those of St. Sylvester, Pope St. Dionysius, Pope, St. Anterus, Pope and Martyr, and in St. Melchiadis are those of Sts. Calocerius and Parthenius, Martyrs, St. Lucius. Pope and Martyr, St. Pigmenius, Bishop and Martyr, St. Cajus, Pope and Martyr, St. Melitis, Martyr, Sts. Chrysanthus, Trason, Daria and Valerius, Martyrs, St. Quirinus, Martyr, Sts. Triphonis, and Calocerius, St. Zepherinus, Pope and Martyr St. Tharcisius, Sts. Cyriacus, Largus and Smaragdus, Martyrs, St. Hypolitus, Martyr, St. Gorgonius, Martyr, St. Januarius, St. Pamphilius and Paul, Martyrs, etc. Sts. Projectus and Severius Martyrs, St. Concilia, Virgin and Martyr, Sts. Optatus and Policanus, St. Nemesius, Deacon, St. Menia and Julian, Martyrs, St. Sophia and her three daughters, St. Faith, St. Triphonia, Martyr, St. Cysilla, Virgin and Martyr, St. Charity, St. Hope, St. Arthemia, Virgin and Martyr. On three days of the year the feast is kept of the Saints, whose names God alone knows, and on another day the feast of twenty-five Martyrs is celebrated.

Under the altar of St. Paul are the following relics: A part of the dress of our Lady, some relics of St. John Baptist, a relic of St. Peter, St. Andrew the Apostle, St. Simon the Apostle, St. Luke the Evangelist, St. Valentino Priest and Martyr, St. Blasius Bishop and Martyr, St. Pri-

mus, Martyr, St. Valerius Martyr, St. Gloriosus, Priest and Martyr, St. Eustachius, Martyr, St. Agapitus, Martyr, St. Superantius, Martyr. Sts. Processus and Martinianus, Martyrs, St. Vincent, Sts. Felicissimus and Agapitus, Sts, Protho and Hyacinth, Martyrs, St. Savino, Bishop and Martyr, St. Timothy, Martyr, St. Gregory Nazianzen, St. Clement, Pope and Martyr, St. Gregory, Pope, St. Urban, Pope, St. Marcello, Pope and Martyr, St Stephen, Pope and Martyr, St. Celestinus, Pope and Confessor, St. Dionysius, Pope and Confessor, St. Eusebius, Pope and of the Holy Innocents,

St. Patricianus Martyr, St. Ursus, Abbot, St. Ephaim Confessor, St. Julian, Virgin, St. Margherita Virgin and Martyr. St. Elizabeth, St. Scholastica, St. Felicita, Sts. Rufina and Secunda, Virgins and Martyrs, St. Theodora, Virgin and Martyr, St. Susanna Virgin, and Martyr. St. Petronilla, Sts. Prassede and Pudentiana, St. Cyriaca, St. Fusta St. Eugenia, St. Martina, part of the sepulchre of our Lord and a stone of Mountainl Calvary.

Part of the hair and clothes of the Blessed Virgin Mary; powder of the bones of Sts. Peter and Paul; of the head of St. Jacob; part of the head shoulderbone and bones of St. Mathew the Apostle and Evangelist; part of the head of St. Stephen Pope and Martyr; of the arm of St. Valentino Priest and Martyr; part of the body of St. Sylvester, Pope and Confessor; St. Marcellus Pope; Relics of St. Conrad Bishop of Constantinople;of the cappa of St. Francis; of the powder of the bones of many holy martyrs. In a glass phial in addition to a portion of the wood of the True Cross are relics of the apostles Andrew and Bartolomey, of Sts. Cosmas and Damian, Martyrs, of St. Agathius and S. Valentine, of S. Julian and S. Victor of S. Arthemia, the Holy Innocents and the Ten Thousand Martyrs.

31 FRIDAY.

S. EUSEBIO.

One of the most remarkable Christian monuments on the Esquiline. Its date is unknown to us, but tradition tells that here existed the house of Eusebius, the Roman priest, who was put to death by the Emperor Constance (son of Constantine) for his unrelenting war against the Arian heresy.

Rebuilt in 750 by Pope Zachary, and restored by different Popes, in the year 1238 it was newly consecrated by Gregory IX. and the name of St. Vincent associated with that of St Eusebius in the title may be read, inscribed under the portico.

There are likewise here relics of SS. Orosius and Paulinus, companions of St. Eusebius.

Under the High Altar are the bodies of SS. Eusebius and Orosius. The relics to be seen are: the head of S. Valentine, M., and that of S. Eusebius, M.; relics of the following martyrs: S. Faustinus, S. Benedict, S. Fortunatus, S. Boniface (an arm and bones), S. Tranquillinus, S. Vincent, S. Victor, S. Theodore, S. Maximus, S. Placidus, S. Constance (one side of the body), S. Faustinus (one side of the body), S. Vincent (the entire body, under one of the altars).

(2) S. BIBIANA

This church on the Esquiline, near the gate of San Lorenzo, was called by ancient writers *ad ursum pileatum*.

Flavian, once Prefect of Rome, and Daphrosa his wife, both martyrs for the faith under Julian the apostate, were the parents of SS. Bibiana and Demetria. These maidens were deprived of their property, and tempted in every way that they might renounce their faith. They remained constant, however. Demetria died a natural death; Bibiana was bound to a column (still shown in the church) and scourged until life was extinct.

She was buried in this place, and a church erected in her honour, in 363 and consecrated by Pope Simplicius, in the year 470. It was restored in 1220, and again in 1625 by Urban VIII., who added the façade after plans by Bernini.

The bodies of SS. Bibiana, Demetria and Daphrosa repose in an alabaster urn under the high altar. The statue, a fine work, is by Bernini. The frescoes, detailing the life of the Saint, are by Ciampelli, and P. da Cortona.

Near the gate of the church, the column to which the Saint and her sister, S. Demetria, were bound, previous to their scourging, is to be seen. Under the High Altar is the body of the Saint. The relics to be seen are of the following martyrs — S. Faustus (a leg), S. Victoire (a leg), S. Victor (a bone), S. Boniface (a bone), S. Theodora (a leg), S. Colomba (a bone), S. Flavian (a leg), S. Lucida (the head), S. Magnus (the head), S. Reparatus (the head), S. Redemptus (the lower jaw-bone), S. Jucundinus (the head), S. Felicita (the head), S. Amantius (a portion of the jaw-bone), portions of the clothing, hair and body of S. Pius, V., portions of the body of S. Philip Neri; six entire bodies of martyrs under a side altar, with glass vessels containing their blood; and a number of bones of martyrs whose names are unknown.

32. SATURDAY.

S. NICCOLO' IN CARCERE.

(near Piazza Montanara)

This church is said to have been consecrated to S. Nicholas, bishop of Mira (who lived in the time of Diocletian and Constantine, and whose body is at Bari, in Apulia) by S. Nicholas II, in the 8th century. The church, however, is as early as the 6th century. Most recent restorations were made by Pius IX in 1865.

The church is divided by 14 marble columns; is built over the substructions of three temples, dedicated probably to Spes, Juno Sospiter and Pietas, which stood side by side. The central altar is very fine; the columns that support the baldachino are of Oriental alabaster. Underneath is the magnificent urn of green porphyry.

The frescoes concerning the Saint's history are by Guidi, those in the apse by Pasqualoni. In the Baptistery is a fine Immaculate Conception by Guido Reni.

Here can be seen an arm of the Saint, a finger of S. Sebastian, and relics of S. Alexis and S. Anthony.

S. NICCOLO' DEI LORENESI.

(near Piazza Navona)

This ancient church was given to the people of Lorrain by Gregory XV., and in the year 1622, they rebuilt it from the foundations. Its three altars are dedicated to St. Nicholas, St. Catherine (to whom the first church on this ground was dedicated) and to the Visitation.

33. PASSION SUNDAY

(1) ST. PETER'S (see p. 456)

(2) ST. LAZARUS

To the right of the road leading to Monte Mario this church still exists. It was destined as a chapel to the neighbouring hospital for leprosy and other contagions diseases. Built in the twelfth century, when, towards the end of the crusades, the dreadful diseases alluded to began to invade the West. It was rebuilt by Dominic Garison in 1536.

Here are to be seen a bone of S. Alphonsus de Liguori and relics of S. Hyacinthe of Mariscotti, of S. Joseph, of S. Lucy and S. Barbara.

34. MONDAY.

S. CRISOGONO.

This saint suffered martyrdom under Diocletian.

The basilica erected in his honour goes back to the time of Constantine. Restorations were made in the eighth century and many times since.

This magnificent edifice is divided by 22 granite columns of different styles. The greater arch has two rare columns of porphyry, rare for their material and their proportions. On the vault is a copy of the remarkable painting by Guercino, representing the titular saint. The original was sold and carried to England. The B. Virgin over the choir is by Guercino. At the end of the right aisle is the tomb of the venerable Anna Maria Taigi, who died in Rome in 1837.

There is a curious natural figuret in the marble on the floor of the church of our Lady and Child.

Stephen Langton, archbishop of Canterbury, was Titular Cardinal of this church, in the time of Innocent and of Honorius III.

Amongst the relics exposed are a portion of the True Cross, the head of St. Chrysogonus, and relics of St. Sabina, the Holy Innocents, St. Modestus, St. Lawrence, part of the tomb of our Saviour, and part of the clothing of our Lady.

35. TUESDAY.

(1) ST. CYRIACUS

Whilst the foundations of the Palazzo delle Finanze (Via Venti Settembre) were being laid, the remains of this church were unearthed. It had been one of the very oldest in Rome. The body of its titular saint (martyr under Diocletian) is in St. Maria in Via Lata; one of his

arms only being in this church, together with relics of Sts. Vincent Ferrer, Charus, and Julitta.

(2) St. MARIA IN VIA LATA.

This church is built on the remains of the « Septa Julia. » It was rebuilt by Pope Sergius I. in the seventh century and restored by Innocent VIII. The façade was constructed by Alexander VII.

Underneath the church is shown the place where it is supposed that St. Paul with St. Luke the Evangelist passed two years as a prisoner; and the spring of water that burst forth, to serve the Apostles in baptising the pagans.

The bodies of SS. Largus, Smaragdus, Cyriacus and their companions here repose; there- are also relics of St Blaise, Francesca Romana, Felician, Felicissima, Bonaventure, Prisca, Felix, Callixtus, Helena, Ursula, Stephen (Pope), Silvester, Urban I, Hippolytus and Marcellinus.

(4) St. QUIRICUS

St. Quiricus was a child of Tharsis in Cilicia, who, for having wept at seeing his mother tortured, in the persecution by Diocletian, was ordered by the judge to be dashed against the steps of the tribunal, and thus passed to a better life.

The church bearing his name (and that of his mother Julietta) is very old. It was rebuilt by Vigilius in the sixth century.

36. WEDNESDAY.

St. MARCELLUS (Corso)

Tradition relates that here stood the dwelling of the noble matron Lucina, which was turned by the Emperor Maxentius into a stable, in which St. Marcellus was obliged to labour.

The church is very old and is said to have been built in 305 A. D. and has been frequently restored; the latest improvements made on it were in 1867, by Vespignani.

In a basalt urn under the high altar is the body of Pope St. Marcellus; there are also relics of other saints, notably St. Longinus.

The statue in the third chapel on the right is supposed to be by Michael Angelo; in the same chapel is the tomb of Cardinal Weld whose titular church St. Marcellus was. In the next chapel the paintings are partly by Pierin del Vaga and partly by Daniel da Volterra.

37. THURSDAY.

St. APOLLINARIS.

Supposed to stand on the site of a temple of Apollo which was turned into a Christian church by St. Sytvester.

It was rebuilt by Pope Adrian I., in the eighth century and reconstructed by Benedict XIV., who added the vestibule, wherein is the chapel of the Blessed Virgin, with the much venerated picture.

The high altar is rich in marble and gilded metal. The picture represents the titular saint, who was consecrated bishop of Ravenna by St. Peter himself.

The painting on the roof is by Stephen Pozzi, and the statue of St Francis Xaviers by le Gros. Underneath the presbytery are the crypt and altar of the Holy Martyrs, St Eustratius and Companions.

By Julius III. this church was given to St. Ignatius Loyola. The latter founded there the German College, and for its use, Gregory XIII. built the two adjoining palaces. Leo XII. placed there the Roman Seminary as well as the offices of the Vicariate.

Amongst the relics exposed are part of the cassock

of saint Charles Borromeo and many relics of St. Pius V., including his crucifix.

To day the Lipsanotheca is open to the public; here are kept relics of all the Saints, whence the Cardinal Vicar distributes them to churches and individuals who have need; especially may be mentioned the bodies of the martyrs which were taken out of the catacombs by Pius IX.

38. Friday.

St. STEPHEN IN MONTE CELIO (S. Stefano Rotondo).

The church bearing this name was judged by many scholars, from the sixteenh century onwards, to have been originally a pagan temple or an arsenal. The singularity of its form led them to this belief. To day, however, we have proof that it was planned and built in the fifth century (468-482) by Pope Simplicius, in honour of St. Stephen. The church was of great magnificence. Besides the 64 columns of granite and marble that we see, there was an outer row but the intervening space was filled up in 1452. Adjoining the church was the famous monastery of St. Erasmus. It was to this monastery that Pope St. Leo III., who had his eyes and tongue torn out before the High Altar of St. Silvestro in Capite, was brought; here he was imprisoned until finally liberated by his faithful servant Albinus, after having his eyes and tongue miraculously restored.

The church was restored by Innocent VIII., in 1488, and later on by Gregory XIII., who handed it over to the care of the Jesuit Fathers of the Germanic College.

The tabernacle in the centre, is hardly in harmony with the building.

The frescoes showing the various species of martyrdom that the saints underwent are by Pomarancio and Tempesta.

39. SATURDAY.

(1) ST. JOHN BEFORE THE LATIN GATE.

This illustrious basilica, situated just within the Latin Gate, was erected by Gelasius I., in 772. It had a chapter of its own, but Leo II. joined it to that of St. John Lateran. Celestine III. in 1190 renewed the consecration.

The neighbouring chapel, called " St. John in the Oil," supposed to be the exact spot where the Evangelist, before his banishment to Patmos, suffered the torture of immersion in boiling oil, was reconstructed in 1509, at the expense of the French prelate Adam, whose arms are above the door with the motto: " Au plaisir de Dieu. "

The church has three naves of different marbles. In the garden is the ancient well of the vestibule, with an inscription of the tenth century.

The church is now in the keeping of the French African missionaries of the Third Order of St. Francis. Amongst the relics exposed are those of St. Vincent de Paul, St. Andrew the Apostle, and others.

(2) CESARIO IN PALATIO.

St. Cesarius, deacon, was remarkable for his works of mercy, and was especially remembered for having buried the bodies of SS. Nereus, Achilleus and Flavia Domitilla. He was tortured and thrown into the sea at Terracina.

This church (which has been confounded with others dedicated to the same saint), existed already in the year 600. From the tenth to the fifteenth century it was held by monks of the Greek rite, and here the Latins themselves, as we know from a document of the time,

communicated in leavened bread. This is a striking testimony of the falseness of the asserted intolerance of Rome towards the Oriental rite.

At one time when ruin, menaced the church the body of the titular Saint was transferred to Holy Cross of Jerusalem. Here are exposed relics of St. Cesarius, St. Alphonsus de Liguori, St. Joseph of Cupertino, St. Lucy, St. Clement, St. Barbara and St. Fortuna.

40. PALM SUNDAY.

St. JOHN LATERAN.
(See page 447).

41. MONDAY.

S. PRASSEDE.

This church was founded on the site of the oratory built by Pius I. in 160 A.D. A church was in existence on this ground in the year 490. Paschal I. in 822 renewed it, or more probably built an entirely new church. That which we see today. He transferred to it, from the different cemeteries, the bodies of 2300 martyres, and amongst others those of the holy sisters Sts. Praxed and Pudentiana.

St. Charles Borromeo having this church as his title when Cardinal, built the front and made vast improvements in the interior.

Under the high altar, the baldachino, which is upheld by four pillars of porphyry, are the chief relics of the Saints. In the Chapel of St. Zeno, which dates from the ninth century and has remarkable mosaics, is the pillar, brought in 1223 from Jerusalem by Cardinal Giovanni Colonna and believed to be that at which our Saviour was scourged. Towards the end of the church, in the centre, is the head of the well brought from S. Puden-

tiana wherein St. Praxedes used to deposit the blood of the martyrs, which she had gathered up in sponges and cloths.

The picture of St. Paschal in the apse bears proofs that it was made in his lifetime. The fine picture in the sacristy, representing the Flagellation, is by Julius Romanus. The Olgiati chapel (opposite that of St. Zeno) has paintings by the Cav. di Arpino and Zuccheri. A marble slab is shown in the left aisle, on which St. Praxedes is said have taken her repose.

The fine steps of old red marble leading up to the altar are remarkable. Remarkable too as one of the oldest and most interesting of its kind, is the painted tower or belfry. This church is one of the richest in Rome in relics. It contains the bodies of St. Zoe, St. Feldian, St. Candid, St. Basile, St. Celestine I., Pope, St. Nicomedius; besides which the following relics;

1. Some of the Body of St. Charles Borromeo.
2. Some of the habits of St. Benedict, and St. John Gualbert, Abbots.
3. The head and bones of St. Paulina, Virgin and Martyr.
4. Relics of St. Nicholas of Bari.
5. Some of the arm of St. Prassede, and of the sponge with which she gathered the blood of the Martyrs, which she placed in a well in her house.
6. Image of our Saviour, given by St. Peter to the Senator Pudens.
7. Some of the arm of St. Stephen.
8. Bones of St. Laurence.
9. Some of the head and other relics of St. Luke.
10. Some of the arm of St. Matthew.
11. Some of the head of St. Bartholomew.
12. Part of a rib, and other relics of St. Philip.
13. Portion of the cross of St. Andrew.
14. A tooth of St. Peter, and one of St. Paul, and some relics of the holy Apostles.
15. Relics of St. John the Baptist.
16. Some of the garments, and a piece of the tomb of the Blessed Virgin.
17. A piece of the seamless garment of our Lord Jesus Christ.

18. Three thorns of the « Crown » of our Lord Jesus Christ.
19. Four morsels of wood from the True Cross and many bodies.

42. TUESDAY.

S. PRISCA.

On the eastern slope of the Aventine rises this interesting church, whose origin is connected with the Apostles themselves. Here stood the house of Aquila, and Priscilla his wife, to whom St. Paul alludes in his Epistle to the Romans; and here it is said, St. Peter used to come to meet the assembled Christians, to instruct and baptise the neophytes.

We read that in 280 St. Eutichius, Pope, brought hither the body of St. Prisca, and dedicated the church in her honour.

The church has three naves with fourteen columns, embedded, for their better solidity, in pilasters. The frescoes on the walls are by Fontebuono; the Baptism of the saint, over the altar, by Passignani. Steps lead down to the « Confession, »where there is a mosaic picture of St. Peter, dating from the thirteenth century, and also the vessel from which he was erroneously believed to have baptised the pagans.

In the church the side altars are dedicated, on the right to S. John Gualberto and to the B. Virgin; and on the left, to our Saviour crucified, and to St. Anthony of Padua.

The adjoining monastery was built, in the 8th century by Greek monks. In 1062 it passed into the hands of the Benedictines. After 1414 it was given to the Augustinians; the body of St. Prisca reposes in this church.

(2) STA. MARIA DEL POPOLO.

A chapel was here erected in 1099 by Pope Paschal II., on the spot where Nero was believed to be buried, and

as it were to purify the ground. In 1227 this chapel was transformed into the present magnificent church. Different Popes have repaired and embellished the church, and a whole volume would not exhaust its literary and artistic history. The brush and chisel of great masters have been here employed, as Pinturicchio, Gargi, Maratta, Caracci, Caravaggio, Sebastian del Piombo, Raphael and Sansovino. Amongst the number of illustrious men here buried are; — Cardinals John de Castro, Christopher della Rovere, John Bapt. Pallavicino, Podocatharus of Cyprus, Alexander and Laurence Cibo, etc.

To this church the Pope used to come with great ceremony on the feast of the Nativity of the Blessed Virgin. The picture of our Lady'so much venerated, and attributed even to St. Luke, was brought hither from the Lateran basilica by Gregory IX.

It contains the crucifix said to have spoken to St. Philip Neri; the relics of one of the order of St. Ursuline; the arm of St. Innocent, martyr, and soldier of the Theban Legion; relics of St. Honorius, M., an arm of St. Ignatius, bishop and martyr; a bone of St. Victorinus M., of St. Christina, martyr, of St. Ireneus, M., of St. Constance, M., of St. Liberata, M., of St. Felicissima M., a relic of the body of St. Faustina M., relics of the martyrs of Treves who suffered under Rictivarus.

43. WEDNESDAY.

ST. MARY MAJORS.
(V. See p. 452)

44. HOLY THURSDAY.

ST. JOHN LATERAN
(V. See p. 447)

45. GOOD FRIDAY.

HOLY CROSS OF JERUSALEM.
(V. See p. 480)

46. HOLY SATURDAY.

ST. JOHN LATERAN.
(V. See p. 447)

N.B. Inasmuch as there is a Station every day in Lent, in the churches of the Holy Name of Mary, and of St. John of the Florentines, we will now make a short mention of these two.

MOST HOLY NAME OF MARY.

A chapel here existed dedicated to St. Bernard. In memory of the victory over the Turks in 1693, a confraternity was shortly afterwards founded under the appellation of the most Holy Name of Mary. To its members were given this church of St. Bernard, and here they erected, after plans by a French architect, the present church under the new title. This was in 1736. It has since been restored by the architect, Gabet.

Over the high altar is revered an ancient picture of the B. Virgin, brought from the oratory of St. Laurence in Lateran.

S. JOHN OF THE FLORENTINES.

The « Compagnia della Pietà », composed of Florentines, was formed in Rome in 1448, to render charitable services to those stricken by a pestilence then raging. Later on they built on this ground — where a chapel previously existed in honour of St. Pataleon — the present church, finished in 1588. The first plans were made by Michael Angelo ; but they were not put into execution,

being too costly. It has three naves; and was but recently restored.

The high altar, rich in marbles, was designed by Pietro da Cortona. The painting on the roof is by Lanfranchi. The fine picture of the martyrdom of SS. Cosmas and Damian is by Salvator Rosa. Other pictures are by Passignani, Pomarancio, Tempesta, Santi di Tito, and many skilful artists. Over the door of the sacristy is the remarkable statuette of St. John the Baptist, attributed to Donatello. In the adjoining presbytery dwelt St. Philip Neri, and in this church he wrought wonders on the population of Rome. It contains the bodies of St. Protus and of St. Hyacinth.

EASTER STATIONS.

EASTER SUNDAY - St. Mary Major (See page 452)

EASTER MONDAY.

(1) St. Peter in Chains (See page 451)

(2) St. ONOFRIO (on the Janiculum).

This church and the adjoining convent were founded in 1435 by the Blessed Nicholas of Forca Palena, whose body reposes in the chapel at the entrance. In the same entrance are frescoes painted by Domenichino, representing the events of St. Jerome's life (the monks of St. Jerome had been brought here by B. Nicholas shortly after the foundation) and there also, on the altar of the Blessed Virgin, is a picture by the celebrated Bassano.

The church is in one nave and has two chapels. The first to the right is dedicated to St. Onofrius, one of the Fathers of the Desert, towards the end of the fourth century. The second has a picture representing the Madonna of Loreto, by Annibale Caracci. Over the high altar the

frescoes are, in the lower part by Peruzzi, higher up by Pinturicchio.

In this church is buried Tasso the poet, and there is a sumptuous monument, raised to him under Pius IX. In the grounds outside the church, remarkable for the magnificent panorama they command over Rome, is still seen the oak, now blighted by the storm, that sheltered the immortal singer of " Jerusalem Delivered " and that sheltered too the great St. Philip Neri, when he brought hither the youth of Rome for innocent recreation.

In the church is also the tomb of the marvellous linguist, Cardinal Mezzofanti, whose body, when being re-exposed in 1889, was found in a wonderful state of preservation. Others buried here are John Barclay, the Scotch man-of-letters; Alexander Guidi, the poet, and Celentano, the illustrious painter.

In the adjoining monastery, where Tasso died, are many interesting relics. There, likewise, is a fresco by Leonardo da Vinci. The arm of St Onofrius is preserved in the sacristy; and the body of B. Nicolas of Forca Palena under the high altar.

EASTER TUESDAY - St. PAULS. (See page 484)

WEDNESDAY - St. LAURENCE. (See page 482)

THURSDAY - HOLY APOSTLES. (See page 454)

(1) FRIDAY.

S. MARIA AD MARTYRES. (Pantheon)

Of this magnificent temple the Portico at least was built by Agrippa, 27 years before the coming of our Saviour. It was restored by successive emperors, and finally was given over in the year 608 by Phocas to Boniface IV.

This Pope converted it into a church, and dedicated it to the Mother of God and to all the holy martyrs.

It is one of the finest pieces of architecture that the world has known, the portico in particular being considered of incomparable strength and beauty.

The vast and elegant interior has little remarkable in the way of painting or sculpture. It contains however the tombs of several illustrious artists, such as Annibale Caracci, Pierin del Vaga, and above all, the immortal Raphael. The striking inscription to his memory is by Cardinal Bembo.

(2) ST. MARIA SOPRA MINERVA.

Near a temple dedicated on this ground by Pompey to the goddess Minerva, stood, from ancient date, a Christian chapel. It was given to the Dominican Fathers in the thirteenth century, and they, by the aid of pious donations, erected in Gothic architecture, the magnificent church we behold to day.

It is rich in works of art and in tombs of illustrious persons. Under the high altar — a work of galvanoplastic metal gilding of great value — reposes the body of St. Catherine of Siena, and in the fine lateral chapel to the right of it, part of the body of St. Thomas Aquinas. Fra Angelico has his resting-place in the passage to the left leading to an exit. The humble sepulchre of Cardinal Bembo is under the pavement of the choir.

The remarkable statue of our Saviour to the left of the high altar is by Michael Angelo; that of St. John the Baptist, to the right, by *Obici* (1885.)

The paintings, sculptures and decorations by distinguished artists are too numerous to mention, even were they within the purpose of the present account.

SATURDAY.

ST. JOHN LATERAN.
(See p. 447)

SUNDAY « IN ALBIS. »

(1) S. PANCRAZIO.

This church was erected probably in the fourth century to the noble Phrygian youth, Pancratius, who came to Rome under Diocletian and received the palm of martyrodom at the early age of fourteen years. This church was reconstructed or restored by Pope Symmacus about the year 500. To the tomb of this saint, Gregory of Tours tells us, the people of Rome used to come to take and ratify their oaths, in the belief that on this spot the sin of perjury would be visited with death.

Restored at various epochs, this basilica was destroyed in the stormy days that ended the last century, and was rebuilt in the beginning of the present one. Little consequently remains of its antiquities. Even the relics were to some extent scattered but it is believed that under the high altar repose the bodies of the titular Saint and of his uncle St. Dionysius, also of St. Victor, and of another St. Pancratius, martyr and bishop of Taormina in Sicily.

In the adjoining catacombs of St. Pancras, or cemetery of Calepodius, so frequently mentioned in the acts of the martyrs, great depredations have likewise been made and the principal marbles and inscriptions carried away.

(2) S. MARIA DELLA SCALA.

Erected in 1492, and entrusted some five years later to the Carmelites, who still hold it, this church draws its name from a picture of the Blessed Virgin painted

over the stairs of a house in Trastevere and concerning which many prodigies were related, it was afterwards brought hither. Francesco da Volterra was the architect of the building, and Ottavio Mascherino of its façade.

Over the door of the church is a statue of the B. Virgin and Child by Valloni. The interior has a single nave. The high altar is from plans by Rainaldi, and most precious is the tabernacle, ornamented with precious stones and with sixteen small columns of Oriental jaspar.

The statues of St. Joseph and of St. Theresa over the choir door are attributed to Bernini. In the first chapel to the right is the exceedingly fine painting of the Beheading of St. John the Baptist, by Gherardo della Notti.

The foot of St. Theresa is here preserved with great veneration, also a piece of the altar of the Presentation; the head of one of the Ursulines Martyrs and some of the relics of the Three Wise Kings, Gaspar, Balthasat and Melchior. The body of St Placidus M. is under the altar of the choir.

The adjoining monastery has been in great part transformed into a police depot.

THE VISIT

OF THE SEVEN CHURCHES
OF ROME

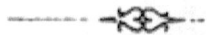

The devout practice known as the visit of the Seven Churches goes back farther than we can trace in history, but the vast development it received during the last few centuries dates from the days of St. Philip Neri. This Saint was profoundly convinced of the spiritual profit of meditating on the combat and victory of the Athletes of Christ, especially on the spot where their relics repose. It was his custom, at first, to pass whole nights in the Cemetery of St. Callixtus, as it was that of St. Charles Borromeo to pass them in the Catacomb of St. Sebastian. St. Philip subsequently varied his devotion by visiting the seven basilicas. Gradually a nucleus of imitators formed itself around him and grew in proportions. A set form was then given to the pious pilgrimage — for such it really was. It received the sanction and encouragement of the ecclesiastical authorities, and from that time succeeding Popes vied with each other in enriching it with indulgences. Pius IX. added greatly to the store.

The round of the Churches may be made, and the indulgences gained by persons singly or collectively. For the plenary indulgences, the usual conditions are required, viz, the intention of acquiring them, and the reception of the sacraments of Penance and the Holy Eucharist and

the prayers for the intentions of the Holy Father the Pope. It suffices to pray in each church at the altar of the Blessed Sacrament. The visit of the other altars pertains to each one's private devotion.

It has been the custom of the faithful, to propose to themselves in this pious journey the triumph of the Church, the extirpation of heresy, the acquirement of virtue, in particular of the seven gifts of the Holy Ghost, and liberation from sin — and especially from the seven capital sins. It has likewise been the custom to pray on the way; to reflect on the seven sorrowful journeys made by our Saviour and on the seven occasions on which his Precious Blood was shed for us; and to read a short account of each church and its relics, before entering.

The reading is done by the head of the group, when there is a certain number.

The method we here give is one of the oldest and best commended.

The following are the seven churches, with the order in which they are visited.
1. St. Peter's (Vatican).
2. St. Paul's (Outside the Walls).
3. St. Sebastian (Via Appia).
4. St. John Lateran.
5. Holy Cross of Jerusalem.
6. St Lawrence (Campo Verano).
7. St. Mary Major.

First Visit.

St. PETER'S.

The visit to this basilica is usually performed the day before that to the others.

PRACTICE. — On the way, meditate on our Saviour's journey, in company with his Apostles, from the Cenaculum to the Garden of Olives, and on the first effusion of his blood, when presented in the Temple. Pray for

deliverance from the vice of gluttony; and beg the holy fear of God.

BEFORE ENTERING. — Read the account of the basilica given above (p.. 456), and reflect on the reverence we should have for this holy shrine, which the Goths and Vandals themselves were accustomed to respect; reverence we owe it, from its origin, from the inestimable number and value of the relics it contains, and from the rich indulgences attached to it. Great saints were accustomed to pay devout visits to this basilica, and even to come from the longest distances for the purpose. We may mention, St. Peter Damian, St. Birgid, St. Catherine of Siena, St. Bernard, St. Francis, St. Sominic, St. Thomas Aquinas, St. Ignatius, St. Joseph Calasanctius, St. Philipp Neri.

Here recite the following psalm and prayer.]

Psalmus 6.

Domine, ne in furore tuo arguas me, * neque in ira tua corripias me.

Miserere mei, Domine, quoniam infirmus sum; sana me Domine, quoniam conturbata sunt ossa mea.

Et anima mea turbata est valde: * sed tu, Domine, usquequo?

Convertere, Domine, et eripe animam meam; * salvum me fac propter misericordiam tuam.

Quoniam non est in morte, qui memor sit tui; * in inferno autem quis confitebitur tibi?

Laboravi in gemitu meo, lavabo per singulas noctes lectum meum, * lacrymis meis stratum meum rigabo.

Turbatus est a furore oculus meus, * inveteravi inter omnes inimicos meos.

Discedite a me omnes, qui operamini iniquitatem, * quoniam exaudivit Dominus vocem fletus mei.

Exaudivit Dominus deprecationem meam, * Dominus orationem meam suscepit.

Erubescant et conturbentur vehementer omnes inimici mei, * convertantur et erubescant valde velociter. Requiem etc.

   Kyrie Eleison.
   Christe Eleison.
   Kyrie Eleison.

Psalm 6.

1 O Lord, rebuke me not in thine indignation: nor chastise me in thy wrath.

2 Have mercy upon me, O Lord, for I am weak: heal me, O Lord, for my bones are troubled.

3 My soul also is troubled exceedingly: but thou O Lord, how long?

4 Turn thee, O Lord, and deliver my soul: O save me for thy mercy's sake.

5 For in death there is no one that remembereth thee: and who will give thee thanks in hell?

6 I have laboured in my groanings, every night will I wash my bed; and water my couch with my tears.

7 Mine eye is troubled through indignation; I have grown old among all mine enemies.

8 Depart from me, all ye that work iniquity: for the Lord hath heard the voice of my weeping.

9 The Lord hath heard my supplication: the Lord hath received my prayer.

10 Let all mine enemies be ashamed and sore vexed: let them be turned back, and be ashamed very speedily.

   Gloria etc.
   Lord have mercy on us,
   Christ have mercy on us.
   Lord have mercy on us.

Pater noster.
Et ne nos etc.
V. Ego dixi Domine miserere mei.
R. Sana animam meam quia peccavi tibi.
V. Domine non secundum peccata nostra facias nobis.
R. Neque secundum iniquitates nostras retribuas nobis.
V. Domine, exaudi orationem meam.
R. Et clamor meus ad te veniat.

Oremus.

Omnipotens, et mitissime Deus, qui sitienti populo fontem viventis aquae de petra produxisti; educ de cordis nostri duritia lacrymas compunctionis, ut peccata nostra plangere valeamus, remissionemque eorum, te miserante, mereamur accipere, per Christum Dominum nostrum.
Amen.

Our Father.
Lead us not, etc.
V. I said, Lord have mercy upon me.
R. Heal my soul for I have sinned against thee.
V. O Lord, deal not with us according to our sins.
R. Do not measure out to us according to our iniquities.
V. O Lord hear my prayer.
R. And let my cry come unto thee.

Let us pray.

O Almighty and most merciful God, who from a rock didst produce for a thirsting people a fountain of living water, call forth now from the hardness of our hearts tears of compunction, that we may be able to weep for our sins, and merit through thy mercy to receive forgiveness of them. through Christ our Lord, Amen.

Let us then make a short meditation on the sufferings of Jesus for our salvation. As yet an infant He shed His Blood for us; and we Christians think only of joys and satisfactions. If we are to rejoice with Jesus in Heaven, we must suffer, after His example, on earth. Let us strive after the mortification of our appetites, and say this prayer.

O my Lord Jesus Christ, I adore and thank Thee for all the painful journeys Thou didst make for my sake, and for the shedding of Thy blood whilst yet an infant. I implore of thee to grant me the mortification of my appetites and the gift of thy holy fear. Amen.

Inside: at the altar of the Blessed Sacrament, let us make an act of contrition, say five Our Fathers, five Hail Marys, five Glorias, and the Apostles Creed, and ask our Redeemer's blessing in the Holy Eucharist.

At the altar of the B. V. M. three Hail Marys, and the Hail Holy Queen.

At the tomb of the Apostles, three Our Fathers, three Hail Marys, three Glorias, and the Creed.

An Our Father, and a Hail Mary to all the Saints whose relics are preserved in this basilica.

Second Visit.

ST PAUL'S (Outside the Walls)

Practice. Reflect on the journey made by Jesus, when, bound with cords, he was led from the Garden of Olives; also on the second effusion of His blood, viz, in the sweat of blood in the Garden; and ask freedom from the vice of anger, and the gift of piety.

(*Note.* As the visit to St. Peter's is supposed to have been made for convenience sake on the day before, we begin by the prayers called *Itinerarium,* or prayers on setting out on a journey. If however S. Peter's is visited on the same day as the others, then the Itinerarium is recited first of all.).

Setting out, say the following prayers.

Ant. In viam pacis, et prosperitatis dirigat nos omnipotens, et misericors Dominus, et Angelus Raphael comitetur nobiscum in via, ut cum pace, salute, et gaudio revertamur ad propria.

Benedictus Dominus Deus Israel: * quia visitavit, et fecit redemptionem plebis suae.

Anth. May the omnipotent and merciful Lord direct us in the path of peace and prosperity, and may the Angel Raphael accompany us on the way, so that with peace, well-being, and joy we may return to our own.

1 Blessed be the Lord God of Israel: for he hath visited and wrought the redemption of his people.

Et erexit cornu salutis nobis, * in domo David pueri sui.

Sicut locutus est per os sanctorum, * qui a saeculo sunt Prophetarum ejus.
Salutem ex inimicis nostris, * et de manu omnium qui oderunt nos.
Ad faciendam misericordiam cum patribus nostris, * et memorari testamenti sui sancti.
Jusjurandum quod juravit ad Abraham patrem nostrum, * daturum se nobis.
Ut sine timore, de manu inimicorum nostrorum liberati, * serviamus illi.

In sanctitate et justitia coram ipso, * omnibus diebus nostris.
Et tu, puer, Propheta Altissimi vocaberis; * praeibis enim ante faciem Domini, parare vias ejus.

Ad dandam scientiam salutis plebi ejus; * in remissionem peccatorum eorum.

Per viscera misericordiae Dei nostri; * in quibus visitavit nos oriens ex alto.

Illuminare his, qui in tenebris et in umbra mortis sedent; * ad dirigendos pedes nostros in viam pacis.
Gloria, etc.
Ant. In viam pacis (ut supra).

2 And hath raised up a horn of salvation to us; in the house of his servant David.
3 As he spake by the mouth of his holy prophets: who are from the beginning.
4 Salvation from our enemies; and from the hand of all that hate us.
5 To perform mercy to our fathers; and to remember his holy testament,
6 The oath that he swore to Abraham our father: that he would grant unto us;
7 That being delivered from the hands of our enemies; we may serve him without fear.
8 In holiness and justice before him: all the days of our life.
9 And thou, child, shalt be called the Prophet of the Highest; for thou shalt go before the face of the Lord to prepare his ways.
10 To give knowledge of salvation unto his people: for the remission of their sins.
11 Through the bowels of the mercy of our God: whereby the orient from on high hath visited us.
12 To enlighten them that sit in darkness, and in the shadow of death: to direct our feet into the way of peace. Glory etc.
Anth. May the omnipotent, etc. (as above).

Kyrie Eleison.
Christe Eleison.
Kyrie Eleison.
Pater noster.
V. Et ne nos inducas in tentationem.
R. Sed libera nos a malo.
V. Salvos fac servos tuos.
R. Deus meus sperantes in te.
V. Mitte nobis Domine auxilium de sancto.
R. Et de Sion tuere nos.

V. Esto nobis Domine turris fortitudinis.
R. A facie inimici.

V. Nihil proficiat inimicus in nobis.
R. Et filius iniquitatis non apponat nocere nobis.
V. Benedictus Dominus die quotidie.
R. Prosperum iter faciat nobis Deus salutarium nostrorum.
V. Vias tuas Domine demonstra nobis.
R. Et semitas tuas edoce nos.
V. Utinam dirigantur viae nostrae.
R. Ad custodiendas justificationes tuas.
V. Erunt prava in directa.

R. Et aspera in vias planas.
V. Angelis suis Deus mandavit de te.
R. Ut custodiant te in omnibus viis tuis.

Lord have mercy on us.
Christ have mercy on us,
Lord have mercy on us.
Our Father,
V. Lead us not into temptation.
R. But deliver us from evil.
V. Save thy servants.
R. My God, who hope in thee.
V. Lend us help, O Lord, from the holy place.
R. And from Sion protect us,
V. Be to us O Lord, a tower of strength.
R. Against the face of the enemy.
V. Let the enemy prevail not against us.
R. And the son of iniquity no undertake to injure us.
V. Blessed be the Lord each day.
R. May the God of our safety, grant us a prosperous journey.
V. Show us O Lord, thy ways.
R. And teach us thy paths.
V. May our steps be directed.
R. To guarding thy just decrees,
V. The devious will be made straight.
R. And the rugged turned into smooth ways.
V. God has given thee in trust to his Angels.
R. That they may guard thee in all thy ways.

V. Domine exaudi orationem meam.

R. Et clamor meus ad te veniat.

V. Dominus vobiscum.

R. Et cum Spiritu tuo.

Oremus.

Deus, qui filios Israel per maris medium sicco vestigio ire fecisti, quique tribus magis iter ad te, stella duce, pandidisti: tribue prosperum, tempusque tranquillum, ut Angelo tuo sancto comite, ad eum, quo pergimus locum, ac demum ad aeternae salutis portum pervenire feliciter valeamus.

Deus, qui Abraham puerum tuum, de Ur Chaldaeorum eductum, per omn s suae peregrinationis vias, illaesum custodisti: quaesumus, ut nos famulos tuos custodire digneris: Esto nobis Domine in procinctu suffragium, in via solatium, in pluvia et frigore tegumentum, in lassitudine vehiculum, in adversitate praesidium, in lubrico baculus, in naufragio portus; ut te duce, quo tendimus prospere perveniamus, e demum incolumes ad propria redeamus.

Adesto, quaesumus Domine, supplicationibus nostris:

V. Lord hear my prayer.

R. And let my cry come unto thee.

V. The Lord be with you.

R. And with thy spirit.

Let us pray.

O God, thou who through the sea didst make the sons of Israel walk with dry footsteps, and who by the guidance of a star, didst show the three kings the way to thee, grant us, we beseech thee, a successful journey, and calm weather, so that, accompanied by the holy Angel we may be able to happily reach the place whither we tend, and finally the harbour of eternal salvation.

O God, who didst bring they servant Abraham out of Ur of the Chaldees, and didst preserve him safe through all his wanderings, deign, we beseech thee, to grant us thy servants; be to us, O Lord, a source of strength in peril, a consolation in journeying, a shade in heat, a shelter in rain and cold, a vehicle in fatigue, a help in adversity, a support in slippery places, placed as a harbour in shipwreck, so that, under thy guidance, we may successfully reach our destination, and afterwards safely return to our own.

Favour, O Lord, we beseech thee, our supplications, and

et viam famulorum tuorum in salutis tuae prosperitate dispone: ut inter omnes viae et vitae hujus varietates tuo semper protegamur auxilio.

Praesta, quaesumus omnipotens Deus. ut familia tua per viam salutis incedat, et B. Joannis praecursoris tui hortamenta sectando, ad eum, quem praedixit, secura perveniat Dominum nostrum Jesum Christum Filium tuum, qui tecum vivit et regnat in unitate Spiritus Sancti Deus, per omnia saecula saeculorum, Amen.

V. Procedamus in pace.
R. In nomine Christi.
Amen.

dispose the path of thy servants in the prosperity of thy salvation so that amongst all the vicissitudes of this life and journey, we may constantly be protected by thy assistance.

Grant, we beseech thee, Almighty God, that thy family may walk in the paths of salvation, and that, following the precepts of the precursor, safely reach him, whom Saint John foretold, our Lord Jesus Christ, thy son, who with thee and the Holy Ghost, lives and reigns one God, world without end, Amen.

V. Let us proceed in peace.
R. In the name of Christ.
Amen.

(Here ends the *Itinerarium*, properly so called. Continue with the following prayers.)

Actiones nostras, quaesumus Domine, aspirando praeveni, et adjuvando prosequere, ut cuncta nostra oratio et operatio a te semper incipiat, et per te coepta finiatur. Per Christum Dominum nostrum.
R. Amen.

Veni Creator Spiritus,
Mentes tuorum visita,
Imple superna gratia,
Quae tu creasti pectora.

Anticipate. O Lord, we beseech Thee, our actions, and accompany them by Thy help, so that our every prayer and work may in Thee have its beginning and in Thee its end. Through Christ our Lord. Amen.

Come, O Creator Spirit blest!
And in our souls take up thy rest;
Come, with thy grace and heavenly aid,
To fill the hearts which thou hast made.

VISIT TO THE SEVEN CHURCHES

Qui diceris Paraclitus,
Altissimi donum Dei,
Fons vivus, ignis, charitas,
Et spiritalis unctio.

Great Paraclete! to thee we cry;
O highest gift of God most high!
O fount of life! O fire of love!
And sweet anointing from above!

Tu septiformis munere,
Digitus Paternae dexterae,
Tu rite promissum Patris,
Sermone ditans guttura.

Thou in thy sevenfold gifts art known;
The finger of God's hand we own;
The promise of the Father thou!
Who dost the tongue with pow'r endow.

Accende lumen sensibus,
Infunde amorem cordibus,
Infirma nostri corporis.
Virtute firmans perpeti.

Kindle our senses from above,
And make our hearts o'rflow with love; [high,
With patience firm, and virtue
The weakness of our flesh supply.

Hostem repellas longius,
Pacemque dones protinus;
Ductore sic te praevio
Vitemus omne noxium.

Far from us drive the foe we dread,
And grant us thy true peace instead, [guide,
So shall we not, with thee for
Turn from the path of life aside.

Per te sciamus da Patrem,
Noscamus atque Filium,
Teque utriusque Spiritum
Credamus omni tempore.

Oh, may thy grace on us bestow,
The Father and the Son to know,
And thee through endless times confess'd
Of both th'eternal Spirit blest.

Deo Patri sit gloria,
Et Filio qui a mortuis
Surrexit, ac Paraclito,
In saeculorum saecula.
    Amen.

All glory while the ages run
Be to the Father, and the Son
Who rose from death; the same to thee,
O Holy Ghost, eternally.
    Amen.

Veni, Sancte Spiritus reple

Come, O Holy Spirit, fill

tuorum corda fidelium, et tui amoris in eis ignem accende.

℣. Emitte Spiritum tuum, et creabuntur.
℟. Et renovabis faciem terrae.

Oremus

Deus, qui corda fidelium dancti Spiritus illustratione Socuisti; da nobis in eodem Spiritu recta sapere, et de ejus semper consolatione gaudere. Per Christum Dominum nostrum. ℟. Amen.

the hearts of Thy faithful and enkindle in them the fire of Thy love.

℣. Send forth Thy Spirit, and They shall be created.
℟. And Thou shalt renew the face of he earth.

Let us pray

O God, who hast taught the hearts of Thy faithful by the light of the Holy Spirit, grant us by the same Spirit to think the thing that be right, and ever to rejoice in His consolations; through Christ our Lord Amen.

Leaving the Porta S. Paolo, we recite the first five decades of the Rosary, viz. The Joyful Mysteries. After that, the *De Profundis* for the faithful departed.

De profundis clamavi ad te, Domine; * Domine, exaudi vocem meam.

Fiant aures tuae intendentes * in vocem deprecationis meae.

Si iniquitates observaveris, Domine, * Domine, quis sustinebit?

Quia apud te propitiatio est: * et propter legem tuam sustinui te, Domine.

Sustinuit anima mea in verbo ejus, * speravit anima mea in Domino.

A custodia matutina usque ad noctem * speret Israël in Domino.

Quia apud Dominum mi-

1 Out of the depths have I cried unto thee, O Lord: Lord, hear my voice.

2 Oh, let thine ears consider well: the voice of my supplication.

3 If thou, O Lord, shalt mark iniquities: Lord, who shall abide it?

4 For with thee there is propitiation; and because of thy law I have waited for thee, O Lord.

5 My soul hath waited on his word: my soul hath hoped in the Lord.

6 From the morning watch even until night: let Israel hope in the Lord.

7 For with the Lord there

sericordia, * et copiosa apud eum redemptio.
Et ipse redimet Israël * ex omnibus iniquitatibus eius.

is mercy: and with him is plenteous redemption.
8 And he shall redeem Israel; from all his iniquities.
Glory etc.

THE MISERERE

Ant. Exultabunt Domino ossa humiliata.
Miserere mei, Deus : * secundum magnam misericordiam tuam.
Et secundum multitudinem miserationum tuarum: * dele iniquitatem meam.
Amplius lava me ab iniquitate mea : * et a peccato meo munda me.
Quoniam iniquitatem meam ego cognosco: * et peccatum meum contra me est semper.
Tibi soli peccavi, et malum coram te feci : * ut iustificeris in sermonibus tuis, et vincas cum iudicaris.

Ecce enim in iniquitatibus conceptus sum: * et in peccatis concepit me mater mea.

Ecce enim veritatem dilexisti : * incerta et occulta sapientiae tuae manifestasti mihi.

Asperges me hyssopo, et mundabor : * lavabis me, et super nivem dealbabor.

Auditui meo dabis gaudium

Anth. The bones that were humbled shall rejoice.
1 Have mercy upon me, O God: according to thy great mercy.
2 And according to the multitude of thy tender mercies: blot my iniquity.
3 Wash me yet more from my iniquity: and cleanse me from my sin.
4 For I acknowledge my iniquity: and my sin is always before me.
5 Against thee only have I sinned, and done evil in thy sight : that thou mayest be justified in thy words, and mayest overcome when thou art judged.
6 For behold, I was conceived in iniquities: and in sins did my mother conceive me.
7 For behold, thou hast loved truth: the uncertain and hidden things of thy wisdom thou hast made manifest unto me.
8 Thou shalt sprinkle me with hyssop, and I shall be cleansed: thou shalt wash me and I shall be made whiter than snow.
9 Thou shalt make me hear

et laetitiam: * et exultabunt ossa humiliata.

Averte faciem tuam a peccatis meis: * et omnes iniquitates meas dele.

Cor mundum crea in me, Deus: * et spiritum rectum innova in visceribus meis.

Ne projicias me a facie tua:* et Spiritum sanctum tuum ne auferas a me.

Redde mihi laetitiam salutaris tui: * et spiritu principali confirma me.

Docebo iniquos vias tuas: * et impii ad te convertentur.

Libera me de sanguinibus, Deus, Deus salutis meae: * et exultabit lingua mea iustitiam tuam.

Domine, labia mea aperies: * et os meum annuntiabit laudem tuam.

Quoniam si voluisses sacrificium, dedissem utique: * holocaustis non delectaberis.

Sacrificium Deo spiritus contribulatus: * cor contritum et humiliatum, Deus, non despicies.

Benigne fac, Domine, in bona voluntate tua Sion: * ut aedificentur muri Jerusalem.

Tunc acceptabis sacrificium iustitiae, oblationes, et holocausta: * tunc imponent super altare tuum vitulos.

Gloria Patri, etc.

of joy and gladness: and the bones that were humbled shall rejoice.

10 Turn away thy face from my sins: and blot out all my iniquities.

11 Create in me a clean heart, O God: and renew a right spirit within my bowels.

12 Cast me not away from thy presence: and take not thy holy Spirit from me.

13 Restore unto me the joy of thy salvation: and strengthen me with a perfect spirit.

14 I will teach the unjust thy ways: and the wicked shall be converted unto thee.

15 Deliver me from blood, O God, thou God of my salvation: and my tongue shall extol thy justice.

16 Thou shalt open my lips, O Lord: and my mouth shall declare thy praise.

17 For if thou hadst desired sacrifice, I would surely have given it: with burnt-offerings thou wilt not be delighted.

18 The sacrifice to God is an afflicted spirit: a contrite and humble heart, O God, thou wilt not despise.

19 Deal favourably, O Lord, in thy good will with Sion: that the walls of Jerusalem may be built up.

20 Then shalt thou accept the sacrifices of justice, oblations and whole burnt-offerings; then shall they lay calves upon thine altars.

Glory, etc.

Ant. Exultabunt (ut supra).

Ant. Si iniquitates observaveris, Domine, Domine quis sustinebit.
Ps. De profundis etc.
Ant. Si iniquitates (ut supra).
Kyrie Eleison.
Christe Eleison.
Kyrie Eleison.
Pater noster.
V. Et ne nos inducas in tentationem.
R. Sed libera nos a malo.

V. A porta inferi.
R. Erue Domine animas eorum.
V. Requiescant in pace.
R. Amen.
V. Domine exaudi orationem meam.
R. Et clamor meus ad te veniat.

Oremus.

Fidelium, Deus, omnium conditor et Redemptor, animabus famulorum, famularumque tuarum, remissionem cunctorum tribue peccatorum: ut indulgentiam, quam semper optaverunt, piis supplicationibus consequantur. Qui vivis et regnas.
Amen.

Anth. The bones (as above)

Anth. If thou, O Lord, shalt mark iniquities: Lord, who shall abide it?
Ps. Out of the depths, etc.
Anth. If thou (as above)

Lord have mercy on us.
Christ have mercy on us.
Lord have mercy on us.
Our Father.
V. Lead as not into temptation.
R. But deliver us from evil.

V. From the gates of hell,
R. Deliver O Lord their souls.
V. May they rest in peace.
R. Amen.
V. O Lord, hear my prayer.
R. And let my cry come unto thee.

Let us pray.

Oh God, the Creator and Redeemer of all the faithful, grant to the souls of thy servants departed the remission of all their sins, that they may obtain through pious supplications, that mercy which they have always desired. Who livest world without end Amen.

Arrived at the Portico of St. Paul's, let us read what is given above (p. 484) concerning this basilica. The number of relics it contains, and of indulgences it is endowed with is very great. In the chapel of the Blessed Sacrament is the miraculous crucifix, and immediately beneath it, the

picture of Our Lady, before which St. Ignatius Loyola and his companions, made the first solemn religious profession of his order. Let us resolve to visit this august sanctuary with all the devotion possible, and to fervently pray the great apostle of the gentiles that he may obtain for us a spark of that zeal and charity with which he burned for the salvation of souls. Let us pray too, that we may be delivered from those earthly attachments that lead us to offend our loving Redeemer.

Entering, we now say the second penitential psalm:

Psalmus 31.

Beati quorum remissae sunt iniquitates, * et quorum tecta sunt peccata.

Beatus vir, cui non imputavit Dominus peccatum; * nec est in spiritu ejus dolus.

Quoniam tacui, inveteraverunt ossa mea, * dum clamarem tota die.

Quoniam die ac nocte gravata est super me manus tua,* conversus sum in aerumna mea, dum configitur spina.

Delictum meum cognitum tibi feci, * et injustitiam meam non abscondi.

Dixi: Confitebor adversum me injustitiam meam Domino: * et tu remisisti impietatem peccati mei.

Pro hac orabit ad te omnis sanctus * in tempore opportuno.

Verumtamen in diluvio aquarum multarum * ad cum non approximabunt.

Psalm 31.

1 Blessed are they whose iniquities are forgiven: and whose sins are covered.

2 Blessed is the man to whom the Lord hath not imputed sin: and in whose spirit there is no guile.

3 Because I was silent, my bones grew old: while I cried aloud all the day long.

4 For day and night thy hand was heavy upon me: I turned in my anguish, while the thorn was fastened in me.

5 I have acknowledged my sin unto thee: and my injustice I have not concealed.

6 I said I will confess against myself my injustice to the Lord: and thou forgavest the wickedness of my sin.

7 For this shall every one that is holy pray unto thee: in a seasonable time.

8 And yet in a flood of many waters they shall not come nigh unto him.

Tu es refugium meum a tribulatione, quae circumdedit me: * exsultatio mea, erue me a circumdantibus me.

Intellectum tibi dabo, et instruam te in via hac, qua gradieris: * firmabo super te oculos meos.

Nolite fieri sicut equus et mulus, * quibus non est intellectus.

In camo et freno maxillas eorum constringe, * qui non approximant ad te.

Multa flagella peccatoris: * sperantem autem in Domine misericordia circumdabit.

Laetamini in Domino et exsultate, justi; * et gloriamini, omnes recti corde.

Gloria Patri, et Filio, etc.

Kyrie eleison.
Christe eleison.
Kyrie eleison.
Pater noster.
V. Et ne nos inducas in tentationem.
R. Ego dixi Domine etc. (ut supra p.   ).

Oremus.

Deus, qui nullum respuis, sed quantumvis peccantibus per poenitentiam pia miseratione placaris: respice propitius ad preces humilitatis nostrae, et illumina corda nostra ut tua valeamus implere

9 Thou art my refuge from the trouble which hath surrounded me: my joy, deliver me from them that compass me about.

10 I will give thee understanding, and will instruct thee in the way, wherein thou shalt go: I will fix mine eyes upon thee.

11 Be ye not like unto horse and mule: which have no understanding.

12 With bit and bridle bind fast the jaws of those: who come not nigh unto thee.

13 Many are the scourges of the sinner; but mercy shall compass him about that hopeth in the Lord.

14 Be glad in the Lord and rejoice ye just, and glory all ye right of heart.

Glory, etc.

Lord have mercy on us.
Christ have mercy on us.
Lord have mercy on us.
Our Father.
V. Lead us not into temptation.
R. But deliver us from evil.
V. I said to. (as above p.)

Let us pray.

O God, who rejectest no one, but in thy divine mercy dost become lenient even towards sinners, when they do penance; look down propitiously on the prayers of our lowliness, and illuminate

praecepta. Per Christum Dominum nostrum. Amen.

our hearts, that we may be able to fulfil thy precepts.
Through Christ our Lord. Amen.

Let us here pause, meditate a while, and make a mental prayer in some such words as these: —

My Lord Jesus, I adore thee; and I thank thee for all the painful journeys thou didst make for my sake, and especially for that ignominious one thou madest, bound with cords, from the Garden to the house of Annas. I thank thee likewise for shedding thy blood for me in the Garden of Olives. I implore of thee to grant me the virtue of patience, and the spirit of piety.

At the altar of the Blessed Sacrament. Make an Act of contrition, and then recite this Hymn:

HYMNUS.
Tantum ergo Sacramentum
Veneremur cernui:
Et antiquum documentum
Novo cedat ritui;
Praestet fides supplementum
Sensuum defectui.

HYMN.
Lowly bending, deep adoring,
Lo! the Sacrament we hail;
Types and shadows have their ending,
Newer rites of grace prevail;
Faith for all defects supplying.
Where the feeble senses fail.

Genitori, Genitoque
Laus et jubilatio,
Salus, honor, virtus quoque
Sit et benedictio:
Procedenti ab utroque
Compar sit laudatio. Amen.

Glory, honour, might, dominion,
Be unto our God most high;
To the Father, Son, and Spirit,
Ever blessed Trinity,
Praise be given, and power eternal,
Unto all eternity.

V. Panem de coelo praestitisti eis.
R. Omne delectamentum in se habentem.

Oremus

Deus, qui nobis sub Sacramento mirabili, passionis tuae memoriam reliquisti: tribue, quaesumus, ita nos corporis et sanguinis tui sacra mysteria venerari, ut redemptionis tuae fructum in nobis jugiter sentiamus. Qui vivis, etc.

Amen.

V. Thou didst give them bread from heaven.
R. Containing in itself all sweetness,

Let us pray

O God, who, under a wonderful Sacrament, hast left us a memorial of thy passion: grant us, we beseech thee, so to venerate the sacred mysteries of thy body and blood, that we may ever feel within us the fruit of thy redemption. Who livest, &c.

Amen.

Then five Pater, Ave, and Glorias; an Act of the love of God; and a prayer for the blessing of Jesus from the Holy Eucharist. (And thus at the altar of the Blessed Sacrament in all the churches.)

Before the Miraculous Crucifix.

V. Christus factus est pro nobis obediens usque ad mortem, mortem autem Crucis. Propter quod et Deus exaltavit illum, et dedit illi nomen, quod est super omne nomen. Popule meus, quid feci tibi? Aut in quo contristavi te? Responde mihi.

Ant. O Crux splendidior cunctis astris, mundo celebris, hominibus multum amabilis, sanctior universis, quae sola fuisti digna portare talentum mundi: dulce lignum, dulces clavos, dulcia ferens pondera: salva praesentem catervam,

V. Christ was made for us obedient unto death, even to the death of the Cross. On account of which God exalted him, and gave him a name which is above every name. My people, what have I done to you? Or in what way did I grieve you? Answer me.

Anth. O Cross, more resplendent than all the stars, renowned throughout the world, exceedingly beloved of men, more holy than other things, in as much as thou wast made worthy to bear the price of the world. Prec-

in tuis hodie laudibus congregatam.

V. Hoc signum Crucis erit in Coelo.
R. Cum Dominus ad judicandum venerit.
Oremus.
Perpetua nobis, quaesumus Domine, pace custodi, quos per lignum S. Crucis redimere dignatus es. Qui vivis et regnas in saecula saeculorum. Amen.

ious wood, precious nails, that bore such a precious burden. Save the present gathering, assembled to-day to chant thy praises.
V. This sign of the Cross will be in the heavens.
R. When the Lord shall come to judge.
Let us Pray.
Guard, O Lord, we beseech thee, in perpetual peace, us whom thou didst deign to reedem by the wood of the holy Cross. Who livest and reignest world without end. Amen.

Three Pater, Ave, and Glorias,

At the " Confession, ,, or Papal Altar.

One Pater, Ave and Gloria.

Ant. Gloriosi principes terrae, quomodo in vita sua dilexerunt se, ita et in morte non sunt separati.

V. In omnem terram exivit sonus eorum.
R. Et in fines orbis terrae verba eorum,
Oremus.
Protege, Domine, populum tuum, et Apostolorum tuorum Petri et Pauli patrocinio confidentem perpetua defensione conserva. Per Christum Dominum nostrum. Amen.

Anth. These glorious princes of the earth, as in their life time they loved each other, so in death they are not separated.

V. Throughout the whole earth spread their sounds.
R. And to the ends of the world their words.
Let us Pray
Protect, O Lord, thy people, and under thy constant guard preserve it, relying on the patronage of thy Apostles, Peter and Paul. Through Christ our Lord. Amen.

APOSTLES' CREED.

Credo in Deum, Patrem omnipotentem, Creatorem coeli et terrae. Et in Jesum Christum, Filium ejus unicum, Dominum nostrum; qui conceptus est de Spiritu Sancto, natus ex Maria Virgine, passus sub Pontio Pilato, crucifixus, mortuus, et sepultus; descendit ad inferos; tertia die resurrexit a mortuis; ascendit ad coelos, sedet ad dexteram Dei Patris omnipotentis; inde venturus est judicare vivos et mortuos. Credo in Spiritum Sanctum, sanctam Ecclesiam Catholicam, Sanctorum communionem, remissionem peccatorum, carnis resurrectionem, vitam aeternam. Amen.

I believe in God, the Father Almighty, Creator of heaven and earth. And in Jesus Christ, His only Son, our Lord; who was conceived by the Holy Ghost, born of the Virgin Mary, suffered under Pontius Pilate, was crucified, dead, and buried; he descended into hell; the third day he rose again from the dead; he ascended into heaven, and sitteth at the right hand of God, the Father Almighty; from thence he shall come to judge the living and the dead. I believe in the Holy Ghost, the Holy Catholic Church, the communion of Saints, the forgiveness of sins, the resurrection of the body, and the life everlasting. Amen.

To all the Saints whose relics repose here,

Pater, Ave, Gloria.

Ant. Sancti Dei omnes intercedete pro nostra omniumque salute.

V. Laetamini in Domino et exultate justi.

R. Et gloriamini omnes recti corde.

Oremus.

Concede, quaesumus omnipotens Deus, ut intercessio nos sanctae Dei Genitricis Mariae, sanctorumque omnium, quorum corpora et reliquiae in hac sacrosancta basilica requiescunt, ubique

Ant. Saints of God, intercede for the salvation of us and all.

V. Rejoice in the Lord, and exult, O ye just.

R. And be glad, all ye right of heart.

Let us pray.

Grant, we beseech thee, O omnipotent God, that the intercession of Mary the holy Mother of God, and of all the saints whose bodies and relics repose in this holy basilica, may be everywhere

laetificet, ut dum eorum merita recolimus patrocinia sentiamus. Per Christum Dominum nostrum. Amen.

a source of gladness, so that whilst we reflect on their merits, we may experience their patronage. Through.

At Our Lady's Altar.

HYMNUS.
Ave maris stella,
Dei Mater alma,
Atque semper virgo,
Felix coeli porta.

Sumens illud Ave
Gabrielis ore,
Funda nos in pace,
Mutans Evae nomen.

Solve vincla reis,
Profer lumen caecis,
Mala nostra pelle,
Bona cuncta posce.

Monstra te esse matrem,
Sumat per te preces
Qui pro nobis natus,
Tulit esse tuus.

Virgo singularis,
Inter omnes mitis,
Nos culpis solutos,
Mites fac et castos.

Vitam praesta puram,
Iter para tutum,
Ut videntes Jesum,
Semper collaetemur.

Sit laus Deo Patri,
Summo Christo decus,
Spiritui Sancto,
Tribus honor unus. Amen.

V. Ora pro nobis sancta Dei Genitrix.

R. Ut digni efficiamur promissionibus Christi.

Oremus.
Defende, quaesumus Domine, Beata Maria semper Vir-

HYMN.
Hail, bright Star of ocean,
God's own Mother blest,
Ever-sinless Virgin.
Gate of heav'nly rest;

Taking that sweet Ave
Which from Gabriel came,
Peace confirm within us,
Changing Eva's name.

Break the captive's fetters;
Light on blindness pour;
All our ills expelling,
Ev'ry bliss implore.

Shew thyself a mother;
May the Word divine,
Born for us thine infant,
Hear our prayers thro' thine.

Virgin all excelling,
Mildest of the mild,
Freed from guilt, preserve us
Meek and undefiled;

Keep our life all spotless,
Make our way secure,
Till we find in Jesus
Joy for evermore.

Through the highest heaven
To the Almighty Three,
Father, Son, and Spirit,
One same glory be. Amen.

V. Pray for us, O holy Mother of God.

R. That we may be made worthy of the promises of Christ.

Let us pray.
Defend, O Lord, we beseech thee, through the in-

gine intercedente, istam ab omni adversitate familiam; et toto corde tibi prostratam ab hostium propitius tuere clementer insidiis. Per Christum Dominum nostrum. Amen.

tercession of the Blessed Mary ever Virgin, this family from all adversity, and mercifully guard it, prostrated before Thee with humble heart, all snares. Through. Amen.

THIRD VISIT.

ST. SEBASTIAN.

Practice. Reflect on our Saviour's journey from the house of Annas to that of Caiphas; also on the third effusion of His blood, in the scourging at the pillar; and ask the virtue of purity and the gift of knowledge.

On the way from St. Paul's to the church of St. Sebastian say Matins and Lauds of the Little Office of the Blessed Virgin, or the second part of the Rosary, that is, the Sorrowful Mysteries.

In the Porch, read the following account.

This basilica is believed to have been first erected by Constantine over the Catacombs and dedicated by Pope Sylvester. It was reconstructed by St. Damasus, in 367, and some half a century later received a new consecration from Innocent I. It was rebuilt in 1611.

The interior has a single nave. In the first chapel to the right are many precious relics; here St. Gregory preached his 37th Homily.

The chapel opposite is dedicated to the titular saint. There is still preserved part of his body, the column at which he was scourged, and an arrow, with which he was transfixed.

This church has been endowed by the supreme Pontiffs with many extraordinary indulgences, and the esteem in which it has been held by the faithful has always been very great, especially for the reason that for many years the bodies of St. Peter and St. Paul were concealed for safety in the Platonia, during the persecution under Valerian

in 258. Hither, on Good Friday, as far back as the days of Paschal II., the people were accustomed to come barefooted, reciting prayers and singing hymns.

In the basilica is an altar dedicated to St. Charles Borromeo, and another in the neighbourhood to St. Philip Neri. These saints were, as we have said, in the habit of spending whole nights in prayer in the Catacombs of St. Sebastian and of St. Callixtus, respectively; and St. Charles is here represented, in the painting that adorns his altar, in the act of gathering and venerating the bones and relics of the holy martyrs.

Entering the sacred edifice we should try to be inspired with the sentiments of these two saints. How tepid and indevout we are when compared with them! Let us approach with humility and contrition the God of Hosts and ask his mercy and compassion.

Here recite as follows:

Psalmus.

Domine, ne in furore tuo arguas me, * neque in ira tua corripias me.

Quoniam sagittae tuae infixae sunt mihi: * et confirmasti super me manum tuam.

Non est sanitas in carne mea a facie irae tuae: * non est pax ossibus meis a facie peccatorum meorum.

Quoniam iniquitates meae supergressae sunt caput meum: * et sicut onus grave gravatae sunt super me.

Putruerunt et corruptae sunt cicatrices meae, * a facie insipientiae meae.

Miser factus sum et curvatus sum usque in finem: * tota die contristatus ingrediebar.

Psalm.

1. O Lord rebuke me not in thine indignation: nor chastise me in thy wrath.

2. For thine arrows stick fast in me: and thou hast laid thy hand heavily upon me.

3. There is no health in my flesh because of thy wrath: there is no rest to my bones because of my sins.

4. For my iniquities are gone over my head: and, like a heavy burden, press sorely upon me.

5. My wounds have putrified and are corrupt: because of my foolishness.

6. I am become miserable, and am bowed down even to the end: I go sorrowfully all the day long.

Quoniam lumbi mei impleti sunt illusionibus; * et non est sanitas in carne mea.

Afflictus sum et humiliatus sum nimis: * rugiebam a gemitu cordis mei.

Domine, ante te omne desiderium meum: * et gemitus meus a te non est absconditus.

Cor meum conturbatum est, dereliquit me virtus mea: * et lumen oculorum meorum, et ipsum non est mecum.

Amici mei, et proximi mei * adversum me appropinquaverunt, et steterunt.

Et qui juxta me erant, de longe steterunt; * et vim faciebant qui quaerebant animam meam.

Et qui inquirebant mala mihi, locuti sunt vanitates, * et dolos tota die meditabantur.

Ego autem tamquam surdus non audiebam: * et sicut mutus non aperiens os suum.

Et factus sum sicut homo non audiens, * et non habens in ore suo redargutiones.

Quoniam in te, Domine, speravi: * tu exaudies me Domine Deus meus.

Quia dixi: Nequando supergaudeant mihi inimici mei * et dum commoventur pedes mei, super me magna locuti sunt.

Quoniam ego in flagella paratus sum: * et dolor meus in conspectu meo semper.

7. For my loins are filled with illusions: and there is no soundness in my flesh.

8. I am afflicted and humbled exceedingly: I have roared for the groaning of my heart.

9. Lord, all my desire is before thee; and my groaning is not hidden from thee.

10. My heart is troubled, my strength hath failed me: the very light of mine eyes is gone from me.

11. My friends and my neighbours drew near, and stood up against me.

12. They that were once nigh me stood afar off: and they that sought after my soul did violence against me.

13. And they that sought to do me evil talked vanities; and imaginend deceits all the day long.

14. But I, as a deaf man, heard not: and as one that is dumb, who openeth not his mouth.

15. I became as a man that heareth not: and that hath no reproofs in his mouth.

16. For in thee, O Lord, have I hoped: thou wilt hear me, O Lord my God.

17. For I said, Let not mine enemies at any time triumph over me: and when my feet slip, they have spoken great things against me.

18. For I am prepared for scourges: and my sorrow is always before me.

Quoniam iniquitatem meam annuntiabo; * et cogitabo pro peccato meo.

Inimici autem mei vivunt, et confirmati sunt super me: * et multiplicati sunt qui oderunt me inique.

Qui retribuunt mala pro bonis, detrahebant mihi: * quoniam sequebar bonitatem.

Ne derelinquas me Domine Deus meus: * ne discesseris a me.

Intende in adjutorium meum, * Domine, Deus salutis meae.

Gloria Patri, etc.

Oremus.

Omnipotens sempiterne Deus, confitentibus tibi famulis tuis, pro tua pietate relaxa peccata: ut non amplius eis noceat conscientiae reatus ad poenam, quam indulgentia tuae propitiationis prosit ad veniam. Per Christum Dominum nostrum. Amen.

19. For I will confess mine iniquity; and will think upon my sin.

20. But mine enemies live, and are strengthened against me: and they that hate me wrongfully are multiplied.

21. They that render evil for good spake against me, because I followed goodness.

22. Forsake me not, O Lord my God: go not thou far from me.

23. Haste thee to my help, O Lord God of my salvation.

Glory, etc

Let us pray.

Almighty and eternal God, pardon, in thy mercy, the sins of thy servants who confess unto thee, so that the faults of their conscience may no further injure them in the way of punishment, than thy indulgent justice may require for forgiveness. Through Christ our Lord. Amen.

Let us meditate briefly on the sufferings of Jesus in his journey from the house of Annas to that of Caiphas; and pray as before, for the virtues proposed, in this instance, the virtue of purity and the gift of knowledge. Let us likewise seek the intercession of some saint remarkable for them, such as St. Philip Neri, or St. Aloysius Gonzaga.

At the altar of the Blessed Sacrament, as before pag. 526.

At the altar of St. Philip Neri.

HYMNUS.
Iste Confessor Domini, colentes

HYMN.
The Confessor of Christ, from shore to shore,

Quem pie laudant populi per orbem:
Hac die laetus meruit beatas
 Scandere sedes.

Qui pius, prudens, humilis, pudicus,
Sobriam duxit sine labe vitam,
Donec humanos animavit aurae
 Spiritus artus.

Cujus ob praestans meritum frequenter,
Ægra quae passim jacuere membra,
Viribus morbi domitis, saluti
 Restituuntur.

Noster hinc illi chorus obsequentem
Concinit laudem, celebresque palmas;
Ut piis ejus precibus juvemur
 Omne per aevum.

Sit salus illi, decus, atque virtus,
Qui super coeli solio coruscans,
Totius mundi seriem gubernat.
 Trinus et unus. Amen.
 V. Ora pro nobis, sancte Philippe.
 R. Ut digni efficiamur promissionibus Christi.

Oremus.
Precibus nostris, quaesumus Domine, intende placa-

Worshipped with solemn rite,
This day went up with joy,
 his labours o'er,
To his blest seat in light.

Holy and innocent were all his ways;
Sweet, temperate, unstained
His life was prayer, his every breath was praise,
 While breath to him remained.

Ofttimes his merits high in every land,
In cures have been displayed;
And still does health return at his command
To many a frame decayed.

Therefore to him triumphant praise we pay,
And yearly songs renew;
Praying our glorious Saint for us to pray,
All the long ages through.

To God, of all the centre and the source,
Be power and glory given;
Who sways the mighty world through all its course,
From the bright throne of heaven. Amen.
V. Pray for us, O holy Philip.
R. That we may be made worthy of the promises of Christ.
Let us pray.
Attend benignantly, we beseech thee, O Lord, to our

tus, et praesta: ut illo nos igne Spiritus Sanctus inflammet, quo Beati Philippi cor mirabiliter penetravit. Per Christum Dominum nostrum, Amen.

prayers, and grant that the Holy Spirit may inflame us with that fire, which he wonderfully aroused in the heart of the blessed Philip. Through Christ. Amen.

At the altar of St. Sebastian,

Pater, Ave, Gloria.

Ant. Gaudent in coelis animae sanctorum, qui Christi vestigia sunt secuti: et quia pro ejus amore sanguinem suum fuderunt, ideo cum Christo exultant sine fine.

Ant. The souls of the saints, who followed Christ's footsteps, rejoice in heaven: and because they shed their blood through love of Him, therefore they exult with Christ unceasingly.

V. Exsultabunt sancti in gloria.
R. Laetabuntur in cubilibus suis.

V. The saints shall rejoice in glory.
R. They shall be glad in their restingplaces.

Oremus.
Infirmitatem nostram respice omnipotens Deus, et quia pondus propriae actionis gravat, beatorum martyrum Fabiani et Sebastiani intercessio gloriosa nos protegat. Per Christum Dominum nostrum. Amen.

Let us pray.
Look down, almighty God, on our infirmity, and inasmuch as our own actions weigh down upon us, let the intercession of the holy martyrs Fabian and Sebastian protect us. Through Christ our Lord. Amen.

FOURTH VISIT.

ST. JOHN LATERAN.

Practice. Contemplate the painful journey of Jesus from the house of Caiphas to that of Pilate, and the fourth effusion for us of His Precious Blood, in the crowning with thorns. Ask deliverance from the vice of avarice and beg the gift of counsel.

On the way, recite the Little Hours of the Office of the

Blessed Virgin or the last five decades of the Rosary, those, namely, of the Glorious Mysteries.

This done, say the Litany of the Saints, with accompanying Psalm, responses, and prayers, page 432.

In the portico, read the account given above (p. 448) of this basilica; and note especially that there are preserved, in the apartments annexed to the building, the cloth with which our Saviour wiped the apostles' feet, the purple garment He wore in Pilate's house, the sponge with which He was given vinegar and gall to drink, a cloth that served to cover his sacred Face in the tomb and which has some traces of His blood; relics of the B. V. Mary, of St. John the Baptist and of his father Zachary, of St. John the Evangelist, of St. Laurence and of St. Pancras.

The number of indulgences here obtainable, is so great that, in the words of Innocent X, it is known to God alone.

Entering, recite as follows:

Int. Exultabunt Domino ossa humiliata.

Miserere mei, Deus, * secundum magnam misericordiam tuam.

Et secundum multitudinem miserationum tuarum, * dele iniquitatem meam.

Amplius lava me ab iniquitate mea: * et a peccato meo munda me.

Quoniam iniquitatem meam ego cognosco: * et peccatum meum contra me est semper.

Tibi soli peccavi, et malum coram te feci: * ut justificeris in sermonibus tuis, et vincas cum judicaris.

Ant. The bones that were humbled shall rejoice.

1. Have mercy upon me, O God, according to thy great mercy.

2. And according to the multitude of thy tender mercies, blot out my iniquity.

3. Wash me yet more from my iniquity: and cleanse me from my sin.

4. For I acknowledge my iniquity: and my sin is always before me.

5. Against thee only have I sinned, and done evil in thy sight: that thou mayest be justified in thy words, and mayest overcome when thou art judged.

Ecce enim in iniquitatibus conceptus sum: * et in peccatis concepit me mater mea.

Ecce enim veritatem dilexisti: * incerta et occulta sapientiae tuae manifestasti mihi.

Asperges me hyssopo, et mundabor: * lavabis me, et super nivem dealbabor.

Auditui meo dabis gaudium et laetitiam: * et exultabunt ossa humiliata.

Averte faciem tuam a peccatis meis: * et omnes iniquitates meas dele.

Cor mundum crea in me, Deus: * et spiritum rectum innova in visceribus meis.

Ne projicias me a facie tua:* et Spiritum sanctum tuum ne auferas a me.

Redde mihi laetitiam salutaris tui: * et spiritu principali confirma me.

Docebo iniquos vias tuas: * et impii ad te convertentur.

Libera me de sanguinibus, Deus, Deus salutis meae: * et exultabit lingua mea justitiam tuam.

Domine, labia mea aperies: * et os meum annuntiabit laudem tuam.

Quoniam si voluisses sacrificium, dedissem utique: * holocaustis non delectaberis.

6. For behold, I was conceived in iniquities: and in sins did my mother conceive me.

7. For lo thou hast loved truth: the uncertain and hidden things of thy wisdom thou hast made manifest to me.

8. Thou shalt sprinkle me with hyssop, and I shall be cleansed: thou shalt wash me and I shall be made whiter than snow.

9. Thou shalt make me hear of joy and gladness: and the bones that were humbled shall rejoice.

10. Turn away thy face from my sins: and blot out all my iniquities.

11. Create in me a clean heart, O God: and renew a right spirit within my bowels.

12. Cast me not away from thy presence: and take not thy holy spirit from me.

13. Restore unto me the joy of thy salvation: and strengthen me with a perfect spirit.

14. I will teach the unjust thy ways: and the wicked shall be converted unto thee.

15. Deliver me from blood, O God, thou God of my salvation: and my tongue shall extol thy justice.

16. Thou shalt open my lips, O Lord: and my mouth shall declare thy praise.

17. For if thou hadst desired sacrifice, I would surely have given it: with burnt-offerings thou wilt not be delighted.

Sacrificium Deo spiritus contribulatus : * cor contritum et humiliatum, Deus, non despicies.

Benigne fac, Domine, in bona voluntate tua Sion : * ut aedificentur muri Jerusalem.

Tunc acceptabis sacrificium justitiae, oblationes, et holocausta : * tunc imponent super altare tuum vitulos.

Gloria Patri, etc.

18. The sacrifice to God is an afflicted spirit : a contrite and humble heart, O God, thou wilt not despise.

19. Deal favourably, O Lord, in thy good will with Sion : that the walls of Jerusalem may be built up.

20. Then shalt thou accept the sacrifices of justice, oblations and whole burnt-offerings; then shall they lay calves upon thine altars.

Glory, etc.

Kyrie Eleison, etc., *as above, pag. 512.*

Oremus.

Exaudi, quaesumus Domine supplicum preces et confitentium tibi parce peccatis; ut pariter nobis indulgentiam tribuas benignus, et pacem. Per Christum Dominum nostrum. Amen.

Let us pray.

Hear, we beseech thee, O Lord, the prayers of thy suppliants, and spare the sins of those who confess to thee, so that thou mayest benignantly grant us indulgence as well as peace. Through Christ our Lord. Amen.

Let each one here make a short reflection on the passage of Jesus from the house of Caiphas to that of Pilate, and on the crowning with thorns; then make a short prayer as before, and with humble and contrite heart beg for the virtue of liberality as opposed to avarice, and the gift of counsel as opposed to precipitation.

Inside the church, say the following prayers to St. John the Baptist, and to St. John the Evangelist.

Pater, Ave, Gloria *to each; then:*

Antiph. Salvator mundi salva nos omnes, et praecursoris inclyti discipulique devota memoria vota nostra perducat in patriam.

Ant. O Saviour of the world, save us all, and may the pious memory of thy illustrious precursor and beloved disciple lead us accor-

V. Salvos fac servos tuos,
R. Deus meus, sperantes in te.

Oremus.

Omnipotens sempiterne Deus, qui hanc sacratissimam Constantinianam basilicam in tuo, et utriusque Joannis nomine dedicatam, cunctarum Urbis et Orbis Ecclesiarum decorasti primatu: concede nobis famulis tuis, ut amborum meritis et precibus a nostris reatibus expiati ad te Salvatorem nostrum pervenire valeamus. Qui vivis et regnas in saecula saeculorum. Amen.

ding to our desire to our heavenly country.
V. Save thy servants,
R. My God, who hope in thee.

Let us pray.

Almighty and eternal God, who hast adorned with the primacy of all the churches in the city and in the world this sacred basilica, dedicated in first place to Thee and then to the two sain's John: grant us thy servants, that being freed from our guilt by the merits and prayers of these two saints, we may be able to come to thee our Saviour. Who livest and reignest. Amen.

Approaching the altar of the Blessed Sacrament we say the prayers, as above, page 526; at the Papal altar as at p. 528; at our Lady's altar as at page 514, with this anthem.

Antiph. Santa Maria succurre miseris, juva pusillanimes, refove flebiles, ora pro populo, interveni pro clero, intercede pro devoto foemineo sexu; sentiant omnes tuum juvamen, quicumque celebrant tuam sanctam commemorationem.

Ant. Holy Mary, come to the aid of the wretched, help the wavering, cherish the tearful, pray for the people, intervene for the clergy, intercede for the devout female sex; let all whoever celebrate thy holy commemoration experience thy assistance.

Three Ave Marias.

FIFTH VISIT.

HOLY CROSS OF JERUSALEM.

Practice. Consider our Saviour's painful journey from Pilate to Herod, and the fifth effusion of His blood, in the nailing of his hands to the cross. Also ask freedom from the vice of sloth and beg the gift of fortitude.

VISIT TO THE SEVEN CHURCHES

On the way recite the "Stages of our Saviour's Passion," as follows.

Jesu dulcissime, in horto moestus, Patrem orans, et in agonia positus, sanguineum sudorem effundens, miserere nobis.

V. Miserere nostri, Domine, miserere nostri.

Jesu dulcissime, osculo traditoris in manus impiorum traditus, tanquam latro captus et ligatus, et a discipulis derelictus, miserere nobis.

R. Miserere nostri, Domine, etc.

Jesu dulcissime, ab iniquo Judaeorum concilio reus mortis acclamatus, ad Pilatum tamquam malefactor ductus, ab iniquo Herode spretus et delusus, miserere nobis.

R. Miserere, etc.

Jesu dulcissime, vestibus denudatus, et ad columnam crudelissime flagellatus, miserere nobis.

R. Miserere, etc.

Jesu dulcissime, spinis coronatus, colaphis caesus, arundine percussus, facie velatus, veste purpurea circumdatus, multipliciter derisus, et opprobriis salutatus, miserere nobis.

R. Miserere nostri, etc.

Jesu dulcissime, latroni Barabbae postpositus, a Judaeis reprobatus, et ad mortem cru-

Most sweet Jesus, sad and sorrowful in the garden, praying to thy Father, entering into agony, and pouring forth a sweat of blood, have mercy on us.

R. Have mercy on us, O Lord, have mercy on us.

Most sweet Jesus, betrayed by a traitor's kiss into the hands of the impious, seized and bound as if a robber, abandoned by thy disciples, have mercy on us.

R. Have mercy on us, O Lord, have mercy on us.

Most sweet Jesus, pronounced deserving of death by the impious council of the Jews, led as a malefactor to Pilate, despised and mocked at by the impious Herod, have mercy on us.

R. Have mercy, etc.

Most sweet Jesus, stripped of thy garments, and most cruelly scourged at the pillar, have mercy on us.

R. Have mercy, etc.

Most sweet Jesus, crowned with thorns, wounded with blows, struck with a reed, blindfolded, covered with a purple garment, in many ways derided, and saturated with insults, have mercy on us.

R. Have mercy, etc.

Most sweet Jesus, esteemed less than the robber Barabbas, rejected by the Jews, and

cis injuste condemnatus, miserere nobis.

℟. Miserere nostri, etc.

Jesu dulcissime, ligno crucis oneratus, et ad locum supplicii tanquam ovis ad occisionem ductus, miserere nobis.

℟. Miserere nobis, etc.

Jesu dulcissime, inter latrones deputatus, blasphematus, et derisus, felle et aceto potatus, et horribilibus tormentis ab hora sexta usque ad horam nonam in ligno cruciatus, miserere nobis.

℟. Miserere nostri, etc.

Jesu dulcissime, in patibulo crucis mortuus, et coram tua sancta matre lancea perforatus, simul sanguinem et aquam emittens, miserere nobis.

℟. Miserere nostri, etc.

Jesu dulcissime, de cruce depositus, et lacrimis maestissimae Virginis Matris tuae perfusus, miserere nobis.

℟. Miserere nostri, etc.

Jesu dulcissime, plagis circumdatus, quinque vulneribus signatus, aromatibus conditus, et in sepulchro repositus, miserere nobis.

℟. Miserere nostri, etc.,

℣. Vere languores nostros ipse tulit.

℟. Et dolores nostros ipse portavit.

unjustly condemned to the death of the cross, have mercy on us.

℟. Have mercy, etc.

Most sweet Jesus, burdened with the wood of the cross, and led to the place of punishment like a sheep to the slaughter, have mercy on us.

℟. Have mercy, etc.

Most sweet Jesus, reputed amongst robbers, blasphemed and derided, slaked with vinegar and gall, and tortured on the tree of the cross with the most horrible torments, from the sixth to the ninth hour, have mercy on us.

℟. Have mercy, etc.

Most sweet Jesus, dead on the gibbet of the cross, and, in the presence of thy holy Mother, pierced with a lance, giving forth both blood and water, have mercy on us.

℟. Have mercy, etc.

Most sweet Jesus, taken down from the cross, and covered with the tears of thy most sorrowful Virgin Mother, have mercy on us.

℟. Have mercy, etc.

Most sweet Jesus, covered with sores, marked with five wounds, embalmed with unguents and laid in the sepulchre, have mercy on us.

℟. Have mercy, etc.

℣. Truly he took up our infirmities.

℟. And he bore our sorrows.

Oremus.

Deus, qui pro redemptione mundi voluisti nasci, circumcidi, a Judaeis reprobari, a Juda traditore osculo tradi, vinculis alligari, sicut agnus innocens ad victimam duci atque conspectibus Annae Caiphae, Pilati, et Herodis indecenter offerri, a falsis testibus accusari, flagellis et opprobriis vexari, sputis conspui, spinis coronari, colaphis caedi, arundine percuti, facie velari, vestibus spoliari, cruci clavis affigi, in cruce levari, in'er latrones deputari, felle et aceto potari et lancea vulnerari, Tu Domine, per has sanctissimas poenas, quas indigni recolimus, et per sanctissimam crucem, et mortem tuam, libera nos a poenis inferni, et perducere digneris, quo perduxisti latronem tecum crucifixum. Qui cum Patre et Spiritu Sancto vivis et regnas Deus in saecula saeculorum. Amen.

Let us pray.

O God, who for the redemption of the world wast willing to be born, to receive circumcision, to be reproved by the Jews, to be betrayed by the traitor Judas's kiss, to be bound with cords, to be led like an innocent lamb to immolation, to be unbecomingly dragged to the presence of Annas, Caiphas, Herod and Pilate, to be accused by false witnesses, to be scourged and buffetted, to be outraged with insults, to be spit upon, to be crowned with thorns, to be stripped of thy garments, to be fastened with nails to a cross, to be raised up on the cross, to be reputed among robbers, to have thy thirst quenched with vinegar and gall, to be wounded with a spear. do Thou, O Lord, through these most holy sufferings of thine, which we, though unworthy, bring back to memory, and through thy most holy cross, and through thy death, deliver us from the pains of hell, and deign to lead us whither thou didst lead the thief who was crucified with thee. Who with the Father, and the Holy Ghost, livest and reignest one God, world without end. Amen.

Under the portico, read the description above (p. 480) of this basilica. Many indulgences are gained by visiting

it, and also in particular by visiting the subterranean chapel of St. Helena and venerating the sacred relics of the Passion of our Lord. To this basilica, also, the faithful used to repair, barefooted, on Good Friday.

Entering, recite as follows:

Psalmus.	*Psalm.*

Domine, exaudi orationem meam, auribus percipe obsecrationem meam in veritate tua: exaudi me in tua justitia.

1. Hear my prayer, O Lord: give ear to my supplication in thy truth: hearken unto me for thy justice' sake.

Et non in'res in judicium cum servo tuo: * quia non justificabitur in conspectu tuo omnis vivens.

2. And enter not into judgment with thy servant: for in thy sight shall no man living be justified.

Quia persecutus est inimicus animam meam: * humiliavit in terram vitam meam.

3. For the enemy hath persecuted my soul: he hath brought my life down unto the ground.

Collocavit me in obscuris sicut mortuos saeculi: * et anxiatus est super me spiritus meus, in me turbatum est cor meum.

4. He hath made me to dwell in darkness, as those that have been long dead: and my spirit is vexed within me, my heart within me is troubled.

Memor fui dierum antiquorum, meditatus sum in omnibus operibus tuis; * in factis manuum tuarum meditabar.

5. I have remembered the days of old, I have mused upon all thy works: I have mused upon the works of thy hands.

Expandi manus meas ad te: * anima mea sicut terra sine aqua tibi.

6. I have stretched forth my hands unto thee: my soul gaspeth unto thee, as a land where no water is.

Velociter exaudi me, Domine: * defecit spiritus meus.

7. Hear me speedily, O Lord: my spirit hath fainted away.

Non avertas faciem tuam a me: * et similis ero descendentibus in lacum.

8. Turn not away thy face from me: lest I be like unto them that go down into the pit.

Auditam fac mihi mane mi-

9. Make me to hear thy

sericordiam tuam : * quia in te speravi.
Notam fac mihi viam in qua ambulem : * quia ad te levavi animam meam.

Eripe me de inimicis meis, Domine, ad te confugi: * doce me facere voluntatem tuam, quia Deus meus es tu.

Spiritus tuus bonus deducet me in terram rectam : * propter nomen tuum, Domine, vivificabis me in aequitate tua.

Educes de tribulatione animam meam : * et in misericordia tua disperdes inimicos meos.

Et perdes qui tribulant animam meam : * quoniam ego servus tuus sum.
Gloria Patri, etc.
Ant. Ne reminiscaris, Domine, delicta nostra, vel parentum nostrorum, neque vindictam sumas de peccatis nostris.

mercy in the morning: for in thee have I hoped.
10. Make me to know the way wherein I should walk: for to thee have I lifted up my soul.
11. Deliver me from mine enemies, O Lord; unto thee have I fled: teach me to do thy will, for thou art my God.
12. Thy good spirit shall lead me into the right land: for thy name's sake, O Lord, thou shalt quicken me in thy justice.
13. Thou shalt bring my soul out of trouble: and in thy mercy thou shalt destroy mine enemies.
14. Thou shalt destroy all them that afflict my soul; for I am thy servant.
Glory, etc.
Ant. Remember not, O Lord, our offences, nor those of our parents : neither take thou vengeance of our sins.

Kyrie Eleison, etc. *(as above, pag. 512)*

Oremus.
Ineffabilem nobis, Domine, misericordiam tuam clementer ostende ; ut simul nos et a peccatis omnibus exuas, et a poenis quas pro his mereamur eripias. Per Christum Dominum nostrum. Amen.

Let us pray.
Indulgently show to us, O Lord, thy ineffable mercy, so that thou mayest at once free us from all sins, and deliver us from the penalties we have deserved on their account. Through. Amen.

A brief reflection on the journey from the house of Pilate to that of Herod, and on the fifth effusion of blood

in the cruel nailing, on account of our sins, of our Divine Saviour's hands to the cross. Let us not by our ill deeds crucify him anew. A prayer to be freed from sloth, and to be granted the gift of fortitude, even unto martyrdom.

Inside. At the Altar of the Blessed Sacrament as above, page 526; to the Holy Relics here preserved,

Pater, Ave, Gloria.

V. Christus factus est. *V*. Christ was made.
(*ut supra p. 304*) (*as above, p. 304*)

In the subterranean Chapel of the *Pietà:*

HYMNUS.
Stabat Mater dolorosa
Juxta crucem lacrymosa,
Dum pendebat Filius.

Cujus animam gementem,
Contristatam et dolentem,
Pertransivit gladius.

O quam tristis et afflicta
Fuit illa benedicta
Mater Unigeniti!

Quae moerebat, et dolebat,
Pia Mater dum videbat
Nati poenas inclyti.

Quis est homo qui non fleret,
Matrem Christi si videret
In tanto supplicio?
Quis non posset contristari,
Christi Matrem contemplari
Dolentem cum Filio?

HYMN.
At the Cross her station keeping,
Stood the mournful Mother weeping,
Close to Jesus to the last.
Through her heart His sorrow sharing,
All His bitter anguish bearing,
Lo, the piercing sword had passed.
Oh, how sad and sore distressed,
Now was she, that Mother blessed
Of the sole-begotten One;
Woe-begone, with heart's prostration,
Mother meek, the bitter Passion
Saw she of her glorious Son.
Who could mark, from tears refraining,
Christ's dear Mother uncomplaining,
In so great a sorrow bow'd?
Who unmov'd behold her languish

Pro peccatis suae gentis
Vidit Jesum in tormentis,
Et flagellis subditum.

Vidit suum dulcem natum
Moriendo desolatum,
Dum emisit spiritum.

Eja, Mater, fons amoris,
Me sentire vim doloris
Fac, ut tecum lugeam.

Fac, ut ardeat cor meum
In amando Christum Deum,
Ut sibi complaceam.

Sancta Mater, istud agas,
Crucifixi fige plagas
Cordi meo valide.

Tui nati vulnerati,
Tam dignati pro me pati,
Poenas mecum divide.

Fac me tecum pie flere,
Crucifixo condolere,
Donec ego vixero.
Juxta crucem tecum stare,
Et me tibi sociare,
In planctu desidero.

Underneath His Cross of anguish,
 'Mid the fierce unpitying crowd?
In His people's sins rejected,
She her Jesus, unprotected,
 Saw with thorns, with scourges rent:

Saw her Son from judgment taken,
Her belov'd in death forsaken,
 Till His spirit forth He sent.

Fount of love and holy sorrow,
Mother, may my spirit borrow
 Somewhat of thy woe profound.

Unto Christ, with pure emotion,
Raise my contrite heart's devotion,
 Love to read in every wound

Those five wounds of Jesus smitten,
Mother, in my heart be written,
 Deep as in thine own they be:

Thou, my Saviour's cross who bearest,
Thou, thy Son's rebuke who sharest,
 Let me share them both with thee.

In the Passion of my Maker
Be my sinful soul partaker,
 Weep till death, and weep with thee;
Mine with thee be that sad station,

Virgo virginum praeclara,
Mihi jam non sis amara,
Fac me tecum plangere.

Fac ut portem Christi mortem,
Passionis fac consortem,
Et plagas recolere.
Fac, me plagis vulnerari,
Fac me cruce inebriari,
Et cruore Filii.

Flammis ne urar succensus,
Per te, Virgo, sim defensus
In die judicii.
Christe, cum sit hinc exire,
Da per Matrem me venire
Ad palmam victoriae.

Quando corpus morietur,
Fac ut animae donetur
Paradisi gloria. Amen.

V. Tuam ipsius animam doloris gladius pertransivit.
R. Ut revelentur ex multis cordibus cogitationes.

Oremus.

Interveniat pro nobis, quaesumus Domine Jesu Christe, nunc et in hora mortis nostrae apud tuam clementiam beata Virgo Maria Mater tua, cujus sacratissimam animam, in hora tuae passionis doloris gla-

There to watch the great salvation
Wrought upon th' atoning tree.
Virgin of all Virgins best!
Listen to my fond request:
Let me share thy grief divine:
Let me, to my latest breath,
In my body bear the death
Of that dying Son of thine.

Wounded with this every wound,
Steep my soul till it hath swooned
In His very blood away:
Be to me, O Virgin nigh,
Lest in flames I burn and die,
In His awful judgment day.
When in death my limbs are failing,
Let Thy Mother's prayer prevailing
Lift me, Jesu! to Thy throne:
To my parting soul be given
Entrance through the gate of heaven;
There confess me for Thine own.

V. The sword of grief hath pierced thy soul.
R. That the thoughts of many hearts may be revealed.

Let us pray.

O Lord Jesus Christ, we beseech thee of thy mercy, that the blessed Virgin Mary thy Mother, whose most holy soul was pierced through by the sword of grief in the hour of thy passion, may intercede

dius pertransivit. Per te, Jesu Christe, Salvator mundi, qui cum Patre et Spiritu Sancto vivis, et regnas in saecula saeculorum.
R. Amen.

for us now, and in the hour of our death. Through Thee, O Christ Jesus, Redeemer of the world, who with the Father and the Holy Ghost livest and reignest for ever and ever. Amen.

In the subterranean chapel of St. Helena:

Psalmus.
De profundis clamavi ad te, Domine: * Domine, exaudi vocem meam.

Fiant aures tuae intendentes * in vocem deprecationis meae.

Si iniquitates observaveris, Domine, * Domine, quis sustinebit?

Quia apud te propitiatio est: * et propter legem tuam sustinui te, Domine.

Sustinuit anima mea in verbo eius, * speravit anima mea in Domino.

A custodia matutina usque ad noctem * speret Israel in Domino.

Qui apud Dominum misericordia, * et copiosa apud eum redemptio.

Et ipse redimet Israel * ex omnibus iniquitatibus eius.

Requiem etc.

Psalm.
1. Out of the depths I have cried to thee, O Lord: Lord hear my voice.

2. Let thy ears be attentive to the voice of my supplication.

3. If thou, O Lord, wilt mark iniquities, Lord who shall abide it?

4. For with thee there is merciful forgiveness: and by reason of thy law, I have waited for thee, O Lord.

5. My soul hath relied on his word: my soul hath hoped in the Lord.

6. From the morning watch even until night, let Israel hope in the Lord.

7. Because with the Lord there is mercy, and with him plentiful redemption.

8. And he shall redeem Israel from all his iniquities.

Glory be to the Father, etc.

(Note — An interval of rest is usually taken before the next two visits.)

Sixth Visit.

ST. LAURENCE.

Practice. Consider the contemptuous rejection of Jesus by Herod, and the journey back to Pilate again, also the sixth effusion of His Blood for us, in the fastening of his feet. Let us pray for freedom from the vice of envy and ask the gift of understanding.

On the way, Vespers and Complin of the Little Office of the Blessed Virgin can be recited.

Under the portico, read the account of the basilica (p. 482) Besides the relics of the two great saints, Laurence and Stephen, there are relics of our Saviour's Passion, of the Blessed Virgin, of St. Justin, of St. Barbara and of others. The indulgences that may be gained, here especially in the subterranean chapel of the Suffering Souls, are very great.

Entering, recite the De Profundis, page 550, the Kyrie eleison, p. 512, to the prayer, then,

Oremus.	Let us pray.
Deus cui proprium est misereri semper et parcere, suscipe deprecationem nostram, ut nos et omnes famulos tuos quos delictorum catena constringit, miseratio tuae pietatis clementer absolvat. Qui vivis et regnas in saecula saeculorum. Amen.	O God, whose property is to be merciful always and to spare, receive our prayer, so that thy affectionate compassion may mercifully deliver us, thy servants, from the bonds of sin. Who livest and reignest world without end. Amen.

A short consideration on the second passing of Jesus between the houses of Herod and Pilate, and on the nailing of his feet for us to the cross. Let us resolve to love our neighbour.

Prayer for the virtue of charity as opposed to envy and for the gift of understanding, especially with regard to celestial things.

Inside at the Altar of the Blessed Sacrament, as above, page 514.

To St. Laurence.

Ant. Levita Laurentius bonum opus operatus est, qui per signum crucis caecos illuminavit, et thesauros Ecclesiae dedit pauperibus.

V. Dispersit dedit pauperibus.

R. Justitia ejus manet in saeculum saeculi.

Oremus.

Da nobis quaesumus omnipotens Deus, vitiorum nostrorum flammas extinguere; qui beato Laurentio tribuisti tormentorum suorum incendia superare. Per Christum Dominum nostrum. Amen.

Ant. The levite Laurence performed good work, for with the sign of the cross he gave sight to the blind, and he distributed the treasures of the Church to the poor.

V. He distributed, gave to the poor.

R. His justice remains for ever and ever.

Let us pray.

Grant us we beseech thee, almighty God, to extinguish the flames of our vices, who didst give to the blessed Laurence to triumph over the fire of his torments, Through Christ our Lord. Amen.

At the altars endowed with special indulgences, an Act of Contrition. To all the Saints whose relics here repose: Pater, Ave, Gloria.

At the altar of the Souls Departed, the *De Profundis*.

Prayer at the tomb of Pius IX.

Psalmus 129.

De profundis clamavi ad te, Domine; * Domine, exaudi vocem meam.

Fiant aures tuae intendentes * in vocem deprecationis meae.

Si iniquitates observaveris, Domine, * Domine, quis sustinebit?

Quia apud te propitiatio est: * et propter legem tuam sustinui te, Domine.

Sustinuit anima mea in

Psalm 129.

1. Out of the depths have I cried unto thee, O Lord: Lord, hear my voice.

2. Oh, let thine ears consider well the voice of my supplication.

3. If thou, O Lord, shalt mark iniquities: Lord, who shall abide it?

4. For with thee there is propitiation; and because of thy law I have waited for thee, O Lord.

5. My soul hath waited on

verbo ejus, * speravit anima mea in Domino.

A custodia matutina usque ad noctem * speret Israël in Domino.

Quia apud Dominum misericordia: * et copiosa apud eum redemptio.

Et ipse redimet Israel, * ex omnibus iniquitatibus ejus.

V. Requiem aeternam dona ei, Domine:
R. Et lux perpetua luceat ei.

V. A porta inferi.
R. Erue, Domine, animam ejus.
V. Requiescat in pace.
R. Amen.
V. Dominus vobiscum.
R. Et cum spiritu tuo.

Oremus.

Deus, qui inter summos sacerdotes, famulum tuum Pium ineffabili tua dispositione connumerari voluisti, praesta quaesumus; ut qui unigeniti Filii tui vices in terris gerebat, sanctorum tuorum pontificum consortio perpetuo aggregetur. Per eumdem Christum Dominum nostrum. Amen.

V. Requiem aeternam dona ei, Domine.
R. Et lux perpetua luceat ei.
V. Requiescat in pace.
R. Amen.
V. Anima ejus et animae omnium fidelium defunctorum per misericordiam Dei requiescant in pace. R. Amen.

his word: my soul hath hoped in the Lord.

6. From the morning watch even until night: let Israel hope in the Lord.

7. For with the Lord there is mercy: and with him is plenteous redemption.

8. And he shall redeem Israel from all his iniquities.

V. Eternal rest give to him O Lord.
R. And let perpetual light shine upon him.

V. From the gates of hell.
R. Deliver his soul, O Lord.
V. May he rest in peace.
R. Amen.
V. The Lord be with you.
R. And with thy Spirit.

Let us pray.

O God, who by thy ineffable providence didst will to count thy servant Pius amongst thy highpriests, grant we beseech thee, that he who took the place of thy only-begotten Son on earth, may be associated to the perpetual company of thy holy pontiffs. Through the same Christ our Lord. Amen.

V. Eternal rest give to him, O Lord.
R. And let perpetual light shine upon him.
V. May he rest in peace.
R. Amen.
V. May his soul and the souls of all the faithful departed through the mercy of God rest in peace. R. Amen.

Seventh Visit.

ST. MARY MAJOR.

Practice. Consider our Saviour's grievous journey to Mount Calvary, and the seventh shedding of His Blood for us, in the transpiercing of his side. Let us ask freedom from the vice of pride, and beg the gift of wisdom.

On the way recite the Hymn *Te Deum.*

Te Deum.

Te Deum laudamus: te Dominum confitemur.

Te aeternum Patrem omnis terra veneratur.

Tibi omnes angeli, tibi coeli, et universae potestates:

Tibi cherubim et seraphim, incessabili voce proclamant:

Sanctus, sanctus, sanctus, Dominus Deus Sabaoth;

Pleni sunt coeli et terra, majestatis gloriae tuae.

Te gloriosus Apostolorum chorus.

Te Prophetarum laudabilis numerus.

Te Martyrum candidatus laudat exercitus.

Te per orbem terrarum sancta confitetur Ecclesia.

Patrem immensae majestatis.

Venerandum tuum verum et unicum Filium.

Sanctum quoque Paraclitum Spiritum,

We praise thee, O God: we acknowledge thee to be the Lord.

Thee, the Father everlasting, all the earth doth worship.

To thee, all angels; to thee, the heavens and all the powers.

To thee, the cherubim and seraphim continually cry:

Holy, holy, holy, Lord God of Sabaoth:

The heavens and the earth are full of the majesty of thy glory.

Thee, the glorious choir of Apostles:

Thee, the admirable company of Prophets:

Thee, the white-robed army of Martyrs praise.

Thee, the Holy Church throughout the world doth acknowledge,

The Father of infinite majesty:

Thine adorable, true, and only Son:

Also the Holy Ghost, the Paraclete,

Tu Rex gloriae, Christe.

Tu Patris sempiternus es Filius.

Tu ad liberandum suscepturus hominem, non horruisti Virginis uterum.

Tu devicto mortis aculeo, aperuisti credentibus regna coelorum.

Tu ad dexteram Dei sedes, in gloria Patris.

Judex crederis esse venturus.

Te ergo quaesumus, tuis famulis subveni, quos pretioso sanguine redemisti.

Æterna fac cum sanctis tuis, in gloria numerari.

Salvum fac populum tuum, Domine, et benedic haereditati tuae.

Et rege eos, et extolle illos, usque in aeternum.

Per singulos dies benedicimus te.

Et laudamus nomen tuum in saeculum, et in saeculum saeculi.

Dignare, Domine, die isto, sine peccato nos custodire.

Miserere nostri, Domine, miserere nostri.

Fiat misericordia tua, Domine, super nos: quemadmodum speravimus in te.

In te, Domine, speravi; non confundar in aeternum.

Thou, O Christ, art the King of Glory.
Thou art the everlasting Son of the Father.
Thou, having taken upon thee to deliver man, didst not abhor the Virgin's womb.
Thou, having overcome the sting of death, hast opened to believers the kingdom of heaven.
Thou sittest at the right hand of God, in the glory of the Father.
Thou, we believe, art the Judge to come.
We beseech thee therefore to help thy servants, whom thou hast redeemed with thy precious blood.
Make them to be numbered with thy saints in glory everlasting.
O Lord, save thy people: and bless thine inheritance.

And govern them and lift them up, for ever.
Day by day, we bless thee.

And we praise thy name for ever: yea, for ever and ever.
Vouchsafe, O Lord, this day: to keep us without sin.
Have mercy upon us, O Lord: have mercy upon us.
Let thy mercy, O Lord, be upon us: as we have trusted in thee.
In thee, O Lord, have I trusted: let me never be confounded.

Oremus.

Deus, cujus misericordiae non est numerus, et bonitatis infinitus est thesaurus; piissimae majestati tuae pro collatis donis gratias agimus, tuam semper clementiam exorantes; ut qui petentibus postulata concedis, eosdem non deserens, ad praemia futura disponas. Per Christum Dominum nostrum. Amen.

Let us pray.

O God, of whose mercy there is no calculation, and whose treasure of goodness is infinite, we give thanks to thy most loving majesty for the gifts conferred, and we continue to pray thy clemency, that as Thou grantest what they ask to those who implore, thou mayest not desert us but conduct us to the future rewards. Through Christ our Lord. Amen.

Litany of the Blessed Virgin.

Sub tuum praesidium confugimus, sancta Dei Genitrix: nostras deprecationes ne despicias in necessitatibus nostris, sed a periculis cunctis libera nos semper, Virgo gloriosa et benedicta.

We fly to thy patronage, O holy Mother of God: despise not our petitions in our necessities, but deliver us always from all dangers, O glorious and blessed Virgin.

Kyrie eleison.	Lord have mercy.
Kyrie eleison.	Lord have mercy.
Christe eleison.	Christ have mercy.
Christe eleison.	Christ have mercy.
Kyrie eleison.	Lord have mercy.
Kyrie eleison.	Lord have mercy.
Christe audi nos.	Christ hear us.
Christe exaudi nos.	Christ graciously hear us.
Pater de coelis Deus,	God the Father of heaven,
Fili Redemptor mundi Deus,	God the Son, Redeemer of the world,
Spiritus Sancte Deus,	God the Holy Ghost,
Sancta Trinitas, unus Deus,	Holy Trinity, one God,
Sancta Maria,	Holy Mary,
Sancta Dei Genitrix,	Holy Mother of God,
Sancta Virgo virginum,	Holy Virgin of virgins,
Mater Christi,	Mother of Christ,
Mater divinae gratiae,	Mother of divine grace,
Mater purissima,	Mother post pure,

Miserere nobis. / *Have mercy on us.*

Latin	English
Mater castissima,	Mother most chaste,
Mater inviolata,	Mother inviolate,
Mater intemerata,	Mother undefiled,
Mater amabilis,	Mother most amiable,
Mater admirabilis,	Mother most admirable,
Mater Creatoris,	Mother of our Creator,
Mater Salvatoris,	Mother of our Saviour,
Virgo prudentissima,	Virgin most prudent,
Virgo veneranda,	Virgin most venerable,
Virgo praedicanda,	Virgin most renowned,
Virgo potens,	Virgin most powerful,
Virgo clemens,	Virgin most merciful,
Virgo fidelis,	Virgin most faithful,
Speculum justitiae,	Mirror of justice,
Sedes sapientiae,	Seat of wisdom,
Causa nostrae laetitiae,	Cause of our joy,
Vas spirituale,	Spiritual vessel,
Vas honorabile,	Vessel of honour,
Vas insigne devotionis,	Vessel of singular devotion,
Rosa mystica,	Mystical rose,
Turris Davidica,	Tower of David,
Turris eburnea,	Tower of ivory,
Domus aurea,	House of gold,
Fœderis arca,	Ark of the covenant,
Janua cœli,	Gate of heaven,
Stella matutina,	Morning star,
Salus infirmorum,	Health of the sick,
Refugium peccatorum,	Refuge of sinners,
Consolatrix afflictorum,	Conforter of the afflicted,
Auxilium Christianorum,	Help of Christians,
Regina Angelorum,	Queen of Angels,
Regina Patriarcharum,	Queen of Patriarchs,
Regina Prophetarum,	Queen of Prophets,
Regina Apostolorum,	Queen of Apostles,
Regina Martyrum,	Queen of Martyrs,
Regina Confessorum,	Queen of Confessors,
Regina Virginum,	Queen of Virgins,
Regina Sanctorum omnium,	Queen of all Saints,
Regina sine labe originali concepta.	Queen conceived without original sin,
Regina sacratissimi Rosarii	Queen of the most holy Rosary,

(Ora pro nobis. / Pray for us.)

Agnus Dei, qui tollis peccata   Lamb of God, who takest

mundi,
Parce nobis Domine.
Agnus Dei, qui tollis peccata mundi,
Exaudi nos Domine.
Agnus Dei, qui tollis peccata mundi,
Miserere nobis.
Christe audi nos,
Christe exaudi nos.
V. Ora pro nobis, sancta Dei Genitrix.
R. Ut digni efficiamur promissionibus Christi.

Oremus.

Gratiam tuam, quaesumus Domine, mentibus nostris infunde; ut qui, angelo nuntiante, Christi Filii Tui incarnationem cognovimus, per passionem ejus et crucem ad resurrectionis gloriam perducamur. Per eundem Christum Dominum nostrum. Amen.

away the sins of the world,
Spare us, O Lord.
Lamb of God, who takest away the sins of the world,
Graciously hear us, O Lord.
Lamb of God, who takest away the sins of the world,
Have mercy on us.
Christ hear us,
Christ graciously hear us.
V. Pray for us, O holy Mother of God.
R. That we may be made worthy of the promises of Christ.

Let us pray.

Pour forth, we beseech Thee, O Lord, thy grace into our hearts, that we, to whom the incarnation of Christ thy Son was made known by the message of an angel, may through his passion and cross be brought to the glory of the resurrection. Through the same Christ our Lord. Amen.

Ave Maris Stella, as at p. 530.

In the Portico, read the description of the basilica given above (p. 452), and note, that beside the relics there enumerated, many others are here preserved. Under the high altar are the bodies of St. Matthias, Apostle and of others; in the Chapel of the Crucifix, relics of the Passion of our Lord, of our Blessed Lady, of the Apostles Matthew and Matthias, of St Luke, of St Bibiana. In this basilica, besides partial indulgences a daily plenary indulgence can be gained. Here St. Philip Neri used to pray with great fervour, and to receive those extraordinary supernatural consolations, which made him at times cry out: " Enough, my God, enough! "

Entering, recite as follows:

Psalmus.

Domine, exaudi orationem meam: auribus percipe obsecrationem meam in veritate tua : * exaudi me in justitia.

Et non intres in judicium cum servo tuo: * quia non justificabitur in conspectu tuo omnis vivens.

Quia persecutus est inimicus animam meam : * humiliavit in terra vitam meam.

Collocavit me in obscuris sicut mortuos saeculi : * et anxiatus est super me spiritus meus, in me turbatum est cor meum.

Memor fui dierum antiquorum, meditatus sum in omnibus operibus tuis: * in factis manuum tuarum meditabar.

Expandi manus meas ad te: * anima mea sicut terra sine aqua tibi.

Velociter exaudi me, Domine: defecit spiritus meus.

Non avertas faciem tuam a me, * et similis ero descendentibus in lacum.

Auditam fac mihi mane misericordiam tuam: * quia in te speravi.

Notam fac mihi viam, in qua ambulem: * quia ad te levavi animam meam.

Eripe me de inimicis meis Domine, ad te confugi : * doce

Psalm.

1. O Lord, hear my prayer: give ear to my petition in thy truth : hear me in thy justice.

2. And enter not into judgment with thy servant : for in thy sight no man shall be justified.

3. For the enemy hath persecuted my soul : he hath humbled my life to the earth.

4. He hath made me dwell in darkness, as those who have been dead of old: my spirit is in anguish upon me: and my heart is troubled within me.

5. I remember the days of old; I meditated on thy works; on the works of thy hands did I meditate.

6. I stretched forth my hands to thee: unto thee my soul is as earth without water.

7. Hear me speedily, O Lord; my spirit hath fainted away.

8. Turn not away thy face from me, lest I be like unto them that go down into the pit.

9. Cause me to hear thy mercy in the morning; for I have hoped in thee.

10. Make the way known to me wherein I shall walk; for I have lifted up my soul to thee.

11. Deliver me from mine enemies, O Lord; to thee have

me facere voluntatem tuam, quia Deus meus es tu.

Spiritus tuus bonus deducet me in terram rectam: * propter nomen tuum, Domine, vivificabis me aequitate tua.

Educes de tribulatione animam meam, * et in misericordia tua disperdes inimicos meos.

Et perdes omnes qui tribulant animam meam; * quoniam ego servus tuus sum.

Oremus.

Deus qui justificas impium et non vis mortem peccatoris, majestatem tuam suppliciter deprecamur: ut famulos tuos de tua misericordia confidentes coelesti protegas benignus auxilio, et assidua protectione conserves, ut tibi jugiter famulentur, et nullis tentationibus a te separentur. Per Christum Dominum nostrum. Amen.

I fled: teach me to do thy will, for thou art my God.

12. Thy good spirit shall conduct me into the way of righteousness: for thy name's sake, O Lord thou wilt quicken me in thy justice.

13. Thou wilt bring forth my soul out of tribulation: and in thy mercy thou wilt destroy mine enemies.

14. And thou wilt destroy all those that afflict my soul: for I am thy servant.

Let us pray.

O God, who dost justify the impious, and who willest not the death of the sinner, we suppliantly implore thy majesty, that thou mayest benignantly protect with celestial help thy servants who confide in thy mercy, that thou mayest preserve them with continual watchfulness, that they may be always faithful to thee, and be separated from thee by no temptations. Through Christ our Lord. Amen.

A brief reflection on the journey to Mount Calvary and on the transpiercing of our Divine Redeemer's side. After Jesus, Mary is our model of virtue. Short prayer for the virtue of humility as opposed to pride, and for the gift of wisdom in heavenly things.

Inside, at altar of Blessed Sacrament, as before, page 514.

At the altar of our Lady, three Aves, and Anthem,

as above, p. 432. *In honour of St. Matthias*, say, *at the Papal Altar* Pater, Ave, and Gloria; then,

Ant. Estote fortes in bello, et pugnate cum antiquo serpente: et accipietis regnum aeternum.

V. Annuntiaverunt opera Dei.

R. Et facta ejus intellexerunt.

Oremus.

Deus, qui beatum Mathiam Apostolorum tuorum collegio sociasti: tribue quaesumus, ut ejus interventione tuae circa nos pietatis semper viscera sentiamus. Per Christum Dominum nostrum. Amen.

Ant. Be strong in warfare, and fight with the ancient serpent, and you shall receive the eternal kingdom.

V. They announced the works of God.

R. And understood his deeds.

Let us pray.

O God, who didst associate the blessed Matthias to the college of thy apostles, grant, we beseech thee, that by his intercession, we may always experience the fulness of thy mercy in our regard. Through Christ. Amen.

To all the Saints whose relics here repose, Pater, Ave, Gloria, with anthem and prayer as above, page 529.

In conclusion the Creed, with Te Deum and prayer as above, page 553.

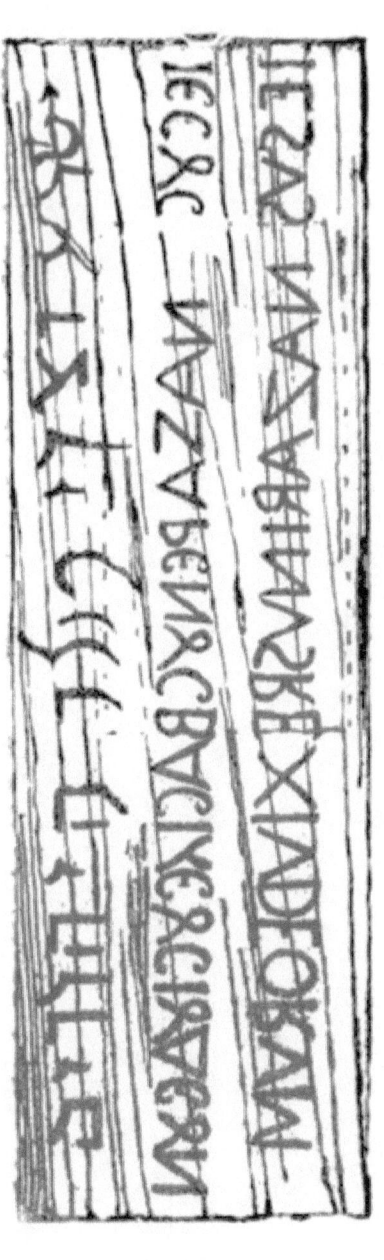

Facsimile of the Title of the Cross as it originally stood in Hebrew, Greek and Latin.

NOTICE

ON THE

SCALA SANTA.

From the time of St. Gregory the Great we have frequent reference to an oratory dedicated to St. Laurence in the Lateran patriarchate, or pontifical palace. In this oratory the most precious relics were generally exposed, and their accumulation, in the course of time, became so great, that Leo III., in 850, thought good to have the words *Sancta Sanctorum*—Holy of Holies—carved on a cypress-wood reliquary there contained. This designation has been ever since attached to the oratory.

In the thirteenth century Honorius III. and Nicholas III., between them, entirely renewed the chapel. Such as we know it, it is of their epoch. And from the point of view of architecture (Gothic-Lombard), painting or marble-work (of the celebrated Cosmati), we could hardly imagine anything more beautiful.

A rare treasure it contains is the picture of our Saviour on the wall behind the altar. This is either the original painting itself, or a very ancient copy of the painting, which, as we read in Moses Corenesus, the Armenian historian of the fifth century, was called *acheropita*, or 'not made by the hand of man.' St. Luke himself was said to have commenced and an angel to have finished the work.

The present picture came from the East, sent by St. Germanus, patriarch of Constantinople, to Gregory II., to save it from the hands of the Iconoclasts. The story is that he launched it on the waters, and that of itself it sped directly over towards Italy; that the Pope in a vision was apprised of a great arrival, and that he went out processionally to the port and found the picture. However

it may be, the very greatest veneration was shown to it from those early days. Stephen II., in 752, to gain the Divine aid against the Lombard invasion, formed a procession, and carried this picture round the city on his own shoulders. It became the custom too, on the feast of the Assumption of the Blessed Virgin, for the Holy Father with the clergy and people to assemble at this Chapel, to take out the picture and proceed with great ceremony to St. Mary Major's. The idea was to bring the picture of the Son to that of the Mother, so that assumed into Heaven she might intercede with Him and obtain favours and graces for the faithful. This devout procession continued down to the sixteenth century, when the factions and disputes of the time caused it to be discontinued.

The Lateran Palace having been damaged by earthquake and fire, Sixtus V. undertook to rebuild it. New arrangements were made for means of transit in the locality, and, as a consequence of the opening of a new street, this sacred oratory found itself isolated.

To form an ascent to it, the Pope thought of placing the *Scala Pilati*, which had hitherto been venerated before the portico of the palace. This *Scala Pilati*, or *Scala Santa*, had been brought from Jerusalem by St. Helena, the mother of Constantine, and had been, as its name indicates, the staircase of Pilate's house, which our Saviour must have ascended and descended more than once, and which was sprinkled with His Precious Blood.

Sixtus V., accordingly, had the twenty-eight steps it is composed of put in position and placed here; and he reconstructed the front of the building to cover it. To the veneration of this memorial of our Lord's Passion immense indulgences had already been attached. Pope Sixtus increased them, and succeeding pontiffs have added to their number. Amongst others, we may mention that of three-hundred days, obtainable for the ascent of each step with the recitation of a Pater and Ave.

So great became the concourse of the faithful ascending on their knees, that two other staircases were added, one on each side, to the ascent of which the same indulgences were attached.

The effective sculptures in the vestibule are due to the chisel of Jacometti and were executed by order of Pius IX. The sacred edifice is in the care of the Passionist Fathers.

As the gaining of the indulgences must depend in great measure on our inward dispositions, we must in the first place remember that the Son of God, in working out our Redemption, ascended and descended these same Steps, bound with cords, derided, spat upon, cruelly torn with stripes and bleeding at every pore. Let every one then, who is about to ascend these holy Steps, imagine that he hears Jesus Christ inviting him to follow Him with the words: — « If any man will come after me let him deny himself and take up his cross and follow me » — and let him promptly answer: « O Lord, I am ready to go with Thee even unto death, but since I know my own weakness, I pray Thee to stretch forth the hand of thy grace, without which I can do nothing. »

Before ascending we may excite ourselves to sorrow for past sins and devoutly say the following prayer.

PRAYER.

O most merciful Jesus, who for the salvation of the world, of thine own will wast cruelly scourged, and crowned with thorns, and then ignominiously dragged by wicked men up these steps before Pilate, we humbly beseech Thee, that whilst we devoutly worship the bloodstains of thy sacred feet, we through the merits of thy Passion may ascend by the steps of thy grace, and happily reach the throne of thy infinite glory, where with the Father and the Holy Ghost Thou livest and reignest for ever and ever. Amen.

THE SCALA SANTA

In going up the Holy Steps it is not necessary to stay long; nor to recite long prayers at each Step. It is sufficient to ascend devoutly from one to the other, thinking meanwhile on the Passion of our Lord, or reciting the Our Father or Hail Mary, so as not to hinder or disturb those who follow. To such however as may wish to meditate with fruit and in order on the Passion of our Redeemer, the following pious considerations and prayers taken from the Gospel history are proposed.

MEDITATION

For the first Step. " He went according to his custom to the Mount of Olives and kneeling down He prayed. ,, (*St. Luke 22. 39-41*)

My dearest Jesus, I contemplate Thee, when after the Last Supper thou didst bid farewell to thy disciples and begin thy most bitter passion by going to the Mount of Olives to pray to thy Eternal Father: give me grace always to begin my actions by seeking for thy divine assistance in prayer.

MEDITATION

For the second Step. " And his sweat became as drops of blood trickling down upon the ground. ,, *(St. Luke 22. 24)*.

My most compassionate Jesus, who, through the intimate knowledge of all thy own pains, and of my sins, didst suffer so intense an agony, that a bloody sweat flowed from all thy sacred body, and ran down upon the ground: give me grace always to remember that I by my sins have been the guilty cause of this thy abundant sweat of blood.

MEDITATION

For the third Step. " Judas drew near to Jesus to kiss Him. And Jesus said to him; Judas, dost thou betray the Son of Man with a kiss? ,, *(St. Luke 22. 47-48)*

My sweetest Jesus, who didst treat the traitor Judas, after his treacherous kiss, not only with meekness, but didst

even reprove him with love, to show him that his treason was known to Thee under that sign of friendship: give me grace in all I do to act with simplicity, that I may never injure my neighbour by any kind of deceit.

MEDITATION

For the fourth Step. " The servants of the Jews took Jesus and bound Him." *(St. John 18. 12)*

My beloved Jesus, who wast seized by the soldiers, bound with cords, dragged from the garden to Jerusalem and treated with every kind of cruelty, like the most infamous of men: give me grace to conceive a true and sincere sorrow for my sins, that being freed from all attachment to them I may remain faithful to Thee unto death.

MEDITATION

For the fifth Step. " And they led Him away to Annas first." *(St. John 18. 13)*

My most humble Jesus, who didst willingly submit thyself to Annas, Caiphas, Herod and Pilate — most wicked judges — and to be led backwards and forwards to their tribunals in such great ignominy: give me grace readily to submit myself for thy love's sake to the judgment of my superiors and to bear in peace the reproofs and rebukes which they from time to time may give me for my correction.

MEDITATION

For the sixth Step. " Then they dit spit in His face and buffeted Him and others struck His face with the palms of their hands *(St. Matthew 26. 67)*

My most patient Jesus, who didst bear from the sacrilegious soldiers their filthy spittle upon thy adorable face on

whose majesty angels fear to look, and didst endure the shame of being blindfolded and buffeted with blows: give me grace to enter seriously into the thought of my sins, that full of humble confusion and holy shame I may excite my hard heart to a true sorrow for having offended Thee.

MEDITATION

For the seventh Step. " And they brought Him bound and delivered Him to Pontius Pilate the governor." *(St. Matth. 27.2)*

My most meek Jesus, who as a malefactor, bound with cords, wast led up and down these Steps, which I unworthy am ascending and which Thou didst in many places stain with thy most precious blood: give me grace to ascend by the steps of true repentance to the eternal glory of heaven, which Thou hast purchased for me by the shedding of this very blood.

MEDITATION

For the eighth Step. " Pilate saith to them: I find no cause in Him. " *(St. John 18. 38)*

My most holy Jesus, who being maliciously accused by false witnesses wast nevertheless declared innocent by Pilate: give me grace to free myself from the persecution of my enemies and from false witnesses, that I may thus be always bound to render Thee unceasing thanks and praises for thy innumerable benefits.

MEDITATION

For the ninth Step. " And Herod with his army set Him at naught, and mocked Him, putting on Him a white garment. *(St. Luke 23. 11)*

My most loving Jesus, who didst allow thyself for love of me to be mocked and derided by the wicked Herod

and wast clothed in scorn with a white garment; give me grace ever to preserve the white robe of purity, until I shall be presented before thy divine tribunal.

MEDITATION

For the tenth Step. " And he sent Him back to Pilate. " *(St. Luke 23. 11)*

My most innocent Jesus, who as a meek lamb didst allow thyself to be led into the courtyard of Pilate's palace, where thou wast stripped and left naked, in the presence of a great multitude, and then wast fast bound to a pillar; give me grace to strip my soul of all affection for the false pleasures of this world and to clothe it with holy virtues by weeping bitterly for my sins, that thus I may not appear before Thee in death without the nuptial robe of thy divine grace.

MEDITATION

For the eleventh Step. " Then Pilate took Jesus and scourged Him. " *(St. John 19. 1)*

My Jesus grievously tormented, who wast scourged so sorely and in so many ways, until thy most pure flesh was wounded and torn and Thou couldst say with the Prophet, " They have numbered all my bones: " give me grace to suffer patiently all the afflictions and pains, both spiritual and temporal, which Thou mayest send me, that I may be able with the Prophet to say unto Thee, " I am ready for stripes. " *(Ps. 37. 18)*

MEDITATION

For the twelfth Step. " And the soldiers platting a crown of thorns put it upon His head; and they put on Him a purple garment. " *(St. John 19. 2)*

My most sorrowful Jesus, whose most sacred Head was with extreme and unheard-of barbarity crowned and

pierced by the wicked Jews with sharpest thorns and who wast then in derision clothed in a ragged purple garment: give me grace to expel my sinful thoughts by the thought of thy most piercing wounds, and to clothe my wretched soul with the robe of an ardent love for Thee and for my neighbour, that I may deserve to be eternally loved by Thee in heaven.

MEDITATION

For the thirteenth Step. " They put a reed in his right hand. And bowing the knee before Him they mocked Him, saying: Hail King of the Jews. And spitting upon Him, they took the reed and struck his head. " *(St. Matthew 27. 29-30)*

My most benign Jesus, who didst allow thy scornful executioners to place a reed in thy hand for a sceptre; to mock Thee saluting Thee as King of the Jews; to befoul thee with spittle; to buffet Thee with blows, and to strike thy head with the reed: give me grace to bear for thy love the injuries and insults which I may at any time endure from my neighbour, in the thought that I may thus in some measure become like to Thee.

MEDITATION

For the fourteenth Step. " Pilate therefore went forth again, and saith to them: Behold the Man. " *(St. John 19. 4-5)*

My most afflicted Jesus, who being covered with so many wounds and so many sorrows wast brought forth by Pilate to the people to move them to compassion: give me grace to contemplate Thee continually thus wounded and bruised by my sins, that bitterly bewailing them, I may share thy sufferings and not offend Thee more.

MEDITATION

For the fifteenth Step. " The governor said to them: Whether will you of the two to be released unto you? But they said:

Barabbas. Pilate saith to them: What shall I do then with Jesus that is called Christ? They say all: Let Him be crucified." *(St. Matthew 27. 21-23)*

My most loving Jesus, I contemplate Thee put on a level with Barabbas, a robber and murderer, in the sight of all that multitude, who cried out that he should be set free and Thou crucified: give me grace always to prefer to the dictates of a foolish world those of thy divine law, that despising the wicked maxims of the world I may persevere in the fulfilment of thy divine commandments.

MEDITATION

For the sixteenth Step. " And Pilate gave sentence that it should be as they required." *(St. Luke 23. 24)*

My outraged Jesus, who for me wast given over by the unjust Pilate into the hands of the Jews, that they might do to Thee whatever their diabolical fury might devise: give me grace that, aided by thy divine help, I may always resist my evil inclinations and conform myself to thy most holy will.

MEDITATION

For the seventeenth Step. " And Jesus bearing His own cross went forth to that place which is called Calvary." *(St. John 19. 17)*

My wearied Jesus, who burning with infinite love for the salvation of mankind didst embrace the cross so much longed for by Thee, and with the same love didst carry it to Mount Calvary: give me grace to bear with patience, and resignation the cross of tribulations which Thou dost lay on me, yea, even to rejoice in following Thee, that I may come one day to reign with Thee.

MEDITATION

For the eighteenth Step. " And there followed Him a great multitude of people, and of women who bewailed and lamented Him." *(St. Luke 23. 27)*

My sorrowing Jesus, who when pitied by those women that beheld Thee thus cruelly treated on thy way to death, exhorted them to weep rather over themselves: give me grace that in contemplating thy sorrowful journey to Calvary to be crucified, I may weep over my own grievous sins which were the cause of thy manifold and most bitter sufferings.

MEDITATION

For the nineteenth Step. " And they gave Him to drink wine mingled with myrrh. " *(St. Mark 15. 23)*

My suffering Jesus, who for support in thy excessive faintness didst receive into thy parched mouth from the perfidious Jews the bitter drink of wine mingled with myrrh: give me grace, in my trials and sorrows, not to seek the vain consolations of the world but only the never-ending joys of Paradise.

MEDITATION

For the twentieth Step. " But they dividing His garments, cast lots." *(St. Luke 23. 34)*

My meek Jesus, who didst allow thyself to be stripped with such fury by the cruel executioners, who then divided thy garments by lot: give me grace that divested of all affection for the fleeting joys of this world I may desire and love only the everlasting joys of heaven.

MEDITATION

For the twenty-first Step. " And they crucified Him and with Him two others, one on each side, and Jesus in the midst." *(St. John 19. 18)*

My suffering Jesus, who wast fastened to the cross with hard nails by thy tender hands and feet, and then raised up on it between two thieves: give me grace to remain crucified to my passions by a true spirit of penance, that united with Thee on the cross here on earth, I may remain united with Thee likewise in the glory of heaven.

MEDITATION

For the twenty-second Step. "And Jesus said: Father, forgive them, for they know not what they do." *(St. Luke 23. 34)*

My dying Jesus, who full of infinite charity didst pray to the Eternal Father to forgive thy inhuman crucifiers and didst solovingly excuse their most frightful sin: give me grace, after thy example and for thy love's sake alone, to pardon also the offences received from my neighbour and, so far from seeking satisfaction, like Thee to return good for evil.

MEDITATION

For the twenty-third Step. " And Jesus said to him: Amen I say to thee, this day thou shalt be with me in paradise." *(St. Luke 23. 43)*

Most merciful Jesus, who at the approach of death didst bestow on the penitent thief an eternal kingdom: give me grace to be sincerely sorry for my sins at the last moment of my life, that I too may hear from thy mouth the invitation to the glory of Paradise.

MEDITATION

For the twenty-fourth Step. " And immediately one of them running, took a sponge, and filled it with vinegar, and put it on a reed, and gave Him to drink." *(St. Matthew 27. 48)*

My abandoned Jesus, who languishing on the cross with a burning thirst from the shedding of all thy innocent blood but, still more with the desire of suffering new torments for the salvation of sinners, didst have presented to thy parched lips a sponge filled with vinegar, which when tasted did but add to thy bitter suffering: give me grace for thy love to mortify my taste by the thought of this loathsome drink and still more by a truly Christian life to correspond with the ardent desire Thou hast shewn for my salvation.

MEDITATION

For the twenty-fifth Step. " And Jesus crying with a loud voice, said: Father, into thy hands I commend my spirit." *(St. Luke 23. 46)*

My agonising Jesus, who when expiring on the cross didst commend thy most holy soul into the hands of thy heavenly Father: give me grace to understand well the great truth, that it will avail me nothing to gain the whole world if I lose my soul, that so giving it over wholly to Thee, as I do from this day forth by an irrevocable gift, I may place it for ever in security from its enemies.

MEDITATION

For the twenty-sixth Step. " One of the soldiers with a spear opened his side, and immediately there came out blood and water." *(St. John 19. 34)*

My crucified Jesus, who having yielded up thy blessed

soul, wast to the unspeakable grief of thy Virgin Mother wounded with a lance in the side, whence issued blood and water: give me grace to choose that sacred opening as an abiding resting-place, that so my unclean soul, cleansed by that water and that precious blood, may find in itself the power and efficacy of the Most Holy Sacrament.

MEDITATION

For the twenty-seventh Step. "Joseph of Arimathea besought Pilate that he might take away the body of Jesus. And Pilate gave leave. He came therefore and took away the body of Jesus." *(St. John 19. 38)*

My loving Jesus, who when taken down from the cross wast placed in the arms of thy most afflicted Mother; give me grace to cast myself into the arms of thy infinite mercy, that grieving from my heart for having kept Thee so long on the cross by my sins, I may have time solely to weep over and detest them.

MEDITATION

For the twenty-eighth Step. "And Joseph taking the body wrapt it up in a clean linen cloth." *(St. Matthew 27. 59)*

My adorable Jesus, who didst wish that thy sacred body should be wrapt by Joseph of Arimathea in a clean white cloth and placed in a new sepulchre: give me grace to cleanse my soul from all foulness of sin and to preserve it white and unspotted unto death. Amen.

Having thus reached the sacred Chapel of the Sancta Sanctorum *we may excite ourselves to more devotion, and say the following prayer.*

PRAYER

O dearest Lord, stir up, we beseech Thee, our hearts, and raise them up to thy holy love and to the fervour of thy faith, that by means of the sacred image of the Saviour of the world which we devoutly venerate here on earth, and through the merits of the saints whose bodies and relics lie in this holy Chapel, we may become worthy to serve Thee with minds cleansed from all stain of sin; and this we beg through the merits of the same Jesus Christ thy Son our Lord, who with Thee in the unity of the Holy Ghost liveth and reigneth for ever and ever. Amen.

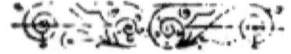

GLOSSARY.

Abstinence — is the depriving ourselves of different kinds of food and drink for the good of our souls. It imports a limit as to the *nature* of the food, not as to the *quantity*. It is *fast* that limits the quantity (see the word). A day of abstinence is not necessarily a fast day and viceversa. The days of abstinence are, according to the general law of the Church, Fridays and Saturdays thoughout the year (in most countries the Saturday abstinence has been dispensed), except the Friday (or Saturday) on which Christmas may fall; Ember days; vigils of certain great feasts; Saturdays and in some countries Wednesdays) in Lent; and Saturdays in Advent.

Absolution — a setting free from crime or penalty. *Absolution from sin* is the remission of sin which a priest, by authority received from Christ, makes to a person rightly disposed in the sacrament of penance. *Absolution from censures* is a removal of penalties imposed by the Church, and reconciliation of the offender with her. *Absolution for the dead* is a form of prayer imploring eternal rest, and so indirectly a remission of the temporal penalties of sin. Absolution is likewise the name applied to certain short prayers in the Breviary, asking forgiveness of sin and a blessing.

Adoration of the Cross, is the term applied to the religious ceremony on Good Friday, when reverence is made to the

cross being the symbol of the ignominious death that our Saviour was pleased to suffer for us. As a general rule, however, we reserve the word *adoration* to correspond to the Greek (and then ecclesiastical Latin) word *latria*, and denote the service, or worship due to God alone.

Agape, a name given to the brotherly feasts of the early Christians.

Agnus Dei, (1) a prayer in the Mass, (2) the figure of a lamb (*agnus*) stamped on pieces of wax taken from the Paschal Candles, and blessed by the Pope on the Saturday after Easter in the first and seventh years of his pontificate.

Alleluia. A Hebrew word meaning, " Praise the Lord, " of very frequent use in the Old Testament. St. John heard angels singing it in heaven. St. Jerome says children in his time were taught it among their first words. It is of very frequent use in the Church on occasions of joy, and especially at Easter-tide.

Altar, stripping of, a ceremony performed after Mass on Holy Thursday, to remind Christians of the way their Master was stripped of his garments, and to signify the desolation of the Church.

Altar of Repose, is an altar set apart on Holy Thursday for the reception of the Sacred Host which is reserved for the Mass of the Presanctified said on the following day. Its necessity comes from the fact that the chief altar has been stripped, in accordance with the ceremony mentioned above; and the great adornment given it is in commemoration of the institution of the Holy Eucharist, which took place on the eve of our Saviour's Passion.

Anglican Church. The national institution formed on the separation of England from the communion of the Catholic Church. This institution retained the old titles of the Catholic sees the church lands, the tithes and a portion of the ecclesiastical discipline. Its establishment was gradually effected from the year 1533, when Henry VIII. claimed the title of supreme head of the Church, to the year 1563, when the thirty-nine Articles were adopted by the Convocation of the province of Canterbury, at the very moment that the Council of Trent was holding its sittings.

Antipopes. Men who at different periods of the history of the Church, either in good faith or fraudulently, claimed the title of Pope, or even usurped the prerogatives of the Holy See, without having been duly elected.

Apocrypha — in general, those books claiming an origin that might entitle them to a place in the canon, or once supposed to be Scripture, but finally rejected by the Church. Non-Catholics, contrary to the faith and traditions of the Church, treat the books, Wisdom, Maccabees and others as apocrypha. See *Canon of the Scripture* and *Deutero-Canonical*.

Ash Wednesday — the first day of the forty days fast of Lent. The name is taken from the solemn ceremony — the imposition of ashes as a sign of penance — with which the office of the day opens. The administration of ashes was originally made to public penitents alone, but other members of the faithful offering themselves out of humility, the institution was soon made universal.

Attrition, as contrasted with contrition is an imperfect sorrow for sin. Contrition is the sorrow that has for its motive the love of God, who has been offended; attrition has a motive likewise supernatural but inferior to this. The motive of attrition may be, for instance, the fear of hell, the loss of heaven, the turpitude of sin, as revealed by faith. Contrition justifies without the actual reception of the sacrament of Penance; attrition justifies, not by itself, but with the sacrament.

Baldacchino, a canopy over the high altar of a church, either suspended from the ceiling, or supported by pillars; also the canopy held over the priest who bears the Blessed Sacrament in procession. The baldacchino in the first sense goes back to the time of Constantine. From its interior a cord hung down, by which was suspended the vessel in which the Holy Eucharist was placed. Cardinals, Roman princes and ambassadors have the right of the baldacchino; so also have the Roman marquises, Theodoli, Cavalieri, Massimo, Costaguti and Patrizi; hence they are called " marchesi di baldacchino. " There is one count who has the same privilege, Count Soderini, of the noble Florentine family connected by marriage with the Medici.

Baptism, is the sacrament wherein by water and the words of the sacramental form we are made Christians, children of God, members of the Church and heirs of heaven. The sign or symbol is physical cleansing and the interior grace which this symbolises is the cause of interior cleansing or spiritual regeneration. The seven sacraments symbolise also the new life of man, and by the first of them, baptism, we

are born to that new life. The descent into the water signifies burial with Christ (Rom. vi. 4. Baptism in Apostolic times was by immersion), the coming forth again signifies the new birth.

Baptism is absolutely necessary for all, not excepting even infants. " Unless a man be born again of water and of the Holy Ghost, he cannot enter into the kingdom of heaven ,, (John iii-5). Children, therefore, who die unbaptised, cannot enjoy the beatific vision of the Deity. Nevertheless, we need not suppose that they suffer any positive pain; on the contrary, it seems most probable that they enjoy all the bliss of which they are capable. In excluding them from heaven God does them no wrong, for they never had a right to go there; heaven is a free gift, and in no sense due to us by nature. The case of adults is somewhat different. For them, where the actual reception of the sacrament is impossible, an act of perfect charity, which includes the desire of it, will suffice for salvation.

Again, martyrdom, which is the highest act of charity, has always been held to supply the place of baptism. We may say then, that there are three kinds of baptism: 1. The baptism of water, which is the sacrament; 2. The baptism of the spirit, which is an act of charity, including a desire for the sacrament; 3. The baptism of blood, which is martyrdom.

Basilica. This name began to be applied to Christian churches about the beginning of the fourth century. It was used previously among the Romans to denote large halls for t e purposes of justice or commerce. The Christian basilicas were of a uniform type, with, on the outside, surrounding wall, portico, atrium or quadrangle, area or open central space; inside, nave and two flanking aisles without transept, ambo, rails, vaulted apse with altar just in front. The term basilica is loosely applied to the large churches of Rome in general. Strictly, in Rome there are five greater or patriarchal basilicas: St. John's, St. Peter's, St. Mary Major's, St. Paul's, St. Laurence's; and eight smaller ones: Sta. Maria in Trastevere, St. Laurence in Damasus, Sta. Maria in Cosmedin, Sta. Maria del Popolo, Sta. Maria sopra Minerva, St. Sebastian, Holy Cross, Sta. Sabina, of which the first five are called the minor basilicas.

Beatification is the act of declaring a person or persons de-

ceased to be among the number of the Blessed, and consequently worthy of public honour in the Church. See Saint.

Beatific Vision, the sight of God face to face, which constitutes the essential bliss of angels and men.

Benediction of the Blessed Sacrament, is the exposition of the Holy Eucharist, and the making the sign of the cross therewith over the people. The rite is comparatively modern. Processions and expositions of the Blessed Sacrament were, we know, in use in the beginning of the fourteenth century, but the blessing dates back not much more than three hundred years. The custom of singing the " O Salutaris Hostia " at the Elevation in Mass (and afterwards in the expositions) was introduced by Louis XII. of France, when harassed by enemies, shortly before his death in 1515.

Bible is the book containing the inspired writings. The Catholic Church defends the authority of this written word of God but likewise holds that there is also an unwritten word of God, tradition. The Catholic Church holds that its interpretation belongs to herself and not to the individual; likewise, though she is anxious for all persons to know this word of God, she holds that not all parts of the Bible may be usefully read by certain classes, by the very young, for instance, and by the ignorant.

Bishop, the ecclesiastical dignitary who has received the plenitude of the sacerdotal power and is invested with authority to rule a diocese as its chief pastor.

Bishops, Suffragan, the members forming the college of bishops under a metropolitan or archbishop. *Suffragan* is taken in another sense, to denote a bishop elected to assist another bishop in the administration of his diocese, but he (unlike the *coadjutor*) cannot thereby exercise any jurisdiction.

Bishop in partibus, (infidelium,) the term applied to a bishop consecrated to a see that formerly existed, but which has been lost to Christendom. The Propaganda decreed in 1882 this term *in partibus infidelium* abolished, and the designation of non-resident bishops henceforth to be « *titular* » bishops of their sees.

Breviary. Breviary means compendium. It is a word of mediaeval origin, but the custom of reciting the divine office goes back to the very beginning of the Church. The office of the breviary is the highest formulary of prayer.

It is divided into seven parts or *hours* (Matins with Lauds, Prime, Terce, Sext, None, Vespers, and Complin), and is obligatory for all clerics who have received the order of subdeaconship.

Brief, a letter from the court of Rome, subscribed by the Pope's secretary of Briefs, and sealed with the Pope's signetring, the seal of the Fisherman.

Bull, a document issued from the court of Rome, signed by the functionaries of the Papal Chancery, and sealed with the *bulla*, or round leaden seal, having on one side a representation of SS. Peter and Paul, and on the other the name of the reigning Pope, and fastened to the document by a string of silk, if it be a Bull of Grace; by hemp if a Bull of Justice. It is of a more formal and weighty character than the Brief, and generally contains some memorable decision or condemnation.

Bussolanti, the ushers of the Apostolic palace. They wear a violet soutane and cincture.

Candles, in times of persecution were necessary as Christian assemblies were then mostly held by night or underground. The symbolism of candles has made their usage be retained in the services of the Church. At Masses and Benedictions their number is prescribed. In Rome the candles are white wax, long and tapering. It is customary to paint and adorn the massive ones used on solemn occasions. The yellow wax indicates mourning and is used at funerals, and in certain offices during Holy Week. On the feast of Candlemas, the superiors and representatives of the ecclesiastical institutions and religious orders in Rome present a candle to the Holy Father.

Canon of the Scripture. The list of the sacred books. Among the Jews a canon of the Old Testament had been arranged by Esdras long before our Saviour's coming. The canon of the New Testament began to be settled in the fourth century. Finally, the Council of Trent has decided authoritatively and definitively on the matter. The principle on which the canon of Scripture rests for Catholics is the infallible authority of the Church, and not the « self-evidencing light » of the Scripture, or the critical investigation of the books — theories put forward by non-Catholics, who forget that Scripture itself rests on Tradition and that they have received it precisely from the Catholic Church.

Capella Papale = Papal Chapel, the term applied to the cere-

mony when the Pope, surrounded by the cardinals, officiates or assists at the offices or processions on the principal festivals of the year. The Papal chapels are fifty-eight in number.

Cardinal, a dignitary of the highest rank in the Church. The cardinalate does not import a sacerdotal power, though according to modern Canon Law, to be named cardinal one must be in Holy Orders and at least a deacon. The number of cardinals is limited to seventy. They owe their appointment solely to the Pope, of whom they are the advisers. They have an active part in the government of the universal Church; and on the vacancy of the Holy See, to them pertains the right of electing the new Pope.

Cardinal Legate. See below the word *Legate*.

Cardinal Protector, a cardinal who is accepted at the court of Rome as consultor or referee in questions affecting the interests of the nation to which he belongs, or of the individuals of that nation. There are also, with the same functions, Cardinal Protectors of the religious orders, the colleges, etc.

Cardinal Vicar. The cardinal who represents the Pope, the Bishop of Rome, as regards the ecclesiastical administration of the city.

Catacombs. Subterranean passages hollowed out in the granular tufa, with which the environs of Rome abound, for the purposes of worship and sepulture in the early days when the Christians were harassed or persecuted. When liberty came, in the fourth century, the catacombs were made a centre of pilgrimage. In the seventh and eighth centuries they were plundered and damaged by the Lombards. Then the remains of the Popes and of the principal martyrs and confessors were transferred to the churches of Rome. The catacombs were outside the city and generally under the property of some wealthy Christian. They are found on every side of Rome, but clustered most thickly at the south east corner of the city. The most noteworthy is that of San Callisto, close to the Appian Way; near it are those of St. Praetextatus, St. Sebastian, and St. Soteris. Very remarkable also are those of St. Agnes on the Via Nomentana, Sta. Priscilla on the Via Salaria, and SS. Nereus and Achilleus on the Via Ardeatina.

Cathedra, ex. Cathedra is used to signify not merely the chair in which the bishop sits, or the authority of the bish-

op who occupies the chair, but also authoritative doctrinal teaching in general. In this last sense our Saviour himself uses it when speaking of the Scribes and Pharisees. The expression *ex cathedra* has thence been used by the theologians to denote those definitions in faith and morals, which the Pope as teacher of all Christians imposes on their belief. The Vatican Council declares that the Pope is infallible " when he speaks *ex cathedra*," i.e. when, in the exercise of his office as the pastor and teacher of all Christians, he, in virtue of his supreme Apostolic authority, defines a doctrine concerning faith and morals to be held by the whole Church. Were it possible that the Pope, *in his capacity of supreme Pastor of the Church, speaking ex cathedra*, could teach error, it might be argued, 1st, that the prayer of our Lord for St. Peter was not granted; 2nd, that the special provision which Jesus Christ made for securing His Church from error, instead of preserving it from erring in faith or in morals, would, at least in certain cases, only serve to draw the whole Church into error, and be an advantage for Satan, not a means of defence to the Church against him.

Cathedral — that church in a diocese where a bishop has his chair or seat; whence *see*, the English form of *siège*.

Catholic, means universal, and has been applied from the very earliest times — from the days of St. Ignatius of Antioch, disciple of St. Peter — to distinguish the true Church from heretical sects. Catholic also came to be applied to the individual Christian. Lastly, " Catholic " is used of the faith which the Church of God holds. It has subsidiary senses in phrases like " Catholic epistle," Catholic king, etc.

Censure, a spiritual penalty, imposed for the correction and amendment of offenders, by which a baptised person, who has committed a crime and is contumacious, is deprived by ecclesiastical authority of the use of certain spiritual advantages. The use of censures dates from the infancy of the Church.

Chair of St. Peter. At the further end of the apse of St. Peter's is a fine piece of bronze workmanship representing four Fathers of the Church upholding a chair. Within this outer chair is another with a hollow seat, with ivory bas-reliefs on the front, representing the constellations and the labours of Hercules. This interior chair, according to tradition, was the curule seat of Pudens, and served St. Peter,

at the time of his residence in the senator's house, on the Viminal, during the celebration of the holy mysteries. The feast of St. Peter's Chair at Rome occurs on January 18; that of St. Peter's Chair at Antioch on February 22.

Chrism, olive oil mixed with balm, blessed by the bishop and used by the Church in confirmation as well as in baptism, ordination, consecration of altar stones, chalices, churches and in the blessing of baptismal water. Oil signifies the fulness of grace, for oil signifies diffusion, and balm incorruption and the " good odour of Christ. " The chrism is blessed on Holy Thursday.

Chamberlain, Secret, attendant of the Holy Father. Four secret chamberlains are *participanti* (participating), and three of them have particular functions (at solemn repasts when the Pope is present, at the reception of foreign sovereigns, and with regard to the papal wardrobe); the others are supernumerary, and do service when the Holy Father gives audience, or performs papal functions.

Chant, Plain, the Church music, perfected by St Gregory the Great, whence called Gregorian, and still dominant in Christian worship in all western lands. It is " plain, " that is, not figured or florid, admitting melody but not harmony, and distinct from modern five-lined music of a sacred character. It abhors the ostentatious displays and tawdry decorations that form so prominent a feature in secular music.

Colours, Papal. The Papal colours were yellow and red, but Napoleon I. having adopted these colours for his troops in Italy, Pius VII., in 1808, chose white and yellow, and these have since been retained. The municipality of Rome affects the yellow and red.

Confession. For sacramental confession see *Penance*. Confession is also used in a technical sense, and in early times denoted the tomb of a martyr. Later on it was applied to the altar placed immediately over the martyr's tomb. The most famous Confession is in St. Peter's. The Confession is mostly a central detached altar.

Congregations, Sacred, the bodies or councils into which the cardinals are distributed to aid the Holy Father in the transaction of business. The principal Roman Congregations are those of the Consistory; the Holy Office or the Inquisition; the Index; Rites; Immunities; the Fabric (for the Basilica of St Peter's); the Council (for the interpretation

of disciplinary decrees of the Council of Trent): Bishops and Regulars; Discipline (of religious orders); the Propaganda and Indulgences.

Consanguinity, blood-relationship, as contrasted with *affinity*, relationship by marriage. The Church forbids marriage between blood-relations to the fourth degree inclusively.

Consultors of Sacred Congregations. Prelates, ecclesiastics or religious, attached to the various Sacred Congregations, and who on all questions that arise, give information and enlightenment, and emit a *votum* or opinion, which the cardinals generally take into account in their decisions.

Consecration, the form of words by which the bread and wine in the Mass are changed into Christ's body and blood. Consecration is also taken to indicate that part of the Mass at which these words are pronounced.

Consistory, is at present accepted to denote the assembly of the whole body of cardinals, under the presidency of the Pope, for the transaction of the important business of the Church. Public consistories are held mostly on the occasion of the promulgation of new cardinals.

Contrition, grief of mind and detestation of sin committed, with a purpose of sinning no more. This is the wide sense. More restrictedly, contrition denotes either a part of the sacrament of Penance (which see,) or, as when contrasted with attrition, that sorrow for sin founded on the highest and purest of motives, the love of God, whom sin has offended. This perfect contrition, we may note, is not necessarily more sensitively intense than other and natural sorrow.

Convent, an abode of a religious community. The parts of a convent are: the church; the choir; the chapter-house; the cells; the refectory; the dormitory; the infirmary; the parlour or reception-room; the library; the cloister and the crypt.

Corpus Christi. The institution of the Eucharist has from Apostolic times been celebrated on the Thursday in Holy Week. But another feast of the Blessed Sacrament, which should occur outside of Passion-time, seeming an object to be desired, Pope Urban IV., in 1364, published a Bull commanding the celebration of the feast on the Thursday following the first Sunday after Pentecost. The office of the feast was composed by St. Thomas Aquinas; and the carrying of the Blessed Sacrament in procession seems

to have been a recognized part of the ceremonial almost from the first.

Creation. The fourth Lateran Council defines that God created, or made out of nothing, the whole universe, which is not eternal but had a beginning. God created it by his free act and without any change in His own nature. The Biblical " days of creation " are diversely interpreted, either as denoting our days of twenty-four hours, or more probably longer periods of time, or else, as having (as St. Augustine and Cajetan suggest) a figurative and mystical sense.

Creation of Cardinals, the ceremony according to which the exalted dignity of Prince of the Church is conferred on new individuals. The Pope assembles the cardinals in secret consistory and mentions the new members on whom he purposes to confer the purple. The cardinals signify their adhesion, and then the Holy Father declares them duly named. Sometimes the Pope elects a cardinal without publishing his name. He is said to reserve it *in petto.* After the private consistory comes the public one, and with different ceremonies and at different times the new cardinal receives his ring, his red *zucchetto*, red hat, and red berretta, and takes formal possession of his titular church.

Cross, Pectoral, the cross which a bishop or abbot wears on his breast. For the former, it is suspended by a gold chain or by a green silk cord interwoven with gold, and for the latter, by a silk cord of violet colour. Cardinal-priests wear it in their titular church.

Crucifix. We cannot prove historically that the habit of representing our Saviour hanging on the cross dates back further than the sixth century. In the preceding centuries a lamb took the place of the human figure, in order not to give scandal to the Pagans, who frequently came to the churches, as crucifixion was the punishment meted out to the worst criminals; they frequently used crosses inlaid with gems, but never with the figure of our Lord upon them.

Crucifix, Miraculous. More than one is preserved in Rome. The most remarkable is that in St. Paul's, which, it is said, held frequent converse with St. Birgitta. Others are in the Mamertine Prison, in St. Marcellus, in St. Laurence in Damasus, and Sta. Maria del Popolo.

Crypt, an apartment under a church designed for burial pur-

poses, and to keep the Church dry, and also frequently serving for Divine Worship.

Deacon. The word means minister or servant. The deaconship is a part of Holy Orders, conferring the right to minister to the priest in the celebration of the Holy Eucharist, to baptise and to preach. The first seven who received this ordination are mentioned as having been chosen to administer the alms of the Church. But not for that alone; as they must be " full of the Holy Ghost and of wisdom, ,, and we find Stephen, one of their number, preaching and instructing, and Philip. another of them, baptising.

Deaconesses, pious women who in the early ages of the Church performed certain functions. They assisted at the baptism of the women, then by immersion. They gave private instruction to women ; visited them in sickness and in prison; kept order in the women's part of the church; assisted the bride at marriages, etc. In the tenth century the office had become extinct in the west. In Constantinople it was contined up to the twelfth, and it is still preserved among the Syrians.

Defender of the Faith, (Defensor Fidei) the title conferred on Henry VIII. and his successors by Leo X. in 1521, in recompense fo the former's book defending the seven sacraments against Luther.

Defenders of the Holy See. In 1856 Pius IX found in the Chapel of the Seminario Pio a daily Mass *in perpetuum*, for those who, in the actual vicissitudes of the Church, defend the Holy See by their prayers, writings, arms or donations.

Desecration. A church, altar, chalice, etc. becomes desecrated when it has lost its sacred character and has become unfit for sacred uses. This may happen by the deterioration of the object itself, or by the committal of certain crimes or abuses in its regard.

Devil, the evil spirit, of whose existence we have most abundant testimony, especially in the New Testament. Though condemned, and that irrevocably, to the flames of hell, still from time to time devils wander in the air and over the earth. Wherever devils go, for they are many, they are tortured by the fires of hell, but the exact manner of that torture is not clearly known by theologians.

Deutero-Canonical, those books of the canon of Scripture which did not always belong to the canon, but about whose authenticity doubt was at some time expressed,

Dimissorials, letters giving leave to be ordained, and containing or implying testimony to fitness. Tyey may be furnished in general by the Roman Pontiff, by a bishop for his subjects, and by abbots and superiors of orders for their own rel gious.

Dispensation, the relaxation of a law in a particular case. There is no dispensation from the natural law. The Pope can dispense from obligations to God which a man has incurred of is own free will i. e. by oath or vow.

Distinguish dispensation from interpretation of the law. Thus a person too ill to fast needs no dispensation, as by the nature of the case he is exempt from the law.

Divorce, In the Catholic Church is a separation between man and wife, on sufficient grounds and by lawful authority. The Pope nor any human power can dissolve the bond of marriage when rightfully and lawfully ratified and consumated between baptised persons.

Doctors of the Church, must, according to Benedict XIV, be of eminent learning, of heroic sanctity, and declared Doctors by a Pope or Council and with the Pope. The four great doctors of the Greek Church are SS. Athanias, Chrisostom, Basil and Gregory of Nazianzan. Of the Latin Church are SS. Ambrose, Augustine, Jerome, Gregory the Great. Pius V added St Thomas Aquinas to the number. Succeeding pontiffs have decreed the title to St Bonaventure, St Isidore of Seville, St Peter Chrysologus, St Leo the Great, St Peter Damian, St Hilary and ultimately Pius IX proclaimed it for St Alphonsus Liguori and St Francis of Sales.

Dove, the symbol of the Holy Ghost, who appeared under that form at Our Saviour's baptism. The dove is also a figure of peace and reconciliation, as we read in Genesis; also of innocence, and the souls of saints are sometimes represented as flying to heaven in the form of a dove. In the Eastern Churches a vessel in the form of a dove is suspended over the altar and used as a repository for the Blessed Sacrament.

Doxology Strictly speaking is the formula for celebrating the praise of the Holy Trinity. There are two doxologies, the greater, which is the " Gloria in Excelsis " and the lesser, which is the " Gloria Patri. " Of the " Gloria Patri, " the second part, viz. " As is was in the beginning etc. " seems to have come into use only in the end of the fifth century.

Duel. Severe penalties have been decreed by the Church against duelling, especially by the Councils of Valence (855) and of Trent and by Popes Clement VIII and Benedict XIV. The combatants, seconds, abettors, spectators are excommunicated; and the person who dies from the effects of a duel is deprived of Christian burial.

Ember Days. The Wednesday, Friday and Saturday that follow the 13th of December, the First Sunday in Lent, the feast of Pentecost and the 14th of September, are days of fasting and abstinence and called in Latin " *quatuor tempora,*" in English " quarter tense " or Ember Days. Their observance was in use in the time of St. Augustine, and is ascribed by St. Leo to Apostolic institution. The clergy are regularly ordained on the saturdays of the Ember weeks, while the whole church fasts and prays.

Empire, Holy Roman, the title given to the central Empire of Europe, which was supposed to continue that founded by Charlemagne with the aid of the Roman Pontiffs, and to combine in itself the chief temporal power, always to be used in the advancement of Christianity. This supreme dominion and centralization was in reality but a mere figment. By " *command* " of Napoleon I in 1806, the ancient title was dropped, and the reigning Emperor took the title of Emperor of Austria.

Encyclical, a circular letter addressed by the pope to all the bishops in which he condemns prevalent errors, or informs them of impediments made in particular cases to the mission of the Church, or explains the line of conduct to be taken with regard to such practical questions as education, or the relations between church and state, or the liberty of the Holy See.

Epistle, a portion of scripture read after the Collects and before the Gospel in the Mass. It is frequently taken from the Epistles of the apostles, whence the name.

Eucharist, Holy, the true Body and Blood of Jesus Christ under the outward appearance of bread and wine. It is both a sacrament and a sacrifice. A sacrament it was instituted by Jesus on the night before His Passion. The bread and wine are the matter, the words of consecration are the form. A sacrifice it continues in an unbloody manner that consummated on mount Calvary.

Excommunication, an ecclesiastical censure by which a christian is separated from the communion of the church. " If he will

not hear the church" says our Saviour "let him be to thee as the heathen and publican." Excommunications are greater and lesser; and excommunicated persons are *non tolerati*, i. e. to be avoided, or *tolerati*, not necessarily to be avoided. To incur the greater excommunication (excommunicatus vitandus) one has to be excommunicated by *name*.

Execration, is taken in the same sense with regard to churches, cemeteries, sacred objects etc, as *desecration*.

Exemption, a privilege by which persons and places are withdrawn from the jurisdiction of the ordinary and subjected immediately to the Holy See. In this way the religious of regular orders (Congregations and Institutes enjoying the privileges of the Regular Orders) are in many particulars exempted.

Exequatur, the right claimed on behalf of bishops or temporal rulers to examine Papal bulls and constitutions and judge of the expediency of admitting them, before allowing them to take effect in their dioceses or territories. A bishop may to prevent serious inconvenience, withhold for a while the execution of a particular Constitution in his diocese, until he has laid the circumstances before the pope. With regard to temporal rulers the Holy See has never admitted their right to impede the execution of Papal rescripts but in practice, to prevent greater evils, it has often acquiesced in the exercise of this power,

Exercises, spiritual, name given by St. Ignatius Lojola to a series of meditations he composed on the truths of religion. These are commonly used for retreats, and are a work of marvellous comprehension.

Exposition of the Blessed Sacrament. It would appear that it was only in the second half of the fourteenth century that the Blessed Sacrament was exposed in the processions on the feast of Corpus Christi. In the sixteenth Century it became common to expose the sacred Host on solemn occasions, times of public distress etc,, and generally for forty continuous hours. These forty hours represented the time Our Lord spent in the tomb. Clement VIII in 1592 provided for the public and perpetual adoration of the Blessed Sacrament under this form of the forty hour's exposition in the different Churches of Rome.

Extreme Unction, the Sacrament in which the sick in danger of death are annointed by a priest for the health of soul

and body, the annointing being accompanied by a set form
of words. We have special mention of it in S. James, ch. v.
The sacrament can only be received in danger of death
arising from sickness, and only once in the same dangerous
illness.

Ex voto, offering made for the accomplishment of a desire.
They generally consist of little objects in silver or of small
pictures, and are appended to the walls of the church near
some particular shrine. The letters P. G. R., that often
accompany them, mean, *pro gratia recepta*, for grace (or
favour) received.

Faith, is the undoubting assent given to revealed truths,
on account of the authority of God who has revealed
them. It excludes all doubt; it concerns the things that we
see not. Without faith it is impossible to please God or
be saved.

Family, Pope's, those who compose the pontifical household, and render service to the Pope, but not menial service. It consists of several cardinals, prelates, clerics, chamberlains, and military officers.

Fan. In early times two deacons stood by the altar, from
the offertory to the communion in the Mass, and held
fans of linen or feathers with which to drive away insects
and prevent them from touching the sacred vessels. When
the Pope is carried in solemn processions magnificent
fans (*flabelli*) of peacock and ostrich feathers are borne
on each side.

Fanon, a special form of double mozzetta, reserved exclu-
sively to the Holy Father. Fanon (Lat. *fano*) likewise signifies maniple.

Fast. We distinguish the natural fast from the ecclesiastical
fast. The former consists in total abstinence from food
or drink and is imposed upon those who are about to
communicate. The ecclesiastical fast limits the quantity of
food to one full meal in the day. It likewise generally
puts some restriction on the quality of the food, forbidding,
for instance, that fish and fleshmeat be partaken of at
the same repast. The full meal, must not be taken before
midday.

Besides it, the Church permits a collation of about eight
ounces of food, from which flesh and white-meats are
excluded; custom, moreover, allows some two ounces of
bread for breakfast. Simple liquids as a rule do not break

the ecclesiastical fast. The days of fasting are: all the days of Lent, with the exception of Sundays; generally, two days a week in Advent; the Ember Days and the vigils of certain great feasts.

Feria, a name given in the ecclesiastical calendar to all the days of the week except Sunday (*Dies Dominica*) and Saturday (*Sabbatum*). The Church terms feria a day that is free, or on which no feast is celebrated.

Ferula, a golden rod surmounted by a cross, which the Pope holds in guise of a crosier in ceremonies of consecration.

Fisherman's Ring, a signet engraved with the effigy of St. Peter in the act of fishing, and with the name of the reigning Pope. With it Apostolic briefs are sealed. It is broken at the Pope's death.

Forty Hours, see above *Exposition of the Blessed Sacrament*.

Free Will, the power of choosing, the power man has of being able to accept an object when he might have rejected it.

It supposes freedom from impulsion from within and from without. The Reformers, and after them the Jansenists, denied man's possession of free will, but their doctrines on the point have been condemned by the Church. See *Predestination*.

Freemasonry, the system of that secret order which professes by means of a symbolical language and certain ceremonies of initiation and promotion, to lay down a code of morality founded on the brotherhood of humanity. Its origin is obscure. During the last hundred and fifty years it has been intimately connected with most of the revolutionary and atheistical movements on the continent of Europe. In England and the United States the baneful principles of the sect do not so openly transpire. It has been condemned by the bulls of various Popes.

The Catholic Church condemns all secret societies in general, and does not make exceptions for individual cases, or special countries, where possibly less evil is done by persons joining secret societies.

Funeral. The funeral rites, as prescribed by the Roman ritual begins with a procession, with lights, of the corpse to the church. The coffin is placed in the middle of the church with the feet to the altar if the dead person was a layman, the head if he was a priest. Candles are lighted

round the coffin, and the office and Mass of the dead, followed by the absolution with sprinkling and incensing of the coffin, are said. Then another procession, and the corpse is carried to the tomb. This ceremonial is very ancient. The procession is mentioned by SS. Gregory Nazianzen, Jerome, and Chrysostom. For infants the funeral rites are very different. White is the colour used, flowers are placed on the coffin, no prayer is said for the repose of the soul, psalms of praise and thanksgiving are sung, and the church bells are not rung, or else rung with a joyful tone. The custom of heaping the coffin of adults with wreaths and ribbons is discountenanced by the Church.

Galileo, much has been written and disserted on the condemnation to which Galileo in the first half of the seventeenth century was subjected for teaching the heliocentric theory of revolution, which theory had already been put forth by the priest Nicholas Cusa and by the immortal Copernicus. The conduct of Galileo was censurable in as much as he tried to prove his theory from the Holy scripture, asserting that portions of the scripture could not be satisfactorily explained unless his system was admitted. A phrase of Milton has led some to the erroneous belief that Galileo was put in prison in a dungeon.

The phrase attributed to Galileo "*eppur si muove*" "and yet it (the earth) does move" is a myth.

Ghost, Holy. To the Ghost, the third person of the most Holy Trinity which proceeds from the Father and the Son, is attributed the work of love which is our sanctification. The great schism of the Greek was mainly founded on their erroneous holding that the Holy Ghost proceeded from the Father alone. The symbol of the Holy Ghost is the dove as under that form he appeared at our Saviour's baptism in the Jordan.

Gnosticism, the doctrine of several sects of heretics that sprung up in the end of the first century, and endured all through the second. They rejected faith and ecclesiastical authority and founded their teachings on "superior knowledge". They denied the dogmas of the creation of the world from nothing, of the resurrection of the body, of salvation through the sufferings and death of Christ the Son of God. The world, according to them, was made by inferior powers ("aeons") more or less in antagonism with the supreme God. These were the chief tenets, though the variety of

minor holdings was infinite. The chief Gnostics were Simon Magus, Menander, Saturninus, Cerinthus, Basilides, Valentinus, and Marcion.

God, is a pure spirit, infinitely perfect, distinct from the universe which He has created. He is infinitely blessed in Himself and from Himself. From the consideration of created things we can come to a knowledge of His existence. St. Thomas Aquinas gives five philosophical proofs of the existence of God, proofs drawn from motion, causality, contingency moral order, and design. As to God's nature, human reason can also deduce something, by removing from God the imperfection of creatures, and by applying to him, though in a different manner, all true perfection of which we see traces in created things. The consequence of natural reason being able to know God as the author of the world is that all who have come to the use of reason are bound to know, love and obey God.

Golden Rose, originally a single flower of wrought gold, coloured red, at present a branch with leaves and thorns with nine or ten small flowers and with a large one on the top, the branch being set in a vase of rich workmanship. The Pope blesses it on the Fourth Sunday in Lent, incenses it and places some musk and Peruvian essence in the heart of the principal flower. The Golden Rose symbolises the joys of the heavenly garden, and the Pope sends it as a present generally to a Catholic Queen, but sometimes (especially formerly) to Catholic kings, to Catholic cities or republics, to illustrious General or to noted Churches and Sanctuaries. Henry VIII received it thrice. His daughter, Queen Mary, was likewise the recipient of it.

Good Friday, the day on which the Church commemorate the Passion of our saviour. During the sacred office take place the " adoration ", during which are sung the *improperia*, or " reproaches " of Jesus to the Jewish people. Afterwards is celebrated the Mass of the Presanctified, that is the Mass with the Host consecrated on the preceding day; for on the day on which Christ was offered as a bleeding victim for our sins, the Church abstains from consecrating. Communion on this day is not given to the faithful except in case of sickness. In Rome the morning office is at Holy Cross of Jerusalem, where the relics of the Passion are exposed. In the afternoon is celebrated in several Churches the Tree Hour's Agony of our Saviour, by sermons

intermingled with appropriate music. In the Vatican Basilica, exposal of the relics, *Tenebrae* Office, and hearing of confessions by the Cardinal Gran Penitentiary. This Friday is called good, on account of the immense Good brought to mankind by our Saviour's great work of love and mercy.

Gospel. A passage from the Sacred Scriptures, read during Mass; we have mention of it from the very earliest ages. In High Masses the deacon sings it, lights and incense being used. In former times he sang or recited it from the *ambon*, which custom is still preserved in some ancient basilicas of Rome.

Grace, the supernatural aid that God freely bestows on man, that he may be able to attain the supernatural end to which he is destined, namely, the eternal enjoyment of God. We are bound to believe that to all men God gives sufficient grace to be saved; and, further, that under the motion of grace we are free, so that it is in our power to resist it. The word grace is also used in minor senses, and even to denote a blessing or an expression of thanks, as Grace before meals.

Greek Church, the so-called orthodox, in reality, schismatic. The Greek Church consists of those Christians who refuse to admit the supremacy of the Pope and acknowledge (or have acknowledged) that of the Patriarch of Constantinople. The schism that brought about the separation of these Christians from the communion of Rome, was originated in 858, when Ignatius, the lawful patriarch of Constantinople was banished by the Emperor Michael III., and his place usurped by Photius, a man of great learning but ambitious and unscrupulous. Pope Nicholas I. condemned Photius, but the latter convoked a council and delivered sentence of deposition and excommunication against the Pope himself. He likewise accused the Latin Church of heresy for asserting the procession of the Holy Ghost, not from the Father alone, but from the Son also. He likewise repudiated certain usages of the Latins, and among others, the celibacy of the clergy. After much difficulty, things were, towards the end of the century again composed. In 1053 Michael Cerularius, Patriarch of Constantinople, renewed the schism, and since then it has practically endured, although union was temporarily effected by the Councils of Lyons (1274) and of Florence (1439).

The Greek and Latin Churches differ on but few points of doctrine, though their ritual and discipline are widely diverse. The schismatic Greeks have always repudiated the doctrines of the so-called Reformation.

Gregorian Music, see *Chant*.

Gremiale, a brocaded cloth placed on a bishop's knees when he sits during Mass or during ordinations. That worn by the Pope is called *a subcinctorium*.

Halo, the glowing tints with which Christian artists surround the head or whole figure of those they represent in sacred pictures. With theologians a halo or aureole, denotes a special reward attributed in Heaven to martyrs, virgins, and doctors, for their triumph over the world, the flesh and the devil.

Heaven, the abode of the blessed, where they enjoy God face to face. Its locality is unknown to us, but we learn from Scripture that it is beyond this earth.

Hell, the abode of the devils and of those who die enemies of God, where they are for all eternity punished with the loss of God and the pain of fire — "Depart from me, ye cursed, into everlasting fire, prepared for the devil and his angels." The endlessness of the punishment has always been according to the general belief of the Church and has been affirmed by the fourth Lateran Council (1215).

Heresy, the rejection by a Christian, professing Christian truth, of an article or articles of faith. Against formal heresy the Church pronounces the greater excommunication. Protestants who are in good faith are not formally heretical, as they do not pertinaciously oppose the doctrine of the true Church, but are only materially so, their tenets being heretical, and consequently may belong to the "soul" of the church.

Hermits, monks who lead a solitary life. Anchorite has the same meaning. In the first centuries, when this mode of life was not uncommon, the monks generally did not go out at once to the desert, but first spent some years of trial and preparation in a religious community. In the seventh century, St. Cuthbert lived as a hermit for nine years in Farne Island. In the twelfth flourished the hermits Bartholomew of Farne, St. Godric of Finchale, and St. Wulfric of Haslebury.

Hierarchy, the organised order of superiors and inferiors

whose office it is to teach and administer in the Church. Of this hierarchy the divinely-constituted head is the Pope, as is defined by the Council of Trent.

Holy Water, water mingled with salt, blessed by a priest, and used by Christians as a symbol of spiritual purification. Holy Water does not of itself give grace, but in virtue of the prayers of the Church it helps to excite in the soul good dispositions, which obtain for us the remission of venial sin and render us more pleasing in the sight of God.

Holy Week, the week (beginning from the Monday) in which the Church celebrates the Passion of our Saviour. On the Wednesday, Thursday and Friday in the evening is sung the *tenebrae* or office of Matins and Lauds for the succeeding day. For the offices proper to *Maundy Thursday*, *Good Friday*, and *Holy Saturday*, see under those words. The celebration of Holy Week is mentioned by Irenaeus in the end of the second century, and is believed to be of Apostolic institution.

Homily, a familiar sermon, wherein the Holy Scripture is explained so as to bring out its moral lessons. The first homilies we have are those of Origen. In the matin office of the breviary, whenever the lesson is taken from the Gospels, the words of the text are explained by a homily from one of the Fathers, which is appended.

Homousion, ' of one substance or nature, ' a term used by the Nicene Council with regard to the Father and Son in the Blessed Trinity, and opposed to the word of the heretics *homoousion*, or ' of like substance. '

Honorary Canons, as contrasted with titular or residentiary canons, is a dignity confered in many dioceses, especially in France, Austria and Prussia, on priests who have deserved well of the diocese. This title imports no obligations with regard to the cathedral church, though it sometimes brings a small emolument.

Honorius. This Pope, who succeeded to the pontificate in 625, is said to have been condemned by the sixth General Council, for his remissness in coping with the Monothelite heresy, which asserted that in Christ there was but one will, the Divine will. This censure, it can be conclusively shown, makes no argument against papal infallibility, for anti-Infallibilists would have to prove the assembled Fathers of the sixth General Council and Pope Leo II., who confirmed

it, intended to declare as a dogmatic fact that the letters of Pope Honorius to Sergius, in which the heresy is alleged to be, contained heresy. Moreover, they should have to prove that Honorius intended to define something in faith or morals, to be held by the whole Church.

Host, the bread which is to be changed into the body of Christ, or Christ present under the form of bread. In the Latin rite the host is of unleavened, whereas with the Greeks it is of leavened bread. A controversy exists as to which of these our Saviour used at the institution of the Holy Eucharist. In Mass the consecrated Host is broken, as at the Last Supper. A portion of it is also put into the chalice that holds the Precious Blood.

Hymn, in a wide sense is sometimes taken to denote a song of praise, including, for instance, the psalms and canticles. More restrictedly it means a religious song in metre. Of hymn-writers whose work survives, the earliest amongst the Greeks is St. Clement of Alexandria; amongst the Latins, St. Hilary of Poictiers. Other Latin hymn-writers are St. Ambrose, Fortunatus, St. Gregory the Great, Venerable Bede, St. Bernard, St. Thomas Aquinas, etc. Hymns in both senses given above enter largely into the office of the Breviary.

Hypostatic Union, the union of the human nature to the Divine nature in the Second Person of the Blessed Trinity made man, Jesus Christ.

Iconoclasts, the "image-breakers," those who opposed the use of images in religious worship. The trouble arose in 716 by Leo the Isaurian publishing an edict against images. He was condemned in Rome by Pope Gregory II. He found many adherents, however, and convened a Council at Constantinople, in which many decrees were promulgated against the images. A term of peace ensued and an oecumenical Council was held at Nicaea, in which the Catholic faith in the matter was defined. The Iconoclast fury was renewed by Leo the Armenian about 815; but it was finally subdued in 841, when Theodora, widow of the Emperor Theophilus, brought back in triumph the images to the principal church in Constantinople. The date is still celebrated as a festival, the Feast of Orthodoxy, by the Greeks.

Idolatry, the worship of inanimate objects as divinities or in general the worship of false gods. The worship of the

golden calf, although meant for the true God, was idolatrous, as it conveyed false notions of God.

Images. Their correct use is laid down by the second Council of Nicaea against the Iconoclasts, and also by the Council of Trent. The Images have no virtue or dignity in themselves; it is not they that are honoured and reverenced but the prototypes or objects which they represent. Their use is very ancient, as we know from the discoveries in the catacombs. Although the images have no power in themselves, Almighty God may deem good to grant particular favours at certain shrines.

Immaculate Conception. That the Blessed Virgin Mary was, by a special privilege and through the merits of Christ, exempted from the stain of original sin is a dogma of faith, defined by Pius IX., on the 8th December 1854. The definition was to the effect that the Immaculate Conception of Mary was a truth contained in the original teaching of the Apostles. As a matter of fact we have evidences of this belief from the earliest times. St. Ephrem, in the fourth century, implies that it was the belief of the Church. As Benedict XIV. says, the belief appeared to be that of the Church, though as yet it was not defined as an article of faith. The feast of the Conception of the Blessed Virgin was celebrated in the Greek Church, at least as early as the twelfth century, and in the Latin Church we have mention of it in the fourteenth, England, it would seem, being the first of Western countries to celebrate it. Finally, Pius IX. defined it an article of Catholic belief, which it would be heresy to reject. This dogma, far from detracting from the Redemption of Christ, adds, on the contrary, a new lustre to it, for it shows Christ's merits to be efficacious, not only in effacing the stain of original sin already contracted, but also in preserving from the contracting of it. A great many who are in dissidence with the See of Rome have misconstrued the tendency of this definition. We may therefore explain that the Church referred to the *passive*, as contrasted with the *active* conception. The *passive* conception is the union of the human soul, created by God, to the body already conceived in the womb. It is in this union that the soul is defiled by original sin; and from this defilement the Mother of God was exempted. Her *active* conception was of course like that of other human beings.

Immortality. The human soul is immortal, because being of a spiritual nature it has not in itself a motive of corruption. It can only cease by annihilation as it began by creation. God alone is capable of that annihilation, and as He gives his creatures no privilege in vain, human reason may conclude that he does not intend to annihilate the soul but that it is immortal. The same doctrine is revealed as an article of faith.

Immunity, freedom from burden or secular obligation. Most canonists vindicate for the clergy this privilege, founding it on divine right. As a matter of fact, however, the clergy have often renounced their right to the exemption by submitting to tribute and taxation, for instance, as our Saviour advised Peter to do, lest scandal should be given. An unwarrantable violation of personal immunity is inflicted on ecclesiastics in France and Italy by their being made to endure the military service.

Impediments of Marriage, either arise from the natural law or from the institution of the Church, which has this right, inasmuch as marriage between baptised persons is a sacrament and therefore falls under ecclesiastical jurisdiction. They are, moreover, such as render the marriage merely illicit or unlawful, and such as render it entirely null and void. The following impediments are *impedientia,* that is, render the marriage illicit (if permission has not previously been obtained): 1. *Undue time,* e.g. in Advent (to Epiphany) or Lent (to Low Sunday); *heresy* of one of the party; *simple vow of chastity; previous engagement,* not mutually rescinded. Impediments that are *dirimentia,* that is, render the marriage null and void, are *error* and *condition,* affecting the substance of the contract; *solemn vow of chastity; consanguinity* and *affinity; public decorum; crime; difference of religion,* that is, a baptised with an unbaptised person; *grave fear; another marriage; defect of age; clandestinity,* i. e. not in the face of the Church, (in England, however, and in Protestant countries generally, this last impediment does not apply, the decree of the Council of Trent imposing it not having been promulgated there); *impotentia* and *raptus.* The Church can dispense from impediments of ecclesiastical origin.

Imposition of hands, a rite of the Church, symbolising the transmission of grace and power. In ordination and in confirmation it has sacramental efficacy. In the Mass the priest

extends his hands over the bread and wine, as in the Old Law the priest imposed hands on the victim.

Incarnation, the assuming of a human body and soul by the second Person of the Blessed Trinity. By becoming man the Eternal Word did not lay aside His divine nature, but, remaining what He had ever been from all eternity, took upon Himself human nature without a human personality, so that from the first moment of His Incarnation there was in Him, and there ever will be, not one only but two natures, the divine and the human, *united* in His divine personality, the Person of God the Son.

The Divine nature of Jesus is one and the same as that of God the Father and of the Holy Spirit, and His human nature is in all things like ours, sin and tendency to sin excepted. He is equal to the Father as to His Godhead, and less than the Father as to His Manhood.

Our Lord Jesus Christ suffered and died in His human nature on Mount Calvary, and thereby effectually interposed His atonement between His Eternal Father and man. He thus made a plentiful expiation and paid a full ransom to the Eternal justice for the sins of the whole world.

Incense, is used in many religious functions, during High Mass, solemn Vespers, at funerals, etc. It symbolises the ascent of prayer, the odour of virtue, the consuming zeal of the Christian. The works of Dionysius the Areopagite, first quoted in the year 532, make mention of it.

Index (expurgatorius,) the list of prohibited books. Persons reading them without permission, incur forthwith excommunication. Certain classes of books are condemned (independently of mention in the Index) for their origin or nature, such as works of heresiarchs, books expressly opposed to faith and morals, etc. The Sacred Congregation of the Index was founded by S. Pius V. in 1574, and has for secretary a Dominican friar, though the prohibition of certain books has at all times been practiced in the Church.

Indulgence. By an Indulgence is meant not the forgiveness of a sin, nor a permission to commit a sin, but the *remission*, through the merits of *Jesus Christ, of the whole or part of the debt of temporal punishment due to a sin*, the *guilt* and *everlasting punishment* of which sin have, through the merits of *Jesus Christ*, been already forgiven in the sacrament of penance. Indulgences do not secure heaven, but hasten the time of entering it to those who

GLOSSARY

have already secured heaven by having obtained forgiveness of their sins and put themselves in a state of grace before death.

To gain an indulgence it is necessary to be in the state of grace, and, generally, to do some good work; to gain fully a plenary indulgence one is further required to detest sin and be so disposed as to be unwilling to commit even the slightest venial offence, also, as a general rule, to have confessed and communicated and to pray for the Pope's intention. Five Paters and Aves suffice for this last purpose. It is consequently evident that indulgences are a strong incentive to virtue and repentance. Indulgences are not, as was represented by Luther, a mere remission of canonical penance, but a full and satisfactory remission of punishment due before God, and to be otherwise expiated, either in this world or in the next (in Purgatory). Of the practice of granting indulgences in the Church we have constant and continuous testimony. The right is founded on the power of the Keys: " And whatsoever thou shalt loose upon earth, shall be loosed also in heaven." On the criminal Corinthian St. Paul imposed penance " with the power of the Lord Jesus, " and afterwards relaxed it " in the person of Christ.,, Tertullian and St. Cyprian make mention of indulgences. In the Pope is invested the right to grant indulgences. This power he may delegate. The most famous plenary indulgences are those attached to the Jubilee, Seven Churches of Rome, Holy Land, Compostella, Portiuncula, Way of the Cross and Blue Scapular.

Indulgentia pro vivis et defunctis, means an indulgence applicable to the living or the dead. By application of an indulgence to the dead is meant, not a direct remission in their regard, for they are beyond that power of the Church, but an offering to God of the merits of Christ with the supplication that having respect to them, He will mercifully remit the whole or part of the punishment still due to the soul or souls in Purgatory.

Indulgentia Quotidiana, is one that may be gained every day.

Indulgentia toties quoties, one that is gained as often as the conditions laid down are fulfilled; consequently not merely once in the same day.

Indult, permission given by the Pope authorising exemption from some ordinary law of the church. Thus the Lenten

indults authorise the bishops to dispense more or less with the rigour of the fast.

Infallibility. The Vatican Council on the 18th July, 1870, declared that the Pope cannot err when he speaks *ex cathedra*, that is, when as pastor and doctor of all Christians he defines a doctrine of faith or morals to be held by the whole church. This follows from Christ constituting the Church the infallible witness of truth, " the pillar and ground of truth, " against which the gates of hell shall not prevail, ,, in whose interest Jesus said, " I will ask the Father and He shall give you another Paraclete, that He may abide with you for ever, " and concerning which He declared, " He that heareth you heareth Me, and he that despiseth you, despiseth Me. " Jesus establishing Peter declares him the rock on which He builds His Church, the pastor of all His lambs and sheep. " Simon, Simon, " he says again, " behold Satan hath desired to have you, that he may sift you as wheat. But I have prayed for thee that thy faith fail not: and thou being once converted, confirm thy brethren. " Of the infallibility of the Supreme Pontiff we have the most explicit testimony in the writings of the Fathers from the earliest times. Human reason requires the same infallibility as in Peter. He is the rock, the foundation on which the Church is built, he is to confirm his brethren, to feed the lambs and sheep. Is it conceivable that God would allow such a one to be, in these very functions, the mouthpiece of falsehood? The Pope may be a sinful man, he may err in matters purely historical or scientific, he may err in all matters as a private doctor, but when he defines in matters of faith and morals and imposes a belief on the universal Church, it is utterly repugnant, seeing his position in the infallible Church of Christ, that God should not protect him from error.

Inquisition. When in the thirteenth century the secular arm ceased to aid the Church in repressing those who maliciously and wantonly opposed it, the Church itself established tribunals for dealing with the culprits. At first the bishops of the dioceses were entrusted with the wielding of the law, but afterwards the responsibility was made over to the Dominican Order. It was principally in France and Spain that the tribunals were firmly established. The Spanish Inquisition was abolished only in 1813. Its main object was

to deal with the Jews and Saracens, who there, feigning Christianity, molested the Church. Much evil has been said about it. But the authority of the profligate Llorente, the author of all the serious allegations against the Spanish Inquisition, has been conclusively proved worthless.

Interdict, an ecclesiastical censure, debarring from the use of certain sacraments, from divine offices and from Christian burial. An interdict may apply to persons, or to places, or to both. England was placed under interdict in the reign of King John.

Invito Sacro, an episcopal mandate, publicly placarded, concerning the celebration of festivals, or other church notices.

Invocation of Saints, Special. The intercession of certain saints is in particular applied to for aid on certain occasions; thus, for a good death, St. Joseph; in child-birth, St. Anne; apoplexy, St. Andrew Avellino; epilepsy, St. Bibiana; lightning and tempest, St. Peter; hydrophobia, St. Guy; storm, St. Thomas Aquinas; earthquakes, St. Francis of Solano; smallpox, St. Bonosa; for the eyes, St. Lucy; the throat, St. Blase; cholera, St. Roch; plague, St. Sebastian; convulsions, St. Erasmus; the womb and breasts, St. Agatha; the teeth, St. Apollonia; gout, St. Trophimus; sickness, St. Theodore; lost property, St. Antony of Padua; welfare of animals, St. Antony.

Januarius, St., bishop of Benevento, martyred under Diocletian. In his church in Naples, there is, on the occasion of his feast, the standing miracle of the liquefaction and ebullition of his blood, on its being brought near his head, contained in a rich reliquary. The miracle takes place the 1st Saturday in May and the 19th September of every year, these being the days that the phial containing his blood is brought publicly with much solemnity to the church where his head is preserved.

Joseph, St., the husband of the Virgin Mother, and the foster-father of Jesus. In 1871 Pius IX. declared St. Joseph patron and protector of the universal Church. His feast is celebrated on the 19th of March; the feast of his Patronage on the third Sunday after Easter.

Jubilee, a term taken from the Jewish Church, a year of remission, granted ordinarily every twenty-five years, and extraordinarily at any time (though not generally for a whole year.) The ordinary jubilee occurs at Rome the year — from Christmas to Christmas — before that on which

it is granted to the rest of the Church. The Jubilee imports a plenary indulgence, and increased powers of absolution for ordinary confessors. The first jubilee was granted in 1300, by Boniface VIII.

Judgment, General, the bringing together all men and angels at the last day, that Christ may decide on their lot. Its motive is to manifest the justice of God, the majesty of Christ, the glory of the just, and the shame of the wicked. It has been a popular belief that it will take place in the valley of Jehosaphat, near Jerusalem, but this does not seem well founded on Scripture. The General Judgment is the motive of Michael Angelo's celebrated fresco in the Sixtine Chapel.

Judgment, Particular, the judgment that takes place immediately after death, and according to which the soul is admitted to glory — either at once, or after a term of expiation in Purgatory — or sent to reprobation.

Jurisdiction, the power of one who has public authority over others for their rule and government. Bishops have in their diocese ordinary (as opposed to delegated) jurisdiction from Christ, but through Peter and in subjection to Peter. To validly absolve (except in the point of death) a priest must have jurisdiction *in foro interno.*

Justification, the restoration of the sinner to God's friendship. The Protestant doctrine differs widely from that of the Catholic Church on this point, as it asserts that man is no free but is moved irresistibly by the grace that gives him justification. They likewise distinguish not only in concept but also in time and existence between justification and sanctification.

Kings, Prayers for, are commanded by St. Paul, and their use is proved from Tertullian, Athanasius, etc. In the middle ages the sovereign's name was inserted in the missal, but in the modern Roman missal it is omitted.

Kiss of Peace. The kiss among the ancients was very frequent, as a sign of friendship or good-will. From the earliest times it was given during Mass, the men giving it to the men, and the women to the women. At present the kiss of peace is restricted to High Mass, is given in the form of an embrace, and is limited to the clergy within the sanctuary.

Kyrie Eleison, Christe Eleison, etc. These Greek words, meaning " Lord have mercy on us; Christ have mercy on

us " are of very ancient use in the Mass and in the offices of the Latin Church.

Lacticinia, or " white-meats, " eggs, milk, butter, cheese, etc. Their use is forbidden during the Lenten fast. At present however they are generally allowed at the full meal, and in Northern countries, generally also at the collation.

Laetare Sunday, Mid-Lent or Refreshment Sunday, the fourth Sunday in Lent. On this Sunday the altar is decked with flowers, the organ played, and the High Mass sung in rose-coloured, instead of violet, vestments. It is called " Laetare " from the first words of the Introit, " Rejoice, O Jerusalem. " Formerly on this day, the station being at the church of the Holy Cross of Jerusalem, the Pope used to pontificate there, and hold in his hand the Golden Rose, the symbol of the joys of the heavenly garden, the mystical Jerusalem.

Lamps. Their symbolic use is very ancient, as we know from the discoveries made in the catacombs. It is prescribed that before the Blessed Sacrament a lamp should burn with olive oil day and night.

Language of the Church. Mass is not said in any language still spoken. Latin, Coptic, Æthiopic are dead languages, the Greek, Syriac, Armenian, Slavonic, used in the liturgy, are entirely different from the modern tongues of the same name. The reason of this is that the Church holds firmly to a liturgy once established and in her unchangeableness has outlived many centuries the languages she naturally adopted of the countries into which the Apostles and their successors went.

Lapsi, lapsed, or apostate, the name given to those who in the early Church, after having embraced Christianity, fell away from the faith under persecution. The repentant apostates were divided into five categories: (1) *Libellatici*, those who had received from the authorities a certificate attesting that they had sacrificed to the gods, although it was not true; (2) *Mittentes*, senders, those who had deputed someone to sacrifice in their place; (3) *Thurificati*, offerers of incense, those who had offered incense to the idols; (4) *Sacrificati*, sacrificers, those who had taken part in the sacrifices of the idolaters; (5) *Blasphemi*, blasphemers, those who had formally denied Christ or had sworn by the false gods. The name of *Lapsi* was also given to those who delivered the Sacred Scriptures to the pagans to be burned. They were subjected by the Church to very

long and severe penance. Confessors or martyrs in prison had the privilege of interceding for them, and helping to restore them to the peace of the Church.

Latin, the liturgical language in the west. The Church preserves it, on account of its antiquity, as a means of unity, and in as much as it can suffer no change or misinterpretation. The faithful have translations of the service in their prayer-books.

Latria, a Greek word used in Latin theology to denote that supreme worship due to God alone. The chief act of Latria is the Mass.

Lay Brothers, the members of religious orders who, having a vocation to the religious, but not to the ecclesiastical state, are employed in manual labour and are exempt from the duties of choir and from studying.

Legate, a representative of the Holy See, having authority. Legates are either: (1) legates *a latere*, who are cardinals deputed to govern provinces belonging to the Holy See, or sent on extraordinary occasions to foreign courts; (2) *legati missi* or nuncios, who correspond to ambassadors or ministers in foreign capitals; and (3) *legati nati*, or legates by virtue of their office, certain archbishops, namely, to whose sees the authority of legate permanently belonged, and of whom the archbishop of Canterbury in England was one.

Lent, a fast of forty days preparatory to the feast of Easter, and commemorative of our Saviour's fast. A fast before Easter was common even in Apostolic times; from the commencement of the fourth century the number of days was gradually fixed. Lent was a time of penance, of almsgiving, of mourning. Festivities were avoided. Penitents were reconciled to the Church. Emperors pardoned prisoners, masters their slaves and enemies became friends.

Liberius, Pope from 352 to 366. Much controversy has taken place in his regard as to the relation of his conduct with Papal infallibility when, having been exiled by the Emperor Constantius, he recovered his freedom by signing certain documents which, contrary it would appear to his knowledge, savoured of semi-Arianism. The act was committed in ignorance and under fear. The case, according to the illustration of Cardinal Newman, was as if an English chief justice were hurried away by bandits, kept without notes, books or counsel, and forced, under terror

of death, to decide a legal case in a particular way. Nobody would pretend that there the decision was valid.

Limbo, the place, called also *Limbus Infantium*, inhabited by infants who die without baptism. There, according to the theologians, they exist in perfect natural but not supernatural happiness. *Limbus Patrum* was the place where those who died in God's friendship were detained, until Heaven was opened to them by our Saviour's Passion.

Liturgical Colours. The colours which the liturgy prescribes for the vestments, at Mass are:

White, on feasts of our Saviour, of the Blessed Virgin, of Confessors, Virgins, Holy Women.

Red, for the Passion, Martyrs, the Holy Ghost.

Violet. Lent and Advent.

Rose. Fourth Sunday of Lent, and third of Advent.

Green, for Sundays having no fixed colour, as those after Pentecost.

Black, for the dead.

(Gold vestments replace any colour but black)

Loreto, the town near Ancona that holds the celebrated shrine of the *Casa Santa* or Holy House, the abode of the Blessed Virgin, St. Joseph and the Holy Child, where the Word was made flesh. In the year 1291 and precisely in the night of the 10th May, it was miraculously transferred from Nazareth, then at the mercy of the infidels, to the Illyrian coast. Three years and half later, 10th December 1294, it was removed, in the same wonderful manner, to the opposite side of the Adriatic, and finally in December 1295 took up the position it now occupies. The enemies of the Catholic Church have tried in many ways to destroy or weaken the authority of this narration, but all in vain.

Magro Stretto, corresponds to the English " black fast, " and is the fast of those days on which the use is forbidden, not only of flesh meat, but also of white-meats. The days of *magro stretto* in Rome are: Ash Wednesday; the last three days of Holy week; Ember days and the vigils of the principal feasts.

Majordomo, Pope's, the prelate who superintends the Pontifical household; he has the privilege of partially quartering the Papal arms with his own.

Mantelletta, a sleeveless vestment of red or violet, reaching nearly to the knees and open in front, worn by cardinals in Rome, by bishops outside their diocese, and by certain *prelates* who have the privilege.

Marriage, a natural contract between man and woman, which between baptised persons is likewise a sacrament. It binds the contracting parties to an undivided and indissoluble union during life. The contracting parties themselves are the ministers of the sacrament.

Martyr. The term, after the middle of the third century, was reserved to signify those who died for Christ. Great honour was in early times paid to the martyrs. A martyr, according to Benedict XIV. the definition of, is one who voluntarily endures death for the faith or for some other virtue relating to God.

Mary, B. V., the Virgin Mother of God, she from whom the Word, born of the Father before all ages, took flesh and became man in time.

Mary is one of God's creatures, wholly dependent on Him and indebted to Him for all her graces, privileges and glory, but it is nevertheless true that she really is the *Mother of God*, in as much as He, who from her took His human nature, has no human personality, but only the divine. To God alone is supreme devotion due, and between God and man Christ is the "one mediator," that is, the sole author of our redemption; but the exalted dignity to which Mary has been raised, makes her intercession obviously of the greatest weight with her Divine Son, and the honour and reverence which Catholics pay her have at all times been according to the spirit of the Church.

Mass. The sacrifice of the Mass is the supreme act of worship paid to God. It is the continuation or repetition in an unbloody manner of the sacrifice which was consummated in a bloody manner on the Cross. This sacrifice was foretold in the Old Testament; it was distinctly declared fulfilled by our Saviour, at the moment of its anticipated institution on the eve of His Passion; it has at all times and in all places been recognized within the Church. The sacrifice of the Mass has the same priest and victim as that of the Cross, and is a means of applying Christ's redemption to men.

In the Holy Eucharist, the victim, namely, Jesus Christ, is truly present, therefore He can be offered up, and He is truly offered up, as an oblation to His Eternal Father; and although the death of the victim does not occur in *reality*, yet it takes place *mystically*, the Body of Christ being made present, as though separated from the Blood,

since by the power of the consecrating words, first, the body of Christ is caused to be present under the *species* (or what appears to the senses) of bread, and then His Blood is caused to be present under the *species* of wine. This *mystical death*, by *seeming* separation of the Blood from Christ's Body, joined with the true *offering* of Jesus Christ, who is truly present living and entire under each *species*, can and does constitute a real sacrifice commemorative of that of the Cross.

This two fold consecration is by *Christ's institution* so essential for the sacrificial act, that if there were *only* a consecration of the bread, or *only* a consecration of the wine, our Lord would be present, but not as a *sacrifice*, because in these cases the mystical immolation would not be complete.

The Holy Sacrifice of the Mass does not differ *in its essence* from the sacrifice offered up upon Mount Calvary. As we find on Calvary and in the Mass the same identical victim and the same principal offerer, Jesus Christ, the two sacrifices are *essentially* the same. The two sacrifices only differ in *non-essentials*, because only the manner of offering is different. One was offered by Christ personally, the other is offered by Him through His ministers. That was offered with real suffering, real shedding of blood and real death of the victim; this with only a mystical suffering, a mystical shedding of blood, and a mystical death of the same victim. Therefore the priest, at the time of the consecration, does not say, "This is the body of Christ," but acting in the person of Christ, says, "This is my body," according to the Divine command, "Do this" or as these words might be rendered, Offer up this. It is on account of this sacrifice offered daily on our altars by Christ that our Lord is called "A priest for ever, according to the order of Melchisedech."

Master of the Chamber, *Maestro di Camera*, the prelate who admits visitors to an audience of the Pope. He has the custody of the Fisherman's Ring, and generally becomes *Majordomo*, when the latter is created Cardinal.

Master of the Sacred Palace, a Dominican friar, who superintends the licensing of books, the conferring of degrees in theology and philosophy, the preaching in the papal chapel, and who is Consultor to several congregations.

Maundy Thursday, the Thursday in Holy Week, so called from the Latin word *mandatum*, which begins the anthem

that is sung during the ceremony of the washing of the feet. On this day the Church commemorates the institution of the Holy Eucharist. The Sacred Host which has been consecrated for the Mass of the Presanctified of the following day is carried in solemn procession and placed on the altar of repose. The high altar is stripped in sign of mourning, and the principal priest washes the feet of twelve poor persons. The bishop on this day consecrates the holy oils. The faithful devoutly visit, in the different churches, the altars of repose (improperly called sepulchres).

Mediator, St. Paul says Christ is the one mediator between God and man, " for there is no other name under heaven given to men whereby we must be saved " than that of JESUS (*Acts.* iv. 12); and when we call the Blessed Virgin, or any other saint, a mediator, it is not in the sense of mediator of Redemption, attributed to our Saviour, but in the sense of *intercessor* or *pleader*, in which sense a Christian may be called a mediator, whenever he intercedes, or mediates between God and his fellow-man, as Abraham and Moses and St. Paul did, and thus prays for his neighbour.

Melchites, members of a distinct Oriental rite, who, however, from a dogmatic and liturgical point of view are merely Greeks living in Egypt and Syria. The name comes from a Semitic word meaning " royalists. ,, Most Melchites are schismatic.

Mental Prayer, the elevation of the soul that takes place in the contemplation of moral or religious truth and in the subsequent affective movement by which the soul goes straight to God, without the need of spoken words. St. Ignatius reduced the rules of mental prayer and meditation as a part of all religious rule, and it is highly recommended to all the faithful.

Metropolitan, an archbishop who has suffragans. The metropolitan has certain jurisdictional rights over all his province. Like all archbishops, he has the privilege of the *pallium* and of the *double cross*. A metropolitan is the same as an archbishop, except that the latter does not now imply the existence of suffragans, whereas the former does.

Miracles, effects that cannot be accounted for by natural causes; they are deviations from, but not violations of, the laws of nature. God, the author of these laws of nature, is not so bound down to them that it is impossible for Him to produce effects independently of them.

Missal, the book containing the complete service for Mass throughout the year. Formerly not one book but different books were used at different parts of the Mass.

Mitre, the head-gear worn by bishops and abbots when they solemnly officiate. The mitres are of three classes ; those adorned with precious stones, those in cloth of gold, those in white cloth (for the Pope, in silver.) These last are used in funeral services.

Mixed Marriages, those between persons of different religions. Between a baptised person and an unbaptised person they are invalid. Between a Catholic and a person of another communion, e.g., a Protestant, without a dispensation from the proper authorities, they are unlawful ; there must be a reason for the marriage and it be understood that the Catholic party shall be unmolested in the practice of religion, and that all the children be brought up Catholics.

Monastery. (See under *Convent*) Different orders chose different sites for their monasteries. The descendants of St. Columba preferred islands or lonely places — witness Iona, Lindisfarne, Old Melrose; the Benedictines chose hill-sites; the Cistercians quiet valleys; the Mendicant orders, the towns. One of the chief regulations concerning monasteries is the law of enclosure, forbidding intercourse from without.

Monk, one who devotes himself to a religious life in community. The first religious lived a solitary life. St. Anthony (250-356) gathered many of them around him, and St. Pachomius, about 315, built the first monastery. In St. Jerome's time Rome had many monasteries of monks and nuns. Various rules existed, but the coming of St. Benedict, and the establishing of his rule, in 529, entirely altered the face of monastic life, and for centuries all Western monks were Benedictines. In the tenth and eleventh centuries the Order of Cluny, the Camaldoli, the Carthusians and the Cistercians formed new branches. In the thirteenth century came the friars (Dominicans and Franciscans), and in the sixteenth the Theatines, and Jesuits; and thenceforward the number of new Congregations formed has been considerable.

Mortal Sin, is a grievous offence against God, which man commits when he deliberately violates God's Commandments. It severs the sinner entirely from God's friendship, and mer-

its everlasting punishment, and is therefore called mortal or deadly. For the forgiveness of sin our merciful Saviour has instituted the sacrament of penance, but even without the sacrament, an act of perfect contrition reconciles us to God, for "Charity never falleth away." If the sacrament, however, can be resorted to, it is a matter of precept and obligation.

Mozzetta, a cape with hood, of various colours and texture, worn by the Pope, by cardinals, bishops, abbots and "prelati" who have the privilege, when not officiating.

National Churches and Establishments in Rome;

  American, North, church with college at via dell' Umiltà.

  American, South, church with college, in Prati di Castello.

  Armenian, church and college, St. Nicola da Tolentino.

  Belgian, church with college, Via del Quirinale.

  English, church of St. Thomas with college (Via Monserrato); church of St. Sylvester in Capite, held by the Pallottine Fathers.

  French, St. Louis, St. Yves, St. Nicholas dei Lorrenesi, St. Denis, St. Claude, church of St. Clare with college, Piazza Sta. Chiara.

  German, church of Sta. Maria dell'Anima; German College, via St. Nicola da Tolentino.

  Greek, church of St. Athanasius with college.

  Irish, church of St. Agatha with college; St. Isidore, of the Irish Franciscans; St. Patrick of the Irish Augustinians.

  Portuguese, church of St. Anthony.

  Scotch, church of St. Andrew with college.

  Spanish, church of St. Maria of Monserrato; chapel, with college in the Altemps Palace.

Neophyte, in the primitive Church, a convert newly baptised. They wore white garments for eight days after their baptism. The west-Saxon king Cedwalla died in Rome, whilst still wearing the white robe.

Nimbus. The halo or aureole around the head in Christian painting. In early times a square nimbus was accorded to illustrious and saintly persons still alive.

Noble Guard, the immediate body-guard of the Pope; a corps of officers taken from the Roman nobility. A newly-elected cardinal, who resides out of Rome, has his nomination and the red zucchetto conveyed to him by a member of the noble guard.

Nocturn, a third portion of the matins office in the Breviary.

It consists, on feast days, of three psalms and three lessons. It is called nocturn because recited by the monks during the night. On ferias and on certain solemn feasts matins has but one nocturn.

Nomination, the way in which bishops are designated in France, Spain, Portugal, Austria, the monarch proposing the subject to the Pope. The Pope then confirms or rejects the nomination. The ordinary mode by which a bishop is designated to a see is election by the chapter.

Novice, one who is undergoing probation for the religious life. The term of probation is at least a year. A novice cannot make profession under sixteen years of age. Novices have certain of the privileges of the order in which they make their noviciate.

Nun, a female consecrated to God and living in a convent. The first mention we have of a nunnery or convent of women is in the life of St. Anthony, who when entering the desert placed his sister in a house of virgins. The cutting of the hair is mentioned in the fourth century. On entering, the postulant receives the white veil of reception; at the end of the noviciate she receives the veil (white or black, according to the order) of profession. Some nuns with solemn vows are under the direction of the Sacred Congregation of Bishops and Regulars; others are under the bishop of the diocese.

Nuncio, a permanent official, representative of the Holy See at a foreign court. (See *Legate*) Papal nuncios had formerly an extensive jurisdiction in the country where they resided. Their tribunals were courts of appeal from the ordinary ecclesiastical courts. Nuncios on being withdrawn are usually elevated to the cardinalate.

Oath, the calling of God to witness the truth of a statement or the binding nature of a promise. An oath is always lawful when taken with judgment (and for a grave reason), in justice and in truth. An oath taken to commit a crime does not bind. Superiors may often annul the promissory oaths of their inferiors, parents those of their children. The "corporal" oath of the middle ages, was the rendering of an oath more solemn by the touching of some sacred object.

Octave, the celebration of certain solemn feasts as continued till the eighth or octave-day.

Offering of the Roman Senate. The Roman senate and people

were accustomed to offer chalices and lights to different churches on certain feast days. These offerings were exposed all day on the altar.

Offertory, a part of the Mass, before the consecration, at which the bread and wine are offered to Christ that he may make them His body and blood. The word is also taken to mean the antiphon sung during this offertory. In St. Augustine's time verses of the psalms were then sung.

Oils, Holy, are of three classes. The oil of catechumens for baptism, consecrations of churches, etc.; oil of chrism for confirmation, consecration of bishops; oil of the sick for extreme unction. They are blessed by the bishop on Holy Thursday and kept in silver vessels.

Old Catholics, a name taken by some priests and lay-people in Germany, who, headed by a Dr. Döllinger, protested against the declaration of Papal infallibility and formed a schism. The German government under Prince Bismark showed them great favour, and handed over to them several churches. But the sect, having in various synods modified many important points of dogma, fell into gradual discredit and is now almost extinct.

Ombrellino, a canopy in form a of large umbrella, carried over the Blessed Sacrament, in which case it is of white silk; over the Pope is it of red silk; over cardinals and bishops, of red or violet silk.

Orders, Holy, the sacrament that confers spiritual power and grace for the performance of sacred duties. The bishop is the ordinary minister of this sacrament, and the recipient may be any baptised male capable of intending to receive it. However, the Church exacts great care in the selection of those to be ordained. She requires likewise a title, or means of subsistence, and imposes an interval between certain of the orders. This is one of three sacraments which imprint an indelible character on the soul of the recipient.

Orders, Religious. Originally each monastery was complete in itself and independent. With the branching-off of the Carthusians, Cistercians and others, after the tenth century, many houses began to obey the rule of one superior, and the word *order* comes into use. After the Benedictines (sixth century) and their branches from Cluny, Camaldoli, Chartreuse and Citeaux, we may mention the Trinitarians (twelfth century); Mercedists (1218); Franciscan, Dominican,

Carmelite, and Augustinian friars (thirteenth cent.); Servites (recognized in 1487); Minims (1473); Theatines (1524;) Capuchins (1528); Jesuits (1440); Discalced Carmelites (1580); Trappists (1662).

Orders of Knighthood conferred by the Pope: The Order of Malta; Order of the Holy Sepulchre; Order of Pius IX.; Order of St. Gregory the Great; Order of St. Sylvester, to which is added that of the Golden Spur.

Ordinary. A bishop is called the *ordinary* of his diocese, for there "jure ordinario," by common right, he accomplishes the divine work of the sanctification of the faithful.

Ordo Romanus, originally a collection of rubrics and ritual instructions; at present an annual publication, indicating the office for each day of the year.

Organ. It is mentioned by St. Augustine. Tertullian alludes to one, the bellows of which were worked by water. It would seem that the organ was introduced into church service not by Pope Damasus, as has been asserted, but in the time of Charlemagne. The Greeks and Orientals have never adopted it.

Original Sin, the sin we inherit from our first parents. It is deleted by baptism. The doctrine on the subject is clearly and emphatically laid down by St. Paul, and developed by St Augustine. We all sinned in Adam, but the way in which we participated in Adam's sin or had it transmitted to us, is a matter of much controversy among theologians.

Orthodox Church. The Schismatic Greek Church arrogates this title. (See *Greek Church*)

Palafrenieri, the attendants who, dressed in red damask with crimson stockings, carry on their shoulders the Holy Father seated in his chair, when he goes to the Papal chapels.

Pallium, a band of white wool worn on the shoulders, and the mark of patriarchal and of archiepiscopal authority. It is conferred also, however, by special privilege, on a few bishops. Archbishops and patriarchs must ask the Holy See for it before beginning to exercise their functions. The wool of which it is made is taken from the white lambs annually blessed in the church of St. Agnes outside the city.

Palm Sunday, the Sunday before Easter, on which the Church commemorates our Saviour's triumphal entry into Jerusalem, when the people strewed palms in his way, and cried: "Hosannah to the Son of David."

Papal Altar, one at which the Pope alone can say Mass or officiate. The confessions, or central altars, of St Peter's, St. Paul's, St. John Lateran and St. Laurence outside the Walls are papal altars. That any other but the Pope should there say Mass a special indult is required.

Papal Benediction. On special occasions and on the festivals of Easter and of SS. Peter and Paul, the Pope before 1870 solemnly blessed the people. To this blessing a plenary indulgence is attached. By virtue of a special indult bishops sometimes receive the privilege of giving this papal benediction. In that case the bishop gives it after Mass, the Apostolic letters having been previously read to the public.

Papal Blessing, a blessing given by the Pope, and generally accompanied by a plenary indulgence at the hour of death. In Rome, forms are to be had, which may be filled up and sent to the Vatican, petitioning for this blessing. They are afterwards returned duly signed by the authorities.

Papal Procession. When the Pope pontificates on unusually solemn occasions, he is carried in on the *sedia gestatoria* with exceeding pomp, being preceded by a long line of chaplains and dignitaries and followed by another equally imposing. A similar entry is called the papal procession.

Paradise, the heavenly garden, the abode of the blessed, where they enjoy God face to face. The garden of Eden, where our first parents were originally placed, is called the earthly paradise.

Parishes, Roman, are 54 in number and are divided into three classes, secular, regular and suburban. In the Vatican palace there is a parish, as there was also in the Lateran and in the Quirinal palaces.

Paschal Candle, a candle, usually of large dimensions, blessed on Holy Saturday and burned at solemn functions until Trinity Sunday. It symbolises the rising of Christ, the light of light, the "sun in his strength." It goes so far back at least as the time of Pope Zosimus, 417.

Paschal Precept, the precept of the Church obliging all Christians to communicate at least once a year, and that about Easter time. It was first imposed by the fourth Lateran Council in 1215. In Rome the time for fulfilling the paschal precept is from Palm Sunday to Low Sunday.

Passion, the suffering and death of our Saviour, commemorated by the Church in the week preceding Easter.

Passion Sunday, the Sunday before Palm Sunday, and consequently the second Sunday before Easter. With it the more solemn part of Lent begins, and the crosses and images are covered with violet until the Resurrection day.

Paten, the circular plate of gold, or silver always gilded, for the consecrated Host at Mass.

Pater Noster, the Lord's Prayer. It is recited in the Mass and in the breviary. A pope, it is believed St. Gregory the Great, was once celebrating at St. John Lateran, and as he uttered the last words of the Pater: " Sed libera nos a malo," angels were distinctly heard to answer, *Amen*. Since then at the Pope's Mass on the feast of Easter the answer *Amen* is no longer made to the Our Father.

Patriarch. The hierarchy of jurisdiction is thus composed: the Pope, Patriarchs, Primates, Metropolitans or Archbishops, Bishops, etc. Patriarch received its present use in the fifth century. The Patriarchates are Rome, Alexandria, Antioch (with a Latin, a Maronite, a Syrian, and Melchite Patriarch), Constantinople, Jerusalem, Cilicia (Armenian rite). Babylon (Chaldaic rite); and the three minor patriarchates are the Indies, Lisbon and Venice.

Patrimony of St. Peter, designated the Papal province, extending some fifty miles along the coast north of Rome, which alone was left to the Holy See after the battle of Castelfidardo (1860). It also with the capital, Rome, was torn from the Pope in 1870.

Pavilion, a conical canopy of red and yellow stripes, which the basilicas (before the Piedmontese occupation) used in processions, and with which they still accompany the seal of their armorial bearings. The same term is also applied to the veil that covers the tabernacle, and to that (always white) which covers the ciborium.

Pax, a plate engraved with the figure of Christ on the Cross, kissed first by the clergy and then by the people. It was introduced in the thirteenth century to replace the real Pax, or kiss of peace, given mutually by the faithful, but it soon fell into disuse, owing to the contentions for precedence to which it gave rise.

Penance, the virtue which inclines those who have sinned to be sorry for it, and to be disposed to make due amends; also the outward act of sorrow; and, finally, the sacrament by which sins committed after baptism are forgiven. On the sinner's part three acts are required for the due

reception of this sacrament: contrition, confession and satisfaction. In cases of necessity the sacrament is not absolutely necessary, and perfect contrition, with the intention of confession when possible, suffices for the forgiveness of sin. As to the act of confession, all mortal sins must be declared, and the contrition or attrition applied to all of them.

Pentecost, from a Greek word, meaning fifty, the feast of the Descent of the Holy Ghost on the Apostles, the fiftieth day after Easter. During the interval between these two feasts the faithful in ancient time prayed erect.

Persecutions, against the faithful, took place chiefly during the first six centuries. The greatest prejudice existed against the Christians from the beginning. "If the Tiber overflows," says Tertullian; "if the Nile does not; if there is a drought, an earthquake, a famine or a pestilence, at once the cry is: 'The Christians to the lions'".

The principal persecutions were those of Trajan (98-117), of Decius (303), of Julian (361-363). In the fifth and sixth centuries the Catholics of Africa were persecuted by the Vandals, and those of Spain by the Visigoths.

Peter's Chains. The chains by which St. Peter was bound in Jerusalem, and those which were attached to him in Rome, miraculously joined together, are kept in the church of St. Peter in Vinculis. The chains from Jerusalem were sent by the Empress Eudoxia to her daughter Eudoxia, wife of Valentinian III, and the latter built this basilica to hold them.

Peter-Pence, or Rome-scot, a tribute of one penny for each house in England, levied at midsummer and paid, from the very earliest times, to the see of Rome. The modern Peter-pence is a voluntary offering made by the faithful for the maintenance of the Pope, especially since his spoliation in 1870.

Pilgrim, one who makes a journey to a holy shrine. The motives of this journey are generally, to quicken the faith, to fulfil a vow or a penance, to seek spiritual or temporal aid. The chief pilgrimages are: the Holy Land; those of our Lady, such as Lourdes, Loreto, Montserrato; those of the Angels, as St. Michael on Monte Gargano; those of Saints, as SS. Peter and Paul in Rome, St. James of Compostella, the Portiuncula, St. Thomas of Canterbury.

Pontifical Cortège, when the Pope was free, was very magni-

ficent, the papal carriage being preceded and surrounded by gorgeously dressed soldiers, and attended by prelates and chamberlains in rich and variegated costumes.

Pontifical of the Pope. When the Pope solemnly officiates at High Mass the ceremonial is very varied and elaborate. Every time that he reads out of the missal, an archbishop or patriarch supports it; every time he sings from it, it is held by a cardinal.

Pope, the successor of St. Peter, the divinely constituted Head of the Church, he who is the rock on which Christ built his Church, against which the gates of hell shall not prevail, and with which Christ is present until the consummation of the world; he who is to confirm his brethren, and to feed Christ's lambs and sheep. The Pope is bishop of Rome, but the administration of his diocese he entrusts for the most part to his cardinal vicar. The Pope is elected by the college of cardinals, but not necessarily from their number.

Porta Sancta, or Holy Door, name given to a walled-up door on the right part of the façade of the patriarchal basilicas. It is distinguished with a cross, which the faithful kiss through devotion. This door is opened and closed in the jubilee year, at St. Peter's by the Pope, at St. Paul's by the dean of the cardinals, at St. John Lateran and St. Mary Major's by the respective cardinal archpriests. The cardinals who fulfil this function are afterwards named legates *a latere.*

Portiuncula, a church at Assisi, repaired by St. Francis, where our Saviour appeared to the Saint, and bade him go to Rome to the Pope, who would give a plenary indulgence to all penitents visiting that church. The same privilege, called" of the Portiuncula," was extended later on to the other Franciscan churches and also to some special churches not Franciscan.

Portraits. In the interior of the churches which are Cardinals' titles are hung portraits of the reigning Pope and of the cardinal whose title the church actually is.

Predestination, is defined by St. Augustine," God's prevision and preparation of benefit, by which those who are freed (from eternal death) are most certainly freed." God wishes all men to come to the knowledge of truth and be saved, and accordingly he gives grace enough to all. But man having free-will can resist that grace; and some are saved,

others lost. God foresaw from all eternity those who were to be saved. These are the predestined.

Prelate, any ecclesiastical dignitary, and in particular the dignitaries of the Pope's court and household.

Presanctified. The chief office of Good Friday is called the Mass of the Presanctified, because celebrated with a Host consecrated on the preceding day. St. John the Baptist is said to have been presanctified, as he was cleansed from the stain of original sin whilst still in the womb.

Primate, a bishop holding a lofty position in the Church. Nowadays the jurisdiction of primates, as such, has almost entirely disappeared and primates properly so called are only those to whose see the dignity of vicar of the Holy See was formerly attached. Such are Armagh, Arles, Lyons and Pisa.

Princes at the Throne. The princely families of Colonna and Orsini have the perpetual privilege of standing near the Pontifical throne, when the Pope holds a Papal Chapel.

Prior, is used to denote either the superior of an independent monastery or the second in authority to an abbot. The word for superior in Venerable Bede's time was *praepositus* (provost).

Prisoners. Under the Popes there existed a commission, whose function it was to go round the prisons at Christmas and Easter, question those there detained, hear their complaints or observations, take the governors' reports, and thereupon draw up an account to be submitted to the Pope, whose desire it was to extend clemency to the incarcerated in the largest measure possible, without injuring the interests of society.

Privileged Altar, an altar with which is connected a plenary indulgence, applicable to one soul in purgatory and attached to all Masses there said. The word also applies to altars such as the seven in St Peter's, by visiting which certain indulgences may be gained.

Procurator, in general the "proxy," or representative of another. The Procurator General of a religious order is its representative in Rome before the Sacred Congregations.

Propaganda. Gregory XV., in 1622, established the Sacred Congregation de Propaganda Fide to direct and promote the foreign missions. Urban VIII. established the college for young men of all nations destined to the priesthood,

and built the present edifice in the Piazza di Spagna after plans by Bernini.

Protestant, name given to those who, holding the principles of the so-called Reformation, are separated from the communion of Rome. The word comes from the *protest* raised by the Lutheran minority in the second Diet of Spires (1529) against a decree enforcing the toleration of the Holy Sacrifice of the Mass.

Protonotaries, prelates, whose function it is to register pontifical acts, and keep the official records. St. Clement in the first century established seven notaries in Rome to register the Acts of the Martyrs, etc. The word protonotary was used in Constantinople in the seventh century, and in the West a century later.

Provincial, the superior who has charge of all the monasteries within the conventual district called a province. He is named by the superior general of the order, or by a chapter.

Purgatory, a place where those souls who die in venial sin, or with the temporal punishment due to mortal sin not yet undergone, suffer for a time before going to heaven. The councils of Florence and Trent define that the souls in purgatory profit by our prayers and good works, and every ancient liturgy contains prayers for the dead. The suffering souls cannot help themselves and must remain there till "the last farthing," *novissimus quadrans*, is paid.

Pyx, a vessel for holding the Blessed Sacrament. It should be of gold or silver gilt within, and covered with a veil. It is not consecrated by a bishop.

Reception into the Church. A convert from an heretical sect, if there is a well-founded doubt about his previous baptism, is conditionally baptised, after first making the abjuration or profession of faith. He then makes his sacramental confession, and receives absolution from a priest having power to absolve from censures. The reception may take place publicly or privately.

Regulars, the monks or nuns belonging to religious orders in which solemn vows are made.

Relics, parts of the bodies of the saints, and the objects that belonged to them, or had some connection with them. The bodies of the saints have been the temples of the Holy Ghost, and will one day indue immortality. They are consequently worthy of all reverence. Besides, God is often pleased to

make use of the relics of the saints as instruments in healing and other miracles.

Requiem. A Requiem Mass is a Mass for the dead, the name being taken from the first words of the Introit: "Eternal rest give to them, O Lord," *Requiem aeternam dona,* etc.

Reserved Cases, are generally more serious crimes, for the absolution of which the ordinary tribunal of penance is not competent, but which are reserved for a superior jurisdiction, that, namely, of the Pope, of the bishop of the diocese, or of the prelate of a religious order. The want of competence referred to comes merely from the want of jurisdiction.

Retreat, a short period of days taken from the cares of this world and devoted to religious exercises, to the meditation, that is, of the primary truths of our religion, to the reviewal of one's past life, and to the formation of resolutions for stricter conformity to the will of God and greater striving after perfection for the future.

Ring. The ring is one of the emblems of the dignity of the Pope, of cardinals, of bishops, of abbots and of protonotaries. It is usual to kiss the cardinal's or bishop's ring immediately before receiving Holy Communion from their hands, also on being admitted to their audience. (For *Fisherman's Ring,* see above)

Rod of Penitentiaries. The penitentiaries of the patriarchal basilicas in the confessional hold a rod with which they touch persons who kneel down before them. To this act of humility is attached an indulgence of twenty days. The cardinal grand-penitentiary who sits in St. Mary Major's on the Wednesday and in St. Peter's on the Thursday and Friday of Holy Week, confers 100 days indulgence.

Rogation Days, the Monday, Tuesday and Wednesday before Ascension Day. They are days of special prayer, and are called Rogation (*rogatio* is equivalent to litany) because the Litany of the Saints is each day recited. Their origin goes back to the beginning of the sixth century.

Rooms dwelt in by Saints. In Rome may be seen the room of St. Ignatius at the Gesù; of St. Aloysius at St. Ignatius'; of St. Stanislaus at St. Andrew on the Quirinal; of St. Philip Neri at the Chiesa Nuova; of St. Dominic at Sta. Sabina; of St. Camillus of Lellis at St. Magdalen; of St. Catherine of Siena at the Minerva, etc.

Rosary, a form of prayer recited on beads. The full Rosary

consists of fifteen decades of Aves, each decade preceded by a Pater and followed by a Gloria. Each decade corresponds to a mystery of religion, which is contemplated during the recital of the decade. The beads usually consist of only five decades. This precise form of prayer is said to have been revealed by the Blessed Virgin to St. Dominic.

Sacristy, an apartment annexed to a church, where the sacred vessels and the vestments are kept, and where the clergy robe for the sacred functions. Among the most remarkable sacristies in Rome are those of St. Peter's, St. John Lateran, the Gesù and St. Andrea della Valle.

Saints, invocation of. The Council of Trent says that the saints reigning with God offer their prayers to him for men, and that it is good and useful to ask their intercession. That they hear our prayers was held by the Fathers as certain. The saints in heaven with the souls in purgatory and the faithful on earth are all members of Christ, bound together as in one body, and so able to influence and aid each other when necessary or possible. This is called the Communion of Saints.

Salt, is symbolical of incorruption. It is used in the ceremonies of baptism and in the blessing of holy water.

Sandals. Formerly sandals formed part of the liturgical dress of all the orders of the clergy; now they are confined as such to bishops alone.

Sarum Use. Bishops, in olden times, having much power in regulating the public worship, minor differences often crept into the liturgical observances, whence the " Uses " or varieties of Liturgy we find mention of in England, and of which the Salisbury or Sarum use was one.

Satan, our adversary the devil, who, as St. Peter says, goes about like a roaring lion, seeking whom he may devour, an evil spirit thrust out of heaven for his pride, the cause of death in the world through his pride; he has a certain power over the other evil spirits; God uses him to try the just and to punish the wicked.

Schism, a formal separation from the unity of the Church. Against this enemy from within, the Church has had to struggle from the earliest times. Schismatics do not lose their power of *orders* but they lose all jurisdiction. Priests consequently can consecrate but not absolve.

Separation. Husband and wife may separate by mutual con-

sent. If one party is to the other a great danger, either as to body or soul, or commits adultery, the other party may obtain a judicial separation.

Sin, a thought, word or deed contrary to the law of God. Sin is original, that which we inherit, or actual, that which we ourselves commit. It is mortal or venial, according as it destroys God's friendship with the soul, or only lessens that friendship. It is the greatest of all evils for man.

Soul, the principle of life. Man has in himself the three degrees of life, the vegetative, the sensitive, the intellectual, but only one soul as the principle of them all. That soul is united to the body as its substantial form, and is immaterial, that is, not corporeal; spiritual, that is, independent in its essential operations; and immortal, that is, not destined to perish. The soul of each man is directly created by God.

Sovereigns, reception of. Catholic Sovereigns, attended by the Pope's majordomo, make the three customary genuflections and kiss the Holy Father's foot. The Holy Father embraces the kings and princes, and salutes the queens and princesses, and holds converse with them. When they retire, the Pope accompanies them to the middle of the next apartment. Sovereigns and royal princes, when they visit a church or religious house are met at the entrance of the church or religioushouse by the superior, who presents them with the holy water. Sovereigns have the right to enter and remain in the sanctuary during Mass or other church functions, and also to enter the *clausura* or enclosure of monks or nuns.

Spiritualism, an outcome of mesmerism, animal magnetism, was the pretended calling-up and conversing with "spirits" or persons departed. It was originated, apparently, in the year 1839, in New York. It is forbidden by the Church.

States of the Church, the territory possessed by the Holy See. From the days of Constantine the Church came to acquire landed estates, which quickly grew to considerable size. The exarchate of Ravenna was bestowed on the Pope by King Pepin. His son, Charlemagne, confirmed the gift. Thenceforward the papal possessions increased. They were very considerable in 1849; from then till 1870 they have been ruthlessly torn from their rightful possessor, the Pope.

Stations, a gathering of the faithful to certain churches on certain days for the purposes of prayer and religious exer-

cis s. In ancient days there was a solemn procession to the stational church, the Pope himself walking barefooted. In the church, the Holy Father sang High Mass and delivered a homily. With the absence of the Popes at Avignon the procession ceased and was never restored. The Popes, however, still greatly encourage the practice of the stations. When a station happens in a church, the principal relics are exposed on the High Altar and the Mass of the feria is said in the morning; in the afternoon, the stational prayers with the Litany of the Saints are recited publicly (see page 425).

Stations of the Cross, a series of fourteen pictures or images, placed around the interior of a church, or in other devout places, and representing fourteen different scenes in our Saviour's Passion. The faithful visit them consecutively, meditate and pray at each station, and to this devout practice the Church has granted a whole treasure of indulgences (see page 600). The devotion of the Way of the Cross began in the Franciscan Order.

Suffragan see under *Bishop*, (*Suffragan*). The bishops of a province are called suffragans relatively to the metropolitan of that province.

Sunday. The observance of the Sunday is of ecclesiastical institution, dating from apostolic times; and the day is chosen in memory of our Saviour's Resurrection. The synods of the fourth century exhort the Christians to rest on Sunday, if they can.

Suspension, the censure inflicted on a cleric, which forbids him the exercise of his orders or the enjoyment of his benefice. This punishment, temporary or perpetual, has been in use from the earliest times.

Synod, a council of bishops, met under a primate, a metropolitan or a patriarch, or a council of the clergy of a diocese met under the bishop. The latter is called a diocesan synod. The members of the synod discuss with a view to the improvement, government, administration and well-being of all within their jurisdiction.

Synod, Holy, is, in the Greek Schismatic Church, the Patriarch's council, consisting of twelve metropolitans. It was by the institution of the Holy Governing Synod in 1721, that the Russian branch of the Greek Church finally asserted its independence from the supremacy of the patriarch of Constantinople.

Tabernacle, the case for reserving the Blessed Sacrament. Constantine presented one to St. Peter's in the form of a turret with a dove on the top. To this turret shape succeeded that of a covered cup or of small vessels suspended over the altar. In France these vessels commonly had the form of a dove, and were hung from the roof or from the centre of the canopy. A magnificent specimen of a tabernacle is to be seen in St. Mary Major's.

Tantum Ergo, the last two strophes of the liturgical hymn Pange Lingua, composed by St. Thomas Aquinas for the feast of Corpus Christi. The Tantum Ergo is universally sung at Benediction of the Blessed Sacrament.

Te Deum, the hymn of praise or thanksgiving. It is a canticle in the form of a psalm and its origin is ascribed to St. Ambrose and St. Augustine at the baptism of the latter. It is recited in the matin office, on all feast days, except that of the Holy Innocents? and on all Sundays, outside of the penitential seasons.

Tenebrae, the public office of Matins and Lauds on the Wednesday, Thursday and Friday of Holy Week. Part of the ceremonial is the gradual extinguishing of the lights on a triangular candelabrum holding thirteen candles. The one at the summit is left lighted, but, after the singing of the Benedictus, it is taken away and hidden behind the altar. The darkness (*tenebrae*) here figured signified the hiding of the Light of lights at the death of Christ but had not victory over Christ, and this last candle is not extinguished but is brought back and reinstated in its place. The noise and clapping made at the end of the office signify the confusion of nature at the death of Jesus.

Tertiaries. St. Francis of Assisi, after founding his own order of monks and the order of Poor Clares, instituted, in 1221, a "third order" of persons who, living in the world, should practice, as far as possible, the observances of the religious life. Many tertiaries afterwards joined in community life, made perpetual vows, received the approbation of Rome, and thus formed the religious congregations of the Third Orders, such as the Third Order of Franciscans, of Dominicans, etc. Tertiaries, however, according to their original institution are still attached to a number of religious orders.

Thorns from our Lord's Crown. Of these Rome possesses twenty-five. Amongst other churches holding these pre-

cious relics may be mentioned St. Peter's, Holy Cross of Jerusalem and St. Sylvester in Capite, in each of which two thorns are kept.

Thurible, the vessel in which is burned the incense used in the sacred functions. The use is very ancient. Constantine presented two thuribles of pure gold to the Lateran basilica. The vessel in which the incense is carried is called the " boat ", in Latin *navicula*.

Tiara, a cylindrical head-dress, with three crowns superposed, worn by the pope as the symbol of his sovereignty. The three crowns denote the threefold office of the Pope, as Father, as King and as Vicar of Jesus Christ. The Pope possesses several tiaras, some of them of great magnificence, notably that given by Napoleon I. to Pius VII. (worth 10,000 pounds sterling, and that given by the Queen of Spain in 1854 to Pius IX, worth 15,000 pounds sterling.

Title to Orders. The Church requires that her clergy should have the means of suitably maintaining themselves. She consequently exacts from them the possession of a benefice or a patrimony, the promise of a continued sustenance from without, or religious profession in a mendicant order or religious congregation, as a "title" to ordination.

Titular Bishop. (under *Bishop* see page 579).

Tituli, are the oldest and principal churches in Rome which are under the Jurisdiction of cardinal priests and deacons. The titular church gives its cardinal a " title " of cure or denomination. A cardinal in his titular church has rights of jurisdiction similar to those of a bishop in his diocese.

Tonsure, the mark of the cleric and the first step in entering the ecclesiastical state; the shaving of the crown of the head in a circle. It symbolises the crown of thorns and was common in France in the fifth century. Some monks, instead of a circle on the crown, have the whole head shaved, leaving as it were, a ring of hair round the head.

Tradition, the unwritten word of God, transmitted by word of mouth. It is in addition to the Scriptures, and was alone left to the Church by Christ. That a doctrine be held a dogma of faith on the virtue of tradition, it must have been the constant and uniform belief of the universal Church.

Transubstantiation, is the changing in the Mass of the whole substance of the bread into the body, and the whole substance of the wine into the blood of our Lord and

Saviour Jesus Christ. Nothing of the substance of the bread and wine remains. There is no new production and there is no annihilation. The accidents or appearances lose the respect or relationship they had to the substance of the bread and wine, and acquire a relationship to the body and blood of Christ, into which the substance of bread and wine has been changed.

Treasure of merits. The superabundant merits of Christ, and of the saints who did more penitential works than they themselves had need of, constitute in the hands of the Church a store of which others may avail. This store, which we have refered to in speaking of the Communion of Saints *(Invocation of the Saints)*, is called the treasure of meri's and is drawn from by the Church when she grants indulgences.

Trinity, Holy, the most recondite mystery of our religion; the existence of the Divine essence, which is one and indivisible, in three Persons, really distinct from each other, and yet each identical with the same Divine essence. This mystery is taught clearly in the New Testament. We cannot fully comprehend it, but it is not repugnant to human reason.

Tube, Golden, used by the Pope in Solemn Mass when he receives the Precious Blood. It is done by putting one end of the tube in the chalice and the other in the mouth, thus drawing the Precious Blood through the tube.

University, a school for higher instruction. The first deserving of the name was the university of Paris, which reached this higher stage of development in the eleventh century. Shortly after, the universities of Oxford and Cambridge began. The complete university had the four Faculties of Arts, Theology, Jurisprudence and Medicine.

Unum ex septem. These words over an altar in the patriarchal basilicas and principal churches indicate that it is " one of the seven " privileged altars. By praying before them indulgences may be gained as are gained before one of the seven privileged altars of St. Peter's. which are of Our Lady called the Gregoriano, SS. Processus and Martinianus, St. Michael, St. Petronilla, Madonna della Colonna, SS. Simon and Jude and St. Gregory.

Unleavened bread. The Latin Church, consecrates in bread unleavened or unfermented, and made simply from wheaten flower and water. The Greek Church, on the contrary

consecrates in fermented or leavened bread, and a controversy exists as to which our Saviour used at the institution of the Holy Eucharist.

Urbi et Orbi, " to the city (Rome) and to the world," an expression used in the proclamation of Papal rescripts, to denote the universal range of their promulgation.

Vatican, the hill on which St. Peter was crucified, where a shrine was raised and the Papal palace afterwards built. This palace in reality a number of palaces, is the vastest and richest the world contains.

Vatican Council, was convened by Pius IX. and met on December 8, 1869. It sat in the basilica of St. Peter's, was prorogued, and is not yet terminated. It made a number of definitions concerning questions that had arisen in the troublous times Europe has known since the beginning of the century, but the most important by far of its definitions was tnat of Papal Infallibility (July 18, 1870). No General Council had been held since that of Trent, three hundred years before.

Venial Sin, that sin which does not destroy but lessens God's friendship with the soul. It may he remitted independently of the sacrament of Penance.

Veronica's Veil, the veil with which the holy woman from the crowd wiped our Lord's face on His way to Calvary, and on which the impression of His sacred features was miraculously imprinted. It is preserved in St. Peter's.

Vespers, the part of the Breviary office to be recited in the evening (*vespere*). It may be said in the after noon, and, during the fast of Lent, before the full meal, even though tha meal be partaken of at noon.

Viaticum. The Latin word means provision for a journey, whence provision for the journey of life, the Holy Communion received in danger of death. For its reception the obligation of the natural fast does not bind.

Vicar Apostolic, an ecclesiastic to whom, by Papal brief is entrusted episcopal jurisdiction in a region where a bishop does not exist. Nowadays almost all Vicars Apostolic are titular bishops.

Vicar General, an ecclesiastic chosen by a bishop to aid in the discharge of episcopal duties. His jurisdiction comes from the bishop. The Pope's vicar general is the Cardinal Vicar.

Vicegerent in Rome is a titular bishop or archbishop, ge-

nerally a patriarch; who is suffragan or assistant to the Cardinal Vicar in the administration of the diocese of Rome.

Vigils, the eves of the principal festivals, which are days of fast and abstinence. Originally, the Christians spent the night before a festival in public prayer. In England, the fast on all vigils, except those of SS. Peter and Paul, the Assumption and All Saints, has been transferred to the Wednesdays and Fridays of Advent. The abstinence, however may remain with the vigil.

Visitatio Liminum Apostolorum. The visit of bishops to the tombs of the Apostles and, consequently, to the See of Rome, was, in 1585, regulated by a Constitution of Sixtus V. They are bound to come, or to send a fitting representative, every three, four, five, or ten years, according to the country in which they live and its distance from Rome. In this visit they make a report of the state of their diocese, and it serves to strengthen their communion with the head of the Church.

Visitation, a feast celebrated on the 2nd February, in commemoration of the visit paid by our Blessed Lady to her cousin St. Elisabeth.

Vocation, the call to a particular state of life, and generally to the ecclesiastical or religious state. Vocation comes from God, and is manifested by one's aptitudes, tendencies and desires.

Vows, a promise made to God of something more perfect. To be valid it must be free, deliberate and emitted by a person capable of doing so. All vows are either directly or indirectly made to God. Vows may be solemn or simple, temporary or perpetual. Vows may be dispensed with or commuted by the Pope, and, in certain cases, by bishops and superiors having jurisdiction.

Vulgate, or " common " edition of the Bible, the version on which St. Jerome worked. It supplanted the old Latin version and has been authorised by the Church in the Council of Trent.

Washing of Hands. The rubrics direct the priest to wash his hands in the sacristy before and after the celebration of Mass. During the Mass he likewise washes his fingers, before the Offertory and after the Communion.

Washing of Feet. Among the ceremonies of Maundy Thursday is the washing, by the chief officiating priest, of the

feet of twelve poor persons. It is called *mandatum* from the first words of the antiphon then sung: "A new commandment (*mandatum*) I give to you," etc. From *mandatum* comes the English word maundy. When the Pope used to officiate in St. Peter's he washed the feet of twelve priests, and presented each of them with a bunch of flowers and with a gold and a silver medal.

Whitsunday, Pentecost, the feast of the visible descent of the Holy Ghost on the Apostles. The Anglo-Saxon name "White Sunday", probably referred to the white garments of the newly baptised, Pentecost like Easter (cf. *Dominica in Albis*, the Latin name for Low Sunday) being the constituted time for receiving that sacrament.

Will, Free (see under *Free Will*).

Worship, a general term for veneration, but now mostly reserved for application to the supreme *cultus* due to God alone, and which theologians call *latria*. The term they give to the veneration or *cultus* paid to the saints is *dulia*, and to that given the Blessed Virgin, *hyperdulia*, a more intense *dulia* or veneration.

Proprietà Letteraria.

CONTENTS.

GUIDE TO THE FUNCTIONS OF HOLY WEEK IN ROME.	VII
EXPLANATION OF CEREMONIES	1
OFFICE OF HOLY WEEK	17
PALM SUNDAY	84
MONDAY IN HOLY WEEK	92
TUESDAY IN " "	119
WEDNESDAY IN "	134
MAUNDY THURSDAY	
WASHING OF THE FEET	213
GOOD FRIDAY	218
HOLY SATURDAY	304
EASTER SUNDAY	404
PRAYERS TO THE BLESSED SACRAMENT	410
LENTEN STATIONS	417
INTRODUCTORY NOTICE	419
LIST OF THE STATIONS	420
PRAYERS TO BE RECITED IN VISITING THE CHURCHES OF THE STATION	425
SHORT HISTORY OF THE STATIONAL CHURCHES	442
THE VISIT TO THE SEVEN CHURCHES OF ROME	506
PRAYERS FOR THE VISIT OF THE SCALA SANTA	561
GLOSSARY	575